Translation of the
Memorial Book of the Community
of Augustow and Vicinity
(Augustów, Poland)

Original Book edited by:
Y. Aleksandroni
Published in Tel Aviv, 1966

Published by JewishGen

An Affiliate of the Museum of Jewish Heritage—A Living Memorial to the Holocaust
New York

Memorial Book of the Community of Augustow and Vicinity
(Augustów, Poland)
Translation of *Sefer Yizkor le-kehilat Augustow ve-ha-seviva*

Editor of Original Yizkor Book: Y. Aleksandroni
Project Coordinator: Jeanette Garretty Reinhard
Hebrew Translator, Translation Project Editor, and Indexing: Rabbi Molly Karp
Yiddish Translators: Daniel Kennedy and Oliver Elkus
Reproduction of Photographs: Jonah Karp Hurst
Cover Design: Rachel Kolokoff Hopper

Published by JewishGen, Inc.
An Affiliate of the Museum of Jewish Heritage
A Living Memorial to the Holocaust
36 Battery Place, New York, NY 10280

JewishGen, Inc. is not responsible for inaccuracies or omissions in the original work and makes no representations regarding the accuracy of this translation. Digital images of the original book's contents can be seen online at the New York Public Library website.

The mission of the JewishGen organization is to produce a translation of the original work, and we cannot verify the accuracy of statements or alter facts cited.

Printed in the United States of America by Lightning Source, Inc.

Library of Congress Control Number (LCCN): 2021942557

ISBN: 978-1-954176-15-7 (hard cover: 576 pages, alk. paper)

Credits for and Explanation of the Augustow Memorial Book Cover

It was not enough for the Nazis and their eager helpers to obliterate all traces of the Jews and the vibrant Jewish life that once thrived in the city of Augustow. They had to also obliterate all traces of the Jews in their deaths as well. Cruel enough that the remains of loved ones murdered by the Nazis were scattered to the winds and buried in unmarked mass graves, survivors of the Holocaust who returned to Augustow discovered that the graves of loved ones who died and were buried before the war had been desecrated and erased by the removal of the grave-stones that had marked their final resting places. These monuments were used as paving stones for streets, steps, and retaining walls throughout the city, and any other construction purpose that could be imagined. In some cases sand was spread on the stones, which were often used face up, to help hasten the erasure of the inscriptions on them.

The legible stone on the heap of stones in the photograph on the front cover is the monument of Avraham the son of Meyrim Soloveitchik. Avraham's son, Meyrim Soloveitchik, named for this grandfather, survived the Holocaust, and is one of the many voices included in this book that tells of the Jewish life of Augustow, memories of loved ones lost and the story of the destruction.

The gravestone inscription reads:

He left life to all the living in the 78th (?) year…
On Rosh Hashanah 5628 [1 October 1867].
Reb (Mr.) Avraham son of Reb (Mr.) Meyrim Soloveitzik,
His soul is in Eden.
There is heavy mourning in our tent
With the taking of the crown of our heads,
Our joy has become distant from us,
Isn't he our teacher, our father!
The light of our eyes, and our splendor.
May his soul be bound in the bundle of life
(Translation by Rabbi Molly Karp)

The great theme of Jewish history— indeed, of Jewish prayers and the Torah itself — is the interwoven and inseparable relationship of the individual and the community. In this spirit, the mourning for the individual, expressed on the gravestone, can be read as giving voice to the mourning for the collective, the mourning of Khilat Augustow.

The poem on the back cover of the book, "On an Ancestral Grave," was written by Fania Bergstein. Born in Szczuczyn, near Lomza, Poland, Fania made aliyah to Palestine before the war, and wrote this poem when she learned of the fate of her family and her community in the Holocaust. The photograph and the poem together perfectly depict the fate of the Jews of Augustow, indeed of all of Eastern Europe, whose lives and deaths the Nazis and their helpers attempted to entirely obliterate.

Jeanette Reinhard and Rabbi Molly Karp

Front cover: Gravestone of Reb Avraham son of Meyrim Soloveitchik, p. 424.
Back cover: On an Ancestral Grave from "Four Songs for My Father" by Fania Bergstein, p. 436.

JewishGen
Yizkor-Books-in-Print Project

This book has been published by the **Yizkor-Books-in-Print Project**, as part of the **Yizkor Book Project** of JewishGen, Inc.

JewishGen, Inc. is a non-profit organization founded in 1987 as a resource for Jewish genealogy. Its website [www.jewishgen.org] serves as an international clearinghouse and resource center to assist individuals who are researching the history of their Jewish families and the places where they lived. JewishGen provides databases, facilitates discussion groups, and coordinates projects relating to Jewish genealogy and the history of the Jewish people. In 2003, JewishGen became an affiliate of the **Museum of Jewish Heritage—A Living Memorial to the Holocaust** in New York.

The **JewishGen Yizkor Book Project** was organized to make more widely known the existence of Yizkor (Memorial) Books written by survivors and former residents of various Jewish communities throughout the world. Later, volunteers connected to the different destroyed communities began cooperating to have these books translated from the original language— usually Hebrew or Yiddish—into English, thus enabling a wider audience to have access to the valuable information contained within them. As each chapter of these books was translated, it was posted on the JewishGen website and made available to the public.

The **Yizkor-Books-in-Print Project** began in 2011 as an initiative to print and publish Yizkor Books that had been fully translated, so that hard copies would be available for purchase by the descendants of these communities and by scholars, universities, synagogues, libraries, and museums.

These translated Yizkor books have been produced almost entirely through the volunteer effort of researchers from around the world, assisted by donations from private individuals. The books are printed and sold at near cost, to make them as affordable as possible. Our goal is to make this important genre of Jewish literature and history available in English in book form, so that people can have the personal histories of their ancestral towns on their bookshelves for themselves and for their children and grandchildren.

A list of all published translated Yizkor Books in the project with prices and ordering information can be found at: http://www.jewishgen.org/Yizkor/ybip.html

Yizkor Books Project Manager: Lance Ackerfeld
Yizkor-Books-in-Print Project Coordinator: Joel Alpert
Yizkor-Books-in-Print Associate Project Coordinator: Susan Rosin

Please send donations to: Yizkor Book Project, JewishGen, Inc., 36 Battery Place, New York, NY, 1280

JewishGen, Inc. is an Affiliate of the
Museum of Jewish Heritage - A Living Memorial to the Holocaust

Notes to the Reader

The images in the original book were made from photographs that at the time of original publication were already of poor quality, being pre-war and thus already at least 30 or more years old and somewhat decomposed. A special process of photographing the photographs in the book produced images that in many cases were significantly improved from the original book, and for that we thank our photographer.

A reader can view the original scans of the book on the web sites listed below.

The original book can be seen online at the New York Public Library site:

https://digitalcollections.nypl.org/items/212a4a90-2287-0133-c359-58d385a7b928

or

at the Yiddish Book Center web site:

https://www.yiddishbookcenter.org/collections/yizkor-books/yzk-nybc313679/alexandroni-yaakov-sefer-yizkor-li-kehilat-ogustov-veha-sevivah

In order to obtain a list of all Shoah victims from Augustow, the reader should access the Yad Vashem web site listed below; one can also search for specific family names using family name option. These lists are continually updated by Yad Vashem, so it is worthwhile to periodically search these lists.

There is much valuable information available on this web site, including the Pages of Testimony, etc. http://yvng.yadvashem.org

A list of this book and all books available in the Yizkor-Book-In-Print Project along with prices is available at: http://www.jewishgen.org/Yizkor/ybip.html

Geopolitical Information:

	Town	District	Province	Country
Before WWI (c. 1900):	Augustów	Augustów	Suwałki	Russian Empire
Between the wars (c. 1930):	Augustów	Augustów	Białystok	Poland
After WWII (c. 1950):	Augustów			Poland
Today (c. 2000):	Augustów			Poland

Alternate names of the Town:

Augustów [Pol], Ogustove [Yiddish], Avgustov [Rus], Augustavas [Lithuanian], Augustuva [Latvian], Agustov, Augustov, Oygstova, Yagestov, Yagistov, Yagustova, Tobiasville [Yiddish]

Nearby Jewish Communities:

Sztabin 12 miles SSE
Raczki 13 miles NW
Rajgród 15 miles SW
Suwałki 17 miles N
Lipsk 18 miles ESE
Suchowola 19 miles SSE
Dąbrowa Białostocka 19 miles SE
Krasnopol 20 miles NNE
Bakałarzewo 22 miles NW
Sejny 22 miles NE
Kaletnik 23 miles N
Hałynka, Belarus 24 miles E

Jeleniewo 24 miles N
Berżniki 25 miles NE
Grajewo 26 miles WSW
Sapotskin, Belarus 27 miles E
Ełk 27 miles W
Sidra 27 miles SE
Nowy Dwór 27 miles ESE
Goniądz 27 miles SSW
Filipów 28 miles NW
Korycin 28 miles S
Janów Sokolski 28 miles SSE
Kapčiamiestis, Lithuania 28 miles ENE
Puńsk 29 miles NNE

Jewish Population: 3,637 (in 1897), 2,397 (in 1931)

קהלת
אוגוסטוב

Community
of
Augustow

ס פ ר י ז כ ו ר

לקהילת אוגוסטוב והסביבה

העורך י. אלכסנדרוני

הוצאת ארגון יוצאי אוגוסטוב והסביבה בישראל
תל-אביב, תשכ"ז

Yizkor Book

The community of Augustow and Vicinity

Editor: Y. Aleksandroni

Published by the Organization of Former Residents of Augustow and Vicinity

Tel Aviv 5726 – 1966

Augustow postcard circa 1915

1

"Der Krieg im Osten Strassenbild in Augustowo"
The War in the East Street Scene in Augustow (1916).

Photo not in the original book - Courtesy of JewishGen.org

The Augustow Community

The Memorial Book of The Augustow Community and the Region

The Editor Y. Aleksandroni

Project Coordinator: Jeanette Garretty Reinhard
Hebrew Translator, Translation Project Editor, and Indexing: Rabbi Molly Karp
Yiddish Translators: Daniel Kennedy and Oliver Elkus
Reproduction of Photographs: Jonah Karp Hurst
Cover Design: Rachel Kolokoff Hopper

A Publication of the Organization of Natives of Augustow and the Region in Israel
Tel Aviv, 5726 [1966]

Khilat Augustow

Printed by "ORLY" Printing, Tel Aviv
The Plates Prepared in Zincography "Tagluf"
The Binding Was Done by the Binding Co-op. Tel Aviv

Acknowledgements

This English translation of the Augustow Yizkor Book is the result of the perseverance of two remarkable women and one generous grandson of the town. When Jeanette Reinhard initially approached Rabbi Molly Karp in 2019 regarding the translation project, Rabbi Karp's time was fully committed to her duties as a pulpit rabbi, Jewish day-school teacher, and translator on another Yizkor book. In early 2020, however, Rabbi Karp thought to pose a simple question to Jeanette as to the status of the Augustow translation, and from that – combined with the unwanted but valued gift of time from the coronavirus pandemic constrictions – the translation took flight. A plethora of emails, supporting a multitude of decisions large and small, went back and forth, often accompanied by personal stories and holiday greetings marking the passage of the Jewish calendar. For both Rabbi Karp and Jeanette Reinhard, this sad and often bitter memorial of death became part of the rhythm of life. The visions of two women who had never met quickly became a relationship of shared purpose. Throughout, Jeanette's husband, Eli Reinhard, asked how he could help and always provided the financial support for the answers. Photography by Jonah Karp Hurst that enabled the faithful reproductions of the Yizkor Book's many pictures, exceptional translations of the Hebrew by Rabbi Karp, of the Yiddish by Daniel Kennedy in France, assisted by Oliver Elkus, and extensive footnotes contributed by Rabbi Karp's own research, all serve as testimony to Eli's vision of a Yizkor Book more widely accessible by current and future generations, honoring the town and way of life of the grandparents he never met, Avraham Eliezer and Rochla Powembrovski.

For more than forty years, Rabbi Karp's work has been devoted to the Jewish people, helping to tend to its past, present, and future. The translation of Sefer Augustow has been Rabbi Karp's way of serving a Jewish world that once was, and is no more. For Rabbi Karp, the translation of Sefer Augustow has been sacred work, work that allows the last voices of a murdered community to be accessible to and heard by generations to come, generations who may not have access to Hebrew or Yiddish, but who are interested in the stories of what was, and who may be searching for their own family members who were tragically murdered. Faithfulness to and love of Jewish language and vernacular prompted Rabbi Karp to leave most Hebrew and Yiddish words and phrases untranslated in the body of the translation, giving a sense of the sound and flavor of Jewish language that are generally lost in translation. A glossary of these words at the end of the book provides their meaning, while leaving the language intact.

An interesting development in the completion of the translation project was the provision of written and photographic material from the Soloveitchik family of Augustow (now primarily living in Israel) that had been intended for inclusion in the original book. Rav Soloveitchik had prepared the text and then, at the last moment and after some soul searching, concluded that it was still too soon (in the early 1960s) for him to be speaking of the dead. His granddaughter asked us to find some way to include it in this book, which we have done as an addendum, with photographs of the family. The text and this story of its omission are both quite poignant.

We would also like to thank two first cousins once removed: Randy Fishbein, for his always helpful guidance and support on questions of format and content, and Arnan Finkelstein, for his much-traveled copy of the original book which motivated Jeanette and Eli to pursue an English translation and which, at the very end, provided the photos that Jonah Karp Hurst was able to reproduce photographically.

Translation Editor's Note: *In translating Sefer Augustow, we made a number of editorial decisions. There are Hebrew, Yiddish, and Aramaic terms and expressions in the book that we felt were best left in the original. A glossary of these terms has been appended to the end of the book for easy reference. Certain Russian and Polish terms are likewise left in their original languages, and are footnoted, but not included in the glossary.*

The names of Jewish organizations, periodicals, and books have also been left in their original languages. These are italicized, with a translation of the name given in a footnote the first time each appears.

Hebrew, and Yiddish, are challenging to transliterate because the pronunciation of certain letters varies. Lacking vocalization in the text, it is impossible to know, for example, if a letter is to be read sh or s, b or v, p or f, o or u, and so on. The transliteration of names has been made largely uniform throughout the text.

Names and terms written in the Hebrew sections of the book have been transliterated according to contemporary Israeli pronunciation, known as Sephardi Hebrew. Names and terms written in the Yiddish sections of the book have been transliterated according to the pronunciation used in spoken Yiddish, known as Ashkenazi.

All Hebrew sections were translated by me, Rabbi Molly Karp. The translator for each Yiddish section is identified in the Table of Contents by initials: DK, for Daniel Kennedy, or OE, for Oliver Elkus.

Page numbers at the bottom of each page are the page numbers for this edition. Within the text the reader will note "{p. #}" standing ahead of or within a paragraph. This indicates the page number of the original book. In some places, portions of the text have been placed ahead of photographs on later pages, to avoid large sections of blank pages. Page numbers for all text remain sequential.

The index, which is not original to the book, is paginated according to the translation's page numbers, not the page numbers of the original work.

Rabbi Molly Karp

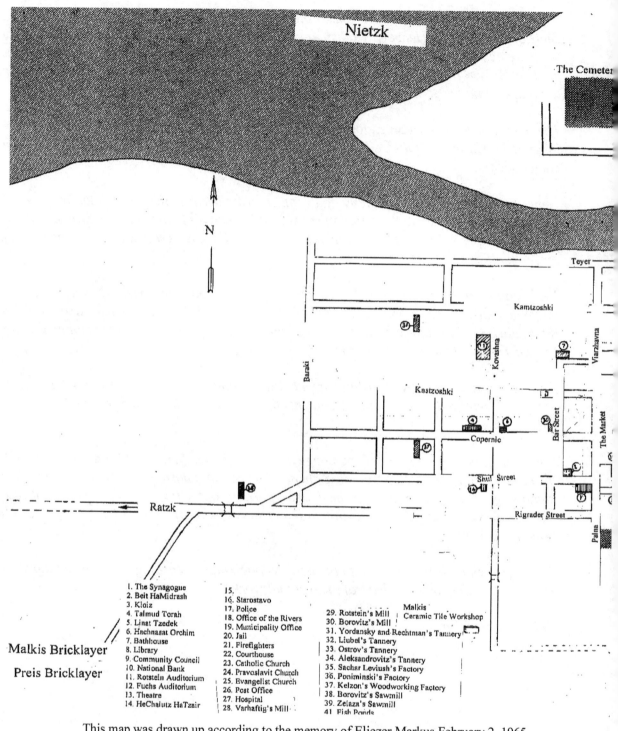

Nietzk

The Cemeter

N

Teyer

Kamtzoshki

Baraki

Kastzoshki

Kovashna

Viarzhavna

The Market

Copernic

Bar Street

Shul Street

Ratzk

Rigrader Street

Palna

Malkis Bricklayer

Preis Bricklayer

1. The Synagogue
2. Beit HaMidrash
3. Kloiz
4. Talmud Torah
5. Linat Tzedek
6. Hachnasat Orchim
7. Bathhouse
8. Library
9. Community Council
10. National Bank
11. Rotstein Auditorium
12. Fuchs Auditorium
13. Theatre
14. HeChalutz HaTzair

15.
16. Starostavo
17. Police
18. Office of the Rivers
19. Municipality Office
20. Jail
21. Firefighters
22. Courthouse
23. Catholic Church
24. Pravoslavit Church
25. Evangelist Church
26. Post Office
27. Hospital
28. Varhaftig's Mill

29. Rotstein's Mill
30. Borovitz's Mill
31. Yordansky and Rechtman's Tannery
32. Liubel's Tannery
33. Ostrov's Tannery
34. Aleksandrovitz's Tannery
35. Sachar Leviush's Factory
36. Poniminski's Factory
37. Kelzon's Woodworking Factory
38. Borovitz's Sawmill
39. Zelaza's Sawmill
41. Fish Ponds

Malkis
Ceramic Tile Workshop

This map was drawn up according to the memory of Eliezer Markus February 2, 1965

8

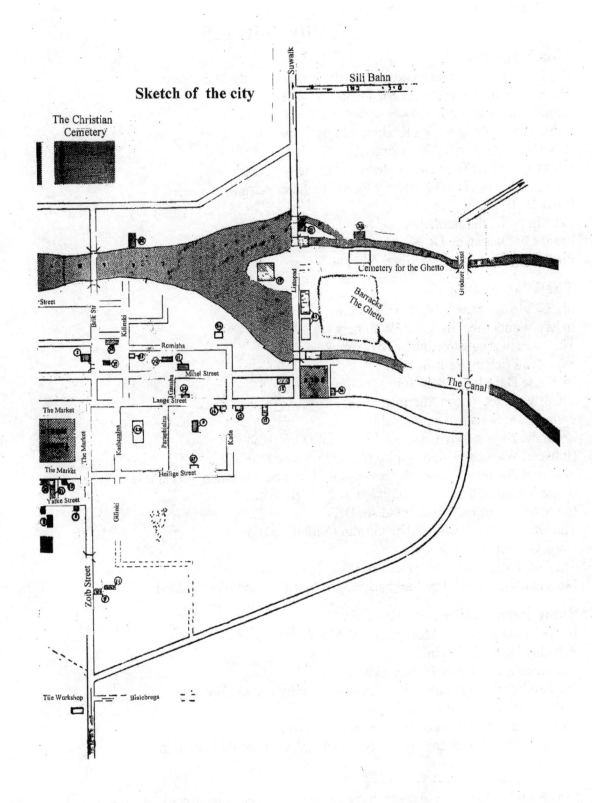

Sketch of the city

The Christian Cemetery

Suwalk

Sili Bahn

Cemetery for the Ghetto

Barracks
The Ghetto

Grodner Shassi

The Canal

Listopad

Street

Brik Str

Kilinski

Romisha

Mihel Street

Gansha

Lange Street

The Market

Kashzalna

Paraphialna

Kada

The Market

The Market

Yatke Street

Gilinki

Heilige Street

Zoib Street

Tile Workshop

Bialobrega

9

Table of Contents

---

[1] This is a biblical phrase, used to introduce a new story or section, as in Genesis 2:4, "This is the story of heaven and earth when they were created. When the LORD God made earth and heaven…"
[2] "HaRav," literally "the Rabbi," is used for the title that in English is rendered simply as "Rabbi"
[3] Literally, students of sages.

---

[4] Immigrating to the land of Israel is always described by the word "ascent."
[5] "The Land" without any other qualifiers generally refers to the land of Israel.
[6] Using the biblical form of the word "how" that is both the opening word and the name of the book of Lamentations, which laments the destruction of Jerusalem and the Temple.

11

List of Photographs and Illustrations

---

[7] This is identified in the Hebrew text as a lake, but it is referring to Svoboda Lock, the 7th lock on the Augustow Canal.

15

Foreword - The editor
Y. Aleksandroni

With awe and reverence, we present the book "The Community of Augustów"[8] for the survivors of the town in the land[9] and in the Diaspora - and for the historian who in the future will write the story of the Jews of Poland, and their history – in the most terrible period of the lives of the Jews in the exile.

For about three years we attended to the collecting of the material. At memorial gatherings, which took place every year, the question was always asked: "When will we erect the literary "Mound of Witness"[10] to our ancestors, our brothers and sisters who were sacrificed on the pyre?" We asked ourselves: "Are we unable to do what emigrants of so many towns and villages have done?" The mission was indeed onerous. The first immensely difficult problem that we faced was – where would the material be found? The community ledgers, party archives, government records and documents – there are none – they were all "gone with the wind."

We turned to all the natives of Augustów in Israel and the Diaspora; we searched in libraries, we gathered them one by one and linked one to the other, and we erected this memorial to those lives that were annihilated – a monument of witness for eternal memory.

It is clear to us that we have not succeeded in giving a complete picture of the life of the town. Even the last chapter of its life is lacking. There remain only a few firebrands saved from the fire and they were not able to reply to our requests to leave reliable testimony for future generations about what the 20th-century Amalek[11] did to the Jews of Augustów.

*

Public life in the town teemed with liveliness and effervescence. We hope that our children, grandchildren, and great-grandchildren will read the book and be filled with pride for their ancestors, and the ancestors of their ancestors, who knew – in spite of the difficulties of life in the Diaspora – to found lifestyles and organizations that can serve as impressive examples even for a normal nation. Without means of coercion and despite the agendas of the authorities, they succeeded in creating a "nation within a nation."

---

[8] Ogustove.

[9] Of Israel.

[10] This term appears in Genesis 31:48 "And Laban declared, "This mound is a witness between you and me this day." That is why it was named Gal-ed."

[11] According to the *Torah*, Amalek was a tribe that harassed the children of Israel in the wilderness, and is identified by the Bible as the ancestor of Haman, the villain of the *Purim* story in the book of Esther. Hitler too is referred to as Amalek, as a vile enemy of the Jewish people.

The Jews had almost no need of the courts of the gentiles[12] – rather, they had their own; they established a network of *"Chadarim,"*[13] *"Talmud Torahs,"*[14] and *"Yeshivot"*[15] - before {p. 12} the authorities had founded schools; even before the gentiles knew what a fund for the sick was – the Jews had organized *"Linat Tzedek"*[16] and *"Bikkur Cholim*[17] and free clinics for the poorest among the people; before the gentiles had created a welfare bureau, our ancestors had supported the needy by means of secret giving, *"Hachnasat Kallah,"*[18] *"Ma'ote Chittin,"*[19] *"Hachnasat Orchim,"*[20] distribution of daily meals for *Torah* students, etc. In a later period, amateur bands of adults and of children, a choir, a sports association, a library etc.; there were established lessons for the "religious" and literary receptions; all this, in a community where the number of its Jews was like the numbers in a small agricultural village in the land.[21] It is worth noting and emphasizing that there were no drunkards among the Jews in spite of the fact that they were tavern owners; there was no Jewish murderer and no youthful wildness.

There was no explanation for it, but an idyll prevailed over the lives of the Jews. There were arguments within the community; there were power struggles for positions within the community between synagogue managers and rabbis; there were jealousies and reasonless enmity; there were rich and there were poor. However, there is no doubt that the light was infinitely greater than the shadow.

And with respect to the period of destruction: there is no judging them for not revealing greater opposition when they were few against the many and the strong; unarmed amidst a sea of alienation – and facing them, a mighty force armed with the most modern weaponry before whom they fell in the blink of an eye; indeed a "Maginot line" and Jewish confidence – both of which failed to stand the test on the day of the command.

From our illustrious community, there remains just a pile of rubble. Even the cemeteries were destroyed and erased to the foundation, and the burial place of our murdered ones is unknown. Our state will be the monument to our loved one, and we will strengthen and fortify it until it becomes a safe refuge for our nation forever.

*

The book is the collective creation of the remnants of the community. It has been mostly written by people who are not writers by trade. There are repetitions, inaccuracies, and perhaps even contradictions. There is no one to survey the organizations of *"Tzeirei Tzion"*[22] *"Poalei Tzion,"*[23] and *"Mizrachi,"*[24] the activities of the Community Council and representatives of the Jewish community on the City Council and so on. We did the best that we could, but time was not on our side and our resources were insufficient. If we had delayed publishing the book for some time there is no doubt it would have been more enhanced in both content and in style.

---

[12] While the Hebrew word *"goyim"* literally means "nations," in Yiddish vernacular it refers to non-Jews, and carries a pejorative sense.

[13] Plural form of *cheder*, literally a room, a school for Jewish children that taught Hebrew and religious knowledge.

[14] A Jewish school that places special emphasis on religious education. Some *Talmud Torah*s concentrate on Talmudic studies as a preparation for entrance into a *yeshiva*.

[15] A school of higher Jewish learning.

[16] Hostels for the poor.

[17] Home visits to the sick.

[18] Creating a bridal dowry.

[19] Flour for *Pesach matzot*.

[20] Welcoming guests.

[21] Of Israel.

[22] Zion Youth.

[23] Workers of Zion

[24] An Orthodox Zionist movement whose name was derived from the words *merkaz ruchani* (spiritual center), and whose slogan was "the Land of Israel for the People of Israel according to the *Torah* of Israel."

However, we were pressed by our aged team to hurry because they wanted to see the finished book with their own eyes. Indeed, there were some who didn't get there. We wish to remember Reuven Levi and his wife Miriam, Gad Zaklikovski, Yaakov Bergstein, Abba Gordin and others – may their memories be for a blessing.

I did not, as editor, use my authority to exclude material. Every note and photograph that were of public interest that came to hand – I have included.

The book is mostly in Hebrew, and a little Yiddish. We adopted a rule that the words of each one {p. 13} would be published in the language of its author. Nothing was translated (an exception was "The Town is Burning"). Because of the paucity of material in Yiddish there was no reason to divide the book by language. The division is therefore topical, but we concentrated the Yiddish sections at the end of each section.

*

There were no famous people in our town. At various times, to our good fortune, there lived in it, at different times, the writers Yaakov Frenkel, Abba Gordin, and – may he be set apart for a [long] life - Tzvi. Z. Weinberg, who described in their creations the way of life in the city at the end of the last century and the beginning of the 20th century. The writer, Yosef Steinberg (may his memory be for a blessing), edited the story of Tzvi Z. Weinberg's "The Mournful Roads," saying that the writer conveys the spirit of the time; another writer noted that the book had documentary-historical value; in other comments Tzvi Z. Weinberg reliably described the Augustów people. Abba Gordin, whose father served for ten years as the rabbi of our town, offered lovely details of events and personalities in Augustów at the beginning of the century. To our joy, we found a manuscript of Meir Meizler (may his memory be for a blessing) from which we extracted notes that described the beginning of the professional organization of the teachers, and in another the difficulties encountered by the public library that donated much through the years to the development of the intelligentsia in town. The eldest emigrant of the city, Akiva Glikstein, a Jerusalemite of youthful spirit and wonderful sense of humor - who is still distinguished today after heroic years - in reading the works of Shalom Aleichem – participates in the book with some of his memories.

*

Our thanks to all those who helped us with spirit and material in publishing the book. Our thanks go especially to the brothers Mordechai, Avraham and Moshe Goldshmid whose generous donation made possible the realization of this memorial to the glorious community that is no more.

May all of them, all of them, come to blessing.
Tel-Aviv 25th Shevat 5726, 15th February 1966.

The Goldshmid Family

The Grandmother Ita and the Grandfather Ze'ev

The Mother Sarah-Malkah and the Father Shmuel-Meir

A City In Its Life

Map of the Region

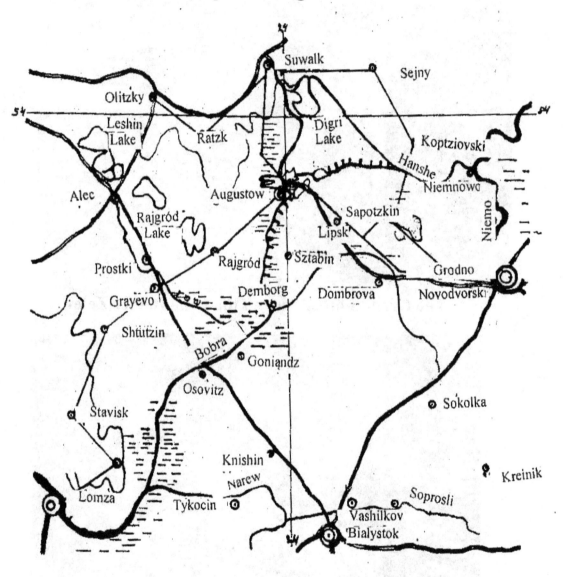

This is the Story[25]

The History of the Town and Its Jewish Community
by M.S. Geshori

Augustów knew ups and downs. Its beginning - a village. About four hundred years ago, it became a city. At a later period, it is mentioned as the provincial capital town. In 1816 when the Russian government divided Poland into new regions they fixed Augustów as the district capital, with Suwalki and Lomza subordinate to her. Afterwards the wheel turned. Augustów was included in the "*gubernia*" (district) of Suwalki. After the First World War the Polish government fixed the seat of the "*voivodstavo*" (region) in the city of Bialystok and Augustów, Suwalki and Lomza were removed from its supervision and authority. Since then it is the Regional capital.

The town was established by the Polish King Zygmunt II August in 1561 and named for him. At the time of the partioning of Poland by the powers that encircled it, Augustów fell to Prussia and afterwards to Russia who ruled it until the First World War. Already at the beginning of the war Germany conquered the town and held it until its defeat in 1918. With the rise of independent Poland the city passed to her hands. After about two years Poland the Russians again conquered it (the Bolsheviks) for a short time, and then the Poles returned again and continue to hold it until today. Only three days after the Bolsheviks left, and the Poles barely had time to enter it, the Lithuanians took hold of the city, claiming that from a historical point of view Augustów belonged to them. The name of the town also went through changes; at the time of the Russians it was known as Avgostow or Avgostovo, while the Germans called it Augostowa – the Poles – Augustów, while the Jewish people called it Yagusto, Yagostov, or Augustov. We found articles in newspapers from "Avgostow."

Chapter One: In the First Days of the City[26]
Foundation of the City in the Days of the Polish-Lithuanian Union – the Area of the City Until 1386 – Forests, Marshes and Rivers – Abandoned Territory – Turning the Village of Mustaka into the City of Augustów – the Year of the Establishment – 1561 – the Founder Zygmunt II – the Granting of the Magdeburg Rights, Fairs and Market Days – the Building of a Bridge by the City – Additional Rights at the Hands of the Coming Kings – the City Boundaries – the Burning of Augustów 1658 by the Enemy – the Division of Poland.

Augustów was founded in the period of the unification of Poland and Places:Lithuania. The territory of Augustow and the surrounding area was, until 1386, part of the Principality of Greater Lithuania. From that same year it passed to the authority of the Kingdom of {p. 18}Poland. But the wars between Lithuania and Poland on one side and the Prussians on the other didn't cease – not before then and not after. After every war, they would make new agreements, which at the first opportunity were broken by one side or the other. In the Melno Peace Treaty of 1422, it was clearly stated that the territory belonged to Lithuania-Poland. Until the 14th Century, the territory

---

[25] This is a biblical phrase used to introduce a new story or section, as in Genesis 2:4, "This is the story of heaven and earth when they were created. When the LORD God made earth and heaven."

[26] Original footnote 1. The history of the city is brought truly in "The Geographic Dictionary of the Kingdom of Poland" in "The General Encyclopedia of the Brothers Orgelbrand" from Warsaw, in "Encyclopedia Gutenberg," which appeared in Krakow, in the book "The Old Poland," of Balinski and Lipinski. However, in no place does there come detail as in the book of the Polish historian Yan Yarnotovski from Lomza (October 1860).

on which were, afterwards, Augustów, Suwalki and the rest of the villages, was covered in primeval virgin forests, large swamps, and many streams.

The conquest of the Visla's exit from the hands of the Teutonic Order preceded the establishment of Augustów. The use of the port of Danzig (Gdańsk) as an exit port from Poland caused an economic revolution for the State.

In 1410, the armed forces of Poland and Lithuania won a significant victory against the Teutonic Order at the Battle of Grunwald. But the Poles did not succeed in immediately seizing the opportunities that opened before them after this victory. However, the Order never recovered from the blows it received after the blow that it absorbed in that war, and during the second half of that century Poland succeeded in annexing a considerable part to the area of their domain, from the shores of the Baltic Sea, with the port city of Gdańsk. Poland and Lithuania had large expanses of agricultural land and also a workforce that was large and cheap, which enabled them to become large suppliers of agricultural products to the Western European countries, where there was a great demand for this produce. With the capture of the outlet of the Viszla River, and the opening of the way to the sea, all the obstacles to continental transportation were removed. Commerce, especially commerce in produce, grew to enormous dimensions. The opening of the sea-route elevated the economic importance of all those centers that could establish a direct connection with the port of Danzig via the river. The importance of the waterways will be demonstrated by the fact that the farmlands of the nobility, the main marketers of the agricultural produce, were concentrated first of all along the waterways. Thus, the economic importance of Augustów, which sat at the center of immense agricultural farmlands and adjacent to the waterways that allowed it a direct connection to Danzig, became great.

The number of people living in the area continued to decrease as a result of the incessant wars between Poland, Russia and Prussia. At the end of the 13th century (1280), the local inhabitants disappeared entirely, and all of the surrounding area became one large wilderness. The chronicles of Germany from the 14th century indicate that the area was a desolate wasteland. The entire territory, which was larger than the region of the future Augustów, in a German chronicle was called Sudova in Latin, and in German "Suduan." The Great Lithuanian Prince Vitold mentions it one time by the Lithuanian name "Terrara Sodarum." In the middle of the 17th century, it was nicknamed by the Poles "Krai Zaproczanski" (abandoned land) and later on, the entire area became known as the "Zaproczanski Tract." According to the Columbia Encyclopedia, Lithuanian criminals, who sought a place where the arm of the law would not reach them, founded the first settlement in that area – from which, afterwards, the town Augustów developed. That thickly forested area was an ideal hiding place for those, who for various reasons had fled from their regular homes.

The city was founded on the land of the village of Mostaki in the former Podlasie region, once part of Bielsk on the banks of the Netta river between the three lakes Nitzko, Sajno and Biala, all found within close range to each other. This land belonged in the past to the royal lands of the village of Knyszyn within the economy of Grodno. Sigmund August II – the son of Sigmund I and Bona the Queen of the Italian House of Sforza, the second wife of Sigmund the Old – became the Grand Duke of Lithuania, while his father was still alive. When his father died, he was chosen as King.

{p. 19} In order to develop the new city that he had founded, the King agreed to grant rights to its inhabitants, according to instructions which were given by him on 16th May 1561:

A) The "Magdeburg Law"[27] – according to which they were freed from all County and Regional jurisdiction;

B) The introduction of weights and measures, butcher shops, bakeries, salt-warehouses and wool-weaving;

C) Two Fairs free of tax payments in ten years, and after that period a one-time payment only for Holy pewter;

D) Two market days a week- Wednesday and Thursday;

E). Free right to fish in Lake Nitzko as far as the river Netta.

The first area of the town was 200 "*tzamday sadeh,*"[28] and according to the instruction of June 21, 1564 from the Bielsk *Sejm*, the King added three additional forest areas[29] whose names are given: Czarnowo, Torovka, and Biernatki. These contained 74 *tzemadim* of land, and included tree-bark fibers and pasture-land in proximity to the town, mills on the other bank of the Netta on the edges of the Grodno prairie, from the city bridge as far as the Kolnicza stream that emerges from the Kolna Lake and joins the Netta River. A quarter mile of tangled forest across the Netta, opposite the forest, has been set aside for many years as a sheep pasture. All this for the obligation of a regular tax payment and six pennies to the priest, instead of the tithe.

Since the city had built the bridge with its own money, it was given the right to set a "bridge tax" and to use the income for its own needs. At the end of this order the King commanded that all the villages adjacent to the town were forbidden to manufacture for themselves beer, brandy, honey or to allow them to be brought in from outside, except – from the city of Augustów.

The rights mentioned above were approved by the kings of Poland: Stephen Báthory in 1578, Zigmund III in the year 1661, Wladyslaw IV in the year 1638, Michal Korybut in the year 1669, Jan Sobieski III in the year 1677, August II in the year 1702, August III in the year 1744. Finally, Stanislaw August confirmed all the articles and conditions.

In accordance with the stated rights the town limits were set: on the eastern side – the State forests beyond the river Netta; on the western side the village of the Noble House of Grabowo and the small Kamenny Brod River; on the north side, the place of the Kosvitza assemblies and Lake Necko; on the south side the villages of Netta, Kolnitza, Yayaziyurka, and Lake Sosnova. Over the course of time these borders were greatly reduced.

The founder of the city, King Sigmund August, rose to the throne of Poland in the year 1548, which is 13 years prior to the establishment of Augustow. He aspired to bring the east close to the west, and encouraged the coming of Jews from the lands west of Poland. From the time of his rule there remain documents that teach about his good relations with the Jews of Lithuania.

Augustów lies a distance of about sixty kilometers to the west of Grodno, which is first mentioned in 1128. Grodno had always been a crossroads and an important strategic point. Already in the 12th century it was known as a capital city of the early Russian princes.[30]

The rise of Stephen Báthory to the throne in 1576 and his choice of Grodno as his beloved Seat {p. 20} brought a flourishing period not only to the town and its Jewish community but also

* *Tzemed Sadeh* = 165 dunam.
** *Machog-Yaar* –

---

[27] Original footnote 2. According to the Magdeburg Law it was permitted for the cities to choose an autonomous municipal council, a municipal judge, and to organize merchants' associations and trade guilds for artisans.

[28] A "field pair"; that is, a tract of land that could be plowed by a pair of oxen in a day. An asterisk in the original indicates a note at the end of the page.

[29] Two asterisks in the original indicates a note at the end of the page.

[30] Original footnote 3. See "Lithuanian Jewry," published by "Am Oved" Ltd., Tel Aviv, 5708 [1948], First Volume.

to the nearby cities in the area, among them – Augustów.

At the time of its founding the new city was situated among lakes, primeval forests, and prairie. It was a broad expanse of forest-land that sprawled between the Augustow Canal in the west, the River Bobra on the southern side, the River Niemica on the eastern side, and the water system of the Black Hańcza River on the northern side. On the edges of this flat area stood the cities of Augustów, Lipsk, Sapotskin, and Grodno. Apart from a small number of tiny settlements of asphalt workers, there was no significant population there.

A number of small brooks and rivers led the waters of the forests into the Bóbr and Black Hańcza rivers. The houses were built of wood, and were easily ignited, and the winds in the area helped much in spreading the tongues of fire. The residents were accustomed to the fires, and excelled in their speed in rebuilding their house anew.

In 1658, that is to say less than one hundred years after its foundation, Augustów went up in flames at the hands of the enemy. The King, Jan Kazimierz gave an order (June 15, 1658) to provide trees from the prairies belonging to the Grodno area to rebuild the town and its church.

Like other cities, Augustów also had various misfortunes, attacks and battles, robbery and destruction, as it is possible to see in the documents of government officials, which are found in the city ledger of Wąsosz. Hodkiewicz, the great military commander of the Principality of Lithuania, who prepared for the attacks against Turkey, prepared barracks for the army in Augustów and Goniądz. His order is recorded in the Land Book of Wąsosz.

In Augustów, in 1621, in the presence of Krzysztof Radziwiłł the village head of Augustów, Jan Karol Hodkiewicz the magnate from Shklow on a mission in Byczów on behalf of the Greater Vilna Voivodeship in the Principality of Lithuania and at the same time as the responsible State military representative dispatched to wage war against the Turkish army, etc., etc....

A second event is reflected in a manifest written in the town of Briańsk:

"Whereas Tatar forces went up against Prussia and returning from there robbed Augustów and her suburbs, taken as prisoners about five hundred souls and removed them to Crimea, and set the town on fire, burning various documents, among them an order concerning the Black Forest of the Nobleman Jardowski, documents of rights and other documents."

The document was signed by Maciej Zaskowski, the head of the city of Augostow, by the will and with the support of, the town residents.

Apart from this, the city suffered other burdensome acts. The respected Weiczyk Klimontowski, a citizen of the city of Augustow, protested against the actions of Franczysk Synduk Reimond, the Government Quartermaster of the battalion under the command of Jan Gorzhimaski, burst into the city and its suburb Biernatki and without any justification took 170 gold Polish Rubles in spite of the fact that they had in their possession a receipt proving payment of the debt. In addition to that, he ordered the beating of the head of the city and the town's elders and took much property. Attached to this was a list of the items and their prices (municipal documents of Vansosh number 44 page 229: stalk of oats, wagons of hay, grain, brandy, beer, pork, pepper, oil, salted fish, butter fish, salt, candles, geese, hens, piglets and other articles to the value of 103 gold coins and 18 cents.)

General View of Augustów

Lake Biala

{p. 22}

Lake Necko

Lake Necko

{p. 23} In the war in the north, the Augustów region was trampled on by various regiments. The agreement between August II and Peter the Great to attack Sweden incited Sweden to invade Kurland, Lithuania, and Poland. At the beginning of 1702 Karl the 12th conquered Zamut, Kovno, Vilna and all of Lithuania and from there he turned to Poland and captured Warsaw and Krakow. The Swedes laid heavy victory taxes on the conquered towns. In 1705 Peter the Great conquered Kurland, Vilna, Grodno and the surrounding area and he, too, laid heavy taxes on the population, especially on the Jews. About a year later, Karl forced the Russians to retreat eastwards. During the battles the civilians suffered greatly and the "cup of tribulation" even passed over Augustów. In 1707 the Russian armies passed through Lithuania and the following year Karl XII returned from Saxony to Poland and Lithuania and after he was beaten at Poltava the Moscow armies returned to Poland and Lithuania, Augustus II was returned to his post. These years were years of great suffering to the nation, years of hunger and plagues, that greatly diminished the entire population, especially that of the Jews.[31]

In the days of the last king of Poland and Lithuania, Stanisław August Poniatowski (1764-1795), efforts were made to correct the rotten State regime in the nation, to disseminate Enlightenment, to develop industry and to be freed of intervention by the neighboring great powers. The attempts were not crowned with success; the fate of the nation was decided by her neighbors, who sparked disagreement, bribed, and did in the state as they did in their own. In 1772, they split up the country, dividing the spoils among themselves. Russia annexed for itself the eastern part of Lithuania and more. In the years 1788-1792 an attempt was made, with the help of Prussia by the united nations, Poland and Lithuania,[32] to effect corrections and be freed, with the help of Prussia, from Russian interference. However, that attempt also did not succeed. In the year 1793, Russia and Prussia again divided up between themselves significant tracts of the nation. The Polish and Lithuanian patriots under the leadership of Kościuszko and Jasiński raised the banner of the rebellion and liberated Vilna and Warsaw. It was the final kindling of the conflagration, which was quickly extinguished. Russia and Prussia suppressed the revolt and conquered the entire nation and together with Austria finally divided the country between them. Russia annexed for itself most of Lithuania; Prussia took for itself the Lithuanian territories that were west of the River Niemen, and in them Augustów and Suwalki. The State of Poland ceased to exist.

Chapter Two: The Rivers of Augustów

Rivers and streams – The waterway junctions – The Augustow Canal –
The connection between the Visla and the Niemen – Digging the canal
1824-1839 – Dams and Bridges on the canal – The Administrative Office in
Augustów – the Loss of Importance With the Building of the Railway Line.

Augustów – flowing with rivers and streams, surrounded by lakes and marshes. The founding of the town alongside vast stretches of water did not come about by chance but was premeditated. Then, at the time of the founding of the city, before there were in the country paved roads or railroads, mail transport throughout the country by horseback was customary for hundreds of years. This transport was mostly in the hands of Jews who knew how to supply excellent horses that could gallop fast, and who saw to it that the roads were maintained. Even transport on the rivers was mainly in the hands of the Jews. By way of rafts and boats they would transport loads of wood and various produce

---

[31] Original footnote 4. Ibid.
[32] Original footnote 5. See "Poland in the Period of the Reforms and Partitions" in the book "The History of the Jews in Poland" by Raphael Mahler, The Workers' Library, Merchaviah.

The Augustow Canal

The Augustów Dam

The Bystry Canal

{p. 26} to the ports of the Baltic Sea by way of the city of Danzig and from there – to other commercial centers that were in Prussia, Russia and the Baltic countries.

The town of Augustów served as an important crossroads of water distribution on the rivers and also mail distribution by horses. However, the water route was significantly more expensive than that of the land routes for transporting merchandise, especially since the vast primeval forests covered the town on all sides.

Let's describe the rivers and their lines of transportation that brought benefit to the town as distribution routes.

A. The Netta River [33]

This river emerges from Lake Necko on the northwest side of the city, and constitutes part of the Augustow Canal. Past Dębowo, it falls on its right bank into the Biebrza. Between Falkiv and Dębowo a second river channel splits off on the southwestern side, which flows by the name of Kofitovka behind Kofitkov, arriving at Szczuczyn province and falling into the Bobra about five viorsts[34] lower on the south side of the main stream. From its right bank, it gathers into itself the waters of the Turówka, Węgrów, Barilovka, and Tończa; on the left bank the Siovnicza, the Kolniczanka and the Olszanka. The Netta flows for its entire course through marshy ground.

B. Lake Biala[35]

This lake is situated in the northeast of the city. Its length from west to east is about 5.5 viorsts and its width between 300 yards and 800 yards,* its area 600 millimeters, or 3.8 square viorsts, and its depth up to 70 feet. At its western end, it merges with Lake Necko while its eastern boundary merges with Lake Studzieniczne and all of it is included as part of the Augustow Canal system. The water is soft, and colored white. The fish present in the lake are: carp, pike, akunas, avduma, whitefish, and more.

C. Lake Augustów or Knyszyn[36]

The lake is situated in the County of Bialystok, south-east of Knyszyn, and is also called by the name Czikovizna. Its digging is attributed to prisoners of war in the time of Zigmund August. According to accepted local legend Twardowski dug it overnight with the assistance of evil spirits.

D. Lake Necko[37]

The lake is situated a distance of one viorst northwest of the city. It lies among the plains dotted with hillocks ranging from 420-450 feet above sea-level. Its banks are high and covered with reeds. The Augustow Canal crosses this lake and connects it with Lake Biala and Studzieniczne. There are no villages on the banks of this lake except for one small village by the name of Shlipesk.

E. River Biebrza (Bobra, Bóbr)[38]

The importance of this small stream is that it is an important factor in the network of transportation between the River Niemen

---

[33] Original footnote 6. See "The Geographical Dictionary of the Kingdom of Poland."
[34] A little longer than a kilometer.
[35] Original footnote 7. Ibid.
[36] Original footnote 8. Ibid.
[37] Original footnote 9. Ibid. This lake used to be described in its time as of great value.
[38] Original footnote 10. See "General Encyclopedia" of the Brothers Orgelbrand, and in it more details about this river.

32

{p. 27}

Lake Sejny

Lake Rospuda

Lake Swoboda

{p. 29}and the Visla (the Augustow Canal exits from the Niemen River). As a result of preparing the River Netta for shipping it joins with the Biebrza. From there it continues by way of the Biebrza, which falls into the Narew, which grew bigger and wider as a result of the addition of the waters of the Bug and other smaller rivers, and falls into the Visla near the Novoyavorivsk Fortress (Modlin). The head of the Biebrza is in the marshlands called "Yotlitza," which are found in the district of Augustów close to the (former) Imperial Tsarist Russian border; it follows the border for its whole length until it falls into the Narew, the border between the Kingdom of Poland and the Russian Empire. At its head, it flows from the north side to the south side. At a distance of 2 viorsts from its source it returns to the western side. From Osovitz it tends more and more to the south and it continues to flow in that direction until the village of Okrasin, which sits on the border of the districts of Augustów and Lomza. Near the village Ruś it falls into the Narew River. At the times when the water is high, it floods the villages that sit along its banks. The waters are mostly frozen in December; the average thickness of the ice is about two feet. The ice melts in March or April.

The marshes of Biebrza[39] are the largest and widest in Poland. They start in the area of Lipsk, which sits on the edge of dry land. They are made up of a sort of peninsula surrounded on three sides by muddy marshes. The extent of the marsh on occasion reaches about 18 viorsts and the area of the biggest marsh extends between Augustów, Suchowola, Goniądz and Rajgród. These marshes spread over a large area measuring about 28 viorsts from west to east and 15 viorsts from the north side to the south side. The Augustow Canal did much to dry the marshes by bringing their waters into the canal. These rivers and lakes were naturally created in the days of creation.

F. The Augustow Canal[40]

The digging of the canal which is called by the name of the town Augustow came to establish a direct connection link between the rivers Visla and Niemen for the purpose of protecting the trade of the Kingdom from obstacles and restrictions which were expected from the Prussian customs authorities. The causes of the implementation of the creation of the canal mentioned in the Handbook of Standards of the canal management are: the protection of the export-trade of the Kingdom of Poland from the influence of foreign States; the freeing of the kingdom's agricultural and industrial produce from burdensome transfer-taxes imposed by the Prussian authorities; the easing of the trade connections between the northern regions of Tsarist Russia via the network of the artificial waterways connecting the port of Windau with the Niemen and the Visla; and lastly – the reduction of internal trading life. The digging of the canal began by the directive of the Viceroy Konstantin the Great on July 27, 1824.

The Augustow Canal was not the first of its kind. It came as the continuation of the aspiration for improvements by the Polish government that began in the reign of the last king, Stanislaw Poniatowski and continued especially energetically after the First Partition of Poland. Members of the nobility lent their hands in improving the lot of the farmers, the development of the country by founding industries, and by advancing trade with improvements in transportation. Then they began paving roads, and digging connecting canals between different rivers. The Oginski Canal was dug, which connected the Dneiper and Niemen rivers and a second canal, which connected the Bug and the Pripyat Rivers.

---

[39] Original footnote 11. The Bobra swamp was considered to be one of the works of the creation of the world.

[40] Original footnote 12. More details about the Augustow Canal are found in the encyclopedias, maybe because of its great economic value to the state in its time. In "The Geographical Dictionary" comes a concise survey of this canal, whereas in Orgelbrand it is described more. Since there existed a connection between the canal and the rivers and lakes in proximity to it, details are brought in it about the waterways.

Then the digging of the Augustow Canal was put on the agenda, which was needed to serve as a connection between the two great rivers: the Visla, which was the largest river in Poland, and the Niemen. Since the whole area {p. 31} was abundant with forests, the Augustow Canal served as an excellent waterway for barge and raft transport. The logs, which were bound together, were floated along the water by way of the Augustow Canal to the Niemen and from there to the Baltic Sea.

According to the original plan, the cost of establishing this undertaking should have been 7,681,587 Polish Gulden. All the expenditures that were made for this need by the authority of the War Ministry up until the year 1830 reached 10,121,990 Polish Gulden, without taking into account the value of the timber given without cost by the government forestry agency, 19,513,325 Polish Gulden, and without taking into account the wages and daily sustenance of the Engineers' Battalion under the primary command of General Malletski.

The water level of the canal was much higher than the waters of the rivers. For that reason, twenty-one locks were constructed along the Canal: Dembovo Lock, Sosnova Lock, Borki Lock, Bialovzhigi Lock, Augustów Lock, Przewięź Lock, Svoboda Lock, Gorczyca Lock, Panievo Lock, Perkutz Lock, Mikaszówka Lock, Sosónwek Lock, Tartak Lock, Kudrynki Lock, Kurzyniec Lock, Wołkuszek Lock, Dombrovka Lock, and Niemnowo Lock. There is a double lock at Gorczyca and a triple one at the Niemnowo. The length of each lock is 150 feet and the width 20 feet.[41] The office of the canal is located in Augustów.

Despite all that, the digging of the canal did not fulfill the hopes pinned on it. After the laying of the railroad line it began to lose its importance and continued to be used for internal commerce, which was very weak, since the lack of water made it impossible for bigger ships to traverse it, and to move at the required speed.

---

[41] Original footnote 13. The workings of the locks are told about by one native of the place, that above the river Netta there was a bridge suspended by chains. The canal was there. On one side of the bridge the river flowed with the dry land. On its second side, there was a deep valley. The difference in height was about 100 feet. Were it not for the lock there would have been created a beautiful waterfall. When rafts would reach the bridge, they would fill the canal with water until it became level with the face of the river in a flat plane. They would put the rafts into the canal and gradually allow the water to go out, until the face of the water would become level with the river in depth. Then they would open the gate of the lock, and bring out the rafts to go on their way.

Kolnitza Augustów Area

Water Authority Administrative Center – Augustów

Chapter Three. The Jewish Settlement in Town

The Beginning of the Jewish Settlement in Augustów – The Relationship of the Founder of the City to the Jews – 18 *Tzemdas* of Land to a Jew in the City as a Gratuity for his Efforts – Two Daring Jews in the City - Fishing in the Lakes and Rivers – The Jewish Census in 1765.

The Jews of Lithuania – and included in it the Jews of Augustów – were not persecuted much, and not restricted as in other parts of Europe. The "Jewish Laws," the restrictions and decrees that operated in Lithuania according to the Polish model, were lighter here, in effect, than in Poland. The Jews of Lithuania were expelled only once, in 1495, about seventy years before the founding of Augustów. By means of this expulsion the Nobility and the government itself wanted, since they owed much money to Jewish lenders, to be freed from payment of debts. This expulsion only lasted eighty years. In 1503, the Jewish people were allowed to return to Lithuania and their homes, as well as their synagogues and cemeteries, were returned to them. From then, and until the middle of the years of the reign of Zigmund III, (1587-1682), there were no extraordinary bad decrees made on the Jews of Lithuania. In the days of his son, Władysław IV (1632-1648) and also in the days of the kings Jan Kazimierz (1648-1668), Michał Wiśniewski (1660-1673) and Jan Sobieski (1674-1696), the situation of the Lithuanian Jewish people even improved.

In the days of Zigmund-August, the Jewish communities in Lithuania continued to develop. The Jews also penetrated the Capital, where their settlement had been forbidden by Zigmund the Elder. In the important communities, neighborhoods of Jews were built with beautiful synagogues, public institutions, hospitals and so on. In Grodno, we find in 1560 three streets of Jewish homes: the street of the Jews, the street of the synagogue {p. 32} and the lane of the Jews. In the days of Zigmund August the joint representative of all the communities of Lithuania was organized. It was called the "The Lithuanian State Committee." Appointees from all the communities chose nine heads of state and three Rabbis to oversee the interests of the Lithuanian Jewish people.

In the first order of 16th May 1561, which served as the basis for turning the village of Mostka into the city of Augustów, and granted various rights that enabled the city to develop, (the Magdeburg Rights, various revenues, Market and Fair days and the right to fish in Lake Necko), the Jews were not mentioned. The second order, that of 21st June 1564, on behalf of the *Sejm* of Bielsk, extended the borders of the town and contained important information. It stated that "one Jewish resident had been granted 18 portions[42] of land as a reward for activities on behalf of the King," without mentioning his name.

Later information tells of two Jews who dared to ignore an order of the town's bylaws. This "crime" served as a reason for a complaint that was brought to King Jan III in accordance with the request of the head of the city, Marcin Pulchaski, dated June 27, 1683.

What were the causes that drew the Jews to settle in Augustów? It was truly not easy to dwell in broad expanses of empty unsettled areas that provided none of their needs, but in Augustów there were not insignificant sources of existence and financial support. Since its founding, the immense forests that spread over large areas were a main source of livelihood for its residents. Lumbering continued during the entire winter period, and the Jews were engaged in transporting the lumber by raft and boat to the port of Danzig.[43]

---

[42] See footnote 3 above

[43] Original footnote 14. The Jewish people of the city and the surrounding area traded primarily in trees. The local people would cut trees in the forests of Augustow. The Jews bought the trees, bound them to barges, and transferred them by way of the Niemen and the Vistula to Danzig.

The land surrounding the forests was distinguished in its fertility, because of its being bisected by rivers and springs that ran all around it. The aspiration to settle on rivers and streams was what brought the Jews to settle in Augustów.

Augustów earned a brief description on the book of Gauguin[44] in a description he wrote: "The town is new and all the houses are built of wood. It is in a process of broad expansion. It was founded by King Zigmund-August and it carries his name. It is 20 miles from Bielsk."

During the rule of Stephan Báthory, an ordinance permitted the creation of associations of professional Christian artisans; these were called guilds. This was among other ordinances for the improvement of the economic situation of artisans, such as fair competition, over-charging, mutual assistance, professional knowledge, and so on. There was also a decree that it was forbidden to accept non-Christian craftspeople into the guild. They could not, actually, forbid Jews from engaging in their profession; therefore, they decreed that a Jew could practice his profession only among Jews, but they would pay taxes to the Christian guild of 6 gulden a year and supply one barrel of gun-powder or brandy, and a specific amount of wax to manufacture candles for the Christian church.[45] In Augustów there was just one guild of fishermen, while the tailors and shoemakers were not organized, because these trades were in the hands of the Jews. This, apparently, seems to be the source of the proverb: "Shoemakers and tailors are not within the category of "humans"" – because they are Jews.

Throughout the 17th Century, which was distinguished by the "The Council of Four Lands,"[46] Augustów is mentioned only a few times in connection to payments.

In the 18th Century, a Jewish "community" existed in Augustów and the Jews of the surrounding area were subject to it. No details of the community's origins in the early days are preserved. No "ledgers" from the city's congregation or from the first societies remain. Apparently, the many fires in the city destroyed {p. 33} the ledgers. The heads of the community were elected each year during the intermediate days of *Pesach* by a small group of scholars and town worthies belonging to the association of "Rabbis, *Chazzanim*[47] and *Dayanim*."[48] The "*Kahal*"[49] administered all community matters, represented the Jewish community before the government, collected and paid the taxes to the government, attended to cleanliness in the Jewish quarter and the health of the Jewish population, supported the poor, took care of the orphaned, education and the like, erected a synagogue, *Beit Midrash*,[50] cemetery and bathhouse. The maintenance of these community institutions and those who served it (rabbi, *shochet*,[51] *chazzan* and clerks), required considerable financial resources. The more the number of people bearing the load increased, the easier it became to sustain them, and improve the services. A large community could allow itself to engage a famous Rabbi who would officiate elegantly. And if a community was small and poor, it would have to make do with a less famous rabbi or join with another community.

"The Council of the Four Lands" was the central Jewish institution of autonomous governance in Poland and Lithuania. It began to operate in the middle of the 16th century and its authority was cancelled by the authorities in 1764. At first the "Council of Lands" was established in Poland, and later was the "State Council" of the Lithuanian communities. It is understood that

---

[44] The Hebrew name quite definitely transliterates as Gauguin. But by the date it cannot be the artist Paul Gauguin. No other "Gauguin" or similar name via web or specifically Jewish sources has been found.
[45] Original footnote 15. See "The City Augustow" Yan Yarnotovski from Loma (in Polish).
[46] Great Poland, Little Poland, Polish or Red Russia, and Volhynia.
[47] Cantors.
[48] Judges.
[49] Head of the community.
[50] Study House.
[51] Kosher slaughterer.

the laws and customs that were discussed, determined, and made into "the law which may not be transgressed" in Jewish settlements – their power also applied in the Augustów community. From the "Ledger of the Council of The Four Lands"[52] we learn that the Community of Augustów participated in it. The "Lithuanian State Council" was established in a meeting that took place on 9 Elul 5383 (September 4, 1623) in Brisk of Lithuania. However, Augustów did not join the Lithuanian council, but continued to maintain its connection with the Council of Poland. In the "Ledger" mentioned above the name Augustów is mentioned only a few times. We will bring a source from there, since not many sources about the community remain for us.

Augustów, the Year (5)434 [1673]:

In Article 342 comes an account of the Holy Community of Tykocin here in Warsaw in 5434 and there is mentioned as follows: (without indicating the day or month) *It seems that the account is made between April 20 and June 9 (14 Nissan – 5 Sivan 1674), with the sitting of the Polish Sejm for the election of the King and also those appointed to the Council of the Lands came to Warsaw to pursue Jewish matters. Among the account totals are mentioned: thirty gulden to Gershon of Siemiatycze for services in the synagogue and graves of Augusti.*[*][53]

Augustów, the Year (5)450 [1690]:

In the article numbered 456: *The officials and leaders in the Holy Community of Tykocin raised a considerable cry of resistance at being forced by the Four Lands to expand the building for the amount of 3,100 Gulden of the above Holy Community of Jarosław in 5447 (1687) after it had been rebuilt after the fire in 5445 (1685) and the trustworthy officials collected from the above-mentioned sum 1,000 gulden to be shared among the Four Lands insisting they owed only 333 gulden.* Well, what is past is past and in the matter of the money that is owed for the above-mentioned renovation, the 24 leaders paid the 333 gulden on Tuesday 24 *Tishrei* 5450.

In Article 457, we find a copy of the distributions of Royal Head Tax of Lvov (that is to say the Lvov in Ignishka) which began on January 21, 1688 - 19th Shvat 5448, and a Royal Head Tax of 21 gulden was imposed on the community of Tykocin according to their wish not to impose {p. 34} anything, only 60 gulden on the Lvov region. And among the rest it is written: The Royal tax in Augustów was 1,659 gulden.

In a second place in the same section is written: a distribution of the Head Tax of Augusti Yaroslav.[54]

In Section 870, number 83, page 81 Augustow is mentioned in a land[55][*] list regarding Fairs taking place in Tykocin. From this it is proven that Augustów participated in various payments of the Council of the Four Lands, without there being found there the name of any representative who would speak on behalf of its community in meetings that generally took place once every two years. At these "council" meetings representatives from all the "lands" participated: rabbis, writers and synagogue sextons, and in the periods between the meetings there were lobbyists ("who had the power to stand in the hall of the king and officers"), representing the communities before the central powers in Warsaw, defending their interests before "the tribunal and the leadership" tribunals and avert the evil of the decrees by means of gifts and prayer.

The Jews of the community of Augustów paid all the general taxes that every Jew was

---

[52] Original footnote 16. "The Ledger of the Council of Four Lands" by Yisrael Halpern.
[53] Original footnote 17. See Halpern, *"Tarbitz,"* Year 6 pp. 217-218 from within the ledger of Tiktin p. 269.
[*] Augusti is Augustow.
[54] Original footnote 18. See the Ledger of the Council of Four Lands.
[55] [*] *zamestavo* - land

obligated to pay. First among them was the head-tax that was levied on the Jews at the Polish *Sejm* sitting of 1581, in addition to the Communal Tax (*korovka*), Right of Settlement in the town tax (*povrotani*), the Drinks Tax (*tzofuba*) and others.

From time to time in the Kingdom of Poland there were censuses (*lustratziot*). According to the Census of the year 1765 there were counted in Augustów and the surrounding area 279 Jewish people (excluding children under the age of one year), and there were in the city 218 houses. To the treasury of the Starosta,[56] there were deposited 3,003 *groschen*.[57]

The taxes levied upon the Jews tended to impoverish them. According to a decision of the Sejm from the year 1764, central and regional Jewish autonomy was nullified and only the local community autonomy remained. The Jews were obligated to pay a head tax of 2 gulden per annum for each soul above the age of one year, and in place of a total of 220,000 gulden paid by the Jewish population of all Poland from 1717, they were obliged to pay nearly 860,000 gulden. In the year 1775, the head-tax on the Jews was again increased to three gulden for each soul and yet again in 1789 the Sejm decided to increase it by 50%.

Chapter Four. Augustów During Partitions and Conquests
The First Partition of Poland – the Second Partition in 1792 –
The Third Partition in 1795 – "Jews are not wanted" – Assembly of Rabbis and
Community Activists in Kaliczeva – Napoleon's Conquest of Poland –
Augustów in the "Principality of Warsaw" – Augustów under Russian Rule.

The difficult events suffered by Poland at the time of its partition left a deep impression also on the status of Augustów and its Jewish population. The war and revolutions that came following {p. 35} an awakening of Nationalism produced disquiet that undermined the stability and also laid a heavy financial burden on the community. Nevertheless, growth and development continued.

The First Partition of the Kingdom of Poland (1772) left Augustów within the borders of Poland. After the First Partition, the country was quiet for twenty years. During that period, cultural and economic change occurred in the country.

In the summer of 1792, Russian armies invaded the State. Prussia did not come to its aid, and the Polish armies, under the leadership of Tadeusz Kościuszko were unable to withstand the invader. Within half a year, at the beginning of 1793, Russia and Prussia divided between them additional parts of Lithuania and Poland.

The leaders of the revolution laid a heavy burden of taxes on the Jews, as on all the population, and the communities were forced to participate with large sums to equip the army of the revolution. The community of Augustów was not exempt from this. The Jews participated with loans and communal and private donations, with money and goods. The Kościuszko rebellion ended in defeat; the final revolt of Poland was drowned in rivers of blood. On the third of January 1795, Russia, Prussia, and Austria signed the Third Partition of Poland, dividing between them the last surviving portions that still remained of the Lithuanian-Polish state, which had already been cut up twice. Russia annexed most of the Lithuanian territory east of the Niemen River and southwards as far as Brisk, while Prussia took for itself the district of Suwalk west of the Niemen, including Augustów.

The Prussian regime over the conquered territory lasted for twelve years (1795-1807). As soon as they entered the area, they began a reorganization of the entire country. Over the course of about two years, an administrative infrastructure of a sovereign nature with a large staff of clerks

---

[56] A community elder whose role was to administer the assets of a clan or family estates.

[57] Original footnote 19. About the number and dispersion of the Jews in Poland in the 18th century see in the book "The History of the Jews in Poland," by Raphael Mahler.

41

was in operation. Indeed, during this period the Prussians worked hard to develop the country both culturally and economically; even a special newspaper was founded in Bialystok called "The New East-Prussian Intelligence Paper" in German and Polish. They even printed "Instructions" on how to govern the population in general with special instructions regarding the Jews. It was a document entitled "An Extract of Laws and Instructions for the New South-Eastern Prussia in 1795-1808."

The Prussians improved the transport of the mail. In 1796, the post operated twice weekly in both directions: Bialystok-Warsaw, and Bialystok-Poltosk via Augustów and Suwalk. Letters intended for abroad were sent from Poltosk to Berlin. The Medical-Sanitary Office attended to the health of the population.

The Prussians also improved fire-extinguishing in the entire area. They created a special fire-watch. Every citizen was obliged to immediately report any outbreak of fire to the fire-watch and the fire-watch would announce the fire to the public by means of bellringing, trumpets, and the beating of drums.

At the same time the Prussians began to reorganize the schools and distance them from the Polish language. The level of learning rose. The Prussians were insistent about cleanliness in the homes, the streets, and all public places.

However, the Prussians' evil was great in their relationship towards the Jews. The head-tax was a significant source of income in Poland, and the Prussians doubled it. Among the other taxes there was a special tax on the Jewish trade ledgers. These taxes provoked extreme anger. Regarding the Jews, the Prussians were not satisfied {p. 36} with extorting various taxes, but also restricted their rights. In order to crush the spirit of the Jews, Friedrich-Wilhelm II[58]* enacted an order in Berlin on April 17, 1797, "General Orders for the Jews of New South-East Prussia" which was printed in Breslau, which came to serve as a guide on how to behave with "unwanted Jews."[59] In the introduction to the "Order of Laws" to the Jews it said:

"Since it is known to us that the number of Jews in the conquered territory is greater than their numbers in other Christian states and they bring damage to our faithful Christian citizens in trade with interest, and negotiation accompanied by deception and corruption – we find it fitting and good to determine and instruct, according to these regulations, how to act towards them and relate to them."

Therefore, between the former "Regulations of the Organization of Jewish Communities" and the Prussian legislation for Jews, there was a great difference. The Prussian legislature was saturated with the poison of hatred and contempt for the Jews and their national and religious institutions, and recognized the Christian population as the sole lords and masters of the state. The Jews were thought of as foreigners, harmful parasites, and fundamentally exploitive, whose activities in trade and in the land should be restricted. According to the legislation, the Jews should be driven from the villages to the cities, forbidden to peddle in the villages, forbidden to buy land from farmers, and even forbidden to trade with them in the barter of products.

In essence, this Prussian legislation cut, as if with a scalpel, the living flesh – the primary artery of the lives of the Jews in the Diaspora, destroying in one fell swoop all the Jewish communal organization that had developed and become entrenched in Poland over the course of centuries. Jewish communal organization in Poland gave the Jews the possibility of withstanding all the terrible persecutions. The Jewish Community was their fortress, which defended them from destruction and assimilation. The satanic Prussian legislation came to completely destroy the

---

[58] Original note: * To this king were added the adjectives "The Great" and "The Philosopher."
[59] Original footnote 20. On "The Prussian Period" see in "The Bialystok Ledger" by Avraham Shmuel Hirschberg, First book, New York 1949.

independent community by handing over the communal, religious, judicial, and school functions to the control of the municipalities and Christian churches.

This Jewish legislation awoke fear and mourning among all the Jews of East Prussia.[60] They could see it as a collection of evil decrees harking back to the Middle-ages, whose purpose was to bring ruin and destruction on Jewish economic life.

All the great rabbis and community leaders gathered for a meeting on 8 *Elul*, 5557 (August 30, 1797), in the city of Kaliczeva for the purpose of searching for means to defend themselves against the new restrictive laws that affected the fate of a Jewish population of more than 160,000 souls.[61]

The edicts concerning trade hurt the Jews because in the entire area, trade and artisanry were in Jewish hands. The purchase of raw materials was entirely in Jewish hands; the Jew who was a peddler, a shoemaker and the Jewish tailor would take their work to the door of the farmer and their wages would mostly be in the form of produce of the land. The tenant would also pander to the estate owner. The Prussian legislation, that came to uproot the Jews from the village, blocked the main source of Jewish income.

The assembly in Kaliczeva found that the legislation was likely to destroy the economic and religious existence {p. 37} of the Jews in two new areas. It destroys the old communal organization, removes from the hands of the Jews the right to debate and judge, made it a goal to abolish the study of the *Talmud* and in addition to all that, levied heavy taxes on trade. The Kaliczeva assembly decided to turn with a request to the King, that his advisors would conduct an inquiry into the Jewish issues, and it hopes that "the King's advisors will spread their wings of graciousness that the pillars of the faith of the Jews would remain on their foundations and that the source of their sustenance not be blocked."

The plea of the Jews to cancel the evil of the decree found a sympathetic ear among the German officials and even among the citizens – and against the will of the King Friedrich-Wilhelm. The assembly levied a head-tax on all the communities to cover the required expenses, especially for "undetermined expenses."

The Ministry's reply, signed by a senior minister, was pleasing. For the Jews of the new South and East Prussia there were dispensations that greatly weakened and lightened the severities that were in the legislation, especially in the area of the peddlers' trade.[62] Little by little the harsh decrees were cancelled, and also the decree on the Rabbinate and the *Shamashim* requiring them to know how to write and speak in Polish was nullified.

The Prussians did not long enjoy their authority over the newly acquired territories. In 1807 Napoleon conquered Prussia, and hope arose in Augustów. Various rumors spread. From the Jewish mail (thus one by the name of Sikorsky wrote in those days), it was made known that French battalions were approaching. Suddenly, the Prussian army began leaving the area and the French, who were received with great joy by all the residents, came after them. In the Tilsit Agreement it was agreed to establish, from Polish territory that had been in Prussian control, "The Duchy of Poland." The Duchy was divided according to the French style, into six departments. The Saxon King Friedrich-August was placed at the head of the Duchy. Augustów was one of these departments. The population happily received Napoleon's army and welcomed and

---

[60] Original footnote 21. P. Bloch, The Year 1793, *Yudenvezen* [Judaism] p. 606.
[61] Original footnote 22. A. Tz. From Hulsha: Geography and Statistics from West-Side and New East Prussia, Berlin, 1802, 2B, p. 266.
[62] Original footnote 23. Still at the beginning of 1790 the Jewish representatives in Berlin and other communities attempted, under the leadership of David Friedlander, to nullify the severity of the decrees of Friedrich's Orders of the Jews.

applauded the principal official of the Department Lassutzky, Napoleon's appointee.[63] According to Napoleon's decree of June 22, 1807, the rights of all citizens were made equal – the Jews among them.[64]

The French army quickly crossed the Russian border, and began a massive and daring attack. In the area were seen the faces of the victorious French Generals and army officers, advancing on Moscow. But all this continued for only a few months. Napoleon's strength was broken and his army hastily retreated. Augustów suffered from the war of 1812, in spite of being far from the battlefield. The French inflicted much damage everywhere, confiscating all kinds of merchandise, without passing over[65] the Jews. According to the Vienna Agreement of April 21, 1815, the Duchy of Poland, including Augustów, was annexed by Russia.

In the year 1815, a new chapter was opened in the history of the town. The King of Russia, Alexander I, was liberal. It is possible that out of intentions to "divide and conquer," he extended kindness also to the Jews, and did not always pay attention to the suggestions of the "Kingdom of Poland." Tsarist Russia ruled over Augustów about one hundred years, until the First World War in 1914.

On March 2, 1816, the High Commissioner of the "Kingdom of Poland," General Zajączek promulgated an order to support foreign artisans and traders wishing to take root in Poland in order to rehabilitate her towns and to awaken her desolate areas. These traders and artisans were freed of taxes for six years and they were also not drafted into military service.

{p. 38} Chapter Five. Augustów Under Russian Rule

Elevation of Augustów to Regional Capital – The Population According
to Race and Religion – Transfer of Capital from Augustów to
Suwalki and Lomza - Agriculture and the Production of Food in the Region

The Russians specifically took favorable notice of Augustów, which since the time of its founding had remained a small town, when they came to elevate it and turn it into a primary city in the civil and governmental administration. During the years 1815-1830, Congress Poland was under Russian domination as an autonomous sub-district with a national administration under the *Sejm* legislature. The State was divided at that time into five *voivodstavo* (provinces). From the year 1816 Augustów was the capital city of the Augustów *voivodstavo,* until 1837 when Russia changed the names of the "*voivodstavo*" to "*guberniyas.*" From then and until 1866 Augustów remained the capital of the Augustów *guberniya.* To the Augustow *voivodstavo* (or "department" in Russian), belonged a few Polish cities and also towns that previously belonged to Lithuania.[66]

Augustów District (*voivodstavo*) was one of the five districts according to which the previous Kingdom of Poland was divided. Its borders: on the north and east side – the Kovno, Vilna and Grodno districts; on the west side – Prussia and from the south side – Plock district. The area of the Augustów Department was 341.91 square miles.

For administrative purposes this district was divided into five regions: Mariampol, Kalvaria, Sejny, Augustów and Lomza. In general, this district consisted of a plain which on its

---

[63] Original footnote 24. Memorial Book of the Community of Lomza, 5713 [1953].

[64] Original footnote 25. Until today an old house stands in Augustow at the corner of the market and the German street, that was not touched in all the revolutions. In this house Napoleon the Great lodged while he was in the city, and it remains as the only memory of that period, which confused all of the countries of Europe and blurred their geographical boundaries.

[65] An allusion to God passing over the Israelites, from Exodus 12:13 "And the blood on the houses where you are staying shall be a sign for you: when I see the blood I will pass over you, so that no plague will destroy you when I strike the land of Egypt."

[66] Original footnote 26. See "The Geographical Dictionary of the Kingdom of Poland," and also "The General Encyclopedia" of the Orgelbrand brothers.

northern side was flat and beyond that, on the south side, hillocked. The type of soil changes and is mostly sandy. Nevertheless, here and there were areas of dark rich fertile earth, with a foundation that is a mixture of sand and stones, clay, and quicksand.

In the lakes and rivers of the entire area there are various kinds of fish: pike, eels, bream, carp, dory, and others.

The surroundings of Augustów were rich in forests that were divided into three regions. Most are evergreens, but there are also poplars, firs, oak, elms, and others.

The amount of wildlife in the forests continued to decrease. There remained rabbits, and also deer. Occasionally one might encounter stags, wild boar or fallow deer. Among the predators are found wolves, foxes, martens, and badgers; game birds found locally - wild fowl and partridge.

The climate of the region was temperate but colder than other regions in the country. In general, the climate was more temperate in the Lomza district and the southern part of the Augustów region, than in the other part of the Augustów district and districts of Sejny, Kalvaria and Mariampol, in which the winter begins in the middle of November and, more than once, continued though the end of March. The temperature can drop to -32^0. In the summer the maximum temperature rarely rises above 27^0.[67] Strong winds only rarely blow here, but the northwest winds, when they blow in September, are often liable to damage crops and trees.

There are 44 cities in the Augustów district, among them: 9 national cities, 4 privately-owned ones; in Lomza {p. 39} 5 national cities, 6 privately owned, in Kalvaria: 7 national towns, in Mariampol: 6 national and 3 private towns, in Sejny 4 national towns. In three towns, the population numbered from 500 to 1000 souls: 20 towns counted a population from 1,000 to 2,000 souls, 10 towns are populated by 2,000 to 3,000 souls and 4 from 3,000 to 4,000. Only three towns were populated by more than 8,000 souls.

The total population of the district was 624,061, giving a population density of 1,825 souls per square mile. The distribution of the population in 1860 was as follows: Men – 303,502, women -320,559. By ethnicity: Slavs - 275,790; Lithuanians -213,310; Germans – 13,751; Jews – 102,955; Tatars – 168; Gypsies -19. Apart from that there were some tens of English and French people. The Slavs were divided into Poles, Rusinis[68] and Kurpie.[69] The Rusinis were divided by their religion into Pravoslavs,[70] Roman Catholic, Members of the Covenant[71] or Pilifones, united with the Pravoslavic Church and lacking priests, or members of the old faith. The Poles, Germans and Jews settled throughout the entire district while the Rusinis settled in Sejny, Augustów and Lomza regions; the Kurpie in Lomza, the Lithuanians in Mariampol. Only a few tens of them were found in Augustów.

The Augustów region spread over 85 square miles, of which the designated agricultural use was as follows: wheat – 165 *tzemed*, cereal – 3328, barley – 498, oats – 1410, peas – 324, buckwheat – 228, potatoes – 1025, flax - 78, cannabis – 25 and some smaller areas for sowing of millet and more. The total population of the region in the year 1860 was 127,304 souls of whom there were 62,565 men and 62,539 women; their ethnic background was as follows: Slavs – 99,657, Lithuanians – 97, Germans – 4051, Jews – 24,481, Tatars – 6 and a few English and French. By religion: Roman Catholic – 10,919, Pravoslavis – 81, Greek Uniate -7,412, Pilifones – 1,354, Augsburg Evangelists – 4.042, Reform Evangelists – 9, Jews – 24,481, Moslems – 8. 40,082 dwelt in the cities while 88,222 dwelt in villages. In Augustów: Poles and Russians – 4,500, Germans – 133, Jews – 3,686.

---

[67] Centigrade.
[68] An East Slavic people who speak the Rusyn language.
[69] Kurpie is an ethnic region in Poland.
[70] Members of the Russian Orthodox church.
[71] An early Syriac Christian sect.

According to the new partition of Congress Poland in the year 1866, which came after Poland's failed second revolt against Tsarist Russia and also as a form of punishment of the Polish people, the Augustów district was dismantled and in its place, two districts were created: Suwalki and Lomza. Until the year 1866 they had both been part of the district of Augustów.

The Augustów district was not generally considered for its agricultural land-usage or advanced in other aspects.

Industry in Augustów was found at that time at a low level. In addition to a brandy distillery and brewery that existed in Sztabin there was a foundry for forging agricultural equipment. Handcrafting was limited to the local supply of very simple needs. The farmers engaged in weaving and the production of tar. Commerce was centered in Augustów.

From the point of view of trade, the town was distinguished by several advantages. Besides the paved road between Warsaw and Petersburg via Augustów, the town nestled between the borders of Prussia and Russia at a distance of 28 viorst from Suwalki and 238 viorst from Warsaw. From Augustów to Sopotkin was 49 viorst and from there to Grodno – 21 viorst. Commerce was in the hands of the Jews, who used every opportunity to their advantage.

{p. 40} **Chapter Six: Rights and Restrictions**

Census of Jews in Augustów and the Surroundings in 1765 –
Liberal Attitude of Russia to the Jews – Worsening Change in Attitude
Nikolai I – Kidnapping of Youth for Cantonist Army Service –
Nullification of Edict under Alexander II – Polish Revolt of 1831 –
Murder and Hangings of Jews – Cholera epidemic – Expulsion of Jews -
Augustow Canal Opened to Traffic – Increase of Jews in Augustów Region –
Under Alexander II – Election of Jews to the Regional Council
Description of Augustów in 1860 – The Economy in Jewish Hands –
Second Polish Revolt in 1863 – Nullification of the Korovka Tax in 1863 -
Extreme Hunger.

We mentioned above that according to the census of 1765, 279 Jews were counted. It was not a regular, general state-wide census of the population, but a special one of the Jews and the first to be held since 1550.

According to the law of 1764, a census like this should be carried out once every five years. In 1768, the law was changed, and it was decided that the Jewish officials should conduct a census once every twenty years. Yet, already in 1775, after the first Partition (in the year 1772), a law was enacted to conduct a census of the Jews that same year and subsequently every three years (the head-tax was then increased to three guilders per person). Since then a new census of the Jews was carried out in 1778, 1781, 1784, 1787, and 1790. After the Second Partition of Poland in 1793, the government disintegrated and the census' of the Jews were no longer conducted.

Five years after the Warsaw Duchy was turned over to Russia, according to a decision of the Vienna Congress (1815), the first general census was established. According to it, the number of residents in Augustow were: Christians – 1504; Jews – 1167; other religions – 254. In the suburbs of the city: Chernovo – Christians, 285; Jews – 18. In Turovka – Christians, 189; Jews, 3. In Birnetki: Christians, 285; Jews, 24. In the city at that time there were 5 mansions, 385 wooden houses. It turned out, therefore, that the number of Jews in the city reached 33% of all the residents of the city.

In the first years of the annexation of Augustów by the Russian government, a liberal wind blew among the officials, who dealt with the Jews with tolerance. Catherine II, in the early part of her reign, adopted a stance of "Enlightened Absolutism." She granted to urban dwellers the right of elected self-governance, added the Jews to the status of town dwellers and traders, made the Jews equal to the Christians in the payment of taxes, granted them the right to vote and be elected to city councils. In no state in Europe at that time did the Jews enjoy rights such as these. On the other hand, the Jews were permitted to dwell only in the regions in which they lived during the time of the Polish government, or the southern regions earmarked for settlement ("New Russia"). Alexander I promised in his first manifesto to citizens not to touch their rights, but when Nikolai I, his brother, rose to the throne of the Tsar (1825-1855), a bitter period began for the Jews. This period is considered the darkest in Jewish history.

In the year 1827, Jews were forbidden to settle in Augustów because it was located adjacent to the border {p. 41} of Prussia. That is to say, for those who were already resident in Augustow, they were permitted to continue to dwell there, but entry to it was forbidden for Jews from other places who wished to settle there – and not only Augustów – but in all the places that were in the entire strip along the border with Germany and Austria.

On August 26, 1827, the despotic Nikolai enacted the cruel law enlisting young men into the army that negatively impacted the life of the individual and the collective. During the Kingdom of Poland era, the Jews were entirely exempted from military service because in Poland there was no obligatory service. Service in the military was considered a right of the noble class and farmers, who were considered property of the nobility. All the Jews belonged to the merchant class, and as such were exempt from military service. According to orders from September 1794 and January 1796 a tax of 500 rubles was levied as "ransom" on everyone reaching the age of military service. However, according to an order dated 26 August 1827 (5587), the Jewish community was obligated to fulfil the obligation to serve in the military with people and not through monetary payments. The "community" was given the right to turn over to the army any Jew who committed the crimes of not paying taxes, lack of employment, lack of identity papers, and the like. This order served as a dangerous means in the hands of the decision-makers of the community, who could turn over to the army anyone that they wanted, and they attempted to extricate from this trouble only the children of the wealthy and privileged. Army service lasted for 25 years, starting at age 25. Yet according to the order of the right-hand man of Nikolai, the Minister of the Secret Police Beckendorf, they would also take into the army Jewish children from the age of 12, who were detained in Cantonist[72] barracks. The despotic Beckendorf intended by this to achieve two purposes: a) generally reduce the number of Jews and b) force the Jews to convert. This awful and tragic decree hit most strongly on the children of the poor. The rich and powerful knew how to extricate themselves from this trouble. It would make one's hair stand on end to hear the descriptions of the actions of the Jewish "kidnappers." Hired by the community, they would steal young children, tender and weak, from the arms of their mothers. They would send the children to Cantonist regiments in Siberia, and there force them, by persecution and terrible tortures, to convert. The children would die of starvation by the thousands either on the way to Siberia or in the barracks. This decree affected all the communities. Even Augustów was not exempt from it. The elders of the surviving refugees in the land of Israel or other countries mention these Cantonists who served 25 years in the army, and were able to survive the difficult experience and returned to their homes and their towns, and they would always recount to the young ones of their towns what happened to them in the depths of Siberia and how great was the danger. Nevertheless, they did not leave the faith of their ancestors, and remained faithful to the ancestral tradition.[73]

---

[72] Jewish children who were conscripted to military institutions in czarist Russia with the intention that the conditions in which they were placed would force them to adopt Christianity.

[73] Original footnote 27. On the period of the Cantonists and "Nikolai's Service" an extensive literature has been created. In the book *"Zikhron Yaakov"* Rabbi Yaakov Lifshitz describes the tragedy of the boys and young men that were kidnapped from the laps of their parents for Russian military service and the bitterness of their fate. The *Rebbetzin*

According to the known numbers from the years 1833-1854, about 70,000 Jewish children fell victim to the Cantonist decree. The Jewish soldiers were sent back after 25 years of military service and were not permitted to remain in their homes in distant Russia.

At the time of the Polish revolution that broke out in November 1830 the Jewish population was "between the hammer and the anvil." They had no interest in assisting the Polish nobility in its war with the Russian government. On the other hand, the harsh decrees of the Russian government lay heavy upon the Jews. The Polish rebels decided in the main not to attack the Jews, in order not to push them to the Russian side. The revolutionaries knew of the bitterness that existed among the Jews against the Russian government. Revolutionary councils called the Jews in various cities to come to their aid. The rebels swore the Jews not to reveal their secrets to the enemy, but the opposite; that they would inform them of the movements of the Russians. Nevertheless, there were some Jews who transmitted information to the Russians on the concentrations of the rebels, their movements, and their activities. The rebels, {p. 42} on the other hand, hanged Jews in the Augustów region without investigation or trial.[74] A company of Polish fighters, who met a cart full of Jews on their way to a wedding, murdered them all. This murder stirred up the emotions of the Jews of Lithuania. The years of the rebellion rocked the unstable economic situation of the Jews of Augustów who endured stress and poverty.

Apart from the troubles that were caused to the Jews of the Augustow area by the revolt, in the year 5591 (1831) a disaster struck them that befell almost the whole of Lithuania and the areas of Poland adjacent to it. Over the course of more than half a year, an epidemic of cholera raged that had been brought by the Russian army, and struck down many victims in the city. The sick were stricken with diarrhea and abdominal pain, and dropped like flies.[75]

In April 1843, the cruel Nikolai promulgated a law stating: "All the Jews living within 50 *viorst* of the Austrian-Prussian border must soon leave their places of residence and move to Russian areas more distant from the border." It was a very harsh decree that struck thousands of Jews in the Augustów region. The Jews, of course, began to investigate means of nullifying the decree. The Jewish communities of the region were the first to fight against this decree. The community of Konigsberg helped them with this, because a portion of its Jews were connected by family or economically with village Jews in this region. Johann Jakobi, one of the chief fighters from Konigsberg in the fight against the decree of expulsion, had family connections in the town of Neustadt, where his father was born. The Russian emissary in Konigsberg at the time was Jacob von Edelstein from the village of Yurburg. Despite being a convert, he was unable to remain passive in the face of the edict against the Jews of his area. He helped his friend Johann Jakobi and indeed the edict was effectively not carried out.

In spite of the edict, in 1851 there were in Augustów and the surroundings 677 Jewish families.

In 1839, the famous Augustow Canal was opened, which developed new trade routes. Augustów merchants opened new trade connections from Minsk to Prussia and from Kovno to Danzig.

The Jews in Poland, and among them the Jews in the Augustow area, tried to bring to life the saying "...and the more they afflicted them, the more they grew."[76] According to one newspaper

---

Zelda Edelstein-Koshelevski remembers Mordechai-Gershon, a teacher of young children from Augustow, who participated in the Crimean War (1853-1855) and after his return he would always tell of the adventures of the war.

[74] Original footnote 28. See "Lithuanian Jewry" p. 84.

[75] Original footnote 29. Also in Augustow they were using means at that time for the quieting of the epidemic that were accepted in every place, such as: fast days, the recitation of Psalms, the smoking of *shemot* [documents on which God's name was written] in the street, and willow branches.

[76] Exodus 1:12

account, 100,007 Jews were added to the population of the Augustów district over the course of the forty years, from the year 5617 – 5577 (1817-1857).

Alexander II, the son of Nikolai, rose to the throne in the midst of the days of the defeat in the Crimean War. His reign (1855-1881) began with signs of liberalism. The good wind that began to blow in government circles was felt also on the Jewish street. The retreat away from his tyrannical father's method of cruel edicts began with the repeal of the Cantonment decree. On August 26, 1856, the edict that had so repressed the Jews of Russia and Lithuania for years was nullified.

There also came important relief from the decree expelling the Jews from the 50-*viorst* strip along the border that affected the Jews of Augustów as well, if less than other communities. The expulsion of 120,000 Jews from the border areas was stopped in the spring of the year 1858.

According to the new rights that the new Tsar granted to the residents, the nation was permitted to choose municipal and regional advisors from within. Even to the Jews was given the right to be counted among these electees. Elections were held in many places. Among 615 advisors and their deputies elected for the Department, from the Jews, 26 advisors and 27 deputies were chosen. The total number of Town advisors and deputies reached 184, of them 28 {p. 43} advisors were Jewish and forty were deputies. In the Augustów district Yitzchak Bialystotzki and Binyamin Biskovitz were elected to the Regional Council and as Deputy, Eliyahu Rosental.

The Hebrew press knew to inform that Jewish Augustów gave much aid to the neighboring communities in the time of trouble. After a blaze that occurred in nearby Szczuczyn, in April 1858, many Jews remained without a roof over their heads, hungry and naked. All the neighboring towns, including Augustów, rushed to provide food and clothing.

Augustów of the year 1860 was briefly described by a Polish historian (Yan Yarnotovski); according to him the area of the town, according to a map from 1822, that was produced by Yablonski – 537 *tzamday sadeh*, 28 small plots of land[77]* and 266 *shevet*.[78]**

The population was divided in 1859 according to religion: Catholics – 4,418; Evangelists – 113; Jews – 3,764 (that is – 45.3% of the total population). 15 mansions of more than one story were found in the city, one-story houses – 9, wooden houses – 504. In the city, there was a Catholic church built with two steeples and one – old and built of wood and also an Evangelical Augsburg church and a prayer-room for Uniates; 3 hotels, 5 hostels built of wood, 12 pubs, 1 candy store. Government offices: Office of the Provincial Governor, the Municipality, office of the 13th Area Regional land and water transport authority, the office of the district head of water transport, office of the treasurer, office of the citizen class, salt warehouse, office of the gendarmes, post office, primary school and a pharmacy.

The town had much land, fertile and good for pasture, and consequently many residents were engaged in agriculture. The city had twenty streets. The village of Bialovzhiga was a part of the city. Six Fairs were held annually; market days - twice a week, on Tuesdays and Fridays.

On the canals and river mainly produce from Russia was transported. In the last years of transport movement different vessels arrived in Augustów: 10 – Berlinki;[79] various vessels – 46. The total value – 150,000 Rubles.

With the opening of the Augustow Canal to public river transport a new class of Jewish merchants developed who dared to traverse enormous distances of the vast Russian State as merchants and agents for import and export. A significant part of the trade in fruit and horses was

---

[77] Original note: *a small plot of land – *moreg* – *dunam*. A unit of land area used especially in the state of Israel equal to 1000 square meters or about ¼ acre.
[78] Original note: ** *shevet* - *pret*
[79] A kind of small transport ship.

by Jews. In their hands were the mills, tanning, distilleries of hard liquor and beer. Also, the most important product of the region, wood, was almost entirely in the hands of the Jews.

In the year 1843, the number of Jewish shopkeepers and merchants in the Augustów region was the smallest of all the other regions in Poland. In contrast to that, the number of laborers grew. Shoe-makers – 576; wagon-masters – 109; Jewish black-smiths – 297. Comparing this with Jewish smiths in the other regions, it is possible to see the position of Augustow in this area: In Mazovyetsk region – 8, in Sandomierz region – 12, in Kieltz region – 6 ...and the like. The number of tar-workers in the Augustów region was the greatest – 39, (in Mazowiecka region – 6, Kieltz – 18). The same applies to Jewish builders whose numbers were – 48, (in Plock region -9, Sandomierz – 6, {p. 44} Kalish – 11...and so on). In the second half of the 19th Century Augustów district had a great number of Jewish textile workers. Already at the beginning of the fourth decade, the Jews controlled the general economic life in the district, such that the Provincial Governor found it necessary to warn the government not to place the obligation of military service on the Jews, because that was likely to cause economic destruction in the area. In a report of the district Minister in Augustow from 1865, he again indicated that the Jews filled a crucial role in the external commerce of the region. In 1861 there were established in a number of places in Augustow a "Farmers' House," where residents from the villages would sell their produce or receive loans. However, this competition for Jewish trade did not last long.

In the year 1861, in Poland, waves of a spirit of revolution began to strike. In these provincial towns, fraternities were created of Poles and Jews who inscribed on their banners the motto "One God created us, one fate is hidden for us from the hands of the Russian enslaver." In Paris there dwelt the famous Polish writer and historian Joachim Lelewel, who had acquired for himself a name also among the Jews, for his idea of the freedom of nations, on complete equal rights for Jews in a free Poland, on the awakening of the Hebrew nation, who would arise and build their historical homeland the Land of Israel and such. The ideas of Lelewel found a strong echo in the groups of the enlightened Jews in Poland and especially among the members of the enlightenment that dwelled along the Prussian border in the Augustów region.

In the Second Polish Revolution of 1863 the Jews of Augustow were found again, as in the year 1831, "between the hammer and the anvil." The Jews had strong ties with their Polish neighbors while the Russian government wanted to draw them to their side. The easing of restrictions that the government of Alexander II had made, in comparison to the decrees of Nikolai I aroused hope among the Jews, whose situation was improving. Many Jews in the Augustów area remained neutral and only a few willingly helped the Poles. Since most of the Jews did not reveal willingness to aid the rebels, the rebels threatened them with revenge. In some places the rebels carried out their threats; they shot and hanged Jews whom they suspected of supporting the Russians.

On the road between Suwalki and Augustów, the rebels caught a Jewish man and tried to hang him on a tree, saying he had revealed their secrets to the Russian army.

But he got lucky. When they hung him on the tree the branch broke under the load of his weight and he fell to the ground. The leader of the rebels told the Jew to go on his way, for he saw this as a sign that God was with him (October 1863). During this revolution, Rabbi Shlomo Margalit (Perla), a *Moreh Tzedek*[80] from Lomza who was known in Augustów, was killed by the rebels, and its Jews mourned for him as if he were one of their own residents.[81]

---

[80] Righteous teacher, that is, a decisor of Jewish law.
[81] Original footnote 30. "*HaMaggid*" 25 *Tevet* 5623 (January 15, 1863).

The Jews of Augustów suffered like all the Jews of Poland from the "Korovka" tax that burdened them, in their paying a tax for every pound of kosher meat that they ate. This tax was nullified at the beginning of 1863, and for the Jews there was relief.

After the Polish Revolution failed again, the Russian Government took punitive measures against those who participated in it. As one of these means came a declaration, by order of the government, to annex the Province of Augustów to the Empire of Russia (November 1863). Until then the Province was an intermediate province, doubtfully part of Poland and part of Lithuania. This doubt came to be realized in the languages, the ways of life of the inhabitants, and the like.

In the years 1867-1869 (5627-5629), there was heavy famine hunger in the districts of Lithuania and the Polish provinces {p. 45} that were within it. At the end of 1868 a committee of Lithuanian exiles from Prussian Memel came to their rescue. Its secretary was the rabbi of Memel Dr. Yitzchak Rilf, a journalist and thinker who was very active for the affected in Prussia, and from then on, he hastened to the assistance of all Jews across the border in all cases of distress, fires, or persecutions. In a call for help from the "Memel Committee" for the "assistance of their brethren in the western Russian provinces" and in Jewish German newspapers that were across the border of Prussia, Memel and Tilsit, the terrible conditions of the Jews in the Suwalki and Augustów areas were described. The newspaper "HaMaggid"[82] that appeared in Lek, a village adjacent to Augustów, especially raised "and they cried out"[83] about the suffering of the famine. A special committee from "HaMaggid" sent hundreds of rubles to the Jews who were suffering from the famine. Indeed, not only the nearby cities, but the whole Jewish world awoke to relieve the terrible suffering.[84]

Adolphe Crémieux, the director of the association "Alliance Israelite Universelle," described the hunger as follows: "In the streets, in the synagogues and study halls hundreds of hunched over people wander around, and without strength hundreds of people who are dying of hunger; people who are mere shadows appear and beg that their lives should end. In the schools the children are dying before their parents' eyes, and the young girls weep and complain in front of their friends." The main committee in Konigsberg engaged, among other activities, in sending Jewish orphans from the suffering areas to German towns in order to educate them and teach them a trade. It was clear that such a terrible hunger greatly shook the economic foundations of Augustów and the surrounding area. Among those who perished was the "Maggid"[85] of Kloiz.[86] This Maggid was one of the major opponents to the new rabbi Yehuda Leib Gordin, who worked to remove the new rabbi and to return Rabbi Katriel to his seat. The death of the Maggid became a major talking point in town because he was brought low during a sermon in which he cast aspersions against the rabbi. He boiled with anger and was stricken, apparently, with a heart attack. But the new rabbi's followers saw in his sudden death the finger of G-d and proof of the righteousness of the new rabbi.[87]

---

[82] The Storyteller.

[83] Exodus 14:10 "As Pharaoh drew near, the Israelites caught sight of the Egyptians advancing upon them. Greatly frightened, the Israelites cried out to the LORD."

[84] Original footnote 31. The famine in Augustow was written about in "HaMaggid" 49 Nisan 5628 [1868] in the form of an announcement, according to which the typhus disease came as a result of the famine.

[85] A traditional Jewish religious itinerant preacher, skilled as a narrator of Torah and religious stories. (Hence the name of the newspaper cited above).

[86] A "Beit Midrash" (Study House) associated with and led by a recognized and accepted strictly orthodox and scholarly rabbi usually as part of the synagogue complex.

[87] Original footnote 32. In the book "Thirty Years in Lithuania and Poland" (Yiddish) written by Abba Gordin, he brings a few details on this chapter, together with the dismay in the city because of the famine and the cholera epidemic.

Chapter Seven: The Murder of Alexander II and Its Outcomes for the Jews
The Knowledge of the Murder – Oaths of Loyalty for the New Tsar –
Alexander III Hater of Israel – Awakening to Nationalist Activity –
Vows for the Good of the Settlement in the Land[88]

The first of March 1881 fell on *Purim* day. The morning of that day arrived with stunning news from Petersburg for the Governor of the Province – that Alexander II, the Tsar of Russia, had been murdered. In Augustów panic and confusion prevailed. The community leaders instructed the Jewish residents to refrain from joy and from the celebration of a holy day, according to the law of the day, and certainly not to do it publicly. They should not sing, or dance or wear masks[89] lest they bring upon themselves slander and libel. It would make them odious in the eyes of their gentile haters, the members of the Russian people, to see them rejoicing over the calamity. It was advertised that the following morning during prayers in the synagogue every Jew must swear an oath of loyalty to the new Tsar.

The following morning was *Shushan Purim;*[90] the synagogue was filled from end to end with men, women, and children. The Ministers, governors and police all came. Rabbi Gordin read the oath from the document, first in Russian then in Hebrew translation, and all the people repeated after him word for word. On the table of the reader's platform a *Torah*[91] scroll lay open; the *Aron Kodesh*[92] was also open. The police warned {p. 46} everyone that any person who failed to come and participate in the oath-taking ceremony would be severely punished to the full extent of the law as a rebel against the State; more than that, they further warned specifically that they – the police – would very carefully supervise to ensure that every Jew would repeat accurately the entire contents of the oath. Anyone who sinned by incorrectly pronouncing the words or who refrained from saying them would be fined.

Concerning the new Tsar, Alexander III, at the time, all they knew was this: that he was decisive in his views, brave, courageous, and steadfast, a clear hater of Israel, surrounded by evil advisors, wicked men, and bitter enemies of Jews.

Immediately after the festival of *Pesach*, saddening rumors began to arrive of attacks against the Jews in Alita, Belozirka, Yelisavetgrad, and several other cities in southern Russia.

Although there were no pogroms in Augustów after the murder of Alexander II, lawless people set fire to the town and on the bitter day, nothing remained of the toil of many years.

At that time a new heralding voice arrived that one great philanthropist, a wealthy Jewish financier, with great wealth, – Baron Hirsch was his name – whose only son had died young, decided to create a memorial monument to his only son. With that purpose in mind he acquired a large tract of land in Argentina, intending to settle it with Russian Jewish exiles impacted by the pogroms, so that they could build new lives for themselves. However, at the same time, a pamphlet appeared, authored by a medical doctor in Odessa - Leon Pinsker – entitled "Self-liberation" (Auto-Emancipation), and the motto of the pamphlet was : "If I am not for me then who will be for me?"[93] Dr. Pinsker explains and proves with evidence and proof that there is no hope of improving the condition of the Jews of Russia and Rumania while they are dependent on the "table of others" and live by the kindness of rulers and ministers who are not generous to them; that the matter of pogroms is not a passing thing, but a plague that spreads and fells many slain. There is

---

[88] Of Israel.
[89] All of these would be customary *Purim* activities.
[90] *Shushan Purim* falls on Adar 15 and is the day on which Jews in Jerusalem celebrate *Purim*.
[91] The Five Books of Moses, or Pentateuch.
[92] Holy ark.
[93] Hillel in *Pirkei Avot* 1:14 "If I am not for myself, who will be for me? If I am not for others, what am I? And if not now, when?"

no recommendation therefore but to gather together the far-flung of Israel to one place, where it will be possible to build a new life on new foundations, where the Jews would stand on their own, and in that way the Jewish problem would be solved. Jewish writers of the day – M. L. Lilienblum,[94] David Gordon,[95] Peretz Smolenskin[96] and others were seized by this idea and began publishing articles in "*HaMelitz,*"[97, 98] "*HaMaggid,*"[99] and *HaShachar,*"[100] all of one opinion, that only by settling the Land of Israel would the redemption of the Jews arise.

The newspapers were also reporting that in Paris an exceptionally rich person, wishing for the moment to remain anonymous, and hiding behind the name "The well-known philanthropist" was the one who was offering his opinion and his pocket for the settlement of the land of Israel.

When these stories reached the ears of the young people among the Jews in Poland and Russia, they aroused within them the aspiration for freedom and liberty. When the distinguished officer Sir Moses Montefiore[101] celebrated his one-hundredth birthday, the Warsaw branch of "*Chovevei Tzion* "[102] published his photograph, accompanied by a laudatory poem composed by the national poet Y. L. Gordon.[103] That photograph was distributed by the young people of Augustów and there was almost no home that did not have the Montefiore picture hung in it. The income was entirely dedicated to the fund for working the land[104] in the land of Israel. They adopted a new custom that on each and every *Shabbat*, those who were called for the reading of the *Torah* would pledge a donation towards the settlement of the country. Also, on the eve of *Yom Kippur*, they would place a bowl for the good of the redemption of the land, and each Jew who gave *tzedakah*,[105] a redemption for the soul, on the eve of *Yom HaDin*[106] contributed from a desire to give a proper donation for this lofty and sacred purpose.

The pogroms in Russia spilled much blood, and caused much grief and agony. However, they also aroused the people from a deep sleep to a new life. Also, our land, which was sunk in a long sleep, the sleep of Honi the Circle-Maker,[107] {p. 47} now awoke for revival. No longer will it

---

[94] Moshe Leib Lilienblum, 1843- 1910, was a Jewish scholar and author

[95] Aharon David Gordon, 1856–1922, Zionist thinker.

[96] Peretz Smolenskin, 1842–1885, Zionist writer and thinker of the Jewish enlightenment, founder and editor of the Hebrew journal *HaShachar* (The Dawn).

[97] "The Advocate."

[98] The oldest Hebrew newspaper in Russia, founded by Aleksander Zederbaum, in Odessa, in 1860.

[99] A Hebrew-language weekly published first in Prussia and afterward in Berlin, Krakow, and Vienna from 1856 to 1903.

[100] "The Dawn," a Hebrew journal which was published and edited in Vienna by Peretz Smolenskin from 1868 to 1884.

[101] Sir Moses Chaim Montefiore, 1784 – 1885, was a British financier and banker, activist, philanthropist and Sheriff of London. Sir Moses Montefiore's activities on behalf of the Jews in the land of Israel included plans to acquire land to help them become self-sufficient. He also attempted to bring industry to the country by introducing a printing press and a textile factory. He inspired the founding of several agricultural settlements; Yemin Moshe, a settlement outside of Jerusalem's Old City, was named for him.

[102] Lovers of Zion.

[103] Yehudah Leib Gordon 1831–1892, the most important Hebrew poet of the nineteenth century and a leading figure of the Russian enlightenment movement.

[104] Working the land with their own hands was an important principal in the thinking of the early Zionists.

[105] The word "*tzedakah*," while frequently translated as "charity," actually means "righteousness," because giving to a cause or a needy person is considered a commandment, the righteous thing to do, not out of the goodness of one's heart, as the word "charity" implies.

[106] *Yom Kippur*.

[107] Babylonian *Talmud Taanit* 23a: "… All the days of the life of that righteous man, Ḥoni, he was distressed over the meaning of this verse: "A song of Ascents: When the Lord brought back those who returned to Zion, we were like those who dream" (Psalms 126:1). He said to himself: Is there really a person who can sleep and dream for seventy years? How is it possible to compare the seventy-year exile in Babylonia to a dream? One day, he was walking along

be said "the land of the dead," where only the elderly and the aged come to stretch themselves out over the graves of ancestors and for the privilege of being buried in the dust of the Holy Land when their time comes, but rather, it will be called the "land of the living," because the strength of the young, strength full of power and vitality, will enliven it, and they will plant eternal life within it.[108]

Chapter Eight. Blood and Fire and Pillars of Smoke[109,110]

Christian and Jewish Fire-brigades – An Invisible Hand of the Igniters of Pogroms - Jewish Guard Posts Night and Day - Two Thousand Jewish Families Without a Roof – Help from the Neighboring Towns and from Dr. Rilf of Memel – Unexpected Help From the Cossacks.

One of the most common events in many Jewish towns during the summer days was to be an eyewitness to the sight of fires that were ignited, intentionally or unintentionally. The announcers and heralds were the large bells in the churches. These were the bells that sounded a mighty and powerful sound, from one side of town to the other; these were the bells that would herald good days and bad days, holidays, or the occurrence of fire. The fire-fighters are already ringing the bells with clanging cymbals and with loud-clashing cymbals,[111] going through the city with their vehicles loaded with equipment to extinguish fires: tanks of water, hoses coiled like snakes across entire streets, iron ladders whose legs are set on the ground,[112] and whose tops reach the highest story in town, the brass helmets on their heads, axes and probes on their thighs, steel vests on their chests, hurrying to save whoever it was still possible to save; working with fire and water without fear or terror; jumping and leaping from place to place and extricating its prey from the jaws of the blaze.

In cities where the population was mostly Jewish, most of the firefighters were also of the children of Israel. Artisans, butchers, but also the reckless and good-for-nothings who loved to glorify themselves and dress themselves up in the uniform of the fire workers. The children and the youths admired and respected them a lot and when there was a line of fire, the youths would run quickly after them to increase the commotion. And when they were in cities where most of the

---

the road when he saw a certain man planting a carob tree. Ḥoni said to him: This tree, after how many years will it bear fruit? The man said to him: It will not produce fruit until seventy years have passed. Ḥoni said to him: Is it obvious to you that you will live seventy years, that you expect to benefit from this tree? He said to him: That man himself found a world full of carob trees. Just as my ancestors planted for me, I too am planting for my descendants. Sleep overcame him and he slept. A cliff formed around him, and he disappeared from sight and slept for seventy years. When he awoke, he saw a certain man gathering carobs from that tree. Ḥoni said to him: Are you the one who planted this tree? The man said to him: I am his son's son. Ḥoni said to him: I can learn from this that I have slept for seventy years..."

[108] From the blessing recited after the *Torah* reading: "Blessed are You, Adonai our God, Sovereign of the universe, who has given us a *Torah* of truth, and implanted eternal life within us..."

[109] Original footnote 33. Information about the fires in Augustow came from the Hebrew weekly "*HaTzefirah*," five times one after another, with different signatures: On 10 *Sivan* 5641 [1881] with the signature of Avraham Yaakov Ilsheski and Shabtai Rosental; on 17 *Sivan* 5641, with the signature of the writer Avraham Mordechai Piyurko, from Grayevo, the government-appointed Rabbi Y. Stein; on 8 *Tammuz* 5641 with the signature of Avraham Yaakov Gatsky and Rabbi Katriel Aharon Natan ; on 28 *Av* 5641 Shabtai Rosental, Naphtali Trovesh, and Yehudah Kahana; and on 2 *Mar Cheshvan* 5642 [1882] the four previous signatures. Also in "*HaMelitz*" there twice came information about the fires: on 17 *Tammuz* 5641, with the signature of Yisrael Yitzchak Ivri , and on 22 *Tammuz* 5641 with the signature of Rabbi Katriel Aharon Natan. Information about the fires in the city also came in other newspapers.

[110] Joel 3:3 "Before the great and terrible day of the LORD comes, I will set portents in the sky and on earth: blood and fire and pillars of smoke."

[111] Psalm 150:5 "Praise Him with clanging cymbals; praise Him with loud-clashing cymbals."

[112] Genesis 28:12 "He had a dream; a stairway was set on the ground and its top reached to the sky, and angels of God were going up and down on it."

population was Christian, most of the firemen were Christians also and the homes and property of the Jews were "...as clay in the hands of the Creator."[113] They did not always hurry to fulfill their duty to extinguish the fires in the house of the village, without difference in religion or race. Here too the hand of hatred of the Jews filled no small role.

According to the law, every resident of the town was indeed obligated to have ready in his house a hose and a fire-axe, or any other implement for extinguishing a fire. But that was only according to the law, and no one did it. When a fire broke out in town, they went from door to door looking for the equipment that was required by law to be in each house. It so happened that there was an outbreak of fire in a near-by town, and they summoned the firefighters from Augustów. They went in haste, taking with them the only hose of the city that they had that would send water to most. When they arrived at the site of the tragedy a miracle occurred; it became clear that the hose discharged not water but spirit-water.[114] (In secret ways like this they would transport brandy or other strong drink into the city, and they had not yet had time to empty it and convey it to the clients.)

That same summer there were many fires in the towns and the Jewish residents were left naked {p. 48} and lacking everything, without a roof over their heads and without covering for their bodies. Those burnt out of their homes cried out for help, turning to the communities with announcements and public appeal in newspapers, asking for food and lodging.

It is possible to suppose that an invisible hand arranged these fires. Augustów, whose population at that time was mainly Christian, suffered greatly from the damage of the fires. The firefighters, who were mostly Christians, tried to save the homes of the Christians, and skipped over the homes of the Jews. In "*HaTzefirah*"[115] (18 *Iyar* 5635 [May 23, 1875]), we find a report from the son of the town's Rabbi of a fire that broke out in one house, and like a destroying angel, in a few moments swept over the many wooden houses surrounding it. From there the blaze reached mansions, and warehouses full of merchandise. About sixty homes went up in flames on the pyre and left the residents destitute. The reporter continues to say that it was terrible to see the unfortunate ones wandering around in the streets without shelter.

Since then about three years passed. It is not known how the victims of the blaze were restored, who gave them assistance, or how many homes were rebuilt. But again, in the month of *Sivan* 5641 (1881) at the end of *Shabbat*, again a fire broke out {p. 49} in a cowshed belonging to a Jew. The informer of this in the newspaper reports on the mood of the town's Jewish people after they read of the pogroms that broke out against the Jews in southern Russia, and the good people of the Jewish population of Augustów were aroused by the cry of brokenness to collect donations for the unfortunate and devastated. In a moment, the wheel turned for them, the town was engulfed in flame, and the donors became the receivers. Within the space of half an hour, more than three hundred houses had gone up in flames, and among them the great *Beit Midrash* , that was built magnificently, with all the holy books. Only the *Torah* scrolls were saved. Even the rabbi's home and the government school, and all the *cheders* of the poor were lost. There were also losses of human souls. A Jewish child was burnt to death and even his bones were not found; many old and young people were severely burned on their hands and faces by the flames. Over six hundred families, about a thousand people, were left naked and lacking everything.

---

[113] Jeremiah 18:6 "… Just like clay in the hands of the potter, so are you in My hands, O House of Israel!"
[114] Alcohol.
[115] The Claxon.

The Fire Brigade

Standing from right to left:
M. Tanenbaum; Denmark, G.; Rotenberg, M.; Rechtman, Y.; Lonshel.; Y. Strozinski;
Second row: L. Lonshel; M. Goldshmidt ; Unknown; Y. Zeligzon;
Third row: Unknown; Unknown; L. Rechtman; M. Kolfenitzki; Domovitz; Unknown; M. Rechtman's daughter.

The Road to Suwalki

Even before the winds had died down from the fire at the end of *Shabbat*, the following Wednesday a fire again broke out. This time a hundred homes were consumed by fire. To great panic, a fire also broke out in the nearby town of Szczuczyn, and there too, about twenty houses burned in one street, large mansions, among the nicest in the town, and also the great library of Rabbi Shlomo Katzprovski of Szczuczyn. Again, hundreds of families were left dwelling under the dome of the sky, children and old people, women and babies, with no cover from the heat of a blazing sun or from the rain from the heavens. Even those that remained as a remnant couldn't stay in their homes because the fear of a further outbreak by the hands of criminals had turned the residents' nights into days.

{p. 50} The night had become a time for watching and the day – a time for recovery. The fire equipment of the brigades stood ready in the market square for any trouble, may it not come. Trade stopped entirely. The buyer didn't buy for lack of means and the vendor was full of worry.

In a note that came about a month later in the same newspaper, the writer points out that: "They did not know the reason for the first fire in Augustów, and they thought that it was simply by chance. However, afterwards they were convinced that it was not by chance, but that the hands of foreign enemies were accomplices. The same criminal hands just a few days later ignited the fire in the Jewish man's cow shed. As a result of that fire almost all of the houses of "The Long Street" were burned, most of them the houses of Jews, among them a *kloiz*.[116] Panic was rife in the town. The faces of the residents of the city showed worry of what might be coming. Five days later, after the second fire, suddenly again the shouted warning: "Fire! Fire in Krakovska Street." To our joy, three Christians who had lit the fire were caught at the scene. Even after, the evildoers did not stop carrying out their plots, and the following day tried yet again to set a fire on Krakovska Street, but this time they missed the target "because in these hard days we gave no rest to our eyes, and all work in our city ceased, and day and night we were on guard, for only a moment,[117] until the fire was put out and no damage was done." Indeed, the Psalmist has said: "unless the LORD watches over the city, the watchman keeps vigil in vain."[118] About two weeks after this, at midnight, the evil doers again carried out their plans in Krakovska Street and this time caused complete destruction in our city, and from the whole town nothing remained but the Great Synagogue, and one *kloiz,* and about forty Jewish houses scattered here and there. After all this, the reckless ones continued with their threats, with their hands reaching out to destroy our homes so that we would leave their country. Two thousand Jewish families in Augustów have been left naked and lacking everything, while those wandering the streets openly expect starvation from lack of support." The writer highly praises the Jews of Tovalk who did so much for the Jews of Augustow in these terrible times, in sending them wagons loaded with bread and food and clothing, in addition to hundreds of rubles.

Seven weeks passed, and in the same newspaper again a note told that within one month alone, five fires had broken out in Augustów, one after the other, and from all the houses of the Jews there remained just a few embers rescued from the fire. Many were aroused from the near and far cities to send aid to them. Even though the small amount did not fulfill the needs of the many, it was possible to speedily dispatch some assistance to the needy. Transports of bread, food and articles were received from many towns, including cash. Among the donors who contributed were included the names of respected Christians, like the nobleman Markovitz from Netta, the nobleman Bokovski from Pomian, the estate owner Shveida in Kolnitza, the Justice of the Peace, the notary. Donations were also received from Warsaw, Rigrod, Grayevo, Sapotzkin, Lomza, Szczuczyn, Sejny, Sztabin, Filipova, Halinka, Prirushla Stavisk, Lek, Kalvaria, Mariampol, Lipsk,

---

[116] A place of study for adult Jewish men.
[117] Proverbs 12:19 "Truthful speech abides forever, A lying tongue for but a moment."
[118] Psalm 127:1.

Ludvinova, Lazdie, Vilkovitz, Seirijai, Sidra, Šakiai, Dombrova. Also, there entered into the burden of the help the wise Rabbi Rilf from the city of Memel, who sent a significant sum of money with a promise to produce additional money.

In an additional report in the same paper about two months later it was told that the help coming from the many near and far towns and villages had decreased. They had done their part in the early days of the tragedy of the fires – and then stopped. In contrast to that, Rabbi Dr. Rilf from the city of Memel continued to see to means for the purpose of rehabilitation {p. 51} of those affected in Augustów with the cooperation of his friends, Luria and Yechiya Vitkind, who from time to time sent significant sums of money to the town, out of consideration that the *Yamim Nora'im, Rosh Hashanah* and *Yom Kippur*, and the festivals, were approaching. Even Baron Ginzburg from Peterburg showed an interest in the situation of those affected in the city, and contributed 5000 rubles for their welfare. Likewise, the noble "well-known philanthropist," Sir Moses Montefiore in London, was kind enough to send his donation.

The frequent fires of course confused the Jews of the city. Families began to roam from apartment to apartment in the few houses that remained, or they left "until the fury passes," in their finding shelter in the nearby towns.

The heads of the *yeshivot* and rabbis of the local towns would visit from time to time, and showed interest in the youth of the place who arrived for years of learning, and transferred them to various institutes of learning, according to their abilities. The historians of these towns record that only thanks to the fires that from time to time befell the wooden houses that filled the villages, the residents arrived at the conclusion that it was better to change from wooden structures to walled houses made of stone and other materials, and many villages, thanks to that, became nicer, with tall houses among them, and also some houses built with multiple stories.

The rehabilitation of the houses of the Jews of Augustów was not done in one fell swoop. The damage was too great. For a long time, most of the streets stood full of mounds of destruction, heaps of sooty bricks, charred wood, and ash. People wandered around stooped over and searched through the ashes.

The economic situation after the frequent fires that engulfed virtually all the houses in town was very bad. However, precisely at that time that a new battalion of Cossacks were stationed in the barracks who were good customers; they bought whatever came to hand. Apparently, they came from a distant region of Siberia where there was nothing to be had even for money; here they found a selection of items and products to buy. Indeed, there were no shops, for they had all been burned. In their place the shopkeepers put up "kiosks" (a temporary stall of a table with a fabric cover against the rains). The proceeds were good enough, until they would be able to get the shopkeepers, economically, back on their feet, and to rehabilitate many of the people of the city, who saw it as help from heaven.

The frequent fires served as dates for births and deaths. The women, when they were talking about the age of acquaintances or relatives, would say: this one was born at the time of the first fire, this one at the second fire, this one at the third, and so on.

On the other hand, the fires aroused the thought among the Jewish residents to seek a more secure place to live outside of the city borders, either by internal migration or by migration to another country. The question was – to where?

Chapter Nine: With the Death of Alexander III (1894)

The Memorial for Rabbi Gordin in the Synagogue - A Big Market and a
Municipal Garden – A Synagogue and a *Beit Midrash* – Rabbis of the City,
Geonim[119] and Scholars – Russian Army Stationed in the City – Jewish
Soldiers in the Guard Corps – The Event of a Jewish Soldier Who Married a
Young Woman – Rabbi Gordin's Halakhic[120] Response – The Mourning in
Augustów Over the Death of the Kovno Rabbi.

In Augustow there was felt seriousness and restrained joy. The heart was full to its banks
with happiness, together with a feeling of concern not to display the feelings publicly. This tension
was especially felt in the home of Rabbi Yehuda Leib Gordin, who was also the government-
appointed rabbi. About an hour ago, the Mayor of the town visited him, a patriotic Polish Christian,
but he knew to hide his affection for the Homeland. He entered the rabbi's house with a grimacing
face affecting sadness. "Our Tsar is dead" he stated in a restrained tone, full of restrained joy and
affected grief – "We must announce from tomorrow the days of mourning." The rabbi agreed with
him that the Russian Homeland had suffered a great loss.

The Polish residents of the town rejoiced. They knew that the Jews were no less happy
than they were, but everyone was concerned not to reveal their joy openly. The fear was especially
great of the "angry ones" in the city. The rabbi immediately informed all of the family heads in
the city, to all the synagogue *shammashim*[121] and *gabbaim*.[122] The next day candles were lit in all
prayer houses. The rabbi ordered the community to recite Psalm 109.[123] All the government
officials came. The large *Beit Midrash* was full to overflowing. The rabbi himself concluded with
sorrowful moaning devotion, with heavenly tones in his baritone voice the verses of the Psalm:

"9: May his children be orphans, his wife a widow. 10: May his children wander from their
hovels, begging in search of [bread]. 11: May his creditor seize all his possessions; may

---

[119] The Hebrew word *gaon* (plural: *geonim*) literally means "genius", but in this context, it is used as an honorific for
the spiritual leader of the town, who decided questions of Jewish law, headed the Jewish courts and rabbinical
academies, and ultimately had the final say in the religious life of the Jewish community.

[120] *Halakhah* is Jewish law.

[121] The Hebrew word used here, *shamash,* refers to the sexton, or caretaker of a synagogue. It is also the word used
for the candle with which we light the eight candles of *Chanukah.*

[122] The term *gabbai* means "collector." In this context, it was the title given to a person charged with collecting funds.

[123] Quite an ironic choice: "For the leader. Of David. A psalm. O God of my praise, do not keep aloof, 2: for the
wicked and the deceitful open their mouth against me; they speak to me with lying tongue. 3: They encircle me with
words of hate; they attack me without cause. 4: They answer my love with accusation 5: They repay me with evil for
good, with hatred for my love. 6: Appoint a wicked man over him; may an accuser stand at his right side; 7: may he
be tried and convicted; may he be judged and found guilty. 8: May his days be few; may another take over his
position...13: may his posterity be cut off; may their names be blotted out in the next generation. 14: May God be
ever mindful of his father's iniquity, and may the sin of his mother not be blotted out. 15: May the LORD be aware
of them always and cause their names to be cut off from the earth, 16: because he was not minded to act kindly, and
hounded to death the poor and needy man, one crushed in spirit. 17: He loved to curse—may a curse come upon him!
He would not bless—may blessing be far from him! 18: May he be clothed in a curse like a garment, may it enter his
body like water, his bones like oil. 19: Let it be like the cloak he wraps around him, like the belt he always wears. 20:
May the LORD thus repay my accusers, all those who speak evil against me. 21: Now You, O God, my Lord, act on
my behalf as befits Your name. Good and faithful as You are, save me. 22: For I am poor and needy, and my heart is
pierced within me. 23: I fade away like a lengthening shadow; I am shaken off like locusts. 24: My knees give way
from fasting; my flesh is lean, has lost its fat. 25: I am the object of their scorn; when they see me, they shake their
head. 26: Help me, O LORD, my God; save me in accord with Your faithfulness, 27: that men may know that it is
Your hand, that You, O LORD, have done it. 28: Let them curse, but You bless; let them rise up, but come to grief,
while Your servant rejoices. 29: My accusers shall be clothed in shame, wrapped in their disgrace as in a robe. 30: My
mouth shall sing much praise to the LORD; I will acclaim Him in the midst of a throng, 31: because He stands at the
right hand of the needy, to save him from those who would condemn him."

strangers plunder his wealth. 12: May no one show him mercy; may none pity his orphans…"

The rabbi finished reciting the whole chapter and the head of the city almost entirely poured himself out with grief…[124]

Nevertheless, the city of Augustów continued to develop as it had done since coming under the yoke of Russian rule. Its population continued to grow bigger. What did the city look like during the second half of the 19th Century? We find a few details about this in the book whose author[125]* spent the years of his youth there and knew it well.

Augustów was then a clean and beautiful city surrounded by forests. The city center was the market and in its center there was a city park with a podium for military bands.

In the city were found all the Jewish institutions common to Jewish communities all over the world and in Israel. First of all, a magnificent synagogue, the first in the city, which was in the fortieth year of the 19th Century. The synagogue was erected a long time after there was already a "congregation" in the town. The synagogue had a large courtyard in the front. The youth and the children were afraid to walk past this respected and admired building at night because of their belief that the dead congregated there at night to pray. In the *Beit Midrash*, they were engaged, {p. 53} as was the pattern in all the cities and towns in those days, in prayer and in the study of the *Torah*. There was a *Talmud* society, and a *Mishnah* society, a society for the study of the *Kuzari*[126] and "*Chovevot HaLevavot*,"[127] "*Ein Yaakov*,"[128] and the recitation of the Psalms, to which belonged "*amcha*."[129] The *Beit Midrash* was packed full in the evenings. At the beginning of the twentieth century, there were five synagogues in Augustów in addition to the *kloizim*. We can get a general idea of the *Kloizim,* from the list of signatories of various societies: "The Bridge *Kloiz*" – its Treasurer son of Reb[130] Betzalel son of Reb Yaakov; "the New *Kloiz*" - its Treasurer Reb Ze'ev the son of Reb Dovid the Levi; "the *Torah* Society *Kloiz*" – its Treasurer Reb Dovid son of Reb Eliyahu Dobovski; "the Society of the Scripture *Kloiz*" – its Treasurer Reb Moshe son of Reb Shlomo; "the *Chevre Kadisha Kloiz*"[131] – its Treasurer Reb Shachne Kostinski; "the *Kloiz* of the *Chayei Adam* Society"[132] - its Treasurer Reb Peretz, *shochet u'bodek;*[133] the Great *Beit Midrash* - its Treasurer Reb Sholom Berkovitz; the Hospital – Reb Zanvil Leib Varhaftig; The *Tiferet Bachurim* Society;[134] The "*Ein Yaakov*" group of the Bridge *Kloiz*; the *Kloiz* of the Long Street; the *Kloiz* of the *Chassidim*.[135] And also the treasurers are mentioned: Reb Chaim Breiman, Reb Yom-Tov Lipman the prayer leader, Reb Kaddish son of Reb Mordechai Arieh, *shochet u'bodek.*

---

[124] Original footnote 34. A portion of this is told by Abba Gordin in his book, mentioned above. Part I recorded from the mouth of *Rebbetzin* [the title of a rabbi's wife] Zelda Edelstein-Koshelevski, and part I found in Hebrew newspapers in the form of news.

[125] Original note: *Abba Gordin

[126] Written by Yehudah HaLevi (1075 – 1141), originally in Arabic, in Spain.

[127] "The Duties of the Heart" is the primary work of the Jewish rabbi and philosopher, Bahya ben Yoseph ibn Pakuda, written in Spain in the 11th century.

[128] "The Well of Jacob," composed in Spain by Levi ibn Habib/Jacob ibn Habib (1490 - c.1550), is a compilation of all the legends found in the *Talmud* together with commentaries.

[129] Literally "your people," this expression refers to "the simple masses." In English one might say "folk."

[130] The honorific "*Reb*" is generally used for all men, and means "Mr." It is not to be confused with the term "*HaRav,*" which means "The Rabbi."

[131] The *Chevra Kadisha*, or "Holy Society," was the name for the Burial Society.

[132] Written by Rabbi Avraham Danzig (1748-1820) in Poland, this book deals with the laws discussed in the *Orech Chaim* section of the *Shulchan Aruch*, which are about daily conduct, prayer, *Shabbat*, and holidays.

[133] Ritual slaughter and meat inspector.

[134] The Splendor of Young Men; a rabbinical academy.

[135] "Pious Ones."

The old cemetery is found really in the middle of the city, next to the *Kloiz* of the *Chassidim* It is clear that at the time of its establishment, it was outside of the city, but over the course of time, the area became filled with dwelling places. The cemetery consisted of a small area with gravestones sunken in the earth. It had already been locked for a long time, from a lack of space, and they would only visit it on *Tisha B'Av*.[136] The new cemetery, founded during the time of the Russian conquest, was far from the city, across the river. Over the course of time it became closer to the city.

One of the heads of the veteran families in the city was Reb Leizer Keinan, a householder among his people, one of the first in the Jewish settlement of the city, and his wife, Feigl. They had six daughters who married the sons of respected families in town, who were at once symbols of the *Torah* and greatness. Over the course of time they became respected public figures. The daughters were all girls of virtue. Leah was married to Arieh Lap, Beila to the Rabbi Dovid Mordechai Markus, Devorah to Zalman Arieh Kopciovski, Channah to Yisrael Grosberg, Zlata to Yaakov Frenkel, who was a writer and *Maskil*.[137] The sixth daughter married a man from the city and they settled in Grodno.

Treasurers and community elders in town in various periods were: Shmuel Eisenstadt, Barukh Leib Otshein, Yisrael Grosberg, Shmuel Grinberg , Binyamin Veirach, Dovid Shlomo Varhaftig, Shimon Varhaftig, Yehuda Kahan, Zalman Leviush, Dovid Slutzky, Yehuda Leib Levatinski (the head of the city at the time of the German conquest), Leib Lap, Yosef Barukh Margoliot, Dovid Mordechai Markus, Zalman Kopciovski, Reuven Rotenberg, Dovid Leib Aleksandrovitz, B. Lieberman. In the Long Street (Długa), there lived a righteous man, Rebbe Shepsel Panos, a shop owner who sold each day just enough for him to live on, after which he locked the shop. He was much esteemed in the city, and many children were named for him.

Augustów had a library with a wealth of books in various languages. In the city, there was a strong movement of "*Chovevei Tzion*" and there could be seen in it the first buds of the illegal socialist movement. The elders of the city used to tell that "they" (the socialists), did "something terrible" and on one occasion detectives arrived in a carriage, caught them and led them away, and no one knows where they disappeared to, and it was forbidden to talk too much about it…

Among the Rabbis who, from time to time came to visit the city and to preach to the congregation and disseminate was the well-known rabbi, Yisrael Meir son of Arieh Ze'ev the *Cohain* from Radin, the "*Chofetz Chayim*.[138]

{p. 54}The Lithuanian towns, even the smallest among them, always aspired to seat the most famous rabbis. Even Augustów didn't fall short of the other towns, in that respect. It is interesting to note that the rabbis of Augustów were far from the type referred to by the *Maskilim* as "dark ones."[139] When Augustów searched for a rabbi, the heads of the community first tried to find out if the rabbi understood spirit of the time. The substance of the fact that all these rabbis were more or less close to the hearts of the local *Maskilim* demonstrates the strength of the "*Haskalah*"[140] in Augustów.

Dr. Nachum Slouschz,[141] the great Hebrew researcher and writer, recorded in his impressions of his journeys on the Jews of the area these characterizing words: "They are all

---

[136] The ninth day of the Hebrew month *Av* – the day on which both the First and Second Temples were destroyed.

[137] The *Maskilim* were adherents of the Jewish enlightenment movement that began in Eastern Europe in the early nineteenth century and was active until the rise of the Jewish national movement in the early 1880s.

[138] "*Chafetz Chaim*": seeks life. From Psalm 34:13 "Who is the man who seeks life, loves days to see good?"

[139] Meaning, "not enlightened," or, opposed to progress.

[140] Enlightenment.

[141] Nachum Slouschz (1872-1966) was a Russian-born Israeli writer, translator and archaeologist.

walking on the 'Golden Mean'[142]...There are no great *Torah* scholars, but here there are many house-holders who know *Torah*. There are no outstanding *Maskilim* here but the 'Enlightenment', especially the practical one, has spread everywhere without awakening fanaticism. There is no anarchy here, but neither is there excessive fanaticism."[143]

Owing to the closeness of the Prussian border to the Augustów region, the ideas of Moses Mendelssohn,[144] who lived in Berlin, spread more quickly. Even the writer Y.SH. Weiss (Yehoshua Halivni), who dwelt in the area, relates that the local people had been much influenced by Mendelssohn's ideas. Jews from Augustów visited many towns in the area, in both in the "Pale of Settlement"[145] and outside it, and more than one of them was attracted to some extent to the new ways of life. It also happened that Jews from large cities, in which Jewish life already had a different face, moved to Augustów.

After the failure of the Polish revolution, special barracks to house soldiers were erected in Augustów. It was not a small garrison. There were also found not a small number of Jews in the contingent, some of whom would come and go in the homes of Jews in Augustów. Also, the many soldiers influenced the new way of life.

In the center of the marketplace, they would conduct training exercises for the newly recruited troops. In them they would teach them how to march properly, to stretch themselves out like strings and like stone statues. They taught them how to hold a rifle and carry it on the shoulder, to thrust a bayonet into the heart of a man made of straw, and so on. A large group of adults and youths always gathered to watch the soldiers' training, how they all as one lifted their right leg and lowered it at the same time, all of them together. In the eyes of many it seemed to be an interesting display. In the city there also dwelt Cossacks, among them were some natives of Kalmykia wearing nose-rings and also some black-skinned people. They would host the Jewish soldiers among them in Jewish homes for *Shabbatot* and Festivals.[146] On time, the following event occurred: There was a party in one of the "Swedish" families (by this name was known those who would leave the city for a few months of the year and travel to Sweden to peddle. There were a few such families in Augustów and they were considered wealthy). A Jewish soldier placed a ring on the finger of a mature adult girl and said: "Behold, by this ring you are consecrated to me according to the law of Moses and Israel," in the presence of a few friends, also soldiers, as witnesses.[147] The matter was talked about by everyone. The girl's mother was crying and wailing. The father, one of the so-called "Swedes," was not at home, but he was informed and arrived speedily at home. The match was not to their liking. The girl was her parents' only child, and the man who had wed her was an ignorant uneducated person, {p. 55} the son of simple folk from Odessa. What did they do? They turned to the rabbi of the city, Rabbi Yehuda Leib Gordin, with a request that he come to their aid in this desperate moment and save them from the embarrassment that had been caused them. Meanwhile the Jews of the city were confused by this event, to the point where they were afraid to admit the Jewish soldiers into homes where there were mature daughters. The parents of the girl

---

[142] The middle path.

[143] Original footnote 35. See in the book "A Journey Across Lithuania" by Dr. Nachum Slouschz.

[144] 1729 – 1786.

[145] The territories of the Russian Empire where Jews were permitted to live.

[146] Original footnote 37. In "*HaMelitz*" 23 *Cheshvan* 5657-1896 a thank-you letter published from a Jewish soldier Yosef Tzvi Kantorovitz Maihomon in the name of forty-four Jews who served in the reserve forces in Augustow, to Rabbi Eliezer Shapira and his son Zalman-Tzvi and the rest of the youths who took care of the matter of good *kosher* food over the course of two weeks, after receiving a special permit from the army to organize for them a special kitchen for the festivals.

[147] This is how a wife is acquired in Judaism, by placing a ring on her finger and making the above-mentioned statement, in the presence of two witnesses.

offered the soldier compensatory money on condition that he gave the daughter a *get*,[148] but he refused. Then again: if he gave her a *get*, she would become "divorced," and what respectable young man would agree to marry a divorcée? If so, she would be likely to remain with her virginity until her hair turns white, or she is married to a divorced man or a widower. In short, here was a real problem and the embarrassment was great. Only the "*Mara D'Atra*,[149] the rabbi of the city, would be able to help. Rabbi Gordin shut himself up in a room in the *Beit Din*[150] to raise the matter in the form of "Question and Answer."[151] Eventually he cancelled the marriage[152] of the soldier, since he found a defect in the soldiers who were the witnesses. He saw them smoking on *Shabbat*, which is to say, that they were publicly desecrating the *Shabbat*. They also ate non-kosher food from the garrison kitchens and were "wanton" men.[153,154]

Jewish Soldiers in the Russian Army

The Rabbi didn't want to rely on himself. He found it proper to turn to the well-known rabbi of Kovno, Rabbi Yitzchak Elchanan Spektor, and sent him the response to the question that he had composed, which included his legal decision to nullify the marriage. After a few days, there arrived the Kovno rabbi's agreement with the "Response," the legal decision made by the rabbi from Augustów, and with that, the matter was concluded in the girl's favor. {p. 56} The event was

---

[148] A Jewish divorce.

[149] Aramaic for "the Master of the Place," that is, the local rabbi who has the sole rabbinic authority to decide local cases of Jewish law and practice.

[150] "House of Law," i.e. the rabbinical court.

[151] *"She'ailah ve-Teshuva,"* "Question and Answer," a process by which a question is brought to a rabbi who then studies all the relevant halakhic material to make an informed decision. This literature, also known as *"Responsa"* literature, is extensive and ongoing, even today.

[152] Literally, "sanctification."

[153] Original footnote 38. This event is told about in Abba Gordin's book, and in a halakhic form the event is described in his book "The Responsa of Yehudah" of the rabbi of Augustow, Rabbi Yehudah Leib Gordin, who acts in the role of a rabbi in the explication of the *halakhah*.

[154] And thus, unqualified to serve as witnesses in this case.

63

published in the books of "Questions and Answers" of the rabbi "*Teshuvot Yehuda*"[155] that appeared in Vilna in the year 5668-1908 with a substantiation of the testimony:

"As a panel of *dayanim*, they came before the three of us sitting together as one;[156] the young men, Zerach Kaplan, Chaim Garnist, and the young man Avraham Mattolski. All these young men were in a regiment of the army of His Imperial Majesty in the Augustow Battalion, and testified before us as follows: Avraham Mattolski stated that he saw with his own eyes how the man Shimon Sapozhnikov took in his hand by force the hand of virgin Mrs. Tz., and with his other hand took a silver coin[157] and thrust it by force into the hand of the woman mentioned above, and then saying to her: "Behold you are sanctified to me according to the law of Moses and Israel," and then instantly Shimon, mentioned above, jumped on her hand so that she would not throw the coin away. After a few moments (or minutes), Shimon, mentioned above, asked the woman to return the coin or at least show it to all the witnesses, but she did not wish to do so, but instead clasped her hand even tighter. Then Shimon, mentioned above, opened her hand by force, took the coin from her hand and threw it on the table. The other two witnesses, Zerach Kaplan and Chaim Garnist, also testified that they saw Shimon take hold of the hand of the woman, mentioned above, with compulsion, and by force thrust his hand into her hand and said to her "Behold you are sanctified to me according to the law of Moses and Israel," and after Shimon, mentioned above, had removed his hand from the hand of the woman, mentioned above, he held the woman's hand closed by force. And Shimon, mentioned above, said that he had done so in order that she not throw away the coin that he gave her. Afterwards Shimon asked that she return the coin to him, but she did not listen to his words, rather, she closed her hand even tighter and did not give him the coin. He then opened her hand by force, and from Shimon's hand the coin was flung on the table. Then these last two witnesses said they hadn't made sure to see if Shimon had actually given the coin to the girl or not, they had only seen Shimon thrust his hand into the woman's hand by force. And also afterwards, at the time that Shimon had opened the woman's hand by force, they did not make sure to see if Shimon had removed the coin from her hand or not, because they had not inspected closely to see it with their own eyes. All this the witnesses all testified before us and before the woman Tz., mentioned above, and also before her father. The woman Mrs. Tz. says she held her hand closed all the time walking down the slope of a hill and never saw or felt that any coin had come into her hand. And what the witnesses said, that afterwards that Shimon asked her to give back the coin and that she closed her hand even more tightly, she replied she did that with the intention of showing everyone that her hand was empty and there was nothing in it. The witnesses further testified that before this event occurred they did not speak at all making a match or a wedding. Afterwards, testimony was collected in the city of Horodna in a *Beit Din Tzedek*[158] there, how two "*kosher*"[159] witnesses testified against Avraham Mattolski that long ago they had seen him light a fire, and smoke publicly on the *Shabbat*, in the presence of Zerach Kaplan and Chaim Garnist, mentioned above, and about these last two witnesses there is gossip that they ate pork. Thus, that testimony was not collected according to the religion and law of *Torah*. But the testimony against Avraham, mentioned above, was according to the religion and law of *Torah*." After paragraph 41 came the signature: Yehuda Leib, Community Rabbi, Augustów.

The Rabbi of Kovno, considered to be the *gaon* of the generation in the rabbinic world, and a great influence in Russian government circles, was a kind of trusted colleague of Rabbi

---

[155] "The Answers of Judah."

[156] This is the formal introduction given by a *Beit Din* sitting in judgment on a legal question. This quoted passage is a mixture of Hebrew and Aramaic.

[157] Acceptance of a token of nominal value signifies a bride's agreement to the marriage.

[158] Jewish Court, requiring a panel of three judges.

[159] Fit or proper.

Gordin of Augustów in the matters of his "Questions and Answers," who turned to him on difficult matters, and would also visit him in a personal way. The drought of a few years earlier had not yet been forgotten, and had brought significant hunger, and when *Pesach* arrived the poor people of town had nothing to eat, because the *matzot* were insufficient. Rabbi Gordin reflected much on the problem and produced a pamphlet in the form of {p. 57} a "*Responsum.*" In the end, the *Responsum* concluded with permission to use corn (sorghum) and *kitniyot*[160] in a time of emergency[161] during the days of *Pesach*. But in this matter the local rabbi didn't want to take upon himself all the responsibility for the mentioned permission, and he turned with a "Question and Answer" to Rabbi Yitzchak Elchanan, and he agreed with Rabbi Gordin's decision. In his letter, Rabbi Yitzchak Elchanan included in his letter praise for the rabbi emphasizing the greatness of his learning, his acuity, and his expertise. The letter from Kovno did much to elevate the reputation of the rabbi in his town, Augustów. The letter passed from hand to hand in groups of the important householders. It is no wonder that with the passing of the *Gaon* in Kovno in 1896, it was considered in Rabbi Gordon's house as family mourning, and his home was filled with sorrow. The rabbi eulogized the deceased in the *Beit Midrash*, and enumerated his greatness in the *Torah* and community activity and the enormity of his loss to Judaism at this time. The *Beit Midrash* was full to overflowing, and even the women's section was full. The mourning sermon of the rabbi caused tears to flow from the eyes of the women and men. Rabbi Gordin's influence on all the groups was great. Since he was an excellent speaker, he caused them to stream to hear his substantive sermons. The rabbi also succeeded in drawing to him the *Maskilim* of the town, who were excited at hearing his orations in the Russian language, which was unblemished and rich in expression, that were spoken by him on royal coronation days, when officials of the government and military commanders would also rise early to go to the synagogue in order to hear his sermons.

Chapter Ten. The Years of Revolution and Migration

The Trade and Artisanship in Jewish Hands – *Chassidim* in Augustów –
Jewish Evasion of Induction into the Russian Army – The Beginnings of
Socialism – Meetings, Demonstrations and Arrests – The Exodus from
Augustów, and Migration to Distant Places

Augustów, whose honor as regional capital was removed from her on the heels of new instructions from Peterburg, became a district city with many offices, that arose after the completion of the digging of the Augustow Canal. The population in the villages that surrounded the city were wealthy people, strong, tall in stature, strong as oaks, owners of agricultural property and village land. Every Sunday the nobles would come, by wagons and carriages harnessed to horses, into the city to pray at the church. The enlightened Poles and the Russians, who were especially brought, occupied the important posts in the government offices. The trade and most of the artisan-based occupations were in the hands of Jews. Traders in agricultural produce bought large quantities of grain, wheat, and barley, transferring it to Konigsberg and Danzig. Over the course of time, there were also agents and representatives who traded in exporting butter, geese and turkeys to Germany. The economic situation was improved, but black clouds hung in the skies.

---

[160] Traditionally, only wheat, barley, rye, spelt, and oats may be used for *Pesach*, and are also considered to be the only grains that can become *chametz*, leavened. *Kitnyot*, literally, "little things," is a category of food that one might mistake for these five grains. Although *kitnyot*, foods like rice, beans, corn, etc. cannot become *chametz*, for Ashkenazi Jews, *kitniyot* have traditionally been forbidden for consumption on *Pesach*. This is a rabbinic "fence around the *Torah*," that is, a regulation imposed on top of the actual regulation to prevent accidental violation of the *halakhah*. While in the past most traditional Ashkenazi Jews did not eat *kitniyot* on *Pesach*, Sephardic Jews did, and continue to do, as do many Ashkenazi Jews today.
[161] "In the hour of urgency" is a rabbinic principle that allows *halakhah* to be set aside, generally for the purpose of *Pikuach Nefesh*, the preservation of human life.

It was known that the rioters who had carried out pogroms against the Jews in Russian towns did not do what they did of their own accord, but on orders from on high, from the capital city of Petersburg. It was there for all to see that these wild animals had no terror or fear before their eyes. They carried out their plots in peace, sure that they would not be apprehended for their crimes, and there would be no punishment. Worse: the police and other guards, those responsible for keeping order in the town, were the ones that were disturbing the order and security {p. 58} by turning a blind eye to the tricks of the rioters, and were ready and prepared to help them to stir up one part of the residents against the other. The days approaching *Pesach* were a window of opportunity for the haters of Israel to make baseless accusations, "blood-libels"[162] against the Jews, because at that time it was easy to spread slander and promulgate a rumor about a Christian girl or boy who had disappeared, with the hand of Israel[163] in the middle. In most cases these fabricated stories emanated from their churches, and these fabricated rumors always found for themselves attentive ears among the Polish and Russian unenlightened masses; there were those among them who truthfully believed in their simple hearts all that was told, there were those who knew the truth, but it was convenient for them in this "time of anger"[164] to consume their anger in the Jews, and to enjoy the chaos of a twilight time like this to plunder and loot, to steal Jewish property and to kill and destroy lives from Israel,[165] when the permission was given.

Most of the Jews living in Augustów were religious, and the practices of their ancestors were in their hands. They tended towards the ascetics[166] or the *Mitnagdim*, the disciples of the Vilna *Gaon*,[167] who revealed opposition to the *Chassidic* movement that had arisen during the 18th century. They opposed the rituals and style of prayer and also the way of life of the *chassidim*.

Only a small group of *chassidim* lived in Augustów during the second half of the 19th century, and almost all of them were not born in the city, but had come from other cities and towns, near and far. In town there were about two *minyanim*[168] of *chassidim* from various dynasties: Gur, Amshinov, Kotzk, Sokolov, Kovrin, Slonim. Each had its own *Beit Midrash*, that was called by the people of the city "The *Beit Midrash* of the *Chassidim*." They lived in peace among them, in spite of differences in the courts of the *Admorim*.[169] The *Beit Midrash* of the *Chassidim* on the "Street of the Butchers" was the spiritual center for all the *chassidim* in Augustów. There they would all congregate on *Shabbat* for prayers. They all would gather there for the "three meals" of *Shabbat*. Each one brought with him a slice of *challah*[170] in his pocket. There was always a bottle of brandy ready. Together they would sing hymns and tells stories of the righteous ones of Chassidism. Those who knew to play music would bring new melodies they had heard from the rabbi. They were separated from the rest of the Jewish community of Augustów by their form of prayer, which was according to the Sephardic style, by their faith in "their" rabbi and by their long

---

[162] These were invented stories about Jews kidnapping Christian children to drain their blood and use it to make matzas. These libels were a feature of Christian anti-semitism for centuries.

[163] The Jews.

[164] Aramaic: בעידנא דרתחא – *b'idna deritcha* "at a time of anger." Babylonian *Talmud Menachot* 41a: "Rav Ketina said to him: Do you punish us even for failing to fulfill a positive *mitzvah*? The angel said to him: At a time when there is divine anger and judgment, we punish even for the failure to fulfill a positive *mitzvah*."

[165] Jews.

[166] The Opposers, the disciples of the Vilna *Gaon* who emigrated to the land of Israel in the time of the old *Yishuv*, settlement, prior to the rise of modern Zionism.

[167] Rabbi Elijah ben Solomon Zalman Kremer, 1720-1797.

[168] A Jewish prayer quorum, a *minyan*, requires 10 adult Jews. In this context, they would have been required to be male.

[169] An acrostic for the Hebrew <u>A</u>doneinu <u>M</u>oreinu ve<u>R</u>abeinu – "our Master, our Teacher, our Rabbi."

[170] Loaves of special bread for *Shabbat*.

caftans. They didn't shave their beards or the *peyot*[171] of their heads. They were strict about the laws of slaughtering and family purity.[172] There were among them outstanding people who knew "hidden wisdom"[173] who studied and pondered the *Torah*, openly and covertly, day and night. Especially prominent among the people of the *kloiz* of the *chassidim* was Rabbi Dovid the Righteous, a tanner, of the Gur *chassidim*, who sat and learned in the "*Shas*"[174] Society. He excelled in his dancing ability on *Simchat Torah*,[175] and many came to watch and enjoy his fine dancing.

The *chassidim* were laborers, artisans, and small shopkeepers, absorbed by the burden of material support and economics. They were notable for their friendly loyalty and mutual assistance. They were bound and connected to each other, they were interested in and knew the doings in the house of every *Chassid*, and all of them were always ready to come with advice or help for each other. If there was celebration or joy by one of them, the joy was shared. The opposite was also true; in the event of a tragedy or trouble for one, may the merciful one help us, they all took part and participated in his trouble.

The Jews of Augustów were not exceptional in their negative attitude towards induction into the Russian army. Every Jew made attempts to escape this "hollow of the sling."[176] The pictures are remembered, when mothers and father, relatives and members of the family assembled at the doorway of the testing house for the army. When a member of their household was accepted for military service, they would raise their voices of outcry and eulogy for the one who was going far away, mostly to the Far East {p. 59} to Siberia, to places where no Jewish houses are found. There, he would live like a kind of criminal who was sentenced to hard labor, he would absorb lashes and blows for anything and everything; he was forced to speak in a language not his own, and to forget the customs of his ancestors. He would return – after many years – foreign and strange to the members of his family and his town, with a depressed spirit but with a strong body. It is no surprise that the Jews feared military service so much.

Many young people who were liable for induction were included among those who emigrated abroad. Although it was forbidden for youths of military age to emigrate, the nearness of the Prussian border made it easy for them to overcome this barrier. The evasion reached such magnitude that in 1883 an "appeal to the rabbis of the Suwalki region" went out, warning against it. The author of the appeal was Avraham Barash HaCohain Eizendorf, the inspector of the government Jewish school of Šakiai, Suwalki region. In the appeal, it was written that serious danger hung over the Jewish people because so many of them were evading military service. The rabbis are asked to take care of this problem, and even register before the time of draft the names of the emigres, those that have died, and so on ("The Generation," 1901). From a list in "*Pravitlastvani Visonik*," it becomes clear that out of 637 Jews summoned for induction in Suwalki region in the year 1891, 259 did not appear at all. ("*HaMelitz*" 1891, issue 45). In 1893, the percentage of Jews who failed to appear for induction in Suwalki was even higher: out of 779 who were summoned to appear for induction, 499 completely failed to respond. In his article "About the Bad Shepherds," the author Mordechai son of Hillel HaCohain writes that in 1900, 618 who

---

[171] Literally, the "corners" of their beards. This custom comes from the biblical commandment in Leviticus 19:27 not to round off the corners of one's beard.

[172] These are the laws that forbid having marital relations during or after menstruation.

[173] Jewish mysticism, *kabbalah*.

[174] "Six Orders" of the *Mishnah*.

[175] Literally, "the Joy of the *Torah*," the Jewish holiday that comes at the end of *Sukkot*, when Jews celebrate the conclusion and recommencing of the annual cycle of *Torah* reading.

[176] 1 Samuel 25:29 "And if anyone sets out to pursue you and seek your life, the life of my lord will be bound up in the bundle of life in the care of the LORD; but He will fling away the lives of your enemies as from the hollow of a sling."

were obligated for induction failed to present themselves to the army council, emphasizing in particular that the number of Jewish youths who evaded induction was greater in areas closer to the border. In the Hebrew "*HaMelitz,*" a petition came from Sejny to the heads of the community insisting on the erasure of the names of those who had left the city (1895, issue 38). In a second article from that same year it was reported from Sejny that the police were asking for penalties of 300 rubles from families whose sons that were obligated for military induction did not fulfill their civil obligations (1895, issue 287).

Apparently, the Minister of the Suwalki region didn't hate Jews, because at the time that he transferred to Petrikov (1905), representatives of the community parted from him with affection and friendship, presenting him with a silver-bound copy of the Five Books of Moses. In his words to the leaders of the Jews the Minister said, among other things: "Make sure that the Jews don't evade their induction obligation, because this matter will cause you many troubles." (The "*Plas*" Poltava 5645 [1885], page 255).

By way of the frontier towns of the Prussian border, goods, people, and also forbidden literature were smuggled, which revolutionary Russian groups of political emigres were sending to Russia from abroad. The interesting fact should be pointed out here, that also the Socialist newspaper "*HaEmet*"[177] (in Hebrew), whose editor A.S. Liebermann was born in Suwalki, and passed through Peterburg, Moscow, Odessa and other Russian centers on his way to the frontier towns. Liebermann the editor would send his newspaper to Baklerove and from there it was sent to his grandfather, Rabbi Eliezer Dov Liebermann in Suwalki, who made sure that it was forwarded onwards. In a letter from May 7, 1877 A.S. Liebermann writes: "For now, a practical man has already been found who is prepared to receive a reasonable number of copies of periodicals and in a way that is known to him he will transfer them over the border and deliver them to subscribers of a number of cities. He is himself a writer and agent." K. Marmor, the publisher of "The Writings of A.S. Liebermann" (New York , 1951 page 174), adds that the known writer is Yehuda Vistinsky from Baklerove.

{p. 60} The economic status of Augustów continued to improve with the paving of the Grodno-Suwalki road, which passed through the town. Other roads were also paved, which also contributed to trade connections. Various industrial undertakings were opened up: brickmaking, flourmills, sawmills, cement-works and also the leather factory of Dovid Yurdanski, who employed hundreds of Jewish and Christian workers. The Jews were also tenants, suppliers and marketers to the nobles and private estate owners.

Over the course of time, a non-Jewish class in the city arose and became established, which began to knock the Jews' economic legs out from under them, and the restrictions against them gradually increased. On the heels of this situation, the movement of exodus from Augustów and the surroundings grew, and overseas emigration increased. After this, the nationalist Zionist movement strengthened its influence and imprinted its signature on the life of the Jewish street. At the center of the hopes stood emigration to the lands across the sea, and going up to the land of Israel. There were also limited possibilities, and extreme patience was required over the course to time to arrive at one of the yearned-for goals. As a result of this situation Jewish residence in Augustów decreased. In the year 1897, there were found there only 3,637 Jews in a population of 12,743 souls. At the beginning of the twentieth century, Jewish settlement grew again, and in the year 1909 reached 6,969 Jews, which constituted 59% of the total residents.

The German border was very close to the city, and the Kingdom of Germany did not make it difficult for those who were illegally crossing the border without travel documents. The first pioneers among the emigrants – the success at the ease of the crossing lit up their faces. Over a

---

[177] The Truth.

brief course of time, they were successful in building for themselves a new life, a good life, and so it became possible for them to quickly bring up after them the rest of their family, their relatives, relatives of relatives and even acquaintances and close friends.

Things were happening every day – that townspeople would suddenly get up and leave for America; the people – mostly young, *yeshiva* students. Most of them, like all of them, were fleeing because of the fear of army service, because of economic hardship, or for political reasons. A woman that would travel, it was usually because she longed for her husband who had already been in America for a few years and had gotten lucky to send her from there a ticket for travel. The emigrants mostly went to the United States and South Africa. The stream of *aliyah* to the land of Israel was weak.

Representatives of German communities met in Leipzig to consult on how to help the emigrants. Afterwards, representatives of *"Alliance Israélite Universelle,"* and at their head Adolphe Crémieux, met in Berlin with representatives of German Jewry, and decided to form committees next to the Russian-German border to assist the emigrants. In Konigsberg, a committee was formed under the leadership of the Rabbi Dr. Yitzchak Bamberger. The committees that were created in Stettin, Hamburg and Memel developed important work for the settlement of the emigres and the education of wandering youth by means of learning a profession. The committees ceased their activities in 1873, due to a lack of resources.

Jew from Augustów region arrived in America about 115-120 years ago. Already in 1866, the "Charitable Society for the People of Suwalki and the Surroundings " was founded in New York. The goal was to build a *Beit Midrash* and give support to those who came out of Suwalki and the surrounding area.

On January 19, 1882, a memorandum was presented from the Russian Jews who dwelt in England to Minister Pobedonostov in Hebrew and Russian, in which they presented various claims for the benefit of the rabbis and students and demanding {p. 61} equal rights for the Jews as there were for the rest of the Russians. Among the names who emerged from various cities that appeared as signatories is found also the signature of Barukh Zilberman of Augustów in Hebrew and Russian.

The migration of the Jews sometimes caused family tragedies. Men travelled and forgot the wife and children they had left behind. It was possible to read occasionally in the Jewish and Hebrew newspapers announcements about searches for husbands from Augustow.

On the other hand, there were men and women in Augustów that were living well on the support of their sons and daughters who many years before had wandered over the ocean.

The revolutionary movement in Russia aroused great interest in Poland, which saw the defeat of the Tsar as an opening of hope for her liberation. The Jewish workers, who in society were deprived as both Jews and as workers, were also awakened. In Augustów there were not yet "proletarian" workers, who worked for exploitative "bourgeois" employers. The small employers would exploit themselves and the members of their families in hard labor. The Jewish shoemakers who worked mainly in supplying the Russian army, would employ Christian workers, who over the course of time learned the work and competed with their previous employers when they opened their own workshops. Two tanneries belonging to Yosef Shimon Friedkovski and Yisrael Hagardi (whose wife, Shayne Esther carried the load), employed Christians, and it was the custom in the china and soap factory of Binyamin Lap, from whom it was transferred to Papirovitz. It is no wonder, therefore, that before the Revolution there were no socialists as such in Augustów, although it is possible that there were a few who showed interest solely from a theoretical aspect.

At the beginning of 1905, the revolt against the Tsarist regime in Russia broke out. In all the big cities, there were battles between the workers and the police, and acts of terror against the government officials. In Augustow they would read this news in the newspapers - *"HaMaggid,"*

"*HaMelitz*," "*HaTzefirah*," which were received by a few householders in Augustów, of the groups of *Maskilim* and *Chovevei Tzion*. They read the news and thought that nothing would happen here. Although the shoemakers and the tailors began to feel that their assistants were vanishing in the middle of the day, but they didn't see much of an issue in that.

But slowly, the eyes of the local young people were opened, and not necessarily from among the workers alone, but also among groups of householders and the wealthy. At the head of the revolutionary movement in Jewish Augustów stood several of the intelligentsia who led and educated the youth for revolution, such as Chava Frenkel (the daughter of the writer, Yaakov Frenkel), who was a popular speaker; Chaya Markus (a member of a veteran Zionist family), whose father was a great scholar and whose brothers were Zionists; Natan Varhaftig (son of the lord); Varhaftig (owner of the mill) who tended towards anarchy; Avram'eleh Glikson (the son of Chaim and his mother of the house of Sperling); Shmerl Krinitzki. On *Shabbatot*, they held propaganda meetings, and they organized meetings and assemblies secretly in the forests of Augustów. The propaganda was arranged by the "*Bund*"[178] and the anarchists. The "*Bund*" (founded in Vilna in 1897) was a Socialist Jewish party in the exile. In Russia, it was illegal, but nevertheless succeeded in developing extensive work. Following the Russian-Japanese war and the first Russian Revolution, the "*Bund*" grew, and the number of its members was counted in tens of thousands. Its aims were: a professional war to improve the working conditions of the Jewish workers; a political war for the defeat of the Tsars; the imposition of democracy; the achievement of equal rights for the masses of the Jewish people. It saw the Yiddish language as the sole national language {p. 62} of the Jewish people. They called Hebrew "a dead language," Zionism – "Jewish nationalism." They fought stubbornly against, and with great hatred for, both of them.

Anarchism espouses the negation of every State and government, and aspires to establish a free society of individuals or groups with no leadership and without coercive force; a society based on free agreement protected by goodwill. Anarchism negates not only a state regime, but all government; control of the many by the few, the obligation of the minority to submit to the majority, public discipline. It considers the important of the destruction of the State above all else, because on its ruins it is possible to establish perfect anarchic order. The first two "*chassidim*" of anarchism in Augustów were still during the period of the rabbinate of Rabbi Yehuda Leib Gordin – his two sons, Abba and Ze'ev. The rabbi was wanted by the authorities because of his knowledge of the Russian language and his leanings towards a regime that "loves justice and benevolence." And precisely his sons were extreme in their systems of socialism and their preaching of anarchy that in Russia was considered extremist and extremely dangerous. Every interaction with anarchism brought after it exile to Siberia, if not the death penalty.

In the city, the face of a new Yiddish newspaper was seen, by the name of "*Der Verker*."[179] In it, Jewish cultural autonomy was spoken of, and of direct secret elections. The intelligentsia read "*Der Verker*" with interest, and would teach the workers to understand the difficult words, the new, strange ideas.

From the big cities there began to arrive party speakers. In the beginning, they spoke in hidden places, hiding in the forests that were close to town, and a little later they began to appear in the city as well. People from the local "*Bund*" would burst into the "Great *Beit Midrash*" without the permission of the sextons, close the doors, and hold a meeting or a lecture.

The town was flooded with illegal literature, pamphlets, proclamations and calls to strikes, to fight against the Tsar, against reactionism, for freedom and equality. Many meetings were held in the forests, and they began to prepare for the establishment of self-defense. They

---

[178] The word "*bund*" means federation or union in Yiddish and German.
[179] The Worker.

were gathering money for this purpose, and if someone did not give willingly, they took it by force. The faces of the Jews, who were always worried about the next day, became gloomy. In the city, police were seen with bayonets on their rifles. The householders and the middle class confined themselves to their homes and envisioned with fear what the day would bring. In the meantime, reactionism grew. Information about pogroms against the Jews of Bialystok and other cities had already begun to arrive.

The day of publication of the famous "Constitution" arrived. Everyone was happy. The old people claimed that it wouldn't end well, and the Tsar, with his experience of "with a strong hand," would not surrender quickly before a handful of inexperienced young men and women. The anarchists carried out in the city an armed attack against an important factory. The fear in town of what was to come grew greater and greater. With the declaration of the "Constitution," they celebrated the "victory" in Augustów as well. The youth organized a public demonstration with flags. They filled the large market square, and even occupied the adjoining streets.

But a few days afterwards, a reaction against it began from the side of the police and the army. In the city, searches began for the leaders of the Revolution; many were caught and served time in prison for their transgressions. The Tsar's regime increased their enforcement. As in all of Russia, the Revolution was stamped out here as well. Many of the youth left the city, and emigrated overseas. Augustów began to miss her youngsters who had left her and were gone.

{p. 63} The year 1905 left a deep furrow in the hearts of the Jews. After the suppression of the Revolution, the winds slowly calmed down, but an awakening had begun in the Jewish lives. Under the pressure of the events, the Jews of Augustów had become more politically mature.

The workers' organizations continued their activities, if in secret, from fear of an "evil eye."[180] The Zionist movement went back and forth among the people. The idea of building Zion and Jerusalem aroused great interest in the hearts.

Chapter Eleven: Maskilim and Writers in Augustów
The Enlightenment Movement – Yaakov Frenkel- Yisrael Ze'ev Sperling –
Citron, Sh.L., Teacher of Hebrew – The Teacher and Writer Tz. Z. Weinberg

The "Enlightenment" – the spiritual stream that wished to introduce the beauty of Yaphet into the tents of Shem,[181] quickly began to strike roots in Augustów region. While among most of the residents in the "Pale of Settlement " a "*Maskil*" was still a rare thing, there already were in the cities and in the towns of this region *Maskilim* that fulfilled a role in the life of the Jewish communities. In Augustów there were found a number of *Maskilim* that served with two crowns as one, that of the Enlightenment and that of literature. Of them, Yisrael-Ze'ev Sperling and Yaakov Frenkel found a place at the head.

Yaakov Frenkel was a shop owner for textile products in the city, and his *Torah* was not his craft. In the synagogue, he sat next to the eastern wall, which was reserved everywhere for distinguished people, exalted in wealth and in spirit. He published a poem in Hebrew with many stanzas, with came to disparage a zealous rabbi who debates at length on one passage in the *Gemara*[182] "he fell from the top of a roof and was thrust into a woman,"[183] and other poems that were published in Hebrew magazines of that time.

---

[180] In Aramaic.
[181] Genesis 9:27 "May God enlarge Yaphet, and let him dwell in the tents of Shem…"
[182] A rabbinic commentary on the *Mishnah*. The *Mishnah* and the *Gemara* together comprise the *Talmud*.
[183] Babylonian *Talmud Baba Kama* 27a-b "Rabba says another similar *halakhah*: If a man fell from a roof and while falling was inserted into a woman due to the force of the fall, but he did not have the intention to engage in sexual intercourse, he is liable to pay the four types of indemnity…"

Yisrael-Ze'ev ben Naftali Sperling, a *Maskil*, author, and translator, officiated as the government-appointed rabbi of the town. He managed the registration books of marriages, births and divorces; translated from French to Hebrew the well-known utopia[184] of the French author Jules Verne (1828-1905) by the name "In the Depths of the Sea"[185] (Warsaw 1876), and the book "In the Belly of the Earth"[186] by that same author (Warsaw, 5638-1838). Sperling knew four languages inside and out: Russian, Polish, German and French.

At the beginning of the book "In the Depths of the Sea" a letter from his friend from his city, Yaakov Frenkel, is printed:

"Your copy found favor in my eyes; with the clear language you chose for yourself, and in the style of its pure and simple language, that every reader will understand, even if he has not learned it well. May your hands be strengthened, and be very successful in Hebrew literature, to which you have dedicated the time of your life into ripe old age. May your arms be strengthened to give us other useful compositions like these, to teach the youth of our people to understand and comprehend[187] the mystery of the secrets of nature. It is my hope that like me, all lovers of the language of *Ever*[188] and who are endeared to our literature will cherish you, and that you will come to your reward in peace."

In his forward "To the readers," the translator announces that pending publication is another book by the name of "Wisdom is Profitable to Direct"[189] in two parts, approved of as good and useful by Rabbi Chaim-Zelig Slonimski, the editor of "*HaTzefirah*," but it was not published.

At the beginning of the book "In the Belly of the Earth" the writer A.D. Liebermann enumerates praise for the translator: "...extraordinary insight is added to the translator to clarify and unite his translation, to hone and sharpen every idiom and expression, to the extent that it {p. 64} presents its face with greater force, according to the judgement of most readers with good taste. You are fortunate, my friend, that you chose for yourself Ori Yeshara, who is splendid as a doer and a magnificent person. You are blessed and blessed is your taste, for you have a palate to discern what is good, and what is loved and desired by each and every person. And now, arise and excel in Hebrew literature, expand it and glorify it, and become a name and praise among the lovers of the *lashon kodesh*[190] and those who are gifted in it and hold on to its covenant."

He is also remembered for good by the writer Y. S. Weiss (Yehoshua Halivni) in his book "*Tiltulei Gever*"[191] (Tel Aviv 5691 [1931]).

The writer Weiss spent two days in Augustów. In his book of travels, he describes in his conclusion, in a few lines, the city and its surroundings; that the journey at the end of the summer there is extremely pleasant, and especially when it passes through primeval forests alongside the many rivers and year-round streams. He declares that he will never forget the wonderful sight that he saw as twilight fell on the bridge suspended by its iron chains above the river Bóbr, which is near Augustów, surrounded on both banks by tall pine trees that are reflected in the ruddy waters like legendary giants, and all the river then seems like a river of fire.[192] A wonderful image as this,

---

[184] Used here in the sense of an imagined place.

[185] "20,000 Leagues Under the Sea"

[186] "A Journey to the Center of the Earth."

[187] From the *Ahavah Rabbah* prayer: "put into our hearts to understand and to comprehend"

[188] Hebrew.

[189] Ecclesiastes 10:10 "Thus the advantage of a skill [depends on the exercise of] wisdom."

[190] Holy language – Hebrew.

[191] "The Travels of a Man" Isaiah 22:17 "The LORD is about to shake you severely, fellow, and then wrap you around Himself."

[192] Daniel 7:10, in Aramaic: "A river of fire streamed forth before Him; thousands upon thousands served Him; myriads upon myriads attended Him; The court sat and the books were opened...."

he had never seen in all his days. From Augustów he travelled to Suwalki by way of a shaded thick forest.

Sh. L. Citron[193] was born in Minsk. He was a teacher-pedagogue, and a young Zionist writer for whom a reputation in our literature had already emerged. Zionism and *Chibbat Tzion* [194] became the substance of his life, and he wrote a number of books that were full of interest. He was invited as a Hebrew teacher to the home of the wealthy and educated Varhaftig, who was one of the "faces" in the city, a wealthy man, owner of steam and water mill just outside of town, that was found outside of the city, not far from the army barracks buildings. The Varhaftig family dwelt next to the mill in a fine house that resembled a palace, in the middle of a garden in which a proud peacock with multicolored feathers paraded and strutted pleasurably. From Augustów, Citron would send his articles to various newspapers. It seems that the city found favor in his eyes, and he endeavored to mention the name of the city of Augustow, from time to time, in books that he wrote. He moved from Augustów to Suwalki where he founded a "*Cheder Metukan*,"[195] and engaged in teaching and the dissemination of Hebrew Zionism. His house was the center for all of *Chovevei Tzion* and Hebrews in the city. After a year, Citron moved to Mariampol, but returned to Suwalki, where he married a woman and was head of a private school there until 1897.

Tzvi Zevulun Weinberg, a writer and Hebrew educator, learned in *cheder* and *yeshiva* and in pedagogical courses in Grodno. He engaged in the instruction of Hebrew subjects in Augustów. He was one of the founders of the "Association of Hebrew Writers and Journalists " in Poland, and for some time also its Chairman. In 1934, he went up to the land of Israel and served in teaching. His first story, "*Nisayon*,"*[196] was published in "*HaZman*"[197] in Vilna (1905). Since then his stories were published in various Hebrew magazines. He was among the editors of the monthly "*Kolot* "[198] and "*Rishon*."[199] His realistic stories describe the life of Jews in Poland and, after his *aliyah* to the land of Israel, the land of Israel experience.

Rabbi Avraham Shiff was also counted among the writers in the city, born in Yashinovka, who dwelt in Augustów for a number of years and composed many books. At the beginning of the book "*K'vod HaTorah VeChachameha*"[200] were approvals from the great *Geonim* and Rabbis, among them Chaim Soloveitchik of Brisk and Rabbi Moshe Betzalel Luria of Suwalki, who referred to him with various respectful honorifics.

{p. 65} **Chapter Twelve: The Tribulations of *Chibbat Tzion* and Zionism**

> National Yearning for Going Up to the Land of Israel and for the Revival of Hebrew – The Association of "*Dorshei Tzion*"[201] – Rabbis of the City are Devoted to Zion – The influence of *Haskalah* on the City – Hebrew Learning and the Hebrew Library – The Zionist Movement in the City – Distribution of *Shekels*[202] in the City - Zionist Propaganda by Orators and Preachers – In the Test of the 1905 Revolution – The Relationship of the Authorities in Russia to Zionism – License for Legal Action in the City – "*Poalei Tzion's*" Fear of the Government – Prohibition of Zionism by the Authorities – Zionism in the

---

[193] Shmuel Lev Citron, 1860-1930.
[194] Love of Zion.
[195] An improved school that combined traditional studies in *Torah* and *Talmud* with secular studies taught in Hebrew.
[196] "Experience." Original note: * A story of an act of theft that occurred in Augustow.
[197] "The Time."
[198] "Voices."
[199] "First."
[200] "The Honor of the *Torah* and Its Sages."
[201] Seekers of Zion.
[202] The ancient Hebrew coin, the *shekel,* was introduced at the time of the First Zionist Congress and became an iconic "Membership Badge" of the Zionist movement.

Underground – *Chanukah* Receptions and the Expansion of the Library – The Collection of Funds for the Herzl Forest – The Organization of the Youth – Searches and Arrests in the City

The harsh decrees against the Jews awoke within them national yearnings, an aspiration for going up to the land of Israel, the revival of Hebrew as a living language, and also an aspiration for social improvements.

In 5645 (1885), an association by the name of "*Dorshei Tzion*"[203,] was founded in Augustów. As a result of the powerlessness of the council, the action was ruled with a heavy hand, and there were not many participants in it. After the death of Sir Moses Montefiore, an awakening occurred, and boxes were distributed to gather donations for Zion and in order for them to be able to distinguish between the boxes for Zion and the boxes in the name of Rabbi Meir Ba'al Ha-Ness,[204] they inscribed a special inscription on them "In the Memory of Moses Montefiore, may the memory of the righteous be for a blessing." Within a few days, these boxes were distributed to nearly all the Jewish homes in Augustów. The writer expresses the hope that the association will be approved by the authorities after presenting a request, and then it will be able to operate freely to widen its efforts for the land of Israel.

Chovevei Tzion[205] were collecting donations for the Land of Israel at weddings, circumcisions, when people were called up to the *Torah*, by selling photographs of Moses Montefiore, Jubilee blessings and the like. In the Hebrew newspapers, especially "*HaMelitz*," one could find lists of collections and volunteers for the land of Israel from various cities in the Suwalki region. And not from only one of them came the initiative from the side of the rabbis of the cities in this plan; for aside from all the virtues that sages counted among the rabbis, they were also nationalistic Jews and faithful "Lovers of Zion."

Who is greater to us than Rabbi Yosef Zechariah Stern (5591-5664, 1831-1904), the Rabbi of Shavel who in the years of his youth lived in Augustów? While he was still a young man he surprised all by the difficulty of the talmudic questions that he asked, that the great ones of his generation struggled to explain. His first book "*Zecher Yehosef*"[206] on the "Six Orders of the *Mishnah*" was the "first fruits of his world" (according to his words in the introduction), and all those who understand things understood that he was created for genius. He was a Renaissance man, a treasure, a living library. He left no word in the *Torah*, small or large, unread or unmemorized; he was proficient not only in both the Babylonian and Jerusalem *Talmuds* but clear to him were the paths of the first of the *Rishonim*,[207] the *halakhot* of the early and late *geonim*, the sages of Spain and Germany, the words of the legal decisors with their interpretations, and the instructions of the last of the *Acharonim*.[208] All of the overflowing and extensive rabbinic literature was laid out before him like a map, and he knew every single one of its folds.

---

[203] Original footnote 39. In "*HaMelitz*" 12 *Tishre* 5646-1885, Edition 68, an article was published, signed by YZ"SH on the foundation of the Zionist association. This was before the Russian authorities knew what Zionism was, and did not pay attention. One of the devoted Zionists was Yosef Chaim Ratner, prayer-leader, butcher and meat inspector, who from the time that the voice of Zionism was heard in the camp of Israel protected it from slanderers and if there were found young people who came out against it in newspapers he was included among those who went out against them openly in the newspaper, (*HaMelitz*, 30 *Adar* I, 5662-1902). "Seekers of Zion."

[204] "The Miracle-Worker."

[205] Lovers of Zion.

[206] "In Memory of Yehosef"

[207] The *Rishonim* were the leading rabbis and decisors who lived approximately during the 11th to 15th centuries, in the era before the writing of the *Shulchan Aruch*.

[208] The *Acharonim* are the leading rabbis and decisors living from about the 16th century to the present, and, more specifically, since the writing of the *Shulchan Aruch*.

This rabbi negated the *Diaspora* even before the pogroms and the "storms from the Negev."[209] And when the idea of founding settlements in the "Land of Israel" suddenly appeared, he joined the front line of the builders enthusiastically, who understood that only in the land of Israel would the nation come to the revelation of its full strength, and he saw that the time had arrived for real action for {p. 66} that dream-like idea. He grasped the problem of settling in the country not only from the religious or economic-philanthropic standpoints, as even the best of his generation thought. He was counted among the first and few rabbis who saw the national aspect of it, and it was appropriate for him to be considered among the fathers of national Zionism or, according to the words of S.Y. Yatzkan (in his article on Rabbi Y.Z. Stern in "The Sokolov Annual," Vol. 5): "This was the first political Zionist – in any case among the rabbis, who looked at the settlement from a political standpoint…" He was an enthusiastic Zionist, and the first to forbid the *etrogs*[210] of Corfu and commanded that they be replaced with the *etrogs* of the land of Israel. In the Zionist movement, he saw this as "the footsteps of the Messiah and the beginning of the redemption."[211] He himself would walk for a long time and go from house to house to collect donations for the support of the settlements, and the Hebrew language was his "favorite child."

Rabbi Y.L. Gordin, who officiated as town Rabbi in Augustów from 5646-5657 (1889-1896), was a lover of Zion, and more than once in his sermons expressed the idea that even those who desecrate the *Shabbat* have a place in the world to come, if they build houses and settlements in the Holy Land.

The Jews of Augustów, who had commercial ties with Prussia and with distant cities in Russia and even travelled outside of the country for matters of commerce and finance, were influenced by the *Haskalah* that had begun spreading amidst the Jews of the west. Interest in secular literature existed in a general way in Lithuania even amongst the rabbis who read German books, and among whom were daily readers of the Russian newspaper "*Novosti*,"[212] and the paths of the state and political tactics were clear to them.

Because of this, they found favor in the eyes of the *Maskilim* and the "face" of the city. In contrast to them, the *Charedi*[213] Jews and the religious were unsettled by them. Specifically, their advantage, their extensive knowledge of worldly experience, was considered a disadvantage.

The activities of the *Maskilim* in Berlin, with Moses Mendelssohn at their head, who they approached to publish a translation[214] of the *Torah* (in German), and anthologies in Hebrew, was accepted with popularity in the Lithuanian cities. Here there were many subscribers to the Five Books of *Torah* with its new translation.

And so, the hidden yearnings for Zion, the harsh decrees of the authorities against the Jews, and the inclination towards the Enlightenment – spoke together to advance the *Chibbat Tzion* movement.

In 5650 (1890), there arose among the enlightened Jews of Augustów the desire to learn the Hebrew language, and to endear it to all who were educated. A few of the enlightened among the youth were aroused to found the "Collection House for Hebrew Books."[215] They began with Hebrew books, and then moved on to collect books in the German and Russian languages as well. The Hebrew language became the desired language of the young people, and the wealthy in the

---

[209] Isaiah 21:1 "The "Desert of the Sea" Pronouncement: Like the storms in the Negev, it comes from the desert, The terrible land."

[210] Citron, waved on *Sukkot* together with the *lulav*.

[211] This is an Aramaic phrase from the Talmudic period.

[212] "News."

[213] "Tremblers," or Orthodox Jews.

[214] Although the Hebrew word used here generally means "interpretation, what Mendelssohn published was a German translation of the Torah.

[215] The term "*Beit Eked*," Collection House, was replaced by the word "*sifriyah*," library.

city invited private teachers for the instruction of Hebrew to their children. Among the teachers of Hebrew in Augustów was the writer and teacher SH.L. Citron, TZ. Z. Weinberg, and other respected teachers.

The Zionist Movement in Augustów.

The Zionist idea grew and developed from the *Chibbat Tzion* movement, which drew the Jewish masses after it.

At the Second Zionist Congress (Warsaw, summer 5658 [1898]), it was decided to require the Zionists to learn Hebrew, and especially that they should teach Hebrew to their children and that they should educate them in the spirit of nationalism. In the summer of 5659 [1899], a regional council was assembled in Vilna, under the authority of Rabbi Sh. Y. Rabinovitz of Sapotskin. 71 delegates from 51 cities and towns attended. Augustów did not send a delegate. According to the report that was transmitted from the regional operations, the number of associations and "holders" of the *shekel* significantly increased, and from 16 the previous year they reached {p. 67} 135 in 5659. According to the report, 974 *shekels* were sold in the County of Suwalki in the year of the fifth Congress in July 1901. Fifty of them were from Augustów.

The tasks that were placed on the Society were: expansion of the movement by distribution of the *shekel* and shares of the "Treasury of Jewish Settlement" ("The Colonial Bank"), the collection of donations to the *Keren Kayemet L'Yisrael*[216] and also for the Odessa committee of the *Chovevei Tzion* and the collecting of books for the National Library in Jerusalem.

The Zionist associations founded libraries and reading rooms, choirs and evening lessons, "*minyanim*"[217] and groups for learning Hebrew Bible, history, the *Mishnah,* and other sacred books, and required every member to acquire and hold the Zionist *shekel*. At the end of every *Shabbat* the members would assemble and read the "circulars" of the regional authority and news of what was happening in Zionism and the Jewish world.

The Zionists in Augustów were interested even from the start of the Zionist movement to act in a legal way. Already in 5646 [1885], the local Zionists made attempts to obtain authorization; it is not known whether they succeeded but the activities continued.

Actually, the Russian authorities were aware of Zionist activities almost from their beginning, but they did not interfere. However, a change for the worse occurred. The authorities were convinced that the Zionists were discussing not only going up to the land of Israel and settlement there, but also problems of culture and national education in exile. It was not desirable for them to have a consolidation of the Jewish population in Russia into a unified nationalistic body. Also, the activities of the *"Poalei Tzion"* movement, which used revolutionary slogans, brought about a change in the attitude of the government.

In March 1906, the Government published laws according to which all associations that had a political platform and whose leadership was located abroad, were forbidden. For Zionists wishing to fuse into a unified organization, a brief opportunity was given to present a request to the ruler. On June 1, 1907, a notice was sent by the Ministry of Internal Affairs containing instructions to act against the Zionists who were actively conducting publicity for the *shekel* and the *Keren Kayemet L'Yisrael*. From the year 1910, the authorities began to take a hard line on the law. They arrested the activists and delivered sentences against the editors of Jewish newspapers, until all the publicity activities were impossible. The police followed the Zionists' activities, and they were compelled to hide and camouflage them as much as possible. Council meetings were called "weddings," *shekels* were called "sacks," and the like.

---

[216] The Jewish National Fund, founded in 1901.
[217] Traditionally a prayer quorum of ten men.

The Central Zionist Council in Vilna influenced the Zionist associations in Lithuania to increase their activities. It sent speakers and leaders to the cities and towns. Leib Yaffa[218] moved from Vilna to Grodno and presented himself as the Head of the Regional Committee that developed a wide range of Zionist activities.

In the summer of 5673 [1913], before the 11th Congress, a "wedding" assembled in Suwalki. Representatives of the Central Council and the Regional Council took part. Associations from 14 cities were invited, and delegates came from ten of them: Suwalki, Augustów, Sapotskin, Sejny, Mariampol, Kalvaria, Pilvishok, Simne, Vladislovova, Vilkovitz and Yarblan.

In Leib Yaffa's archive, which was transferred to Jerusalem, letters are preserved from Zionist associations that belonged to the region in the years 1911-1914. In this archive, we found about thirty letters and postcards, vouchers and telegrams from the Augustów Zionist Association that had been sent to the Regional Council in Grodno. Apparently, the archives from earlier years had been lost due to confiscations and constant searches by the police, who, with their eyes peeled, supervised the Zionist activities that were forbidden in public. The letters of Augustów are from the years 1912-1913. It is good that there remains for us at least a little material in writing from the Zionists of {p. 68} Augustów, from which is reflected the serious situation in which the Zionist activists in the city were found in the time of the Russian regime.

We have very few letters from 1912. Apparently, because of the caution, more than a few letters remained without dates, and it is difficult to decide to which year to attribute them. Most of the letters refer to the year 1913.

Chaikl Meyatviar, who dwelt in Augustów, wrote to Grodno on March 28, 1912, in reply to a letter received from there, that he has nothing to answer, since "in the city there is no Zionist association and there is not even one Zionist." He adds that in the past there were also no associations. Nevertheless, he sold a number of *shekel*s among his acquaintances, without there being anything within his ability to correct the situation, first of all from lack of opportunity, and also because "our town is as far from the Zionist idea as east is from west."

In a second letter from June 12, 1912, Chaikl Meyatviar writes to Mr. Margolin in Grodno and informs him that the preacher Avramson had been with them, and he spoke twice. The impression that he had left on the public was very good, and as a result of that several friends had gathered together and decided to turn to the Grodno center with a request to send vouchers for 200 *shekel*s, 200 books from the "*Kopika Biblioteca,*" and 25 collection boxes for the *Keren Kayemet L'Yisrael* to the address of Dovid Arieh Aleksandrovitz. He also mentions that they want to found a Zionist association in town but the regulations are not in their hands. They therefore ask for the regulations to be sent to them, and to let them know about the steps they must take in order to establish and authorize the society.

The third letter, (2 *Tamuz*, without knowing whether the year is 1912 or 1913), opens with the verse "They that sow in tears shall reap in joy."[219] And the writer complains: "…And we did not sow in the hearts of our masses and our enlightened ones the idea of resurrection to all of their departments and branches. And if the latter has some Zionist literature, the masses here have nothing." The writer suggests preaching the abstract idea constantly, early in the morning, and in the evening, and then they will find the love of Zion, and the movement will become national. According to his words, it is the responsibility of the center in Grodno to "create" speakers and to spend much money on it. "The community will not be weakened," and it will introduce the various Zionist institutions. After he spends some time on the problems of the Congress[220] and the sending of delegates, he moves on to writing about the Zionist situation in Augustów, which does not

---

[218] 1876-1948.
[219] Psalm 126:5
[220] The Zionist Congress.

resemble the other cities in which Zionism built branches for itself in the early days, and it continues there without interruption, and it is good to work there, because there are workers in sufficient measure, while in Augustów, everything is strange to them. About two years ago, when the writer came to settle there, he found a town abandoned and desolate in the Yiddish aspect. He didn't find there Hebrew or Jewish cultural institutions, and all spirit was strange to its people. Rabbi Yitzchak Nisenbaum, the famous preacher, came to the city once and preached in the *Beit Midrash*, and not even a *minyan* came to hear. And now here comes Avramson, and he excited the hearts, and began a movement that achieved something, but again got stuck because of lack of supporters. The three Zionist activists were busy all the days with their businesses, and that is the answer why last year was the greatest number of *shekel*s sold in the city, because the effervescence had not yet subsided; and those who gave generously then are not giving today, even ungenerously. But about twenty men bought shares in the "Training for the Settlement of the Land of Israel" with payments for lessons, volunteering in the *Keren Kayemet L'Yisrael*, and the like. He concluded his words: a) to increase preaching Zionism orally and in writing; b) to assemble frequent gatherings of regional association leaders in every city.

The letter from *Tishre* 5673 [1913] informs about some changes for the better. Two months ago a council was elected, and after a few members sensed that it was falling asleep, they called for general meeting and demanded a full report on its activities.

{p. 69} The old Council resigned and a new one was elected. These are the results of its work: a) It organized the collection boxes for the good of the settlement in the land of Israel, and instead of the 12 rubles that were collected last year for the settlement, this year 40 rubles were sent; b) It set up collection bowls for the benefit of the Yemenites in the land of Israel, and about 25 rubles were collected; c) It sold about 100 *shekel*s, in addition to Avramson's *shekel*s, and stands to sell two hundred; d) It organized a *minyan* on *Simchat Torah*, and from the men and women who donated 60 rubles were collected; e) A big meeting was assembled in which one person lectured about the great value of the Yemenites as Ottoman settlers in the Land of Israel, and as workers. The meeting decided to collect 380 rubles for housebuilding for the Yemenites in the Land of Israel. About 60 Rubles had already been deposited in the local "Saving and Loan Society"; f) At a meeting of speakers of Hebrew and those who cherish it, a few members lectured on the enormity of the importance of our language in the past, which needs to also become the language of the future, and that the historic thread should not be severed. Their words made an impression, and immediately they volunteered to donate about 30 rubles, in order to open a branch of the association of Lovers of the Language of *Ever*. A council was elected to engage in its operation. The council decided to organize a party for *Chanukah* in support of the "Fund for the Workers of the Land of Israel" and for the benefit of the Yemenites.

In the letter that came after it, it was said that their work did not come to a stop, and they hope that in the future, too, they will work energetically and with greater vigor. Indeed, various obstacles were laying in the path of a *Chanukah* party with light pictures; but they were not free to refrain from it.[221] They wanted to present on the stage a Jewish spectacle, and to show the pictures of it to the community, and to preach warm words about *Chanukah*. The last act of the performance was to be the most difficult to carry out; first of all, because of a lack of an excellent speaker, and secondly because of the difficulty of obtaining a license from the authority for a nationalist program. For all that, the council decided to try…Four times they wrote to the Council of Lovers of the Language in Peterburg on the founding of a branch of the Lovers of the Language of *Ever* here, and four times – no one answered.

---

[221] *Mishnah Avot* 2:16 "He [Rabbi Tarfon] used to say: It is not your duty to finish the work, but neither are you free to refrain from it;"

In a letter from 5 *Tevet* 5673 [1913] it is told that on one of the Saturday nights after *Shabbat* a general meeting was held, in which about eighty members from all echelons of the city participated, and in it there appeared three speakers about the story of *Chanukah*, on the activities of the association, and on Hebrew as the language of the past and the future. The community was very satisfied, and so they announced that for a few weeks, *Shabbat* lessons had been taking place, and young and old had gathered to hear a chapter from the *Tanakh*[222] and history, and a lecture on our historical heroes. The lessons drew a large congregation, and the people that thronged multiplied. Fifty of the new collection-boxes of the *Keren Kayemet L'Yisrael* were already distributed in the community. The permit authorizing the association was not received.

In a letter of 25 *Shevat* 5673 it was said that the council decided to seek from Grodno a speaker for three lectures on the society for the strengthening of the settlement, its goals, activities and more. Avramson is an excellent speaker and also an activist. He was not satisfied with only lecturing, rather, he was active and founded our association.

In that same letter came information about the Hebrew library in Augustów, that has about two thousand books in Russian, about a thousand in Yiddish, and only 400 in Hebrew. That happened because in the management of the library there was not one of the Zionists who would act to increase the number of Hebrew books. At the moment, efforts are being made to change the management in a general meeting of the library, and then everything will fall into place peacefully.

In a letter dated from *Rosh Chodesh*[223] Nisan 5763, it informed on the results of the activities of the recent weeks. The Zionists achieved complete victory at the general meeting of the library, and its administration passed entirely to their hands. The new council first of all approached to strengthen the Hebrew section of the library, which had been neglected and inadequate, and new Hebrew books had already been received, even before they brought books in Russian and Yiddish. They also informed about the opening {p. 70} of the official branch of "*Chovevei Tzion*" in Odessa, in the hope that under the protection of Odessa they could increase the fruitfulness of the activity, and they had already entered into discussions with Odessa. Another four shares had been acquired in the "Training for the Settlement Society" in the names of: Dovid Boyarski, Rivka Czarnes, Yechezkel Rotenberg and Meir Meizler. It was also decided to send a delegate from Augustów to the 11th Congress. And since in Augustów such pretensions of honor were not appropriate, and it was not within their ability to send him on their own account, it was decided to turn with a request to the center in Grodno that they recommend a suitable and fitting delegate as its emissary, and then they would vote for him, on condition that he come afterwards to Augustów to deliver a report on the work of the Congress.

The lectures that were established on *Shabbat* days in the *Beit Midrash* were cancelled. The *Charedim* of the city sought a pretext to cancel them, and they found one when one of the teachers said, among other things, that the story of Samson the Hero was nothing but a legendary hero. Then they closed the *Beit Midrash* to the lecturers.

In an undated letter, information is given on the sending of funds for the good of "Herzl Forest" in order to plant 12 trees in the name of Augustów, and the remaining three in the names of a) Dovid son of Aharon Tzukerman to mark the day of entering into the covenant of our Father Abraham;[224] b) Reuven son of Avraham the Levite Levine, as a sign of thanks for his work; c) The town's prayer leader Yosef Chaim Ratner, as a sign of appreciation for his Zionist activities.

In another letter, it is reported that the youth of Augustów organized themselves into a special association without yet seeing among them actual deeds, and all their strength lay only in

---

[222] Hebrew Bible.
[223] The first day of the month.
[224] The covenant of circumcision.

the mouth. But their numbers continued to increase. Mr. L. founded an association of 12 members, and as of now, their numbers have doubled.

For the sake of memorializing the names of the Zionist members who worked in the underground in Augustów despite the police investigations and supervision, there is transmitted herein one of the lists of members from Augustów people in the Zionist association. The list, according to the *aleph bet*: Aleksandrovitz, Dovid Leib; Oeron, Mordechai; Olichnovitz, Pinchas; Avramski, Eliezer; Ezerski, Simcha; Eisenstadt, Shmuel; Borovitz, Yaakov; Borovitz, Nisan ; Borovitz, Yosef; Bezant, Zalman Leib ; Bergstein, Dov; Bramzon, Zalman; Boyarski, Dov; Borovski, N.; Boyarski, Dovid; Blacharski, Nachum; Bass, Moshe ; Bidek, Arieh; Bidek, Yaakov ; Beker, Yaakov Yehuda; Borovski, Yisrael Yehuda; Brenman, Yerachmiel ; Glikson, Chaim; Grosberg, Yisrael; Grosberg, Meir; Goldshmidt, Shmuel Meir; Gotstein, B .; Gofenstein, Eliezer; Grinvald, Feigl; Glikson, Dov; Gritzen, S.D.; Grinberg, Shmuel; Denmark, Sarah; Demoratski, Alter; Halperin, Eliezer; Varhaftig, Shimon; Zupnitzki, Shalom; Zeligzon, Shabtai ; Yedvab, Eliezer; Yachnis, Shmaryahu; Lap, Binyamin; Levine, Reuven; Levatinski, Tzvi Boruch ; Leizerovitz, Avraham; Liubel, Shmuel Yitzchak; Lap, Tzvi Arieh; Lap, Chaim; Lozman, Ze'ev; Lozman, Liba; Lozman, Yisrael; Loite, Arieh Leib; Markus, Chaim Yosef; Minsker, L.; Michelson, Shlomo; Madianovski, Isaac; Meizler, Meir; Meiski, W.; Stoliar, Yitzchak; Staviskovski, Yaakov Yosef; Sarna, Sofia; Simner, Dovid; Soloveitchik, S.; Arbstein, Moshe; Frankel, Yisrael; Feinstein Tzvi; Pianka, Yitzchak; Feinstein, Hillel; Feinstein, Menachem Mendel; Tzukerman, Aharon; Czarnes, Tzvi; Mrs. Kantrovitz; Kalson, Shaul; Koptziovski, Zalman Leib; Kleinman, Zalman; Krinitzki, Yitzchak; Kentzuk, Eliyahu; Rotenberg, Chava; Rotenberg, Yitzchak; Rubinstein; Ratzitzky, Yisrael Mordechai; Rotenberg, Moshe; Rosenfeld, Avraham-Dovid ; Rechtman, Nechemiah; Skliar, Rivka; Shumski, Yaakov Tzvi; Rotblit, Yisrael; Rotenberg, Yechezkel; Shreibman, Moshe; Sperling, Shlomo; Shumski, Eliyahu Leib.

{p. 71} In a letter dated 13 *Nissan*, 5673, it is told that it was decided to fix the intermediate days of the festival for the emptying of the donation boxes and for the collection of the appraisal tax that was imposed on them, while the days for distributing the *shekel* is delayed until the "Three Days of Limitation."[225] They will make an effort to disseminate the idea of the *Keren Kayemet L'Yisrael*, and will empty the boxes, without doubt collecting a specific amount to the benefit of the *Keren Kayemet L'Yisrael*. After that, they will make efforts to distribute the *shekels*. They did not engage in gathering donations at *Purim* for the proposed house building for the Yemenites, and in place of it they sent 53 rubles for "the Redemption of Jerusalem," because we could not place the burden on the few public activists to act for the good of various institutions at once, since indeed all of them were necessary and productive, but the members remained confused, asking: "who is deferred for whom? It was better to announce an action each festival for a specific institution. But are our festivals enough for our institutions? Great agitation was felt among the youth in many cities, and that summer, with the visit to us of youth from other cities, much propaganda was spread among them, perhaps with some success.

From letters of the summer months it became clear that the distribution of the *shekel* encountered difficulty, due to the lack of volunteers. A need was felt for speakers, who were invited but did not respond. In the city, there were found a few who were devoted to the Zionist cause with all their hearts and souls, and only by their work was something done until now.

---

[225] The "three days of limitation," which are the three days immediately prior to the giving of the ten commandments, observed at the time of the writing of this book immediately preceding *Shavuot*. Exodus 19:11-12. "Let them be ready for the third day; for on the third day YHVH will come down, in the sight of all the people, on Mount Sinai. You shall set bounds for the people round about, saying, 'Beware of going up the mountain or touching the border of it. Whoever touches the mountain shall be put to death.'"

However, they were very busy. They felt the need for a speaker and preacher for 20 *Tammuz*, the anniversary of Dr. Herzl's death, on which they would be able to collect for the "Herzl Forest." They wanted to hold a memorial, and to arouse the public, and to do something significant, since the ground had already been prepared.

An election war took place for the Zionist Congress. There were three candidates: Dr. Bernstein, Olshatzki from Kalvaria, and the young people put up Mr. Kranatz in the name of B. Goldberg. The first was preferable. On the second, they lacked the knowledge to know if he was appropriate for the honor. Because there lacked 200 *shekel*-holders[226] the Zionists of the city were compelled to join with another city for the purpose of the election of a joint delegate.

A postcard from 20 *Tammuz* 5673 informs that a memorial service for the soul of the leader, Dr. Herzl, was held in the city, in the synagogue. The *Chazzan* with the choir sang "The One Who Dwells in the Hidden Place,"[227] and one of the speakers from the "*Tzeirei Tziyon*" from Vilna spoke about the deeds of Dr. Herzl. A second speaker spoke about the "Herzl Forest," and after that a memorial was conducted. The impression was excellent and exalted. A significant sum of money was collected to benefit the "Herzl Forest."

The secret Zionist activities in Augustów were apparently like "an arrow in Satan's eye,"[228] and perhaps there was the hand of informers in it. In any event, it was known that the hand of the police, which was spread out against the Zionists in other cities recently touched also Augustów and aroused fear. And indeed, the political activists in Augustów were very careful in their dealings with the Regional Council. The name of the writer of the letters is unknown. The essential terms come in the language of *notarikon*[229] and *gematria*.[230] Even the address for the receipt of mail was indirect. And with all this, something happened in the city. Here we read in a letter from September 1913: "...Do not send us any *shekels* or circulars, because here a big investigation is being conducted by the police, on account of the local Zionists, and we have to be very careful. I have also been called there. How the matter will conclude – it is impossible to see in advance. But caution will not hurt. Be careful in our letters."

In a second letter from September 5, 1913 it says: "We received. But my voucher is missing and the matter is suspicious, since scrutiny has been increased. Please answer right away; perhaps the voucher was not included, and the fear is fear in vain. Please don't send the most modest items."

{p. 72} It seems that because of the "evil eye"[231] there was a pause in the exchange of letters between the Center and the association in Augustów.

This pause also brought a halt to the receiving of information, which brought, on December 20, 1913, the question in a letter: "Why have we stopped receiving letters? It is very difficult to get subscriptions for "*HaTzefirah*" and the rest of the newspapers, but it would be good if "*HaTzefirah*" came to the house. We await your letters."

Such was the face of Zionism in Augustów at the end of the year 1913. No letters are found in the archives from the year 1914. That was the year that on 9 *Av* the First World War broke out between Russia and Germany, and the bloody dance began to rage. The period of the Zionist underground in Russia was concluded with the outbreak of the Great War, and with its conclusion there began a new period for Zionism, a period of the Beginning of Redemption.

---

[226] That is, voters.

[227] Psalm 91.

[228] Babylonian *Talmud Menachot* 62a.

[229] Using one word that is composed of the initial letters of an entire phrase.

[230] A code that uses the numerical value of a Hebrew word instead of its letters.

[231] In Aramaic.

Bibliography on Augustow

A. Books

- The Tents of Shem, by Shmuel Noach Gotlib, Pinsk, 1912, p. 364.
- World Encyclopedia,[232] Dovno-Fund, Paris 1934, *Ershter Band* z. 171
- "These I Will Remember," An Anthology of the Martyrs of 5700 – 5705 [1940-1945], Volume 5, New York, 5723 [1963]: The Rabbi Reb Azriel Zelig Noach Koshelevski from Augustow, pp. 123-126
- Encyclopedia Judaica (German), published by "*Eshkol*," Berlin, Volume 3, pp. 602-603
- General Encyclopedia "*Yizra'el*
," Published by *Yizra'el* Books Ltd., Tel Aviv, First Volume, p. 61
- Encyclopedia "*Eshkol*," published by "*Eshkol*," Berlin, First Volume, pp. 19-48
- In the Depths of the Sea, by Jules Verne, translated from French by Yisrael Zev son of Naftali Sperling, Warsaw, 5637-1876
- Breinsk, "Book of Memory," New York 1948: "*Augustower Shul*" in Harlem , p. 161
- Thirty Years in Lithuania and Poland[233] (Autobiography) by Abba Gordin, in Buenos Aires
- The General Hebrew Encyclopedia , published by "Masada," 5719 [1959], Volume A, p. 644
- The Harvest, edited by N[achum] Sokolov, Second year, 5646 [1886], Warsaw, p. 129
- *Zikhron Yaakov*, by Rabbi Yaakov Lifshitz, part 3 pp. 76, 79

{p. 73}
- "Red Beads" by Fania Bergstein, published by the United Kibbutz, 5716 [1956], pp. 175-176
- The Wandering of a Man by Y.Sh. Weiss (Yehoshua Halivni), Tel Aviv, 5691 [1931], pp. 89, 90
- Lithuanian Jewry published by "*Am HaSefer*" Ltd., 5720-1959, Vol. 1, pp. 84, 117, 179, 511, 526
- Suwalk Yizkor Book, New York
- "First Days," 5695 [1935], Memories of A.M. Altschuler
- "The Honor of the *Torah* and Those Who Study Her" , an Interpretation of the Song of Songs, by Avraham son of Shimon Shiff, Bilgoray, 5473 [1713]
- The Almanac of Achiasaph, Fifth year, 5658 [1898], Practical Chart p. 11
- The Almanac of Achiasaph, Sixth year, 5659 [1899], Practical Chart p. 11
- "*Lita*" Compilation,[234] Vilna, 1914, published by Uriah Katzenellenbogen and A.Y. Goldshmidt, p. 984
- "From Lions' Dens," by Rabbi Azriel Ze'ev Koshelevski, Bilgoray, 5688 [1928]
- "Portion of the Ancestors" by Rabbi Levi Yonah Auvtzinsky, the Rabbis of Augustow pp. 36, 46, 51, 82
- The Memory Book of the Community of Ostrov-Mazowiecka , Tel Aviv, 5720 [1960], pp. 22-23
- The Memory Book of the Community of Lomza , 5713 [1953], pp. 17, 20, 25, 105, 115, 317
- "*Ayin Tzofim*"[235] on the Five Books of the *Torah*, by Azriel Zelig Noach Koshelevski, Vilna, 5683 [1923]
- The Bialystok Ledger by A.S. Hershberg, First Volume, New York 5709 [1949], p. 379
- The Ledger of the Council of the Four Lands , edited by Yisrael Halpren, sign 342, 456, no. 83, (of paragraph 843)
- Fania – Thirty at Her Death Gevat 5711 [1951] (In stencil) pp. 5, 11

---

[232] In Yiddish.
[233] In Yiddish.
[234] In Yiddish.
[235] The Eye of the Watchers.

- Culture Carrier of the Yiddish Liturgy,[236] by Eliyahu Zelodkovski, 1930, p. 11
- "The History of One Town" The Scroll of the Flourishing and Destruction of the Community of Sapotzkin, by Aleksander Manor, 5720 [1960]
- Lists, by Fania Bergstein, publication of the United Kibbutz, 5712 [1952], p. 6
- "Questions and Answers" by Rabbi Moshe Yehoshua Yehuda Leib Diskin , Jerusalem, 5671 [1911] paragraph 44
- The History of "The Love of Zion" by Citron, Sh.L., Odessa, Part 1, 5674 [1914], p. 84 edited by Rabbi Shmuel Avigdor, head of the Jewish Court of Augustow and Nesvizh
- The Answers of Yehuda, by Rabbi Yehuda Leib Gordin, Vilna, 5668 [1908] in the Introduction, pp. 144, 152

{p. 74}

B. Periodicals:

- *HaKarmel* edited by SH.Y. Fein
, Vilna, Third year, 5623 [1863], p. 290.
- *HaKarmel* edited by SH.Y. Fein, Sixth year, 5626 [1866], pp. 116, 699.
- *HaMaggid* 5618-1858, Edition 10, 18.
- "   5620-1859, "   41.
- "   5621-1861, "   3, 45.
- "   5623-1863, "   44, 24 *Tevet*, 9 *Shvat*.[237]
- "   5624-1864, "   42.
- "   5625-1865, "   26.
- "   5626-1865, "   47, 50.
- "   5626-1866, "   5, 11.
- "   5627-1867, "   2, 23, 25, 28.
- "   5628-1868, "   14, 16, 19, 31.
- "   5630-1870, "   19, 34.
- "   5631-1871, "   13.
- "   5641- [1881], "   50.
- "   5643-1883, "   25 *Tevet*, 1 *Adar*.
- "   5649-1889, "   21, 26.
- *HaMelitz*   1881, Edition 13, 21, 26
- "   1885, "   68.
- "   1890, "   154.
- "   1896, "   228.
- "   1902, "   46.
- *HaTzefirah*, 5622 [1862], Edition 10, 10 *Nisan*.
- "   5638 [1878], "   19, 18 *Iyar*.
- "   5641 [1881], "   21, 22, 25, 32.
- "   5642 [1882], "   40, 20 *Cheshvan*.
- "   5652-1892, "   79.
- "The Jew," edited by Yitzchak Sobleski, London, Year 3, Edition 35, 17 Section 660 – 1900.
- "A Polish Jew,"[238] New York, Number 19, December 1943, p. 3.

---

[236] In Yiddish.
[237] Names of Hebrew months of publication.
[238] In Yiddish.

Subscribers to Authors' Books

This was formerly a wide-spread custom, that an author of a book who wanted to print it, would collect beforehand as a deposit for the acquisition of the book, an amount of money from "subscribers", who were called by the foreign name "*Prenumeranten*."[239] Lists of the prenumerators that came at the end of a book reflected the cultural aspect of the city and served as important material for the history of Jewish settlement. With this we transmit a number of books in which there were published lists of prenumerators of the Jews of Augustow:

{p. 75}

"Story of the Land," Part 1, Yosef Sheinhak, Warsaw, 5601 [1841].

"The Book of Genealogy of Assyrian Writing ," Yaakov Bachrach, Warsaw, 1954.[240]

"And the Priest Approaches," by Hillel Dovid Trovesh, Vilna, 5642 [1882].

"The Desire of Solomon," by Moshe Shlomo Levinson, Warsaw 1888.

"Produces Pearls," by Duber son of Tzvi Horovitz, Vilna, 5650 [1890].

"The Splendor of a Deer," by Tzvi Hirsh Boyarski,[241] Warsaw, 5653 [1893].

"The One Who Illuminates Forever," by Meir Micha'el Rabinovitz, Vilna, 5663 [1903].

"The Orchard of Wisdom," by Moshe son of Mr. Aharon Maslant, [Sadlikov, 1836].

The Market Square in the Period of the First World War, 1914-1918

---

[239] Prenumerators.

[240] This book was actually published in 1854.

[241] The name is incorrectly written "Tzalvei." The actual name of the author is "Tzvi."

84

{p. 76}

The Municipal Building

The Long Street

The Market Square – The Corner of Mostava (Bridge Street)

---

[242] Notes and References; Translator's Note: All endnotes (numbered 1-39) originally listed on pp. 77-79, have been moved to the bottom of each page of text as footnotes, to facilitate accessibility to them for the reader. They are listed as "original footnote # ...

{p. 80}

The Long Street

The Square Named for Pilsudski

{p. 81}

The Market Square

The Market Square

The Market Square

Reception for the Minister of the Region

Dovid-Arieh Aleksandrovitz, (Head of the Community Council), Rabbi, Nisan Borovitz, the Teacher Y. Bergstein, Domovitz (Secretary of the Community Council)

{p. 83} The Editor:

In their great kindness, the Directors of "The Chief Archive of Old Documents" in Warsaw and the "National Institute in the Name of Osolinsky" in Breslau permitted us to use the microfilms found in the "General Archive for the History of Israel" in Jerusalem. We thank them for it.

It was only possible for us to print a small portion of the microfilms that are found in the archive in Jerusalem.

Two of the photographs, this one and the one that follows it, are a part of a large document that discusses the request of the Jew Leib Kalman (the years 1858-59) to cancel or reduce the fine that was levied on him.

The original is found in "The Chief Archive of Old Documents" in Warsaw
Signature: Sekret. Stanu Krol. Pol. 439/1858
Microfilm: HM 3736

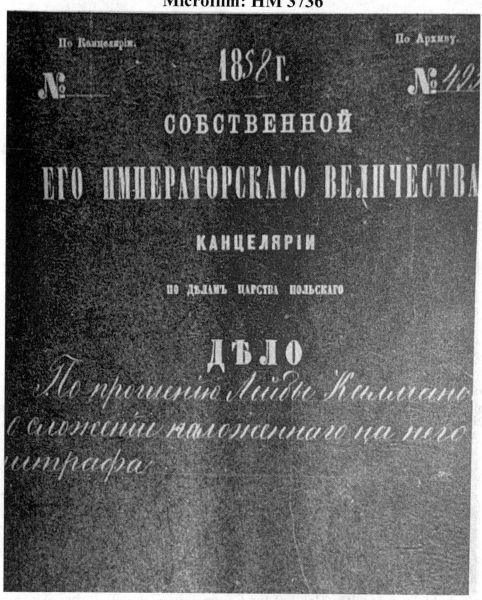

Signature: Sekret. Stanu Krol. Pol. 439/1858
Microfilm: HM 3736

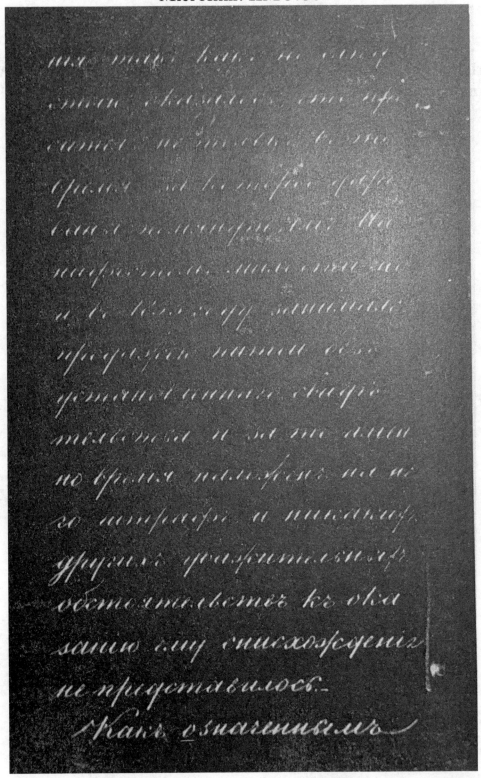

{p. 85} This photograph and the one that follows it are a part of a document that discusses the request of the Jew Yehuda Leib Srulovitz, that the administration of the city pay him for food supplies that he provided in the name of the city in the year 1807 for the French army. The discussion was conducted in the years 1817-1823.

In This Period Augustow was a Regional City
The original is found in "The Chief Archive of Old Documents" in Warsaw
Signature: Kom. Rf. Spr. Wewn. I Policyi 4816 Microfilm: 3590 HM

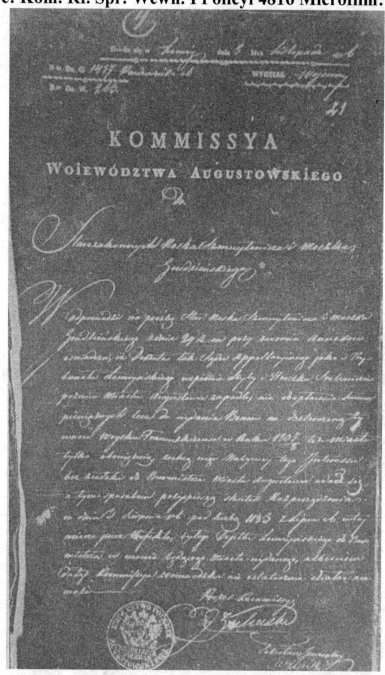

In the matter of the Request of Leib Srulovitz

The original is found in "The Chief Archive of Old Documents" in Warsaw.
Signature: Kom. Rf. Spr. Wewn. I Policyi 4816
Microfilm: 3590 HM

{p. 87} This photograph and the one that follows it are a part of a document from the year 1640 that includes a list of Jewish families that own lands in Augustow.

**The original is found in the
"National Institute in the Name of Osolinsky - Library" in Breslau
Signature: 1640/ III 6650 HM
We received the microfilm from
the "General Archive of the History of Israel" – Jerusalem.**

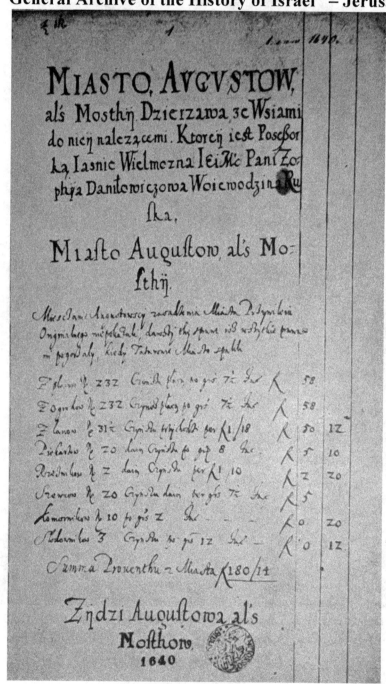

The original is found in
the "National Institute in the Name of Osolinsky - Library" in Breslau
Signature: 1640/ III 6650 HM
Microfilm: 6650/HM

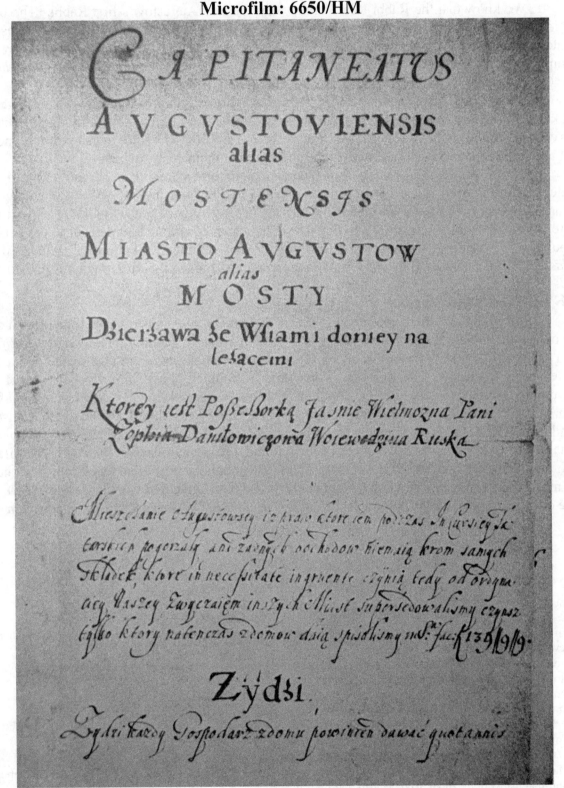

Rabbis of Augustów
By Moshe Tzinovitz

Reb Shalom Shachne – the First Rabbi

We know that the Rabbi Reb Shalom Shachne was Augustów's first Rabbi. The book *"Siftei Yesheinim"*[243] on the *Chumash* serves as proof of that. The author of the book was the righteous Rabbi, Rabbi Shabtai son of the Rabbi Moshe Zalman , an Augustów resident. He refers to himself in the foreword to the book as the grandson of "Rabbi, the famous *Gaon* and *Admor*, Our Great Teacher the Rabbi Shalom Shachne, the *Av Beit Din*[244] of this community.

When exactly did Rabbi Shalom Shachne officiate as Rabbi in Augustów? This matter is not known to us, nor have any details been preserved of the story of the rabbi's life. Nevertheless, it is certain that the period of his officiation began before 5597 (1837), since in that year it is known that another Rabbi was already seated on the chair of the rabbinate in Augustów.

At that same time, the Jewish settlement in Augustów was an important urban Jewish center, according to the ideas of the time. Compared to 239 Jews in 1765 (5526), including the village settlements that were adjacent to it, the Polish government census of 1820 showed that there were already in Augustów 1,167 Jewish souls, which constituted 30 percent of the general population of residents in the city (according to the "Hebrew Encyclopedia" published by *"Masada"*). It is understood that this important community looked forward to famous rabbis.

Reb Yosef son of Reb Barukh

In 5597 (1837) there appeared as "Rabbi *Av Beit Din* of Augustów" the Rabbi Reb Yosef son of Barukh. We are taught this by the book *"Shvil Hayashar"*[245] (the interpretation of *"HaRif"*[246] on Tractate *Brakhot*). [247] In the list of subscribers to this book, there are also mentioned a few names from Augustów. The first one is the rabbi mentioned above, *Rav Av Beit Din* of the community. Among those who come after him, respected householders:[248] Yisrael Dov Varhaftig, Reb Yitzchak *HaCohain*, Reb Eliyahu son of Ezra, Reb Ezra Leib son of Eliyahu of the Reinstein family, and Reb Avraham Charlap. A large number of the offspring of these householders remained to live in this city. A number of them found a respected place in the communal life of their native town. Regarding Reb Avraham Charlap, it should be noted that this family had one of the most respected lineages in Poland-Lithuania. It had a pedigree that went back to King David. One of the members of the family was the *Gaon*[249] Reb Yaakov Moshe Charlap of Jerusalem.

---

[243] The lips of those who sleep. Song of Songs 7:10 "And your mouth like choicest wine. Let it flow to my beloved as new wine gliding over the lips of sleepers."

[244] Head of the Rabbinical Court. *Av Beit Din* designated the principal of the *yeshiva* who made *halakhic* rulings and took part in the communal administration; in particular, it was used as the title of the district rabbi of a large community.

[245] The Straight Path.

[246] Rabbi Yitzchak ben Jacob Alfasi HaCohain (1013–1103).

[247] This is the tractate of the Babylonian *Talmud* that deals with blessings.

[248] In this time period, this generally refers to the middle- and upper-class.

[249] The Hebrew word *gaon* (plural: *geonim*) literally means "genius," but in this context, it is used as an honorific for the spiritual leader of the town, who decided questions of Jewish law, headed the Jewish courts and rabbinical academies, and ultimately had the final say in the religious life of the Jewish community.

The Title Page of "*Siftei Yesheinim*" on the Book of Exodus

ספר

ש פ ת י י ש נ י ם

על ספר

ש מ ו ת

באור חדש מלא ישן. פשטים נעימים טעם זקנים. מאיש אמונים. חכם
ונבון הנבונים. ביסודות חזקים כראי מוצקים. על אדני האמת
בנוים. באמת וישר עשוים. דרושים נפלאים מדבש ונופת מתוקים. על
יסודי אגדות חז"ל ומדרשים. לדעת כי בתורה שבכתב המה חקוקים. מלהיב
לב איש ישראל לאהבת ד' ותורתו הקדושה. אשר יצא מפה קדוש מפיק
מרגליות. ה"ה הרב הגדול צדיק ונשגב חסיד ישר ונאמן לד' ולתורתו
עובד ד' בשמחה מתוך יסורים ומכאובים. במתק שפתיו ונועם לקחו
רבים השיב מעון. מופת היה לרבים. תפלתו וברכתו לכל הבא בצלו
לא שבה ריקם. קדוש יאמר לו כקש"ת אדמו"ר מו"ה **שבתי** זצלה"ה
המחבר ספר **אמרי נועם** על שיר השירים. בן הרב הגדול וכו
מוהר"ר **משה זלמן** זצ"ל לנכד הרב הגאון המפורסם בדורו וכו' אדמו"ר
מו"ה **שלום שכנא** זצלה"ה אב"ד דקק **אוגוסטאוו** יע"א.
גם יבאו בו איזה הגהות וחדושים נעימים בשם **זרע יצחק** מכונים.
מאת המלקט המעתיק והמו"ל ומסדר הרב הגדול וכו' מו"ה **זלמן יצחק**
ראווידאוויטש בן הרב המחבר זצוק"ל זי"ע וע כי"א:

ג ר א י ע ו ו א
בדפוס אברהם מרדכי פיורקא
שנת תרס"ה לפ"ק

СЕФЕРЪ
СИФСЕ IЕШЕНИМЪ
Коментаръ на 5 книжіе Моисея
Часть 2-ая.

ГРАЕВО
Типографія и Стереотипія А. М. Пюрко.
1904 г.

The Title Page of "Siftei Yesheinim" on the Book of Exodus

The Book of
The Lips of Those Who Sleep
On the Book of Exodus
A New Interpretation Full of Old.[250] Pleasant Simple Meanings, The Reason of Elders.[251]
From a Faithful Man. Wise and the Sagest of the Sages.
With Foundations Firm as a Cast Mirror. [252]
Built on the Foundations of Truth. Made with Truth and Honesty.
Wonderful Homilies from Honey and Sweet Nectar.
On the Foundations of the Tales and Legends of Our Sages,
May Their Memories Be for a Blessing.
To Know That They are Engraved in the Written *Torah*.[253]
Rouses the Heart of a Man of Israel to the Love of God and His Holy *Torah*.
That Which Came Out of a Holy Mouth Produces Pearls.
The Respected Lord, the Great Rabbi, Righteous and Exalted, an Honest and Devout Person,
Faithful to God and His *Torah*, Serves God with Joy Out of Agonies and Pains.
With the Sweetness of His Lips and the Pleasantness of His Lesson,
Many Returned from Transgression. He was a Wonder to Many.
Holy They Will Say to Him, Honor is the Holiness of His Splendid Name,
Our Master, Our Teacher, Our Rabbi, **Shabtai**,
May the Memory of the Righteous Be for Life in the World to Come,
The Author of the Book
Pleasant Words on the Song of Songs .
Son of the Great Rabbi etc. Our Teacher the Rabbi, Rabbi **Moshe Zalman** ,
May the Memory of the Righteous Be for a Blessing,
Grandson of The Rabbi the Gaon Famous in His Generation etc.,
Our Master, Our Teacher, Our Rabbi, Rabbi Sholom Shachne,
May the Memory of the Righteous Be for Life in the World to Come,
Av Beit Din of the Holy Congregation of Augustow, May God Protect It.
Also, There Will Come in It a Few Commentaries and Pleasant Innovations
Known by the Name *The Seed of Yitzchak*.
By the Compiler, the Copyist and Organizer
the Great Rabbi etc., Our Teacher the Rabbi **Zalman Yitzchak Ravidovitz**

Son of the Rabbi the Author, May the Memory of the Righteous and the Holy Be for a Blessing,
May His Merit Protect Us, and All God-Fearers.

Grayevo
Printed by Avraham Mordechai Piyurka
In the Year 5665 [1905]

---

[250] *Pirke Avot* 4:20 "there is a new container full of old wine, and an old container in which there is not even new [wine].
[251] Job 12:20 "He deprives trusty men of speech, and takes away the reason of elders."
[252] Job 37:18 "Firm as a mirror of cast metal..."
[253] The *Torah* is the Written *Torah*, and the *Talmud* is the Oral *Torah*.

The Rabbi the *Gaon* Shmuel Avigdor Tosfa'ah – the Third Rabbi

With the beginning of the officiation of the Rabbi, we have in our hands an orderly record of the Augustów Rabbis one after the other, with the exact dates and also the details of the histories of these personalities, and of their spiritual values and their standing in the community.

With the appointment of Rabbi Shmuel Avigdor, the community of Augustów gained a Rabbi *Gaon* who had a reputation in the rabbinic world for his Talmudic[254] greatness and as a distinctive religious author who had enriched rabbinic literature with his interpretation "*Tana Tosefta*"[255] on the "*Toseftot*"[256] of the *Mishnah*.

Rabbi Sh. A. was born (in the year 5566-1806) in Słonim to his father the exalted and well-known Reb Avraham. His father-in-law was the *Gaon* Rabbi Tzvi Hirsh Broidy, *Av Beit Din* of Salant. Already in the springtime of his life Rabbi Shmuel Avigdor became known as a prodigy. When he was 15 years old he dared to write a treatise on the Rambam's[257] "*Hilkhot Edut*,"[258] and the *Geonim* of Lithuania (among them the *Gaon* Rabbi Yaakov Meir Padva, afterwards *Av Beit Din* in Brisk of Lithuania), desired to see this book printed, putting it on the same level with the work by the *Gaon* Rabbi Yehonatan Eibeshutz the "*Tummim.*"[259] Nevertheless, due to financial stress, the matter was not supported. At the age of twenty, he was accepted as Rabbi in "Fahrshtadt" (beyond the river) which is in Horodna, as a replacement for his brother-in-law the *Gaon* Reb Binyamin Diskin (*Av Beit Din* of Volkovisk and *Lomza*). From there he was taken to be the Rabbi of Sislovitz, (Świsłocz, Volkovisk district). From there he moved to Augustów, here he worked as a blessing until 5614 (1854.) In those days, Rabbi Shmuel Avigdor became famous as the writer of a wonderful composition on the "*Shulchan Arukh*"[260] – "*Choshen Mishpat*,"[261] containing excellent innovations on the laws "concluding the tractate according to the *halakhah*."[262] At this same time, he wrote his composition "*Tana Tosefta*," with which he acquired his place in the rabbinic world.

On the importance of Rabbi Shmuel Avigdor in the eyes of the rabbis of his generation, the fact will testify that the *Gaon* Reb Yechiel Haklier,[263] *Av Beit Din* Suwalki, who, in one of his replies to him in his book "*Amudei Or*,"[264] writes of him: "The famous *Gaon*, Sinai and mover of mountains,[265] Light of Israel, the Strong Hammer."

It must be emphasized that in those days they used caution in the distribution of the description "*Gaon*." In the entire book mentioned above, this description is not given to any other rabbi.

---

[254] The *Talmud* is the central text of Rabbinic Judaism and the primary source of Jewish religious law (*halakhah*).

[255] "Teach *Tosefta*."

[256] The *Tosefta (plural Toseftot)* is a compilation of the Jewish oral law from the late 2nd century, the period of the *Mishnah*, that was not included in the *Mishnah*.

[257] Rabbi Moses son of Maimon, Maimonides, 1138-1204.

[258] "The Laws of Testimony."

[259] The *Urim* and the *Tummim* are elements of the *choshen*, the breastplate worn by the High Priest attached to the ephod, and are understood to be oracular devices.

[260] "The Set Table." An influential Jewish code of law written by Joseph Caro (1488-1575).

[261] *Choshen Mishpat*, "the Breastplate of Judgement," is the fourth section of the *Shulchan Aruch*, and deals with laws of finance, financial responsibility, damages, the rules of the *Beit Din*, and the laws of witnesses.

[262] Aramaic.

[263] This appears to be a typographical error. The rabbi in question is Yechiel Heller, the author of the mentioned work.

[264] Pillars of Light.

[265] Babylonian *Talmud Horayot* 14a: "Rabbi Yoḥanan said: Rabban Shimon ben Gamliel and the Rabbis disagreed with regard to this matter. One said: Sinai, i.e., one who is extremely knowledgeable, is preferable; and one said: One who uproots mountains, i.e., one who is extremely incisive, is preferable."

With all the greatness of the *Gaon* Rabbi Sh. A. Tosfa'ah, he did not achieve the rabbinate of Augustow. After several years, he moved to Nyasvizh in place of the Rabbi the *Gaon* Reb Yitzchak Elchanan Spektor, who had accepted the Rabbinate of Novhardok. (He later became famous, while he was the Rabbi of Kovno, as the *Gaon* of his generation). The reason for Rabbi Shmuel Avigdor's leaving Augustów is tied, apparently, to his unwillingness to be under the same roof as one decisive local person, who was an influential "Man of the Century."

This matter is hinted at in the letter to him from the *Gaon* Rabbi Yehoshua Yehuda Leib Diskin, *Av Beit Din* Lomza. The Lomza Rabbi, (the son of Rabbi Sh. A. Tosfa'ah's brother-in-law), was of the opinion that the men of Augustów would prevent their rabbi from leaving them, however he saw that the matter was not so. If so, in hindsight, it was good that his uncle the Rabbi uprooted himself from there because "...if this is what you will call a city and it is given into a single hand, then it is in his hand to overturn a basin and trample and devour and no one to save it from his hand." In connection to that he counseled his uncle the Rabbi in Augustów to decide on his settling down in Nyasvizh, and he sent him "blessing and success" as *Av Beit Din* in his new and important community ("Questions and Answers"). It can be pointed out that from Nyasvizh {p. 92} Reb Shmuel Avigdor went to officiate as Rabbi *Av Beit Din* in the community of Karlin, next to Pinsk, which was famous for its rabbis and *geonim*. He died there in 5626 (1866) when he was only 66 years old. Then, words of appreciation were written about him in the Hebrew newspapers, and they eulogized him in the villages throughout Lithuania and Reisin[266] and the vicinity of Grodno, Bialystok, Lomza and Suwalki. In Augustów, Rabbi Shapira, the local *Av Beit Din,* eulogized him.

The writer of this article heard in his childhood from the elders of the *Beit Midrash* in his hometown of Jedwabne, that Rabbi Shmuel Avigdor and the Rabbi of Suwalki the Kabbalist *Gaon* Rabbi Yitzchak Isaac Chaver – wanted to impose a ban[267] on the Rabbi from Filipova, because he was lenient in matters of what was unkosher, but the *Gaon* Rabbi Arieh Leib Shapira *Av Beit Din* of Kovno, who knew this Rabbi well, dissuaded them from taking this step. He explained to them that the Rabbi is lenient and permits to others from the aspect of sparing the money of Israel, but he himself is highly righteous, abstaining from all the pleasures of this world, honest, hating greed, not accepting any payment for legal decisions, and barely supporting himself on the negligible salary given him by the communities in which he serves as Rabbi. One of the grandsons of Rabbi Shmuel Avigdor, the son of Rabbi Reb Yehoshua Leib Rabinovitz, published a book of his grandfather's, the *Gaon* mentioned above, sermons in 5647 [1887], "*She'airit HaPleitah.*"[268] The Lithuanian *geonim* gave their unqualified approval to the book, and pointed out in their "*haskamot*"[269] that the work contained interesting material for rabbis and preachers. The Rabbis Reb Yitzchak Elchanan Spektor of Kovno, Reb Eliyahu Chaim Meizel of Lodz, and Rabbi Reb Zalman Sender Kahana Shapira of Maltsh, described the author as "The great *Gaon* of his generation – a "Knight of the Shepherds."

The Rabbi Shmuel Avigdor didn't forget Augustów when he was *Av Beit Din* in Karlin. In 5626 [1865], he willingly gave his agreement to the book "*Siftei Yesheinim*" that was written by an Augustow man, Reb Shabtai Ravidovitz, son of Rabbi Moshe Zalman, the grandson of the famous *Gaon Admor*, our great Teacher and Rav-Rabbi Shalom Shachne – May he be remembered for life in the world to come – *Av Beit Din* of the Holy Community of Augustów (we mentioned him earlier as being the first Rabbi of Augustów). This book on the *Torah* was completed in 5601

---

[266] Belarus.

[267] Excommunication.

[268] The surviving remnant.

[269] These *haskamot*, agreements, were letters that appeared at the beginning of a book from various rabbinic authorities, stating their approval of a book. They served as rabbinic seals of approval.

(1841), but its publication was deferred time and again. In *Nissan* 5625 (1865), Rabbi Zalman Yitzchak Ravidovitz, the son of the author, attempted to publish it with the addition of the approvals of the *geonim* of the generation: Reb Yehoshua Leib, *Av Beit Din* of *Lomza*, Rabbi Eliyahu Chaim Meizel, *Av Beit Din* of Pruzhani, and Reb Shmuel Avigdor *Av Beit Din* of Karlin. Rabbi Shmuel Avigdor writes in his approval that he recalls the author from the time that he was a Rabbi in Augustów "who was known for his holiness and abstemiousness, and his prayers were heard, and his teaching was a blessing. He returned many from transgression, and taught through holiness and suffering. This, his book, is built on the foundations of the legends of "*Chazal*"[270] and expositions and on the principles of *Mussar*."[271]

For unknown reasons, the book was published only in 5665 [1905], by the New Hebrew Publishing House of A.M. Piyurka in Grayevo. One of the writer's grandsons, from the Horovitz family, attended to the matter; he attached to the treatise the booklet "*Zera Yitzchak*"[272] from the pen of the author's son, which has in it annotations and innovations. It should be noted that this book, "*Siftei Yesheinim*," is not widely known and is not registered with the "The Book Collection House"[273] of Ch.D. Friedberg. The little that is brought here is according to what I have recorded from this that I found about him in his time at the *Beit Midrash* of my home town, Jedwabne.

Rabbi Yisrael Isser Shapira – the Fourth Rabbi

His father, Reb Dov-Ber, was a scion of the well-known Shapira family of esteemed lineage that had produced many men of repute in Judaism. He was one of the respected men of Augustow about a hundred and fifty years ago. He is described as the "Rabbi Exalted {p. 93} in *Torah* and God-fearing, who walked the straight path with God and people, and pondered the *Torah* day and night. He negotiated with faith; the fear of God was his treasure. His dealings were in tens of thousands, yet his hands did not redeem a penny that was not his. He was also a great sage in matters of the world, and excellent in negotiations; his wise and knowledgeable advice was always trustworthy." He left six sons and two daughters. The sons were all exalted in *Torah*, and especially, the two: Reb Yehoshua Heschel Rabbi of Shaki and Szczuczyn in the *Lomza* region, and Reb Yisrael Isser, who was seen as a *Gaon*, and was *Av Beit Din* in the city of his birth, Augustów.

Reb Dov Ber, son of Rabbi Natan Neta, died in Augustów in the year 5621 [1861] at the age of seventy. His two sons, mentioned above, eulogized him. An appreciation of the respected deceased was published in "*HaMaggid*" (the year 1861 Issue 24) by his grandson, Eliezer Yitzchak Shapira.

Reb Yisrael Isser Shapira was born in Augustów in 5588 [1828]. He was the distinctive student of the *Gaon* Reb Yehuda Bachrach, who established a *Yeshiva* for young men of excellence in the city of his rabbinate, Sejny. He also visited frequently in the *Yeshiva* of Volozhin; there he poured water on the hands of[274] the *Gaon* Reb Yitzchak Barbano Chaim, founder of the renowned *Yeshiva* mentioned above. He heard "lessons" from the two young heads of the *Yeshiva* – the brothers-in-law Rabbi Eliezer Yitzchak Fried and "*HaNatziv*" (Reb Naftali Tzvi Yehuda Berlin). He took for a wife in Vilna the granddaughter of the Righteous Rabbi Yishayahu Grammer, a notable of the city, and returned to the vicinity of his hometown. He was still a young *yeshiva*

---

[270] *Chakhameinu Zikhronam Livrakha*, "Our Sages, may their memory be for a blessing," refers to all Jewish sages of the *Mishnah, Tosefta* and *Gemara*.

[271] The *Mussar* movement was developed in 19th century Lithuania by Rabbi Yisrael Salanter. It promotes the development of inner virtues and characteristics.

[272] Yitzchak's Seed.

[273] Library.

[274] Was a student of. This is similar to the English expression "sat at the feet of..."

student and assisted the *Gaon* Reb Yitzchak Avigdor, the new rabbi of Sejny, in the founding of the new *yeshiva* in this city of his rabbinate, and was already appointed to be a second *yeshiva* teacher in the "telling of lessons" for the students. The Sejny *yeshiva* was planned to be an advanced level academy for the communities of Israel in Poland in the format of the great *yeshiva* of Volozhin in Lithuania, but because of the decrees of the Russian authority, that was not carried out. Rabbi Yitzchak Avigdor was appointed as Rabbi in Kovno in place of the *Gaon* Rabbi Shmuel Avigdor who had moved to Nyasvizh. In Augustów Rabbi Yisrael Isser acted as a blessing during the period of time from 5614-5629 [1854-1869]. Afterwards he moved to serve in Mezeritz as the *Av Beit Din*. There he found his final resting place in the year 5694[1894], at the age of sixty-six.

Rabbi Yisrael Isser Shapira was held to be a scholarly Rabbi; those who knew and admired him considered him the distinguished "best" in instruction; rabbis from near and far rushed "their questions" in serious matters of *halakhah*. The Geonim of Poland and Galicia considered him important and appreciated him; Reb Yisrael Trunk from Kutno, the Rabbi of Bialystok – Reb Yom Tov Lipman, Reb Chaim Eliezer Vax from Kalish (author of "*HaNefesh HaChaya*"),[275] Reb Yosef Shaul Natanson, author of "*HaSho'el U'Meishiv*,"[276] *Av Beit Din* Lvov, Reb Tzvi Hirsh Orenstein, *Av Beit Din* of Brisk of Lithuania, Warsaw and Lvov. His name even reached the land of Israel. Two sages from the Sephardi Tiberias, Rabbi Aharon Alchadif and Rabbi Moshe Yedid, corresponded with him in the year 5633 [1873] about a complicated matter of law regarding a will. Rabbi Yisrael Isser established a *yeshiva* in his home for fine young men and provided them with a lesson every day, and also guided them in learning the books of the "*Shulchan Arukh*" as a team. With all this, his eyes were looking at issues concerning the city. With the awakening of the *Chibbat Tzion*[277] movement at the beginning of the 1880s he, too, joined this movement. He was one of those who preferred the *etrog* of the land of Israel over those that grew in Corfu, which is in the land of Greece, and agreed with all his soul with the *Gaon* Rabbi Chaim Eliezer Vax, who conducted vigorous propaganda in the boycotting of the *etrogs* from Corfu. This matter was indeed to the dissatisfaction of the zealots who saw it as a "hurrying the end"[278] but they did not dare to come out against it openly because Rabbi Yisrael Isser was held, even in the extreme God-fearing groups, and also in the courts of the righteous *Admorim*, as a great God-fearer, punctilious about the *mitzvot*,[279] made do with little, and hated greed, like a squanderer, on matters of *tzedakah*.[280]

{p. 94} The book "*Ezrat Yisrael*"[281] that was published in Warsaw in 5650 [1891] contains *Responsa* by Rabbi Yisrael Isser on issues that are in the four sections of the "*Shulchan Arukh.*" In this book, we find his letters to his two brothers, Rabbi *Gaon* Yehoshua Heschel and Rabbi Reb Nisan, and also to his brother-in-law, Rabbi Aleksander Ziskind Maimon from Seirijai. From the period of his rabbinate in Augustów we find in his book, mentioned above, his replies: to the *Gaon Av Beit Din* of Bialystok, after having been asked to express his opinion on a *get* that had been issued in Rotzk, even though the Rabbi of that town mentioned above was himself a great scholar; to the *Gaon Av Beit Din* of Sharashavi (adjacent to Brisk of Lithuania), the Righteous *Gaon*, God-fearing and complete Reb Ben-Tzion Sternfeld; to the Rabbi Elchanan Tzvi HaCohain Lap, *Moreh Tzedek* in Grayevo, (the father of Reb Arieh Leib Lap, one of the notables of Augustów); to Rabbi Avraham Yoel Abelson *Av Beit Din* of Staviski. And also, his own unique conclusion in the matter

---

[275] The Living Soul.
[276] The Questioner and the Responder.
[277] Love of Zion.
[278] Hastening the end times and the coming of the Messiah.
[279] Commandments.
[280] The righteousness of giving to the needy.
[281] The Helper of Israel.

of a childless widow awaiting levirate marriage to go to market, that occurred in Augustów, the city of his rabbinate (from the year 5624 [1864]).

Rabbi Moshe Yitzchak HaLevi – the Fifth Rabbi.

During his lifetime, he was known in the rabbinic world as Reb Moshe Itzel the Ponevezhi, after the name of the town Ponevezh, a town in the Kovno region, where he served as rabbi for a number of years. He also served as rabbi in Susmaken, Libvi, Golding, Kretinga, Tavrig, and Plungyan in Zamot, where he served as rabbi for a number of years. From there he came to Augustów, the place where he functioned as Rabbi *Av Beit Din* for only about year, and there he found his final resting place in the year 5630 [1870] when he was only 52 years old. The reason Reb Moshe Yitzchak HaLevi had been rabbi in seven communities prior to coming to Augustów is explained by the fact that he was a wealthy merchant and therefore was not dependent on the public. On the other hand, every town wanted a Rabbi who was not in need of a salary. Reb Moshe Itzel was famous as the *Gaon* of the generation, and a significant master of instruction, and also, he excelled at quick comprehension, and had a tremendous memory. The *Gaon Reb* Yisrael Lifshitz, the Rabbi of Danzig, who knew the *Gaon* Reb Moshe Itzel well from the time that this Lithuanian Rabbi was staying in Danzig for his business ventures, wrote praises of him for his well-known interpretations of the *Mishnah*, "*Tiferet Yisrael*."[282] It is also known to us that the Kabbalist *Gaon* Reb Eliyahu Raguler, who was older than him by many years, and who knew him from the time of the rabbinates of the two of them in Zamot, respected and esteemed him, and would publicize his praise among the masses at various opportunities.

Rabbi Moshe Itzel was quick-witted, expert in worldly experiences, witty and sharp. He also guided the members of his community on occupational matters, commerce and purchasing. For the purpose of his business matters, he would be missing from his residence for weeks and even months. It was told that he would say: the community leaders would have already removed me from the rabbinate, but they don't find me at home. Once, two litigants came to him for a deliberation on a burial place. They had both purchased a burial plot in the excellent place, and they were arguing and deliberating with each other. Rabbi Moshe Itzel studied the matter, turned their claim over, and ruled: whoever dies first will have the right to the excellent grave… and they did not argue again.

Rabbi Moshe Itzel would show extra affection to the boys of the *yeshiva* and the schoolchildren. When he would enter the *Beit Midrash* and see a child sitting and engaging in *Torah*, he would hug him and kiss him and give him coins from his pocket. It happened that the *shamash*[283] in the *Beit Midrash*, a difficult and impatient man, got angry at one child and the took the page from his hand by force. The child faltered and fell. When Reb Moshe Itzel noticed the matter, he rushed to the *shamash* and ordered him with a rebuke: "Hurry and kiss the child! You must take it upon yourself as if you threw a book on the ground…"

{p. 95} The Jews of Augustów were given only a short time to enjoy this witty and sharp *Gaon*. In 5629 [1869] he came and in the summer of 5630 [1870] he passed away. A special article about his death and funeral was published in the Hebrew weekly "*HaMaggid*." He was described there as the great *Gaon*, the glory of the generation, who left behind him his writings on the *Mishnah* and decisors, sermons and anthologies, that he left nothing of our Holy *Torah* that he did not interpret by way of its plain sense, and the true homily. (It can be pointed out that from all his writings, only his commentaries on the *Mishnah* were published in Stettin); and that "the land of

---

[282] The Splendor of Israel.
[283] The *shamash* is the sexton, or caretaker of a synagogue.

Zamot conceived and gave birth, and woe is me, said Augustów - for she has lost her precious instrument."[284]

According to the article mentioned above, we know that many rabbis from the surrounding area participated in his funeral. The elderly Rabbi Reb Yehoshua Heschel Eliaszon from Sejny eulogized him in the *Beit Midrash*, and Reb Shmuel Mohilever, who came especially from the city of his rabbinate, Radom, in order to pay final respect to the deceased rabbi. In the cemetery, Rabbi Eliezer Simcha Rabinovitz, the rabbi of Suwalki, eulogized him. The writer of the news item sums up his words, that no one left the cemetery until all the men and leaders of the city of Augustów had signed a rabbinic letter to the late rabbi's son-in-law - Rabbi Katriel Natan – who was dependent at that time on his father-in-law's table.[285]

In addition to Rabbi Katriel Natan, the young son-in-law of Rabbi Moshe Itzel Halevi, he had two other sons-in-law: the well-known Rabbis Reb Ber Wolf Lifshitz and Reb Nachum Shraga Ravel. Reb Ber Wolf was Rabbi in the towns of Ventspils and Shavlin - in Kurland, and Sradnik in Kurland. Reb Nachum Shraga was Rabbi in Blinkovi, (Kovno region) and Prani, (Suwalk region). The son of this rabbi was the Rabbi *Gaon* Dr. Revel-Mashkama of the *Yeshivot* of Rabbi Yitzchak Elchanan in New York, and Head of the *Yeshiva* and Head Administrator for many years, until the day of his death in the year 5701 [1941].

From the family of Reb Moshe Itzel it should be pointed out that his son, Reb Shlomo HaLevi, settled in Augustów and took as a wife one of the daughters of the Augustów notable Reb Eliyahu HaCohain Rosental (the father of Reb Shabtai and Reb Tzvi Rosental). Reb Shlomo Revel died in 5663 [1903] in Konigsberg, East Prussia, when he went there to seek doctors, while he was still in the best of his years. The matter of his death made a great impression in Augustów. The friend of the deceased, Chaim Yosef Markus, published words of appreciation of him by the name of "*Alon Bachut*"[286] in *HaTzefirah* (the year 1903, # 45):

"How very much the terrible news shocked and melted every heart in our city when the telegram came from Konigsberg, on Tuesday, 15 Iyar, that a member of our community like the exalted, sharp, precious, the honored Rabbi, our Teacher, the Rabbi Shlomo Revel, may peace be upon him,[287] had passed away there. The deceased was the son of the *Gaon* Rabbi who knows all secrets,[288] the righteous, as well-known as our teacher and Rabbi Moshe Yitzchak Halevi, may the memory of the righteous be for a blessing, who served with the crown of the rabbinate in the cities of Kurland and Zamot and whose honorable rest is in our city. And even if it is more than thirty years since he went to his rest, nevertheless his great name is still gloriously raised, and with feelings of holiness, everyone will remember his name.

This his son, who in the days of his youth poured water on the hands of his father the *Gaon*, may his memory be for a blessing, apart from the fact that he was exalted in the *Torah*, still inherited from his father, may his memory be for a blessing, noble qualities. He was careful with the *mitzvot*,[289] good-hearted and with a halo of the light of success on his head, for he was a timber

---

[284] Borrowing from the Babylonian *Talmud*, *Megillah* 6a:3 "… when Rabbi Zeira died, a certain eulogizer opened his eulogy for him with these words: The land of Shinar, i.e., Babylonia, Rabbi Zeira's birthplace, conceived and bore him; the land of the deer, i.e., Eretz Yisrael, where Rabbi Zeira lived as an adult and rose to prominence, raised her delights. Woe unto her, said Rakkath, for she has lost her precious instrument."

[285] Supported by him financially.

[286] "Oak of weeping." Genesis 35:8 "Deborah, Rebekah's nurse, died, and was buried under the oak below Bethel; so it was named the oak of weeping."

[287] This is the equivalent of the English "May he rest in peace."

[288] Babylonian *Talmud Brakhot* 58a: "And Rav Hamnuna said: One who sees multitudes of Israel, six hundred thousand Jews, recites: Blessed…Who knows all secrets."

[289] Commandments.

merchant, – he was a very excellent philanthropist. He was the head and the first in all matters of holiness, and his home was wide open to all who sought and asked.

But in his last years God's hand was upon him, and on the occasion of the change for the worse that happened in the timber trade, his situation worsened, and the hard hand of heart disease weighed on him. When the condition of his illness improved a little, he travelled after {p. 96} the Festival of *Pesach* to Konigsberg, to seek the advice of Professor Lichtenheim but he was only in the clinic for five days, and on the fifth day of his arrival there his spirit returned to the one who gave it, in the best of his years. He was 52 years old at his death. May his soul be bound up in the bonds of life. He left for lamenting three daughters and two sons. And as the man was loved and respected in our community, consolation for our wound will not quickly be found, and in the hidden places all who loved and knew him will weep. I too, who writes with a broken heart."

Rabbi Yehuda Leib Gordin – the Sixth Rabbi

The son of Reb Avraham Abba, from among the honored residents of Rezhitse. He received an excellent religious education, and already in his youth he was considered a prodigy. At a young man, he entered into correspondence with Rabbi Yosef Zechariah Stern from Shavli, and Rabbi Shlomo HaCohain from Vilna. After this, he became the distinguished student of Rabbi Moshe Danushevski, the author of *"Be'er Moshe,"*[290] who at that time was *Av Beit Din* in Svir. He also acquired for himself a secular education and learned the Russian language inside and out. In the year 5643 [1883], he was appointed, on the recommendation of his Rabbi, *Av Beit Din* of Michaelishok (Vilna region), and in 5647 [1887] was appointed *Av Beit Din* in Augustów. From here, he moved in the year 5657 [1897] to serve as *Av Beit Din* in the town of Ostrov in the Lomza region. Even though that city was mostly *chassidic*, he was accepted by all the groups. Incidentally, after the community of Ostrov Mazovyetsk sent to Rabbi Gordin the rabbinic letter, as was the accepted practice, doubts were aroused in him if it was worth it for him to move from the peaceful Augustów to the *chassidic* town of Ostrov. They say that at the time, Rabbi Yisrael Meir, the author of *"Chafetz Chaim,"* was visiting Augustów, and Rabbi Gordin revealed his hesitation to him. The *Gaon* from Radin, with a frequent smile on his lips, answered him: "What is the fear of the *chassidim*? And what do they do? Drink a toast to life with a little brandy? So – you drink a glass of brandy with them!"

In the year 5662 [1902] he was appointed *Av Beit Din* in Smorgon. At the beginning of 5674 [1914] he moved to officiate as the Rabbi and *Av Beit Din* in Lomza, and became known throughout the breadth of Poland as one of the greats of the *Torah* and instruction. In Lomza, he was conspicuous as an accomplished public activist, and revealed total devotion for the Jews of his city and the surrounding area. During the emergency years of 5674-5675 [1914-1915], when the lives of the Jews in Poland were forfeited to Russian induction into the army and the Polish population at the same time, he stood at his post and saved the Jews of his community. When the danger of expulsion for the Jews of Lomza, the fortified city, could be seen, he travelled to Vilna, presented himself before the military commander there, and thanks to his, the Jews remained in place. Again, when Jews of Lomza were accused of spying for the Germans by an officer who

---

[290] The Well of Moses

hated Jews, who sought to take them hostage, he endangered his life, and went to the hater, to request that he cancel the order. He was received rudely, but he responded to it {p. 97} proudly; he even offered himself as a hostage. His courage was convincing, and the decree was nullified.

It should be noted that Rabbi Yehuda remained in contact with public activists in Augustów even when he was the rabbi in other towns. It was thanks only to his special recommendation that the *Gaon* Reb Yitzchak Kosovski was accepted as Rabbi *Av Beit Din* in Augustów (and that in accordance with the personal request of the *Gaon* Reb Chaim Ozer Grodzinski from Vilna, the brother-in-law of Reb Yitzchak Kosovski). In the year 5681 [1921], he was accepted as the Rabbi of the Chicago *Kollel*.[291] He succeeded in becoming beloved by all the congregations, and in the unification of the synagogues, which consulted him and listened to his words. He was an active member of the Union of Orthodox Rabbis of the United States and Canada. When Rabbi Yehuda Leib Gordin went to his eternity in Chicago in 5685 [1925], the *Gaon* Rabbi Y. Kosovski eulogized him in the Great *Beit Midrash* in Augustów in the presence of a large assembly.

Rabbi Gordin published three important books: "*Divrei Yehuda*" (Warsaw 5664 [1903]),[292] questions and answers on the *Shulchan Arukh, Orech Chaim*[293] and *Yoreh Deah*;[294] "*Teshuvot of Yehuda*" (Vilna 5668 [1908]), questions and answers on the four parts of the "*Shulchan Arukh*; "*D'var Yehuda,*"[295] part 1 (Warsaw 5664 [1904]) – two sermons: "*Degel HaGadol*"[296] for the Great *Shabbat*,[297] and "*Degel HaMishnah,*"[298] for the conclusion of the Six Orders of the *Mishnah*. In this book, he reveals himself as expert in religious philosophy and possessing a broad general education. He was an excellent preacher; every sermon of his was a public event and assembled an audience from all of the groups.

In the year 5694 [1894], a disgraceful event occurred in Tsarist Russia. A "Jewish criminal," an apostate, sent slander to enrage, to the Tsarist government in Peterburg in which he falsely and despicably accused the *chassidim*, in his description of them as being an illiterate cult that hated the Russian Crown and was likely to endanger its existence. In the Tsarist government, the idea developed to close all the prayer houses of the *chassidim*, and declaring that people who gather frequently in their shadow were an "illegal cult" who should be wiped out. The Government imposed on its Minister of Education to prepare a detailed survey of this movement, its nature and function, in preparation for a government discussion. The Minister of Education turned to Rabbi Yehuda Leib Gordin, who officiated as Rabbi of Augustów, with a request to prepare a detailed memorandum on the subject: "What is *Chassidut?*" The Rabbi fulfilled the important task appointed to him. He composed in Russian a comprehensive overview from a philosophic-scientific point of view, and about the mystery that is in this idea. In his booklet, Rabbi Gordin tastefully described the system of Chassidism, and proved that this was not a separate class of Judaism. Thus, he nullified the claims of the enemies and the libels of the apostates Pfefferkorn, Eisenmenger, Rohling, and others. The fact that a Rabbi in Israel, who had indeed been known for a long time as a distinguished scholar and an excellent preacher, had also succeeded in writing a

---

[291] A *kollel* is a men's institute for full-time advanced study of the *Talmud* and rabbinic literature. While it resembles a *yeshiva* in that it offers lessons, it is different from a *yeshiva* in that most of the students are married.
[292] "Words of Judah."
[293] "The Way of Life" is a section of Rabbi Jacob ben Asher's compilation of *halakhah, Arba'ah Turim,* Four Columns, and deals mostly with the Jewish Calendar.
[294] "Instructor of Knowledge" is a section of the *Arba'ah Turim* that deals with aspects of *halakhah* other than the Jewish calendar.
[295] Word of Judah.
[296] The Great Flag.
[297] The *Shabbat* immediately before *Pesach*.
[298] The Flag of the *Mishnah*

book on *Chassidut* in pure Russian language, made a strong impression also amongst non-Jews. It should be noted that these books of his would be used by the defense attorneys of Mendel Beilis[299] in his famous trial that took place in 1913 in Kiev. Rabbi Gordin also collected all of his speeches that he gave in the Russian language at various opportunities, and published them in the book "*Slova*."[300] He received a letter of appreciation for these books from Tsar Nikolai II. He was also familiar with Russian literature, and was in correspondence with the greatest of the Russian writers, Lev Tolstoy, who suggested to the Jewish rabbi that the rabbi should write a book in Russian volume on the Jewish ethics in the *Talmud*.

{p. 98} Rabbi Yehuda Leib Gordin followed the *Chibbat Tzion* movement, and even favored the national Zionist movement; however, because of the special conditions in which the Polish Rabbis were found, not even Rabbi Gordin could not openly act on behalf of the movements mentioned above.

After the Balfour Declaration (in the year 1917), when he had already been *Av Beit Din* Lomza for four years, he openly joined the Zionist movement and advocated on its behalf in speech and in writing. He became especially active in the religious Zionist "*Mizrachi*" movement that was becoming entrenched in Poland at that time. This matter aroused much attention among the Rabbis of the communities that were adjacent to Lomza, and some of them that secretly in their hearts also were inclined towards affection for the Zionist movement, now joined it openly without fright or fear. Among them were: Rabbi Benyamin Eliyahu Remigolski, the Rabbi of Stavisk, Rabbi Moshe Avigdor Amiel, the Rabbi of Grayevo, (later the Rabbi of Antwerp and lastly the Chief Rabbi of Tel-Aviv-Yafo), Rabbi Shmuel HaCohain Kaplan, the Rabbi of Kolno, and others. Concerning the blessed activities of Rabbi Yehuda Leib Gordin in Augustów, the well-known Hebrew journalist, Mr. Y.Z. Sperling, a resident of this town, wrote in *HaTzefirah* in # 51, 1890 (5650):

"The Rabbi *Gaon* Yehuda Leib Gordin, famously praised, in addition to his great sharpness and expertise in all areas of *Torah*, according to certification of the great ones of our time, still has a name in wisdom and experiences of the world and the national language, enabling him to stand before ministers and the nobility of the land, and address them in their native language. During this present week (February 12), he was called to the test in the knowledge of the Russian language before the council that is appointed in this matter in the Command House of Suwalk region and with God's desire in his hand, he succeeded in withstanding the difficulty. The Head of the Council, who is the deputy of the Minister of the region, together with the teachers (professors), were surprised by his clear speech in the Russian tongue without any error in the rules of grammar and his wonderful ability to formulate in that language every matter that they instructed him to in writing (*sochinenie*),[301] rapidly and without hesitation, also regarding his great expertise in all the laws that touch on the enumeration of the civil situation which are required of him as a government-appointed Rabbi. He was given by the Council a certificate of excellence in experience that will authorize him as a servant of the government-appointed rabbinate, favorably and to the joy of all who knew and loved him."

In 1896, the Jewish soldiers of the 104th Battalion stationed in Augustów decided to celebrate the completion of writing a *Torah* scroll in honor of the coronation of Nikolai II as Tsar. The celebration took place in the home of Leizer Vizhinski. Rabbi Yehuda Leib Gordin invited all the officers of the battalion mentioned above, and also the officers of the Cossack regiment that was also stationed in the city, together with civil servants in the city. He even succeeded in

---

[299] Menachem Mendel Beilis was a Russian Jew accused of a ritual murder in Kiev in a notorious 1913 trial, known as the "Beilis trial" or "Beilis affair."
[300] Russian for "speech."
[301] Russian for an essay, composition, or opus.

including in the celebration the musical troupe of the regiment. Many of the officers and clerks asked the *Sofer Stam* (scribe)[302] to write, in their names, one letter in the *Torah* scroll "and they grasped the quill and offered speeches in honor of the Kaiser, and they blessed the Rabbi…". A "wedding ceremony" was conducted, and a parade of two lines of soldiers, with candles in their hands, left the home of Mr. Vishinski to the Great Synagogue that was illuminated with thousands of candles. The Rabbi expounded in the state language for about an hour on the connection between the coronation holiday and the completion of the writing of a *Torah* scroll. And how all the ministers were amazed to see a Rabbi from the old generation produce such fine words in Russian.

The correspondent mentioned above, in "*HaTzefirah*" (the year 1896 issue 51), brings the thanks of the men of the Augustów community to the notables that assisted in the success of the wonderful celebration: Reuven Rotenberg, Y. Varhaftig, Dovid Mordechai Markus, Yehuda Cohen, Sh. Eisenstadt, Y. Grosberg, Leib Glikstein, Y. A. Reichstein, Yosef Trotsky, Yehuda Shapira and Arieh Leib Lap.

Rabbi Katriel Natan - the Seventh Rabbi

The Rabbi Reb Katriel Aaron Natan was born in the town of Latskovi (Kovno region). His father, Reb {p. 99} Hillel son of Reb Meir, a native of Vilkomir, was one of the greats in *Torah* there. He was modest, humble, and charitable. He engaged in the study of *Torah* for its own sake, and died at the age of 84 in the town mentioned above in the year 5656 [1895] (according to *HaTzefirah*, 1896, #134). His son was Reb Katriel, who became well-known as a *Gaon* already in the spring of his days. The *Gaon* Reb Moshe Itzel the Levite chose him to be his son-in-law. As mentioned above, Reb Katriel was appointed the Rabbi of Augustów in the year 5630 [1870] in place of his father-in-law, and he was but 28 years of age. For fifty-two years, on and off, he served as *Av Beit Din* Augustów.

In the year 5647 [1887], there occurred a rift in the Jewish community. The wealthy and the scholars supported Rabbi Katriel, while *amcha* preferred a preacher rabbi, a quality that the rabbi was missing. This division of hearts caused Rabbi Katriel to leave the city in which he had officiated as rabbi for 17 years, and he became the rabbi in Bodki, and afterwards, in Sopotkin. Nevertheless, when the *Gaon* Rabbi Y.L. Gordin transferred from Augustów to Ostrov, the two sides were reconciled, and Rabbi Katriel Natan was returned with much honor to the seat of his previous rabbinate, and became the teacher and rabbi of all the people of his congregation until the day of his passing in 5682 [1922], when he was 80 years old. His two-volume work, "*Keter HaMelech*,"[303] on the Rambam's "*HaYad HaChazakah*"[304] (Warsaw 5656 [1896]) proves his extensive knowledge of the *Talmud* and its interpreters. Many elements of "*Keter HaMelech*:" regulations concerning *Beit HaBechirah*,[305] the Temple implements, the sacrificial procedures, the perpetual and additional offerings, the disqualification of dedicated items, entering the Temple, prohibitions of the altar and the priesthood – "are a light to the feet[306] of all these who engage in the study of the matters mentioned above from The Order of *Kodoshim*."[307] Well-known *geonim* used these volumes and also members of the "*Kollel Kodoshim*," founded by the righteous *Gaon* Reb Yisrael Meir HaCohain of Raduń, the author of "*Chafetz Chaim*." It is also worth pointing out that in this book "*Keter HaMelech*," the author, Rabbi Katriel, brings many innovations, respecting

---

[302] A *sofer* is a scribe. The acronym *ST"M* stands for the Hebrew words for *sifrei* (scrolls of) *Torah, tefillin* (phylacteries), and *mezzuzot*, the parchments that are affixed to the doorposts of Jewish homes.
[303] "The King's Crown."
[304] "The Strong Hand."
[305] The Temple.
[306] Psalms 119:105 "Your word is a lamp to my feet, a light for my path."
[307] *Seder Kodoshim*, the Order of Holy Things, is one of the six orders of the *Talmud*.

"my teacher and father-in-law the great and well-known *Gaon* Rabbi Moshe Yitzchak the Levi – may the memory of the righteous be for a blessing, who served with the crown of the rabbinate in several towns, Zamot and Kurland and his name was raised for glory, and he left behind him many innovations on the *Talmud*, and the Jerusalem *Talmud*, and legends, many of which have been lost or burnt, may the Merciful one save us, and now I have brought only very few of his innovations on Rambam, may his memory be for a blessing, that which I found written on his edition of the Rambam, or what I heard from his mouth, may his memory be for a blessing, so that will be for him a reminder there shall be a memorial, and his lips mouthing the words in the grave[308] for a name and a memory."

Reb Katriel promises in his foreword to his book, mentioned above, to publish more of the innovations of his father-in-law, the *Gaon* mentioned above, that remained in writing together with his other innovations. However, he did not get to do that. In the meantime, the First World War broke out, and the mind was distracted from these things.

In the period of his officiating as Rabbi, crucial changes in the lives of the Jews: a great migration to America began, the Enlightenment movement, *Chibbat Tzion* and national Zionism sprang up, even the Socialist movements penetrated Augustów. The rabbi that trembled at the unique character of the community attempted to fight the new winds, but when he saw that his splendor would not be on this path, he desisted from it, and consoled himself with his work on his book and his diligence in studying the *Torah*. When Rabbi Katriel passed away – 18 Kislev 5682 [1921] – the Augustów community, published a mourning notice in *HaTzefirah* and the Warsaw "*Heint*" on the death of its teacher and rabbi, "The Rabbi the Righteous *Gaon*, the great one in the generation, Rabbi Katriel Aaron son of Reb Hillel Halevi Natan."

Rabbi Azriel Zelig, the community's *Moreh Tzedek*, eulogized him, and said, among other things, (according to the book "*MiMe'onot Ariot*"),[309] that the late Rabbi was "…a great *Gaon*, a righteous foundation of the world, the glory of the generation," and that he was for the members of his community as a father is to his sons. He took an interest in each and every one of them, took part in our joys and participated in our sorrows, and when {p. 100} he saw a small child saying the *Kaddish*[310] in the synagogue he would investigate and try to find out who was supporting him, and he would speak to him as a father to a son. All the days of his life were days of sorrow and pain, and his book "*Keter HaMelech*," which is a "crown of roses,[311] full of buds and blossoms, has beneath it "a crown of thorns," [312] because he composed it out of sorrow and distress.

They also eulogized the *Gaon* Rabbi Katriel in towns near and far. In Lomza, the *Gaon Av Beit Din* Rabbi Yehuda Leib Gordin eulogized him. In Bialystok, the *maggid* of the city, Rabbi Rapoport, eulogized him in the old *Beit Midrash* where the *Gaon* would pray whenever he came to visit the town. In Jedwabne where they knew Rabbi Katriel well for he often came to visit family there, the Rabbi Eliyahu Bornstein the town's teacher – he was eulogized by the *Gaon*, Rabbi Avigdor Bialystoki.

---

[308] Babylonian *Talmud Yevamot* 97a "With regard to any *Torah* scholar in whose name a matter of *halakhah* is said in this world, his lips mouth the words in the grave…"

[309] "From Lions' Dens."

[310] The prayer for the dead, which is entirely words of praise for God.

[311] Babylonian *Talmud Bava Metzia* 84a "One who wishes to see something resembling the beauty of Rabbi Yochanan should bring a new, shiny silver goblet from the smithy and fill it with red pomegranate seeds and place a crown of red roses…"

[312] Babylonian *Talmud Shabbat* 152a "Youth is a crown of roses; old age is a crown of thorns."

The Rabbi the Gaon Yitzchak Kosovski

The Rabbi, Rabbi Yitzchak Kosovski, may his memory be for a blessing, was born in the year 5637 [1877] in the city of Warsaw, to his father the Rabbi Reb Shaul, may his memory be for a blessing, a descendant of a house that merited two tables, *Torah* and greatness.[313] This was the house of Shachor-Berlin, from Mir, the famous city of *Torah*. In the days of his youth he was educated by and learned *Torah* with his uncle, The Rabbi the *Gaon* Reb Yosef Dovid Shachor, may the memory of the righteous be for a blessing, in Antopol. When he was about thirteen years old, he travelled to study *Torah* in the famous Telz *yeshiva*. He studied with great diligence, he was sharp and proficient in all the tractates of the *Talmud* and the decisors and while he was still young in days he had already acquired for himself a great name throughout Lithuania.

In the year 5660 (1900), he took to wife the daughter of the Rabbi the *Gaon* Reb Dovid Shlomo Grodzinski, may the memory of the righteous be for a blessing, from Ivye (the father of the *Gaon* Reb Chaim Ozer, may the memory of the righteous be for a blessing.)

In the year 5664 (1904), the Rabbi Reb Dovid Shlomo died in good old age, and the Rabbi Reb Yitzchak Koshelevski was chosen to sit on the seat of his father-in-law, while he was still a young *yeshiva* student. He immediately became the spiritual leader of the community. He had a wonderful memory, rapid comprehension, and common sense. His mouth produced pearls. He spoke with lovingkindness, which amazed his listeners with his sermons. He became beloved by the congregation also for his majestic appearance and his pleasant stature. He knew foreign languages, and was expert in the experiences of the world.

As the brother-in-law of the *Gaon* Reb Chaim Ozer Grodzinski, may the memory of the righteous be for a blessing, he took part in his work for the *yeshivot*.

In the year 5674 (1914), with the outbreak of the First World War, he was forced to leave the community of Ivye. He was accepted at the beginning of the year 5676 (1915) as the Rabbi of Mariampol, and officiated there until the end of the war.

{p. 101} In the year 5682 (1922), he was accepted as Rabbi of Augustow, where he was active for three years. In the year 5686 (1925), he was called to sit on the seat of the rabbinate of Volkovisk.

In the year 5694 (1934), he moved to South Africa; there he was appointed rabbi of the Association of Congregations in Johannesburg and the surrounding area. Here too he worked for the teaching of *Torah*, and the strengthening of the religion. Here he was also active for the "*Mizrachi*," and until his final day he served as President of this movement in South Africa.

In the last years, his book, "*Shabbat U'Mo'ed,*"[314] was published in two parts, which included conversations, meditations, and sermons on the weekly portion.

The rabbi's aspiration was to go up to our land. In one of his last letters, to his sister the *Rabbanit*,[315] he wrote, among other things, that Johannesburg served him as only an intermediate station before his *aliyah* to the land. He let her know that he had it in mind to go up to the land and settle there, if the doctors would permit him the journey.

---

[313] Babylonian *Talmud Brakhot* 5a "not every person merits to eat off of two tables, one of wealth and one of *Torah*…"
[314] "Sabbath and Festival."
[315] Rabbi's wife.

But he did not get the chance. On 20 Elul 5711 (1951), he died. He was 74 years old at his death.

(According to an article that we received from the Association of Emigres from Ivye).

Rabbi Azriel Zelig Noach Koshelevski
By Yitzchak Edelstein

Reb Azriel Zelig Noach arrived in Augustow in the year 5645 [1885] when he was 18 years old. After he absorbed *Torah* in the *yeshivot* of Lomza and Stutzin, he decided to travel to Augustow in order to improve the condition of his health. Augustow is a city encircled by forests, and Reb Asher Zelig Noach needed the clear air for the sake of his recuperation. He hoped that in this place he would be able to learn out of the serenity of body and soul.

He received his sustenance, like all young men who learned at that time in the *Beit Midrash* of Augustow, from the hands of righteous women, who respectfully provided food to the young men who were studying. Among these women, Mrs. Chaya Sarah Denmark should be mentioned, who brought his meals to the *Beit Midrash*, where he learned and pondered the *Torah*.

He fixed his regular place for study in the "*Yatke-Kloiz*." They formerly called this place "*Chassidim Kloiz*," since a *minyan* of *chassidim* prayed in it, and they were its founders. Over the course of years, the *chassidim* disappeared from the city, and the *yeshiva* boys took their place. The worshippers of the *kloiz* in those days were householders who were exalted in the *Torah*, and every night they would learn *Talmud* there. The sound of the *Torah* would erupt from within the walls of the *kloiz* until the bitter and hurried day when the Augustow community was destroyed by the vile Nazi.

Reb Azriel Zelig Noach learned with great diligence and deep perseverance in the "*Yatke-Kloiz*." He also gave lessons in *Torah* to the householders, in the hours between the afternoon and evening prayers, in the "Bridge Street *Kloiz*," and the Shoemakers' *Kloiz*, which was located in the vestibule of the Great *Beit Midrash*. Reb Azriel Zelig Noach became much endeared to the congregation of those who listened to him and heard his lessons, because he was gifted with a wonderful power of explanation and a mouth that produced pearls. {p. 102} Reb Azriel Zelig Noach married a woman in Augustow, Mrs. Sarah, the daughter of Reb Yehuda Gilda, one of the important householders in the city, who promised to provide meals on his table for several years, so that he could continue his studies in *Torah*.

ממענות אריות

כולל

הספרים אשר נשאתי במקהלות על גאוני וחכמי ישראל
ועל קדושי האומה, שנספו, שנהרגו ונרצחו בשנות
תרע״ה – תר״פ.

בתקופה הנוראה של המלחמה העולמית.

מאת

עזריאל זעליג נח באאמו״ר מוהרי״ר יצחק צבי ז״ל קושעלעוסקי
מרין באוגוסטאוו

בילגורייא

בדפוס נ. קראנענבערג

ה׳תרפ״ה

SEFER MIMONOS AROJES
t. j. Nekrologi o zmarłych genjuszach Izraela
Druk. N. KRONENBERG
Bilgoraj ziem. Lub. (Polski) 1925

Printed in Poland

From Lions' Dens
Including
Eulogies of the Geonim and Notables of Israel that I gave in assemblies,
And martyrs of the nation who died, were killed and murdered
In the years 5675-5680 [1915-1920].
In the Terrible Period of the World War.
by Azriel Zelig Noach son of My Master, My Father, My Teacher and My Rabbi,
Our Teacher, The Rabbi,
Rav Yitzchak Tzvi, may his memory be for a blessing, Koshelevski
Teacher of Righteousness in Augustow
Bilgoraj
Published by N. Kreinenberg
5685 [1925]

Printed in Poland

A few years after his marriage he travelled to Kovno. For four straight years, he learned in the famous *kollel*, at whose head stood the *Gaon* Reb Tzvi Hirsh Rabinovitz, the *Av Beit Din* of Kovno, and the son of the famous *Gaon*, Reb Yitzchak Elchanan, may the memory of the righteous be for a blessing. Over the course of these years his spiritual image was formed, his personality matured, and he arrived at full knowledge of all areas of the *Torah*. He was endowed with two valuable unique qualities: a wonderful memory, and a rare power of concentration. These abilities of his stood him to be counted among the most excellent young yeshiva students of the Kovno *kollel*. He was ordained for the rabbinate by the *geonim* of Lithuania, with the President of the *kollel*, *Gaon* Reb Tzvi Hirsh Rabinovitz, at their head.

With his return to Augustow he was appointed (in the year 5667 [1907]) as judge and decisor, and over the passing of the years, when the seat of the rabbinate became open, as Rabbi *Av Beit Din*.

Rabbi Azriel Zelig Noach served his community faithfully and without measure[316] for about 40 years. He positioned his special spiritual qualities, and his comprehensive knowledge of

---

[316] There is a typographical error here, but the intended word can only be *shiur*, measure.

112

the *Torah*, as the authority his community. He learned and he taught, spread *Torah* among the masses, taught righteousness, judged the case cases of the poor and the pauper, served in council and guidance.

He was like a father for the people of his community. He took an interest in the situation of each and every one, took part in their joys and participated in their sorrow.

He did not skip over any communal activity. He worried about the existence of the *Talmud Torah* in his city, and took care of the Jewish soldiers {p. 103} that were camped in the city. In the days of Tsar Nikolai, he raised money and gave each Jewish soldier a weekly allowance, in order that they not be defiled by unkosher food. On the Festival of *Pesach*, he arranged a communal "*seder*"[317] for them, and did not go to his house to conduct his own *seder* until the *seder* for the soldiers had been conducted according to law and religion.

Every day he taught a lesson in the *Talmud* society, lectured before the Jewish gymnasiasts,[318] in order to bring them near to *Torah*. He founded the society "*Tiferet Bachurim*" and gave lessons before them. In this way, he molded, in large measure, the spiritual image of his community.

He had a big soul, a noble spirit, a gentle soul; these are the lines that stand out in his personality of many special qualities.

He studied the *Torah* all his days. He learned with great diligence, with his body swaying. The joy of learning captivated all his existence.

He loved humanity, and was beloved by them. He was humble and modest, sensitive, and pure in thought. All of the qualities that Our Sages, may their memory be for a blessing, included in a learned person were combined in him with great grace.

At that time his trust was in God. Still in the days of his youth his trust in God stood him in good stead to roam to places of the *Torah* in a condition of terrible poverty.

His heart was open to all the downtrodden, and he did much in the matters of righteousness and lovingkindness. With a kind face he received the face of a guest, and indeed many were the guests in need of help who found themselves in Augustow, in their knowledge that there was a rabbi there who would stand at their right hand.

His soul longed for Zion. When they brought out for sale the first shares of the National Bank,[319] he collected his last pennies and bought a share. In his twilight days, he wanted to leave his rabbinate and go up to the land of Israel, but crucial reasons prevented him from this step. He was a gifted explainer. The words that came out of his mouth were illuminating and joyful. He went down to the people, to the masses, took care of them, taught them lessons in *Torah*, and succeeded in revealing the hidden light in their souls.

In the year 5682 [1922] he published his book "*Ayin Tzofim*,"[320] explanations and homilies on the *haftarot*[321] for *Shabbat* and the festivals. In this book, he paved a new way in the explication of the words of the prophets, and it constitutes an important asset in homiletical literature.

In the year 5685 [1925], he published his second book "*MiMe'onot Ariot*," eulogies for the *geonim* of Israel that he gave in assemblies, and for the martyrs of the nations that died, were killed or murdered, in the period of the First World War (5675-5680 [1915-1920]). In this book

---

[317] *Pesach* is celebrated with a ritual event that is called a *seder*, order, which follows the order of the *Haggadah*, the book that is used to tell the story of the exodus from Egypt.

[318] Students in the *gymnasia*, a secular college-prep school.

[319] Of the land of Israel.

[320] "The Eye of the Watchers."

[321] *Haftarot* are readings that are excerpted from the Prophets (*Nevi'im*) and accompany each weekly *Shabbat Torah* reading, as well as readings for special *Shabbatot* and festivals.

he stands out as a great national lamenter. Within the book there also came eulogies of notables of the city of Augustow who died in that same period.

In the year 5699 [1939], around the time of the outbreak of the Second World War, he left in the printing press his third book, by the name of "*Levush Adanim*,"[322] innovations on Tractate *Avodah Zarah*.[323] In this book of his he revealed his power in *halakhah*. To our great anguish this book was not disseminated in the community, because in the meantime the war broke out and all the books were lost.

With the outbreak of the Second World War, in September 1939, the city of Augustow was conquered by the Soviets, and in June 1941, by the Nazis, who established a ghetto for the Jews in a suburb of the city, {p. 104} Baraki, on the other side of "the Augustow canal." They took the Poles out of there, and settled them in the dwelling places of the Jews in the city center, and transferred the Jews to Baraki. There they were crowded together and forced into crowded huts.

In one of the huts there, Rabbi Azriel Zelig Noach sat wrapped in a *tallis*[324] and *tefillin*,[325] hunched over his *Gemara*. His clothing crushed, his hat a cap, his shoes tattered. He sat as he swayed with his gaunt body, swaying over the pages of the *Gemara* with strong movements in his usual way. His face was distorted, only his innocent deep blue eyes occasionally twinkling, and asking for the mercy of heaven.

At the beginning of the month of August 1941, 1650 men, from the age of 14 and up, from the Jewish community in Augustow were taken by the Nazis to the Shtzavra Forest. There they were killed by gunshot.

In the month of December 1943 the remnant of the Jewish community in Augustow was transported, elderly, children, and women, on the death train to the gas chamber at Treblinka. Hungry and thirsty, broken and crushed, they were packed together on the train that hastened to the place of the destruction. In the choking compartments, the last group of the Jews of Augustow were packed in and concentrated, surrounding their old dying rabbi.

Great was the pain on the death train when they suddenly discerned that their beloved rabbi was no more, that he died from exhaustion, and his pure soul went up to the hidden places on high.

{p. 104} Scholars in the City
by M. Tzinovitz

Reb Aleksander Ziskind son of Moshe Maimon

The religious sage Reb Aleksander Ziskind was the son-in-law of Reb Dov Ber Shapira and the brother-in-law of the *Gaon* Reb Yisrael Isser Shapira, the local *Av Beit Din*. He resided for a number of years next to his father-in-law in the city of Augustow, and influenced greatly in its unique spiritual-cultural character. However, when he went to live in Seirijai, he would come occasionally to Augustow, and his words on matters of *Torah*, wisdom, and public communal activism were heard by the men of the city as if he was one of the veteran residents of the place. Nevertheless, Reb Aleksander Ziskind was a scholar, upright, one of those who seek the welfare of the faithful in Israel. [326] He would also "pull with the pen of writers." He published religious research articles in the Hebrew weekly "*HaMaggid*," whose editor Dovid Gordon was his friend

---

[322] "Delightful Garb."

[323] Idolatry.

[324] A prayer shawl with *tzitzit*, fringes, on each corner, as described in Numbers 15:38 and Deuteronomy 22:12.

[325] Phylacteries, the embodiment of the commandment found in Exodus 13:9 and 16, Deuteronomy 6:8, and Deuteronomy 11:18 "You shall put these words of mine on your heart and on your soul; and you shall tie them for a sign upon your arm, and they shall be as *totafot* between your eyes."

[326] 2 Samuel 20:19 "I am one of those who seek the welfare of the faithful in Israel."

from the period of their being together in the city of Seirijai. He would sign these articles with the name "*A"Z BR"M*" (initials: Aleksander Ziskind son of Reb Moshe).

{p. 105} Reb Aleksander Ziskind died in the year 5647 [1887] at the age of 78. In "*HaTzefirah*," of the year mentioned above, (No. 158), Y. Broide, a resident of Seirijai from Kelm, published on his memory of the deceased, these words: "the elder deceased was one of the outstanding people of the remnant of the old generation for whom *Torah* and wisdom, wealth and honor, together surrounded and encircled him. His name went out for praise as one of the greats that were in the land, great was his knowledge in the Hebrew literature that he showed quite a bit in the abundance of his articles that were brought in "*HaMaggid*," and he never, until his last day, departed from the tent of *Torah*. And more than Reb Ziskind was wise, he was even more engaged in *mitzvot*, and took part at the head of every good enterprise. He established a house for the study of *Torah* on strong pillars that would not weaken, and also the rest of the charity houses saw light in the light of his face. The end of the matter: he was head and first in all matters and ways of the community, and by his mouth every matter was directed.[327] To this degree his hands were faithful to God, and his witness, until his sunset.[328] And now, woe is me! Who will return his value to us?"

It should be pointed out that Reb Aleksander Ziskind Maimon left in manuscripts "*Kovetz Ma'amarim V'Inyanim Shonim*"[329] that was published (3 5654 [1894]) by a childhood friend, the Sage Yaakov son of Yaakov in Vilna.

It can be added that the words of *Torah* of Reb Aleksander Ziskind Maimon are brought in the book of questions and answers "*Ezrat Yisrael*" of his brother-in-law, the *Gaon* Reb Yisrael Isser Shapira.

The Rabbi the *Gaon* Reb Yehoshua Heschel Shapira

He was born to his father Reb Dov Ber in Augustow and spent the years of his youth and his time as a *yeshiva* student in the tent of the *Torah*, under the supervision of his brother the *Gaon* Reb Yisrael Isser Shapira the local *Av Beit Din*, and also, with his father-in-law the Gaon Reb Lipa Chaim *HaCohain, Av Beit Din* of Zembrova (Lomza region). He officiated afterwards as *Av Beit Din* in the two important communities of Shaki (Suwalk region) and Shtutzin (Lomza region).

In contrast to his brother the *Gaon* Reb Yisrael Isser, Reb Yehoshua Heschel was opposed to the *Chibbat Tzion* movement. On the other hand, he stood at the head of the "Lomza-Suwalki *Kollel*," and did much to strengthen the *Torah* institutions of the old *Yishuv*[330] in Jerusalem. He was the confidant of the *Gaon* Reb Yehoshua Leib Diskin, the Brisker Rabbi, in Jerusalem. There was an event, that when it became known to Reb Heschel, that one of the men of "*the Kollel*" in Jerusalem, Reb Yehoshua Yellin, handed his son over to a modern school – Reb Yehoshua Heschel approved the decision of the men of "*the Kollel*" to expropriate the right of Yehoshua Yellin to benefit from the funds of "*the Kollel*." Attempts by known personages from Suwalk, Lomza, and even from Augustow (Reb Mordechai Markus), did not help to nullify the decision of the zealots of Jerusalem.

When he went to his eternity in the year 5668 [1908], old and full of years, they eulogized him in villages near and far. In Augustow, the city of his birth, the *Dayan* Reb Azriel Zelig Koshelevski eulogized him. Reb Yehoshua's *Torah* innovations are found in other writers' books, especially in the book of questions and answers "*Ezrat Yisrael*" by his brother the *Gaon* Reb

---

[327] Exodus 41:40, Pharaoh speaking to Joseph: "You shall be in charge of my court, and by your mouth shall all my people be directed..."
[328] His death.
[329] "Anthology of Articles and Various Matters."
[330] The Jewish settlement that existed in Israel before the *aliyah* of the modern period.

Yisrael Isser, *Av Beit Din* of Augustow. And also, in the book "*P'nei Arieh HaChai*"[331] by the Rabbi Chaim Leib Rotenberg, who is known by the name "*The Tzaddik*[332] *from Stavisk.*"

{p. 106} **The *Gaon* Reb Yosef Zechariah Stern**[333]*

In the year 5611 [1851], the young *yeshiva* student Reb Yosef Gedaliah Stern, the son of Rabbi Natan, who was *Av Beit Din* Neustadt-Schirwindt, resided in Augustow. Already then, this young *yeshiva* student had become well-known as a prodigy. In the year 5620 [1860], when he was 26 years old, he came to Warsaw to print his first book, "*Zecher Yehosef,*"[334] which contained his innovations on tractates of the *Talmud*. He turned to the two famous rabbis of Warsaw: Reb Yishayahu Moskat, the rabbi of Praga, and Reb Yaakov Gesundheit, *Av Beit Din* of the city, and asked for their agreements, as was the custom of those days, for the printing of his book. Reb Yaakov Gesundheit wrote to him: "I stood trembling and amazed at his sharpness and expertise in the sea of *Talmud*, Babylonian and Jerusalem, *Tosefta* and all the early and late decisors and responsa." Reb Yosef Zechariah spent a short time in Augustow. After some time, we find him as the son-in-law of the *Gaon* Reb Mordechai Gimpel Yaffa – the rabbi of Ruzhany. When he died in the year 5664 [1904], the Hebrew press wrote articles of appreciation in the memory of this great person, who was a living treasury of many bookcases in all fields of the *Torah*, in the new Hebrew literature, in Hebrew linguistics, history, and more. In "*Luach Achiasaph*"[335] for the year 5665 [1905], it is written about him: "Not a day passed that he did not reply with an answer to his questioners, among them – the greats of the rabbis from all the lands."

Reb Yerucham Fishel *HaCohain* Biskovitz

Reb Yerucham Fishel was born of a good family, a scion of a respected rabbinic chain. Reb Yerucham's father the Augustovi – the *Gaon* Reb Kalonymus Kalman - was the son of the *Gaon* Reb Nachman from the town of Orly. Together with his brother, the *Gaon* Reb Shabtai, composed an important book (innovations in the *Talmud*) by the name of "*Shevet Achim*"[336] (printed in the year 5593 [1833]).

Reb Fishel had a son that was sharp in the *Torah*, Reb Yaakov Tzvi Biskovitz, who lived in Stavisk.

In the Biskovitz family of distinguished lineage is also included Rabbi Avraham *HaCohain* Orlianski from Bialystok, who went up to the land in the year 5643 [1883] and was the first rabbi of the mother of the settlements – Petach Tikvah. His son Reb Mendel Orlianski, the rabbi of Zikhron Yaakov (murdered in the riots of 5689 [1929]), was the son-in-law of Rabbi Yekutiel Koshelevski (Azrieli), born in Augustow, who filled the place of his father-in-law in the rabbinate of Zikhron Yaakov.

Reb Tzvi Korkovski [337]** **and His Son Menachem**

Shochet U'bodek in Augustow, and afterwards in Vilkovisk. He was known in the entire area as exalted in the *Torah* and righteous in all his ways. He devoted himself to *Torah* all his days, and to the service of God, and was punctilious about benefiting others.

His son, Reb Menachem Ben-Tzion, one of the greats of the Lithuanian rabbis, served as *Av Beit Din* in Novhardok, and afterwards, Preacher and Teacher of Righteousness in Vilna.

---

[331] Face of the Living Lion.
[332] Righteous person.
[333] Original note: * He is Vofsi in the famous poem of Y.L. Gordon "The Tip of the Yud."
[334] "In Memory of Yehosef."
[335] "The Almanac of Achiasaf."
[336] "The Dwelling of Brothers." Psalm 133:1 "How good and how pleasant it is that brothers dwell together."
[337] ** The uncle of Chaitza Aleksandrovitz.

{p. 107} While he was still a boy, Reb Menachem Ben-Tzion stood out in his vast knowledge in the field of *Torah*, and his intelligence in worldly matters. In the year 5641 [1881], when he was only 11 years old, he was orphaned by his distinguished father. The respected scholars, Reb Dovid Mordechai Markus from Augustow, and Reb Yitzchak Leib Rabinovitz from Vilkovisk, took an interest in his future. At the recommendations of the rabbis Reb Katriel Natan and Reb Yaakov Vilovski (the *Ridvaz*),[338] the Rabbi of Vilkovisk, he was accepted to the famous *yeshiva* of Volozhin, where he was one of its excellent students. The *Gaon* Reb Levi Soloveitchik, head of the *yeshiva*, would consult with him on the preparation of his lessons. While he was in Vilna, he became well-known as an excellent speaker.

Rabbi Yehoshua son of Reb Reuven *HaCohain* Blumental

Born in Augustow, he was a prodigy from his childhood. He learned *Torah* in the yeshiva of the *Gaon* Reb Moshe Sofer in Pressburg; afterwards he received *Torah* from the mouth of the *Gaon* Reb Arieh Leib Zuntz from Plotsk. He also learned with the *Gaon* Reb Yehuda Bachrach *Av Beit Din* Sejny.

In the beginning, he was appointed rabbi in the town of Lazdijai. After a short time, he was accepted as Rabbi in the provincial city of Mariampol. Since he was an extreme zealot in matters of religion, he was not satisfied by this city, in which most were enlightened, who did not accept his authority. He renounced the rabbinate, therefore, and returned to Lazdijai.

After some time, he was appointed as head of the *yeshiva* in Bialystok. When he would give the lesson, the place was too narrow to contain all who came to hear his wonderful analyses, which earned him the name "Yehoshuale the Sharp." He also served as head of the judges in Bialystok. Differences of opinion broke out between him and the second *Moreh Tzedek* in the matter of a legal decision in the case of 18 geese that had been slaughtered together, and in the gizzard of one a nail was found. The geese were mixed together, and they did not know which of them was unkosher.[339] The second *Moreh Tzedek* declared all of the geese unkosher, while Reb Yehoshua declared all of them kosher, except for the one in which the sign of a hole in its side was found. This event caused a great disagreement among the scholars of the city. The matter reached the *Gaon* Reb Shmuel Avigdor Tosfa'ah, who laid his hand on[340] the permission of Reb Yehoshuale. Because of the disagreement, Reb Yehoshua no longer wanted to remain in this city, and moved to officiate as Rabbi in the city of Yanova.

In the year 5627 [1867] he was appointed *Av Beit Din* Kaminetz of Lithuania, where he served with blessing for 13 years. He died in Brisk of Lithuania, when he came there to inquire of physicians, on 11 Shvat 5640 (1880).

Apart from being great in the *Torah*, he was tremendously diligent. Despite the weakness of his health, he would rise every night at the hour of 1:00 after midnight, and would study until the morning prayers. On the night of the holy *Shabbat*, when he would rise at midnight to study, his righteous wife Sarah would rise to sit by his side and watch that he would not knock over the candle.

He had good qualities; there were none like him. He never got angry, and he fled from honor. He never flattered anyone, and he loved every person as himself. He did not turn the poor away empty-handed, even though his income was very insubstantial (his salary was accumulated

---

[338] An acronym for Reb Yaakov David son of Ze'ev.
[339] The presence of a nail in the gizzard would render the goose unkosher.
[340] Supported.

from payments of one *agora*[341] (*kopek*) a week that every householder paid, and not all of them would pay).

Reb Yehoshuale left two famous sons after him: a) the great *Gaon* Reb Avraham Aharon *HaCohain* Burstein – the rabbi of Slobodka, and at the end of his days the head of the *Yeshiva Mercaz HaRav*[342] {p. 108} in Jerusalem. He died in the year 5685;[343]* b) The Rabbi the *Gaon* Reb Reuven Dovid Hachen Burstein *Av Beit Din* Kaminetz of Lithuania, killed in the Holocaust.

Reb Dovid Mordechai Markus

Reb Dovid Mordechai Markus was considered to be the significant scholar of the community of Augustow in the previous generation. He became well-known as a prodigy. He was in correspondence about matters of *Torah* with the *Geonim* of the generation, among them the *Gaon* Reb Yehoshua Leib Diskin (*Av Beit Din* Lomza, Brisk and Lithuania and other communities, and at the end of his life, in Jerusalem), and the *Gaon* Reb Yosef Shaul Natanson *Av Beit Din* Lvov. This Rabbi *Gaon* writes these words about Reb Dovid Mordechai in his well-known book "*Sho'el U'Meishiv*"[344] (Part 1, the year 5628 – 1868): "Let the mountains deliver well-being[345] to the sharp, gifted *K'vod HaRav*[346] Dovid Mordechai from Augustow in the country of Russia." In section 73 in the book mentioned above, the *Gaon* author brings words of *Torah* from the mouth of the Augustovi scholar. Reb Dovid Mordechai was one of the friends and one who had turned his face towards the *Gaon* Reb Shmuel Mohilever, *Av Beit Din* Suwalk, and afterwards, *Av Beit Din* Bialystok. Reb Dovid Mordechai, unlike other zealous scholars, was inclined towards the *Chibbat Tzion* movement, and saw in it rescue and great salvation for the Jewish people. In this matter, he was in complete agreement with the *Maskil* and the Hebrew writer Yosef Ze'ev Sperling from Augustow, although in matters of spirit Reb Dovid Mordechai was completely far from the writer mentioned above.

Reb Dovid Mordechai contributed much for the good of the settlement of the land of Israel, and he was one of the heads of the supporters of the Palestinian[347] Council in Odessa, which acted for the strengthening and establishment of the new settlements in the land of Israel.

Reb Dovid Mordechai Markus died in the year 5670 [1910] at the age of 62. The article of appreciation on his memory appeared in the Hebrew newspaper in Vilna "*Hed HaZman.*"[348]

The Religious *Maskil* Reb Ziskind Arieh Treves

Reb Ziskind Arieh, the son of Naftali Treves from Augustow, poured with his soul the best of his excellent scholarliness into the students of the Lithuanian with a moderate critical approach, according to the methods of the Talmudic sages Reb Tzvi Hirsh Chayut and Reb Shlomo Yehuda Rapoport (*ShI'R*)[349] from Galicia. This pouring can be seen in his important articles on the pages of the Hebrew weekly "*HaMaggid,*" which appeared in the frontier town adjacent to Augustow – Lek. Those who understood the matter saw in this young Augustovian a bright future, however he was plucked from life in the spring of his days. In the year 5633 [1873], Shlomo, the

---

[341] An *agora* is an Israeli coin of the smallest denomination, named from 1 Samuel 2:36 "...every one that is left in your house shall come and crouch to him for a piece [agora] of silver...".

[342] "The Rabbi's Center;" named for Rabbi Abraham Isaac Kook, the first Chief Rabbi of the land of Israel, and the founder of the *yeshiva.*

[343] * His son is the member of the *Knesset*[343] Reuven Barkat.

[344] "Asks and Replies."

[345] Psalms 72:3 "Let the mountains deliver well-being for the people, the hills, the reward of justice."

[346] A title of respect for a Rabbi, along the lines of "Your Honor, the Rabbi."

[347] Pre-state Israel was called Palestine by the Romans, as distinct from the Palestinian people, who first begin to use that appellation after the Six-Day War in 1967.

[348] "Echo of the Time."

[349] An acronym of his name.

son of the *Gaon* Moshe Yitzchak HaLevi, informs us, in the newspaper *"HaMaggid"* (the year 1873, No. 7), that he was distinguished by his excellent memory, that the words of our Sages, may their memory be for a blessing, from the Babylonian and Jerusalem *Talmud*, and legends, were fluent on his tongue, and he succeeded also to create new interpretations, which he had in mind to publish. This scholar was young in days. He died at the age of 25.

We find words of appreciation of his greatness in the *Torah* and the wisdom of Ziskind Arieh Treves in the anthology *"HaPisgah,"*[350] whose editor and publisher was Rabbi Hillel Dovid *HaCohain* Treves – Rabbi of Vileki. On the occasion of his being published in a collection of articles of *Divrei Torah*[351] from the pen of his relative from Augustow by the name of *"Dovev Siftei Yesheinim,"*[352] the Rabbi editor writes these words about the deceased: "The Rabbi, great in *Torah* and wisdom, a treasury of *Torah* who is an ornament of pride[353] and glory, the crown of knowledge, the deceased Reb Arieh Ziskind, may his memory be for a blessing, the exalted son, honored among his people, the elder Reb Naftali Treves, may his light shine,[354] from the city of Augustow, born in the year 5609 [1849]. While he was still[355] young, the great *Torah* scholars were surprised by his deep common sense and by his wonderful memory that caused every heart to tremble and quake. He gathered in the hollow of his hand[356] in the shortness of days in which he lived all the sheaves of *Torah* in all its fields, and like a great leviathan he gulped into his mouth all the water that was in the *Talmud*, and all the talmudic literature, so that there was really no secret that escaped him in the Babylonian and Jerusalem *Talmud*s, the *Toseftot*, the homilies of our Sages, may their memories be for a blessing, and their legends. The greatest of the experts assailed and were astonished by him in their speaking with him, on the greatness of his expertise, which one would have to go far to find one like him, in these last periods in Israel.

The deceased was an energetic and exalted critic until he became one of the great critics in Talmudic literature. If God had not taken him in his youth and we had not lost him, he would have illuminated the land[357] and rays of light from his hand[358] for his light to appear over all the settlements of Israel. He would have been one of the heads of the *geonim* of Israel and one of the singular ones of the generation.

Reb Zalman Arieh Koptziovski

Born in Vishai, Suwalk region. Son of the respected Koptziovski family, among whom are included greats of the Torah, respected merchants, and highly active in Zionism and the settlement of the land of Israel. He took to wife a daughter from the Keinan family in Augustow, became the brother-in-law of Reb Dovid Mordechai Markus and the writer Yaakov Frenkel. Reb Zalman Arieh was a distinguished scholar. After the death of his brother-in-law, Reb Dovid Mordechai, he was considered the head of the scholars in the city. In the days of the First World War, Reb Zalman transferred his dwelling place to Moscow and there he found, in the year 5678 [1918] his final resting place. The Rabbi the *Moreh Tzedek* Reb Arieh Zelig eulogized him in his absence, and these are his words according to his book *"MiMe'onot Ariot."*

---

[350] "The Summit."

[351] "Words of *Torah*."

[352] The lips of those who sleep. Song of Songs 7:10 "And your mouth like choicest wine. Let it flow to my beloved as new wine gliding over the lips of sleepers."

[353] Ezekiel 20:7 "...or out of their beautiful adornments, in which they took pride..."

[354] This expression is used in reference to one who is still alive.

[355] There is a typo here, but in the original book *"HaPisgah"* the word is 'b'odenu."

[356] Proverbs 30:4: "Who has gathered up the wind in the hollow of his hand?"

[357] "*Mei'ir la'aretz*" from the first blessing before the *Shma*: "You illumine the world and its creatures with mercy..."

[358] Habakkuk 3:4: "And rays of light from his hand..."

"One of the notables of our city, exalted in Torah and famous in his name. The walls of the *Beit Midrash* will confirm that his voice reached them like the voice of a lion, and that he would study with desire and vigor. All the worshippers would have already left and he remained alone in the *Beit Midrash* in his fixed place, studying with depth the issue in the serious tractate. In his life he was a wood merchant, and when he would travel outside of the country, he would come beforehand to the *Beit Midrash* and study *Torah*. Sometimes he would go deep into his learning, until he did not sense at all what man was passing before him in the hour of his learning."

Reb Arieh *HaCohain* Lap

Rabbi Azriel Zelig, who eulogized him, describes him with these words:

"He was already considered a learned person and of a good family. He was a community leader for many years, and one of the heads of the community, and all the matters of the city were decided by him. He gave his soul for communal matters and the needs of the city, and he was quick to gather money for the synagogue and the *Beit Midrash*, and a building for guests, and gaining strength like a lion[359] to go to the *Beit Midrash*, even if it was far from his house."

The father of Reb *HaCohain* Lap was Rabbi Elchanan Tzvi, *Av Beit Din* of Vizhnitz and Zablodova; one of his brothers was the Rabbi the *Gaon* Efraim Dov Lap, *Av Beit Din* of Verblova, one of the great of the rabbis of Lithuania, author of the book "*Zivchei Efraim*."[360] With this he was a faithful Zionist and helped Rabbi Y.Y. Reines in establishing the "*Mizrachi*" organization.

{p. 110} Reb Eliyahu Sender *HaCohain*

Rabbi Azriel Zelig, who eulogized him in the year 5677 [1917], describes the deceased as "exalted and precious," a legacy to the *yeshiva* of Volozhin not for the purpose of receiving a reward,[361] and as one who received a letter of thanks from the *Gaon* Naftali Tzvi Yehuda Berlin *Av Beit Din* and Head of the Rabbinical College of Volozhin for his activities there. He was one of the early risers to the *Beit Midrash* for prayer.

Reb Meir Koifman

The father-in-law of the Rabbi *Gaon* Mordechai Eliyahu Rabinovitz, *Av Beit Din* of Vashlikova and Sapotzkin. In his book "*Torat Mordechai*"[362] that was printed in the year 5669 [1909], the Rabbi brings a few pleasant new ideas about *Torah* in the name of his father-in-law. Reb Meir Koifman was the distinguished friend of Rabbi Katriel Natan. He brought the *Mitnagdim*[363] to reconciliation with their rabbi, and to their agreement to return him to their city when Rabbi Yehuda Leib Gordin moved from Augustow to Ostrow-Mazowiecka. He was expert and sharp and served as the teacher of lessons in the *Talmud* Society. Professionally he was a pharmacist, and earned his livelihood from the pharmacy.

Reb Yisrael Barukh Lieberman

He was one of the great scholars of the *yeshiva* of Radin, blessed with ability and with distinguished qualities. He was one of the assistants of the Wise Rabbi Reb Yerucham Lebovitz in *Mussar* studies in the famous *yeshiva* of Mir.

After his wedding, he opened a shop for the sale of fabrics, and engaged in the needs of the public as one of leaders of the community. Before the outbreak of the war, he emigrated to the

---

[359] Babylonian *Talmud Brakhot* 3b:22 "From midnight on, he would gain the strength of a lion."

[360] "Sacrifices of Efraim."

[361] *Pirkei Avot* 1:3 "He used to say: do not be like servants who serve the master in the expectation of receiving a reward, but be like servants who serve the master without the expectation of receiving a reward, and let the fear of Heaven be upon you."

[362] "The Teaching of Mordechai."

[363] Opposers of Chassidism.

United States, but his family was killed in the Holocaust. This crushed his spirit. He shut himself up in his room in the Bronx, which is in metropolitan New York, and engaged in *Torah* day and night.

He likewise spread *Torah* in the *Talmud* and *Mishnah* Societies, not for the purpose of receiving a reward. He died at the end of *Rosh HaShanah*[364] 5722 [1942]. At his funeral heads of *yeshivot*, rabbis, his many friends and students participated. Among others, Reb Dovid Lifshitz, a member of the presidium of the Rabbis' Association, and previously *Av Beit Din* Suwalki, eulogized him.

The article in appreciation of his memory appeared in the rabbinic monthly *"HaMaor"*[365] in New York, *Cheshvan-Kislev* Edition, 5722.

M. Tzinovitz

The Rabbi the *Gaon* Reb Betzalel Ze'ev Gibstein, May the Memory of the Righteous be for a Blessing.

The Rabbi the *Gaon* Reb Betzalel Ze'ev Gibstein was born in Augustow in the year 1883. He learned in the famous *yeshiva* of Volozhin, until his marriage to a daughter of Augustow – Mrs. Kendle Yocheved Povembrovski.

All his days were dedicated to the study of *Torah* and the service of God. He fasted a lot, until he became weak, and he was forced to postpone the wedding and strengthen his body. After he married he continued to fast during all the days of the week. His wife turned to the greats of the *Torah* and to the doctors, and these tried to convince him to stop the self-denials, but to no avail. He continued on this path of his until the day of his death on 8 Sivan 5720 [1960].

Father, may the memory of the righteous be for a blessing, refused to accept on himself the yoke of the rabbinate, and began to engage in the commerce of turpentine, a product of his factory.

{p. 111} When he did not succeed, he switched to trading in hides, wood, and more. When all his money went down the drain, he decided to dedicate all his time to *Torah* study. From then on, his support was from his brother-in-law in the United States. In the years 1926-1929, he served as Director of the *yeshiva* of Slonim. Since he was satisfied with "a *kav*[366] of carobs,"[367] he divided his salary among the *yeshiva* boys, so that they could excel in their studies. For two years, he officiated as rabbi of the small community of Rozhinka, which is next to Grodno. He brother-in-law advised him to emigrate to the United States, but Father, may the memory of the righteous be for a blessing, refused to travel to the *"eretz hatreifa,"*[368] and preferred to go up to the land of his heart's desire all the days, which is the land of Israel. In the year 1931 he fulfilled his dream.

---

[364] The Jewish New Year.

[365] "The Lamp."

[366] About 1.3 liters.

[367] Babylonian Talmud *Chullin* 86a: "The entire world is sustained in the merit of Chanina ben Dosa, my son, and yet for Chanina, my son, a *kav* of carobs, i.e., a very small amount of inferior food, is sufficient to sustain him from one *Shabbat* eve to the next *Shabbat* eve."

[368] The unkosher land.

Da'as Torah Title Page

ספר

דעת תורה

באור על התורה בדרך ההגיון

מאת

הרב יהושע ב"ר בצלאל זאב גיפשטיין

מאבגוסטוב.

Book of Knowledge of Torah
An Explanation of the Torah by Way of Common Sense
By
Rabbi Yehoshua son of Betzalel Ze'ev Gipstein[369]
From Avgustov.

All his days Father was "hidden among the baggage" and fleeing honor. All his time – dedicated to Torah study and writing. Two of his books – "*Pirkei HaGaon*"[370] on Tractate *Avot*, and "*Da'as HaTorah*" Part 1 on the *Torah*, were published while still in Poland. In the land were published: "*Da'as HaTorah*" Part 2 "*Cheker Kohelet*,"[371] and also a booklet published by the center "*Beit Yaakov*" by the name of "*Hishtalmut HaAdam v'HaShabbat*,"[372] and another booklet of interpretations of prayer. He left a manuscript on the *Talmud* that he did not get to complete.

Father was extremely careful in his speech, for fear of "*lashon hara*."[373] Therefore he was nicknamed by many "The Silent One." His love for the land of Israel knew no boundaries; in Zionism he saw "*atchalta de'geulah*."[374] He was a member of the *Mizrachi* movement, which he extremely valued. Father founded the branch of "*HeChalutz HaMizrachi*"[375] in Augustow. The first training groups of "*HeChalutz HaMizrachi*" in the area were organized by the signed, below, with Father's full assistance. Our house served as a lodging place for the first pioneers that reached the training collectives. Father, may the memory of the righteous be for a blessing, was happy that it was within his ability to contribute to the strengthening of the settlement in the land in general, and especially for religious settlement. I remember the first couple that went up to the land from "*HeChalutz HaMizrachi*" {p. 112} in Augustow: Eliyahu and Devorah Gardovski. They were

---

[369] Although the name is spelled "Gibstein" in the Augustow Yizkor Book, the name on the title page of this work is spelled "Gipstein."

[370] "The Chapters of the *Gaon*."

[371] "Study of Ecclesiastes."

[372] "The Perfection of the Human and the Sabbath."

[373] Literally, "evil speech." There is an entire body of *halakhah* that governs speaking about others, even saying nice and/or truthful things, when they are not present; when it is permitted, when it is forbidden, and when it is required.

[374] Babylonian *Talmud Megillah* 17b; the beginning of the redemption.

[375] The *Mizrachi* Pioneer.

approved for *aliyah*[376] by father, may the memory of the righteous be for a blessing, because the center of "*HeChalutz HaMizrachi*" had limitless confidence in him. Father, may the memory of the righteous be for a blessing, was very sensitive to injustice. He aspired to social righteousness. In the *Torah*, he saw the way that would lead to the uprooting of evil and a world that is entirely good.[377] The *Shabbat* and festivals of Israel were in his eyes symbols for this aspiration towards "the complete perfection of humaneness that even righteousness and honesty are only a rung to the final step," and the final goal is "a day that is entirely *Shabbat*."[378] From here was his great admiration for acting for settlement in the land in general, and particularly for the collective settlement.

Betzalel Gibstein   **Rishon L'Tzion, Adar 5726 [1966]**

Reb Chaim Yitzchak Ravidovitz

Born in Augustow to his father Reb Avraham Shlomo and his mother Shayna, most of whose toil and effort went to guiding him on the path of *Torah*. He learned in the *yeshivot* of Mir and Volozhin. He married a woman from Grayevo and fixed his place of residence and trade there. In the year 5675 [1915], he moved with his family to Bialystok. Reb Chaim Yitzchak was a wealthy man. He dealt in exporting merchandise from Russia to Germany. His warehouses were in Prosetkin, which is in eastern Prussia. With the outbreak of the First World War the Russians plundered the warehouses and sent them up in flames. Reb Chaim Yitzchak became impoverished.

In the year 5682 [1922], he went up to the land of Israel, and established the first shack in the settlement of Merchaviah. Despite the difficult conditions, Reb Chaim Yitzchak saw the period of his work in agriculture as the happiest in his life.

Reb Chaim Yitzchak Ravidovitz (in the land of Israel he changed his family name to "Ravid") was a significant scholar. His book "*Merchevei Yitzchak*"[379] will testify to his scholarship, was published in the year 5689 [1929] and included "innovations, explanations, and resolutions in the words of *Rashi*,[380] may his memory be for a blessing, on the order of the *Talmud*." The *Gaon* Reb Avraham Yitzchak *HaCohain* Kook writes in his approval of the composer of this book: "a superior man, greater than many, excellent in his name, in his deeds, and in his place, my comrade and friend the great Rabbi, a clear thinker, a treasury of delight and purity of heart, one of the crown jewels that frequently visits the sacred ground, and among the residents of our holy and renewed settlement. And here is the precious person the rabbi the author, may he merit a good long life, amen, one hand grasping the work to develop and plough the holy soil with the toil of his hands with sacred love and the love of an artist, and his second hand holding the tree of life,[381] in the toil of the *Torah*."

Reb Chaim Yitzchak was the son of Reb Avraham Sholom; Reb Avraham Sholom was born to Reb Shimon; Reb Shimon was the son of Reb Moshe-Zalman; the father of Reb Moshe-Zalman was Reb Sholom Shachne – the first rabbi of Augustow.

Reb Chaim Yitzchak Ravidovitz died in the year 1936 in Merchaviah.

---

[376] Emigrating to Israel is always "ascending."

[377] The world to come. Babylonian *Talmud Chullin* 142a: "this aforementioned verse: "That it may go well with you" (Deuteronomy 5:16), as referring to the World-to-Come."

[378] *Mishnah Kodoshim, Tamid*, 7:4 "On *Shabbat* they used to say: "A psalm, a song for the Sabbath day" (Psalm 92). "A psalm, a song for the time to come, for the day that will be all *Shabbat* and rest for everlasting life."

[379] "*Open Spaces of Yitzchak*." A play on the name of his settlement in Israel, *Merchaviah*.

[380] Rabbi Shlomo Yitzchaki 1040 – 1105. An important commentator on the *Torah* and *Talmud*.

[381] The *Torah*.

Reb Shlomo Tzvi Kalyer

Was born in Bialystok. Ordained for instruction by the famous rabbis Reb Refael Shapira, *Av Beit Din* and Head of the Rabbinical Seminary of Volozhin, Reb Chaim Naftali Hertz Heilpren Rabbi *Av Beit Din* Bialystok, Reb Yitzchak Eliyahu Ginzburg, *Moreh Tzedek* in Bialystok, and Reb Dovid Payence *Av Beit Din* Knishin.

About a year before the outbreak of the First World War, Reb Shlomo Tzvi took to wife the daughter of the Augustovi scholar Reb Avraham Shiff, and he, too, settled in Augustow. After a few years, he moved to Suwalki, to officiate as one of the heads of the *yeshiva* that was there. Afterwards he was appointed *Av Beit Din* of Filipova, and in the year 5684 [1924] he moved to Suchowola, where he officiated as *Av Beit Din* until the days of the Holocaust, when he was killed together with the members of his community.

Rabbi Shlomo Tzvi Kalyer was one of the best rabbis of the young guard that was active between the First and Second World Wars. He preached with lovingkindness, and was active and activating in the field of national-religious education. He was one of the signers of the public appeal of the rabbis' group in Poland to support the "*Keren HaYesod*"[382] with fundraising.

While he was in Augustow he helped the religious Zionists to organize the "*Mizrachi*" Union. He would also preach for the establishment of "*HaMizrachi*" and "*HeChalutz HaMizrachi*" each time that he came from Suchowola to visit his family in Augustow.

Reb Avraham Shiff

His wife had a grocery store in Augustow, and he himself learned *Torah*.

Reb Shiff published 3 books:

a. "*HaTorah Velomdeha*"[383] is a commentary on the Song of Songs by way of the simple meaning. According to the introduction of this book, this is one pamphlet from his book "*Torah VeDerekh Eretz.*"[384]

The book was printed in 5673 (1913) on the Hebrew Press in Bilgoray which is in Lublin region. At the end of his introduction to this book he expresses his thanks to his father-in-law "The Rabbi the *Gaon*, sharp and expert in all areas of the *Torah*, the "*Ma'ayan HaMitgaber,*"[385] wise and complete, Shlomo Tzvi Kalyer, may his light shine, who comes to my aid in my every matter," and he blesses him that God will grant him the privilege of ascending to the heights of success and publish his precious innovations. The book mentioned above is adorned with the agreements of the two *Geonim* of the generation, Reb Chaim *HaLevi* Soloveitchik from Brisk, and Reb Moshe Betzalel Luria from Suwalk, who point out that with the permission of the author, this Reb Avraham son of Reb Shimon from Augustow, there is also a composition on Tractate *Baba Kama* "*Harei Besamim.*"[386]

b. The book "*Derekh Oniyah*,"[387] on "*Eilu Treifot*"[388] which is in Tractate *Chullin* (Bilgoray 5692 [1932]). This book clarifies most of the issues with correct, reasonable, explanations, explanations from the small to the dialectical. And explains most of the disputes of the *Tannaim*[389] and the *Amoraim*.[390]

---

[382] "The Foundation Fund," established in 1920 at the World Zionist Conference in London.

[383] The complete title of this book is "*K'vod HaTorah Velomdeha*," the Honor of the Torah and Its Learners."

[384] "*Torah* and the Way of the World."

[385] An ever-flowing spring: *Pirkei Avot* 2:8 "...Rabbi Eliezer ben Hyrcanus is an ever-flowing spring..."

[386] "Mountains of Spices."

[387] "The Way of a Ship.": Proverbs 30:19 "How a ship makes its way through the high seas..."

[388] "These are Torn" i.e., unkosher.

[389] The Sages of the *Mishnah*, ca. 1st-2nd centuries CE.

[390] The explicators of the *Mishnah*, from the time of the death of the patriarch Rabbi Yehudah HaLevy (219 CE) to the completion of the Babylonian *Talmud* (about 500 CE).

At the end of the book is brought the opinion of the author that shaving the beard by electric mechanisms is a prohibition of shaving really like with a razor, and with it one transgresses the prohibition "do not destroy the corners of your beard."[391] These shaving mechanisms are "new destroyers," and it is forbidden to use them to remove a beard.

{p. 114} The author points out that he has in his possession another 15 books awaiting publication. He requests that whoever wants to print one of his books, mentioned above, at his expense, or to take upon himself the work of selling, should let him know.

The books that were not brought out in print are: "*Oniah B'Lev Hayam*,"[392] "*Sefer HaBrachah*,"[393] "*Mo'Adim L'Simcha*,"[394] a book on Tractate Women "*Milei Nezikin*,"[395] "*Ma'ayan U'Mikvah*,"[396] "*Sefer HaChanukah*,"[397] the book of "*Inyanim Shonim*,"[398] "*Sefer HaMitzvot*,"[399] "*Shofar Gadol*,"[400] "*HaMashal HaKadmoni*,"[401] "*Deluta D'Avraham*."[402]

Learned Men That I Knew in the Days of My Childhood
Rabbi Yekutiel Azrieli

Reb Avraham Shiff, may the memory of the righteous and holy be for a blessing, was a student of the *Gaon* Rabbi Reines, may the memory of the righteous be for a blessing, of Lida. He wrote an interpretation of "The Song of Songs", and a significant book by the name of "*Oniot Socher*"[403] on Tractate *Bava Kamma*. He made a living from a produce shop, but did not stop reading day and night. During his study time in his regular place in the *Vyatka-Kloiz* he did not stop his learning, and when he was forced to stop, he would speak only in *lashon hakodesh*.

Reb Moshe Arbstein, may his memory be for a blessing, was a distinguished student of the Volozhin *yeshiva*, a timber merchant, one of the notables of the town in his time, aroused respect, and was loved by humanity.

Reb Moshe Shmulian, (Shlomo Yashes), may the memory of the righteous and holy be for a blessing, was one of the elite students of the Slobodka *yeshiva* in Kovno. He dedicated most of his time to *Torah*. He was "…one who is modest and humble, who bows and enters and bows and exits…"[404] He fixed his place of study in the *Vyatka-Kloiz*. It is also said of his father that he was also a great in the *Torah*.

Reb Chaim Yoel Grodzin, may the memory of the righteous and holy be for a blessing, the man of the book, learned man, had a shoe store. He preached regularly from the *bima*[405] of the *Beit Midrash* to the "Psalms Society" on *Shabbat* nights in the winter seasons.

The old *shochet u'bodek*, **Reb Shlomo Meitkas**, may his memory be for a blessing, who had an impressive majestic appearance, involved himself in collections for the sake of Heaven for the good of institutions of *Torah* and benevolence in Jerusalem, the Holy City, out of his devotion and incomparable love. He was the initiator of all kinds of ideas to increase the donations. Every

---

[391] Leviticus 19:27.
[392] "A Ship in the Heart of the Sea."
[393] "The Book of Blessing,"
[394] "Festivals of Joy."
[395] "Words of Damages."
[396] "Wells and Pools."
[397] "The Book of Chanukah."
[398] "Various Issues."
[399] "The Book of the Commandments."
[400] "A Great *Shofar*."
[401] "The Ancient Proverb."
[402] "The Door of Abraham."
[403] "Merchant Ships."
[404] Babylonian *Talmud Sanhedrin* 88b.
[405] The raised platform in the synagogue where the prayer leaders, *Torah* readers, and preachers stand.

calendar, or symbolic napkins that came to him from Jerusalem for distribution among the contributors, he would kiss, in order to inhale into himself the holy air of our land that clung to them. {p. 115} His 2 sons-in-law: The *shochet u'bodek*, **Reb Moshe Leib Shidlovski**, may the memory of the righteous and holy be for a blessing, a scholar, one of the distinguished learned men inside and out. "All say "Glory!"[406] from the aspect of "A man's wisdom lights up his face."[407]

The *shochet u'bodek*, **Reb Chaim Zalman Kaplanski,** may the memory of the righteous and holy be for a blessing. A learned man, well-liked by humanity, welcoming to every person, engaged in deeds of *tzedakah* and benevolence.

Reb Gedaliah Gizumski, *shochet u'bodek*, may the memory of the righteous and holy be for a blessing. In his youth, he studied at the Great *Beit Midrash*, and specialized in slaughtering work in our city. He was distinguished by a pleasant voice. He sang pleasantly for many with his prayers. He devoted himself to the *mitzvah* of welcoming guests, for passing impoverished guests.

Written for memory from hearsay: Reb Yisrael Wistinetzer (Gilda), may his memory be for a blessing, the student of the *Gaon* the "*Chatam Sofer*,"[408] in the *yeshiva* in Pressburg, Hungary. He was a teacher of *Gemara* to students in our city more than a hundred years ago; the father of my grandfather on my mother's side.

Lipsk
By B. Efrati

Lipsk was a small town in the region of Augustów on the way to Grodno. With the First World War, there were about fifty Jewish families living among 200 Christian families.

Part of the Jews made their living from agriculture, another part from small business, but most of them were laborers. In the town there was an old wooden synagogue with a triangular roof, and also a *Beit Midrash*, in which there was also the Rabbi's living quarters. Rabbi Y.L. Rozenberg, may his memory be for a blessing, taught *Torah* every day, *Mishnah*, *Ein Yaakov*, and *Gemara* in the congregation of his community. Part of the Rabbi's time he dedicated to acting as a *Shaliach Mitzvah*[409] to surrounding *yeshivot*. The Rabbi's father-in-law was Rabbi Naftali Hertz Kaplan, may his memory be for a blessing, an important person in the town. He was able to go up to the land and to be buried there. He was the grandfather of Shabtai and Daniel Kaplan, may they be distinguished for a long life.

I am reminded of something curious: in Lipsk the Jews read from a *Sefer Torah*[410] in the Christian church. "The incident that took place, took place in this way:"[411] In the year 1915, the Germans conquered Lipsk. They immediately began to gather all the residents, the Jews and the Christians. A rumor spread that they were going to transfer all of us to Germany as prisoners. When I passed by the *Beit Midrash*, I slipped inside to say my farewell to the *Torah* scrolls and the *Beit Midrash*. It crossed my mind to try and rescue at least one *Sefer Torah*, and I took it with me. When we got to the church, a new building with thick walls, the Germans brought all of us inside. It became clear that the intention of the Germans was to find cover for the residents who lived in small wooden houses, and many of whom were being wounded by the shrapnel of the Russian bullets. Yes – that's how the Germans behaved at the time, before they learned the *Torah* of Hitler, may his name be erased. The Jews organized themselves, therefore, {p. 116} in one of

---

[406] Psalm 29:9.

[407] Ecclesiastes 8:1.

[408] Moses Shreiber, 1762–1839, known as Moshe Sofer, also known by his main work *Chatam Sofer*, "Seal of the Scribe," and an acronym for *Chiddushei Torat Moishe Sofer*, "Innovations of the *Torah* of Moshe" Sofer. A *sofer* is a scribe.

[409] An emissary sent to do a *mitzvah*.

[410] *Torah* scroll.

[411] This phrase appears many times in the Babylonian *Talmud*, for example in *Pesachim* 82b.

the corners of the church, prayed, and read from the *Sefer Torah*. After the German retreat, the Russian command expelled the Jews to the Russian interior, suspecting that they were German supporters.

At the end of the war, a few Jews returned to Lipsk and they were there until the murdering Nazis came who annihilated all of them. I raise with this the memory of the Jews of Lipsk: the Kaplan, Feingold, Staviskovski, Strozinski, Brustein, and Berger families, and others. May their memory be blessed.

Sztabin
by Leah Sherman

From among the mists of the past, Sztabin, the town of my birth, rises before me. That same small, picturesque village standing on the banks of the Bobra. Streets with no road or sidewalk. Doubtfully a town, or even a village.

The homes were low and on them were thatched roofs. Here and there – a new house with a roof of wooden tiles. In the village, there dwelt only about a hundred Jewish families, but the lives of the community were conducted as in a large city. All the institutions existed: a synagogue, a *beit midrash*, a *cheder*, a rabbi, a *chazzan*, and a *shochet*. There were in town a few householders who had rabbinic ordination. The Jews supported themselves with commerce and labor. Cultural life was very meagre. The State school, in the national language, had only three classes. We, the youth, learned Hebrew in the *cheder* – specifically with the method of "Hebrew in Hebrew,"[412] and other learning we acquired in the government school.

The First World War almost erased Sztabin from the face of the earth. When we passed by way of the village in 1915, a few orphaned chimneys peeked at us from among the ruins.

{p. 117} From My Diary
by Dr. Nechemiah Aloni

I was born in Warsaw from a "mixed marriage." My father, Naftali Hertz Linda, was a *chassid* born in Warsaw, and my mother, Channah Alta Borovski, a *Mitnagedet*,[413] was born in Sztabin in the Augustów region. While I was a child, six years old, the family moved from Warsaw to Sztabin.

In the year 5674 [1914], the First World War broke out and the family wandered to Suchowola and Jonava, and finally settled in Augustów. In this city I acquired my elementary education, and began high school. I participated in "*HaShomer Trumpeldor*,"[414] "*Hashomer HaTzair*,"[415] "*Yidisher Yugend Bund*"[416] and "*HeChalutz*."[417] In the last

---

[412] An immersion approach to language that teaches Hebrew material while speaking only the Hebrew language.

[413] A follower of the movement that opposed Chassidism.

[414] Yosef Trumpeldor (1880 – 1920, was an early Zionist activist who helped to organize the Zion Mule Corps and bring Jewish immigrants to the land of Israel. Trumpeldor died defending the settlement of Tel Hai in 1920 and subsequently became a Zionist national hero.

[415] "The Young Guard."

[416] "The Jewish Youth Union."

[417] "The Pioneer."

two movements I was counted among the founders. In *Kislev* 5686 - December 16, 1925, I went up to the land.

Sztabin was a small town that was entirely built around the market square. The church occupied the right-hand side, and on the other side, one stone house – the local administrative office, and a few wooden houses. On the small surrounding streets stood low wooden houses with thatched roofs. When a fire broke out, all the houses went up in flames. The streets were not paved, the sand was deep in days of the summer, and a wagon only traversed it with difficulty. There was a Russian government school and "*cheders*" at various levels; one of them was modern and taught the first basics of the language. The synagogue served also as the *beit midrash*, and there was a rabbi who also served as the *chazzan*. An agricultural atmosphere prevailed over the town. Every family had a vegetable garden, some milk cows, a field parcel of land and a forest parcel. I never ate more tasty vegetables in all the days of my life than those cucumbers that were picked in the vegetable garden, wiped on my sleeve or pants, and eaten on the spot. My grandmother, Basha Leah Borovski, a daughter of the Aleksandrovitz family in Suwalki, was a wonderful character. In her room, she had a picture hung of the Western Wall and the holy cities: Jerusalem, Hebron, Tiberius and Safed. When my mother was a little girl, may she live, my grandmother would lift her up and stand her on the heavy chest of drawers, {p. 118} so that she could better see this picture. Mother would spend a long time looking at each and every detail in the picture, and her soul became attached to the soul of the nation, and all her days she longed to go up to the Land, until she was able to, and to this day she lives there, for more than forty years.

On one of the days in 5681 [1920], the writer Gad Zaklikovski arrived in Augustów. He was a Sokolov man, a *chassid* dressed in a long *kapote*,[418] with *peyot* and a beard. He "went out to bad culture,"[419] divorced his wife and left the town of his birth. I met him in Augustów when he was a writer, clean-shaven and with an exquisitely done head of hair, in European dress. He founded the "*Yugend Bund*" and gathered around himself many of the youth. He developed diverse cultural activities. Among others, he staged the play "The Kidnappers." The production that was staged in a public hall was a great success. In the year 5673 [1913], the "*Yugend Bund*" disintegrated, and Zaklikovski assisted in the founding of the "*HeChalutz*" organization.

In the land, together with my brother Joseph, I joined the "*Ma'avar*" group.[420] After a short while, I founded the "*Hitamtzut*"[421] group together with friends from the Augustów region. During the years 5686-5687 [1925-1927], there existed a terrible lack of work in the settlements of Yehuda. I decided, therefore, to turn to studies. I enrolled for studies in the Hebrew *Beit Midrash* for Teachers in Jerusalem. In the period of my studies, I also worked in youth leadership in the "*Noar HaOved*"[422] movement in Petach Tikvah and Machaneh Yehuda, Beit HaKerem and in the "*Bachurot*"[423] movement in Jerusalem.

In the years 5692-5693 [1931-1933], I was in Germany as an emissary of the Labor movement in the land of Israel. For two years in Berlin, I led the youth movements of "*HaBonim*"[424] and "*HaNoar HaOved*," (*Arbeits Kreiz*) and led the branch of "*HeChalutz*." I served as a member of the "*HeChalutz*" center, and secretary of the Hebrew Council in Germany. In these

---

[418] Caftan.

[419] Abandoned the path of chassidism.

[420] A group for workers, largely those newly arrived to the land of Israel, who were looking for work in collective settlements.

[421] "Effort."

[422] "Working Youth."

[423] "Young Women."

[424] "The Builders."

same years, I completed my studies at the Friedrich Wilhelm University and the *Beit Midrash* of Jewish Wisdom in Berlin.

After Hitler's rise to power on January 30, 1933, the British Government agreed to give one thousand certificates to the Jews of Germany. Three hundred of them were transferred to the possession of "*HeChalutz.*" One hundred and fifty went up first in the month of September 1933. I returned to the land at the head of that group.

In the years 5692-5697 [1932-1937] I completed my studies in Hebrew literature, Bible, and language.

After the completion of my studies, I engaged in teaching in high schools in the land. In the year 5704 [1944], I was appointed Scientific Secretary of the Encyclopedia *HaMikra'it*[425] published by the Bialik institute and the Hebrew University.

In the year 5707 [1947], I traveled to England for the first time to investigate Hebrew manuscripts that had been preserved there. I discovered a treasury of language and poetry.

At the end of the summer of 5710 [1950], I was in Jerusalem for the organization of the Institute of Hebrew Manuscripts. The initiator of the project was David Ben Gurion, the Head of the Government and the Minister of Defense. I was engaged with this project of assembling photographs of Hebrew manuscripts that were found in libraries all over the world - for thirteen years. In these years, I visited Austria, Italy, Belgium, Germany, Denmark, Holland, Hungary, Ireland, England, Spain, and Switzerland.

{p. 119} From Days Gone By
by Eliezer Markus

I arrived from Sapotskin, the town of my birth, to Augustów, in the year 1911. Our dwelling place was on the street of the synagogue, in the house of Lazer Freimark (Tzibulkes), opposite the home of Rabbi Chaim Baier (Korek the *Melamed*). In the courtyard of that same house lived an old Jew, a water-drawer, and his two sons who followed in his path. One was "Gali" the blind, who, despite his handicap, would bring water from the river and distribute it in buckets to the houses of the residents. His brother, Avak'eh, would also bring water and, later, became a gravedigger.

Our neighbor on the left side was a welder, and his name was Avraham Yitzchak Cohen, nicknamed "Grovetz." He had two sons: Shimon, and Avraham'eleh the crazy, the city simpleton.

On the right side stood two wooden houses in front, and a wooden house in the courtyard. There lived the Bat-Sheve'le family: in one house Bat-Sheva lived with her husband, and in the second her daughter Rachel-Leah'ke, and in the courtyard, her daughter, Devore'ke. The husbands were fishermen, and the women sold the catch in the market. Devora's husband was also a glazier. Rachel Leah had two daughters and three sons: Aharon - "Noz," Tanchum and Moshe Yitzchak. This last was killed when he was with the Partisans (according to the testimony of Shmuel Zufintzki).

I was placed in the "*cheder*" of Dovid Boyarski, known as "*Der Vishaiyer*," for the name of Vishai, the town of his origin.

---

[425] Biblical.

My friends in the *"cheder"* were: Yitzchak Bezant, Yaakov Cohen, Mordechai Ostrov, Ze'ev Sheinimer, Zerach Finkelstein, Dovid Hillel Kaplan, Arieh Shreibman, Aminadav Grinberg, Dovid Friedman (*Katonti*),[426] Yerachmiel Kaplan, Meir Vezbotzki and Moshe Biyuranski. Those younger than me: Noach Denmark, Mordechai Shreibman, Metushalach Chalupitzki.

The *"cheder"* was in the house of Hershel Denmark, which was in Gelinki Street. In the same house was Yazurski's *"cheder"* for the youth who were more mature than me.

{p. 120} In the city there were other *"chadarim:"* of Pilosky (*Der "Supotzkinner"*);[427] of Rotblit (the *Stavisker*);[428] of Chaim Baier (*Korak*); of Meir Meizler. In 1913, Rabbi Elyakum Levinzon came from Lazdie (*"Der Lazdeiner"*). There was a *"Talmud Torah"* under the management of Rabbi Betzalel Grader. There he taught with his son-in-law, Rabbi Avraham Yitzchak Solnitzki, who had a pleasant voice and had a majestic appearance, and was the *"baal koreh"*[429] in the *Beit Midrash*.

Rabbi Nachman Friedberg, a teacher of Russian literature, was a modest man, "hidden among the baggage." He founded and managed the benevolent fund that developed into a savings and loan fund, lending associations, and eventually to a national bank.

Among the youth there were stories that circulated about the underground and the revolutionaries who would squeeze funds from the people of means in order to finance their activities. The chief activists were: Avram'eleh Glikson and Chava Frenkel.

The priests frequently preached in the churches against the Jews, and spread the poison of anti-Semitism. This situation induced fear among the Jewish population. They began to organize and prepare themselves for the hour of trouble that was likely to come. The Blood Libel against Beilis[430] in Kiev terrified the Jewish settlement throughout Russia. There was great worry for the fate of the Jews in the villages (Olinki, Lipsk, Tzernovroda, Yanovka, etc.), in which a few isolated Jewish families lived among a sea of Christian farmers. Among the youngsters in the *"cheder,"* stories spread of terrors carried out by robbers and thieves, the most famous of whom was one Tzarsky (a robber in the forests of Augustów who had escaped from prison and was executed for armed robbery in the year 1916).

A group was organized, therefore, of householders and tenants for the needs of night-patrols against attacks and arson. Every night, in turn, two men would go out to patrol. Among the activists in this organization, I remember Lazar Freimark and a colorful young man, dressed impeccably, wearing shiny polished boots – Yishaya Tuvia Falk was his name.

When the news was received that Beilis had been freed, the joy was so great that the Jews kissed each other in the streets, and wept from joy. Many celebrated the event with feasting and drinking.

In the association of volunteer fire-fighters, the Jews shared activity with the Polish population. In the lines of firefighters were many Jewish young men. Their band of wind instruments made a great impression. The society was supported with a small amount from the town, while a large part of its budget came from donations and income from receptions that they would hold in the town park in spring and summer.

From time to time, preachers or *maggidim* would come to town who would preach to the congregation. There were among them those with ability who knew how to draw a large audience

---

[426] I am too small. Genesis 32:11 "…I am too small for all the kindness that You have so steadfastly shown Your servant."

[427] From Sapotzkin.

[428] From Stavisk.

[429] The person who reads the *Torah* aloud for the congregation during prayer services.

[430] Menachem Mendel Beilis, 1874 – 1934, was a Russian Jew accused of ritual murder in Kiev in a notorious 1913 trial, known as the "Beilis trial" or "Beilis affair."

130

of eager listeners, men and women. One of them was the "*Maggid*" of Posvola. His sermons were peppered with the sayings of our sages, may their memories be for a blessing, and proverbs that relied on the issues of the day and what was going on in the world. He knew how to make tears flow from the eyes of the women – when speaking of the hardships of making a living, family separations, migrations, etc. The reward for his efforts came from money that everyone would drop into a bowl at the exit, each man according to what his heart moved him to give.[431]

When Theodor Herzl published his historic call, prior to the Zionist Congress in Basle, a great awakening arose in Augustów as well. Among those who stood at the head of the Zionists must be mentioned M. Koifman, the owner of a shop for medicines, Dovid Slutzky, Shmuel Grinberg, a merchant, {p. 121} Arieh Aleksandrovitz, the brothers Chaim Yosef and Binyamin Markus, and Tzvi Feinstein. The authority of the Lithuanian and Belorussian communities was Rabbi Rabinovitz of Sapotskin, a town in the Augustów district.

A central place in the cultural life of the town was held by the Jewish library. At the head of the library at that time stood Mrs. Avramsky and her assistants were: Aharon Zukerman, Atsha Lap, Chaya Markus and Naftali Rubinstein.

The council members also served as volunteer librarians. In the year 1912, the Zionists succeeded in introducing into the library council the teachers Reuven Levi and Dovid Boyarski. The two brought a new spirit into the library. They succeeded in acquiring many Hebrew and Yiddish books, and in the schools conducted publicity to increase reading. For the youth the library was a significant meeting place for getting to know each other, and throughout the evening hours, there was considerable movement. The library served as a very valuable institution for indirect education, for Zionism and Hebrew culture.

On Malinska Street, in Rubinstein's house, there was a silent movie ("Illusion"), owned by Yones-Kaplanski. There was also the "Fuchs" theater, where sometimes wandering troupes of actors would perform; sometimes the local Jewish youth would organize a reception, or a presentation, whose proceeds would be devoted to a charitable institution.

On one of the August days of 1914, when joy reigned in the park, on the occasion of the annual festival to benefit the Fire Brigade, the news came about the general mobilization. The information came down like thunder on a clear day.

With the outbreak of the war, life in the city was disrupted. Great confusion prevailed; studies in the *chadarim* ceased; a few teachers left the city, together with a few other families, believing that the nearness of the border was dangerous during war time.

There were those who distanced themselves by travelling through Russia. Of these, many were the families who did not return with the end of the war.

In effect, the town was captured by the Germans, with a flanking maneuver, a short time after the war began, without causing serious damage. A few lone shells hit a few houses and lightly injured a small number of people. The Germans treated the residents fairly, apart from commandeering supplies for their troops.

At the end of two weeks, the Russians mounted a counterattack and captured the city. The return of the Russian army was accompanied by incidents of imprisonment, robbery, and false accusations against the Jewish population. As a result of one accusation two Jews, Reb Yisrael Grosberg and Shaul Kilzon were imprisoned. In Czarny-Brod, seven Jews were hanged by the military authorities when there was no guilt on their hands. The wave of imprisonments and assassinations passed over the Jewish population in all the cities and towns in the border settlements.

---

[431] Exodus 25:2 "…you shall accept gifts for Me from every person whose heart so moves him."

With the receding of the snows, in the spring of 1915, the Germans conducted a great attack along the entire front and Augustów was captured by them for the second time.

Many that lived in wooden houses in the area were brought into our house, which was a house of stone. Soldiers passed through the town and warned people not to light fires in their stoves, because the smoke from the chimneys served as a target for the cannons of the enemy. Indeed, a Mariampol house was hit by a shell, since smoke rose from the chimney.

{p. 122} The Russian soldiers disappeared and the streets were emptied of any person. The city resembled a ghost-town. People sat in the houses in groups, full of expectation and fear in anticipation of what was about to happen.

Not an hour had gone by when large numbers of Russian troops began streaming into the city, and arranged themselves in the market square. The shops remained closed, out of fear lest the Russians would return and consider it shared action with the enemy, as they had experienced after their first retreat.

City matters were subordinate to the military authority. The conquering army published announcements in three languages: German, Polish and Yiddish, by which they sought to calm the population. It was said in them that the German army had come to liberate the oppressed nations from the yoke of the Russian government, and it was incumbent on all residents to continue with their normal lives while obeying the orders of the government. Movement in and out of the city was forbidden, and needed a special license.

With the stabilizing of the front, a military hospital was opened and an officer was appointed who was expected to organize life in the city. The officer began exploring on whom to place the administration of public affairs.

At the head of the Jewish community he placed Reb Yisrael Leib Litinsky and as his alternate, Reb Avraham Veidenbaum. Efraim was elected as the secretary (*Der Bershter*). The appointed heads of the community held meetings and consultations with the heads of the householders, on how to support the town matters so that the Jews would not be harmed – God forbid – in the event that the Russians returned. One of the first directives dealt with the opening of the shops and arrangements for preserving cleanliness in the city. A special order was set that the bakeries should continue with their work, and they were obliged to provide bread to everyone who requested it.

The German conquest did not weigh too heavily on the population. The Jews even felt a certain lightening of the situation after the persecutions and oppressions by the Russians. Instead of second-class citizens, they became citizens with equal rights and obligations with the Christian population.

At the end of 1915, when the Germans advanced into Russian territory, the front moved from the city, which then emerged a little from its geographic isolation. The Germans refurbished the municipal park, repaired the fence, neatened the lawns, and every Sunday a military band played in the center of the park. Two Jewish policemen were appointed: Yitzchak Bialovzetzki ("Russko") and Vasserman.

Senseless persecutions, whose purpose was to cause the population to feel the superiority of the German conquerors, were not lacking. For example, an order was brought out that all the men were obligated to remove their hats when passing a German officer on the street, and transgressors were punished. One of the Polish notables, an estate owner (the *Fritz*) from Garbów, began to walk about on the streets without a hat, and many did as he did. It was also forbidden to sit on the threshold of their homes on the market street, as the residents were used to doing. A sentry was strict about fulfilling the decree.

The Germans appointed a sub-officer who organized a grade school for the children of the Jews. In it, instruction in German was compulsory. The teachers in German were the women:

Niota Yones, Povembrovski, Rabinovitz and Soloveitchik. For the children of the Christians, a separate school was established. The first supervisor of the schools was Officer Tzovak. He was the very epitome of a Prussian officer, and he placed the emphasis on exercise lessons in a military drill structure. The officer that came in his place was a professional teacher, and taught German to the higher classes.

{p. 123} On one of the days an inspector came to visit the schools. How great was the amazement of the children and the teachers when he tested the children on the Bible and read from a Hebrew book with the Sephardic pronunciation.

Although agriculture was advanced in Augustów region, and in the usual years the farmers supplied all the basic food needs of the population (potatoes, vegetables, dairy products, fish, fruit, etc.), during the time of the conquest a lack of many necessities was felt. The Germans took for themselves the agricultural products, and imposed ration-cards. The flour that the Germans earmarked for baking bread was of very bad quality. Of course, a black market was developed. Due to the serious lack of metal in Germany, they confiscated all copper vessels in the city. The soldiers, accompanied by militia, went from house to house collecting all the copper vessels, which were the pride of the housewives. The bells of the Catholic and Pravoslavic churches were also taken down and transported to Germany.

There began to arrive from the Vilna area a number of refugee families, who on most days were absorbed into the city, but the nickname "refugees" clung to them for many years. With the moving of the front from the city, some of the families who had left it at the start of the war returned. With the returnees came the teachers Dovid Boyarski, Reuven Levin, and Pilipinski, whose influence on the young generation was significant.

The Germans began to energetically exploit the forests. They established sawmills in and around town. Across from the "Fuchs" auditorium (which had served as a silent movie house before the war), a sawmill was established in which Russian and French prisoners of war were put to work. For the operation of the sawmills, a large power-station was built which also provided electric light to the residents of the town who until then had used kerosene lamps. They also built, next to the railroad station, a modern factory for the production of tar and turpentine, and a second factory for dehydrating fruit and vegetables. The Germans sent the vegetables back to Germany, which suffered a great lack of food. A few Jewish families earned their living in the factories mentioned above.

One of the big sawmills constructed by the Germans was erected in the village of Blizna, next to the Augustów-Suwalki railroad tracks. For the purpose of administering the forest economy, the forest supervisor, Hoiftman Shreider and his deputy Officer Milke, were located in Augustów. Many Jews, who were expert in the timber trade, found lucrative employment there, and also succeeded in developing private trade in wood.

With the advance of the Germans on the Russian Front, and after the conquest of Warsaw and Brisk of Lithuania, the area where citizens were permitted to move was expanded. Life became a little easier. Trade began to flourish. The Germans made it possible to bring from Germany tobacco products, chocolate, coffee substitutes, preserved fish, etc. For this purpose, the Germans opened a store that supplied merchandise to Jewish wholesalers. This store, which was also responsible for food, was managed by a German Lieutenant whose name was Zaks, who established friendly relations with the merchants of the city.

Activity also increased in the area of cultural life. At the initiative of the teachers Boyarski and Levin, courses for study of the Hebrew language, the Bible and general studies were organized that enjoyed great success. Most of the youth in town took part in these courses.

Literary receptions were also held, with public readings and lectures.

At the initiative of Wolf Ratner, the son of the city's *Chazzan*, an amateur drama group was organized. At his direction, {p. 124} plays from the repertoire of the Jewish theater were brought, with great success and to the pleasure of the audience, the rehearsals and preparations for the theater productions served as an opportunity for meetings of the youth, because tens of the young men and women were involved in the event. The income was dedicated to public institutions: the library, *Linat HaTzedek*,[432] etc. The main activists in the dramatic group were: Yitzchak Varhaftig, Arieh Eizenstat, Yehuda Rotstein, Dovid Stolar, Eliezer Mintz, Rivka Kantorovitz, Niota Yones, Nadia Sarni and Sonia Yones.

Also the library, which had been closed with the capture of the town by the Germans, operated again.

The yearning for cultural and literary activity brought about the publication of a literary collection by Moshe Markus, Ze'ev Sheinmar, Ben-Tzion Boyarski, Shlomo Levinson and Yishayahu Plotzinski. The sole printing-house in town, which was owned by Varhaftig, stood idle. The youth were permitted to organize and print the collection by themselves.

The collection, "*Pinateinu*,"[433] was published and edited by Moshe Markus and contained articles, poems, literary items and a long historical article from the estate of the writer Rabbi Yaakov Frenkel, may his memory be for a blessing, "The Land of *Ophir*."[434]

At the end of the days of the German conquest, when the doctor, Yitzchak, returned to the city, a large meeting of many youth activists was called at the initiative of Chaya Markus, for the sake of expanding medical aid for the poor of the town. A special house was acquired, and instruments, and a permanent clinic was established. Dr. Yitzchak Yurdanski served as the institute's doctor, and the head of the council stood Mrs. Chaya Markus (until her *aliyah* to the land). Her deputy was Liuba Lozman; Mordechai Ratner was engaged as the pharmacist.

The clinic also loaned equipment to the sick and kept ice in the cellar in case of need. With the approach of the time for the German withdrawal, a great national awakening arose within the Polish population. The mood was uplifted. The Jews hoped, that with the declaration of Polish independence they would become integrated into the new state as citizens with equal rights.

At the initiative of the Polish *Intelligentsia,* a great public meeting was called in the courtyard of the Pravoslavic Church. Poles and also Jews spoke. But the harmony did not continue for long. Immediately upon the organization of the Polish Government, the Jews were once again pushed aside into a dark corner. Anti-Semitism again raised its head.

{p. 125} **Avram'eleh "Gruvatz"**

---

[432] A charitable organization that took care of the sick and all their needs, above and beyond medical care.
[433] "Our Corner."
[434] 1 Kings 10:11.

Performance of the Kreitzer Sonata

{p. 126} **Amateur Troupe 1917**

First row from right to left: Shlomo Ratner, Laurent, Berel Rozenhof, Alter Kentzuk, Shmuel Yehuda Loinshel, Feivel Blacharski, Gedaliah Rotenberg.
Second row: Meizler, Chune Lap, Esther Stoliar, Etta Goldring, Yaakov Stein, Sima Shreibman, Kentzuk, Gedaliah Denmark.
Third row: Bergstein, Devorah Bramzon, Volf Ratner, Niuta Yones, (…), Rochel Rubinstein, Dovid Stolar.
Fourth row: Meir Vezbotzki, (…), (…), Abba Stolar.

135

The Dramatic Group (1923-24)

Standing from right to left: Y. Beker, M. Volmir, M. Kolfenitzki, Leah Sherman, VV. Sheinmar, Y. Linda, Y. Plotzinski.
Sitting: S. Yones, L. Markus, Ch. Strozinski, VV. Ratner, D. Lobel, Doron. Bottom: Liza.

{p. 127} Amateur Troupe

First row from right to left: Masha Rozenfeld, Avraham Vezbotzki, Rivka Rozenfeld, Chaya Markus, Dov Friedman.
Second row: Chaya Lev, Eliezer Markus, Channah Lozman, Yishayahu Plotzinski, Channah Strozinski, Niuta Eibeshutz. Bottom: Portnoy, Cohen.

Members of the Choir

Standing from right: Y. Beker, M. Kolfenitzki, Beknovitzki:, (…), (…), A. Tsherman, P. Tsherman, Y. Chalupitzki, T. Linda, B. Rozenhof, M. Stolar.
Second row: Y. Bialovzetzki, B. Ivriyah, Y. Linda, Ch. Bergstein, Ch. Plotzinski.
Third row: Tsherman, S. Ratner, M. Volmir, Volf Ratner, S. Yones, Y. Ignovitz.
Bottom: A. Leizerovitz, (…).

{p. 128} Amateur Choir (1923)

Standing from right to left: Y. Beker, B. Friedman, Y. Zeligzon, M. Goldshmidt, A. Rozenfeld, Y. Lonshel, Y. Sherman, M. Kolfenitzki.
Second row: R. Mistivovski, Avresha, R. Varhaftig, S. Ratner, B. Rabinovitz, Y. Doren, R. Rotenberg.
Third row: A. Markus, Y. Plotzinski.

137

The Dramatic Group, Performance of "The Dybbuk."

{p. 129} The Amateur Troupe

Standing from right" A. Stolar, … M. Lap, Y. Vilkovski, Chaya Markus, M. Elenbogen, Yoel Chalupitzki, …. D. Freitzeit, Nachum Lozovski, M. Kahn.
Second row: M. Mariampolski, M. Goldshmid, L. Markus, Channah Lozman, Plotzinski, … VV. Sheinmar, … B. Friedman.
Third row: Ch. R. Rozenfeld, M. Stolar, Y. Ratzitzki, Leizerovitz.

Way of Life and Lifestyle

My City Augustów
by Akiva Glikstein

I was born in this city in the year 1881. When I was 20, that is, in 1901, after I had completed my service in the Russian army, as a "volunteer" in a foot battalion in my city, I went up to the land of Israel. Just once, when I was in Europe in the year 1921, I visited in it. I found almost none of my friends, for most of them had migrated to the United States, and a few of them had moved to live in larger cities. With a depressed spirit, I left my city after just one day. I stayed for another two days in adjacent Suwalki. Since then I feel no longing for the city of my birth, despite the memories that are tied to it from the days of my childhood.

My parents, who had gone up to the land in 1904 and found their eternal rest in the cemetery of Zikhron Yaakov, were not born in Augustów; they settled in it in the year 1863 for special reasons. In the year 1842, when my father was about 18 years old, he married a girl two years younger than himself. The young couple settled in the Polish town of Czarnovo, which is adjacent to Augustów. My father lacked a profession. He learned in *cheder* and knew a little *Talmud*. With the help of his father, who lived in a small town in the same area, he opened a small shop in the village, with a public house, a trade that was at that time an acceptable occupation for Jews. The village was small and poor. Making a living – as difficult as the splitting of the Reed Sea. Decades after that, when my father was one of the wealthy householders in Augustów, he used to say that in the village it was more difficult to earn two zlotys a week to support the small family than afterwards, hundreds of rubles to support the family that had grown in the meantime. In the year 1863, the Polish revolt broke out against the Tsarist régime. This was the second revolt. The first failed about 30 years before it. My father was the only Jew in the village and the only one who knew how to read and write in Polish. Every night, after midnight, the local commanders of the revolt, who did not know even the shape of a letter, came to his house. My father would close the doors and shutters, sit down with them next to {p. 131} a table, light a small kerosene lamp, and read them the orders that they had received from the higher command. My father knew well that mortal danger hung over this deed of his. Once, when he was in Augustów, he read a government order from the Tsar in Polish and Russian, in which it said that all regional governors had permission to hang, without trial, anyone suspected of supporting the revolt. On the other hand, the Poles also established mobile military tribunals, which would move in the night from place to place and ordering the hanging of anyone who was thought to oppose the revolt. It went without saying that – as always – the Jews were the goats to Azazel.[435] Father related that once such a tribunal arrived in the village and decided to hang a Jew – a carpenter (*shtelmakh*)[436] who prepared planks of wood for wagons. The Polish elders of the village begged them not to hang the Jew, because there was no one to replace him in repairing the wagons. In

---

[435] The scapegoats. Leviticus 16:10 "…while the goat designated by lot for Azazel shall be left standing alive before the LORD, to make expiation with it and to send it off to the wilderness for Azazel."
[436] Yiddish.

place of him, they suggested hanging one of the two blacksmiths in town. And indeed, the judges acquiesced to them. For a few months, my father read the revolutionaries' orders, until the information reached the opposing side. One dark night, two armed Cossacks, mounted on horses, came to my father's house, carrying in their hands an order, according to which it was incumbent on Leib Glikstein to present himself immediately to the general in Vilna. My father was certain that he would be taken out to be killed. While the tired Cossacks and their horses ate and rested, my father wrapped himself in *tallit*[437] and *tefillin*, prayed and said the *Vidui*.[438] Afterwards he parted from his young wife and the two babies, and went with the Cossacks. The journey took three days and at night, they slept in villages. The Cossacks, who were armed from head to toe from fear of the Poles, would tie my father to themselves with a rope. When they arrived at Vilna, they took him immediately to the general, who turned to him with these words: "So, Yid – they tell me that every night you sit there in Czarnovo reading to the Polish traitors the lousy orders they get from their commanders. Do you know that I am obligated to hang you for that?" My father prostrated himself at his feet and said: "Yes, your Excellency! But what could I do? I was between the hammer and the anvil. They knew that I know Polish and if I refuse – they will hang me as they did to many Jews. Do with me as you will." The general, who happened to be in a good mood, ordered my father: "Get up Yid. You must leave the village immediately and move to the adjacent Augustów. Two Cossacks will accompany you, in their hands I will send instructions from me to the governor of the Augustów region, that he supply you with wagons and laborers to transport your family and possessions to Augustów, and that he should also see to a place to live. March!" My father got to his feet. It seemed to him as if he had returned from the world of truth.[439] Thus, he came to settle in Augustów. There arose the question of making a living. It was known to him that they were about to bring a regiment of mounted cavalry, Cossacks from the Don, and that the authorities were encountering difficulties in housing them; he hastened to suggest that the government grant him a suitable plot of its land in the area surrounding the town, and that he would erect all the necessary buildings: barracks, stables for the horses, a hospital, workshops, a prison, etc. After intensive effort, accompanied by a bribe, of course, the work was given to him. He didn't have sufficient money, but the Augustów people knew him as an honest man, and enterprising, and provided him with the means at a monthly interest of 2%. The rate was indeed a reduced one, but the rents he received for his property was so high that he had enough to return the loans and manage a house at a high standard of living. The old people of Augustów remember Leib Glikstein of the "Long" Street and the barracks. Of all this, not a memory remains.

The city was not large and most of the residents were Jewish, and a few Polish and government clerks, and Russian army officers who lived in Jewish houses. The city was noted for the canal that went through it, which was called by the name of the Augustow Canal. Around the city, rivers and lakes full of various kinds of fish. The Jewish population made their living from exporting the fish. Among the fish there was one kind by the name of "*shlibes,*" a tasty fish, {p. 132} and very expensive. In Warsaw, I saw a placard in a fancy shop for delicacies with the name of this fish and the name of my city.

In between the rivers and lakes that spread over tens of square kilometers were huge pine forests.

There were a few factories in the city for processing hides, whose owners and workers were Jewish, and one brewery. By the way, the jokers of that generation used to say that it was permitted to drink the beer on *Pesach*, because the beer was made up of two ingredients, which were not *chametz* – it was composed of just water and excise – (taxes to the government). Nice –

---

[437] Prayer shawl with *tzitzit*, ritual fringes attached to the corners.
[438] The confession said by, or for, a Jew who is about to die.
[439] The world to come.

they protested against them – it was possible that one of the workers who mixed the two ingredients would put a slice of bread into them! A thing like this was not possible! Answered the jokers: the owner of the brewery has no bread in this factory, from where would the worker have it!?

A most important economic factor was the military, especially the Cossack regiment. It was a one-of-a-kind army. The Tsar's government relationship to the residents of the Don was "respect him and suspect him." Because most of the revolutionaries in the Tsar's regime were Cossacks (Pugachev, Stenker Razin and others), the government tried to bribe them, and granted them rights that other Russian residents did not have: freedom from taxes, the right to wear uniforms for life, the right to keep riding horses, cold weapons,[440] etc. The Cossack would bring with him all the equipment, except for hot weapons,[441] which he would receive from his regiment. Contrary to what was customary in the army, he would not receive clothing and boots from the army. Instead, he received a fixed monthly sum (*ramonet* funds). All the Jewish tailors and shoemakers in town worked for them. It is worth noting that the Cossack, who got his money by robbing and stealing, used to pay his debts to the craftsmen. I knew the Cossacks well, and I must say that I had many friends among them. At the age of 3-4, I spoke "juicy" Russian with the accent of the "quiet Don." I also knew how to curse like them, with the famous 3-story or more curse, in which the Holy Mother is mentioned, precisely not with respect. They always had in their hands the *nagaika* (the Cossacks' whip), which was able to kill a person with one blow. Our big house stood adjacent to the barracks, and there was not a day that Cossacks didn't come in to see my father. Mother would say to the maid: "Watch him very carefully – he is a *lakchan*" (an expression in Yiddish for a thief).[442] Yet for all that, something almost always went missing. One time, my father forgot the *tefillin* on the table in the kitchen. A Cossack came in and in the blink of an eye – the *tefillin* were in his pocket. When he realized that the leather of the straps was not strong enough to make a bit for his horse, he went to the market to sell them. A Jewish man met him, who as it is known had to redeem the holy article from the hands of a Christian, and asked him: Where did you get these?" The Cossack answered: "I'm a shoemaker by profession and I made them." The Jew paid him a few kopeks and brought the *tefillin* to my father. My mother prepared tens of fowls for *kapparot*,[443] and when she came on the eve of the *Yom Kippur*, she did not find in the coop even one of the birds alive. Scattered on the floor were the heads and intestines. She realized that the hand of the Cossack was in the matter. When my father met the battalion commander, he told him about the event, in the hope that he would punish those who were guilty. The colonel asked him: "When did it happen?" My father answered, "In the autumn, before our Great Fast." "Ah," said the colonel, "Yes that's possible, the Cossacks love poultry meat in the autumn." When the officer punished a Cossack who he caught stealing, he would add: "I'm punishing you not because you stole – but because you got caught."

At the age of 8 I learned to ride a horse like them. Once a year, the regiment would leave the city and moved to adjacent villages in order to feed the horses on green grass. My father would {p. 133} take advantage of this period to repair the barracks. For me and my friends these were holidays. We would roam about the barracks and the stables collecting "finds:" metal buttons, live bullets, wallets, etc. One time a Cossack asked me if I wanted to learn to ride a horse like Cossacks ride at my age. "Certainly I want to," was my reply. I already knew how to ride a workhorse without a saddle, because we had 3 or 4 teams of horses for hauling building materials, but I had never ridden a Cossack horse with a saddle. The Cossack brought his horse out of the stable, put

---

[440] Weapons that do not involve fire or explosive power.

[441] Weapons that do involve the use of fire or explosives.

[442] "A taker." This is a Hebrew word that was used previously to refer to a thief.

[443] Literally, expiations. This is a riddance ritual where a Jew symbolically transfers their sins onto a chicken, in advance of *Yom Kippur*.

the wooden, chair-shaped saddle on it, tied some cushions filled with pigs' hair to it, took off from his belly a long soft woolen belt, sat me on the saddle, tied my legs together under the horse's belly with the woolen belt, and pulled the saddle straps tight so that I, the saddle, and the horse were like one body. He put the bit in the horse's mouth, placed the reins in my hands, and said a few words of encouragement to me: "Don't be afraid, don't fall, be a man!" He stroked the horse's neck and called him by name: "Vasra, don't misbehave!" When he left the reins in my hands, the horse felt that the rider was not a Cossack. He shook his head vigorously and the reins fell from my hands. The horse reared up on his hind legs and shook his rear quarters to send me flying. When he didn't succeed, he stood on his forelegs…the Cossack watched but did not move. He wanted me to overcome the situation with my own strength. A great fear fell on me when the horse suddenly began to run as fast as the wind. I didn't shout because I was embarrassed. When the horse had gone some distance the Cossack put two fingers in his mouth, whistled, and the horse immediately returned, tired and quiet. The Cossack freed me from the saddle, kissed me on the forehead and said: "You are brave; you'll grow up and become a fearless Cossack."

Generally speaking, the relationship between the Cossacks and the Jews was all right. At the beginning of each year, young Cossacks came from the Don who had never in their lives seen Jews, and then it was happy in the city. The Cossacks would stroll around town distributing to our lads (girls were too shy to talk to the Cossacks) dried cherries, small hard crackers, and water-melon seeds.

From the Mouth of A. Glikstein

In our city there were, as is known, two public gardens: an old one, where the citizens, mostly Jewish, strolled – the gentiles didn't have time for strolls, and there was another garden, a new one, that had been planted on the occasion of an important event. Tsar Alexander III travelled by train, and the revolutionaries had laid a bomb under the tracks. To the sorrow of the Russian people (and also, of course, to the sorrow of the Jews), the train passed peacefully. The garden was planted in memory of the event.

They told at that time that the Jews were sitting in the synagogue talking about the event and regretting that the Tsar, who hated the Jews, had not been killed. There was among them one who shouted: "These revolutionaries, may their names be erased, all the troubles come only because of them; they have to be extracted by the roots." They asked him: "Reb Nachum, were you really sorry that this dog wasn't killed?" "Of course not!" Nachum fumed. "I'm just saying that if you're doing something – then do it properly; one should not scrimp on explosive materials!"

{p. 134} **In My Wanderings**
by Tz. Z. Weinberg

I wandered around all the days in the streets of the town (Ostrow Mazowiecka) to search after matter and deed – and I returned almost always with disappointment, despairing and annoyed. My wife hinted to me about the little one, Sonia, whose entire creation sang with the abundance of forces, as if saying this to banish my sorrow and diminish my bitterness. I bent over her out of pleasure and joy, and immediately there jumped on me her anger of livelihood, and from the girl's whispering eyes, as if she protested the many times more responsibility: "You are a father! You are obligated to worry for us, for me and for Momma, and to produce our sustenance!"

On one of these gloomy days one of my friends appeared like a rescuing angel, Aharon Tzukerman, who had moved around years before for his trade to one of the towns in Lithuania and he had been very successful. He spoke to my heart to transfer my dwelling place from Ostrow Mazowiecka, and to move to the place where he was living and try my luck there.

At the beginning of the fall season, I went out to my new place. I spent a full day in the loathsome and filthy train car, and the annoying leak, that babbled all day and all night onto the windowpanes, tainted my mood, and muddied the remnant of hope that sparkled in the hidden places of my soul.

However, the town of Augustow welcomed me warmly. It was entirely washed with the brightness of the sun of an awakening fall day. The town danced before me the whole way, from the station to its small white houses that were engulfed in the green of the fields and the shading trees, and opened before me a gate to a new period of life. It was as if all the suffering and hardship of yesterday's rains, which had always been beside me, were removed, and from now on new skies would shine on my head, and a new land would stretch out under my feet.

I was transformed overnight into a veteran teacher, experienced and comfortable. My friend, a man engaged with those around him, offered me private Hebrew and *Talmud* lessons, and advertised for me in the city. Quickly I acquired a reputation among my male and female students, and the work hours were filled more than enough. My livelihood was established, my mood also improved. I found satisfaction in my work, and in teaching my students I myself learned. I also tried in my free hours to complete my education in general studies. The residents of the town of Augustow were far from excessive *chassidim*, and the young people and the *Maskilim* of the city found something in my friendship.

The little comfort in my life opened before new horizons. From the field of the book, study, and the abstract, I passed to the real and the concrete, which feeds a person's senses. Constricted adolescence, which was restrained as if in a splint, left its bounds, as if it had completed now at one stroke what had been lacking for it for a long time. I became devoted to swimming in the river, sailing in a boat, trips and tours in the near and far surroundings, to gymnastic exercises, and all kinds of sport, to happy parties of man and woman, as if I had been instructed {p. 135} in all of these from the dawn of my childhood. From now I became a witness to all echo of play, chasing after every hint of companionship, joining the youth as if I were one of them, as a brother to every laugh, mischief and wild behavior.

Accompanied by my new friends and acquaintances, we would go boating from time to time, especially on *Shabbat* days and school vacation days, to the surrounding area of the town, a place of forests and shady groves, streams and lakes, which gurgled from beneath the land and filling the landscape with a wonderful mysterious cooing.

We were equipped with food and drink and wandered around all the day all over the place. The members of the convoy were given to conversations during the journeys, of which my ears did not catch almost anything at all. They, in the area and in the place, were distracted by the beauty of the landscape and the lovely sights, and found a desire to converse, in these hidden places, about their concerns, about the revealed and the hidden things, that accumulated for them during the ordinary days, and sought their solutions. And I, thirsty for what my eyes could see, shaking with all my senses to the wonders of the surroundings, did not turn at first to their conversations and deliberations.

On the winter journeys, on a surface of a covering of snow and frost, when the members of the company, wrapped in their cloaks, deepened their conversation mostly with new travelers, I escaped from the group by myself, and took myself far away, clearing myself a path, entirely given over to the brilliance of the sparkling snow, and imitating with pleasure the sound of the "kra" of the crow, that jumped from branch to branch, shaking the snowflakes to the ground.

Only once, at the beginning of the spring, when I joined the company on one of the trips, and we sat down {p. 136} among the trees for a shared meal, and the girls spread a white tablecloth

A Group of Revolutionaries (1905)

out on the grassy surface, and set out the food and the drinks, and set a place for each one of us to sit, a setting of place that had in it, as it were, a special intention, and I found myself sitting next to one guest, who I saw from time to time in our group, but only now did I understand him and his nature, and I leaned over so that I would not miss a word of all that was spoken, and all that served the depiction of the debate, at the time of the meal and afterwards, the content of the conversations and deliberations during all of the journeys of the fall and winter seasons became clear to me at one stroke, which, while they were happening, I had unintentionally ignored, and I had not dwelt on them at all.

At once the matter became clear to me "... the conditions, the unconsciousness of the masses, the regime of the brute..." the speaker, who sat next to me, revealed human suffering with pure and clear language, and piercing logic, and came to an explicit conclusion, understood by all the assembled, that there was nothing for us but to travel with the line of courageous fighters blazing a trail for human emancipation.

Now I knew exactly who my companions were and to where they were heading, and for what these long journeys were intended, and what the meaning of the secrets and the whispers and the concealed hints were, that were woven around me all the time, in which I did not participate at all. It was as if the cataract had been removed from my eye, and a new light shone on me through the passageway of the heavens and the green of the trees and the grasses. My confusion was transformed, as they began to break through in Russia, piercing with their first rays of light also into this distant corner.

*

One of the active members of the revolutionary underground, Bluma Sapir, clung to me as a special guide, penetrated into my house and befriended my wife, and taught us a chapter of the law of national economics, and the ruling regime.

I taught Hebrew to her younger sister, and I was a frequent visitor in her parents' house. This was a destroyed family. Her father, an important merchant, and stout, lived separately from his wife, in one of the isolated rooms in his big house. He always quarreled with his older daughters, who stood on the side of their quiet and delicate mother, whose hair had gone prematurely white from great sorrow and disgrace, and her posture was stooped over as if from old age. The father would also bring prostitutes to his room, and then the argument would erupt all the more forcefully. The woman would flee from the house to members of her family, and the adult daughters would attack their father with insults and cursing. He would listen to his daughters' reproaches in disobedient silence, and with ridicule, protest their opposition with one fell swoop: "Momma, Momma… always Momma…and I need a woman and not a Momma…"

He was a heartless person, both in his house and in his business. But just as people discerned that he was bad, so they increased their lauding of the members of his household, and spoke in praise of his daughters, goodhearted and broad-minded, on whom true nobility was poured. They especially praised Bluma, his youngest daughter.

Excess affection was known to Bluma by her revolutionary friends. With a warm temperament, animated, quick, she was the living spirit in all the meetings and interviews that met on behalf of the center of the "movement." She was also occupied with the goings on at home, in matters of the "movement" and her father's business, for with her, her father would {p. 137} conduct himself pleasantly, and give through her the support of the house. With all this, she also contributed several hours to my wife and me, for frequent visits, for prolonged propaganda for her sacred idea. We got used to her as to a member of the household. My wife travelled with our daughter for a week to Ostrow Mazowiecka, to visit her father and the members of her family, and Bluma did not stop coming to my house, to prepare my bread for me, and to see to all that I was missing. On one of the evenings she brought a small group into my house, among them one of the emissaries that had come for a special task. The emissary was an angry man, gloomy, one of the downtrodden people of the nation. He negotiated with Bluma in a whisper, on an issue that was on the agenda, and at last joined into the general conversation on the matter of the status of the workers and the worldview of the proletarian person.

"And as for me" asserted Bluma "the matter does not depend on the status and not on the condition of the status. I am a daughter of a bourgeois against my will, but my psychology is one of a complete proletarian…"

"There is still something to be suspicious of in the matter…" the emissary grumbled with his eyes lowered.

"Father is a bourgeois" Bluma apologized "however I am also formally on the side of the working person, an abused handmaiden in the house, a subjugated servant to Father in his business!"

"That's what I said" her friend Batya supported her "and if I am busy an entire day in Father's warehouse, and sell wine and spirits to customers, am I not a proletarian?"

In her eyes the flash of victory sparkled; her friends were secretly chuckling.

The emissary's head was down to the ground, and a look of scorn came over his face.

The conversation stopped, and the friends began to scatter. Bluma remained alone with me.

"The hour is late…" I said.

"And what of it?" "she protested, and remained in the house, and began to make order in the rooms and to prepare what was needed for the next day.

I sprawled on the bench, for I was very tired, and I waited for Bluma to finish the organizing, so I could lock the door behind her. I waited a long time in vain. My eyes stayed closed. I dozed off for a while. Suddenly I awoke to the touch of a soft body.

"Bluma?"

She was pressed up against me, and was moaning a quiet moan, resembling an extended snore from between her teeth.

"Bluma…."

145

For a moment, I clung to her with hugs, and an abundance of kisses, but within a minute a bitter thought like a sharp skewer was stuck in my brain, my heart was quieted, and all of my limbs trembled from passing cold. The picture of my wife and daughter stood before me.

I forcefully shook myself off, jumped off the bench. I turned up the light of the dimmed lamp. I approached her without pause and I said:

"Bluma! Go home! Go in a hurry!"

She arose, rubbed her eyes, pulled herself together, glanced at me and said, slapping me on my shoulder:

"Brother – you, you are a revolutionary, pretending to belong to the revolutionaries, but you are nothing but a rabbit, a worthless rabbit...."

She wrapped herself in her coat, patiently put on her hat, and went out.

I stood silently in place for a few moments. My blood came to a boil again, licked my body and burned {p. 138} my flesh. My blood was pounding in my temples, as if reproaching me: "idiot, complete idiot..." Only when I stretched out on the bench and lowered my head on the pillow, did feelings of resolution begin to caress the fabric of my scorched skin, and a sweet calming wrapped its arms around me: "good, good this way, good this way, good..."

*

On the next day, in the afternoon, my students came from the Sapir house and told me in the name of its father that from that day on they would not learn Hebrew from me.

Bluma too agreed – added the student – there is no need for Hebrew. Hebrew was only an extra burden, extraneous learning. And he glanced at my face with *chutzpah*.[444] I groaned silently inside of myself, and I turned the back of my neck to him, until he left the room.

That same evening, it became known to me that Bluma went out with the emissary from "the movement," in order to not return again.

My wife gave birth to the second child almost unintentionally, when we were sitting at a house party, in the company of our many acquaintances. The joy in the house became almost endless. The women took care of the birthing mother, and the tender one who had been born, according to watches that they organized amongst themselves, and I hurried to the post office to announce the good news to Mother.

The post office hummed with its visitors: Jews assembled at the small window of the office and stood in line. Even next to the telegraph window many stood and waited for their turn to come, and exchanged conversation between them. I stood in the middle of the long line, looking at those who were standing and those who were walking around on the side, who were humming with an extended hum, like a swarm of bees, each one carrying within themselves some matter that gladdened them or pained them, and hiding it from the others, and I am one among them who is holding back the joy of my heart, and my warm feelings that are bubbling within me like new wine. And here, at the time of this standing, almost without moving, a group of Cossacks, some of the local soldiers, forced its way into the office, and took their place next to the windows in a parallel line, as was customary for army men. The people's conversation immediately stopped, as if terror had entered the hall; and the Cossacks, as if they were not paying attention to the many people in the office, continued their conversation about "the hunt for maidens" and their skirmishes in the area, how they taught a lesson to this Jew and that shopkeeper, who "tried to trick them and take advantage of them," and how "they cleaned the noses and the faces" of the Moshes and the Itziks until they bled. The Jews stood silent, trembling in their places, putting on faces as if they

---

[444] Cheek, insolence, audacity. The classic definition of *chutzpah* is the one who kills both his parents, and then asks the judge for mercy because he is an orphan.

were not listening to their exchange of words, and began, as if out of a defensive feeling, to cover the fear with conversation on an unrelated topic. And the Cossacks, as if offended by the *chutzpah* of the Jews, hurled curses towards the lines, as distractions amongst themselves: "these cursed *Zhids*,[445] always with their screaming, their shrieks, even in the post office, a government office..." And one short Cossack, solid and sturdy, with a black mustache and aggressive eyes, whose prominent forelock and single nose-ring rustled, as if with arrogance,[446] who stood across from me the whole time and did not take part in his friends' conversation, suddenly sent a predatory look at me, and sweetened his strange laugh towards me, which danced on his mustache and his jaws, and was hidden in his eye sockets.

And I, I... finally, he hid his expression from his friends, but the laugh did not leave his lips.

{p. 139} "I would like to crush the face of this naïve "*Yehuduni*,"[447] for his face, and his trace of a beard, and his virgin eyes..."

"And who's stopping you?" The second one patted him on his shoulder with a wry smile.

"Certainly!" The Cossack took courage, with all his body dancing with evil intent, "I really slashed a *Yehuduni* like this with my sword at the times of the riots in Minsk, and like squashed porridge he was thrown, soaked in his blood, into one of the sewers..."

"It's worth it! It's worth it!" his friends urged him, erupting in laughter.

"Of course it's worth it!" The Cossack was enthusiastic. *Yehudunis* like these, innocent faces like these, they, they are the ones who are carrying within themselves the seed of the "*Karmola*..."[448]

I did not hear his last words. Those standing in the line and outside surrounded me in a heap, and secretly pushed me from the hall. Outside, the Hebrew-Russian teacher Feldsher accompanied me, and hurriedly drew me to one side of the yard and took me to his house by a shortcut.

"It's good that we took him out of there" he told his wife, "one should not discount the words of a Cossack after the Minsk slaughter. And apparently, this Cossack participated in the slaughter, and the truth was in his mouth."

His wife Rivka glanced at me with compassion, and diminished the chill that attacked my body, and removed the nervousness and the tremor in my limbs.

I stayed in Feldsher's house for a long time, until my spirit returned to me. From the great fear and panic that arose around me, my blood froze in my veins, and like one turned to stone, I was brought by my escort, this Feldsher, by way of the alleys and shortcuts to my house.

Feldsher expressed his resentment of the fires that burn in the common people, which are like a stumbling block to all development and advancement, and he continued to attach logical reasons to the course of history and the mysterious path of the Russian storm that was suddenly approaching.

"How many more days of horror are prepared for the righteous fighters on this sorrowful soil, which transforms the children of the nation, actually pillars of revolution, into malicious people and predators?!"

*

The unrest in this small village was great. Almost every evening Cossacks burst with whips and drawn swords into groups of young people who were walking in the streets, and drove

---

[445] An anti-semitic term for Jews, which is common to Russian, Polish, and other Slavic languages.
[446] There seems to be a typographical error here, a switch of one letter, perhaps an intentional pun, where the text spells "intense murder," עזות רצח but the known idiom is "arrogance" עזות מצח.
[447] Another anti-semitic term for a Jew.
[448] The Kremlin. Anti-Tsarist communists.

them off the sidewalks and paths, while waving their whips and swords at them, and chasing after them with laughter and terrible cursing. Only the elderly and the sons of the wealthy they did not touch for evil. Things continued this way for some time, and the streets in the evenings were emptied of strolling young men and women, and the Cossacks returned in the end with empty hands. Then they began rounding up and attacking the sons of the wealthy also, and then very slowly they moved on to old men and women. Only then did the community leaders become agitated, and they turned to the authorities. And when their complaints were ineffective, they grasped onto their fathers' deeds, and bribed the Cossack officers and their commander for the full price, and the attacks in the evenings stopped.

The quiet returned as before. The Cossacks were mostly confined to the barracks, and the only ones permitted to go out {p. 140} were the ones who were known for their good manners, and even these only in the afternoon, but not in darkness. Their officers found interest in the Jews' cowardice, and extracted from them security taxes, and became regular visitors in the houses of the notables, and ate their bread and fish, and drank their wine. Since the quiet of the atmosphere from outside and in trade broke out as in the beginning, and the Jews enjoyed their cunning which stood them in good stead "to trap the Cossack in a sack," so the destroyers argued and stormed in secret, and the tapestry of the revolution was woven in the dead of night, and the erosion of "Tsarism" continued incessantly and indefatigably, also in the hiding places of the small town.

Every day I walked a long way to my lessons in instruction, to a suburb of the city, a large neighborhood of houses of workers and clerks that sprawled around a broad field between the water mill and a lumber mill that stood next to the canal.

In the area of this place, from the side that was next to the forest, stood the headquarters' hut of the Cossacks. From there nothing bad was expected to happen to the by-passer. Even in the days of the disturbance, when danger was expected for the one who passed by the Cossack barracks, a person could walk carefree and safe in this place, for nothing bad would happen to him. The officers of the soldiers, who worked in the headquarters, would encounter each person with courtesy, and would sometimes pleasantly offer a blessing of peace. Even I was used to taking a moderate walk, tarrying and looking at the huts and the yards that were next to the officers' houses. And behold one day, when I passed by, minding my own business, in front of one of the huts, I noticed one Cossack standing in the yard, holding a dagger in his hand, sharpening it with his sharpener. He sees me pass by, throws a glance my way, and immediately he is shooting glance after glance at me, like white-hot skewers, which pass entirely through me. I recognize in him with an internal sensation, almost without seeing, the same dwarf Cossack that was in the post office, the one preying on my life, the same barbed mustache, and the same aggressive eyes. I begin suddenly to take rough strides, as all my limbs are trembling and freezing within me, when I suddenly bump into an acquaintance of mine who is coming towards me, and I stop him and hint to him, almost without language and without turning my head, that he should turn on his heel and accompany me. He lifts up his eyes, and immediately he turns and begins to run with all his might, and me after him, and the Cossack is chasing us with his sword unsheathed, and his voice erupting and exerting himself on the backs of our necks: "You spoke ill of the King, of God! *Karmolniks!*[449] Destroyer of the Tsar! Infidels! Traitors!" - - - And as long as there is breath in me I am following behind my acquaintance, and while the breath of life is in our nostrils we burst through the gate of the mill, fleeing towards the first man that we meet on our way: Save us!! Hide us!! Within the mill a few firefighters are working, who saw the performance through the window, and with the speed of lightening they bring us into the mill, hide us in one of the holes, and the Cossack meanwhile bursts into the yard, and in full voice screams: "Where are the *Karmolniks*? Where are

---

[449] Kremlinites; communist opponents of the Tsar.

they? They came in here!!" And the clerks are calming him down, and claiming: "Indeed they fled by way of the yard, but they went out through the second open gate." But the Cossack does not believe it, searches in the yard, checks in the office, bursts into the mill, goes upstairs and downstairs, and returns angry and cursing, walks and approaches the second gate, peers at the empty road, and turns on his heel, walking and grumbling, one minute furious, and the next minute quiet: "*Karmolniks, Karmolniks.*" - - - -

I was taken out of the hiding place while my spirit was still in me. Workers brought me home in a wagon, and I fell into my bed for many days. Residents of the city, from the elders to the youth, came to visit me. This event took place a few days before May 1st.[450] The order was given by the head of the Cossacks that no Cossack should dare to touch any person, unless "if he explicitly hears the name of the Tsar or God damned by his mouth," therefore the Cossack shouted while chasing {p. 141} after us, in his fury "You spoke ill of the King, of God!..." The Jews saw an ominous sign in this. They came and atoned before the "Head" with a gift, noses to the ground, and the first day in May passed peacefully. The Cossacks did not step outside the entrance of the barracks. The small demonstration that the daring young people organized, to fulfill the obligation of the day, went by easily, with no effort by the town police. They too, with their clubs and swords, learned the work of the Cossacks inside and out, and decreed on the right and the left, and obtained their rewards. The District Governor expressed to them afterwards "deep thanks," in the name of the Tsar and the homeland.

*

The unrest of the fear that was in the town aroused the residents to supervise their sons and daughters extremely well. And the *yeshiva* students, who caught on to the revolution openly or secretly, needed accompanying protection from their faithful wives, who guarded their steps and confined them only when spirits were excited. The *gendarme* police that were in the town also became alert and sensitive to any changes in the air, and once they had a taste of this, and the unsheathed dagger, they made these their constant entertainment, and at convenient and inconvenient times they entertained themselves with these precious things on the heads of the young men and women, to the pleasure of the isolated Cossacks who left the barracks, who stood on the side and delivered encouraging voices: "It is fitting and proper!"

My wife was the only one who was not worried about meetings of young people in her house, and did not oppose it if I joined them for one of the forbidden meetings. She only required one thing from me, that I should not go to the suburb of the city by way of the mill and the barracks, and that I not accompany the suspects more than to the top of the street. I obeyed and I didn't obey my wife's instructions. And when at first there hung in the air of the city the matter of the planned pogroms, which the hand of the "black forces" in the city was preparing with a secret agreement between the police and the secret police, I was swept up among the first to the defense company, and I taught my hands to grasp hot and cold weapons, to the delight of my friends, who always looked at me with scorn.

In this season, I made a request to the authority for an instruction permit to teach in one of the *cheders* that were in the town. I was invited to the police in order to fill out a questionnaire. A *gendarme* came and to visit me in my house. The visit was known to me ahead of time. Both the police officer and the *gendarme* were bribed ahead of time by one of the "intermediaries" for that same matter. However, my wife bore no grudge the whole time, and offered the *gendarme* the honor of a drink of brandy, and pastries. The *gendarme* assailed me with his questions, and I trembled with every question that came out of his mouth. When he had conducted and arranged

---

[450] May 1st is International Workers' Day, established in 1889 by the Marxist International Socialist Congress.

everything, and drank a mouthful of what was prepared for him, he softened and intimated offhandedly in hinting language:

"Indeed, even a young man like you isn't entirely within the bounds of legitimacy... there are also those who are talking about you... but for the present time there is still no suspicion about you..."

In parting from my wife, he whispered to her with a voice of honey.

"Watch out for him, watch out for him very carefully... he is young. His eyes twinkle too much... and you have tender children... watch out for him..."

A sly fox was this *gendarme*, an old rake whose teeth had fallen out, and who knew how to walk around among people and buy their hearts. My wife was agitated to the core, his words penetrated deep into her heart, and the abyss of life had been revealed to her, as if all at once. She began to ask insistently that I should leave Augustow for a while, in order to remove any suspicion from myself. I went out to the adjacent village, to rest there a little, as it were, for the sake of the repair of {p. 142} my health. And when I returned I found the town in turmoil. The most suspected youths were imprisoned. The rest of the members were scattered in every direction, some of them fled, and some of them were hidden in their holes and did not step outside the doors of their houses. My wife's face shone with joy, since by means of a real miracle she had saved me from all evil, as if she had foreseen with the spirit of prophecy what would occur. And when once we met that *gendarme*, on one of our trips, he bowed his head with respect towards my wife, and his lips smiled in her direction, as if saying: "My advice was useful, isn't it so? This time my advice was useful..."

I reached army age. The days of summer passed over me with worry and fear. Mother's many letters, which were equipped with hints and crammed full of advice, confused me and disrupted my spirit. She travelled a few times to the district city Vengrov, the place where I was registered on the list of those summoned to the army, to consult with the rabbi of the city, one of the members of our family, and to find through him a way to the members of the military council.

Uncle Elimelech accompanied Mother on her trips, and together with the agent that was in the place she prepared the "plan" for how to bribe the members of the council and how to conduct the entire matter from beginning to end, so that no mishap would occur, God forbid, from the side of the informers and the few members of the council that did not take bribes.

I was called to Warsaw for the purpose of being advised on this serious matter by the experts in this area. They advised me to mutilate my body; they advised me to starve myself until my body became gaunt, but this too was not accepted by my heart. Uncle Elimelech objected scornfully, distorting his face in anger: "Foolish and obstinate!" And Mother looked at me with restrained compassion. Her inflamed face and the passion that was in her eyes testified to the great war that was taking place inside her, since she did not know how to take counsel in her soul, how to save her son from this approaching danger, and how to support him in the presence of these violent men: Uncle Elimelech and the various experts.

I travelled back to Augustow with a broken heart. The strange advice with which I was stuffed in Warsaw was a resentment to me. In Warsaw I now saw the poor position of Mother in the house of Uncle Elimelech and Aunt Gittele, and I couldn't help. I advised Mother to leave Warsaw and Gittele's house, and move immediately with me to my house in Augustow, but she did not agree in any way. "At this difficult time," she said, "at the time when I need to stand guard, to save you, my place is here... there is no relying on anyone, and behold I need to gather money, lots of money, for this purpose..."

I accepted additional work, and I saved every penny, to come to Mother's aid, who had loaded onto herself a load too heavy to carry. I knew also what was expected for me, if I was not freed from the yoke of the army sooner or later: "forced labor over the course of continuous years,

150

without any benefit or enjoyment, and to leave for this a wife and children for years with no means of livelihood. For what? And why?"

The time of the army was growing nearer. The fall was already on the land. The heart was crushed: "What will be? What will be?..." I am waiting for news from Mother. And suddenly my brother Shmuel appears as an emissary from Mother and Uncle Elimelech. He grew, matured, from the matter with intelligence and good sense, and it seemed that he disagreed with all of the plans of Uncle Elimelech and the experts, that, had it not been so, they would not have relied on him with this honored mission. Their explicit decision was: "to defer the day that I presented myself before the military council, to the second or third season, since then it would be possible to free me easily." It was necessary to obtain here, in Augustow, a "Certificate of Disease," and to deliver it to the required place.

My friend arranged this matter with great ability and secrecy. I moved to his house, which was surrounded by a broad yard, {p. 143} full of piles of wood and building equipment, since he traded in them. The house stood at the end of the yard, on the side, isolated and set apart. The day was set in which the health council would visit me, the doctor accompanied by the head of the city and his secretary. The doctor and the secretary of the town had been bribed. I lay in bed all day in the narrow back room, pretending to be ill, waiting impatiently for the members of the council to come, until I got sick of it, and I went out to the adjoining rooms, to spend a little time at a party of the household, who sat at the table and played cards. The day went by. Darkness wrapped the house in a gloomy fall covering. Outside, an endless dripping.[451] The lamp was lit. Tea and biscuits were served. The mistress of the house, Biederman's wife, and her sisters were betting fiercely on the card game, to banish my sorrow a little. Suddenly, Shmuel, who had gone intermittently to watch for Biederman's arrival, burst into the room, and announced in panic that the members of the council had already entered the yard.

I ran hastily to the bed. From an abundance of haste and confusion, I did not have time to properly undress again, and I thrust myself into the bed with my shoes and my pants and I covered myself with the blanket. The faint light of a small night lantern was lit. On the night table that was next to the bed bottles of medicines were displayed, on the nearby chair lay bandaging material. On my head an icebag was placed, filled with lukewarm water. I lay motionless for a few minutes, my heart pounding... the members of the council entered the adjacent room, and the head of the city exchanged a few words with the lady of the house. Afterwards they came into me one by one after the lady, who went at the head. The doctor approached the bed, studied the bottles, and attempted to speak to me: "You are still sick, you have still not returned to your strength?" I did not reply. I groaned in a weak voice. He approached near me, felt my head, opened my robe, bent over my chest, listened to the sound of my heartbeat, intended to remove the blanket from upon me, and to check the rest of the parts of my body, but I grabbed his hand from under the blanket and did not allow him to turn it over. He understood my intention, dropped his hand under the blanket, touched my pants and immediately took his hand out, bent himself over my chest a second time, removed his hand and turned to the head of the city: "There is no need for additional examination. The situation is clear. He is burning with fire. He is unconscious, it seems, he requires rest..." And to Biederman and his wife he said in a commanding voice: "You must periodically replace the ice bag. And if something should occur, knock on the door of my house even at night..." And he turned to go out, and his friends went out after him. The sounds of the room accompanied him in silence. Their whispering voices quickly disappeared. And only Shmuel and Biederman returned from accompanying those who were leaving to the gate. The card game continued in the adjacent room, and I got off my bed pale-faced and with stumbling limbs. After I

---

[451] Proverbs 27:16 "An endless dripping on a rainy day…"

drank a cup of wine to dispel the remainder of the fear and the shuddering that still shook in my body, I joined the group.

*

After two months, I went out to Vengrov to present myself to the military council. A hard and angry winter prevailed in full force. I arrived at the place a week in advance. I was a guest at the rabbi's house. Mother and Shmuel also came there. Everything was prepared ahead of time. Only the head of the council – the District Governor – and the Agricultural Commissar, who was respected among the members of the council, only they did not take bribes, and they did not know all that was developing around them. The District Governor, a simple man and not overly bright, was like clay in the hands of his sly secretary, who knew how to spin him with lies. The Agricultural Commissar was a powerful man, and as hard as iron, and hated any extraneous commotion for any Jewish recruit {p. 144} who came with pain in hand. Towards a Jew he was frequently stubborn, and disqualified any injury that he had as doubtful. "He will work in the army and get healthy! These *Yehudunis* are lazy! Lazy!" No one dared to oppose him except in obvious cases that were visible to the eye, and he also decided negatively, for they were afraid of him lest he submit a complaint about them in a high place.

Mother demanded insistently that I reduce what I was eating, and that I should drink a lot of coffee, a folk remedy for weakening the heart and losing weight. The rabbi read a chapter of Psalms with me and sections from *Mussar* books every day, as a shield against calamity. The members of the household looked at me with pitying eyes, as one judged for the gallows. Even Mother sometimes hid her look, and her eyes welled up with tears.

Shabbat morning was appointed by the council for checking the disabled recruits from the whole district. By the light of that day, that is Friday in the evening, the rabbi read with me songs from the Psalms, after the *Shabbat* meal, and indicated to me that I should get into my bed with "thoughts of repentance." Towards morning the rabbi woke me, placed me in his "judgement room," and began to read with me verses of Psalms, verse after verse, in study, with intention and great devotion, until I forgot the bitterness of my situation, and a relieved spirit came over me. Mother also, in the adjacent room, read the verses of the Psalms in a whisper after us.

That same hour there was a terrible ice storm. The windows whistled and rattled and wailed, as if devils and demons from *Sheol*[452] arose to destroy the world and to swallow it up together with our pleasant recitation. Dawn broke. From hymns of Psalms we went on to the prayers upon arising, and the study of a chapter of *Mishnah*, from the matters of the day, which the rabbi chose, as if the entire outside world did not exist before him, or all his "family below."[453] When we finished, Mother served me a mug of hot tea that had been kept for me, and the rabbi and the members of his household blessed me for the journey, and I went out on my way, accompanied by Mother and Shmuel.

The strong wind and the cold and the blowing snowflakes struck our faces and froze our limbs. With difficulty we reached the place. Mother entered the hallway while there was till breath in her nostrils. In the waiting room, in the army office, we, ten young men, waited a long time for the members of the council to arrive. The bad weather had prevented them from coming on time. Only the Agricultural Commissar was missing, who did not come since he had a cold, and due to the difficulty of the day. And again, the council's consultation went on for about a full hour, whether to begin the meeting in the Commissar's absence, or to defer it. Mother retreated to a secluded corner and stood in prayer. Finally, it became known that the meeting would not be deferred. We took off our clothes, and went in two by two. Before me entered a few who had been

---

[452] The place underneath the ground where the Bible believes people go when they die.

[453] From the Zohar, פמליא דלתתא, "*Famalia d'l'tata*," Family down below (on earth), vs. the ministering angels on high.

summoned, Christians and Jews. All of them were judged fit for the army. I entered accompanied by one Christian, gaunt as a dried fig, with a face as pale as lime, who had risen, injured in his heart, from a hard illness of pox. They examined him quickly and released him. My examination began. The secretary of the council measured my height and my width, weighed me, and indicated for me to pass naked before the members of the council. They all fixed their glances on me. The District Governor looked at me through his glasses with a neutral gaze, and moaned to himself: "A pleasant lad, a proper lad!" And immediately the doctors approached, the Russian Army doctor, and the district doctor, a Pole, to examine my body. The Polish doctor, an old man, with a wrinkled, sickly, face, checked me for some time in my heart, in my lungs, in all my limbs, shrugged his shoulders, said something that was half in Russian and half in Latin, and turned me over to his colleague the Russian doctor, a young man with a thick face, and clumsy, who emitted the smell of brandy and nicotine from his nostrils, and he did as his fellow had done, and he too shrugged his shoulders, and nodded his head as if in agreement with the words of the Polish doctor. The members of the council sat meanwhile and had a general conversation. Only when the Polish doctor approached and told the District Governor, {p. 145} the head of the Council, the results of the examination, he recoiled, shook his head and asked a second and third time: "to such an extent?" He got up and approached me, struck me, and on my chest, lifted his doubtful gaze, returned to his place and groaned to himself: Behold it is so, behold it is so." He listened for some time to the words of the doctors, as if to learn from them and their wisdom, until he delivered to their hands the registry to list the results of their examination, and bowed himself afterwards to confirm the protocol with his signature. Now I felt the cold that melted in my bones, and my spirit returned to me. I looked at the white head and frightened eyes of the Polish doctor, downcast, to the side of the head, completely serious. "A person stands on the threshold of the grave, and because of lucre he taught his tongue to speak deception with this extensive deviousness." I glanced at the rest of the members of the council, who seemed to be innocently talking amongst themselves, and at the sly secretary who had buried his head in the papers that were spread out before him, and immediately the drunken eyes of the Russian doctor rose to me, and pierced me like needles. "Completely released!" the Governor announced, and I was pushed into the other room to dress. I came out of there hastily, half dressed, and fell into Mother's arms, who wet the hairs of my head and my face with tears of joy and with sighs of relief.

We spent three days at the nearby station, me and Mother and Shmuel, at a filthy, dirty inn, suffering from cold and hardship, but we could not continue on our journey. The snowstorm that took place with powerful force on the day of my journey, created destruction in the area and covered all the roads and pathways and the train, with no exit, until finally the workers came and returned the train to service, and we left the place with a feeling of those redeemed from captivity. At the crossroads, I parted from Mother and Shmuel. They returned to Warsaw, and I to Augustow. In my house, they welcomed me with great joy. My wife and her acquaintances prepared pastries and sweets for a party. From every side, they blessed me "On my salvation from the hands of the *goyim*."

At the party, at the beginning of the celebration, I felt a shuddering in all my limbs. I held back the weakness and participated in the party. However, after a short while, my head became very heavy and a strong dizziness attacked me. The implements of the room and its furniture began dancing, with me in the middle, and in the middle of the dance I saw my wife going out in a dance arm in arm with the District Governor, and the Polish doctor, bald head, white beard, and eyes in a jealous rage, dancing towards them with the chubby, tipsy, Russian doctor. He's secretly pulling on my wife's sleeve, at the end of her dress, to get her away from the Governor; and I am dancing wildly across from him, and whispering in his ear, out of a desire for revenge: "Ai, disobedient old man! Does it burn well enough for you? See, really see, my wife is telling all your doings to the

153

Governor...!" I woke up in the middle of the night in my bed. My senses had returned to me. My wife and her friends stood next to my bed. An ice bag lay heavy on my head, and I was entirely burning up with fever. In the second room burned a dim oil lamp on the table, which was set with every good thing, which almost no hand had touched. I searched for the guests with my exhausted eyes....

"Where are they all?" I mumbled.

"Lay down, lay down and rest..." my wife warned me.

"Thank God." She let out, sighing softly to her friends.

"What happened?" I tried again to ask.

"Lay down, lay down and rest..." my wife calmed me – "a mild illness - the doctor was here. You have a little fever."

{p. 146} I stopped asking further. Again a cloud of fatigue enveloped me. With my confusion, the dawn awakened me. My wife lay slumped on her bed in her clothing. In the second room, next to the children's cribs, her friend also lay in her clothes, stretched out on the bench, snoring by herself, in a deep sleep now after a sleepless night. My mind became clear. I felt the ice bag that was falling off my head to the side of the pillow. I cast an eye through the window. The weak light of the day pricked my eyes. I turned my face towards the room. Medicine bottles that were on the nearby chair silently waved to me. I lifted the thermometer that was out, placed on the chair, and my eyes fastened on it in amazement: "more than 41 degrees?"[454] Now all became clear to me. I felt my forehead, my pulse. My flesh burned on me, my pulse beat rapidly with great haste. - - -

After a few days, it became clear to the doctor what the nature of the illness had been. On my skin, reddish spots had broken out, and after a few days all of my skin was covered, from the top of my head to the soles of my feet, blossoms of pox blisters, and the disease spread on my body with all its strength and heat. The disease came over me, it seems, from my neighbor in the examination on the day of army. From now there was placed on my house a full quarantine. For my wife and my children blisters again formed. The windows of my room were covered with a black fabric so that the light would not penetrate into it. Food and drink necessities were served to my household to the threshold of the corridor, and my wife was left alone, with her two children and her sick husband. Only from time to time did the doctor visit me, wrapping over his clothing a white cloak and a white headscarf wrapped like a turban on his head, and his hands covered with white gloves. When he came, he brought with him the medical necessities that were required, spoke a few words with my wife, and left. Also, one old woman who dwelt in the suburb, who lived apart from any person and was supported by *tzedakah*, came each day from the "*Linat HaTzedek*" to help my wife with the housework and watching the children, and brought with her a little of the news of the day, and brought a little comfort into the house.

On one of the hard days of the illness my weakness reached the end of its limits. I had managed to whisper to my wife: "the doctor..." and I sunk down into a foggy sleep. When I opened my eyes a little, I noticed the doctor, who had delayed his departure, by the door of the other room. I saw him stand and hold out his palms, and my wife was standing next to him and crying. The echo of a hoarse, dry voice pounded on my ears: "The disease is severe. Her help is in God..." The door swung on its hinges. My wife dropped onto the sofa, leaned her head on the children's crib, and silently sobbed. I tried to call out to her, but the speech was lost from my mouth. My eyes closed, my lips stuck together, and from somewhere a whisper welled up from deep inside me, that spilled out and touched my lips, one of the verses of Psalms, that I sang by the morning light on that same *Shabbat*, on the day of deliverance, with the rabbi from Vengrov: " A prayer of the

---

[454] About 105.5 degrees Fahrenheit.

lowly man when he is faint and pours forth his plea before YHVH,"[455] and again I sunk down into a deep, prolonged, sleep, free of pain, as if an invisible hand was sent to me and brought healing for me.

*

When I regained my strength, my wife told me the events of a mother in the days of the illness: "the irritation and the constant anxiety, and her many responsibilities, in which she became entangled again on the occasion of my redemption from the army, shook her strength. When she heard the news about my deadly disease, she fell to the bed as if with a stroke, and the doctors could not figure out the nature of her illness. Now her health had improved a little, and she was intermittently walking around the house and returning to bed. There was no cure for it."

{p. 147} Mother's letters and my wife's words whispered to me in mute language some of the pain of her soul: "I have one request of God, that he return your health to you, and guard you from all evil, you and Shmuel here and my Yoel in a foreign land…"

Shmuel, who came at Mother's direction to visit me, later filled in my wife's words, and I expressed to them my idea to move Mother to my house without delay. They both thanked me.

*

We moved Mother from Warsaw to Augustow. She was stooped and sorrowful when we got her into her bed, which my wife had prepared for her ahead of time. Her hair had turned white, her face had yellowed, her bones were worn, and her eyes burned with the fire of a fever. She rested peacefully, without complaint, as if at peace with her fate. Light emanated from her face, and a smile slipped onto her lips every time her grandchildren approached. Her thin hands were smooth, and a tear of contentment ran down her cheeks.

Shmuel stayed with us for a number of weeks, taking counsel with us alternately on the matter of his desire to leave the country, awaiting a propitious time, so that he would be able to speak with Mother and part from her with a blessing.

"Travel in peace…" Mother hugged Shmuel in parting from him – "I do not want to interfere with your path in life. Don't worry about me – it's good for me this way, good…"

I was doing exhausting work, in order to restore the position of my household, which had become impoverished, and to support my sick Mother. Besides this, there had developed in the past a full series of debts, in addition to debts from my illness and army debts. I did not know what was right. My wife was helping me in silence and with a cheerful face. Mother was being checked each time by the local doctor, who would shrug his shoulders and go out in the same way that he came. Most of the day she had fun with the children, who were hanging around her bed, and sometimes she would get up, take care of them at their cradle with strained efforts, and return to her bed. Yoel and Shmuel would rush their letters to her, and she would wrap them up in a special wrapper and hide them in the pillow at her head. Yoel began to send a monthly gift to Mother. The contribution made it easier for me, and lifted Mother's spirits. At free moments, my wife and I would sit at her bed, talking with her and enjoying her alertness, her wit, and the vitality that flowed in her words. It was difficult then to find any similarity between her fluent, lively, speech, and the collapse of her destroyed body.

I am making Mother's bed when I find, wrapped up alone, one letter from Yoel, in which he informs that "He cannot travel to Father in America, since his new wife has born him a daughter, he is unable to depart to his house…" I return the letter to its place and ponder from time to time how Mother unties this binding, studies the letter, and wraps it up again. My heart aches inside of me at this sight. One visitor from America, a passer-by, who enjoys himself and his words, brings

---

[455] Psalm 102.

155

greetings from Father in America and from Yoel in London. He sits next to Mother's bed and tells about Father's lifestyle, and about his visit to Yoel.

"I told Jozef (Yoel) this: "Why is he spending time in London, and doesn't set out for America, to his father? And his father is wealthy and capable, and his situation is strong..." and Jozef says at once: "No! No! Nonsense, really!"

I pull on the guest's sleeve, stop him from his verbose speech, and step aside with him to the corner. He tells me additional details about Yoel, and is amazed to hear about the amounts of money that he sends to Mother: "From where? He lives a life of poverty, he wears rags, he sells oranges and bananas in the street, and from what he sends it seems it must be more than half of his earnings..."

Mother's illness is getting worse. She sleeps for days at a time without moving or speaking. The doctor finds in her a change for the worse. The American chatterbox has caused this. I persuade Mother with words, and finally succeed in putting a smile on her lips. Slowly, slowly, her speech and her laughter and her interest in the children return to her. I am happy. However, her strength is leaving her. Again she is unable to stand on her feet. I am happy to serve her, to make things easier for her and fulfill her desire. In the day, during work hours, she is entirely loaded onto my wife. Only in the evenings, during free time, I don't move from her bed, and I don't allow my wife to be troubled with her. At night, I get up from time to time to help with the bed, and one prayer is in my mouth to the God of heaven: "let this please continue all the days of my life, provided that she remain alive." And my wife jumps from her bed, returns me to my bed, and says: "You are a working man, you toil for a piece of bread, it is forbidden for you to disturb your sleep, and it will not hurt me." And I peek into my wife's face, and see the charming maternal spark, which erupts from the slits of her eyes, and I accede to her. I now feel our shared fate, that harnessed us together to one yoke, the human fate, that emerged from the path of youth and entered onto the long and difficult road of life....

The Writer Tzvi Zevulun Weinberg

Tz. Z. Weinberg was born on 6 Sivan 5644, May 30, 1884, in Praga, a suburb of Warsaw. Fate did not spoil him. His childhood days were exceedingly difficult. Hunger, cold, illness and mental anguish, were his fate. Also, the days of his youth, as well as the days that came after them, did not improve for him. In the year 1902 he took to wife the daughter of the Head of the *yeshiva* in Ostrov. From Ostrov he moved to Augustow. He lived there for three years (1903-1906); when the situation of his livelihood worsened, he moved to the adjacent Suwalk. While living there he completed, with the help of friends, the pedagogic courses in Grodno.

In the year 1920 he went up to the land and directed the school in Zikhron Yaakov. He founded the Association of Writers and Hebrew Journalists in Poland, and served as Head of the association. In the year 5694, 1934, he returned to the land with the members of his family, and was accepted as a teacher in the school at Tel Mond.

His first story was published in 1905, while he was living in Augustow, in "*HaZman,*"[456] which came out in Vilna. In the years 1913-1914 (5673-5674), two collections of his were

---

[456] "The Time."

published: "*Sippurim v'Tziyurim.*"[457] In the year 1932 there appeared "*Bayit v'Rechov.*"[458] In the year 5702 [1942] his book "*Bidrachim Aveilut*"[459] was published; in 5703 [1943] "*Mechitzot*;"[460] in 5711 [1951] "*Asher Avar*"[461] Volumes 1 and 2; in 5714 [1954] a collection of his stories "*Sham u'foh*;[462] in 5716 [1956] a collection of his stories, "*Asher Avar*" Volume 3 and a collection of his articles "*Adam be'Ohalo*"[463] Volume 4. In the year 5717 [1957] a collection of his stories and his notes on the slain of the settlement bloc of Tel Mond "*Haym Halchu;*"[464] in 5725 [1965] his last book, "*Echad Mi-hem*"[465] was published. Now, when he is 82 years old, but young {p. 149}in spirit, he is working on publishing his writings, since he is supported by a council that was established at the initiative of the President of the State, Zalman Shazar.[466]

Tz. Z. Weinberg is an honored member of the settlement of Tel Mond.

*

In the meeting that was held this week in the framework of the decade celebration of the local council of Tel Mond, honorary citizenship was granted to the veteran writer and teacher Tz. Z. Weinberg, on his reaching the age of strength,[467] and to mark the occasion of the publication of his book, "*Echad Mi-hem.*"

Present at the ceremony were representatives of the Writers' Association and the Teachers' Union. Among the guests were Professor Tz. Sharfstein from the United States and Professor R. Mahler.

The parchment certificate was presented to the guest of honor[468] by the Head of the Council N. Din, who pointed out on his remarks Weinberg's diligence in the work of instruction, over the course of the 30 years that he lived in the settlement. Osnat Levi read the scroll that expresses "In respect for his many practical deeds and his devotion in the fields of education, literature, and public activism." The Head of the Local Council A. Avrech, Rabbi A. Zemel, A. Margalit, D. Gilboa, A. Astrin, G. Kaduri, B. Freiber, and the Professors Sharfstein and Mahler, blessed the guest of honor. Blessings in writing were received from the Minister of the Treasury, the Head of the Writers' Association, and the Secretary of the Writers' Association.

The double celebration of the veteran writer and teacher, Tz. Z. Weinberg, at his reaching the age of 80 and the appearance of his new book "*Echad Mi-hem*," was celebrated with great audience by the residents of the Tel Mond bloc (Hadar HaSharon). Writers and public personalities came to the party, which was held in his honor in the house named for Rivka Ziv in Tel Mond.

The party, which was held on behalf of the Regional Council Hadar HaSharon, was opened by the Head of the Council A. Avrech, who blessed the author, who succeeded in elevating in his new book the epic of one of the settlement blocs, one of whose buildings served as the backdrop for a book that is a song of praise for a son of the land and a son of the settlement.

---

[457] "Stories and Illustrations."

[458] "House and Street."

[459] "Paths of Mourning."

[460] "Divisions."

[461] "What's Passed."

[462] "There and Here."

[463] "A Person at Home."

[464] "They Went."

[465] "One of Them."

[466] Zalman Shazar was President of Israel for two terms, 1963-1973.

[467] Psalms 90:10. "The span of our life is seventy years, or, given the strength, eighty years…"

[468] The guest of honor is frequently referred to as the groom, which is the expression used here.

The Jews in Augustow[469]*
by Yaakov Frenkel

Yaakov Frenkel was the brother-in-law of Yisrael Grosberg. The two of them had stores for the selling of fabrics. On this basis competition developed between them. In addition to this, Grosberg short-changed Frenkel in the division of the inheritance. Against this background, the relations between the brothers-in-law sharpened greatly. The story "The Jews in Augustow" came to punish the brother-in-law and an additional competitor, who also had a shop for the selling of manufacturing, Barukh Margolis. Incidentally, we learn about the atmosphere, trade relations, and way of life in that period.

The Matters of the Disputes and Debates, the Frenzies and Events
That Raged Around Me in Storm and Tempest

{p. 150} My eyes looked about for a short time, for the honored guest who came in the gate of Lodz with bundles of his melodies loaded on his shoulder to delight us for free was Reb Shealtiel,[470]** the splendor of whose voice I heard in his passing before the ark. I will remember him and all the events that happened to him from the day of his existence until this day. Prepare please to greet me, dear reader, and I, here I am wearing pride and genius[471] to present myself before you as a distinguished person. With the desire of Divine Providence, which pays a man his reward many times, more than what is proper for him, according to the measure of his deeds, it has fallen to my lot[472] to be honored with a great honor, much greater than my worth, to know Reb Shealtiel the musician[473] who prays face to face,[474] being one who knows him and sees his face, for the reason that in the city Madmannah[475,476]*** I too dwelt in honor for about two decades. There I buried the best days of my youth. There I was one of the silk[477] yeshiva students in whom all the righteous women of the city would be blessed. There I took for myself a wife, before I knew how to find my daily bread,[478] and I fathered sons and daughters while I was supported by my father-in-law,[479] as was the customary practice in Madmannah, where the father-in-law makes an agreement with his son-in-law like the partnership of Zevulun and Issachar.[480] The father-in-law engages in trade, and the son-in-law sits in the tent of *Torah;* the father-in-law provides meagre bread and scant water,[481] and the groom pays him as his recompense with difficult and challenging debates about the *Torah* that even with great difficulty it is impossible to resolve them or find their correct meaning. There my hand grasped great commerce whose bundle was established not on earth or in the heavens, not on a simple foundation, but on keen and focused debate that I took out of my study houses, as a law for all *yeshiva* students of Israel after the completion of their years of hospitality, to do trade and acquisition according to the 13 attributes[482] that the *Torah* demands

---

[469] Original note: * From his book "The Jews in Lodz."

[470] Original note: ** Margolis

[471] From the commentary of Malbim, Meir Loeb Ben Yechiel Michel, a Russian-born rabbi and scholar of Hebrew, 1809-1879, on Proverbs 20:11.

[472] Psalms 16:6 "Delightful country has fallen to my lot; lovely indeed is my estate..."

[473] This form of the word appears only in the *Zohar*, section 2, 143b.

[474] Deuteronomy 34:10 "Never again did there arise in Israel a prophet like Moses—whom YHVH knew face to face."

[475] A city mentioned multiple times in the Bible, including Joshua 15:31, Isaiah 25:10, and Chronicles 2:49.

[476] Original note: ***Augustow

[477] "Men of Silk" is a reference to *chassidim*. See the book "Men of Silk," by Glenn Dynner.

[478] Proverbs 30:8 "...Give me neither poverty nor riches, but provide me with my daily bread."

[479] Literally, dependent on my father-in-law's table.

[480] Genesis *Rabbah* 99:9 "Zevulun engaged in trade, and Issachar engaged in Torah, and Zevulun came and fed him."

[481] Isaiah 30:20 "My Lord will provide for you meager bread and scant water..."

[482] This is a reference to the 13 Divine attributes found in Exodus 34:6-7 "... "YHVH! YHVH! a God compassionate and gracious, slow to anger, abounding in kindness and faithfulness, extending kindness to the thousandth generation,

of them, until they lose the money of their dowry. Then their eyes will be opened to see that the debate was their destroyer, and then they will begin to deepen with great study to find the simplicity of commerce. However, then the order will be reversed for them, and instead of that which was before, that their pockets were full to brimming and their minds were empty, they are now experienced and expert as is proper. Their minds will be full of knowledge of the simplicity of commerce, but aha! Because their pockets are empty. There I enjoyed myself for many years in the company of the national and enthusiastic residents of Madmannah, who spend all their days in national allegiance, in their always making every day a national festival in memory of the Exodus from Egypt. Their bread is the bread of affliction[483] and bitter herbs,[484] and sometimes also affliction without bread, the bread that they eat bound[485] with grief and bitter herbs, but simple bread and the taste of simple food will not enter their mouths, because their words are as simple as these: "bread to eat, and also to suck out enjoyment from the comforts in life, are only for simple people, who live for the sake of living, but not for the residents of Madmannah, who live only because the time of their command to die has not yet come."

Indeed, I knew Reb Shealtiel when he was still one of the young students of the *Beit Midrash*, sitting for his enjoyment near the oven and working diligently over his stories in the long winter nights, telling of miracles and wonders of the *golem* that the *Gaon* of Prague[486] created, and awesome deeds that happened to Napoleon I. His meals were given to him at that time by seven people, one day of the week in the house of each one. I knew Reb Shealtiel when the *Torah* shone its face towards him to find him all good, that is, a woman with a double hump, in front of her and behind her, with a dowry of 100 *shekels* in cash, and meals seven days a week in the house of one person, in the house of his father-in-law, over the course of three years. I knew Reb Shealtiel when success shone its face towards him again to take his humped wife off his head and to give him in exchange for her {p. 151} younger sister who was dark and comely,[487] and an additional allotment of new dowry money, 50 *shekels* his reward for the exchange and the substitution, and the eyes of all the silk *yeshiva* students who were envious of his wealth and his success, seeing and yearning. I knew Reb Shealtiel in his standing on the height of the summit[488] of happiness, when his business greatly burst out and in the pride of his wealth, which was not according to nature, and the women of Madmannah unanimously told that the demons brought him much money each and every night by way of the chimneys through the egg stew that he would arrange for them under his table. This is the evidence, that Reb Shealtiel's wife always bought many eggs, more than a mouth could eat. I knew Reb Shealtiel when he passed before the ark[489] on the *Yamim Nora'im*,[490] with the choir of his composers at his command, they are the tailors who stand at their posts in his store, and expect

---

forgiving iniquity, transgression, and sin; yet He does not remit all punishment, but visits the iniquity of parents upon children and children's children, upon the third and fourth generations."

[483] *Matzah.*

[484] Eaten at the *Pesach seder* as a symbol of the bitterness of bondage.

[485] This is a reference to *Korech*, the "Hillel sandwich," eaten at the *Pesach seder*, which substitutes *charoset* for the Pascal lamb, based on Exodus 12:8 "They shall eat the flesh that same night; they shall eat it roasted over the fire, with unleavened bread and with bitter herbs."

[486] In Jewish tradition, the *golem* is a creature created by magic, often to serve its creator. Legend holds that Rabbi Judah Loew ben Bezalel, the Maharal of Prague (1513-1609), created a *golem* out of clay to protect the Jewish community from the Blood Libel.

[487] Song of Songs 1:5 "I am dark, but comely, O daughters of Jerusalem— Like the tents of Kedar, Like the pavilions of Solomon."

[488] Pisgah, the mountain where Moses goes to die. "Moses went up from the steppes of Moab to Mount Nebo, to the summit of Pisgah," Deuteronomy 34:1

[489] "To pass before the ark" means to lead the *Amidah,* the standing prayer, also known as the 18 benedictions or the *Shemonah Esray*.

[490] The Days of Awe, also called the High Holy Days.

to obtain work there that God would make happen for them from the purchasers of the fabric merchandise. And then Reb Shealtiel found for himself the propitious time to arrange together with them the melodies that his intelligence and understanding innovated, which in the future would be conducted at the time of prayer before the congregation of worshippers.

I especially will raise before me the memory of Reb Shealtiel in his image and unique true style at the time of his passing before the ark. How awesome was Reb Shealtiel then! More dreadful than the *Yamim Nora'im* themselves!

His eyes protruded from their sockets, the hairs of his beard were askew and bristly like a rabbi's, and with his thundering voice he made the world and all that fills it[491] tremble. He especially knew to build ascents and descents[492] with his strong voice, and the composition of his melodies according to what suited the meaning of the words. In the hour that he used to scream and shout "And fear of you on all that you created,"[493] a dark terror would fall on the congregation of his listeners, until their souls took flight from the sound of his fear. At the time that he said "Strength is in your hand,"[494] he would sob in a gentle voice like a baby goat,[495] until he himself believed that he was showing the strength that was in His hand to the eyes of the congregation, for however strong Reb Shealtiel was in his city, in his knowledge of the correct meanings of the words he was weak and powerless.[496]* In the hour that he was thundering "Rebuke Satan that he not accuse me,"[497] the posts that the house was standing on trembled from the sound of his reprimand. Outstanding people before whom were revealed the secrets of the mystery of all that is done behind the heavenly curtain[498] in the house of Reb Shealtiel decided that his intention was not on the devil against whom, in general, all the emissaries of our people the House of Israel fight in every generation but have not bested him, but rather on the private demon that God established for him alone here on earth, in the image of Reb Lemel.[499]** Reb Lemel competes with him in his business, to hunt with his fishing net all the customers in the city, until there did not remain anything for Reb Shealtiel, and will further oppose him every time that he is found before the factory owners, so that they will not give their merchandise to Reb Shealtiel on credit, for the reason that it is correct for the slipping of a foot or debt forgiveness.

All of the praiseworthy values and virtues that we counted for Reb Shealtiel are also found in Reb Lemel, the man who is his accuser[500] in content, and also surpassed him in his outward qualities. Reb Shealtiel was short in stature, lean in flesh, and thin bellied, like all who dwelt in Madmannah who fast and deny themselves physical pleasures all the days from lack and distress and also from miserliness.

On the other hand, Reb Lemel was full-bodied and fat, tall of stature and thick in the belly; his cheeks and his neck were fattened, his eyes shone like torches and his face was ruddy, and the whole shape of his torso was sunken in a ring of fat and from the fat of his flesh. The chest like this of a healthy man was a strange sight in the city of Madmannah. Why was this {p. 152} Reb Lemel different from all the residents of Madmannah? And why was only he exceptional? The circumstance for this is very simple. Reb Lemel grew up in the city of Zafrona[501]* in the house

---

[491] Psalms 50:12 "Were I hungry, I would not tell you, for Mine is the world and all that fills it."

[492] Babylonian *Talmud Eruvin* 22b. "...perhaps you spoke of the ascents and descents of the land of Israel..."

[493] From the High Holy Day Liturgy.

[494] Also from the High Holy Day Liturgy.

[495] The Hebrew word עז, ez, or baby goat, is spelled the same as the word עז, oze, strength.

[496] Original note: * In an Ashkenazi accent the pronunciation of *oze* would have sounded like *ez*.

[497] From the *Rosh Hashanah Musaf* service.

[498] Babylonian *Talmud Brakhot* 18b "...My friend, let us roam the world and hear from behind the heavenly curtain..."

[499] Original note: ** Yisrael Grosberg.

[500] Job 31:35 "...Or my accuser draw up a true bill!"

[501] Original note: **Trastina.

of his wealthy father whose business in pig's hair expanded greatly outside of the country, and the needs of his business encouraged him to travel frequently to the country of Germany, and to reside there from time to time for a long period of time, and especially for the market days in Leipzig, in order to sell his merchandise there, and when he dwelt there he endangered himself in the way of the Germans by satisfying his soul with eating and drinking gluttonously, and this pleasant tendency he planted in his house as well. For about ten years Reb Lemel was supported by his wealthy father-in-law's table, and he broadened like a fattened calf at a table full of rich food and pleasure, which his modest wife Shprintza the barren set before him in her father's house. She took care of everything in his store and his business, for she was his daughter of old age. Shprintza saw herself as happy because she succeeded in acquiring the family lineage of her husband for the price of her dowry. The elder father of her husband, so it was said by her in her boasting in her neighbors' houses. He lived long, until 100 years old, he brought seven wives to graves in his life, and all of them bore him sons and daughters. The number of issue from his loins multiplied like locusts, and all of them grasped their fathers' deeds in their hands and were merchants in pigs' hair. All of her neighbors envied her because she had achieved such greatness. And she spoiled him with a gluttonous economy as was the law that came out of the place. In order to balance the scales of the economy of the household, in order not to tremendously elevate the expenses, out of fear that her father would shut his hand, she afflicted her soul daily with dry bread and legumes, like Daniel in his time,[502] and on Mondays and Thursday of the week she also fasted, and with this if she did not succeed in reconciling the lack she fasted again on the eve of the new month.

Reb Lemel gave his money with interest, and with this knew how to speak a word,[503] because interest and principal were always coincident topics. Also, Reb Lemel fulfilled with a diligent hand the law of determining the scale in favor of the receiver according to the laws that are clarified in the *halakhah* of weight, because Reb Lemel was from his youth God-fearing and observant of the *mitzvot*, and also in all matters of harmful exploitation and robbery, he put the words of the decisors as a line.

Suddenly new mourning: the old man, his father-in-law, died after a protracted illness. Reb Lemel, who in order to please himself, considered money as nothing in his eyes, became very stingy in expenses to support the illness of the patient, in his closing the door before doctors and pharmacists, so as to not reduce his inheritance.

But the old man closed his eyes, and Reb Lemel waved his innocent hands to search in the holes and cracks to remove each and every penny from the fortune of the deceased, before a second heir could come and divide the inheritance with him. "Is it really so" – Reb Lemel said to himself - "that also my brother-in-law[504]** the heretic and the *apikores*[505] for whom books of enlightenment drop from his lap, will inherit a portion of the wealth of my God-fearing and trembling at the word of God father-in-law? Is it really so that the wealth of a righteous man should be stored up for the wicked?[506] Was this the intention of our *Torah* in the law of inheritance? It is a conclusive law[507] that the heretics and the *apikorsim* do not inherit a share of an inheritance." Reb Lemel, all of whose devious tricks were founded on the holy purity, put this holy thought into

---

[502] Daniel 1:16 "So the guard kept on removing their food, and the wine they were supposed to drink, and gave them legumes."

[503] Isaiah 50:4 "The Lord GOD gave me a skilled tongue, to know how to speak timely words to the weary...."

[504] Original note: ** The author Yaakov Frenkel.

[505] A Greek word from the *Mishnah*, literally an epicurean, but used by the *Mishnah* to refer to a heretic. Babylonian *Talmud Shabbat 99b* "The *Mishnah* teaches that those who have no share in the World-to-Come include an *epikoros*. Rav and Rabbi Chanina both say: This is one who treats a *Torah* scholar with contempt."

[506] The opposite of the statement in Proverbs 13:22 "A good man has what to bequeath to his grandchildren, for the wealth of sinners is stored up for the righteous."

[507] Babylonian *Talmud Berakhot* 31a "And the *Gemara* asks: What is an example of a conclusive *halakhah*?"

deeds, in his taking for himself every good and fat piece, and every whole piece that tasted good, and he left for his brother-in-law the *apikores* only small crumbs under the table, as a kind of leftovers from the banquet of the righteous. And Shprintza was happy with her lot,[508] because God blessed her with wealth and possessions from her father's estate, and also a good advocate on high, in addition to honor and family lineage, and {p. 153} her husband, a capable man,[509] who knows how to use every fit opportunity to increase his fortune and to profit by hurting others.

Before, Reb Shealtiel and Reb Lemel dwelt together in safety[510] and were loving companions. And if in the qualities of their souls they were far from each other, as the goat is from the tiger, in one way they were equal, and that is in the wisdom of music, in which this one was like that one, they both boasted[511] of knowing it, and it was the point of contact in which they met together, and that brought them closer to each other. Please don't imagine for yourself, my dear reader, that the wisdom of music which all of us loved was wallowing in the trash heaps in the city of Madmannah; in the role of an ear witness behold I promise that the sound and the sense of the music of the two of them mixed in the palate of the listener like the sounds of frogs peeping in the rivers of water on a summer day, but others were silent. And they tried to stand before the ark on the days of the festival, to show the majesty of their music before it to all who came to the gates of their city, and if lords like this were praying, how can their music not find favor in the eyes of the nation bowing beneath them?

So lasted their association for many days, but with Reb Lemel's malice the bundle broke apart. Reb Lemel set the tiger's eye[512] on the business of Reb Shealtiel, his friend and loved one, and established for himself as well a warehouse for selling all kinds of weaving and fabric, facing the entrance to Reb Shealtiel's house and his store. In order to conquer his opponent and defeat him on the field of competition, Reb Lemel set up his wife the businesswoman, the woman of valor,[513] at her post at the entrance to Reb Shealtiel's shop, and when some customer passed by, she would grab hold of the corner of his garment and drag him by force into her shop. In a place where her right hand[514] did not save her, she was helped by the freewill offering of her mouth,[515] and the grace of her lips and her multiplying of temptations and entreaties, and she would promise to every customer to give them large discounts, only for him and his honor. Enchantment was spilled on Shprintza's lips to promise to each and every person to fulfill his heart's desires and his lacks as he wished, from her knowledge of them and what touched their hearts. To Reb Tzivon the sucker whose lack of money irritated him seven times over every day, she always promised to loan money at low interest, 3 percent a month, on condition that he bring a pledge whose value was double the money of his debt. To Reb Tzadok the widower whose eyes were lifted to the one who dwelt in heaven because she was precious before him, an important woman, in order to use her dowry money for the blessings of his failing business, she recommended a *shidduch*[516] with a young maiden with a large dowry, from the family of her well-pedigreed husband. To Gronah the leather worker, the hand of whose compassionate and gracious husband fell on her ten times a day, hitting and hurting her, she promised to enforce on her husband by order of the rabbi and the heads

---

[508] *Pirke Avot* 4:1 "Who is rich? He who is happy with in his lot…"

[509] Exodus 18:21 "You shall also seek out from among all the people capable men who fear God…"

[510] 1 Kings 5:5 "All the days of Solomon, Judah and Israel from Dan to Beersheva dwelt in safety, everyone under his own vine and under his own fig tree."

[511] Psalm 94:4 "How long shall the wicked, O LORD, how long shall the wicked exult, shall they utter insolent speech, shall all evildoers boast about themselves?"

[512] Job 16:9 "… My foe stabs me with his eyes."

[513] Proverbs 31:10 "A woman of valor who can find? Far more than pearls is her worth."

[514] Psalm 44:3 "…their arm did not give them victory, but Your right hand…"

[515] Psalm 119:108 "Accept, O LORD, the freewill offerings of my mouth; teach me Your rules."

[516] An arranged marriage.

of the community a decree to lighten his hand from upon her. To the Lady Matilda who oppressed her servant girls ruthlessly, and harassed them incessantly with aggressive curses, and therefore they were fleeing from her house on the first day that they arrived, she offered a submissive servant who was diligent in her work, and at a low price. To Reb Gamliel, the baker who practiced asceticism all his life, and drank wine to satiation only once a year (that is, from the beginning of the year until its end), who every day made the sound of a great noise to disturb the rest of the heads of the community, in his upsetting the order of community behavior which were not always right in his eyes – to this Reb Gamliel the baker (and there are versions that say "the pourer"), she would promise that the hand of her powerful husband would plan to be of one mind and opinion with him in matters of the community's behavior. To Reb Elyakum the shopkeeper, whose business ledgers were arranged according to the method of the system of double business ledgers, where he would sell to his customer on credit once and write in his ledger twice, she promised to bring him customers who would specifically buy on credit. With one word! She was founded in her goodness to fulfill the desire of every man, to do for him all that his heart desired, only in order to satisfy his desire, and with this, hope could be seen in her, for she drew it with cords of desire to her shop, and he inclined his heart towards her merchandise.

{p. 154} And Reb Shealtiel did not also stand coolly in opposition to Shprintza's capturing of his acquaintances that came to his store, across from the doorway of his shop, and he too did not delay in pulling them by force into his shop. The joke was to see, sometimes, how when some customer passed by, and Shprintza was pulling him by the corner of his coat from this side, and Reb Shealtiel held onto the other corner of his coat, until the two corners of his coat were torn from the force of the pulling, and the embarrassed customer, ashamed to go naked and in torn clothing in the street of the city, would run home, like the fox fleeing from the hunters' bow, to change clothing, and the two rivals, when they saw that the customer fled from their hands like a bird from a snare, would be aggravated, and curse each other, and from arguing they would find themselves coming to blows and punches. From time to time when Shprintza and Reb Shealtiel would encounter each other around some customer, Shprintza's hand would be thrust in her opponent's beard, and also his hands would grab her braids, and the members of their households would join them.

On account of this tremendous competition, cursing took place in Reb Shealtiel's shop, which sapped his strength to oppose Reb Lemel and Shprintza, who were stronger than him. Reb Lemel brought slander about his opponent to the factory owners who were giving their merchandise to Reb Shealtiel at a discount, and every place he spoke, an agreement (credit) came, and in most cases it did not miss the mark.

And time does its own. The moments of time move forward according to their order, and are swallowed up in the realm of eternity. Winter marches in the cycle of the season of the year, the month of Shvat arrives, and soon the days of the festivals are about to come. Reb Shealtiel gathered the remainder of his fortune and took his money in his hand and travelled to Lodz to buy the necessary merchandise for the time of the days of the festivals. As was the custom of all the Lithuanian shopkeepers, he stayed at the house of the man that he had chosen to be his intermediary (commissioner) H. Shmelkin. What was a commissioner in the city of Lodz? Listen closely, dear reader, and hear.

The commissioner is a very great necessity for the Lithuanian shopkeepers that buy their merchandise in Lodz. Without him the shopkeeper would not lift his hand or foot.[517] He is the mischievous lad who takes hold of the blind man and misdirects him to the place that he is seeking.

---

[517] Genesis 41:44 "Pharaoh said to Joseph, "I am Pharaoh; yet without you, no one shall lift up hand or foot in all the land of Egypt.""

The commissioner is not a buyer or a seller, not a fabricator or a shopkeeper, yet he is equal to them all, and takes the wage of all of them combined. The mission of the commissioner in the world of commerce here resembles in all its aspects the mission of the Hebrew teacher. This one is like that one; they don't take anything, not the reward for their wisdom which they do not know, not the wages of their work which they do not do, but the wages of their idleness, that is, their laziness. And according to the many levels of their idleness, their wage is according to what they do. The teachers are loafers on a low level, and therefore they will be on the cliff and under pressure, and the commissioners in Lodz who are accomplished in this attribute live a life of wealth and honor. A parable is carried on the lips of the people. The father advises his son, who doesn't know how to read or write, not *Torah* and not knowledge and not the way of the world, that there is only one path before him to find the source of his livelihood, that he should be a teacher. Resembling this, our eyes see that here, too, a Lithuanian Jew who comes to Lodz with an empty plate, without proper knowledge of the nature of commerce and its character, without knowledge and understanding, he is the one who is chosen to be commissioner. However, while the teacher still takes only the wages of idleness and nothing much more, and sometimes they do not pay him even the wages of idleness, as is practiced in these days of ours, the commissioner would take 5 things: only the wage of idleness, only the wage of lifting[518] hand and foot, only the twisting of his lips,[519] only the wage of the bite of the fabricators, and only the wage of the bite of the customers. There are many commissioners in every city that has much commerce, but here in Lodz they surpass all members of their kind, because here the ground is capable of growing these seedlings.

{p. 155} For them to prosper, because the prices are not fixed appropriately, fixed and not fixed are the same, inflated and hollow inside and in their content, and a simple man from the market does not get to see the depth of their hollowness. The price of the known merchandise of *Ploni*[520]is a full silver ruble, the price is the price, but there is a discount here, and a man had not yet been let into the secret to know the measure of the discount and its quantity. The commissioner Reb *Ploni* calculates the price for his customers according to what it is, without a discount, and Reb *Almoni*, who casts his net to hunt the allies of Reb *Ploni* and to draw them to him, offers to discount the price by 10% on a hundred, but has not yet divulged that for the third he deducts 15%, and for the fourth he expands his position to reach 25%. This wild regimen in the setting of prices is a source of salvation for the commissioners, to give them the ability to earn whatever their hand can reach, and to blind the eyes of the customers with a great and awesome discount.

Reb Shealtiel consulted with his guide and administrator Mr. Shmelkin, and paid him the allotment of money that he owed him previously, to take in exchange for it a fine portion as is fitting for a very old shopkeeper like him, who buys his merchandise from the first hour with a promissory note and not with money, and no disaster has happened to him yet. Mr. Shmelkin was agreeable to this. Since Reb Shealtiel was one of his best customers, and Reb Shealtiel would purchase merchandise when the spirit moved him, Mr. Shmelkin gave his guarantee on his behalf. Mr. Shmelkin brought the purchased merchandise home to wrap in secure bundles, and to rush it onto the railroad, and between this and that the *Shabbat* day arrived, and because of that the shipment was stopped.

Happy and with a heart full of pride on the splendor of the glory of his music that he played before a large congregation in his passing before the ark, Reb Shealtiel returned home from

---

[518] A typographical error here substitutes one letter in the word for "lifting."

[519] Babylonian *Talmud Sanhedrin* 65a "The *Gemara* answers: The twisting of his lips while he speaks is considered an action."

[520] "*Ploni Almoni*" is the Hebrew expression for "so and so," used together and separately. It is first attested in Ruth 4:1 "He called, "Come over and sit down here, So-and-so!" And he came over and sat down."

the prayer house and sat down to eat bread together with the family of Mr. Shmelkin. And while they were eating and gladdening their hearts, a messenger from the house of runners[521]* brought a letter to Mr. Shmelkin. Without any malice aforethought Reb Shealtiel looked innocently at the letter's envelope, and he saw the address of his enemy who grieved his soul, Reb Lemel, printed on it, and his spirit was agitated[522] within him, in his knowing that some matter was hidden in the letter that would cause him to be made odious in the eyes of Mr. Shmelkin also, who was his last only hope and his one heart's desire, to hold on to his trade, which was collapsing on its foundation, after all the merchants and factory owners in Moscow in whom his heart had trusted before had locked their faith away from him on account of the slander that Reb Lemel had maliciously brought before them. With sorrow and emptiness Reb Shealtiel finished his meal and came to his room that the master of the house had designated for him, but his rest was robbed the whole night. He sprawled unmoving on his bed like a block of wood and acted like a deep sleep had fallen upon him, his ears attentive to every sound of thin silence[523] that the members of the household were whispering in the room that was near his bedroom.

Reb Shealtiel's shipment arrived. The letter that was hurried by Reb Lemel was full of bitterness and words of accusation about Reb Shealtiel, that this purchase would be the last, a little more and he would go bankrupt to his creditors. But Mr. Shmelkin set his eyes to read it and his face became pale.

In the room that was next to Reb Shealtiel's bedroom, Mr. Shmelkin sat on his chair upholstered with silk fabric, and under the soles of his feet were lovely carpets of silk tapestry made in the style of the land of the east. He was leaning back against the back of the chair. His right leg was placed over his left leg, his head was tipped to the side, and his eyes were directed motionlessly to the letter that was in his hand. He read it ten times, as if he refused {p. 156} to believe what his eyes were seeing, as if he was trying to find what was hidden in it between the lines, and as if he was attempting to find the correct way to determine the falsehood of the words of the letter, and to nullify its words, because parting from Reb Shealtiel would be difficult for him, since he had been connected with him in the fetters[524] of commerce for many years, and he had been as a milk cow for him this long. Hah! Now here is the time to shear his sheep, and his heart was pained, as if he was forced to send an unshorn lamb from his hand. Next to him sits his magnificent wife in fancy clothes, adorned with precious jewels. She clings to him fondly, passes the palm of her hand over the locks of hair on his head, and waits impatiently for him to finish his reading, in order to remind him that the time for the play to begin in the Playhouse[525]* was fast approaching, and it was not right to delay further. Each and every minute is like an eternity in her eyes. She restrains herself with great power from disturbing his work, and feels bitter and very angry about it in the secret place in her heart. When will he finish his reading? When will the end come? He read the letter until its end, and sat to read it a second time. Now the strength of her patience failed.

"What do you in see in this letter, my darling, that you so diligently read it over again, as if the secrets of the world are hidden in it? Don't we still have to go to the Playhouse?" Her words express a kind of silent complaint. She takes out her watch from her pocket and looks at it.

---

[521] Original footnote: *Mail

[522] Genesis 41:8 "Next morning, his spirit was agitated, and he sent for all the magicians of Egypt…"

[523] 1 Kings 19:12 "After the earthquake—fire; but the LORD was not in the fire. And after the fire—a sound of thin silence."

[524] Isaiah 58:6 "No, this is the fast I desire: To unlock fetters of wickedness…"

[525] *Theatre.

"This letter was rushed to me from my acquaintance Reb Lemel, a respected merchant who has treasures from the city of Madmannah, in which he warns me against placing my trust in Reb Shealtiel and his promissory notes, because his circumstance has very much worsened, and he is about to claim bankruptcy to his creditors. Thank God that the letter arrived while there is still time, while the merchandise is still in my house. Let Reb Shealtiel return to his house by himself, with his promissory notes that will be useful now to cover the mouth of the flask.[526] I will not give him my merchandise. And what do you say about this my darling? Is my way in this right in your eyes?"

"Your counsel is good and correct; do as you have said."

Her shining face expressed a feeling of joy, that the matter had reached its end, and her advice was accepted in a moment, before they had been late for the starting time of the play. She looked at her watch and said:

"The ninth hour is approaching."

"And maybe only with malice and treachery Reb Lemel rushed this letter, only in order to throw his opponent who competes with him on the field of commerce into a pit that he dug for him. The shopkeepers in the small cities in Lithuania are as shrewd as snakes,[527] and every matter of guile and malicious evil will not stop them from carrying out their schemes, only in order to find a benefit for their souls."

"Indeed, there is no end to the evil of these swindlers."

"But Reb Lemel's letter is not an empty matter this time. Reb Shealtiel is very suspicious in my eyes. I see that a wicked matter is hidden inside him at this time, that he purchases merchandise from all who come to hand, without considering the paths of his purchase, and also that he expands the extent of the purchase more than he has been accustomed to always doing."

"That being the case, the matter is as right as sun at noon."

"But didn't I know Reb Shealtiel from before as an honest man, and believe that he would spread out his net at my feet?"

{p. 157} "So, I too will express my opinion. A man like him would not claim bankruptcy to his creditors."

"And maybe…it would frighten me to endanger my fortune. Also, without this the ground would sway under the soles of my feet, on account of the blows with which I was stricken last year, and if this time a disaster were to happen to me, then my downfall would be complete."

"So I too would predict. It is forbidden to us to put our heads into a place of danger – look, it's 5 minutes after 9:00."

"And who knows if we would not lose much goodness. To break my agreement with Reb Shealtiel is to walk away from a large salary, 500 *shekels* a year. And what will you say, my dear?"

"Do not, my man, afflict me with your counsels this time, at the time that the minutes are few. The *Shabbat* day is still long, we will still take counsel on the matter. See, a little more and we will be late for the time of the play. Let's go."

She forcefully took hold of his arm and got him up from his chair, and they turned their faces towards the door.

"My contract with Reb Shealtiel is broken, I will not give him even one *kesitah*."[528]

So spoke Mr. Shmelkin as he got up from his chair, and his face expressed grief and bitter disappointment over his large salary that was subtracted from him.

---

[526] That is, having no value. Babylonia *Talmud Bava Metzia* 7b "…Does he need half of the document to cover the opening of his flask? Having half a promissory note is of no legal consequence."

[527] Genesis 3:1 "Now the snake was the shrewdest of all the wild beasts…"

[528] A unit of money mentioned in the Bible. Genesis 33:18 "The parcel of land where he pitched his tent he purchased from the children of Hamor, Shechem's father, for a hundred *kesitahs*."

They went to the theatre house to see the play that was being presented there.

And Reb Shealtiel lay on his bed, and his ears were paying attention to every utterance that came out of their mouths. Reb Shealtiel's blood froze in his veins, and the hair on his head stood on edge from fear, his spirit was deeply moved inside him, like a sinner liable for death who stands before his judges and waits for his sentence and his law to emerge from them, whether he will live or he will die.

"Where will I go?" The unfortunate one imagined in his heart, "to return to Madmannah with empty hands?"

What will I answer my wife and my nine children who await my arrival with bundles of new merchandise?

The night covered with a dark shroud the tears of the unfortunate one who was abused for no reason by the hands of a man who was the adversary and enemy.[529] Deep silence and darkness all around, and no one hears his bitter groans, none see the warm outpouring of tears from his eyes.

Night went by with all the storms of his fear and panic. Morning came. The sun sent its rays, rays of gold, pouring precious light into the window of my bedroom.

And behold my friend came and said:

"Did you know? Reb Shealtiel who trilled with his throat is hanging by his neck. He died by strangulation in suicide."

My soul suffered greatly over the unfortunate Reb Shealtiel, who could not summon the strength to carry life's suffering, and my soul troubled me for the ridicule and contempt with which all who knew him slandered him, instead of nodding and expressing a feeling of sorrow over the death of a human soul, even if he had killed himself. It was not his fault that he committed suicide, but the fault of this generation that conducted this bloody practice and joined him to the laws of the mode.[530]*

{p. 158} My Memories
By Reuven Levi

At the beginning of 5672 (1912), my wife, of the house of Sperling, and I, came to Augustów in order to settle down there and found a Hebrew school in it. The name Augustów was not foreign to my wife's family, the Sperling family. My wife's grandfather, Reb Ze'ev Sperling, was the government-appointed rabbi and a municipal worker. He became known as the translator of two books by Jules Verne from French into Hebrew: "In the Depths of the Sea"[531] and "In the Belly of the Earth."[532] In addition, he engaged in the study of astronomy and wrote a book on this topic. However, the manuscript, along with other manuscripts was burned in one of the many fires that struck Augustów. His son, Dov Ber Sperling, also dwelt in Augustów and directed a *cheder* in it. He moved to Suwalki after his house was burned down twice. Another writer, Yaakov Frenkel, was also known to us, not personally, however, but from the literature.

---

[529] Esther 7:6 "The adversary and enemy," replied Esther, "is this evil Haman…"
[530] Original note: *Fashion.
[531] "20,000 Leagues under the Sea."
[532] "Journey to the Center of the Earth."

We chose to settle in Augustów because we knew that many people in town knew the Sperling family, and our hope was that we would find a living there and also room for a broad range of cultural and Zionist activities. Our hopes were not disappointed.

What was the cultural and intellectual situation in the town when we arrived there? There were two educational institutions for Jewish children, where they taught mainly Jewish studies, and they educated for the fear of Heaven and fulfillment of the *mitzvot*. In those days, there existed in the eastern European Jewish communities the *talmud torah* and the *cheder*. The *talmud torah* was a public institution funded and supervised by the community, and the *cheder*, a private institution funded by tuition paid by the parents of the children who learned there. The *talmud torah* didn't have a good reputation, not as a teaching institution and not as an educational institution. Only those who were unable to pay tuition for this learning sent their children to the *talmud torah*, out of necessity. The people who had the ability would send their sons to the *cheder*. There were various *chadarim*: elementary (learning the aleph-bet and reading), the *Chumash*[533] with Rashi, {p. 159} and the *Gemara*. The father would choose the *cheder* that was most suited to his son according to its world view. There were poor people who scrimped on their meagre bread so that their sons could learn in the *cheder*.

In Augustow at that time there existed only one educational institution – the *talmud torah*, in which all the town's boys learned. It was actually both *cheder* and *talmud torah* in one. Those who were able paid tuition, and the poor children learned at the expense of the community. The institution had a good name; at its head stood Reb Betzalel, may his memory be for a blessing, a God-fearing scholar who was modest in his manner. There was no Hebrew educational establishment in which those who completed their years at the *talmud torah* could continue their studies.

A few travelled to other cities to study in a *yeshiva* or in a general school. Others studied Hebrew and Russian with private teachers, but most remained uneducated and uncultured. The teachers of Hebrew were Mr. M. Meizler, a grammarian and expert in the *Tanakh* and its interpreters (he himself had written an interpretation on the *Tanakh*; it is not known to me if it was published), and Mr. Dovid Boyarski, who was a modern teacher that taught literature and history in addition to grammar and *Tanakh*. Both of them were distinctive teachers, but they did not establish an educational institution, and in addition to the lessons, a tightly knit society was created.

The benevolent institutions that existed then were: *Gemilut Chassadim,*[534] *Linat HaTzedek, Matan B'Seter,*[535] etc. These institutions, which were found in all Jewish communities, were also in Augustów, but I did not know them. However, one very valuable institution, with which not every town was blessed, we found in Augustów: a Jewish public library. This library had been founded at the initiative of the wife of Doctor Avramsky and Chitza Markus. Aharon Zukerman and Utzi Lap were active in its administration. Every adult who paid an annual fee of two *rubles* had the right to vote and be elected. Every year a new administration was elected by a majority vote. The library occupied two rooms. In the first were shelves, and on them the books stood in fine order. The second room was designated for meetings of the administration. One of the members of the administration would always sit at the time when books were being borrowed, and would answer the readers' questions. It was a magnificent institution. In this library there were books in Russian (the majority), Yiddish and Polish. There were no Hebrew books. I found a printed announcement in the library that read: "If twenty people register their names as wishing to read Hebrew books, the administration will try to acquire books in that language as well."

---

[533] A book containing the five books of the *Torah*.
[534] Acts of lovingkindness; providing for the needy, often with interest-free loans.
[535] Giving in secret.

In the city there existed a Zionist association headed by Shmuel Grinberg. The association engaged in selling the "*shekels*" and collecting donations for the *Keren Kayemet L'Yisrael*, for *brises*,[536] weddings, and collection bowls in the synagogues on the evening of *Yom Kippur*. They did not engage in cultural activities or Zionist propaganda; they lacked, apparently, active people among the members of the association.

Thus I found the city when we arrived to live there. The saying is known: "A guest arrives one minute - and finds a fault the next." I found in Augustów quiet residents, ready to help the one who asks, alert to public affairs. This was proven in the field of education and culture, and Zionist activism in the years 1912-1914.

My wife opened a school for girls, and I gave private lessons for one year. In the second year, we – I and Mr. D. Boyarski, founded a *Cheder Metukan* using the method of "Hebrew in Hebrew" and Sephardic pronunciation; the Russian language was taught by another teacher. We saw to it that the Zionist association would contribute to the take-over of the public library by the assimilated and members of the "*Bund.*" Instruction was given to members that registered for the library and paid the membership fee. All the new members came to the annual general meeting of the library and elected to the administration the candidates of the Zionist association. Of the members of the previous administration there remained only the doctor's wife and Chitza Markus. However, they both resigned {p. 160} as a sign of solidarity with the rejected candidates. Chitza returned afterwards and was more active than any of us, and cooperated with us. The new administration acquired hundreds of Hebrew books, and books in Yiddish and Russian on national topics. Hebrew readers multiplied to the degree that the number of new books multiplied. The Augustów public library was famous throughout the area and its influence on the youth of the city was tremendous. It was open to the community five days a week, Sunday through Thursday, in the evening. When the Germans captured the city in the First World War (February 1915), they quartered some of their soldiers in the library's apartment. In order to warm themselves on the cold winter days, the soldiers began to light the stove by burning the shelves and also the books. When this became known to Chaya Markus, she enlisted a few young people and coachmen who transferred the remaining books to the Markus family's storerooms. Until the library returned to its regular dwelling place, many came to the Markus house to borrow books.

Chaya Markus   **Yishayahu Plotzinski**

---

[536] Circumcisions.

The success of the action for the conquering of the library encouraged the Zionist association to widen their cultural activities. It was the custom that on every Friday night a lecture would take place in one of the Study Houses, on Jewish history of the people on the land of Israel in the past and in the future, or on the *Torah* portion of the week. These lectures became a regular institution; the audience continued to increase until the space available was too small to contain them, insufficient, and late comers stood in the vestibule. It is especially to be pointed out that a close connection was formed between the lecturers and the audience, and after every lecture, questions would be asked by the audience. The lecturers were the three teachers, and sometimes, also someone from among the one of the educated leaders of the town. Thanks to the intensive activity, the atmosphere in the city was changed. Interest in Zionism and in the land grew. The association decided, therefore, to rent {p. 161} an apartment. The club was open every evening except *Shabbat* evening. The council gathered there once a week for a meeting, people came to talk with each other and to read the newspapers and circulars, and the youth – for practical work.

In addition to the collection of funds for the benefit of the *Keren Kayemet L'Yisrael*, as was the custom previously, and now more vigorously, the association ordered the *Keren Kayemet L'Yisrael* boxes.[537]

The youth that undertook the work distributed the boxes to the houses, and would empty them every three months. They would send the money and the list of donors to the center in Vilna. Another project that the association initiated with the help of the youth was the sale of shares in the Jewish Colonial Trust, in London. Contribution cards were distributed to the purchasers of the shares, and every day the youth went and collected the payments (20 *agorot*); a *Keren Kayemet L'Yisrael* stamp was stuck onto the card as proof of payment. Every month the money was sent to the center, in order for them to transfer it to the chief administration that was in London. Tens of the investors in the shares had not yet received them when the war broke out. A portion of the monetary payments remained in the Loan & Savings bank in Augustów, who with the outbreak of the war transferred it to Russia, and all those savings were lost. Part were transferred to the center in Vilna and to London.

An additional activity of the Zionist association in the area of culture was the establishment of Hebrew courses. The instruction was conducted using the method of "Hebrew in Hebrew" and in Sephardic pronunciation. The classes took place each evening for two or three hours, except Friday night and Saturday. The teachers were the writer of these lines, and Mr. D. Boyarski. The courses lasted for about two years. In the second year, there were two classes. The studies included: Hebrew language and literature (the works and the study of literature), Jewish history, the geography of the Land of Israel, Zionism, festivals and holidays, etc. In order that the youth would become accustomed to speaking Hebrew also outside the hours of lessons, we established a "*minyan*" for Hebrew speakers on *Shabbatot* and festivals in the girls' school. The meetings on every *Shabbat* morning were for a blessing, and served to encourage Zionist activity. On festivals, festive parties would be held after prayers. The main party was held on *Simchat Torah*.

The growing Zionist activity aroused the opposition of the *Bundists*, who brought propagandists from the outside. There were stormy arguments, but we had the upper hand, because the Zionist spirit that prevailed in the city encouraged our debaters, and their words that came from the emotional heart aroused a storm of agreement from the congregation. In light of their success, our association also began to bring propogandists from outside, and the ferment was tremendous. There came on the agenda a plan to open a Hebrew kindergarten. There were also those who dreamed of a Hebrew gymnasium. Hebrew performances were held, and the cantor's son, Wolf

---

[537] The blue and white collection boxes that have been distributed by JNF since its inception.

Ratner, organized a choir from the students in the courses, and they sang very pleasantly at the parties.

At that time, a few students from the course went to study in the Hebrew gymnasium in Mariampol and Kovno. In those days, information was publicized in the newspaper that the Hebrew gymnasium in Jerusalem was interested in opening a guest house next to the gymnasium for students from outside of the land, and it was desired that its proprietor would be a teacher who could help the students. This matter enchanted us, my wife and me. We presented ourselves as candidates and received a positive reply. We published an announcement in the press that we were accepting youths for the guest house that we were about to establish, and that they would go up with us to the land of Israel. From Augustów about ten youths registered. Suddenly the war broke out, and the whole thing was cancelled.

{p. 162} With the outbreak of war, all the Zionist activity was finished, but the deep plowing that was done in the prior years gave its fruit.

*

The Library Activists

From right to left: M. Lap, Liza Aleksandrovitz, M. Stolar, A. Chalupitzki, Channah Chalupitzki, M. Stein, Alter Aleksandrovitz, Genya Rosianska, Z. Sheinmar, Z. Kentzuk.

After the completion of the First World War and with the arrival of the information that there existed a possibility to go up to the land, a group of ten people in our city was organized for *aliyah*. As secretary of the Zionist association, and the organizer of the group, I travelled to the *aliyah* bureau in Warsaw with the list of the members and the required documents. After standing in line for a few hours, I was received by Mr. M. Marminski (Marom). He told me clearly, after looking at the list of members, that only tradesmen receive entry permits for the land. That is to say - builders, carpenters, plasterers, white-washers, shoemakers, tailors, and the like; every one of them needed to have a certificate of permission from the guild (the Tradesmen's Union of a particular profession), to show that he was a certified tradesman and a member of the guild. Marminski returned all the documents to me, and added: "If you want your group to travel in the up-coming convoy, tomorrow before noon you have to present at the bureau certificates signed

171

with the approval of the guild according to the law." I answered with agitation: "Is that possible? Isn't the trip to Augustów and back a matter of two days and how?..." Mr. M. calmly interrupted my words and said: "I didn't say how to do it, but what to do. Go and do it!"

{p. 163} I did it, although in fear and worry, because there was no one to guide me as to whom to turn to in carrying out this task. By chance I turned to the respectable Jews. I wandered around in the streets and I found a Jew that makes seals sitting alone in the shop. At my request he showed me examples of the seals of the guilds and I ordered five or six various professions. I also found a Jewish office for writing and duplication. The following day at 10 in the morning, I stood in line to hand in the documents. Mr. M received me with a smile and said: "Be ready! When you get a telegram from us you must come immediately." The telegram was received after a few days, and they all went up – except me! The members of my wife's family blockaded the house and announced that they would not let me travel to "a land of desolation, diseases, and plagues" – and I did not travel. From then on, I did not know a resting place for my soul. I walked around as if in a daze. My wife saw my depressed mood; she came to me and said: "Go!" I went secretly without even parting from the family.

On 22 *Tammuz*,[538] the ship anchored in Jaffa Harbor with about 300 immigrants from Alexandria to the land of Israel. From Trieste to Alexandria, we travelled on a large beautiful ship; in Alexandria, we sat for a week without a connection to transportation to the land of Israel, because the ship-owners were worried about the danger of mines that floated in the Mediterranean Sea from the days of the World War. Finally, the owner of an old tiny ship, with no minimum amenities, agreed to bring us to the land. Many people warned us, and also the bureau did not hide their concern from us about the danger involved in this trip. But not one of the immigrants was deterred. We sailed – and arrived safely.

After I spent a few days in Tel-Aviv, I went up to Jerusalem, the Holy City, the ancient historic city. From Jerusalem, I travelled to the group of people from Augustów, in Merchaviah, which served as a place for agricultural training, the vestibule[539] for settlement. We were not yet engaged in agriculture itself. For the time being we dismantled old buildings that interfered with the agricultural area, we dug ditches, laid water-pipes from the well of the Merchaviah cooperative to the Merchaviah *Moshav*,[540] which was about a kilometer away from us. The relationship between us was good. They guided us in the work, and the women taught us cooking and baking. The training group at that time numbered about thirty people.

After the festival of *Sukkot*, we received instructions to leave the place, because the training had been terminated. They transferred us to the Afula road, under the administration of "*HaPoel HaTzair*." The first course of our first meal (and all the remaining ones too), was quinine.[541] We did contract work; the young women broke the large rocks into gravel, and we, the young men, dug ditches. Our allowance for food, drink and lodging amounted to about 20 *grush*[542] a day. The ground in this period, at the end of the summer, was very hard, we were unable to earn from our work, in spite of all our physical efforts, the 20 *grush* a day… The deficit continued to grow. The days of rain came; three days of torrential rain came down, accompanied by stormy winds, without letup. The tents collapsed. The bread supplied to us by *Moshav* Tel Adashim did

---

[538] In the summer.

[539] *Pirke Avot* 4:16 "Rabbi Jacob said: this world is like a vestibule [*prozdor*] before the world to come; prepare yourself in the vestibule, so that you may enter the banqueting-hall."

[540] A collective settlement. It is similar to the *kibbutz* in that labor is communal, but in contrast to the *kibbutz*, farms in a *moshav* tended to be individually owned but are equal in size.

[541] The traditional treatment for malaria for nearly 400 years until the 1940's. Until the late 19th Century the south-eastern half of the Jezreel Valley was a pestilential swamp; the graveyards of the various *moshavim* and *kibbutzim* show was full of the graves not only of the early, young pioneering settlers themselves but of their children.

[542] The smallest denomination of Israeli coin, no longer in use. The linguistic equivalent of a penny.

not arrive, because of the swamp that stood between the *moshav* and the road. Only on the fourth day, when the ground began to dry a little, we climbed the hills and went up to Nazareth, where we bought some pita and the like.

When we again began to work, the ground was as soft as butter and the productivity of our work increased significantly. We covered our debts, and there remained some left over in our favor. Our group organized itself for the purpose of settling did not want to continue with the road work. We hoped that we would attain settlement, so we decided to look for a suitable place for agricultural training. In my hands was a letter of recommendation to Mr. Chaim Margolit-Kaloriski, and he gave me a letter to Mr. Eizenberg, the manager of the groves in Rechovot. Mr. Eizenberg received me graciously {p. 164} and agreed to accept all of us for work. All of our group then moved to Rechovot except one, Zalman Bezant, may his memory be for a blessing, who had died in Merchaviah from yellow fever. In Rechovot the situation of the Hebrew workers was no better. A few citrus growers hired only Jewish workers, while others employed a few Jews and many Arabs. But the lion's share of the citrus growers – the foot of a Jewish worker did not step on their property. Also in the orchards under Eizenberg's management there was intermingled work. The work was exhausting; at the head of the row stood a strong Arab used to working with a hoe.[543] In order not to cause pleasure for the Arabs and shame to our brothers, we exerted ourselves with our last reserves of strength and we did not lag behind. After a few days, when the Arabs were convinced that we were not defeated, they slowed the pace of the work a little and gave us a break. The citrus growers who opposed Hebrew work composed a song:

> Hear our voice, O Lord our God, oy, oy, oy.
> Do not send here the pioneers, oy, oy, oy.
> At half-past seven they go out to work, oy, oy, oy.
> At half-past four they are already returning, oy, oy, oy.
> Working, working, that's a year for them,[544] oy, oy, oy.
> If you don't believe go out and see, oy, oy, oy.

In those same days, The Association of Lithuanian Immigrants was formed for *kibbutz* settlement (they completed Kibbutz Degania 'A'). I also joined that association, telling so to my wife. She responded that she would not go to a *kibbutz*, because she had no idea about agriculture, and demanded that I find work in the city. I moved, therefore, to Tel Aviv. I bought a pair of mules and a wagon and started to work, with a partner, in the port of Jaffa transporting building materials. We built a cabin with two rooms in the Bordani citrus grove – today it is Tchernichovsky Street – and a stable for the mules.

At *Chanukah* 5682 [1922] my wife, my eldest daughter Shulamit, our son Yisrael, and youngest daughter Bat-Tzion arrived in the land.

Tel Aviv in 1922 was a small town, next to the larger city of Jaffa. Herzl Street, the main street for walking and meeting people, and spending time in coffee houses, began at Ahad Ha'am Street and ended at Petach Tikvah Road. Across the street were orchards and Arab houses. The parallel road to Herzl Street was Nachlat Binyamin Road; its houses reached Gruzenberg Street. On Yehuda HaLevi Street, a few houses had already been built. In that street was the Chaskina kindergarten. A boys' school and a girls' school were located in Neve Tzedek. Bat-Tzion was registered in the Chaskina kindergarten. It was quite a long way, but she was nicely familiar with the way. Shulamit studied in the girls' school in Neve Tzedek and Yisrael, since he did not speak Hebrew was not accepted for school.

---

[543] The word used here for "hoe" is the Arabic word *turiah*.
[544] This line is in Yiddish.

{p. 165} In Those Days
by Noach Borovitz

I parted from our city in the year 1920, two weeks after *Pesach*. I had been drafted into the Polish army seven weeks before that. Before I had time to become a soldier in the fullest sense of the word, I deserted to Lithuania because I did not agree to be sent to Kiev to fight against the Bolsheviks. We felt good in the army because we excelled in the training. In my platoon, there was someone from Augustów – Reuvka Beker (a shoemaker's son), who produced a profusion of joke stories, and knew how to play the harmonica and dance Polish dances. Among other things, he did amazing dancing on his hands to the rhythm of a tune on the harmonica. The Poles very much loved him. Thanks to Reuvka, who was short but solid, healthy and cheerful, not one soldier dared to offend a Jewish soldier. When the officers informed us that they were about to send us to an attack on Kiev, they added that the Jews will certainly flee from the front. From that moment, the anti-Semitism began to raise its head. Our gentile friends began to besmirch Jews. In a moment, we became stepchildren. I went out from the area of the military camp, therefore, at night, by way of the torn wire fence, and I reached home. I exchanged the army clothes for civilian clothes and travelled to Suwalk. On the next day, at night, I crossed the border and arrived at Mariampol, which is in Lithuania.

At that time, "*HeChalutz*" was founded, whose center was in Kovno. I joined the "*HeChalutz*" organization. We worked on an agricultural farm. All those who excelled in the work advanced their *aliyah* to the land. At *Chanukah* in the year 1920, I left Kovno. I arrived in Tel-Aviv by way of Egypt on a train from Qantara, together with a group from Lithuania, in January 1921. Since then I have not again seen Poland.

After three years of my being in the land, I brought my sister Miriam up to the land. After a short time I also brought my sister's groom from Warsaw. In the year 1924, I also brought my parents up to the land, may their memories be for a blessing. I also brought a young woman from Augustów. My sister Miriam didn't succeed in getting along in the land, and immigrated to America with all the members of her family.

I will return to the days of my youth in Augustów. We lived across from the Great Study House. We visited there three times a day for prayers. We were very tied with all the fiber of our being to Judaism, to *Yiddishkeit*.[545] In its time it made an indelible impression on me. One *Yom Kippur* night in the period of the Beilis trial, *Yom Kippur*, when after *Kol Nidre*[546] {p. 166} Rabbi Katriel spoke in the Great Synagogue in front of the magnificent Holy Ark. I have never seen another like it in beauty and majestic holiness. He opened the Holy Ark while weeping for the libels of which accused us, and all of the tremendous congregation wept with him. Everyone's prayer was that it would come out in the light of justice, and, blessed is God, our prayer was accepted, because that afternoon, our judgement and our righteousness appeared.

Who in Augustów didn't know the name Borovitz? A glorious family. The eldest of the Borovitz's was the grandfather, Reb Chanoch Henech, may his memory be for a blessing. He was

---

[545] Jewishness.

[546] "All Vows." The prayer for which the *Yom Kippur* evening service is named, which asks that all vows made in the coming year be nullified.

an honest and God-fearing man, as careful with the light commandments as he was with the serious ones. His brother was Reb Tzvi Borovitz, an energetic man,[547] a big merchant and God-fearing, cheerful and happy. His sons Reb Shmuel Borovitz, Reb Yaakov Borovitz, and Reb Nisan Borovitz, died here in the land; all of them were energetic men.[548] Nisan and Yaakov had wandered to Siberia during the Holocaust, but were privileged to finish their lives in the land. Reb Shmuel had greater privilege, for he arrived in the land before the Holocaust and died there at a good old age, with most of the members of his family around him.

The years of my youth in Augustów were bound with two close friends. Together we studied, together we hiked and spent our free time. One of them was the son of the *Dayan*[549] Rabbi Reb Yekutiel Azrieli, and the second, Tzvi Stolnitzki, the son of Avraham Yitzchak, the teacher in the *talmud torah*. The father was the "*ba'al tefillah*"[550] in the Great Study House throughout the year, and also the "*ba'al kriah*."[551] He was a wonderful man. His son Tzvi currently officiates as a rabbi in Miami Beach, which is in the United States. The *Dayan*, may his memory be for a blessing, Reb Azriel Zelig, frequently taught us lessons in *Gemara* and *Tosafot* in the Great Study House. In the days of summer, towards evening, we strolled through the forests of Augustów. How pleasant it was. I will not forget the chirping of all kinds of birds, and the deep soft grass. The three of us together somewhat resembled "A threefold cord is not quickly broken."[552] In about the year 1924, my friends also came to the land. Mr. Yekutiel studied in the Hebron *Yeshiva*, and Tzvi in the *Mizrachi* seminar in Jerusalem. My friend Tzvi went down to America, and joined his parents, who were there. My father, Reb Dovid Yitzchak, may his memory be for a blessing, was God-fearing, proficient in the *Tanakh*, and a "*baal koreh*." He fulfilled the verse: "This book of the *Torah* shall not depart out of your mouth."[553] His brother, Reb Moshe the baker, was devoted to observing the *mitzvot*, and was as careful with the light commandments as he was with the serious ones. There remains engraved in my memory an event that happened at the time of the First World War, when the Germans controlled Augustów. At that time, there was a tremendous shortage of food. By chance, the Germans brought a large basket of bottles of rum (schnapps) to Reb Moshe, and other kinds of food, just before the *Pesach* festival. Reb Moshe bought from them, but didn't have time to sell them before the festival. He went to the rabbi to ask if it would be permitted to use the *chametz* after the festival. The rabbi, of course, prohibited him from using food over which *Pesach* had passed.[554] Then Reb Moshe, may his memory be for a blessing, on the intermediate days of the festival took the bottles of rum out and smashed them all on a big rock, and the rest of the food he burned. Reb Moshe the baker was killed in the Holocaust, together with all of the rest of the members of his family. May God avenge their blood.

I remember the festivals from the days of my youth that the Russians held on the birthday of the King, or the Queen, or the Prince, in the large square facing the church. The Cossacks and the Russian soldiers, the men of the band and the officers all dressed in their ceremonial clothing, held fine parades, accompanied by the band and the priests all dressed in their priestly robes. These

---

[547] It is highly likely that there is a typographical error here, resulting in exactly the opposite of what seems to have been intended. What is written, בל מרץ "bal meretz," means "lacking energy," while the writer seems to have intended בעל מרץ "ba'al meretz," having energy, or energetic. It is an omission of a single letter ayin.

[548] Here the phrase discussed in the previous note is spelled correctly.

[549] A rabbinical judge.

[550] The prayer leader.

[551] A *Torah* reader in liturgical contexts.

[552] Ecclesiastes 4:12

[553] Joshua 1:8

[554] Which had been in a Jew's possession over *Pesach*. *Mishnah Pesachim* 2:2 "*Chametz* which belongs to a gentile over which *Pesach* has passed is permitted for benefit; But that of an Israelite is forbidden for benefit, as it is said, "No leavened bread shall be found with you."

festivals left a strong impression on the school children who had been freed from their studies. The Jews would also hold a celebration, in this instance, in the *Beit Midrash*. There were {p. 166} two Russian flags hung at the entrance, and Chazzan Ratner with the choir sang "God Will Protect the King" and "The One Who Gives Salvation to Kings,"[555] and at the end the Russian anthem.

There Was...
by Leah Sherman

A small town surrounded by forests and lakes was Augustów. Because of its natural beauty, many tourists and summer vacationers came in the summer, to rest in the shade of its thick forests, or to enjoy boating on its lakes. More than half its population was Jewish. Some of them were wealthy. The youth were talented and enthusiastic. In the city there was, however, no high school, but many nevertheless continued their education by various means. In the city, there were courses for Hebrew in which a large part of the young people studied. Others studied with teachers in private lessons, and there were those who travelled to larger cities in order to study in high schools and professional schools. Only a few continued their studies in schools of higher learning. The youth were mostly Zionist, and did wonderful things for the *Keren Kayemet*,[556] *Keren HaYesod*, and the *Kapai*: *Kupah L'Poalei Eretz Yisrael*,[557] etc. The pioneering youth movements (*HeChalutz*, *HeChalutz HaDati*,[558] *HeChalutz HaTzair*,[559] and *HaShomer HaTza'ir*),[560] were well-organized with many members. In their clubs, diverse cultural activity was conducted. At the initiative of Sheima Zak (the husband of Rachel Yevreiski, may God avenge her blood), the *Maccabi* sports association was created, "In a healthy body, a healthy soul" was its motto. Sheima Zak devoted himself to this activity heart and soul, and succeeded in gathering around himself many of the young people who trained in the evenings on gymnastic equipment and in other sports areas. Over the course of time, the members of the association demonstrated their achievements to the public at sports evenings. The success was tremendous. A drama group and a chorus were also organized, and they too gathered many young people. They appeared in presentations and reaped much applause. The activities in the various associations filled the youths' free time, and gave flavor to their lives. The evenings, the Shabbatot and the festivals were full of interest. In the clubs, it was warm and good, but outside an entirely different atmosphere prevailed. Anti-Semitism was increasing; the lack of any chance for Jewish youth to integrate into the economic life of the exile grew from year to year. Most of the youth saw their future in the Land of Israel. Indeed, each year tens of pioneers went up to the land. They were absorbed into the country in various areas of life, and brought forth children and children's children. The great sadness that many, a great many, were unable to realize their soul's desire.

---

[555] Psalm 144:10 "to You who give victory to kings, who rescue His servant David from the deadly sword..."
[556] Short for *Keren Kayemet L'Yisrael*, the Jewish National Fund.
[557] The Fund for the Workers of the Land of Israel
[558] The Religious Pioneer.
[559] The Young Pioneer.
[560] The Young Guard.

{p. 168} **The Party of the Founding of the Maccabi Branch**

The Members of the Maccabi Branch with Their Guide Sh. Zak

The Soccer Group

Standing from right to left: R. Tsherman, Sh. Plotzinski, D. Linda (Aloni), A. Leizerovitz.
Second row: A. Chalupitzki, Ch. Kestin, Moshe Goldshmidt, Channah Goldstein, B. Sherman.

{p. 170} **Fathers and Sons**
by Daniel Kaplan, Kfar Saba

Augustów. A Jewish community that, in spite of all the difficulties, continued its existence and traditional customs. A lively Jewish town with *kloizim*, study houses, schools and institutions of benevolence and *tzedakah* in it. The non-Jewish residents of the surrounding villages also accorded it respect.

The most difficult day of the week was Friday. It was as if Satan himself had ordained it to be the market day in order to test the Jews. On that day the work was much greater than on a regular day; preparations for *Shabbat* and attention to customers out of precision about the closing the doors of the shops before the entrance of *Shabbat*. For me, who was still a youth, this was the most interesting day of all the days of the week. Father hurried the village shoppers while I peered outside. When I saw the city's *Dayan* striding past with his head held high, his yellowish beard, parted and well-kept for years, descending on his shining, long black silk caftan, all of him bespeaking respect, I knew that the time had arrived to greet *Shabbat*, the Queen.[561]

Inside the house, a white tablecloth was spread on the long table. My sister Sarah was setting the table tastefully and quickly. Mother was waving her hands three times over the lighted

---

[561] Babylonian *Talmud Bava Kamma* 32b "Come and go out to greet the bride, the queen. And some say: To greet the Sabbath, the bride, the queen. R. Yannai would cover himself and say Come, bride; come, bride."

candlesticks and blessing in a whisper. Only her lips were moving. The number of candles - as the number of children. This was her custom, that she inherited from her mother. Two large *challot*[562] were ready for the father and grandfather, and a small one for each child. This was mother's handiwork, to be proud of. After the prayers that welcomed *Shabbat*, when we returned from the *kloiz* that was on Bridge Street, sometimes with a guest, Father and Grandfather would open with "*Eshet Chayil Mi Yimtzah*"[563] and we would all repeat[564] loudly after them, singing in a chorus of appreciation to Mother. Grandmother would add her low hoarse voice, casting glances of joy and happiness at us. The set table and the home testified that Mother was an "*Eshet Chayil*," and everything in it said "*Shabbat*." She began the preparations for *Shabbat* early on Thursday morning, when she lit the baking oven. Afterwards she would knead the dough and shape it for baking. She put in it the spirit of her soul. The next day she would be busy preparing the cooked dishes for *Shabbat*. This was not easy work, but Mother found satisfaction in it, because the sanctification of the *Shabbat* was embedded in her. The *Shabbat* day was a day of complete rest – "even the Sambatyon rests on *Shabbat*"[565] Mother used to say.

*

{p. 171} "*Lange Strass*" was its name[566] – the long street. On its two sides, old houses, in which dwelt Jews toiling away to make their living that they received as their inheritance. The generation that was going also transmitted a spiritual heritage to the generation that was coming after it. The tradition of ancestors and the hope for redemption. Our house stood at the beginning of the street. Not far from it on a broad lot stood the Christian church, which was prominent with its pointed spire and cross. At the times when the bells rang and the melodies of the choir were accompanied by the organ, it would spill outside. Then the music of Israel and Hebrew songs would burst out from Father's house. It was not in Satan's power to confuse us. All the members of the household would join in the songs of the grandfather and the father, from the youngest to the oldest, in order to overcome the sounds from outside. Sometimes the sounds would mix together. It seemed as if they were blending together with the ringing of the bells. Together they seemed to be levelling a path to the heavens. Occasionally the songs of Israel grew stronger and won. The bells ceased their monotonous ringing and the organ music faded and grew quiet. In the house, we sat around the long set table, and continued to sing chants, praising and glorifying the Creator of the universe.

When our uncle asked to sell the half of the house that belonged to him, my mother did not want to reconcile herself to it. She begged that her brother would not do injustice to those who sleep in the dust.[567] "One does not sell the inheritance of ancestors, unless one needs the money to go up to the lands of the ancestors" Mother said. Father was active in the Zionist organization. The blue box of *Keren Kayemet L'Yisrael* was fixed to the wall, next to the *mezuzah*[568] at the main entrance, to the house so that the gentiles would see it and know that our eyes were set on our homeland.

---

[562] The special braided loaves traditionally used on *Shabbat*.

[563] Proverbs 31:10-29. "A capable woman, who can find?..."

[564] There seems to be a typographical error here. The word printed is מחרים macharim, which means "ban." The apparently intended word is מחזרים, which in this context means "repeat." This is a difference of one letter.

[565] Babylonian *Talmud Sanhedrin* 65b:12 "Rabbi Akiva said to him: The Sabbatyon River can prove that today is *Shabbat*, as it is calm only on *Shabbat*."

[566] 1 Samuel 25:25 "Please, my lord, pay no attention to that worthless fellow Nabal. For he is as his name: His name is fool and he is a fool..."

[567] Isaiah 26:19 "...Awake and shout for joy, You who dwell in the dust!..."

[568] A parchment affixed to the doorpost of a Jewish home in fulfillment of the commandment to affix the words contained on it to the doorpost of one's house, as instructed in Deuteronomy 6:4–9 and 11:13–21.

179

Grandfather Naftali-Hertz and Grandmother Rivka were old when they merited to receive the demand from their household to go up to the land. All the worshippers of the *kloiz* accompanied them to the railroad station. At home the joy was mixed with a little sorrow that we were unable to join them. We consoled ourselves with the thought that they were clearing the path for us. With the emigration of the elders, the singing became quieter at home. The void was filled with stormy debate among the children, who met at the table with their different outlooks and opinions.

Dovid Hillel, the oldest in the company, was an industrious man. He had a carpentry shop. One of his duties was to teach the trade to those were preparing to go up to the land. He was one of the sustainers of the house, in spite of the fact that he was disqualified from going up by the Mandatory government, because of his disabled hand from a shrapnel injury during the First World War, when he was still a youth. Despite this he continued to train himself to be ready to go up. I was already in a training *kibbutz*, and when I would come home for a break, I would heatedly defend the path I had chosen for myself. And Shabtai, who worked energetically in the branch of *Hashomer HaTzair,* was resolute in his opinion that that was the way to educate and train the young generation.

Thus, we sat at the table and argued. Each one trying to defend the 150 different reasons for the path of the framework to which he belonged. At the head of the table sat Father. It is doubtful if he derived pleasure. With his common sense, he did not understand why we were so divided by arguments when all of our goals were one and the same.

After the gates of the land had been closed for a long period, I at last received a certificate, together with {p. 172} my friends in my training group "*Shachariah* A." To be among the first in the Fifth *Aliyah*[569] was no easy thing. Many waited for a certificate and the number who merited one was small. I passed the physical examination at the sawmills in Nurzec and Dombrova. The cultural examination certainly did not bother me.

On *Shabbat* night, I hurried to leave the table at Father's house. Unusually, I passed up the arguments in the family group. I could not find peace in my soul. I went to the *HeChalutz* club. The large room that was on the top floor on Krakowska Street was full of youth and young adults. Here, they received their education and training from a spiritual perspective – the attention and encouragement for the continuation of the journey. *Shabbat* evenings were dedicated to singing and dancing. In the room girls and boys stood with their arms interlocked. Circles, circles. They reached as far as the stairs. Fania, slim of body and fair-haired, and dark-skinned Breintsa – the two of them demonstrated a new dance that they had learned at a *HeChalutz* seminar. G. Zaklikovski – with a round face, and his broad smile, examining and checking the movement of the feet, to make sure they were in time with the pioneer song. The song conquers the hearts and takes over them all. "On the rock! Strike! Strike![570] The arms intermingle and the couples are entwined, arms interlocked on shoulders, all in one movement, as if they were one body. Slowly, voices became hoarse and fell silent. Midnight. In the empty street the song still reverberated: "Free, a Free Palestine!"[571]

It was like a farewell party from my friends. The day following *Shabbat*, I was to go out on the journey.

The course was difficult, full of suffering and tribulations until we reached the land. But greater was the longing for redemption that our ancestors had bequeathed us. Therefore, borders did not frighten us, and prisons did not deter us.

---

[569] The Fifth *Aliyah* was the fifth wave of Jewish immigration to Palestine from Europe and Asia in 1929-1939.
[570] "On the rock, strike, strike!" An early Zionist song based on the Jewish prayer for rain.
[571] "Frei," Yiddish for "free."

*

The house remained standing on its foundation – so we were told by rescued embers.[572] Not one shell struck it during the First World War also, when the Germans' shells fell in the center of the city and cut short the lives of two family members. Even the flames that occasionally visited the city passed over us. Was it because of the merit of the songs for *Shabbat* and festivals that its walls had absorbed? Even after the great destruction, the house remained standing, bereaved and abandoned. Its rooms were bereaved; its walls wept. The church bells continued to ring, the organ continued to accompany the ringing, but from the Jewish house the song no longer emerged. The voice of Yaakov was silenced. The community of Augustów was destroyed, with the rest of the communities of Israel in Poland.

{p. 173} From the Days of My Childhood
by Chaim ben Abba Orimland

My cradle did not truly stand in Augustow, but I was connected to it from the age of two years, a time that my father settled in it and registered all of the family in the books of the municipality.

In the year 1917, when I was six, I began to learn in a school for boys called "Compulsory School."[573]* The teachers and the students were all Jews, but the supervision was in the hands of the German "Inspector."[574]**

It is not in my ability to judge whether the nature of the school and its educational method were good or bad. What is engraved in my memory and left a deep cut in my soul, are the blows that we absorbed from the hands of the educators. The blows were an inseparable part of the method of learning. They were given arbitrarily, without a thorough examination, or because of inconsequential matters. If you switched, God forbid, a "*kamatz*" for a "*patach*,"[575] or you made a mistake on the multiplication table, you deserved to be punished. What is written is not talking about just blows, but heavy punches that rained down on you without pause. The teacher's rod did not know mercy. More than once the child would be punished by absorbing 25 lashes. That was enough to prevent the child from his sitting in the regular way for a few days... We consulted how to get over the punishment of the rod, and discovered that spreading garlic on it hastened its end. So we did. How great was our joy when at the first blow, the rod broke. We breathed a sigh of relief, but the respite was brief.

Fine writing – "calligraphy" – was considered an important subject. The student that excelled in fine handwriting would move from his bench to the one behind it. And when he reached perfection he would sit on the last bench. Then the teacher would tear out the page from his notebook and hang it up to be seen in the classroom window, in order that "they will see it and take pleasure."

---

[572] Survivors.
[573] In Yiddish, צוואנגס שולע Tzvengas Shule. Original note: * A compulsory school. That is to say, a free compulsory school.
[574] ** Supervisor.
[575] Two Hebrew vowels.

181

I must point out that in addition to secular mandatory learning in the German school, our fathers were concerned that we learn *Torah* and general Jewish studies in the afternoon. There arise before my eyes the spirits of Fridays, the time when I reviewed the weekly *Torah* portion. Frequently my father, may his memory be for a blessing, would also be present, and drew pleasure from my reading. When I would turn the last page in the *Chumash*, I would find a mark.[576]*** "This is a gift of the angel for your diligence" the teacher would explain.

{p. 174} The year 1918. The period between the times. Chaos.[577] One authority is leaving and a second authority is coming. An army comes and an army goes. We benefit from the abandonment. We are wandering around without *Torah* and without work. Left to ourselves, without supervision. When order was reinstated, I found myself in the "*cheder*" of the teacher M. Meizler. A long table and benches on its two sides on which the students are gathered around. It is possible to point out that the easing nightmare indeed has passed by, but in its place appears a bitter enemy of a new kind, which is not inferior to the first. In place of the rod of tyrants, the fist of the *Rebbe*.

The year 1919. I am in the improved school that is on "*Shul* Street" (the street of the synagogue). In this school[578] they also learned, in addition to sacred studies, Russian and German.

This educational institution excelled in its improved arrangements in discipline and in the high level of studies. The organization was in the hands of the administration of the congregation.

I remember the day of the completion of the year of studies, when I received a certificate of completion, a source of pride. At its top was displayed the year "crown," which was 5679.[579] It was signed by the teachers of the institution and at their head the Rabbi of the community, Azriel Zelig Koshelevski, may his memory be for a blessing.

The year 1920. The days of Polish rule. A school opened under the administration of the teacher D. Boyarski, and I am a student in this institution. It is possible to point out that this school was already modern, but the punishment of blows had not yet passed from the world. The "sinner" himself was obligated to bring the rod from the Director's room. After he had absorbed a blow by hand as required, he had to say "thank you" and return the rod to its place. The insult was bigger than the pain of the blow. I continued my learning over the course of two "times," in the *talmud torah*, and I finished them in a Polish elementary school, which had seven classes. This was a school of "compulsory learning." Jews and Poles learned in it together. Here we suffered – from the hatred of Israel.[580] Our friends the "*shkotzim*"[581] harassed us because of our being Jews, and because we surpassed them in our knowledge and ability.

There is certainly in this short survey a kind of mirror to the ways of learning and the methods of education in days gone by.

These memories from that time are precious to me.

---

[576] Original note: *** German paper currency.

[577] The Hebrew phrase "*tohu va'vohu*," the untranslatable phrase used at the beginning of the *Torah*. Genesis 1:2 "the earth being unformed and void…"

[578] Aramaic: בית אולפנא "Beit Ulpana."

[579] The letters that indicate the Hebrew year, תרע"ט, are an anagram for the Hebrew word עטרת "crown."

[580] The Jews.

[581] Non-Jews. The Hebrew word "*sheketz*" means "abomination," and is found in Leviticus 11:13: "The following you shall abominate among the birds—they shall not be eaten, they are an abomination…" It comes into Yiddish as the word "*shaygetz*," used to refer to a non-Jewish man. The female equivalent is "*shiksa*." These words are highly offensive epithets for non-Jews.

Between War and War
by Yishayahu Livni (Bialovitzki)

I remember, the thing was in 1915. I was then a boy of about 5. There was war between the Germans and the Russians at that time. The Germans surrounded our city and attempted to conquer it. Our house was in "Long Street," near the Christian church, which at that time also served as the place of the seat of the Russian command. I remember well the bombs that the Germans dropped on the city. We lay in the basement of our house, and we were subject to great danger. In order to create bedlam and sow panic amongst the residents, the Germans lit the forests surrounding the city on fire. And indeed, they accomplished their goal, making it easier for themselves in conquering the city. The residents began to flee in every possible direction in their attempt to save their lives, some by foot and some on wagons. The bridge over the canal in the direction of Grodno was destroyed, and those fleeing had to make their way by foot. In that same hour the Germans entered the city from the direction of Grayevo. They put up a power station to provide electric current to the city, and opened schools. In 1918 the Germans were expelled by the Poles, who liberated it from the foreign yoke. The maturing youth that was abandoned over the course of a long period now began to plan its life anew. The Jewish community placed its concern for the youth at the head of its activity, and established a Hebrew school, and a "*talmud torah*." The Polish government also established a primary school, in which the children of the Jews and the children of the gentiles learned together. Antisemitism was felt in the school in full force. We suffered greatly. With great difficulty, the community council obtained the arrangement that we would not learn on *Shabbat*. The children who learned in the mixed school visited the *talmud torah* in the afternoon hours, or went to teachers for private lessons, in order to acquire Jewish studies. Antisemitism planted in us the recognition and the thought that our place was in the land of Israel. The youth began to organize in Zionist organizations. "*HeChalutz HaTzair*" had crucial influence in the cultural life of the city. "*HeChalutz Hatzair*" also trained its members in agricultural work, in the vegetable garden that we rented from the Sheintzeit family on the "Long Street." Members of "*HeChalutz HaTzair*" also excelled in the area of sports, and organized a football[582] group. The tremendous activity of the members of our city in all areas highlighted them for good in the life of the Jews of Poland until the last days of their existence.

{p. 176} *Talmud Torah* (1920-1940)
by Elchanan Sarvianski

The "*talmud torah*" building stood on Koprinika Street. This was a religious school, in which almost all of the youth of the city acquired their primary education.

Reb Efraim Wolf officiated in the role of administrator and teacher of *Torah* and *Gemara*. The teacher of Hebrew and history was the teacher Reb Yehoshua Bergstein. The Hebrew teachers in the first grades were Yisrael Yismachovitz and A. Levinson. The teacher for Polish, arithmetic, history and Polish geography was Zilber. In the last years, Wasserman also served as a teacher. In

---

[582] Soccer.

the general Polish school, Dina Soloveitchik and Kupler taught. Of all of these teachers not even one remains. May their memory be blessed!

One Day in the *"Talmud Torah"*

The bell rings. The hour is exactly 8:00 in the morning. The children enter the classroom and seat themselves on the benches, each one in his place. The teacher Yehoshua Bergstein enters the classroom, and immediately silence prevails. With quick hands he opens the journal, and calls the names of the students in Class D alphabetically: Borovitz, Zelig; Brenner, Barukh; Vilovski, Yekutiel; Zlotnizki, Tzvi; Lazdeiski, Chaim; Morzinksi, Ezra; Sarvianski, Elchanan; Pozniak, Tzvi; Kolfenitzki, Pesach; Rozenfeld, Shlomo; and more. When the teacher was convinced that they were all present, he directed that we take out from our satchels the book *"Korot HaIvrim"*[583] part 2 by S. Dubnow. Among the students there were always those who disturbed at the time of the lessons; they fooled around, told jokes, or drew various and sundry pictures. The sharp eye of the teacher fell on the student who was playing. He would command the student to rise, and to tell what was being spoken of in the classroom. Of course, he did not know. The teacher would eject him, in this instance, outside, pull his ear, or strike the student on the palm with a thick wooden yardstick.

With the ring of the bell the students would run outside like crazy people. After the break, they return to the classroom and the teacher Zilberg enters. He was a feeble and hunchbacked man, but an exceptional teacher. He taught Polish language and history, arithmetic and geography, all in the Polish language. And it happened that if the lessons were not interesting, the students would fool around, because they had no fear of the weak teacher. When the ringing of the bell was heard, redemption came for the students and the teacher.

The hours went by. The sixth and last lesson: *Torah*. The teacher Efraim Wolf entered the classroom. A hush was cast in the room. At the time of the lesson it was possible to hear the buzzing of the flies {p. 177} in their flight. With the completion of this lesson, the students packed their rucksacks, put on their coats, and went to their homes, in order to return to the school after two or three hours to learn *Gemara* for two hours, from the teacher Reb Efraim Wolf.

"Tiferet Bachurim"[584]

In Augustow there also existed a group *"Tiferet Bachurim,"* which included religious young men who were members of the religious Zionist party *"HaMizrachi,"* or inclined towards it in their views. They numbered a few *minyanim*,[585] and made a place for themselves at the house of the Rabbi the *Dayan* Reb Azriel Zelig Koshelevski, on Krakovska Street (Zoyb Street), and afterwards, in a more spacious apartment, as the rabbi's family had moved to live in the new building of the baker Brizman. Rabbi Azriel Zelig Noach Koshelevski founded the group, and his son, the deceased Rabbi Reb Yisrael, was the living spirit in it until his death.

The young men of *"Tiferet Bachurim"* routinely prayed in the rabbi's house. A few of them are remembered by me, and I mention them here: Ben-Tzion Filivinsky, Shepsele Bachur-Yeshiva[586] (refugee), Yaakov Blacharski, Aharon Cohen, Yashke Gizumski, Borovski, Moshe Yudke Grodzanz.

---

[583] "The History of the Hebrews," published in Warsaw, 1920.
[584] "The splendor of young men," a rabbinical academy.
[585] Tens.
[586] Literally, *yeshiva* boy.

The *Simchat Torah Hillula*[587] in the Home of the Rabbi

Anyone who did not see *Simchat Torah* in the house of Rabbi Azriel Zelig Koshelevski did not see joy in his days. Already at the end of *Yom HaKippurim*, the members of *"Tiferet Bachurim"* began, with the help of a few of the residents of Augustow, the *mitzvah* of erecting the *sukkah* on the balcony of the rabbi's apartment. All of them worked energetically and diligently, some with a hammer, some with a saw, and some who stuck a nail in their finger.

On *Simchat Torah* there were hundreds of men[588] of the city in the rabbi's house, the householders, and simply poor people who came to gladden their hearts. The long tables, that had white tablecloths on them and simple benches alongside them, were set up one next to another. On the tables there were bowls of peas, fava beans, pickled fish, cucumbers, and all kinds of sweets. There was also brandy, beer, and lemonade; their place was not empty, to fulfill what is written: "wine that gladdens the hearts of men..."[589] Everyone waited for a sign. When the Rabbi took his seat, and next to him his son the mortally ill rabbi, all of the townspeople took their places facing them. The banquet began. The bottles were opened, the lemonade corks flew upward, the brandy was poured into little cups, and the beer, half of it went in cups and half of it onto the white tablecloths. After they enjoyed themselves, they broke into the singing of "purify our hearts,"[590] "*Adon Olam*,"[591] etc. The hands of the clock were moving, and in a little while it was midnight. The old people and the weak ones get up, blessing each other with the blessing "a good year," and a blessing for the happiness of the holiday, part, and go out into the dark night. The perseverers and the young people get up and take the empty dishes off the tables, move the tables to the corners, and lift the benches and the chairs onto their backs. Once they finished their work, they take each other by the hand, and open the *mitzvah* dances.[592] Mouths are opened wide, and the song "Blessed is our God who created us to honor him,"[593] and the like burst out. The feet are lifted up, and the congregation is dancing, dancing, until they tire themselves out. The hands of the clock show the last watch.[594] Quick as a flash they bless each other, each man parts from his friend, and disappear into the dark of night. Soon the dawn will shine.

{p. 178} The Baking of *Matzah*s

Our Sages said: "From the time that *Adar*[595] enters we multiply joy."[596] One of these joys was the baking of the *matzah*s. In our day the matter is simple; we enter the store and we buy packages of *matzah*s. It was not so in those days. Then there were not *matzah*s in the grocery store. Incidentally, their shape too was different: they were not square, but, precisely, round. *Matzah* flour and meal our parents also had to prepare with their own hands.

---

[587] A *Yom Hillula*, day of festivity, is usually another word for *yahrzeit*, the anniversary of a death. It is different from a regular *yahrzeit* in that it refers specifically to the *yahrzeit* of a great *Tzaddik* who taught *Kabbalah* and/or *Chassidism*. Unlike a regular *yahrzeit*, a Yom *Hillula* is commemorated through joy and festive celebration. Here, it seems to refer simply to a celebration which is not connected to a *yahrzeit*.

[588] This was almost certainly an all-male gathering.

[589] Psalm 104:16 "wine that gladdens the hearts of men..."

[590] From *Sefer Chassidim*, The Book of the *Chassidim* 882:1: "Purify our hearts to serve you in truth..."

[591] Lord of the World."

[592] The *mitzvah* dance is generally conducted at a wedding in certain Jewish communities, where the male relatives of the bride dance before her. It is likely that this is done on *Simchat Torah* because of the imagery of the *Torah* as a bride.

[593] From the weekday morning concluding prayers.

[594] Of the night. Exodus 14:24 "At the morning watch, the LORD looked down upon the Egyptian army from a pillar of fire and cloud, and threw the Egyptian army into panic."

[595] The month of *Adar* is the month in which *Purim* falls, and precedes the month of *Nisan*, when *Pesach* occurs.

[596] Babylonian *Talmud Ta'anit* 29a:18

There lived in our city two householders who were not at all bakers, but in their houses they baked the *matzah*s each year. The one – Reb Shimon Eirhohn, a Bialobrega man; and the second, Reb Shimon, a Ratzk man.

And this was the order of the baking of the *matzah*s. About a week after the holiday of *Purim*, the houses of the Shimons filled with men, women, and children who came to roll the dough in order to make it round and thin. When the dough received its correct shape, they transferred it to the perforator who would perforate it with holes with a special wheel that he had in his hand. From him the dough would pass to the oven. After a few minutes they would take the *matzah* out of the oven. One time it would be nice, and one time it would be unimpressive, one time it would be a little burned and one time it would be burned a lot. Everything was dependent on the man who was in charge of the oven, his mood, and his attentiveness. They baked the *matzah*s by families, through mutual assistance between neighbors. When the baking of the *matzah*s was completed, the preparation of *matzah* flour and *matzah* meal would begin. This was difficult handwork. The vessel into which they would put the *matzah*s for the preparation of the flour, was a thick block of wood whose upper part was hollow, and its name was "*stampa*." The second part – it too was a block of wood in a length of about 80 centimeters, and about 25 centimeters thick, round and smooth, and thinner in the middle, fitted to the fingers of the hands. With this block of wood they would forcefully strike the *matzah*s within the "*stampa*," and after some time the *matzah*s would become flour and meal. At the time of the baking of the *matzah*s the joy permeated the house of Reb Shimon Eirhohn. They would sing and tell stories and jokes in order not to fall asleep from exhaustion.

The little children would fall asleep on the beds of the hosts, and would lay that way until the completion of the baking work. They would pack the *matzah*s carefully in special baskets whose height was one meter, awaken the children from their sleep, and with a blessing for happy holiday and a kosher *Pesach*, they would part from each other.

{p. 179} In the Mirror of the Press
Compiled by M. Tzinovitz

An Educational Institution for *Torah* and *Derekh Eretz*[597] in the Year 5624 [1864]

In the Hebrew weekly "*HaCarmel*,"[598] a Hebrew writer who visited in Augustow at that time transmitted to us these words about this interesting phenomenon: "Here too I saw that our brothers the Children of Israel are diligent about doing the will of the government, for while I was walking on the way I turned aside here too to the school which is for the young people of the Children of Israel. Here I saw more than 50 youth sitting and learning the language of Russia. And they turned their backs on the language of Poland, which they and their ancestors had clung to for many years."

The guest mentioned above who visited Augustow and wrote down a gladdening matter like this knows to emphasize that "there is no coercion"[599] by order of the government that the children of the Jews should learn in the school mentioned above. "Only a man, a man according to his desire, sends his sons and his daughters, for their rescue and with all their desire, to follow the government that elevates and seeks good for the peoples that take refuge in its shadow."[600]

---

[597] Literally "the way of the world" this phrase refers to the desired manner of behavior. *Pirke Avot* 3:17 "Rabbi Elazar ben Azariah said: Where there is no *Torah*, there is no right conduct; where there is no right conduct, there is no *Torah*.
[598] Published weekly 1860–1871, and monthly 1871–1880, in Hebrew and Russian, in Vilna, Tsarist Russia.
[599] Esther 1:8 "And the rule for the drinking was, "No compulsion!" For the king had given orders to every palace steward to comply with each man's wishes."
[600] Isaiah 30:2 "To seek refuge with Pharaoh, to seek shelter under the shadow [protection] of Egypt."

The correspondent adds that "Levi Yitzchak Finkelstein, the enlightened teacher, does his work faithfully, and in a number of months the students learned to read well and also the beginnings of grammar in the language of Russia."

He concludes with this language: "How wonderful are sights like these in the eyes of every man who loves his people Israel with eternal love. All the cities around will see, and will hear, teaching themselves to also do this, and their teachers will educate them to draw the hearts of the fathers and the children to hear his lesson."

On the situation of education and the enlightenment in Augustow a number of years after this, the Hebrew local writer Y. Z. Sperling informs us in the Hebrew weekly "*HaMelitz*" from the year 1879 (No. 43) under the pseudonym "Wonderful:" "There are 35 teachers in the city. Of them, two teachers who teach the "translation" of the *Torah* established by Moses Mendelssohn, and these teachers also teach the principles of grammar and interpretation. But these two teachers only have a few students, and they do not earn enough wages to support their households, and the rest learn in the 33 "other *cheders*."

Sperling complains in his article about the local *Av Beit Din* (the intention is to the *Gaon* Rabbi Katriel Natan) who in his homily on *Shabbat Shuvah*[601] 5640 [1880] aggressively rebuked some of the youth from among the children of the congregation, who read Hebrew books by the enlightened Hebrew writers, which are full of heresy, and preached against the study of *Chumash* with the translation mentioned above, and grammar, and also against learning in the gymnasia of Christians. And he attacked those who wear short attire and dance with young women.

{p. 180} The Burial of a Donkey

The writer Sperling informs us about an interesting matter that happened in Augustow in those days: "An event of an 18-year-old young man, Z. Finkelstein, and he writes on behalf of the Secretary of the House of the Justice of the Peace, and he died. For the religious, this was a festival, and they drank and made merry and they buried him in the grave of a donkey." And the reason for this: "He resided in Berlin for a few years, and knew German and Russian, and the work of the "*tzigaren*,"[602] and because of that he did not fulfill the *mitzvot*, and his brother visited in the *Beit Midrash* of the Scientists in Peterburg. The youth of the new generation stood on guard, so as not to humiliate him further."

The correspondent adds: "And what is painful is that he, the Rabbi, reads many external[603] books, and even on *Shabbat* before the prayers, in order to be instructed by them, and nevertheless he conducts his rabbinate at this level, and pursues the enlightened ones." **"*HaMelitz*," 1879**

"Augustow – The First to Affix Boxes for the Purpose of Collecting Donations for the Settlement of the Land of Israel"

"It is about nine moons[604] since the members of our community here attempted to form an association by the name of "*Dorshei Tzion*," to the regret of its administrators, who administered with difficulty, and the participants in it were not many. However, in those days after the death of Moshe the servant of God, may his soul be in Eden, (the intention here is to Sir Moses Montefiore, our righteous savior) the administrators saw that the death of this Shepherd of Israel, may the memory of the righteous be for a blessing, was very dear in the eyes of the members of our community. They refused to be consoled after the crown of their heads had been removed. They attempted to create collection boxes from sheets of tin (tin boxes); the boxes were made in a cube

---

[601] The *Shabbat* of Repentance, which is the *Shabbat* between *Rosh HaShanah* and *Yom Kippur*.
[602] Russian for cigarettes.
[603] Secular.
[604] Months.

shape, in order to distinguish them from the boxes of Reb Meir Ba'al HaNes.[605] Therefore they glued on labels with the seal of the association, and beneath the seal the inscription "As a memorial for Reb Moshe Montefiore, may the memory of the righteous be for a blessing." Not many days went by and the boxes were distributed in almost all the houses of our brothers the Children of Israel here, who received us extremely hospitably, until many came themselves to the house of the association's administrators with a request to give them boxes too. The writer of the article, who is signed "YZ"S" (is he not Yosef Ze'ev Sperling), concludes his words with these enthusiastic words: "From now there is hope that our respected association will establish itself with God's will (with the permission of the government) on a strong foundation and teach us to know that all the community of Israel will easily be able to do this, and redemption will grow from it.

"HaMelitz" the year 1885, No. 68

Kosher Food for Jewish Soldiers Who Are in the Military Camp in Augustow

"Yosef Tzvi Kantrovitz from Aihumen (Minsk District, Military Police) gives his thanks and blessings in the name of the 44 men that worked in Augustow in the Reserve Forces, to the Righteous Dayan by the name of the Rabbi the Gaon Eliezer Shapira, *Shlit'a* [606] and to his son Zalman Tzvi and the rest of the youths in our city that attempted to feed us good kosher food over the course of two weeks. They made this effort on our behalf before the officers of the army, to gain permission for us to cook kosher dishes in our city in the place of military stations that were four parsangs[607] away from the city, and gained us permission to eat in the city, and each and every day they made the effort to come every single morning, and prepared for us good dishes with meat for the noon hour of the day, and they themselves served us the food, {p. 181} like guest house servants, and they restored our souls with this. A blessing from us to those who labored on our behalf in this, that they should be sated with every good. *"HaYom"*[608] (the year 1886), a **Hebrew newspaper that appeared in Peterburg, edited by Dr. L. Kantor.**

The Beginnings of the Library

Yisrael Dov Varhaftig informs from Augustow that in recent days the desire has awakened among the enlightened of the city to learn the language of *Ever* and to make it beloved among all men of letters, and that recently a few enlightened ones from among the youth awakened to found a Hebrew book collection house and also their hands were stretched out to collect in this house every book that touches on questions of the Jews, and also in the German and Russian languages.

"HaMelitz" the year 5650 (1890) No. 154

In *"HaTzefirah"* 1894 (No. 163) Mr. Yam writes in the name of the people of the community of Augustow on the matter of "the excellent doctor Dr. Goldberg who, over the course of 5 years that he dwelt in this city won for himself the love of all the hearts of the city, but who because of the reduction of the number of residents of the city due to the many who are going out to the new land, is said to seek for himself a wide range of activities, and a place more prepared for the work and activity in skilled healing."

The correspondent mentioned above adds that "although our city is not a widow, she is now bereft of doctors. Nevertheless, the notables of the city will remember the name of Dr. Goldberg with longing.[609] Also the heart of the mass of the people followed after him, and his memory is in their mouths for a blessing, because in addition to his being generous and

---

[605] Rabbi Meir Baal HaNes (Rabbi Meir the miracle maker) was a Jewish sage who lived in the time of the *Mishnah*. Various charitable foundations have been named for him.

[606] An acronym for "May he live a good long life, amen."

[607] A parasang is about four miles.

[608] "Today."

[609] Isaiah 26:8 "…We long for the name by which You are called."

participating in the troubles of others, he was amazing at bringing relief[610] to the sick and the wounded, and infected; to these as well, that other doctors said "it is no use"[611] to their illness, and were unable to heal the sores."[612]

A Teacher From Augustow Opens a School in Lomza

In "*HaMelitz*" 1895 (68), P. N. Katz from Lomza informs that the respected pedagogue Mr. Issachar Levinski from Augustow opened a school near them, "happy and hoping from the government for the youth of our brothers who dwell in the city to guide them in the pastures of the *Torah*, knowledge, understanding, and faith on a straight path. And in addition to the students hearing a lesson in God's *Torah*, according to the rules of its language and its grammar, they will also learn there the Russian and German languages, knowledge of accounting, the regions of the land, and the chronicles of the Children of Israel. This school in its founding caused great and awesome noise, and the zealous ones among the teachers and those who hold fast to their hands threw excessive fear on its founding, for they struck it with a tongue lashing, and also attempted to send lampoons to the officials of our city, but it was not at all effective, and now they will admit against their will that there is a blessing in it.

*

A list of the donations that were gathered in Augustow from the *Yom Kippur* eve collection bowl for the settlement of the land of Israel in the year 5659 (1898). In sum, 10.7 rubles; gathered from the worshippers in the synagogue, in the *kloiz* {p. 182} of the street of the butcher shop, in the *kloiz* of Bridge Street, and in the *kloiz* of the Long Street. On *Simchat Torah* the following donated for the good of the settlement of the land of Israel: Reb Arieh Glikstein, 2.70 rubles; Avraham Meir Zenevoski, 3 – (to plant a tree in "Gan Shmuel");[613] Nachum Zechariah Levin, 3; A. Girfalovitz, 3.24; Eisenstadt, Noach, 1.50; Ze'ev Glikzohn, Akiva Glukstein, Yaakov Voisanski, , Avraham Treves, Yechezkel Koptziovski, 1 ruble each; Meir Grosberg, 95 kopek; Yosef Glikzohn, 50 kopek; Reb Barukh Leib Gotstein, 1 ruble; Chaikel Palman, 1.50; Meir Ezra Lerman, 2 rubles; Chaim Shlomo Lap, Avraham Yitzchak Slomon, 1 ruble each; Chaikel Omburg, Chaim Eilender, Beker, Yechezkel Rotenberg, Shmerl Rotenberg, Yehoshua Meltzer, Avraham Barukh Cohen, 50 kopeks each. Avraham Yitzchak Kaplan, 30 kopeks; Nachum Barglovski, Ziskind Preisman, Yaakov Friedkovski, 25 kopeks each.

At the wedding feast of Mr. Shaul Eliezer Lozman with his *beshert*,[614] there were collected among the invited guests 8.82 rubles. And these are the donors: The groom and the bride, Ze'ev, Chaim, Yisrael Yaakov Elchanan, Mendel – of the house of Lozman. Chaim Dov Borovski, the father of the bride, Levatinski Yehuda, Neta Borovski, Tenenboim, Novodvorski, Avraham Smolinski, the mother of the groom - Rayzel, Lozman, Avraham Meir Zanovski, Yeshayah Hershovitz, the maiden Henya Channah Lozman, the brother of the groom, Bidek Tzvi. In sum, 55 rubles. They transferred all the funds mentioned above to the Palestinian Council in Odessa, Moshe Yitzchak Revel, Aharon Platnovski, Chaim Lap, and Binyamin Markus.

"*HaMelitz*," the year 1898, Issue 253

---

[610] Jeremiah 33:6 "I am going to bring her relief and healing…."
[611] Jeremiah 18:12 "But they will say, "It is no use…"
[612] Hosea 5:13 "Yet when Efraim became aware of his sickness, Judah of his sores, Efraim repaired to Assyria— He sent envoys to a patron king! He will never be able to cure you, will not heal you of your sores."
[613] The settlement of Hadera was founded in the land of Israel 1891. In 1895 the settlers there planted a small orchard, which was named "*Gan Shmuel*" - Shmuel's Garden, to commemorate the name of their leader, Rabbi Shmuel Mohilever (1824-1898).
[614] Daughter of destiny.

In *HaTzefirah* 1899 (No. 228), information is brought about the death of the exalted master, the respected merchant, the doer of *tzedakah*, a man of lofty attributes and a compassionate soul, the religious and God-fearing and trembling at the word of God, Reb Dovid Bialystotzki. He was born in the city of Augustow in the year 5598 [1836] and was gathered to his people[615] on 11 Elul 5659 [1899], in the city of Bod-Zaltzvronin (Shalzien). Attached to this information is a long lament styled in rhyme that describe the magnitude of his importance and the blessed activities of the deceased.

*

The Zionists in Augustow, in the year 1900, collected more than 30 rubles for those affected by the famine in Bessarabia. The contributors: Slutzky, Z.L. Koptziovski, Y. Cohen, Y. Stalovski, Ch. Mintz, M. Erbstein, N.Z. Levin, Binyamin Lap, Moshe Glikstein, D.M. Markus, Arieh Lap, V. Grosberg, M. Feinstein, A. Friedberg, Dr. Zelkin, D. Folifovski, T. Burak, Tz. Denmark, Sima Levin, Sternfeld, L. Levita, M. Lozman, Arieh Demeratski, Alter Demeratski, Demeratski, A. Greenvald, G Shumski, Y.G. . Glikstein, L. Avraham Shiff, Rivka Visansky, Sh. Glazer, M. Ch. Glikzohn, Y. Glikzohn, A. V. Solomon, Z. Stein, Y. Meizler, D. Glikzohn, Yanus, A. Davidovitz, M. Meizler, A. Denmark, VV. Aleksandrovitz, Mordechai Bidek, N. Rechtman, A.V. Postvaleski, R. Rotenbeg, Tenenboim, Zanovski, Y. Borovitz, Shayna Borovitz, D. Wolf, M. Freidman, Y. Shapira, Y. Frenkel, Margalit, A. Levinzohn, Kantorovitz, Povembrovski, Arech, {p. 183} Y. Gilda, Z.TZ. Glikzohn, A. Friedman, Ch. Glikzohn, A. Viedenboim, A. Finkelstein, Y. Starazinsky, Sh. Z. Bramzon, Sh. Grinberg, Tz. Borovitz, P. Valovski, A. Levitzky, P. Lifshitz, Cheyne Friedman, D. Levit, Shachne Ampel, A.M. Sigalovitz, G. Blacharski, Liubel, Shustarski, Kalmanovitz, D. Vichenberg, L. Frenkel, A.Y. Kaplan, A. Kentzuk, Sh. Friedman, V. Broman, Y.M. Levitt, D. Dobowski, Tz. Meltzer, Ostrov, D.Y. Otstein, Z. Milkes, A. Leizerovitz, Ch. Liftzianski, Y. Glikstein, N. Vinitzki, Sh.Y. Vergman.   **"*HaTzefirah*" the year 1900, Issue 78**

Members of the association "*Bnei Tzion*,"[616] boys age ten and eleven years, collected among them a total of 9.85 rubles for the hungry in Bessarabia, and these are the names of the donors: Eliezer Koptziovski, Yitzchak Varhaftig, Eliezer Grosberg, Yaakov Grosberg, Shimon Leib Varhaftig, Leib Glikzohn, Simcha Visansky, Eliezer Segal, Natan Mintz, Azriel Cohen, Avraham Kantorovitz, Refael Friedman, Ezra Strankovski, Aharon Eliezer Rotenberg, Yitzchak Rotblit, Raza Markus, Raza Frenkel. These youths, when they received an *agora* from their parents to buy sweets, foreswore sweets and dedicated it for the benefit of the hungry.

"*HaTzefirah*" the year 1900, Issue 171

At the wedding party of Yehuda Bialystotzki with Shifra Katz,[617] Shmuel Katz and Avraham Kaplan solicited donations from the wedding guests for the benefit of the workers of the land of Israel.

"*HaMelitz*" the year 1901, No. 218

In "*HaTzefirah*" 1900 (No. 121), Reb Yosef Chaim Ratner, the local *shaliach tzibur*[618] and *shochet u'bodek* of Augustow, informs about "a big fire that broke out on the evening of *Shavuot*, 5660 [1900]" in the town mentioned above. "More than two hundred families emerged from the fire lacking all of their possessions, and did not save anything of all that they had, for the fire took hold suddenly, until an entire section of the city was like a very terrible bonfire, and those

---

[615] Genesis 49:33 "When Jacob finished his instructions to his sons, he drew his feet into the bed and, breathing his last, he was gathered to his people."
[616] Children of Zion.
[617] The name Katz here is spelled כ"ץ, an abbreviation of "*Cohain Tzaddik*," righteous priest.
[618] The "Public Emissary," which is the term for the prayer leader.

that tried to save any of their belongings were burned by the fire and were brought to the hospital with mortal wounds." He informs that "With the help of the officer of the city, honest among men, a council was established to collect donations for the unfortunate ones," and gives a blessing of thanks to "the donors from the cities of Suwalk, Sapotzkin, and Ratzk, who were so kind in their goodness to send for those impacted by the fire a wagon full of food and provisions. The food was distributed to the Jews and Christians with no distinction. The name of heaven[619] will be sanctified (by this), by them.

*

On the 33rd day of the *omer*[620] 5680 (1920), the community council in our city held a wonderful celebration in honor of the San Remo[621] news. In a proclamation that brought out the call to all the institutions in our city and to all of the Hebrew community to come to the synagogue to participate in the celebration. At 11:00 before noon, all the shops were closed, the students of the schools and the Hebrew courses went as a group through the streets of the city to the synagogue, and all the community

{p. 184} **Title page of Augustower Leben**

פרייז 20 גר.   Augustower Łeben

אויגוסטאוויער

לעבען

אונזערע ג   דער ערשטער פרוב.

א פרוב איז געמאכט געוואָרן צו פאַרוואַנדלען לאַנגיאָריגע חלומות און

---

[619] God.

[620] The 49-day period between the beginning of *Pesach* and the festival of Weeks, *Shavuot*. The *omer* is a period of semi-mourning, when no celebrations take place, but the restrictions are lifted for the 33rd day.

[621] The San Remo Conference was held in San Remo, Italy, in April 1920. It was an international meeting held at the end of World War I, and determined the boundaries for territories captured by the Allies. Great Britain, France, Italy, and Japan participated in the conference, with the United States as a neutral observer. At San Remo, the Allies confirmed the pledge contained in the Balfour Declaration, which concerned the establishment of a Jewish national home in Palestine.

after them. There the students sang Hebrew songs and the following gave addresses: the Head of the Zionist Organization, D. Slutzky, Patek, B. Lieberman, B. Markus, D. Boyarski, and Reb Levin, on the value of the day.

After the assembly, the Community Council held a feast in the Zionist hall for the students of the schools and the courses who participated in the celebration. The Council of the *Keren Kayemet L'Yisrael* held a collection of funds that brought in about 5000 marks.[622] Towards evening the boys and girls among the students gathered again and passed in procession in the streets, singing Hebrew songs. When they arrived at the Zionist hall, they sang "The Oath"[623] and "*Hatikvah,*"[624] they read a proclamation of appreciation in honor of our great ones, and dispersed. Then began a festive Zionist assembly that continued until a late hour of the night. On *Isru Chag Shavuot,*[625] our organization held a public meeting in the synagogue for the benefit of "*Keren HaGeulah,*"[626] in which the Rabbi the *Gaon* and the local *Moreh Tzedek* also participated. With warm words from the *bima* they excited the congregation to donate for the benefit of "*Keren HaGeulah.*" On that same night about 4.000 marks were collected, in addition to various objects. Especially the women increased the amount; they took off their jewelry and dedicated it to the "*Keren HaGeulah.*" This correspondent, who signs with the name "Zionist," concludes that "the collection of money for the benefit of "*Keren HaGeulah*" still continues.   *"HaTzefirah"*

{p. 185} The Beginning of the Migration from Augustow to the United States
Even before the 80s of the previous century, from December 25 1869 until the end of June 1870, the following Jews from the city of Augustow traveled by way of Konigsberg, by means of the first council that was organized for the migration of Jews from Russia: H. Horovitz, M. Horovitz, A. Yarmulinski, M. Sinetzki, V.S. Reitman.

Simkhe Lev, Chapters from Jewish History, New York, 1941.
In Augustow, illegal Zionist gatherings were organized in 1903. One such gathering was raided and Sore Markus was sentenced to two weeks in jail. She served the full term of her sentence, according to a report sent by the governor of Suwalki to the ministry of interior affairs.

New Pogroms in Poland
Warsaw - Pogroms were carried out against the Jews of Augustow which is adjacent to Suwalk, and also in Shirbaz. The government claims that the Jewish leaders control the situation and that the pogroms were organized by haters of the government. Minister of the Interior came to Grodno to investigate the situation. The Jewish minister Rotenstreich protested the pogroms in the Sejm council.

Greeting*[627]
By *Khaye Kalinska*
For a long time now our town has been in need of its own tribune, a publication capable of giving expression to our lives and the creations of our town.

---

[622] The mark is a measure of weight mainly for gold and silver, used throughout Western Europe and is generally equivalent to about eight ounces
[623] By Yehoshua H. Pelovitz, 1912. "We swear by Zion's emblem, to rescue our homeless and oppressed people."
[624] Composed by Naftali Herz Imber, 1877. "The Hope." Now the Israeli National Anthem.
[625] The day immediately following each of the three pilgrimage holidays—*Pesach, Shavuot* and *Sukkot*—is called *Isru Chag*, which literally means "bind [the] festival" since the day is "bound" to the holiday. Psalm 118:27 "The LORD is God; He has given us light; bind the festal offering to the horns of the altar with cords."
[626] The Redemption Fund.
[627] On the 24th of February,1939 a once-off publication appeared in Augustow with the title *Life in Augustow* edited by Yoysef Gizomski. Each entry marked with an asterisk comes from this publication.

Our town, aside from its considerable historic significance, boasts a great deal of natural beauty. Its hills, forests, lakes, the famous Augustow Canal, and the newly refurbished yacht club, which serves as a recreation spot for government workers, as well as a meeting place for foreign dignitaries. In the summer, our town's health resorts are visited by thousands of tourists. Should our town, with its social institutions and facilities, cultural and material resources, heaving and bustling with life, not also have its own voice?

{p. 186} Finally the fateful hour has arrived! With joy and enthusiasm I greeted the news about the publication of *Life in Augustow*. Thanks and acknowledgements are due to the initiators of this project, Messrs. Gizomski and Ben-Tsiyen Levinski. I hope that the seeds which have been planted shall grow and expand, from the initial four printed pages, may they develop in quantity and quality, and from page to page, issue to issue, grow into a life-giving force, nourishing and strengthening our much-needed charities and institutions with its breath and energy.

Rabbinate Elections

As our honored and respected rabbi, Reb Azriel Zelik Noyekh Kushelevski, long may he live, has made the timely decision to leave our town and make aliyah to the Land of Israel—at the behest of his son the rabbi, Reb Yekusiel, long may he live, the rabbi of Zikhron Yaakov—he has thereby renounced his rabbinical office.

Taking into account the departure of the rabbi, the authorities have instructed the congregation to open up a search with the purpose of finding a new rabbi. Of the twenty-odd applications, four were selected as viable candidates to stand in the rabbinical election.

The outcome of this election, which took place on Sunday the 8th of December last year, resulted in the election of Reb Tsvi Hirsh Leyter, long may he live, from Tarnopol, as the new rabbi of Augustow.

Books by Rabbi Kushelevski

Our esteemed rabbi Reb Kushelevski, long may he live, is preparing to release his third treatise, with the title, *Levish Edenim* on Tractate 77.

It is worth taking this opportunity to mention and summarize his two previously published treatises. His first book, *Eyn Tsufim* on various Torah portions, which the author published in the year 5682 was received with praise and interest in the world of religious oratory, containing as it did a wealth of materials for sermons. The author's second book *Mimonos Aroyes* contains a series of eulogies of various famous scholars, notables and martyrs from around the period of the Great War (1915-1920) in our town. In this book of sorrows he explores the tragedy of the Jewish people upon the loss of its best sons.

{p. 187} For these two previous books the author received many letters of thanks from researchers at the "*Dorshey Ha-universita Ha-Ivrit Birushalayim*" among others.

The same volume will include interpretations by the late rabbi, Reb Yisroel Uri of blessed memory.

The author has also produced a manuscript on the topic of indecipherable legends of the Sages.

In order to enable the publication of this last volume there will need to be a sufficient number of pre-orders among the townsfolk. Incidentally, a certain number of people have already made their interest in pre-ordering known to the esteemed author.

The Reception

Reception for the rabbi Reb Tsvi Hirsh Leyter, long may he live.

Thursday January 26th this year saw the welcome reception for our esteemed rabbi, Reb Tsvi Hirsh Leyter, long may be live, and his wife the rebbetzin Mrs. Khaye, long may she live, upon their arrival in Augustow.

To greet the rabbi a group of some dozen townsfolk went to meet him at the station, representatives of the Jewish community accompanied by a delegation of women to greet the esteemed rebbetzin. Stepping off the train, the rabbi was greeted by Nosn Varhaftig, wishing him, on behalf of the town, a heartfelt mazel tov on taking over the position of town rabbi.

Next to the congregation hall the esteemed rabbi was awaited by a large crowd who greeted him with great enthusiasm. Particularly joyous and impressive was the second part of the reception in the meeting hall of the congregation marked by generously laden tables and an elevated intellectual atmosphere. The president of the congregation, Mr. Volmir, opened proceedings, before passing the floor to the honored guest who thanked the townsfolk for their hearty welcome.

The subjects of the day were discussed and the esteemed representatives introduced themselves: Reb Khayim Zalman Kaplanski, Reb Meyer Lazovski, Reb Gedalye Gizumski, Reb Zev Lazman, and Messrs. Derevianski, Zavl; Yeruzolimski, Peysakh; Dr. Grodzienski; Hermanshtadt, Nakhmi; {p. 188} Mr. Shevakh, Uri of the congregation and Mr. Khlupitski, Avrom of the handworkers' union.

Finally—in splendid Hebrew, with spirited form, shot through with pearls of wisdom—the rabbi himself spoke, and the reception ended with the sentiment that the congregation and rabbi should work together harmoniously in all their communal endeavors.

At the same time, a welcome reception for the esteemed rebbetzin was taking place in the house of Mrs. Rubinshteyn where many important local women gathered around well-laden tables.

On behalf of all the ladies Miss Lenzinger greeted the rebbetzin, who thanked them for their heartfelt welcome and reception, promising them her full cooperation in all of the town's communal institutions.

A Girls' Class in the Elementary School

Standing: ... Z. Blacharski, B. Gizumski, S. Kolfenitzki, D. Sherman, D. Borovitz.
Second row sitting: P. Aronovski, S. Berliner, ... Beknovitzki, A. Orimland.
Third Row: ... ...

194

{p. 189} **The Past that Does Not Pass Away**
by Abba Gordin

I have barely any memory of Michaliszki, my place of birth. My father was taken on as a rabbi in Augustow. He emerged from under the wings of Reb Sender, who had aided him economically, and Reb Moyshele, who had aided him spiritually and intellectually. He was now ready to follow his own path, under his own steam, standing on his own two feet. He was a gifted orator and a rabbi with maskilic tendencies, and so he appealed to a wide audience of common folk, the Jewish masses. He was altogether saturated in the spirit of his times. He preached not only about piety, but also touched on "national questions" and spoke in particular of *Chovevei Tzion*.

Before his arrival there was the rabbi in Augustow, Reb Kasriel, who was cut from the old cloth: he distinguished himself with his expertise. He had quite a loyal following in town, composed to a large extent of members of his own extended family. But on account of a quarrel— a common occurrence that plagues Jewish life in small towns—he was forced to leave. He found a rabbinical posting not far from Augustow, in a tiny town which, in comparison, made Augustow look like a bustling metropolis, a major center of Jewish culture. Augustow's notable citizens, the elites, were close relatives of Reb Kasriel, but the common folks had risen up, the handworkers, led by the members of the burial society, led a mutiny and they triumphed. As a result the town's elite were enemies of the new rabbi on principle. They still hoped, by means of some machinations or other, to turn the communal wheel backward, to bring Reb Kasriel back somehow and restore his reign . . . At the time I knew nothing of all this, of course: being all of two years old I had little interest in communal politics.

One of the earliest things in the town that left a lasting impression on me, managing to make an enduring trace on my memory which is still there to this day, was of a curious well. The well was located in a neighboring yard, separated from the yard in which we, the rabbi and his family, lived. The well was fenced off by a railing with spikes along the top. What was most unusual about the well was that it had a hinged lid on the top, not unlike a little door, which was locked.

{p. 190} The man who owned the yard, the house, and the curious well was also Jewish, but he was a fat, mean man prone to melancholy, a veritable dark cloud. He wore a pair of high boots and a hat with a polished visor, like a Gentile. He was such a penny-pinching misanthrope that he could not abide the thought of his neighbors using his water. Twice a day that miser would come out to unlock his well, draw two buckets of water for himself and lock the well again. His yard, too, was closed off, the gate locked: it didn't open from the outside as normal people's gates did.

*

We moved to a new apartment, to a larger, nicer place in a stone building located in the market square. The windows—three large, bright windows—looked right down onto the market itself. I could watch everything that was going on down there, and be seen myself. Everything I observed was so immeasurably interesting: there was the town clock on the facade of the town hall; there were the town gardens, surrounded by iron fences, all laid out with tree-lined promenades, with dark corners of thick shrubbery so perfect for playing games of hide and seek. Right at the very center of the park stood a bandstand for an orchestra. In the summertime the military band would play there every evening. On one side of the park stood a cathedral with proud cupolas which looked for all the world like gigantic onions or turnips.

Next to us lived a young couple: Esne, the eldest daughter of Sheyne Yudis, and her husband. They ran a wholesale grocery store and had their living quarters in the rear of the

195

building: two spacious rooms with a kitchen, all exquisitely furnished. The corridor leading out to the yard, and the back porch were shared between our two apartments.

*

Sheyne Yudis, in addition to her grown up daughter and a son named Nisl who was three years older than me, naturally also had a husband. But she wore the trousers. She was renowned throughout Augustow. Their business was grain, and they had a full granary. I would go there to play with Nisl. What drew me to the granary more than anything was the musty smell, the semi-darkness, the flour dust {p. 191} which hung in the air, the cobwebbed corners which housed full sacks of wheat, corn, barley and rye. Being very small for my age, and flexible, I liked to hide between the sacks where no one could ever find me. But the greatest attraction of all was the tub of peas. I liked to roll around on top of the piled-up peas, enjoying the feeling of having peas run in under my shirt and into my shoes.

In the attic of their hay barn I played with my little sister Masha and a couple of her friends, playing a game we called "mothers and fathers." My sister and the other little girls would take turns pretending to give birth, while I would be a combination father and obstetrician, helping the baby come out into the world and then raise it as my own.

Sheyne Yudis was a pious woman, and word would be passed around the town, with mocking intent, of her morning appeals to God from the Women's synagogue. She would come very early, before *Minyan* prayer service in the men's synagogue had even begun. Sheyne Yudis was on first name terms with the almighty and would speak to him in a very straightforward, familiar manner, not just in prayer, but constantly throughout the day.

— "I, your servant, Sheyne Yudis, am here. My husband, Tsvi Hirsh, is still in his underpants, but he will be along shortly."

*

I was a regular visitor to the prayer house. I would walk around there with other children my age, circling the *bima*, rummaging around in the little pile of torn pages that had accumulated there. In those days, the prayer house in Augustow was always full of people. It was cheerful there—during the *minyan* of course, but also afterwards. The boys of the town, middle-class kids and their parents, would sit there around the long tables, or beside lecterns, reading aloud in a melodic singsong. There were also poor students, from other towns who "ate days" [628] and also a recluse or two. Large mantle lamps over the tables, lit by candles, in whose shine one read and studied the small print of the Rashi script.

The prayer house was filled with the singsong of students learning, but also the sound of mischief. It was more than a place of worship, and more than a house of learning, it was also like a clubhouse. Behind and on top of masonry stoves, slept guests, paupers who had travelled from nearby towns, wandering and begging.

The oven also served as a bed for the town madman Kalman *"Tume veta'are."*[629] He would wander around, {p. 192} disheveled and bedraggled, in filthy rags with holes large enough to show patches of bare skin underneath. The hair on his head and beard was as black as pitch, and matted. His face, with its two glinting eyes, was battered and anguished. He wandered around, mumbling to himself, and the only words of his articulated clearly enough to understand were *"tume"* and *"ta'are."*

*

---

[628] Eating days: A practice whereby meals for poorer *yeshiva* boarding students were provided on a charitable basis by nearby families, whereby students could eat at a different house each day of the week.
[629] Nickname made up of the two words: *Tume*: state of ritual impurity, immorality, sinfulness. *Ta'are*: ritual purification of the body of the deceased before burial; purity.

In the center of the market square, right across from the middle window of the rabbi's apartment, was where they drilled the army recruits, teaching them how to march in the appropriate manner, which meant learning how to "goose step," how to stand tall, stretched as taut as bows, frozen as still as statues. They were also taught how to hold a rifle, how to carry it on their shoulders, and how to pierce a scarecrow with a bayonet. Augustow, being a town not far from the German border, had a large garrison.

*

A regiment of Cossacks was stationed in town including—serving mostly as orderlies, servants to the officers—Kalmyks with earrings.

I was not indifferent to the soldiers' parades on the Russian public holidays. The soldiers and officers would all enter the Orthodox cathedral to linger for an hour or sometimes more. I stood with children my age, and also older children, outside in the market square, waiting patiently for them to reemerge. It was not too difficult in the summertime, but in winter, in the burning frost, waiting was pure torture. Our ears would freeze, our noses ran, our feet were like blocks, our toes began to go numb, our teeth rattled—but through it all I persisted and waited. The spectacle to come was worth all the hardships.

The soldiers, the officers, the colonels emerged, and arranged themselves in straight rows. The drill sergeant gave the signal and they marched back and forth through the square. It was a sight to behold. The military orchestra played, the drummers marching in front, beating their drums. The lead vocalist let out a protracted melody with a soldier's refrain and the whole company sang in response. For me it was a source of jubilation.

{p. 193} I sang along and skipped along after them in time with the drumbeat. I accompanied the soldiers through the town and some of the way out of town until they went into their barracks. Only then—hungry and half-frozen—would I turn around and return home to have something to eat and regain my strength. I wouldn't have missed a military parade for anything in the world.

*

The epidemic that spread over the whole country touched the town of Augustow with its black wings. Terror seized everyone young and old: people were dying, cholera was running rampant through the town and people were dying. The afflicted would start to vomit, get diarrhea, stomach cramps—and fall like flies. This is what the adults were saying, and the children repeated the same words in horror, in fright.

We had to take precautions. I wasn't allowed to eat any raw food—no fruit, no vegetables. I wasn't allowed to drink water that hadn't been boiled first.

Fear hovered over the whole town, a fear with its own peculiar smell that tickled my nostrils: the smell of sawdust and carbolic acid. The cutters were awash with carbolic acid; it was poured on the toilets, on the floors, on the walls—carbolic acid everywhere.

My father was no longer the same person. He no longer sat in the next room writing sermons; no, he donned a strange smock, tied with a leather belt around the hips. He set off to the synagogue early in the mornings. I followed him from a discreet distance. A group of men were waiting for him in the synagogue. They were going from house to house with a bottle of alcohol and various utensils. But before they went to work they prayed quickly and recited a few psalms. They were going to visit the sick, to rub alcohol on them, and in this manner they saved many lives. They were all strong and tall, fearless in the face of the cholera. They were unflappable and indefatigable. My father would come home late, and he too would smell of carbolic acid.

By the market square, no more than a few paces from our house, stood a small shop. The entrance was behind a porch up a flight of steps. An old woman sold leather there to be made into boot soles, gaiters, horse collars and other things. On rare occasions her husband would also make an appearance there. He was an elderly Jew, a *soifer*. I knew him well, I would go into the shop, and peek in through the door at the back, stealing a glance into the living quarters behind, which consisted of a single {p. 194} room with a kitchen. The *soifer* would sit, wrapped in a *tallis* and *tefillin*, writing with a goose feather. He was in the process of writing on a *Torah* scroll, quite a contrast to my father who would jot down snippets of *Torah* on pages of white paper with a steel pen. The *soifer* wrote on yellow parchment and his handwritten was something entirely different.

He was an old, shrunken man, his face a collection of wrinkles bordered by a patchy beard. I knew that the *soifer* was a very pious Jew and that the work he did was holy; he wrote the *Torah* scrolls that were wrapped in a mantel and held in the Ark at the back of the synagogue to be taken out during prayer services and placed on lectern, and that people were called up to read from it. Afterwards the *Torah* scroll would be held aloft for all to see, before placing it, with great ceremony and respect, back into the *Torah* Ark. There it would remain, locked and secured with a *poroykhes*.[630] It does not stay there alone; there are other *Torah* scrolls in there, all decked in beautiful, embroidered mantles.

Torah scrolls just like these were written by the *soifer* Reb Zelig.

When the *soifer* fell ill I learned about it from conversations at home. The little shop would be closed. I would have loved to see what it looked like when someone came down with that curious illness, cholera. But my mother and Zelda[631] would not allow it. A few days later they took the *soifer* from his house and brought him to the cemetery. The old woman who used to stand in the shop wept aloud.

After they removed the *soifer*'s body they burned the bed he had slept on, along with the straw mattress, pillows, blankets and everything else that had come into contact with his sickbed. But I went to have a look anyway; I was not able to get too close. I was surprised: "Why are they burning it all?" I asked an older boy who was standing nearby observing the curious scene. He informed me that cholera was such a contagious disease, that it even infected the bed linens.

I knew by then that in the synagogue yard—which was covered in fresh, green grass as good as the finest lawn, and which could be an excellent playground for me and my little friends—there was a shed which housed the stretcher and the *ta'are* board,[632] two things before which I and the other children trembled in fear, because they were connected to death and the dead. I also knew that there was an Angel of Death {p. 195} who went around armed with a sword. He had many eyes, and he took people's lives and one needed to watch out for him.

I never played in the synagogue courtyard. Not only was I afraid of the *ta'are* board and the stretcher, but I was terror-stricken by the synagogue itself. It was a huge building of stone and brick, with wide stairs leading into the antechamber. From the antechamber it was down another set of large stairs down into the cellar where the main part of the synagogue was. The synagogue was an intimidating place. At night the dead played inside. The old *shammes*—I knew him well—kept the synagogue locked, but naturally that did not deter the dead from coming to pray inside. Every morning the *shammes* would knock on the massive door with his heavy key and ask the dead to leave the premises. As he did so he would repeat three times: "Go to your rest!" Only once the ghosts had had time to leave would he dare to open the synagogue doors for dawn prayers.

I went into the synagogue with my father, Reb Yehuda Leyb, only for *Yom Kippur*. The rest of the year I followed my father into the prayer house. As he walked past the other people stood up. I enjoyed seeing them show honor to my father.

---

[630] The curtain covering the opening of the *Aron Kodesh*.

[631] The maid.

[632] Table for ritual purification of dead bodies.

I went to the synagogue for evening *Yom Kippur* service arriving just before *Kol Nidre*. Before *Kol Nidre* my father, the rabbi, held a short sermon full of spiritual awakening. His call for repentance was met with lamentations. Above all, one could hear the sound of the women weeping and lamenting their past transgressions. There were many lamps, candles and candelabras burning. The synagogue was packed with people. It was so hot and suffocating that it was hard to breathe. The stone walls were sweating condensation. I alternated holding one cheek, then another, against the damp stone walls, in this way cooling them and helping me to catch my breath to avoid fainting.

*

We were all woken up by the alarm. But seeing as the fire was burning on the other side of town we calmed down and went back to sleep. I wanted to go and see the fire for myself, but I was not allowed. The fire burned the grain-merchant granaries on Zoyb Street. I rushed there first thing in the morning. I had missed the flames, but I was determined to see the ruins with my own eyes; there were still a few embers smoldering, while in some places there were only a few wisps of steam.

{p. 196} Mountains of ruined grains lay piled up, alongside bricks from the broken foundations. I found it all so interesting.

*

The rabbi changed apartments again for the third time. Whenever the rabbi went to look at a new apartment he would test it out with his voice; if the acoustics were good, and his voice resounded well in the space, and the resonance was to his liking then he would give his approval and we would move in. Near the rabbi lived an old widow. She had two children. The youngest was only a year older than me. They went around in tattered clothes and were always hungry. I would run around with the youngest; we played together and whenever I had food I would share my last morsel with him. When I was having fun I would forget to eat and drink, and so I had no problem parting with the snacks Zelda had prepared for my playtime. I would spend the long warm summer days running around and would come home exhausted and fall asleep practically as soon as I crossed the threshold. Sleep was as sweet as paradise in those days, as delectable as the finest jams.

My mother, the *Rebbetzin* Khaye Esther Sore, would help the widow whenever she could: with hand-me-down clothing for the children, with food, but above all with credit. She vouched for the widow and arranged for her to buy a whole barrel of herring on credit. The widow would set herself up in the main square during market days selling the herring and paying back the *Rebbetzin* what she owed. The wholesaler, knowing full well that the *Rebbetzin* was doing a *mitzvah* in helping the widow provide for her children, played along by offering a lower price.

In this whole affair I acted as messenger: joyfully, fully aware that I was doing a good deed, I would go to tell Markus that my mother would guarantee the barrel of herring that the widow Rivke would buy from him on credit.

Markus was a *Chasid*, with a reputation as a learned man, and from a respectable family to boot. He had a well-stocked shop, with all manner of dried goods, smoked fish and barrels of herring.

With pleasure and a feeling of satisfaction in playing an important role in doing a good deed, I would take [p. 197} the grubby pouch full of five-kopeck pieces and coppers—which stank of herring—and bring them to Markus on the morning after market day.

*

My mother and father decided that it was time for me to learn in *cheyder*. As teacher they chose Chaim "*Kukuriku*."[633] That's what they called the teacher for beginners. He had earned his nickname thanks to his hoarse voice as he was always coughing and clearing his throat and so the children had granted him this uncharitable moniker. Soon everyone in town called him this; most had forgotten his real surname, and those who knew it chose to ignore it.

Kukuriku had served a full term as a soldier: a strenuous discipline. He carried his discipline over from the barracks to the classroom. He would beat the children without mercy. He gave one child such a thrashing that he fell ill, languishing a few weeks before passing away. But these stories—and they were not just stories but genuine occurrences—did nothing to damage his reputation as a "pedagogue"—in fact, if anything, it had the opposite effect. He gained a reputation as an effective teacher. He was a very good teacher of Hebrew, and not bad at teaching *Chumesh* and *Nevi'im*. Even the fact that he beat the children—was there any other way to make those little devils learn after all? On Mount Sinai the *Torah* had also been received through violence, bending the mountain like a barrel: "Either you accept the *Torah*, or you will be buried here on this spot."[634]

But the *Rebbetzin* was apprehensive: I was a weak child—one proper soldier's slap from Chaim *Kukuriku* and I was a goner. And so the rabbi called the teacher to him and, in my presence, told him, in the words of the angel to Abraham: "Do not lay a hand on the boy, or do anything to him;"[635] and if the teacher did not do as he was told my father told me to come straight home and tell him and I would be taken out of *cheyder*. The teacher was not to touch so much as a hair on my head.

Chaim Kukuriku understood that his reputation as a teacher would only rise with the news that the rabbi had entrusted him with the education of his son; it was a seal of approval for his style of teaching. He also understood what a disaster for his career it would be if the rabbi took his son out of his care. And so, with a heavy heart, he accepted the conditions and promised not to beat me, though in truth he could not imagine {p. 198} how it was possible to teach a boy without a few slaps, or at the very least the threat of them—how is it possible for a child to learn if the cane did not hang over his head? But that is how it had to be; he accepted the rabbi's conditions though he held them to be entirely nonsensical.

They prepared for me to join the *cheyder*. Zelda brought me. She held my hand and led me as far as the threshold, allowing me to cross over by myself to become a schoolboy independently of her.

I went inside and remained standing by the door. In front of me I saw the wrathful teacher, who was in the process of shouting, and a handful of children my age, as well as a few older than me, a mixture of boys and girls. I was dazzled by the noise and commotion.

The teacher's greeting was not especially friendly. He was disappointed that I had been brought by the maid and not by my mother, the *Rebbetzin*. He was standing beside the window. I did not want to take a seat between children I did not know, and then there was the racket which all but tore my ears off. I was afraid, a little Daniel in the lion's den.

I refused to stay if Zelda did not stay with me, and so she stayed. There was not enough space for both of us on the bench, and so the teacher's wife brought out two chairs just for us.

Zelda accompanied me to *cheyder* the whole week. During that first week the teacher taught me nothing. I sat there watching and listening to everything happening around me. Gradually I grew accustomed to my new environment, and I began to make friends with the other children in the *cheyder* and stopped being afraid of them.

---

[633] Literally: cock-a-doodle-doo.

[634] *Midrash Aggadah*, Exodus 19:17:1

[635] Genesis 22:12 "And he said, "Do not raise your hand against the boy, or do anything to him.""

I would stand in the corner of the room, watching the teacher, my whole body trembling, even though I knew that I was protected from his beatings. My teacher would obey the rabbi's wishes. Everyone had to obey my father, the rabbi of the whole town, for whom everyone stands when he enters the prayer house. And yet I trembled, because a teacher is someone to fear, and also someone to honor, or so my mother had told me, and Zelda too, and even my father the rabbi: You must hold your teacher as dear as your own father, because he teaches you *Torah*, God's *Torah*.

From the second week on the *belfer*[636] brought me to *cheyder* in the mornings and brought me back home in the evenings.

{p. 199} The *cheyder* was located on a small side street not far from the edge of the town. On the other side of the street, heading westward, were various gardens, and a little further on was the bathhouse just on the outskirts of town, at the very edge of the world.

With yearning and desire I looked toward the bathhouse and over the roof of the bathhouse. At a slight remove from the bathhouse was already world's end. One time I approached the bathhouse, but as I got closer the edge of the world shifted further away, revealing a new expanse of space—I was afraid. Who knew what kinds of ferocious beasts were lurking out there, and maybe there were even serpents, which are much worse than beasts?

The *cheyder* was made up of one spacious room. The furniture consisted of several benches and a long table that stood in the center of the room; the table was surrounded on three sides by benches for the children, while at its head was a chair for the teacher. The teacher's apartment was made up of a kitchen and one other room where the teacher lived with his wife and two young daughters—one breastfeeding while the other crawled around—as well as three or four chickens.

The *cheyder* was not especially clean, but the other room was positively filthy. The stink of dirty diapers emanated from there along with the sound of crying children and clucking chickens.

The "modern" aspect of the *cheyder* was that the space was entirely dedicated to learning: the teacher and his wife did not sleep in that room. But all day the teacher's wife, their children, and the chickens, wandered back and forth through the cheyder, because their bedroom was too small for them. The cradle along with the bed, pillows, blankets, a few rickety chairs and a commode filled up that room until there was nowhere to move. There was one other noteworthy addition to the *cheyder*, and that was a portrait of the Tsar, which occupied pride of place on the western wall.

I was genuinely terrified by that portrait. The other pupils often talked about the Tsar. They regarded him with great awe, as someone who stood near the heavenly realm, operating with the approval of God himself. I imagined him to be a creature on a higher level than a mere human, more important even than a rabbi, he dwelled somewhere among the angels. The words "*malekh*" and "*meylekh*"— "angel" and "king"—sounded so similar, suggesting to me a link in their meaning as well.

The children would bring food from home to keep them going during the day, though we would return to our homes to eat a warm lunch. I was not much of an eater, and {p. 200} would take no more than the smallest snack to see me through the day.

For the most part the food was sliced bread rolls with butter which the children kept next to them on the benches. The dirt and the food attracted whole swarms of flies such that the buzzing rose above all other sounds. The lays laid siege upon the windows, doing acrobatics and other fly-exercises along the windowpanes.

---

[636] The assistant in a *cheyder*.

The hours in *cheyder* were very long, from early morning until dusk. When boredom grew intolerable we would sneak out into the yard with the excuse of needing to go to the toilet. Instead we would stand in the outhouse, or between the blocks of firewood, trousers undone, talking. We were in no hurry to finish up and go back inside, but we could not linger for too long or else the teacher would come to see what we were doing and drag us back into the *cheyder*.

*

During the second term a whole gang of girls arrived in the *cheyder*, from the large, extended Keynanes family. Blonde girls with red cheeks, beautiful, pure, dressed up almost like dolls; that's how they appeared in my eyes. They would bring large, buttery cakes with them, and bottles of milk. Early in the morning they would start on their provisions, eating with appetite, not because they were hungry, more as a kind of vain bragging, to show that they were rich and could afford to have the very best.

I hated them on principle, and hated them especially for their ostentatious dressing up. My sister, Rokhl, who had now joined the same *cheyder* and sat in the beginners' section, had no love for them either. Fights often broke out between her and the Keynanes girls and I, naturally, always took my sister's side. The weapon of choice in these fights was not their hands—they were not strong after all—but their mouths. Verbal disputes and hurled curses. The most powerful weapon of all, in terms of destructive force, was the employment of nicknames.

It is interesting to note how the animosity that existed between the parents was carried over by the children.

A constant, endless conflict reigned between the Keynanes girls and my sister, while I, as her brother and protector, was always dragged into every verbal duel. As the principal combatants were girls it never came to thrown punches, {p. 201} though the mutual hatred burned all term with no sign of abating.

The Keynanes girls were fast learners, and they could already recite Hebrew loudly and clearly, with pleasant voices. I would have admired them if I could have forgiven their vain arrogance, their pride, their flouting of their fine clothes, their cambric dresses and delicate Ukrainian embroidery.

*

There was very limited time for playing, except between terms during the major holidays. During term we played mostly on Friday afternoons when we had time off from *cheyder*. Then we would play in one of the courtyards as far away from the watchful eyes of our parents as we could.

Like all the children my age I played "soldiers" and "court." A thief or a bandit would be caught and would stand trial and be punished. It turned out I was a good *palant*[637] player, a pasttime that several other children enjoyed.

The game consisted of placing two bricks on the ground, with a length of string between them. A board of wood, sharpened on both ends, would be placed on the bricks. The player would take a narrow, flat plank of wood and knock the sharpened board with it in such a way that it would fly into the air. Once airborne the player would give the board an almighty wallop, hurling it into the distance. We would measure the distance travelled by the board. Meanwhile the second player would try to catch the board with their bare hands and send it back. The closer it landed to the bricks the more points it was worth.

I also liked to go walking with Nisl, the son of Sheyne Yudis, over the fields, through undeveloped lots and unfenced yards collecting stones, which we would carry back to Sheyne Yudis's yard. For me it was just a game, a way of passing the time, without any other motivation,

---

[637] A Polish game similar to baseball.

but that was not the case for Nisl. When Nisl had collected a good pile of stones he would sell them for a few *kopecks* to a man who would come with a wheelbarrow—once even with a horse and cart—to collect the stones. When I realized that my game had been debased by this transaction I was annoyed. I lost all interest in collecting and carrying stones; I stopped helping Nisl. I felt a natural antipathy to the whole business of buying and selling.

{p. 202} I had a friend who lived on the other side of the park. His father had an iron workshop. The child had a tricycle—a contraption with one large wheel in front and two smaller wheels behind. He rode around on that tricycle as if it were a horse, all around the yard. He was a good friend and from time to time he let me have a go on his "iron horse." I was in seventh heaven. Riding was such fun. I all but burst for joy. To this day I can't quite get my head around the idea that fate can gift little children with such intoxicating pleasures. Every Friday, as soon as school was over, I would run at full speed to my friend, in order to snatch a few minutes to ride on his tricycle.

*

On Saturday we would usually play at home. There wasn't much to be done in the yards. Most of the games we would want to play were forbidden on *Shabbes*, as they involved carrying things. It was forbidden to carry anything in our pockets, so the best was to just stay at home.

We played in the parlor, the largest, cleanest and most beautiful room in the whole house. It was rare that anyone would pass through to disturb us there. It was practically the "Holy of Holies" of the house. It stood empty almost all year round. Only the most honored guests would be entertained there. Large mirrors hung on the walls. The furniture consisted of a half dozen upholstered chairs, two sofas equipped with covers to protect them from the dust, a round table topped with a tablecloth; the windowsills were decorated with well-tended and healthy potted plants.

The children gathered there and—crowned a king, a Jewish king. Why did the Gentiles have a Tsar and the Jews had nothing? The Jews should have their own king, and his portrait should hang on the wall. So what if we were in Exile?

An armchair served as a lofty throne.

Who was chosen to be king? Moyshke, the youngest. But you couldn't have a king without a queen, so we made his youngest sister Masha into his queen. And why did we choose Moyshke of all people? There was a certain logic to it. He was the youngest and in that regard he was unsuited for any of the other roles which would have required more understanding, action, initiative and he was entirely unsuitable for them.

{p. 203} To be a Tsar he didn't need to do anything, just sit on the throne with a swelled head like a turkey. That was the only thing he could do; he held court with great poise.

For whatever reason I was chosen to be the chief of the army which did not exist, so I had to play both chief and the whole army.

Even though there wasn't much to do in the game it amused us for the whole day. Everything we had to do, from guarding the throne to bowing before our great king, we did with great ceremony: we were in the presence of royalty.

*

I came home from *cheyder* late in the evening. It was already cold; the days were short, and the streets were covered in slush. We walked home together in a kind of procession, holding lit lamps made of paper, homemade. We children had ourselves folded the paper forming the skeleton of the lanterns. To make the paper transparent, so that the light would shine through to light up the way, we soaked it in fat or kerosene.

The others would walk me as far as the yard, and from there I had to run the short distance inside in darkness. A single lantern was no match for the darkness, barely making a dent in the pitch blackness. I missed the old days when the student from Yedwabne, a boy, would collect me and accompany me home. I arrived inside panting and half-alive.

No one paid any attention to me; it was not like usual when they showed interest in us children and Zelda would prepare me food right away.

I was surprised. I could feel tension in the room, an emotion was being choked back, but it was not sorrow, rather its opposite—a suppressed gaiety. They were overcome with joy, but were afraid to show it in case someone saw.

I have a sixth sense for these things, and I could feel that something important and good had happened.

What was it?

{p. 204} My sister, Rokhl, who had stayed at home this term rather than going to *cheyder* with me, explained what was going on:

"Did you not hear? The Tsar has died."

"How do you know that?"

"Father said."

"Should we celebrate?"

"Of course, he was bad for the Jews."

An hour before, the rabbi had paid a visit to the mayor. He was a Pole, a patriot, but his patriotism was something he hid under lock and key.

He entered with a feigned look of sorrow on his face:

"Our emperor is dead," the mayor announced the news in a voice laden with suppressed joy and feigned sadness.

"We must declare tomorrow and the days that follow as days of mourning."

The rabbi agreed that the fatherland had indeed suffered a great loss.

The rabbi, Reb Yehuda Leyb, was a double rabbi: a real rabbi and a state appointed "official" rabbi. Which meant that he held a small administrative office.

The Poles in town were happy, and they knew full well that the Jews were no less happy, but both groups were wary of expressing their joy in public: particularly they were afraid of the soldiers and the Russian officials garrisoned in the town.

I was overjoyed: I did not have to go to *cheyder* the next morning, and could avoid facing my arch-nemesis—my teacher.

Wouldn't it be great if a different nasty gentile—king or no king—died every day? I hated my teacher, but did not wish him death . . . it was forbidden to curse a fellow Jew, and certainly not a teacher, no matter how bad they were.

The rabbi soon informed all the townsfolk, all the *gabbai*s from the synagogues and all the *shammes*es.

The next day candles burned in every prayer house. The rabbi announced that we should read Psalm 109.

All of the important people in town came down.

The large synagogue was packed. The rabbi declaimed the scripture himself, with a mournful, pious tone in his rich baritone voice: "*Let his children be fatherless, and his wife—a widow. Let his children be continually vagabonds, and beg; let them seek their bread also out of their desolate places . . . Let there be none to extend mercy unto him: neither let there be any to favor his fatherless children . . . Because he remembered not to show mercy, but persecuted the poor and needy man . . .* {p. 205} *as he loved cursing, so let it come unto him: as he delighted not in blessing, so let it be far from him. As he clothed himself with cursing like as with his garment, so let it come into his bowels like water, and like oil into his bones. Let it be unto him as the garment which covers him, and for a girdle wherewith he is girded continually . . ."*

The rabbi recited the whole psalm and the mayor all but dissolved in sorrow . . .

*

I began to see a new teacher, a *Gemara* teacher, an elderly Jew with a dignified face and a grey beard. He was a kind-hearted man, and a sickly man—he suffered from pains in his legs. His wife too was a courteous, refined woman who almost never showed her face in the *cheyder*. She sat in her room, or worked in the kitchen. The teacher had a son-in-law who lived with them. The young couple had their own alcove. The son-in-law would sit all day working, making leather goods; wallets, women's handbags and the like. His work was precise, pure and elegant. He did not have a "patent," that is to say he had not paid the government for a work permit allowing him to earn a living for himself and his bride, the teacher's daughter. Police raids were quite frequent. The police would barge in, trying to catch him in the act. During such raids, the teacher would tremble like a leaf. The son-in-law would quickly hide the material he had been working on. There was not a lot to hide, and he would make himself scarce, escaping out the back window that opened out onto a yard. The searches and raids usually ended with a few carefully deposited coins in the pockets of the tax inspector and the police officer who accompanied him. The fear was considerable, but the teacher did not interrupt his lessons: he did not want to show that it had anything to do with him, to avoid being held responsible for the sins of his son-in-law.

During these raids, my heart all but fell out of my chest. My hatred of the police and the hated regime grew in my soul. Who did they think they were, tormenting my good, kindly teacher? Why did they want to scare him?

The love that a Jewish child usually feels for his spiritual father-figure, the one who teaches him *Torah*, *Mitzveh*s and good deeds, which I had not felt for my first teacher, I now gave two-fold—like a debt with interest—to my new teacher. I truly revered him.

{p. 206} Nisl, Sheyne Yudis's boy, was also a pupil in the same *cheyder*. He was tall, three years older than me, and knew a lot less than I did. It was no wonder. Nisl never listened when the teacher explained the meaning of the words in the *Mishnah* or the Book of Isaiah. During lessons Nisl kept his hands down on the bench, fidgeting with something, hiding a treasure or a booklet of some sort. He had customers for such wares and was paid for them. He always had something he would rather be doing. Nisl was actually more a friend of Velfke,[638] though Velfke learned with a different teacher, one with a reputation as a scholar. He was dark-haired, tall, and thin with a short, trimmed beard, also a sickly man. His name was Reb Abba, but the pupils called him the "Straw Cossack."

*

The *cheyder* shared a large corridor with the neighboring tailor. His name sounded a little strange to my ears: "Kushmender." It's possible it was not a real name at all, but an epithet, containing a little "*shmendrik*"[639] within it. But I had no connection to the tailor and his name, or nickname would not have interested me in the slightest if he hadn't had a son who learned in the same *cheyder* as me.

He was an only child, about two years older than me. The boy was not the brightest, but his father, the tailor, believed that *Torah* was something that could be hammered into you, or forced down your throat like a bitter medicine. He genuinely wanted to make a scholar of his pride and joy. Because he was a high-class tailor, who earned a good living and could afford the fees he

---

[638] Abba's brother.
[639] Yiddish for a stupid person or a fool.

enrolled his only son in a good *cheyder*, approaching my teacher and offering to make it worth his while. He asked my teacher to pay special attention to his son, and in return he would earn an extra bonus on top of the usual fees.

In simpler terms, he had given the teacher to understand that he should not hold back, and could "skin the boy alive" as long as he got results.

The teacher had a section in his *cheyder* where he taught both *Gemara* and the works of the latter prophets as well as the *Ketuvim*. The teacher, unable to refuse his neighbor Kushmender's offer, {p. 207} put the boy in this section, which was much too advanced for him with his limited capacities in Hebrew.

The whole week learning in *cheyder* went according to plan. But on Friday when it came to repeating, that is to say being examined, everything fell apart. The Kushmender boy did not know the meanings of the words from the chapter we'd just finished learning. He could read the lines without difficulty, but when it came to explaining the sentence he was at a loss. The examination began first thing in the morning, and continued into the afternoon when the school day came to an end. For every wrongly explained word there was a slap, resounding slaps.

The beating could not change anything; the teacher's slaps were in vain. It made about as much sense as whipping the benches, or trying to beat milk out of a billy goat. With my instinct for pedagogy I could see it wasn't a matter of the boy not wanting to learn, it was simply that with his soft teeth he could not bite into the tough complexity of the prophets' speech which was aimed at a more sophisticated audience, with a firmer grasp of Hebrew. The expressions were too beautiful, too embellished, too lofty. The young Kushmender had to learn the latter prophets, had to struggle his way through them.

It's possible the teacher knew all this, but renouncing the juicy financial carrot, especially in his financial position, was not an option. Abandoning the boy entirely to his ignorance and incompetence would have been inappropriate: he was paid double for teaching him and goading him on. It would not do to spare the rod, so he continued to whip him in the hope that perhaps a miracle would occur and the colt would be able to pull the overloaded wagon after all. Giving the colt a smaller load, that is to say, teaching the boy easier material was not something he was prepared to do, not just because he did not have the time to teach a separate course, but also because it would undermine his position in the hierarchy of teaching: a *Gemara* teacher has no desire to become a *Chumesh* teacher, that would be a step down. Should he lower himself all for a single peasant? There was only one solution: whipping and beating—he was being paid to break bones after all.

I was a soft-hearted boy. I could not bear to watch the execution. On Fridays, when the teacher was busy with Kushmender's boy I would go out to the toilet and loiter there for as long as possible.

The teacher lost a lot of respect in my eyes from playing the role of a violent man; it was a role that did not suit him.

*

{p. 208} The *cheyder* had a supplementary teacher, and that was the Russian teacher. What was his name? The children did not call him by his name. He was a short man, but as stout as a barrel, almost broader than he was tall, as the expression goes. The boys called him *Bulke*[640]— bread roll. His job was to come into class for an hour or two to teach the boys how to read and write in Russian, along with a little arithmetic.

Both subjects seemed easy to me. Russian was not an unfamiliar language for me. I could understand the Gentiles, the laborers in my grandfather's yard, and they spoke a language that was

---

[640] Yiddish.

very similar to the literary Russian that Bulke taught me. But I truly adored arithmetic. I quickly mastered the multiplication tables which went up as far as a hundred. The numbers were laid out in such a way that you could find the correct answer without having to calculate. All you had to go was to find the numbers in the horizontal and vertical bars and in the place where the lines converged there would be the answer. When I was going to bed I would set up a chair next to my bed, and on the seat I would read arithmetic problems, exercises from a book called *Zadatshnik*[641] (problems).

Two years before I did not yet go to *cheyder* but I would sometimes meet Velfke when he came out of Abba the straw Cossack's *cheyder*. I would bump into Velfke's friends as they were off to eat lunch.

"Where is my brother?"

"Bulke kept him behind, making him miss lunch as a punishment.

"Really?" I was surprised.

The boys told me to go inside where Bulke was currently teaching another class, and ask the teacher: "Bulke, why don't you let my brother Velfke go to eat?" That would surely help, they said.

What one won't do for one's own brother! I did not know that Bulke was a nickname and so I did exactly as the boys had suggested.

I went inside and addressed the teacher with my question, calling him "Bulke."

The teacher turned as red as a beet. The class almost choked with laughter. The pupils had gotten revenge against their hated teacher. I soon realized that I had made a terrible mistake, {p. 209} though I had no way of knowing what I had done wrong. In fright I ran out of the *cheyder* and rushed home.

An hour later I see Bulke is there. He denounced me to my father: what was the meaning of me humiliating him in front of his whole class?

My father did not reprimand me: he was sure that I had acted in complete innocence—as indeed was the case—but when I discovered what I had done, in my foolishness, I felt ashamed. I humiliated a teacher, a person second only to a rabbi in prestige.

After this error I became more cautious. I began to realize that it was better not to do everything that the older boys told me to do.

*

Velfke went off with the widow's son, who was the same age as him—while I tagged along like a calf following a cow—toward the river, or more accurately, to the bridge which was suspended over the River Netta. This was where the river met the canal. On one side of the bridge the river was level with the earth, and on the other side it poured down into a deep valley, a drop of perhaps a hundred feet. If it wasn't for the bridge and the lock there would be quite a waterfall there. When barges approached the bridge from the river, the canal would be filled with water until the water was on the same level as the river. The barge would be let in and then the water would be allowed to gradually flow back out until it was now level with the canal in the valley. The lock gates could then be opened, allowing the barge to continue on its journey.

*

I wasn't much of an eater. It was only with much cajoling that you could even get me to drink half a glass of milk before setting off for *cheyder* in the morning.

To stop me from fainting with hunger I was sometimes given a whole five-kopeck piece, sometimes only one, to buy something to eat.

---

[641] Russian

I would set off in the mornings without any baggage. I did not need to carry any books with me: the *Siddur*, *Tanakh* and *Gemara* were waiting for me in *cheyder* tucked away in the desk drawer.

{p. 210} It was a fine, sunny market day. There were countless wagons parked on the market square. The horses were unhitched, the wagon shafts raised. They looked like dried, branchless trees. The market was abustle with Jews and Gentiles alike. With difficulty I picked my way through the heaving throng, the human sea.

I hold the copper coin tightly in the palm of my hand so as not to drop it and lose it in the bustle. I think about what I'll buy with it, deciding this time not to buy any sweets but some proper food.

I walk past a line of tables, old Jewish women hawking their wares: a veritable cornucopia. I stop, and consider the sweets, the fruit, the various berries. It's hard to resist these distractions and stick to my plan. I hesitate: what should I choose? Should I give in to temptation and buy some sweets? No, I shall not give in. My gaze falls on the cheeses. A bargain: a penny a piece. I know my way around the prices. I'm a seasoned buyer after all; I won't pass up a bargain like this—I buy a piece of cheese.

In *cheyder* I show my classmates the piece of merchandise I purchased for next to nothing. Everyone admires my shrewd acquisition. Several boys ask me where I bought it, as they too would like to get in on the action. But the time it would take to leave the *cheyder*, go to the market, and come back, was not a luxury they had. What's more they could not be sure that the cheese had not all been sold out by now. It was a market after all, with so many customers coming from all over to shop there.

I eat my cheese. Really I only tasted it. I could not eat it. After the first bite I already felt full. I looked at the cheese in my hand and thought: What should I do with this? I can't eat any more. There's no point in taking it back home with me after class. There's no shortage of food in the house. And my mother would surely shout at me for buying food without eating it. Should I throw it away? It is a sin to squander God's bounty. There was only one way out: share it with my classmates. I divided the cheese into four equal parts. I give the first piece to Nisl. All four friends eat their cheese with relish, promising me that when they buy cheese they will share a piece with me. Measure for measure.

*

At that time my father had an appointment to visit the military doctor. My father, like all rabbis in the towns and villages, dedicated a lot of his time and energy, among other things, to {p. 211} attempting to free bright young boys from the clutches of the army. He could not abide if a young man, a potential scholar, was taken away from his *Torah* study to "serve the Tsar" and waste three years of his life on military service. Snatching someone back once he was already in uniform, already conscripted, had one great advantage: one boy's escape would not put another Jew at risk. Every town had to provide a particular quota of recruits. If you succeeded in exempting one Jewish boy by means of bribing a doctor or an official, another Jewish boy would have to take his place. And so a favor for one, would be a dirty deed for another. Rich families freed their sons by offering bribes. Poor scholars were freed in the same way. Pious Jews would pool their money to find the necessary funds, and so the holes in the quota were filled by poor boys and ignoramuses.

But my father did things differently: it is not good to do a kindness at someone else's expense. What he liked to do was take a scholar out of the regiment; that was without doubt a worthy thing. No one, or at least no Jewish young man, suffered because of it. This form of ransom my father performed with his whole heart and soul. Whatever risks he took he justified to himself with the thought that the townsfolk would never allow him to be arrested and sentenced to hard labor in Siberia.

The process was a simple one. The recruit feigns an illness and asks the military doctor to examine him. The chief-doctor would receive a bribe and would confirm that the patient was ill . . . the wording the rabbi, Reb Yehuda Leyb, used in such cases was precise and simple:

"Please, doctor, please help the patient in whatever way you can within the limits of the law (*v predelakh zakona*)."[642] But both the limits and the law were elastic; they could be stretched like rubber if it was to the doctor's advantage.

The meetings between the rabbi and the regiment's chief-doctor always took place in secret, late at night, in the doctor's home. Naturally, it was always better when there was some pretext for the late-night visit. My illness served as such an excuse. The military doctor was considered a good healer, though civilian patients in town rarely called for him, and it is possible he would not have answered if they did.

Reb Yehuda Leyb brought me, his son, with him to the doctor's house. Even though I was with my father I still felt scared {p. 212} when I stepped over the threshold into the doctor's richly furnished parlor, where my father left me to speak to the doctor in private. The parlor was a sight to behold. It was unquestionably more beautiful than the room in which we had crowned Moyshke as a king. Even Dr. Goldberg's apartment paled in comparison to this spacious extravagance. There were such large mirrors hanging on the walls that at first glance I thought there was a second room behind them. I was overwhelmed by the splendor and decorations that I was literally afraid to budge from the chair in which my father had told me to sit. The carpets on the floor were so thick and soft that I had not heard my own footsteps as I came into the room, and this only served to intensify my anxiety.

*

1896. The rabbi's house was engulfed in deep, heartfelt sorrow when the news arrived that Reb Yitskhok Elkhanon Spektor, the rabbi of Kovno, had died. I saw my father weep warm tears, something I had only ever observed on the eve of *Yom Kippur* as he blessed the children. My mother was also in tears as though it had been a family member who had died.

I knew that Reb Yitskhok Elkhanon had been a great scholar, a sort of general Jewish father figure. Mt father, Reb Yehuda Leyb, had gone to Kovno to visit Reb Yitskhok Elkhanon and when he returned he talked a lot about him, and about the hearty welcome he had received there.

A few years before there had been a drought, almost leading to a famine; by the time Passover came around the poor people had nothing to eat, and did not have enough *matzo*.

In our house there had never been a shortage of matzo. My grandfather, Reb Sender, sent us *matzo* flour every year, as well as *matzo farfel*[643] and three pounds of *shmura matzo*. Reb Sender himself supervised the wheat as it was harvested, bound and dried, then ground and baked. We had more than enough *matzo*. We shared our *shmura matzo* with whichever townsfolk asked for some, or even with those who did not ask outright, but sent their holiday wishes in the form of money, wine or cakes. We would send some *shmura matzo* back with the same messenger, and even after all this sharing we still had enough *matzo* left over for the children to eat all year.

{p. 213} But the poor people in town did not have any food, that's what I heard at home. My father put his head down, thought long and hard, consulted scripture, and eventually issued a rabbinical decree permitting maize flour and peas.

In Sheyne Yudis's house they rejoiced when they heard news of the decree. They had a granary full of maize which they had amassed hoping to sell it at high prices and make a good profit.

---

[642] Russian.
[643] Small broken pieces of crumbled matza.

But Reb Yehuda Leyb did not want to stand alone and take sole responsibility for the decree; and so he sent word to Reb Yitskhok Elkhanon asking for his opinion and received word that he approved the plan.

The answer was considered an important event in our household. Reb Yitskhok Elkhanon had said very complimentary things in his letter about Reb Yehuda Leyb's learning, expertise and shrewdness, causing a significant boost to the rabbi's prestige in town, to the annoyance of his enemies. Reb Yitskhok Elkhanon's letter was shown to all the scholars and important townsfolk. I also saw the letter. I was surprised to see such bad handwriting from such an eminent scholar— instead of letters it was scratchings and scribbles. I had good handwriting; Khayim *Kukuriku* was good at teaching handwriting and so my grandparents never tired of praising the letters I sent them twice a year for *Pesach* and *Rosh Hashanah*—letters actually written by my mother, but which I copied out by hand. I believed that a scholar should also know how to write beautifully.

*

In Augustow there was stationed, in the barrack built for that purpose, a large garrison, a division comprising four regiments.

There were quite a large number of Jewish soldiers in the garrison, and they were invited as guests to celebrate *Shabbes* and *Yom Kippur*. Others were invited to the well-off Jewish homes. There was a story going around: during a party in one of the houses of the *shveydaks*, a soldier had taken out a ring and put it on the finger of a girl of marriageable age, and uttered the magic words: "*Behold, you are consecrated to me with this ring according to the law of Moses and Israel,*" with several of his soldier friends as witnesses. A "*shveydak*" was someone who went off to Sweden for several months a year to peddle. There were several such families in Augustow, and all of them were quite well off financially.

{p. 214} The town was turned topsy turvy. Everyone was talking about the incident. The girl's mother wailed and moaned; her father, the *shveydak*, was away on business. But word was sent to him and he came rushing back from Sweden without delay. They were not in favor of the match. What was to be done? They came to the rabbi to save them from their predicament, from the shame and humiliation. The girl was an only child and the soldier, a crude, simple lad, from a humble family in Odessa.

The scandal had the whole town abuzz. People were afraid to let Jewish soldiers into the houses where there were grown daughters.

I knew all the details of the case. I was proud of the knowledge that only my father could rectify the situation.

They offered the soldier money if he would agree to divorce the girl. He rejected the offer. If he offered her a divorce she would of course have the status of divorcée, and what boy from a respectable family would want to marry a divorcée? She would have to, God forbid, sit it out until her hair turned gray, or else marry a divorced man, or a widower. In short the misfortune was considerable, and the shame was no smaller.

Only one person could save them and that was the rabbi, the local rabbinical authority.

My father locked himself away in his rabbinical court, consulting a great many books and engaged in correspondence with other rabbis. In the end my father annulled the marriage, voiding the whole thing by invalidating the witnesses. They had been seen smoking on *Shabbes*, that is to say, they had publicly desecrated the holy *Shabbes*; they had eaten unkosher food at the barracks, and were generally debauched youths.

But it was the same as before: the rabbi did not want to rely on his own authority alone and so he again wrote to Reb Yitskhok Elkhanon explaining his judgement. And again a response arrived addressed to the rabbi with salutations of respect: the letter was addressed to *Harov Hagoen*

210

H"G, the latter part an acronym of *HaGodl.*[644] The acronym made it a little less meaningful than if it were written out in full, nevertheless, to be called a "great genius" was a signal that Reb Yitskhok Elkhanon wished to support and protect the young Reb Yehuda Leyb by lending his full approval.

Young as I was, I was finding my bearings in the rabbinical hierarchy.

In short, Reb Yitskhok Elkhanon counted as practically a member of the family, a kind of spiritual grandfather, and I mourned his passing with great sadness. Naturally, I went to grieve {p. 215} in the synagogue to hear how my father would eulogize the great man. The synagogue was packed. The women's synagogue too was full. Not just women, but young girls too came. Reb Yehuda Leyb performed the funeral oration; the congregation wept, the women lamented and I with them, after which I felt purified, like a blue sky after the rain.

*

I was visiting my grandfather's house.

A young man appeared. He had brought a letter from my mother. He had come all the way from Augustow.

My grandmother was distracted and occupied: how would she cope with so many things to organize, there were only a few hours left before *Shabbes* would begin.

"Get out of here, what are you imagining?" She rubbed her hands, wiped them without a towel and donned her floral headscarf.

"I'm not imagining anything. He's standing outside on the porch."

My grandmother followed me.

The young man handed over the letter.

I read it for my grandmother.

The letter was brief. Clearly written in a hurry. The letter said they were preparing to leave Augustow and move to Ostrow in Lomza Province. It was a big city and also an important rabbinical office.

*

My father brought me with him to Ostrow.

I saw new kinds of Jews. They were nothing like the ones I knew in Augustow; they spoke differently, they dressed differently. If my father was their rabbi then that must mean they were true Jews, genuine Jews, but in my eyes they still seemed a little strange. They were so shabby, with wild, unkempt beards and long *peyes*, and they were all muddy, dusty, dirty.

But curiously, from what I could see my father was fond of those strange Jews. They were always hanging around our house, coming and going. They never left the door closed. By all appearances they needed my father all the time, needed his {p. 216} advice. They were very pious Jews, so said my mother, and that's why they liked my father. But I didn't like them at all. How could I be expected to like them when they didn't like me? They looked at me askance, cut me with their eyes and call me a "*daytsh.*"[645]

I can't begin to imagine how I, a Jewish boy from Michaliszki via Augustow could be a *daytsh* all of a sudden; when you're born Jewish in a rabbi's household can you be any different? How does that work? I don't know how they can come up with such a strange accusation.

I go out in the street and the boys of my age avoid me, look at me like I'm a freak. They wore long caftans; the coattails tangling between their legs—surely an impediment to walking

---

[644] The Great.
[645] A German word commonly used to denote a modern/assimilated Jew.

211

quickly. On their heads they wear such strangely shaped hats. I feel very uncomfortable in the streets. I prefer to sit at home away from watchful eyes. I'm ashamed of my attire.

My mother sent for a tailor. He took my measurements and in a few days' time I would have a long caftan like the others. I don't want to be so different from everyone else that they point their fingers at me. I also want to let my side locks grow so that they'll stop looking at me like I'm a scarecrow.

I was now all fitted out as was expected of me. I wore a long *tales-kotn*, a long caftan and a strange hat. I look at myself in the mirror—I can barely recognize myself. I think: I'm not the only one who has changed; my elder brother Velfke has also changed. The sisters have it easy, they have remained the same.

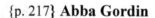

Augustow had quite a lot of *Maskilim*. There was a Hebrew and Yiddish library. The town even boasted two writers. One, named Frenkel, was a shopkeeper with a dry-goods store with his seat on the Eastern wall.[646] He published a long multi-stanza poem in Hebrew, in which he made fun of a fanatical rabbi who was splitting hairs about the line in the *Gemara*: "if a man falls from a roof and, in falling, inserts himself into a woman . . ."[647] The second writer, Shperling, was a helper of the state appointed rabbi, looked after the books of births, deaths, marriages, circumcisions, divorces etc., and had translated Jules Verne's (1828–1905) fantasy *Twenty Thousand Leagues Under the Sea* from French to Hebrew, in which the author predicted the invention of an underwater ship.

{p. 217} Abba Gordin

Abba Gordin was born in 1887. His father, Reb Yehuda Leyb, was a famous rabbi, a scholar of *Talmud* and *Torah*, as well as a *Maskil*.

In 1905–1906 Abba took part in the Russian Revolution and was arrested. In 1908 he founded (along with his brother V. Gordin) a *kheyder mesukn*, modernized religious school, in Smorgon, where he conducted interesting pedagogical experiments. In 1917 he took part in the October Revolution in Moscow where he was seriously wounded. He edited a daily newspaper *Anarkhia* (in Russian), battling Bolshevism. He was sentenced to death by the Cheka. Lenin pardoned him an hour before his scheduled execution. He left Russia illegally. Through Manchuria, China, and Japan he made his way to the United States in 1926.

He wrote in Hebrew, Yiddish, English, and Russian. He contributed to numerous newspapers, including; *Yidisher Kemfer*, *Tsukunft*,

---

[646] Of the synagogue. Closest to Jerusalem, it was a seat of honor.
[647] Babylonian *Talmud Yevamot* 53b.

HaDoar, Mabua, Megillot, Sefer Hashana, Reflex (English), and *Liberation* (Russian) and between 1948–1950 the quarterly periodical *Problems* (English).

His works: *The Children's Organizer, Game Album, Theatrical Garden, Youth* (drama and verse), *The Book of the Exile, Yiddish Grammar: A System of Material and Relative Naturalism* (Russian), *The Imitative Rational Method* (Russian) (these later in collaboration with his brother V. Gordin), *The Message of Transcomprehension* (poem, Russian), *Anarchy of the Spirit, Egotism* (poems), *Interindividualism,* two volumes (Russian), *Communism Unmasked* (English), *Jewish Ethics, The Basic Principles of Judaism, Women and the Bible, The Morality of Jewish Life, Social Superstition and Critique, The Foundations of Society, Memoirs and Musings,* two volumes, *Thirty Years of Jewish life in Poland-Lithuania, The Struggle for Freedom, Thinkers and Poets: Essays, Jewish Life in America, Sh. Yanovski* (biography), *Moses* (historical novel).

At the end of 1958 he settled in Israel. Edited a bimonthly periodical *Problemot—Problemen* (Hebrew/Yiddish). Problems of the Society, The Maharal from Prague, The Ar'I, Rashi. He died at the age of 77 on August 21, 1964.

p. 218 **On the Old Path**
by Eliezer Aronovski

When Borekh Beyle-Dobes walked across the street, from afar one could mistake him for a man without a head. His neck was bent from spending night and day hunched over the holy books. His head merged with his body, as though the *Torah* had drawn it downwards towards its light as sunlight draws plants towards the sun.

The burden of having to earn a living and provide for their four young children, fell upon the man's wife, Beyle-Dode. She was an efficient woman: healthy and solidly built, she ran the bakery. When the children were grown they began to help her with the work. Their baked goods had a reputation, and they made a good living. Their household was one of small-town wealthy bourgeoisie.

The three sisters looked like well-baked bread rolls with tanned cheeks. Two of them had chestnut hair, while the third was a brunette with eyes like black lumps of coal that had been driven into the dough, never to be removed. A fire always burned in those eyes, beautifying her face and hiding her flaws. She had one crippled leg. With her gaze she compelled everyone to look her straight in the eye and not at her limping.

It was rare to see Reb Borekh at home. His natural habitat was the prayer house. His entrance always brought with it a change of atmosphere; like a message from another world—from the world of *Torah* and holiness; of awe and trembling, of *mitzvot* and good deeds. He would greet people with a laborious turn of the head, revealing his gentle, sky-blue eyes. When someone visited his house as a guest he would treat the occasion with a detached solemnity, as though he were not the host, the head of the household, but a messenger for Him that feeds and nourishes all creatures and people in the world, who gives everything their daily bread.

{p. 219 } One could say that he had mixed blessings from his children. His eldest daughter, Khave, who always looked like a *Shabbes challah*—straight from the oven, brown and fresh, just asking to have a *brokhe* said over her—became a widow quite young. Her husband, a rabbi, died a few years after the wedding, without leaving a child behind. She moved back in with her parents.

The second daughter, Khane, never had any luck with betrothals. Perhaps her pale face, half-baked, as though the flames of the oven had sapped the blood from it, and her sour smile, as though smeared in lemon juice, had repelled any would be matches. For all that her body was slim, flexible, shapely—a flowery posterior. She was a kind girl too, one in a million.

She did find a husband though, in the end, admittedly a little late perhaps. He was a *yeshiva* student, Reb Khayim-Zorekh they called him. He possessed not a thing in the world, save perhaps destitution itself.

He was welcomed into such a bourgeois home—cookies and cakes on weekdays; white *challah*, fresh every morning; crystal glassware for tea and mealtimes fit for the Tsar. How could one resist a home like that?

He had no need to worry about making a livelihood, he could sit like his father-in-law, studying the *Torah*, and to top it all off he received a dowry of several thousand dollars. He was no oil painting himself: a redhead, with a freckled face, like a cookie sprinkled with cinnamon. His eyes were dull and watery, topped with sparse eyebrows. The marriage was agreed upon.

Several months after the wedding he was hardly recognizable. He had filled out, put on weight, like a swollen tire. His eyes were smaller and deeper, squinting; his cheeks jutted out, his face wide and round like a rose with its kernel removed—just two eyes, still immature, remained.

Several years after the wedding and the only path he knew was the one leading from the house to the synagogue and the synagogue back to the house.

He sat and studied alone—without great desire. Alone, in solitude, benches and lecterns, in wooden silence the whole day long. His voice was lost in the void, like water poured into a leaky bucket . . .

In the *yeshiva* his voice had blended with a dozen other voices forming a song of praise; but here it was a lone voice in the desert. His only comfort was that his wife took good care of him, and he thanked God for his marriage.

{p. 220} Time marched on and they began to search for a match for Rivke. True, she was crippled, and few cripples could hope to marry in keeping with their station . . . but a more pressing concern was where to put the son-in-law? Two sons-in-law in one house is like two cats in one sack. They had to find a way to get Khayim-Zorekh to go out into the world by himself; there was a whole world of Jewish businessmen out there, why could he not become one of them? They began to plant the idea, gradually, in his mind that he should continue to study as he did now, but only a few hours a week, and during the week he should go out and try to earn a few dollars as most people do it.

When Poland regained its independence as a state, hundreds of Poles came from America to settle in the surrounding towns and villages and from them one could always earn a little money. If the sum is small he can sell here to the local moneylenders, and if it's a larger sum, it would be worth his while traveling to Warsaw and getting 20–30 points more.

Khayim-Zorekh ate his breakfast, said his prayers, donned his coat and strode out the front door right into the market.

In the first moment he was lost. It had been years since he even stepped foot in a market. The shouting and the bustle, the noise and commotion seemed deafening to him. He stumbled his way through, around the wagons. A stallion let out a neigh at the highest octave, as though laughing at everything and everyone. Pigs squealed, tied up in wagons; hens, ducks and geese attempted to shout over the humans at their stands hawking their wares. With difficulty he found his way out from amid the wagons and back onto the sidewalk. He walked around, eyes peeled, searching for an American Pole, but could not find one for love nor money. He looked out for American shoes— an unmistakable hallmark of a returned Pole in those times—but there was neither sight nor sound of any. There was one man who looked like a nobleman and as he circled the perimeter of the market, every quarter of an hour, he looked him right in the face but could not ascertain if he was an American or not. He felt the man beckoning him with his gaze, with a welcoming demeanor. Several times he was on the verge of asking him if he had dollars for sale, but each time he lost his nerve and continued on his way. But how long can someone roam the streets concluding some business? What would they think of him at home? They would surely laugh at him, saying he was a total failure . . . how would that look if, after a whole day traipsing around the market, he came home saying he had not found a single American?

Thinking this he noticed that the nobleman was once again standing near him {p. 221}as though he were waiting to be called. He plucked up his courage and asked him: "*Mocię macie talarow przedać?*"[648]

He responded with a sly expression and nodded, yes. They went together into a nearby yard, behind a gate, and negotiated. The nobleman produced a twenty-dollar bill. Khayim-Zorekh touched it and scrutinized it from all angles to make sure it was not a forgery. He paid in zlotys and the two men re-emerged out onto the street. The nobleman stood still for a moment, and then asked Khayim-Zorekh to come with him. At first Khayim-Zorekh had no idea what was happening; he thought perhaps he was taking him to sell him more dollars. But when the man produced his ID, identifying himself as an undercover policeman, Khayim-Zorekh went weak at the knees. He began to tremble and begged him, half in Polish, half in Yiddish, to let him go.

The policeman choked with laughter at his bad Polish, and led him into the police station like a hardened criminal.

"I've got a new moneychanger for us today!" the policeman announced with triumphant pride.

Across from them, sitting at a desk, was a flaxen-haired sergeant who regarded him with an expression as though all the world belonged to him. From the wall, a portrait of the "old man" Pilsudski, looked down at him alongside a second image—the dead chicken[649]—the emblem and symbol of Polish independence . . .

The two men looked at Reb Khayim-Zorekh with disdain for the crime of dealing in foreign currency . . .

He attempted to explain, with gestures and grimaces more than with words, that he was no moneychanger, but that his sister was traveling to America and he wanted to give her some dollars.

They mocked him even more:

"*Żydowski*[650] brains . . . they have an answer for everything . . ."

Khayim-Zorekh sat frozen still on a chair in the corner. If he could have, he would have taken himself and torn himself apart, anything to avoid the shame that of all the thousand *goyim* wandering around the market he had to choose the undercover policeman!

Khane, his wife, began to worry about him . . . he should have been home from the market long ago. Her heart told her something was not right . . . she sent out her brother Ruven to go to the market and find out what was happening.

It did not take long. The Jewish shopkeepers told him {p. 222} that they had seen his brother-in-law walking with the police. Ruven went to the police station and found Khayim-Zorekh sitting there, pale and listless, looking like death warmed over.

After meeting with one of the fixers who was connected to the police they added another twenty to the twenty dollars and Khayim-Zorekh was free to go.

Khayim-Zorekh did not have a bite to eat that day, only a glass of tea with a slice of lemon. His blood was boiling, his face was aflame: his freckles seemed to merge together into one big fiery blotch. One could barely see his pained, tear-filled eyes.

Dear Khane, that kindly soul, his wife, comforted him as one consoles a sick child, caressing and stroking him, attempting to calm him down.

---

[648] "Do you have dollars to sell?"

[649] Aronovski is of course being ironic here: the symbol referred to is a heraldic eagle, not a dead chicken.

[650] Jewish.

"It will never happen again," she whispered in a motherly tone. "Your place is in the prayer house. I will go out and work for you, like my mother. I'll find some business to do and you'll be free to sit and study. That is my father's path and that will be your path. How had I not realized it sooner? Where was my head that I sent you off into the market? Well, what's done is done. It'll never happen again!"

Her words, like the cooing of a quiet dove, calmed his nerves and settled his troubled spirit. The evening sun shining in through the window encouraged him. It was time for afternoon prayers. He got up, said good day, and went out the back door to go to the synagogue.

Khane followed his progress through the window with pensive, pain-filled eyes. The hidden light of a pure soul radiated from her entire being, breathing sanctity and wisdom. Her lips trembled as though she were kissing his every footstep as he neared the prayer house, on his path—the path of the eternal Jew.

Mottinke the Sweet

Motinke the Sweet is one of the sons from the Kurik family. The Kurik family is a large, extended family of gardeners. Uncomplicated, healthy people, with wide shoulders and ruddy rustic faces. Most of them were blond with freckles {p. 223} and they walked with heavy, steady gaits atop solidly built legs.

They always carried with them the faint odor of the fields, of the gardens and orchards. In the springtime they plowed, tilled, and sowed. They watered the plots, plucked and tore out every weed, pampered every new shoot, every bud, until the plots were teeming in their full ripeness, overflowing with green.

The garden always followed them into the house, on the bare feet of the women, and on the boots of the men, together with the carrots, radishes, cucumbers and potatoes which lay in piles by the table, next to the chairs, in the corners, under the beds, along with clumps of the rich, brown earth itself, as though the garden had moved into the house to live with them.

Mottinke the Sweet was brown haired and of medium height. He looked nothing like his brothers, who were all blond, looking more like his two sisters who were both brunettes.

Mottinke found a girl who resembled himself, a dark-haired, plump girl whom he married and who bore him a daughter nine months after the wedding.

In addition to working in the gardens he also opened a fruit shop. In the summer, his shop also served cold glasses of soda water. In the early years his wife ran the shop and later new employees arrived: his own daughters. With God's grace his wife bore a new child almost every year, and every child, as if to spite their wish for a son, was a girl. Nonetheless their daughters were a source of pride: each was more striking than the last: black eyes, pitch black hair, just as Jewish children should be.

With each passing year his fruit shop became fuller and livelier. His ten daughters stood behind the counter, like a living ladder reaching for the highest shelves.

The older girls began to attract the attention of boys who would gather in the shop in swarms, drinking soda water with chocolate, or buying a bunch of green-gilded cherries; juicy apples; plums so fiery they appeared kissed by the sun; apples as red as frozen girlish cheeks; chaste yellow pears, full of life's juices.

Alongside the fruit, Mottinke's daughters also ripened, like a living orchard of trees. By some their breasts began to grow under their linen blouses like newly ripened plums; others were more like stiff, juicy {p. 224} apples; and some like late summer pears. For this reason, the local boys were drawn to Mottinke the Sweet's fruit shop: not so much for the fruit on the shelves, but to catch a glimpse of the burgeoning harvest of the living orchards . . .

216

Mottinke the Sweet had no great luck in business, but his shop was always jolly and lively and that lightened the burden of his toil.

He spent most of his time traveling around the gardens and orchards, bartering produce in the villages or transporting it to other towns to sell. He never complained of his fate, was always happy with his lot; but deep in his heart he yearned for a son. And as it turned out, God heard his prayer and gifted him with a male child, a boy. His joy and the joy in his home was indescribable. The whole world danced to meet him, everyone wished him *mazel tov*! People he had never dared approach—what right had he, a simple Jew, to bother such learned men? —came to him to shake hands and wish him *mazel tov*!

One scholar said to him:

"*You have sought and you have found*! *Mazel tov* to you!"

"What do you mean by that?" Mottinke asked, not quite understanding the Hebrew words.

"You've done it!"

"Oh," Mottinke cried out, "You think it was as easy as that to have a son? Ten girls it cost me!"

"What do you mean ten girls?" the learned man asked him with a grimace.

"I've been seeking the boy ever since I got married, but everything went downhill."

He realized the gravity of what he had said and added hastily, "Praise be, I have nothing to be ashamed of where my daughters are concerned! Lovely fine children, but it's not the same as having a son. But now, God be praised, my family is complete."

For the ten girls the boy was like a gift from heaven. Day and night they fought over him; each wanted to coddle him, to carry him around in their arms, feed him, play with him. Several times fights broke out between the sisters over whose turn it was to take care of the boy. Sometimes just as one sister was about to raise a fist against her rival {p. 225} their father would come in just at the right moment and cry out:

"Be quiet, you brats! Give the boy to me, he is mine and that's the end of it!"

They were afraid of their father and both rivals would admit defeat and Mottinke would be left with the boy.

The boy was raised by Mottinke the Sweet like a crown prince. The very best of everything that came into the house was reserved for his son. And when Mottinke returned from business in a distant town he would always find some trinket or other to bring home for the boy. Mottinke, his wife, and his daughters—they all treated the boy the same way; guarding him with their lives, keeping him safe from any possible harm.

*

It was a dark late summer's night. The rain was pouring down like buckets, fall had announced its imminent arrival bringing with it death, cold and desolation.

Soaked to the bone, Mottinke made his way home along the path, battered by the wind and rain; it was only thanks to his horse with its animal instinct, homing in on his stable and trough, that Mottinke found his way home in the dark.

He perceived a pale light shining through the window. His heart trembled. How could they not be asleep yet? He quickly untethered the horse, led it into the stable, and entered the house, running straight into the room where he saw his wife and older daughters who were anxiously huddled around the bed of his only son.

"What's wrong?" he struggled to ask.

"The child is not well," his wife said, barely able to speak through the tears.

The child lay in bed with red, cloudy eyes and pink cheeks. Through feverish lips he managed a smile when he saw his father next to him.

"What do we do?" he paced around the room, forgetting that he had been drenched from head to toe by the rain.

"Father!" his eldest daughter tried to console him; "It's nothing, he has a little fever. That's all. The doctor will come tomorrow and he will get well. Go and get out of those wet clothes. You could catch your death yourself, God forbid."

And she began to peel the wet coat from her father's shoulders so that he could get undressed.

{p. 226} The whole night they stayed up without sleeping, every now and then stealing a look at the child's burning face, and as though to spite them, the night stretched ever on, like flowing pitch, as though it did not want to end. Each hour felt like a year. The hands of the clock seemed not to be moving at all. It felt as though an hour ago it had been three o'clock, but now, after what felt like an hour of pain, suffering and dark thoughts, another glance at the clock revealed that it was only ten past three! What was happening? Was the clock broken? —No, it was working! My God, when would the night end!

The doctor warned them not to let any of the other children into the boy's room, only the parents and the eldest daughter were to be allowed in. He wrote a prescription, administered an injection, and told them to call him again if things looked like they were getting worse.

A few days passed where the child was feeble. The household was turned upside down. Every face displayed grief. On the third night the parents had still not slept. The children implored them, but to no avail.

On the fourth night the rain battered the windowpanes, as if demons were tapping with their fingernails, trying to claw their way into the house. The child's face was aflame, like a winter's sun on a frosty day, on the edge of the horizon at dusk. The child's mother sat by one side of the bed, tears flowing from swollen eyes, wringing her hands with worry. The father paced around the room, as though wrestling with someone who wanted to strangle him, unable to shake off his assailant. The child was going out like a light, a flame flickering on the last piece of tallow, one more twitch and the room would be plunged into darkness.

It was midnight. The pouring rain continued to dance in a whirlwind with demons and ghosts, whistling and howling, enveloping the town in black fabric, stretching out into the abyss. Mottinke threw open the door, as though he wanted to give himself up to the Devil, to cast himself into the storm, and set off to fetch the doctor. At first the doctor was hesitant, as though he wanted to extricate himself from his duty, reluctant to give up his warm bed for the wet outside. But when he saw Mottinke's eyes—like two gaping chasms, from which poured a sea of pleading and pity— he put on his smock and coat, picked up his umbrella and they ran through the weeping streets into the howling night.

The doctor tried to give the boy a second injection, perhaps it would help him at the last minute. But it was already too late. Death {p. 227} was already dancing outside. The whole town wept and lamented. The wind carried the lamentations over the world and Mottinke's gift from heaven swallowed up the Earth.

Overnight it was as though he turned gray. Old age crept up on him. People barely recognized him.

After the *shiva* he hitched up his horse and cart, as though he wanted to run away from home, away from the place where his child, his only son, was taken from him, and set off on the road, as though he were trying to find his son somewhere; as though he were not dead, but merely lost, somewhere out there beyond the fields, beyond the forests, trying to find his way home to his parents and sisters, just as his father was searching for him.

But he soon returned from the village with several sacks of grain, a few pounds of potatoes and some winter vegetables. The day was coming to an end. The last rays of sunlight were still coloring the tips of the pine trees, making them appear like bloody needles which had pierced his heart. He was pensive and muttered to himself, alone in the forest:

"What did I do to deserve such a punishment? What was my crime? I have always done only good things! I've never done anyone any harm. If I met a stranger on the road I would always give them a lift on my cart—Jew or Gentile, it made no difference, no need for him to go on foot. I've always given whatever I can: a piece of bread, some fruit, a donation. God knows I've never earned more than I needed to get by, and have never complained, and when the gift came to me from God—my boy—I was happier than could be. The whole world could not match my joy. And then suddenly . . . such a calamity! Such misfortune! I hardly had time to spend with him. Barely six years old and already taken from me. Oh, God! If I encountered you now on the road, and you asked me for a lift, I would not be a Jew if I accepted! . . . that you could create so much pain and anguish for me!

Waves of bitterness tore his heart apart and covered the forest with his grief. Black shadow crept around the trees like snakes, and stretched up to the treetops like cords upon which the day dangled like a hanged man. The surrounding woods were saturated in the terrible grief of Mottinke the Sweet, emanating with the bitterness of bile. The winds carried his lament, his muted howl, like a dark curse—and night fell upon the world.

{p. 228} The Saccharin Man

A dark and handsome boy with lively eyes framed with thick eyebrows, which bordered his nose the way the edge of the forest runs along the riverbank.

A thick head of chestnut hair with a white part by the side and a quiff on top like a brawler.

Short riding breeches, a sports-jacket, a hat whose long visor, half-round, bent like a quarter moon, served to intensify the shadow from which his bright eyes shone like stars.

He turned away from *kheyder, Gemara, yeshiva*. What was one to do? His mother, with her three other children, had just come back from the Soviet Union where she'd been a refugee.

A new state, Poland, had come into being. A mother with four children needed food, needed a home—her old home had gone up in flames on the outbreak of the First World War. From the whole town only two houses and the church survived intact. They went to stay in a neighboring town.

Jews were wheeling and dealing—doing business. Most lived from markets and fairs. Individuals smuggled merchandise from Germany into Poland and further on to the Soviet Union. The largest market was the smuggling of saccharin tablets and crystals.

He was pulled into it. He himself did not know how. Was it poverty? Hunger? Hopelessness?

Around Suwalki there were a line of towns that bordered Eastern Poland. With a simple pass one could cross the border in either direction. The shopkeepers were regular visitors to Germany and they did business both above and below board.

On dark nights when you could not see one step in front of you, when a tree could appear to be a person, and a person a tree, they stole over empty fields with sacks on their shoulder, brought by farmers who lived right next to the border. Sometimes whole carts of smuggled goods were moved out in the open, bold as brass, when the border guards had been bribed on both sides.

On each bridge, by every exit and entry from the town, stood Polish policemen or "canaries'—gendarmes, who searched the vehicles, poking around in the hay, inspecting the seats, covers, baggage etc., only rarely finding any contraband.

The saccharin wagons went with double covers. The wagons, hollowed out inside, hid a few dozen kilograms of saccharin each. The large-scale smugglers operated in this manner. The small-time smugglers contented themselves with {p. 229} carrying the contraband about their person: in sacks on their bodies, under shirts, on their ribcages, hanging down over their bellies.

Others filled the lining of their coats with long thin sacks like sausages, from top to bottom, containing a universe of saccharin.

The young saccharin man wrapped his body in thin sacks which he filled with small boxes containing 100–500 saccharin tablets in each.

Wrapped in this sweet shell he feigned an innocent expression, and always sat up front like a driver's assistant and it never occurred to anyone to imagine that he was a smuggler.

On more than one occasion when all the passengers were taken off and searched, he would stand to one side like an innocent soul that does not understand what is going on. He went on all sorts of trips and missions that an older man would never have dared.

He would find out that on a particular day a certain coachman had been ordered by the government to transport soldiers, or government employees, and in front of everyone's eyes, in the courtyard of the magistrate's building, which was swarming with police and soldiers, he would bring two parcels of saccharin and hide them under the seat of the carriage.

On the bridge over the Black Anshe, no one dared stop the carriage filled with such scoundrels, these princes of the new Poland.

Evening fell. From both sides of the forest glow worms traced luminous arcs over the road, like phosphorus flares lighting up the sky with their threads. A sharp turpentine smell blew in from the pine forests, filling the air with the intoxicating scent of blossoms. The soldiers ordered the carriage to stop, and lay glow worms on top of the hay where they lit up the wagon like flashlights.

He did not always manage to travel so calmly; often his heart pounded louder than the saccharin rattling in the boxes under his breast.

Spring. The woods were teeming with red and black berries. Gentile women with floral head scarves and dresses, their posteriors pointed towards the heavens, picked berries, filling whole baskets and taking them to sell in the town. Blue, matte, enveloped in dew like black beads, shimmering and sparkling to passers-by like wanton girls with dark come-hither eyes.

Fiery, like the flaming lips of ripe youth, the red berries beckoned, calling out to be kissed. During berry season, alongside the normal {p. 230} saccharin contraband which he had on his person, he also brought two large milk cans filled with saccharin at the bottom, and covered on top with a layer of berries. A stroke of luck that the clatter of the wheels and the hooves drowned out the echo of the shaking saccharin boxes against his body. And the policeman, the gendarme, who often sat next to him on the bench did not hear a thing.

Winter. Night. A blizzard sweeping and grinding; thin, silver whips of snow assailing you, making it impossible to open an eye; a wild twisting of frozen white foam enveloping everything and everyone. The horses, who know the way, lead the sleds back home over hills and through the mounds of snow that have erased the roads and pathways.

The cold, the frost, the treacherous weather—none of it deterred the saccharin man. On the contrary, they were his companions . . . they helped him to smuggle. Who would be out in such weather waiting to intercept a sled in the middle of the night?

"*Stój!*"[651] a voice called out from the darkness.

They are here! Like pieces of the blizzard personified with burning faces, ordering him to get down off the sled. Lighting their torches, searching and rummaging—finding nothing.

A muttered curse and a spit in the snow, they begrudgingly stepped back. They had been so sure they had snagged a fish and would make a few zlotys . . .

---

[651] Halt!

Daybreak. The houses huddled up together outside, everything at peace and aslumber. There was already a light burning in Rokhl's window. She was preparing a packed meal for her son's journey.

Like a piece of the night itself, he ran through dark, empty streets, like a cat, to the coachman who was preparing to go to pick up his passengers.

All day long his mother went around with a pounding heart. She did not see anyone. On her lips she whispered a prayer, that God should watch out for him, that he should not be arrested.

In the evenings she lay in bed with cramps, with both daughters lying by her side, her youngest son in the next room on the sleeping bench. Everyone else was asleep but she could not keep her eyes closed. The minutes stretched out interminably. Hours went by like years. All the while she imagined she could hear footsteps on the stairs, the creak of a door; he was done for—policemen like bandits had captured her Khayim and they were raiding the house, forcing the children, weeping in fright, from their beds, searching every nook and cranny, inside the mattresses, under the beds, poking the bedding to find more hidden saccharin . . .

{p. 231} The black night looked in through the window, darkening her fear even more . . .

The things she went through during those night hours! How many terrible thoughts went through her mind? Until finally she would see her son slip back into the house, removing his sacks of saccharin, and her heart would once again know respite . . .

The Polish-Soviet War broke out. The Red Army was already in Warsaw. The town now lay far behind the front in Soviet territory. Prices rose. Food was in short supply. People came from the big cities to buy food in the smaller towns. You couldn't find food at any price; those that had food hid it.

In the house there were several kilograms of saccharin. A young man came from Grodno willing to pay a good price. It would be enough to keep the family alive for several months. But how to get it out of the town?

Yoshke, a fellow townsman and the son of a glazier from Sztabin, stood watch on the bridge over the Augustow Canal. Khayim begged him to let them pass with the saccharin, to make it as far as the train station.

"I'm standing guard. I must follow the orders of the authorities: I'm not letting you or anyone else past"—there was no solution.

A late summer's evening. A blue frame—the forest—enveloped the town. Parallel with the canal, in the forest, two youths walk, avoiding the guard on the way to the train. They pass through without difficulty, and with the money the mother bought wheat, and with a hand-mill attached to the table, he stands there for days on end grinding the wheat: one turn, two turns, three turns, until the flour is a fine powder.

Young, muscular hands knead the doubt in the trough, like a lump of clay, fermenting with abundance and nourishment.

Brown loaves, like wheels, are taken out of the oven. During the short period of the occupation they knew no hunger. The loaves of bread sang from their hiding places, filling the house with peace and happiness.

Over the bridge, for twenty-four hours straight, the Red Army's baggage trains were making their retreat. Iron and stone expressing the moan of human anguish, lending a melancholy flavor to the clatter of the wheels.

At home, ground, kneaded and baked with their own sweat and toil, the loaves shone like radiant suns, illuminating and seemingly offering protection to five lives amid the external deluge of blood and fury . . .

Some Personalities of Our City

In the Company of Meir Meizler and Yaakov Frenkel
by Tz. Z. Weinberg

In the beginning of the fall of 1903, when I had only just moved the members of my family from the religious Ostrov to Augustow, and I breathed easier in the free atmosphere of the area, I found much interest in the company of new acquaintances, the salt of the earth, with whom I became acquainted. I connected with strong friendship with my neighbor Meir Meizler, the Hebrew teacher, whose house I lived across from, as if I had known him for a long time.

The fall and the winter passed for me with hard and exhausting work. My friends and acquaintances offered me private lessons, from which I supported myself with difficulty. The work was plentiful and the salary was small, and Meir Meizler guided me in the ways of instruction and human relations, how to teach and how to come into contact with people, and he became a guardian to me, and he was a help and useful to me. The essence of my strength was in the teaching of *Tanakh* and *Aggadah*[652] and works of literature. In the teaching of language and grammar I was more than a little lame, and each day before the lessons I prepared myself properly and with great effort. I was always worried that I would fail, and so, slowly, I completed my education in this profession also, and in my coming to teach I became a learner.

In the evenings, after difficult and exhausting work, and walking all over from house to house, and from the castigation of the comments from the mothers that supervised my lessons, I arrived home, towards evening, tired and broken. I ate my bread and lay down to rest. By the light of a candle, in my small room, I rose and shook myself off, took hold of the writers' pen, and the fever of writing entirely encompassed me, and liberated me from the bitterness of my day and from carrying my yoke, and in this way I sat and wrote until a late hour of the night.

I developed three stories at the same time, in the fall and winter, the first fruits of my labor, and together with a few things (unripe attempts, that I was able to show to the writer H.D. Numberg, a passing guest in Augustow, who supported them and said to me in these words: "young man, you have talent…") I hid them in my drawer, and I did not reveal them to any person, mostly because of my hesitations and my doubts, and I was embarrassed to articulate[653] that I was a writer.

On the festival of *Purim*, I was invited, me and my wife, to the house of Meir Meizler. We spent an extended time there. After the hearty feast and lively conversation with the company, the group split; the women sat apart on the sofa, and continued with the conversation that was pleasant for them, and Meizler and I went into the other room, and exchanged words on the matters of our profession, teaching, and we touched also on matters of literature. To my great surprise Meizler opened his bookcase, and on its shelves manuscripts were placed, packaged and bound in tens, one upon the next, and with a sarcastic joke, slightly tipsy, he commented to me, with the bitterness of his soul, that all these {p. 233} writings, which my eyes were seeing, he had sent more than once to various publishing houses, but he had not succeeded in publishing them; they sent them back. Oh well – he concluded with a bitter laugh – these evil ones did theirs, and I do mine. I don't despair at all…" And in the middle of this, he took out of the stack of his writings an edition of *HaTzefirah*," bound nicely in thin white paper, opened it and spread it out before me "Here,

---

[652] "Telling," which refers to non-halakhic rabbinic exegetical texts, in the *Talmud* and in works of *Midrash. Aggadah* (sometimes "*Haggadah*") is a corpus of rabbinic texts that includes folklore, historical anecdotes, moral exhortations, and practical advice in various spheres.

[653] Literally, to raise to the door of my lips. Psalms 141:3 "O Lord, set a guard over my mouth, a watch at the door of my lips;"

finally, I won" - he said like a victor – "they printed one of my big articles, and the readers were full of enthusiasm from it."

Because of my manners I read the article in its entirety. Meir Meizler sat across from me and peered at me, and did not take his eyes off me, and when I finished the reading, I said what I said to praise him, and he clapped his hands and his eyes {p. 234} gleamed, and radiated satisfaction at my words, and he added and said: "here you see, the rest of the articles are also not inferior to this… but nevertheless…" he sighed and did not finish, and he drank an additional glass of liquor to banish his sorrow.

The Writers Yaakov Frenkel and Tz. Z. Weinberg (1904)

From right to left: The writer Tzvi Zevulun Weinberg, Meir Meizler, Moshe Ber Eizenstadt, Shmuel Weinberg (1904).

We sat for a long time, until a late hour of the night, and we conversed out of good-heartedness and friendly connection, and when I rose to go, while I was standing on the threshold, there escaped from my mouth, unintentionally, a restrained utterance: "I too write sometimes, I too have manuscripts, but I have not yet sent them anywhere…" When Meir Meizler heard this, he did not let go of me; he accompanied me to my house, and I was compelled in the dead of night to search for my writings and put them in his hands for reading.

On the next day, in the afternoon, *Shushan Purim,*[654] I turned aside again to Meir Meizler's house just to visit, {p. 235} as was my way, since there was also a free day from learning, and incidentally, I was in a hurry to hear his opinion on my writing, which I had turned over to him the day before, and I found in his company the *chazzan* of the town, whom I had met a long time ago, and he was an educated man and a lover of books, and the two of them as one received me with a shout and compliments, and mentioned with praise my story that they had read together, before my arrival, and they advised me to publish it without delay.

---

[654] The holiday of *Purim* is celebrated on the 14th of the month of *Adar*, but the sages instituted that *Shushan* residents perpetually observe *Purim* on the 15th of Adar—the day when the Jews of *Shushan* celebrated. The 15th of *Adar* is hence known as "*Shushan Purim.*"

I sat in their company thrilled and confused,[655] and agitated by their good words, and dubious within myself, lest these friends of mine had exaggerated, and when I sent these stories of mine to a publication, then it would happen that their fate would be like the fate of Meir Meizler's writings. I considered and I restrained my spirit and I did not answer at all. At last I girded strength and I said to them that I was not able to send my writings to a publication, because I feared the great disappointment when they sent my writings back. When they heard my words, the two of them burst out into laughter, and they continued and took counsel between them, and they arrived at a conclusion that these writings should be transmitted to the merchant Yaakov Frenkel, a permanent resident of Augustow, and they would hear what he had to say. I agreed to their suggestion.

This Yaakov Frenkel was known to me. Immediately upon my arrival in Augustow I heard about him a lot. I read something in his books (his translation of "The History of Beliefs and Ideas" and his "Chronicles"). I also encountered his name in various periodicals. In Augustow, there were those who interpreted him for praise and also for reproach. They lauded his ability, his intelligence and his understanding, and criticized his stubbornness, his rigidity, and his vindictiveness, in his book of polemic that he published against his rivals. I saw him a few times on the streets and next to his shop (his wife's manufacturing shop), and also sometimes I stopped by his house to his daughters, in my wife's name, who befriended them, and I peeked into his room, when he was sitting bent over his books and his papers, next to his table, studying, pondering and writing. I felt an internal agitation, a kind of reverence, in my peeking at him; this is what a Hebrew writer looked like in my eyes, sitting on the birthstool[656] in his hidden corner. When he would get up and pass to its end, from his room to the kitchen, and saw me in his daughters' presence, and didn't say anything, and his sparkling eyes as if really redeeming me, I became confused and I hastened to leave the house. He was exalted in my eyes, and I humbled myself to stand in his presence.

Many days went by, and I did not receive any information about my writings that were in his hand. Meir Meizler too did not know what to say: "He is not in a hurry to read" he added "he is busy with his own, there is no hurrying him, this is his way, and it is forbidden to bother and annoy him…" I bit my flesh with my teeth[657] and remained silent, and I didn't ask him again.

A few days after that, Rosa, Yaakov Frenkel's youngest daughter, in talking with my wife, divulged… "I forgot entirely… Father requested that you stop by to see him…" I heard, and my heart pounded inside me, and I thought a lot about the appointed meeting. Quaking I entered Yaakov Frenkel's house, and he rose to greet me, received me hospitably, brought me into his room, seated me across from him, with prolonged deliberateness took my writings out of his drawer, felt them a little, as if weighing their quality, and placed them in my hands. "The stories are written with ability" – he said – "but they are full of mistakes and more than a few flaws…" I lowered my head, and he added "continue, continue to write…you have your own style, and in the end you will succeed…" These last words of his encouraged me. I lifted my head, and I looked straight at him: tucked into the armchair, dressed in a morning robe, the hair of his head graying, his short beard black and gray, he sat before me like an old hunchback, entirely shrunken, as if a chill gripped him, and his high forehead and his inspecting eyes directed at me: "nice, nice" he ended softly – "I have no doubt, you have ability… but it is not enough…you must learn…learn…read a lot…and acquire much information…"

---

[655] There is a little *Purim* humor here, for in the Book of *Esther* we read (3:14) "The king and Haman sat down to feast, but the city of *Shushan* was confused."
[656] Exodus 1:16 "…When you deliver the Hebrew women, look at the birthstool…"
[657] The equivalent of "I bit my tongue."

{p. 236} We parted in friendship. His unyielding tension softened as he stood on the threshold to accompany me, but he did not ask me to stop by to see him again. I heard from Meir Meizler that he spoke favorably of me, but I did not again come into contact with him alone. I encountered him many times on the street, I blessed him with peace, and it was like he veered away to pass by, and did not stop at all. An extended time passed in this way. On one of the days his daughter Roza again informed me that her father requested that I come to him. This time he received me really with warm-heartedness, as if a new light was radiating on him, talked with me at length, asked me in detail about the progress of my work in teaching and writing, made his comments with light humor and good advice. At last, incidentally, he told me the purpose for which he had summoned me: "he had received an invitation from the well-known writer Ben Avigdor[658] to participate in a new newspaper "HaZman," a daily and monthly newspaper, which was about to come out soon in Vilna. He sees, therefore, that he has a pleasant obligation to include my stories that he read a long time ago, in sending his writings to the publication, but that I had to bring them to him together with the additional things that I had written, in order for him to proofread them in advance and prepare them appropriately before sending them for their document."

I was filled with joy after his words, and I became a regular visitor in his house. He sat with me many hours, and he passed his quill over my writing, and did this with pleasure and fury. When he found some expression appropriate or a sentence as it should be, he shriveled with sweet language and an easy breath: "nice, nice, so, so..." And when he encountered a mistake or linguistic flaw, he got angry: "How, young man? How do you write?... This is absolutely not Hebrew..." And when once he found a linguistic distortion, he laughed out loud, and turned to me with his sharp disparagement: "How, young man, how do you confuse the creatures? On the street, I often see you, you know how to distinguish between male and female... you know well how to follow the pretty girls... and here, here in your writing, you are not precise at all... male and female, the two of them are as one, equal in your eyes...is that possible!!??"

I left him in good spirits, my writings in my hand, in order to copy them over cleanly, and transmitted them to him a second time in order to send them to the publication "HaZman." Full hours of the night I sat and copied, and I trembled over every letter and word, to copy them correctly. When I had finished everything, I hurried to Yaakov Frenkel's house, and trembling, gave him the copies. He sat across from me, in his usual way, relaxed, studied my writing and read, read them silently and aloud, and I did not take my eyes off him. I sat like a sentenced person waiting for his judgement. When he finished, he lifted his face, looked at me with wonder, and chuckled: "How, how, young man? Letters like these?!...Lilliputians! Tiny letters!! The editors will poke out their eyes to read them!" He leafed through the pages again, leafed, until he arrived at the last page, and suddenly he burst out in laughter: "so, so, what signature?! What length?! Really a long Sephardi name, long, Tzvi Zevulun Weinberg... what letters! And what size?! Here, inside, small, small, really midgets... and here, at the end, big, big, gigantic really, Tzvi Zevulun Weinberg... you should be ashamed of yourself, young man, is that how one writes?!..."

I shame-facedly took my writings back, and sat again for full nights to copy them over, scrupulously making sure that they were copied and edited according to their proper format, in average writing, according to Frenkel's instructions, and I signed my name with the abbreviation "Tz. Z. Weinberg," in small letters, so that it would not stand out so much. I brought all this to Frenkel, and gave it to him, with trembling hands. He checked my writing cursorily, cast an eye on the writing and on my signature, and laughed lightly, patted me on the shoulder, and was satisfied with my work.

---

[658] Pen-name, Avraham Leib Shalkovich, Russian Hebrew novelist and publisher; born in Zheludok, Vilna, in 1867.

225

I went out from him happy and goodhearted, and everything in me sang within me, but on the way and in my house {p. 237} my doubts gnawed at me, as was my way: "lest Frenkel regrets his decision, and doesn't send my writings... and if he sends them, who at the publication, will pay attention to them? And if they read them, who knows, what will be their fate? They will still send them back to me...so I mulled it over in my doubts, and my soul was disgusted.[659] Over a few days Roza, Frenkel's daughter, came into our house again, and in her hand a package of articles bound up for sending, and her father's letter, which she opened circumspectly out of curiosity, and her laughter filled her mouth. And this is approximately what Frankel wrote, in a summary of his letter to Ben Avigdor: "Surely my opinion of our fine literature, with which we stuff the Hebrew community, is known to you, which, as far as I'm concerned, is in the sense of permissible, and there is no need for it except that the community is enthusiastic about it, and you find interest in it. Here I add, therefore, the stories of the beginning writer Tz. Z. Weinberg, which from each and every line bursts forth great talent, and the material is good according to your taste..." I found great satisfaction these words of Frenkel's, and I calmed down. The company in my house joked about me and my "great talent" that Frenkel found in me, and caused me pleasure.

In my next visits to Frenkel, I pretended not to know about his letter to Ben Avigdor, I brought him new writings to read, and when I asked him, pretending innocence, if he had sent my stories to Ben Avigdor, he answered me with annoyance: "Well then what did you think, that I left them in my house?! Do you have a need for them?!" And he did not continue to speak with me further, read my new writings, went over them with his quill, and poured out on me the fullness of his complaints: "For what purpose is there to write with this kind of contempt, with mistakes like these? Why don't you take pains, young man, to learn something fundamental and write properly, surely there is talent in you, there is!" I did not tell him that I sat seven clean days[660] on everything that I turn over to him for reading. I knew that he would not believe me.

On one of these visits I found Meir Meizler in his house, sitting and discussing with him a thick notebook, that he had given him for reading, and Frenkel had dismissed his article. The purpose of dismissal: "I found nothing of value in it – he said – the Hebrew, however, is not bad, but aside from that there is nothing in it."

"But Reb Yaakov" Meir Meizler argued to defend himself – "here, here" and pointed with his finger to one section in particular, which seemed much in his eyes, "here too, Reb Yaakov, will you say that there is nothing, here too?!" He concluded in amazement, and his face turned red.

But, Reb Meir, Reb Meir, Yaakov Frenkel answered after him, imitating his voice twice – you have put before me a bucket of water, and put into it a sugar cube, will it be sweet? Will it be sweet?! And he concluded his words with annoying laughter. Meizler's face was covered,[661] and I turned my eyes away, so as not to see his failure, and I immediately left the room, as if hurrying on my way.

He was a lonely man, walking on his own path, and strange to the members of his household. His wife was exaggeratedly religious, bound to the synagogue and prayed every day, and he was a freethinker, an *apikores*. His foot did not step into the prayer house, except on *Yom Kippur*. His daughters were blossoming scholars, and his mind did not rest from them. Every day he would rise early, enter the nearby tea house, review the newspapers and return home. He would eat his meal, and seat himself next to the table, and hours upon hours he would sit and read and

---

[659] Job 10:1 "I am disgusted with life..."

[660] Referring to the full week that a woman waits after seeing a drop of menstrual blood before she can immerse in the *mikvah* and resume sexual relations. Babylonian *Talmud Berakhot* 31a "The daughters of Israel were stringent with themselves; to the extent that even if they see a drop of blood corresponding to the size of a mustard seed she sits seven clean days for it..."

[661] Or, downcast. Esther 7:8 "...No sooner did these words leave the king's lips than Haman's face was covered."

write. Only towards evening he would go outside, take a walk, annoy the loafers, and at their posts he would pass the townspeople under the whip of his tongue, those who were hateful to him,[662] and with special venom he would pour the bitterness of his contempt and ridicule on {p. 238}these "stammering faces and twisted backs" with his nicknames for those who were dear to him, to the enjoyment of the listeners, and take leave of them for his walk quiet and calm, as one who had fulfilled his task properly.

I accompanied him on these walks of his more than once, for it was not comfortable for me to disturb him a lot in his house, and he would receive me willingly, and his conversation was gurgling like a babbling spring, and with his sharp expression he harshly criticized world champions and men of letters. He was especially angry and complained about Frishman, who praised Nietzsche and interpreted his words: "this crazy person, with the torturous distorted mind, the degenerate of the 19th century, he is our *Yoreh Deah*?!"[663] He is a paragon for us?!" And he concluded with a sting: "we were influenced by the beauty, the beautiful one of Yafet,[664] and if this beautiful one of his is anointed[665] with poison,[666] he destroys all of our good part in literature and in life."

On one of the *Shabbatot* I came out of the synagogue, on my way home, and Frenkel encountered me and stopped me. He was in a happy mood, and took up his message on nation and humanity as one, and he spoke trembling on the believers who followed in vain and hurled scathing words about the synagogue and those who come to pray within it, and he struck with the staff of his mouth the people of the east and the west as one, and suddenly he glanced at me and discerned my weak position in relation to him, and immediately he changed his tune and added: "these words are not spoken towards you…you appear in my eyes to be honest and a true believer… go, therefore, on this path of yours, and may God be with you…only these…those who trade in God and faith as one…they are abhorred by me, and I am unable to tolerate them and their faith as one…"

I was confused in all my meetings with him, and I was embarrassed to ask him about the fate of my writings. In the meantime, I stood for the army exam and I was released from service, but I was stuck there with a pox illness, and I became very ill, and I was confined to my bed for many, many, months, and when I recovered and recuperated and got out of my bed, I sat and I studied the stories that had then been published in various places, and I compared my stories to them. I did not find that they were inferior to the ones that I read, and I wondered about their delay. I therefore wrote a letter to Frenkel, and I asked him if he had received any information regarding my writing, and he answered me sharply: "Don't you have patience? Do you really think that there at the publication, they have no other matters, only to attend to your writing?!" I became silent and did not ask him again. I carried the pain inside, and the doubt about the value of my writing consumed me.

A few more weeks went by, and when I went outside for the first time after my protracted illness, on *Shabbat* in the morning, leaning on my stick, and all of me throbbing and tipsy from the clear air, I ran into an acquaintance of mine, who informed me that my first story had been published in "*HaZman*." I hurried to his house to see the printed edition, and when my

---

[662] 2 Samuel 5:8 "On that occasion David said, "Those who attack the Jebusites shall reach the water channel and [strike down] the lame and the blind, who are hateful to David…"

[663] The Teacher of Knowledge; the names of one of the four sections of the *Shulchan Aruch*, containing laws about *kashrut*, religious conversion, mourning, laws pertaining to Israel, and family purity

[664] Yafet is the youngest son of Noah, Genesis 5:32. His name is a form of the word "beautiful. He is also considered to be the forebear of the Europeans, and therefore their thought as well.

[665] The Hebrew words "anointed" and "destroy" sound very similar, and one can hear the play on words in the Hebrew.

[666] A pun. The Hebrew word for "beautiful one" is also the word for belladonna, a poisonous flower.

acquaintance held the edition out to me, the headline became blurry before my eyes, (the publication had changed my story "The First Theft" to another name, "Experience.") I turned red and pushed the edition away from myself, because I did not believe that this was my story. My acquaintance held up the newspaper, and the first lines were revealed to the eye, and I recognized that they were mine, and joy and trembling gripped me, and I dropped onto the chair from much weakness, and when I came home I was again confined to my bed for upwards of two weeks.

From an abundance of confusion and a lack of faith in myself, I rushed a letter to the "*HaZman*" publication, inquiring as to the fate of the rest of my stories that were in their hands, and I concluded more or less with this: "and if it is the case that they are not worthy of publication, they should be so kind as to return them to me and let me know the reason for their disqualification." I immediately received a response from one "Domachevitzky" that the second story would come soon, in the edition of the coming *Shabbat*, and the third, although he had not yet read it, indeed was sure {p. 239} that he would find it, too, fit to publish in "*HaZman.*" He invited me to participate regularly in "*HaZman,*" and praised the fitness of my writing. From much excitement and exhaustion of energies, after my protracted illness, I became ill again and fell into my bed for a number of days. When I recovered, and went outside, I stopped by Frenkel's house, and showed him Domachevitzky's letter, and he figured out for me the name of the writer, who was the writer Bershadski.[667] He read his letter forwards and backwards, lowered his head, and sighed: "So, so…" He moaned and said, as if speaking to himself "that's it, that's it, that's what's necessary for them, not true works of literature, but short stories." He almost did not look at me, and I felt a sort of envy in this, his whispered grumbling, and I was embarrassed to remain in the presence of the man, who had been charitable to me, and had done much on my behalf, and it was as if I had been made a competitor to him. I parted from him hastily, and went away from him disappointed, and my conscience troubled me.[668]

From then on, I avoided extraneous meetings with him, and when, occasionally, I met him by chance, I turned the conversation to various matters, and I did not touch on matters of literature at all, and he too avoided speaking about it, as if he was afraid to wound me, and to touch his pain.

Meanwhile, my material situation in Augustow had been significantly weakened and deteriorated drastically. I really did not have bread, I and the members of my household, and I made efforts to move to the district city of Suwalk, where there were many opportunities for me to get sorted out. From an abundance of busy-ness and negotiation on the matter of the move to Suwalk, I neglected meetings with friends and did not visit anyone. And Frenkel, I almost did not see at all. Only before my departure did I go in to part from him, and I was shocked at his appearance. His grim face and his dulled eyes cast terror on me. He sat across from me hunched and withdrawn into himself, and he spoke with me only a little. I hurried to part from him warmly, and I thanked him for all the good that he had done for me, and he extended his hand coldly, and dull indifference slid off his face. I left his house with heartache.

In Suwalk additional details about him became known to me. He was sick with an illness that would not leave him again. The aging and the forgetfulness jumped on him in one stroke, and his mind became faded. He went about despondent all the days, found his shelter in the tea shop that was next to his house, quiet and abandoned and hidden in his corner, sunk in the newspapers that were before him, and when he recovered a little he poured out before those whose encountered him the bitterness of his anger on the order of the world and its inhabitants. In this way, he

---

[667] Isaiah Bershadsky (1872-1908) born Isaiah Domachevitzky, was a Russian novelist.
[668] Psalms 16:7 "I bless the LORD who has guided me; my conscience troubles me at night."

continued day after day, until the years of the First World War, when death came and redeemed him from all his troubles. **Tel Mond, 5725 [1965]**

{p. 240} The Compositions of Yaakov Frenkel

1) "The Natural Inheritance" (Warsaw 5659 [1899]). Published by Tushiah. It discusses the foundations and laws of inheritance and its relationship to Jews and Judaism.

2) "My Region 3" (Warsaw 5660 [1900]). Published by Tushiah. The story of his life and scientific activities.

3) "Nikolai Copernicus" (Warsaw 5660 [1900]). Published by Tushiah. It tells about the story of his life and his scientific activities. Translated from foreign language sources with changes and additions.

4) "The History of the Jews," a popular history for the nation and the youth. This publication of his in its six parts (he composed them while he was dwelling in Lodz) is the crowning glory of his literary work. In its time, the book won enormous distribution and was learned in schools of "Hebrew in Hebrew" and in improved *cheders*. Yaakov Frenkel was assisted in this important work of his by the books of the researchers of the history of Israel written in foreign languages and in Hebrew, however in many matters he was reliant on his own judgement, from his own unique point of view, without being too enslaved to the knowledges of sages who preceded him (from the words of his introduction to this book of his, Part 1).

Part 1 (Tushiah Publication Warsaw, 5657 [1897]), from the first days of the nation until the Babylonian exile;

Part 2 (Tushiah Publication, 5658 [1898]), from the Babylonian exile until the brothers Hyrcanus and Aristobulus;

Part 3 (Tushiah Publication, 5658 [1898]), from the days of the brothers Hyrcanus and Aristobulus until the destruction of the Second Temple;

Part 4 (Tushiah Publication, 5661 [1901]), from the destruction of the Second Temple to the completion of the *Talmud*;

Part 5 (Tushiah Publication, 5662 [1902]), from the period after the completion of the *Talmud* to the rabbinic period;

Part 6 (Tushiah Publication, 5668 [1908]), from the period of the latter Babylonian *Geonim* to the persecutions in the period of the carriers of the Cross.

5) "What is Death" an investigation into the teaching of life (Odessa 5654 [1894]).

6) "The Railroad: Its Invention and Development" Warsaw 5683 [1923].

7) "The Jews in Lodz" Warsaw 5654 [1894].

8) A Translation of "The History of Faiths and Ideas" of A. Menses, 5659-5661 [1899-1901].

His Articles in "*HaTzefirah*"

1876, Edition 11,12, 26-28, 34-35, 36-37, 43-44, 50.

1877, Edition 3-4, 7. 9-10, 18, 33-48.

1878, Edition 13-14, 16, 18, 48-49, 51.

1879, Edition 27-32, 34-35.

1882, Edition 12; 1884 Edition 2.

A Candle for the Soul of the Teacher Meir Meizler

A Penny
by Tz. Z. Weinberg

Melman was short-statured and potbellied; his face was swollen and somewhat embarrassed; he had gaping, flashing eyes. His shoulders lifted up, thrusting his head and short beard upwards, and with his constricted movements it was as if he immersed himself in his poor value. In teaching – he was accustomed to tyrannize his students with force, and in the loan business, he was in a hurry for each and every penny that left his possession to the pockets of his customers. Indeed, the minute that a penny of the fund returns to him with an additional *agora* in interest, or when a student pays tuition in full, then his eyes shine and well up with tears of joy, his shoulders lift higher, and enjoyment of his existence, radiating in his humble ways, stretches over all the lines of his face.

He loves nature. A pleasant meadow, a lovely flower, a bird mating, excite him. He loves literature. A fitting idiom and an apt expression capture his heart. Sometimes when he is teaching his students and he reaches a chapter of *piyyutim*[669] in the *Tanakh*, or one of the poems that is beloved to him, then he forgets his "heads of cabbage" (a nickname for his students), his "loathsome penny" (a nickname for his business), and his voice erupts and pours out his feelings with enthusiasm, to the point of forgetting the essence. His excessive weakness for the fair sex is known. The shape of a delightful woman, the rustling of the hem of a dress, a captivating glance, distract him. And it happens that when one of the poor women who is indebted to him, the glowing ember of her beauty and former femininity dimmed, in bondage to him and exploited by him to the point of depression and resentment, places her last penny in his hand, when she reveals her naked arm from under her worn-out garment, and a spark of hidden beauty flashes before his eyes, then Melman expresses his interest, and his eyes are nourished by a burning excitement from the fading beauty in the filthy garb and the confusion of worry, and he softens and speaks with her pleasantly and forgoes also several of his pennies. But this feeling changes quickly. When the woman just moves away, and the coins are rolling around on the table, his eyes are immediately kindled, and with trembling hands he makes the precious coins dance, and all his senses and attention are on the reverberating sound in the room.

"Sound! Sound! All the world was created for just this sound!"

Melman was entirely different, when he left his house for their daily walk accompanied by his friend Globerman. Then he would break off himself the teacher's yoke, and the troubles of his business, and enjoy himself in God's world in the lap of nature.

{p. 242} In the forest, outside of the city, he is encouraged and shakes off of himself the dust of secularity and the filth of the city, devotes himself to his inner world and communes with his hidden wishes, which yearn for a different shade of life, except for grace and beauty and the elevation of the soul. In this hour, when he is suddenly reminded of his status and his function among people, as a teacher and as a lender at interest, an enormous nausea about himself encompasses him, and he accidentally lets words slip from his mouth: "Uch, life…"

And he turns to his friend Globerman with a dull voice: "how strange is the person, who doesn't live according to his nature, or the inclination of his spirit…"

However, in a moment he recovered, shot his gaze at the surroundings, and was distracted by all this, and returned to equilibrium. A joyful spirit returned to him, and he patted his friend's

---

[669] A *piyyut* is a liturgical poem, from the Greek *poietes*, poem. The word is not usually used to refer to biblical poetry, but it is intelligible in its use here.

shoulder with his usual cheerfulness, as if becoming reconciled with his fate and making peace with his deeds and his role.

"mmm…. Let it be so…" indeed as if agreeing with himself.

And he continued his walk with his friend, as if cutting himself off from the dirty reality, and as if sweetening with it the bitterness of his day. His conversations about life and nature were mostly abstract, covering over internal pressure and profound pain, superficial and not touching straight on, as if deliberately covering up the missing essence. Therefore, Globerman was not surprised at all when he heard once from his friend Melman a bitter lament from which an echo of deep despair erupted, like a person who has nothing more to lose. One relinquishment, that one let go of a firm debt, was that which crushed him to the brink of despair, and like the confession of a deathly ill person, Melman pushed it aside before his friend, this tragedy a portion from the scroll of his life.

"I almost didn't know my parents. My father educated me until the twelfth[670] year, and, because of the reduction of income, sent me from his house, "to worry for my sustenance and to create for myself a path in life." With his blessing, and provisions for the journey,[671] my father aspired for my future, in which he would see me "an exalted man." I went out to the big world alone and abandoned, by myself. I passed through many places in the land. Wandering nights and days of hunger found me. I withstood the troubles and terrors of the world, and I did not believe my father's words, that at some time I would be "an exalted man."

From where? From the bad days, from the pressure of hunger and lack? In all the days of my wandering I struggled to reach some position, any kind of livelihood. I clung to small[672] teaching, and in free time I learned and I added to my knowledge. When I tasted the first taste of profits, an intense desire was aroused in me to add to them and to strengthen my situation. The first coins were for me a source of hope, consolation, and amusement. My hands stirred within the piles of the *dinars*[673] that accumulated on my table, and I played with them incessantly for full hours. I did this, of course, silently, at night, so that no one would see me in my corruption.[674] And in order to add[675] penny to penny and increase my fortune, on many days I became a lender at interest."

Melman stopped speaking, peered at his companion with watery eyes, and added:

"And as you are of the opinion that these two issues are pleasant to me, the exhausting teaching, which sucks the marrow of the bones, and the business of interest, which removes the image of God from a person's face …but there is no choice, my friend…I became a lender at interest, and I engage in this work diligently…I know how to keep on hand and to guard the penny…and if only everything within me would protest, and regret reproach me bitterly, it is impossible to remove from my heart that there is something more important in life and of greater value than the penny…"

---

[670] Written in an unusual Aramaic form.

[671] Genesis 42:25 "Then Joseph gave orders to fill their bags with grain, return each one's money to his sack, and give them provisions for the journey…"

[672] Aramaic.

[673] The *dinar*'s historical antecedent is the gold *dinar*, the main coin of the medieval Islamic empires, issued in 696–697 CE by Caliph Abd al-Malik ibn Marwan. The word "*dinar*" comes from the silver "*denarius*" coin of ancient Rome, first minted about 211 BCE.

[674] Jews are not supposed to lend at interest to Jews, based on Exodus 22:24, and elaborated on extensively in rabbinic literature: "If you lend money to My people, to the poor among you, do not act toward them as a creditor; exact no interest from them."

[675] Numbers 32:14 "And now you, a breed of sinful men, have replaced your fathers, to add still further to the LORD's wrath against Israel."

He fell silent, threw a penetrating look, and suddenly turned his face to his companion and continued:

{p. 243} "And worse than this is the psychological rift…the same perpetual unrest and the strange desire that sometimes entirely agitates you internally, changing from one end to the other and to turn the entire bowl upside down…[676] for after all these what do I have in life, and who do I have? The penny…indeed, without it there is nothing in life, but as far as I'm concerned this is only a deception of the eyes,[677] a kind of lying divination,[678] isn't it so that I do not have any control over it, complete control over it…don't you see how I live and by what I live? And the rest, the rest…my family life…my Miriam, I don't delude myself …this is not what I prayed for…not this…"

His voice began to quiver.

"But nevertheless, there were days…I always hated the ugliness, especially in a woman. I too was not attractive. But when I captured the heart of a young woman, and I myself did not know because of what, consider well…[679] When I learned in the yeshiva, I lodged in a house where there was a young woman whose memory until now has not disappeared from my heart. The curls of her hair were black as a smith,[680] her eyes were breathtaking, as profound as the Holy of Holies,[681] and when she spoke grace spilled from her lips, and great sweetness in all the limbs of her body. Her love, I pondered in dreams and when awake, and I said to myself, that only her would I take for a wife. I befriended her and I pledged allegiance to her, and she, she too returned love to me. I still remember her conversations, her glances, and her encounters. I was happy. I imagined that this would go on forever. But…here too the hand of the penny remained in the middle, together with my great love a bitter thought clung to me, as if casting lead, that turned my feelings to stone and spoiled my happiness: "entirely without a dowry, it is not possible." And since her parents were miserably poor, my love died and slowly faded away, and the package broke apart…"

His voice was strangled by his suppressed groan, he took a breath and added:

"And this wife of mine, my Miriam, as you think, they did not deceive me? They offered before me this "mine," they dropped her dowry on the table, they set up a household. My eyes were drawn to the blue papers and the gleam of the dinars. They counted the money into the hand of the trustee. The rest, the trustee guaranteed. They transmitted a document of debt in my presence. They celebrated the wedding celebration with mazal.[682] And after the wedding, when I demanded what was coming to me, they ridiculed me and my naivete. Even the trustee laughed at my destruction. He was in full agreement with them, as was the custom. And a greater evil than this – the wife and the mother-in-law. The two of them fell to my lot, in one stroke. Wasn't mine beautiful… while her mother was incomparably ugly. Nausea assailed me upon seeing her face, at the times when she spoke moral reproaches to me. But finally I became reconciled. For why

---

[676] Babylonian *Talmud Bava Batra* 16a: "…Rava says: Job sought to turn the bowl upside down…"

[677] Babylonian *Talmud Sanhedrin* 67b: "…One who deceives the eyes is exempt from punishment, but it is prohibited for him to do so…."

[678] Ezekiel 13:7 "It was false visions you prophesied and lying divination you uttered, saying, "Declares the LORD," when I had not spoken."

[679] This phrase appears in the Jerusalem *Talmud* but not the Babylonian *Talmud*, e.g. *Megillah* 25b, *Chagigah* 6a, *Shekalim* 23a:2, and more, as well as frequently in later rabbinic literature.

[680] There is no word in Hebrew or Aramaic spelled this way, or even anything close to it that makes sense. Phonetically it can read "smith" or "semite," but neither really makes sense in this context, and neither is a Hebrew or Aramaic word.

[681] Babylonian *Talmud Berakhot* 7a: "…Rabbi Yishmael ben Elisha, the High Priest, said: Once, on *Yom Kippur*, I entered the innermost sanctum, the Holy of Holies, to offer incense…"

[682] Luck.

should I still be a complaining fool? They added for me years of "*keset*" (food), and I agreed. My fund of money continued to grow larger. My Miriam helped me as a true woman of valor. Like me, she also knew to appreciate the penny. I was content with her, and children were born…"

"And in truth, isn't it the same. Beauty? Of course, this is a tremendous power. A beautiful wife, certainly this is happiness. Love? There is no doubt that this is an exalted emotion. But what – finally, it is all vapor.[683] None of these have honest contact with life. And in essence, it's the same thing,[684] indeed most of my years have already gone by, and if you say, my Miriam, also as a wife….*nu*,[685] do you know, it is possible to love her."

He concluded. A kind of sour taste trickled in his throat, when he wrung out the final expression. His face reddened. His eyes sought a hiding place. He immediately moved his conversation to "The Confusing Trees" to "The Delicate Weather and the Sustainer of Souls" to "Nature, Which has in it Cures for All Suffering" its heart a profusion of colors {p. 244} and images, skipped from topic to topic, and again spoke about the value of beauty in human life. A tired pallor stretched across his cheeks, and his eyes burned.

"And what" he commented offhandedly, "my daughter, Channah, without this" he indicated the coin "would you be able to take to heart?"

And without expecting an answer he exaggerated with his glance, as if speaking with himself "the apple does not fall far from the tree…her nose…her eyes…like mother like daughter…my Channah is not at all beautiful…not like this one…not like this one…"

Again he patted his companion's shoulder, and alluded to his pain in his incidental comments, on the shrubs and the flowers that one encountered along the way. And suddenly, as if he felt the falsity of his words, he fell completely silent, and immersed himself in his ruminations, and communed with a section of one poem, which he repeated a number of times in a special tone:

> For I have loved! And loved you faithfully!
> Also when I returned from behind you
> I did this from love…

In this way, he trudged along after his friend, repeating the section of his poem in his pleasant voice. When they came near to the city, Melman stopped, stood erect in his full height, and deepened in a whisper:

"What a loss…what a loss…ten promissory notes…worth 500 gold coins…business?! I have to "let loose" my Miriam…also Channah will go with her…the two of them as one…maybe they will somehow be useful…maybe they will rescue…they are daughters of valor…and their mouths with them…maybe…*nu*…*nu*…what a loss…oy, what a loss…" **The year 1909**

There were two heads of families in the city: Kalzon and Goldshmid, whose affectionate nickname of the two of them was "Velvel." One was swarthy, and the other, ashen. The eyes of the two of them sparked with fire. Kalzon was outstanding in his scholarliness and sharpness; Goldshmid in his quick wits and restraint. The one – thin and short, his eyes big and penetrating, his chin tuft was pointed and his *peyot*[686] were curled. "Velvel Stirkus" was his name. He was the father of the Kalzon family. The second – swarthy, illuminated by a majestic appearance, "Velvel the Black" was his name. He was the director of the *Chevre Kadisha* of the city.

The two of them were beloved by all the people. Many wanted to be near them. They would always sit in judgement between two people, in the role of chosen arbitrators. They would

---

[683] Ecclesiastes 1:2 "Vapor of vapors —said Kohelet— vapor of vapors! All is vapor!

[684] Aramaic, appearing profusely throughout rabbinic literature.

[685] Yiddish for so? or well?

[686] Traditional Jewish men do not cut of the forelocks of their hair, based on Leviticus 19:27 "You shall not round off the corner of your head, or destroy the corner of your beard." These forelocks are called "*peyot*," corners.

233

argue and debate with sharp and amazing skill, elegant and honest arbitrators, and increasing peace among Jews.

{p. 245} The Keinan Family
by Eliezer Markus

At the end of the previous century and the beginning of the present century, there lived in Augustow five households, who were known by the Jews of the city by the inclusive name: "The Keinan Family," or by the nickname, as was the custom in the towns in those days, "The Tzarska Family."[687]

The beginning of these five families were in a Jew, a man from Augustow by the name Leizer Keinan. He was the son of a baker, who also engaged in the selling of flour. In those days, they used to bring white flour from the areas of Kovno and Vohlin. For the purpose of diversification, he also would import salt and salted fish from Prussia. At the end of his days he also worked at the sale of fabrics and became a big "kol-bo."[688] His commercial connections reached to Konigsberg in Prussia, Kovno which is in Lithuania, Lodz which is in Poland, and the Vohlin region, which is on the Ukrainian border.

He built a big house on the market plaza. In time the house became known as "Markus' Moyer"[689] after the name of one of his sons-in-law.

Reb Leizer Keinan had six beautiful and successful daughters; he had no sons. When the daughters reached marriageable age, he married them off, according to the custom of those days, "royally." To each of his sons-in-law he paid a respectable dowry, and connected him to his table.[690] After the completion of the days of "keset,"[691] he allotted each one a portion of his business.

Since he was wealthy and respected, he was fussy about the selection of his sons-in-law, who would have respectable ancestry and be *Torah* scholars. In this way five respected families were added to the Augustow community (one daughter went out with her husband to Grodno):

1) Reb Yaakov Frenkel, a scholar, *Maskil*, writer, and historian.

2) Reb Arieh Lap, a scholar and a merchant.

3) Reb Dovid Mordechai Markus, a scholar who had rabbinic ordination, who was known as "the *Ilui*"[692] from Kovno.

4) Reb Zalman Leib Kopciovski, a scholar, *Maskil*, and merchant.

5) Reb Shmuel Grosberg, a God-fearing teacher from a rabbinic family.

To the last three he turned over his big house, and a side house. In the side house there was one large room, the roof of which could be raised to turn it into a *sukkah*. During the festival of *Sukkot* he lived in the *sukkah* with his three sons-in-law. There they would take their meals, and also sleep in spacious beds.

Over time the big *sukkah* became one of the living spaces of the Orimland family, the owner of a store for medications.

With the years, the families of the sons-in-law of Reb Leizer Keinan grew.

The Frenkel house had five daughters and one son. The Lap house had three sons and two daughters. The Markus house had three sons and five daughters. The Kopciovski house had four sons and two daughters. The Grosberg house had four sons and four daughters.

---

[687] Yiddish.
[688] Everything in it.
[689] Yiddish, "wall."
[690] Agreed to provide his meals.
[691] Yiddish for "keep."
[692] The Prodigy.

234

The total of Reb Leizer's grandchildren was thirty-three.

{p. 246 } The son and the daughters of the Frenkel family acquired a general education. One of the daughters, Chava Frenkel, was known in the days of her youth as head of the propogandists of the "*Bund*" in the city, and participated in an active way in the revolutionary underground in the days of the rule of the Tsar. One of the daughters remained in Augustow and continued in her parents' fabric business. Her husband, Reb Sh. Chefetz, a man of *Torah* and enlightenment, was appointed afterwards as administrator of the Jewish cooperative bank, and served in this position until the *Shoah*.[693]

The Lap family engaged in the wholesale and retail grocery trade. The store passed afterwards to his son, Binyamin, and to his son-in-law Reb Tuvia Burak.

The Kopciovski family had a big store for iron, iron tools, and metal. All of the children received a Jewish and general education. All of them left the city– part for Lodz, and part for Moscow. Not even one of this family was left after the First World War.

At the end of his days, Reb Yisrael Grosberg bequeathed his business to his daughters, and went up to the land to grace its soil. He died and was buried in Tel Aviv, in the old cemetery.

I was named for Reb Leizer Keinan. My grandfather, Dovid Mordechai, who arrived in Augustow from Goldava, which is next to Kovno, was proficient in *Talmud* and verses, and all the city was blessed in him. Well-known rabbis used to visit him for the purpose of debate and advice. He was a good Jew, friendly, and was pleasant to everyone who turned to him. He administered his many businesses as a merchant in foodstuffs and also found time for his learning.

In his store, there was arranged a special lectern, on which a *Gemara* was always placed, or another book with interpretations, that he studied.

He was also accepted by all of the Christian population as an honest and God-fearing man. He also considered enlightenment studies to be important. The *Chibbat Tzion* movement was also close to his heart.

He saw to it that his eldest son, Chaim Yosef, also learned Russian, German, and French. In time, this son also became one of the administrators of the joint business of the family, and the administrator of the account books of the store. He was an educated man, humble, gentle, and "dwelt in the tent."[694] He sent his second son, Binyamin, to the *yeshiva* of Volozhin, which was one of the well-known *yeshiva*s in those days, and he was ordained for the rabbinate there. He also received additional general education in Russian and German.

My father Reb Binyamin was a sociable person, and active in the public life of the city. For many years, he was the head of the Zionist organization in Augustow, the head of "*Tarbut*,"[695] an activist in "*Keren HaYesod*," and "*Keren Kayemet L'Yisrael*." He was also one of the founders of the Jewish cooperative bank in the city, and the head of its administration. He was accepted by all echelons of the population, the educated and the simple folk alike.

With the death of Reb Meir Koifman, who gave the "lesson" in *Talmud* in the *Beit Midrash*, he filled his place. Sometimes he would lecture before the youth on Zionist topics.

His wife, Rachel, the daughter of Reb Yechezkel Berman, the owner of the leather factory in nearby Sapotzkin, was a quiet and modest woman, a diligent home worker and devoted entirely to the management of the many-person family household. She was compassionate and engaged in *mitzvot*, and giving in secret.[696] The two of them, my father and my mother, were exiled in the

---

[693] Holocaust.

[694] Of Torah.

[695] Culture. The *Tarbut* movement was a network of secular, Hebrew-language schools in parts of the Jewish Pale of Settlement in Poland, Romania and Lithuania.

[696] The highest level of *tzedakah*, according to Maimonides, is when neither the giver nor the recipient knows who is giving or receiving.

days of the Soviet conquest to the town of Suchovola, and remained there until the Nazi invasion. According to what was transmitted, they were transported to Treblinka and placed on the pyre.

The Markus house was open. Everyone was received with great hospitality. The house served {p. 247} as a meeting place and center for the various emissaries that would come to the city on behalf of the Zionist organization, *Keren Kayemet L'Yisrael*, *Keren HaYesod*, etc.

Of the daughters of Reb Dovid Mordechai, the two sisters, Sarah and Chitza, were known to the Augustovi public. Sarah was very active in the family store, whereas Chitza was an active functionary in public institutions. For many years, she stood at the head of the council of the Jewish library, and was one of the founders and administrators of the "*Linat Tzedek*" society. With her *aliyah* to the land she worked as a nurse[697] in Hadassah Hospital in Haifa. She died at a good old age on 29 Adar, 5725 [1965].

Of the descendants of the Keinan family, there are grandchildren of Reb Leizer Keinan in the land:

From the house of Lap: one grandson, Dr. Menachem Burak, a chemist in Ramat Gan.

From the house of Kopciovski: one grandson, Zalman Rozenblum, an official in the electric company in Haifa.

From the house of Grosberg: one grandson, Chanun Kantzok, a merchant in Tel Aviv.

From the house of Markus: 6 grandchildren:

The sons of Reb Binyamin Markus:

Moshe Markus, a doctor of economics and political science;

Eliezer Markus, engineer, Tel Aviv.

The children of Regina Rabinovitz-Markus:

Dr. Ze'ev Rabinovitz, doctor, Haifa;

Nechemiah Rabinovitz, engineer, Tel Aviv.

Beila Greenstein, Haifa.

A daughter of Sarah Saperstein-Markus:

Liza Gonen, chemist.

Binyamin Markus   His wife, Rachel   Dovid Mordechai Markus, his wife Beila of the house of Keinan, their daughter Dr. Roza Markus

---

[697] Literally, a merciful nurse.

{p. 248} My Brother Sender
by Akiva Glikstein

My mother used to say: "Sender was born in a *ketonet*."[698] That is to say, he was lucky.

When I was born my parents had 6 children: 3 sons and 3 daughters. Mother bore more, I do not know exactly how many. I only know that Sender, the oldest in the family – he was about 20 years older than me – was not the first-born. They used to mention sometimes a Reuvele and a Yankele, that were born before him, but they died when they were babies. When they mentioned one of them Mother would knock on the table with a fist and say: "It is forbidden to mention him, he is in the Garden of Eden." I don't know if she didn't want to mention their names because it is forbidden to interfere with their rest there, or because she didn't want them to think that she did not protect them enough and because of that they passed from *Gehenna*, which is on the planet, to the Garden of Eden, a world that is all good. They used to tell about Sender that he was hard to teach, that he had a domineering manner. My father used to say that if only the Tsar had granted the same rights to the Jews that he had to the rest of the subjects, Sender would – lacking an education and having a fist – would have become a *gendarme*, a kind of "*drezimorda*" *broyzer* of Gogol.[699] In his youth he used to spend his time playing cards. He did not want to help Father in his business. It is interesting that the one two years younger than him, Moshe, was exactly his opposite; he was Father's right hand, frugal and also enthusiastic, the only one among the sons. And he, specifically, did not have luck. Already in his first endeavors he lost the dowry that he had received, he had lost his energy, and after that he was a clerk for Sender. Apparently, Sender really was born with a *ketonet*. He began his career in the role of a construction contractor for the army. There were at that time military councils for building, as an example of these, that we had during the Mandate.[700] The head of the council was a general, his assistants – two-three officers, a military engineer, and a number of Sergeants and Corporals. The projects were awarded by auction. The steep prices and the work were fixed in a special booklet as standard prices. The contractor had to make it known what percentage of these prices he required. According to this method the contractor that made the cheapest offer won the work. It is understood that our brothers the Jews would "work it out" with a bribe and become rich. My father was an honest man, the opposite of Sender, and he would scream bloody murder about these "deals."[701] He would say that they hate us not because of our offensive deeds; among the gentiles there are many more criminals. Rather, the gentile would be caught and receive his due - he would sit in prison. The Jew knows how to evade the punishment and continue his deeds. As an example Father would tell: in Russia there was a law, according to which, only sons[702] were exempt from military service. But if the Jew had a few sons, each one of them became an only son. The Jew would find another Jew who had no sons, and for a payment he would agree to adopt him as a son.

{p. 249} So it was possible to encounter brothers from belly and birth, each of whom had a different family name. To the government this thing finally became known, and it nullified the law of only sons relative to the Jews. The exile turned us into people with a deformity from the aspect of the national manner. Because of this we decided to flee from there, to come to the land, to engage in working the soil, in which there is no possibility of doing "deals" of this kind, to live

---

[698] Only two people in the Bible wore a *ketonet*, a cloak. Joseph, in Genesis 37:3 "Now Israel loved Joseph best of all his sons, for he was the child of his old age; and he had made him an ornamented tunic." And Tamar, a daughter of King David; 2 Samuel 13:18 "She was wearing an ornamented tunic, for maiden princesses were customarily dressed in such garments..."

[699] Nikolai Vasilyevich Gogol, 1809 – 1852, was a Russian dramatist of Ukrainian origin.

[700] The British Mandate for Palestine, from the end of WWI and the declaration of Israel's independence.

[701] Yiddish.

[702] Sons with no siblings.

simple lives, healthy lives of austerity. What affects me, and many like me, who came to the land before the second aliyah,[703] the prime cause that brought us here, was the desire to live healthy lives, like the rest of the peoples. Sender, even though he was my brother, was a great parasite. A plant like this could grow and develop only in the rotten regime of the Tsar. In the military council that I mentioned, all of them were taking bribes. It began with the General who was the head and ended with the Corporal, whose power was also great, because he would approve the receipt of the materials. I remember that on Sunday (on this day outside worked ceased, but the office was open), the Corporal would enter as drunk as Lot,[704] and he would say to the clerk: "give me 3 *rubles*, I must drink." (As is known, alcohol is chased from the body by the drinking of additional alcohol). At that same time, the Corporal would throw the receipt ledger on the table, the clerk would fill out receipts for a large sum, and the Corporal would sign them. Only then would the clerk give him 5 *rubles* instead of the 3 *rubles* that he had requested. Thus would the contractors conduct themselves in that period, and so did they act in our time.

It is interesting that Sender was not a miser. He would give a donation generously, and would spend much money on himself and his family. "Making money" was a hobby for him. Father, who was of another kind, even though he too did not do productive work, as the owner of army barracks for a Cossack regiment, supplied wood for heating, etc., did not love Sender, because of his desire for money. He used to say: "Nothing interests him except for money. He is not a member even in "*Chovevei Tzion*," no one of the intelligentsia enters his house, he never read a book, and in the newspaper he is interested only in the financial section, in order to follow the movement of bonds, with which he filled his steel cabinet."

He was a tyrant. His wife was the daughter of a poor family; she was tall and beautiful. She respected only rich people. My father used to call her "cow." Every year she gave birth to a child. Sender had about 12 living children. His wife was deathly afraid of him. He was always busy looking for strategies to increase his wealth. When it happened, sometimes, that an engineer was accepted who despised a bribe, he saw to it that those who were in charge of him would be informed that the man was not qualified, was stupid, did not understand the profession – and they would fire him.

Every year Sender would travel to one of the bathing cities of Europe. By himself, far from his businesses, he did not run around after the money, and resembled a human being. At that time I studied in Germany, and he would send me the expenses for the journey, and he would invite me to him in Carlsbad. I lived with him in an expensive hotel. In the morning I would accompany him to drink mineral water, after which we would go into the expensive coffee house "Pop," and he would feed me every good thing.

Sender had a bank in Suwalk. While I was with him in Carlsbad, he received a telegram from the administrator of the bank, Shmuelke, in which he asked if he should give to *Ploni* a loan of 1000 rubles. Since I knew German he asked that I write the reply. "Write, that he should not give it to him" – he ordered. I wrote "no money was given." "What did you write here?" Sender said, "won't he give him the money, and it's as if he invested in a dubious venture. Write to him "no money not given." "Sender" I said "in German won't {p. 250} the opposite be understood?" "I couldn't care less" he answered. "Indeed. you know German, but I know Shmuelke." And he was right.

---

[703] The Second *Aliyah* that took place between 1904 and 1914. At that time, about 35,000 Jews, mostly from the Russian Empire, immigrated into Ottoman-ruled Palestine.

[704] Genesis 19:31-33 ff. "And the older one said to the younger, "Our father is old, and there is not a man on earth to consort with us in the way of all the world. Come, let us make our father [Lot] drink wine, and let us lie with him, that we may maintain life through our father. That night they made their father drink wine, and the older one went in and lay with her father; he did not know when she lay down or when she rose."

In Suwalk, the city in which Sender lived, there was a very wealthy fabric merchant. His wealth came to him not from the sale of merchandise, but, as was the custom in this type of trade, from bankruptcy. A merchant who respected himself, and so that others would respect him, would declare bankruptcy every two years. In this instance, he would transfer his shop to his wife's name. The previous sign they would place in storage, in order to hang it a second time after he paid his creditors 20%-30% of the amount that was coming to them. Not bad at all. If you think that he would lose credit by means of this, you are mistaken. After the bankruptcy, he was more secure than Rothschild. The owner of the factory in Lodz would himself open for him a large line of credit, for he was sure that in the next two years he would not again declare bankruptcy. Over the course of this period he would reduce his credit. If you think that the factory owner was sorry about this, that he lost 70%-80%, you are nothing but mistaken. He would do the same thing to the suppliers of wool, thread etc. "Don't you see?" – he would say to them – "how *Ploni* destroyed me? From where will I take the money to pay you?" And so forth.

The fabric merchant had a son whose name was Leibke. It seemed that he was a member in the dangerous revolutionary socialists' organization, the men of terror, who took the bitter enemy Plehve[705] out to be killed, and others. The young man was a student. When they would take him out of one university because of his activities, his father would enroll him in another university.

When sometimes Leibke would come to stay as a guest in his parents' house, already on the first night the *gendarmes* would come, conduct a search, and find some illegal pamphlet, and they would, of course, arrest Leibke. His unfortunate father would run, distribute bribes left and right, and free him.

Sender my brother was, according to his acquaintances, a monarchist. Could he become wealthy under a different regime? Only in Tsarist Russia was this possible. With all his heart and soul he loved Nikolai II, who did not know what was being done in his country. After the First World War, and I was already in the land, one of the "*olim*"[706] from Suwalk brought with him the weekly "Illustrated Newspaper,"[707] and in it we see my brother Sender, an amazingly beautiful man, in a black suit, with a top hat on his head, white gloves on his hands, at the head of the community of Suwalk, and the local rabbi, in whose hand is a *Torah* scroll and another Jew with a plate of bread and salt[708] in his hand, welcoming the Tsar, who came to Suwalk.

This brother of mine Sender would scream bloody murder at Leibl: "What does Leibke want? You understand, he wants to teach Tsar Nikolai to run the country. What *chutzpah*! All the troubles and the pogroms come upon us, because our youth engage in politics. Were it not for them – Russia would be "*Gan Eden*"[709] for the Jews."

Many years went by, and I have already been in the land for a long time, the father of children, the year 1926. I arrived by chance in Berlin and I was reminded of Suwalk; from there I took my lifelong friend, who I lost due to the disasters of the present. There were there some relatives of mine, and also of hers. I hoped to see the places I had walked, the city park, wasn't I once young? I wanted to see how the Poles ruled their country, for which they aspired from the time that Poland was divided. I entered the Polish legation, a magnificent building, with many

---

[705] Vyacheslav Konstantinovich von Plehve, 1846 – 1904, was the director of Imperial Russia's police and later Minister of the Interior.

[706] Those who make "*aliyah*," ascent, to the land.

[707] Yiddish "אילוסטרירטא צייטונג."

[708] Bread and salt is used in a welcoming ceremony in several Slavic and other European cultures, and in Middle Eastern cultures.

[709] The Garden of Eden, or paradise.

officials. I approached the clerk; I spoke German. I showed him my *"laissez passe,"*[710] in which it was written that I was born in Augustow. The clerk: "My Lord {p. 151} was a Polish citizen and now the land of Israel, did my Lord receive the permission of our government to renounce Polish citizenship? Me: "When I renounced Russian citizenship, it was in the year 1914, there was not yet a Polish government." "I am sorry" the clerk decided "I am unable to give Your Honor a visa." I asked "Maybe I would be able to receive a transit visa, by way of Warsaw to Danzig?" "To Danzig there is no need for a visa" the clerk explained "it is possible to travel by way of the "passageway" without a visa." I travelled by way of the corridor and I arrived safely in Danzig. There my wife had wealthy influential relatives. They owned a famous cigar factory for all of eastern Prussia. Danzig was then a free city. Despite the fact that this family had lived in Danzig for decades, they did not permit them to become citizens. They remained Polish citizens, and every year they were obligated to request an extension from the Prussian government. I decided to invite my two brothers to a meeting with me in Danzig. I reserved a hotel room and I waited for them at the train station. I have not seen them since the year 1912; for 14 years. In this period, great changes began in the world. Poland; independence. In Germany, the "Kaiser" had been removed. In Russia, the Tsar was taken out to be killed and the Bolsheviks took over. The train came, two old men got off the car. My brother Moshe was religious and bearded; because of this there was not a great change seen in him. Sender had changed completely; stooped over, dressed cleanly, however, but missing the "chic." My brothers and I kissed each other, and entered the hotel. "Nu, Sender" I asked, *Mah nishmah,*[711] how's the situation?" "The Bolsheviks, may their name be erased,"[712] Sender answered, "they took over Russia and they are destroying it. The children remained with them, and are surely dying there of starvation. They took almost everything from me. The Tsar's government owed me millions for barracks that I built for them before the revolution, the Bolsheviks came and released everything. The revenues from the assets that remained with me, a few houses, are not enough for a modest existence. This is the situation! But they will not remain in power for long, they are not successful people, they will destroy the country, etc." I was reminded of Leibke the revolutionary, that he and his friends removed Sender and his kind from their properties.

Sender went to his eternity a long time ago, his children died in Soviet Russia, the rest were destroyed by the enemy in Poland. May they rest in peace. I am reminded of his eldest daughter, wonderfully beautiful, who was married in 1906 to the son of wealthy people from Tula, the city of the "samovars."[713] The groom's father was the son of a cantonist, owner of a mine, factories, forests, - a millionaire. The youth was one of the children of "the golden youth."[714] He and wife wasted thousands of rubles.

In the year 1912 I spent my vacation with my family in Europe. I also visited in Konigsberg. There, by chance, I ran into my brother's daughter, who was on the way to Berlin. She was dazzling in her beauty and in her dress. This daughter of my brother Sender, Asper, concluded her life in Moscow as a corset sewer.

---

[710] Literally: let pass. A document granting unrestricted access or movement to its holder.
[711] A typical Israeli greeting. Literally, "what's heard?" similar to the English "what's doing?" or "what's happening?"
[712] This phrase in generally used for the worst enemies of the Jews, such as Haman, or Hitler.
[713] Tula was a major center of Russian samovar production.
[714] Children of rich, prominent, and successful parents, who usually live on their wealth and connections.

{p. 252} **Lippe the Wagon Master**
by Akiva Glikstein

When I emerged from my mother's womb I felt cold, they wrapped me in diapers and I calmed down. But then I felt terribly hungry. I was the last of the children, and my parents – middle aged. My mother, may her memory be for a blessing, used to tell that she was embarrassed to visit the synagogue during the period of her pregnancy, lest people say: "she is old and isn't embarrassed to engage in nonsense like this." Artificial feeding wasn't known in those times. There were women, Christian and also Jewish, who served as wet nurses for a wage. In our house there lived a widow woman, Michla was her name. My father made it her responsibility to find a wet nurse for me as soon as possible, before I would join my grandfather, who was no longer alive. Michla brought Tzipke. Father signed her to a contract, according to which she was obligated to keep me in her house for a year, and we had the permission to extend the time until I would stand on my feet. The natural food, the milk – she was obligated to provide – the artificial feeding, porridges, etc., was on our account. Father was obligated to supply her with 35 bottles of beer every week, which increased the milk, as is known. The wet nurse wrapped me in a white sheet, took me under her arm as one carries a log, and carried me to her house. There I found a friend my age. We became friends, and divided the field of action between us.

The wet nurse had a father whose name was Reb Lippe. A strong Jew, with a majestic presence, a long beautiful grey beard. He resembled Professor Schreiber in Konigsberg, to whom the wealthy women in the area used to travel. He was expert in the written Torah,[715] loved to season his conversation with verses from the Tanakh with an Ashkenazi accent; he also loved the alcoholic beverage, as it is written: "Drunk and not from wine,"[716] apparently, from brandy. He was an excellent coachman, expert in his profession. His horses had a beautiful appearance. He also engaged in trading horses, but of a special kind. As is known, a merchant, before he sells merchandise, has to acquire it. He never bought a horse, because he would, excuse me, steal it. Lippe had a "principle:"[717] he would never steal a horse from a gentile. A gentile would run to the police, who would then find the horse with him, and they would send him (not the horse) to a sanitarium in Kalvaria (the prison there was less comfortable than today's "Sing-Sing"[718] which is in America.) His family would be left without a breadwinner – not worth it. A Jew, compared with this, as is known, is a "merciful one, son of a merciful one." A Jew would not turn over a Jew, God forbid, to the hands of the gentiles. Informing, for generations, arouses nausea ("to the informers let there be no hope"). [719] A Jew will not place another Jew in trouble because of a horse, which is worth a few tens of rubles. To steal from Jews, therefore, had no danger in it. Lippe was a decent man. He would sell the horse to its legal owner, specifically at a cheap price. I remember him, when he went out to "*penzia*."[720] His sons and his sons' sons worked in his profession. Lippe had a second "principle." He would not steal from the same Jew more than twice a year. He had a ledger, in which was listed: "*Parashat Vayikra*"[721] - next to the owner of the flour mill; *Parashat* {p. 253} "*Acharei Mot*"[722] next to the Polish lord (a young black horse, valuable); and so on. Before midnight he would say to his students: "Group! To work!" Take the "musical

---

[715] The *Tanakh* is the Written *Torah*; the *Talmud* is the Oral *Torah*.

[716] Isaiah 51:21 "…Therefore, listen to this, unhappy one, who is drunk, but not with wine!"

[717] The English word written in Hebrew letters is used here.

[718] Sing Sing Correctional Facility is a maximum-security prison operated by the New York State Department of Corrections and Community Supervision in the village of Ossining, New York. It is not known for its amenities.

[719] Maimonides, Mishneh Torah, The Order of Prayer 2:13, found in the morning service in most Jewish prayerbooks.

[720] Retirement.

[721] The name of the weekly *Torah* portion that was the first one in the book of Leviticus.

[722] The name of the weekly *Torah* Portion "After the Death," also in Leviticus, that begins after the death of the sons of Aaron.

instruments" (that is to say: pliers, scalpel, screwdriver, keys of various shapes and sizes, etc.); be careful of the Ashmedai[723] (The Chief of Police); if they were to fall into the hands of the "angels of destruction"[724] give them "a blow on his side" (that is to say, a ruble). Go in peace and "*Hashem*[725] will help you." They would bring the horse into a secret place. They would give him hardly any food, only enough that he wouldn't die, and wait for his owner to redeem him.

I was a boy of about 10. My father had horses for the purpose of transporting building materials. Especially trees from the forest for his buildings. Two waggoneers worked for us: Shmerke the Jew, and Frank the Pole. Once, early in the morning, as the ox licks,[726] I heard in my bed, that someone was knocking on the shutter of the parents' bedroom, and yelling in Polish: "Mr. Leibnu" (my father's name was Leib), I found the stable open, the lock broken, and the "*bulan*" (a color of horse) gone." "Good" my father answers sleepily in Polish, and adds to himself: "Again the work of Lippe, may his name be erased, Master of the Universe." He got dressed and washed. I understand that he is going to Lippe, and I ask that he take me with him. Lippe's house is known to me, after all I was raised there from age 0 – 1 ½, by his daughter Tzipke. Lippe stands at the eastern wall of the room, wrapped in a *tallis* and *tefillin*,[727] as if he did not see us, totally focused on prayer. Finally he spit, as was the custom, at "*Aleinu*."[728] He finished. Lippe approached my father, entirely surprised. "Peace be to you Reb Leib, what an honor that you came to visit in my house" he says. "Certainly you want me to hitch my "lions" and travel with you to Suwalk (the District city, a distance of 28 kilometers from my city). "This time I did not come for that purpose" - my father says – "Frank woke me and said that my stable was open, the lock was broken, and "the boy was gone,"[729] that is to say, the *bulan*." Lippe: "Am I my brother's keeper?"[730] My father (carefully, so as not to damage his honor), "isn't it known to me that you trade in horses (not steal, God forbid), certainly the thief would bring my horse to you, please ransom it, I will return to you what you are owed." Lippe is tapping quietly with his fingers on the table as if to recite: "cast your bread on the waters and after many days it will return to you."[731] Father: "How much is it?" Lippe: "The more, the more praiseworthy."[732] Father takes his wallet out of his pocket, pulls out of it a blue 5-ruble bill, and puts it on the table. Lippe gently pushes the bill away from himself and says: "Give me some of that red, red, stuff…"[733] (a 10-ruble bill was red). Father says: "Lippe, God be with you, 10 rubles for the *bulan*?" If I sell it, they would not give much more than that; isn't his left eye, not upon you, crossed, and the right hind leg is shorter than the other 3, 10 rubles, aren't you embarrassed?" Lippe gently taps with his right hand on the table, and says: "tell my Lord."[734] Which is to say, "talk to the wall." My father again takes his wallet out of his pocket,

---

[723] The head of the demons in Jewish mythology. Babylonian *Talmud Gittin* 68a: "Solomon brought a male demon and a female demon and tormented them together, and they said: We do not know where to find the shamir. Perhaps Ashmedai, king of the demons, knows."

[724] Babylonian *Talmud Shabbat* 55a: "…And inscribe a *tav* of blood on the foreheads of the wicked as a sign so that the angels of destruction will have dominion over them."

[725] "The Name," a euphemism for God.

[726] Numbers 22:4 ""Now this horde will lick clean all that is about us as an ox licks up the grass of the field."

[727] A prayer shawl and phylacteries.

[728] In this concluding prayer, which begins with the words "It is upon us to praise the Master of all," there is a rare custom of spitting after the words "*lahevel varek*" which literally means: "that they (the gentiles) bow to vapor and emptiness," because the word for emptiness, "*rek*," sounds like "*rok*" which means spit.

[729] Genesis 37:30 "Returning to his brothers, he said, "The boy is gone! Now, what am I to do?""

[730] Genesis 4:9 "The LORD said to Cain, "Where is your brother Abel?" And he said, "I do not know. Am I my brother's keeper?"

[731] Ecclesiastes 11:1

[732] From the Passover *Haggadah*: "The more one tells of the Exodus from Egypt, the more praiseworthy it is."

[733] Genesis 25:30.

[734] 1 Kings 20:9 "So he said to Ben-hadad's messengers, "Tell my lord the king…"

returns the 5-ruble bill to its place, and takes out a 10-ruble bill. Lippe puts the bills in his pocket and says: "Take yourself to your land, and to the land of your birth,"[735] that is to say, that the horse would be returned to the stable that same night. The next day, in the morning, we found the *bulan* next to the trough, as if nothing had happened. My father was a smart and practical Jew. Once he said to Lippe: "Listen, Lippe, let's talk openly. Why do you have to steal a horse twice a year, each time to get 10 liras,[736] in addition to this you cause damage, since you break the lock, and a pair of horses with a coachman are idled? I have a suggestion: leave my horses be, come to my house twice a year, the eve of *Rosh Hashanah* and the eve of *Pesach*, each time you will receive 10 rubles, and peace on Israel, both of us will be satisfied."

{p. 254} Lippe: "*Oy* Reb Leib, aren't you a smart Jew, how can you suggest such a thing to me? What am I in your eyes? A beggar? I should take donations? I receive the money for work, as it written: "By your sweat of your brow you will eat your bread."[737] In Lippe's yard there was a kind of beauty parlor for horses. When they wanted to sell an old horse for a good price, they would bring it to Lippe a few days before the "fair." Lippe would take a small file, a small scalpel, he would place a device into the horse's mouth so that he would not close it, and remove the signs on the edges of the teeth that indicate the true age of the horse. A few hours before the start of the fair, the owner of the horse would again bring his horse to Lippe, and he would spread spicy pepper under its tail. The horse would turn into a war horse, stamping his feet, and swinging his tale like a young horse. The buyer would be very impressed. After an exhausting negotiation, accompanied by pats on the palms of the seller and buyer, the two of them would enter the public house to "wet" the deal (with the expense on the buyer's account). After a few hours the influence of the paprika dissipated, the horse returned to being sad, his head lowered, quiet, ready to be delivered to be "a carcass skinned in the market,"[738] but the money was already in the hand of the seller, and go scream "alive and well." Lippe would also dye stolen horses. A white horse would turn to black with shoe cream, to brown with chicory, to yellow with onion skins, the way they color eggs for *Pesach*. On that night they transfer the horse to the nearby eastern Prussia, and sell it to a farmer at dusk, when vision is weak. On the next day in the morning the farmer would wonder that the black horse from yesterday had turned white. Lippe had a heart of gold. He would give a donation to the poor, buy an "*aliyah*,"[739] precisely the third one on *Simchat Torah*, precisely the "*Chatan Torah*."[740] When a Jew would approach Lippe and say to him" "Lippe, I need to travel to Suwalk, but I have no money," Lippe would smile and say: "If there is no flour there is no *Torah*,"[741] and immediately add "Reb Ploni son of Reb Almoni, we honor you with an *aliyah* to the *Torah* (that is to say, to get up on the wagon), and the price – when conditions improve." He was honored and beloved by all, especially by children. When I began to visit the "*cheder*" at the age of 6, I would encounter Lippe nearly every morning, when he was standing in the market with his wagon master friends. He was always a little tipsy. When he would see me, he would approach with a smile on his lips, would grasp my cheek with the two rough fingers of his right hand (this was a pinch of fondness, of course, that brought tears from my eyes), and he would say: "Do you remember,

---

[735] Genesis 12:1 "The LORD said to Abram, "Go forth from your land and from the place of your birth…"

[736] The currency of the State of Israel from June 9, 1952 until February 23, 1980.

[737] Genesis 3:19.

[738] There is an error in the original, which gives the phrase as "a carcass skinned outside," but the correct expression is found in the Talmud and makes more sense. Babylonian Talmud *Pesachim* 113a: "…Rav further said: Skin a carcass in the market and take payment…"

[739] The honor of being called up to the podium to recite the blessing for the *Torah* reading.

[740] On *Simchat Torah*, after completing the reading of the Torah at the end of the book of Deuteronomy, it is a special honor to receive the last *aliyah* of the Book of Deuteronomy. The person who receives that *aliyah* is called the *Chatan Torah*, the groom of the *Torah*, or *Kallat Torah*, the bride of the Torah, in synagogues where women receive an *aliyah*.

[741] Pirke Avot 3:21.

Kivele, how Tzipke the wicked woman, would let you wail all night like a puppy, and I used to rock your cradle, since I am a Jew. Honor me with a shot cup." Five *kopeks*, the price of the shot cup, were always in my pocket, but I was not able to give it to him, because Lippe owed money in every public house in the city. He did not receive on credit anymore, and if he offered the money in advance they would credit it to his account, but they would not give him a shot cup. I was compelled, therefore, to disturb my honor, to enter the pub, request a shot, and serve it to him. Lippe would make the "that everything is created by his word"[742] blessing. He would upturn the shot into his throat, and he would say: "if only I was a king, I would hang the owner of the factory that manufactures tiny cups like these." He begins to sing loudly from the Passover *Haggadah*: "Who knows two? I know two." Which is to say, it will not hurt at all if Reb Leib's son would pour him another one. Finally, I am not Rothschild. When I was convinced that Lippe was waiting for me every morning, and because of him I couldn't buy a pear or an apple for myself, I began to walk to the "*cheder*" by a circuitous route. But when it became known to him from the mouth of a friend that I continued to attend the "*cheder*," he came, waited until the break, and when I went out to play with my friends, he approached me, smiled, and said: "I raised sons and elevated, and they transgressed against me,"[743] ai, ai {p. 255} not nice." I had no choice, but to continue and supply him with brandy. To my joy, my parents transferred me to a "*cheder*" in the district city of Suwalk, and the unfortunate Lippe remained without worry. My father told about an event that happened with Lippe, which is worth bringing here. In our area there lived a Pole, owner of a large holding, an exalted rich man. He had a carriage, which he ordered specially from outside of the country with all the amenities. His coachman looked like a prince, the bridle with silver ornaments, etc. A pair of horses that he bought in Denmark was harnessed to the carriage. There they had high quality pedigreed horses. He was proud of these horses, because their color was rare, white patches on a brown background. These 2 horses were twins, young, about 3-4 years old, and the patches on their bodies was the same size and arrangement, a very rare thing. Really a wonder. A tragedy happened; one of the horses got sick and died. The "Fritz"[744] mourned as if one of the members of his family died. All his aspiration was to find a matching horse. He photographed the living horse and sent his picture outside of the country to famous horse sellers, but it was all in vain. Finally he bought a less praiseworthy pair of horses for his carriage, and instructed the manager of his farm to sell the orphaned horse at any price, in order not to see him in his sorrow. The matter became known to Lippe. When the Fritz went out for a walk, Lippe entered the property. When the manager of the farm saw him he was very happy to greet him, and offered him the horse at a good price. Lippe tied the horse behind his wagon, and travelled in the direction of the place from where the Fritz had to return to his castle. And here the Fritz appeared in his wonderful carriage with the decorated coachman and his armed bodyguard. Lippe, as usual, lowers his hat, stands and blesses him. The Fritz's eyes lit up. Tied to Lippe's wagon was a horse that he was seeking. In vain, for more than a year now. He doesn't believe what his eyes are seeing, and orders the coachman to get down and check the horse. The coachman gets down, checks the horse, crosses himself, mentions Jesus[745] and the Holy Mother; a miracle happened; a double of the horse which is up for sale has been found. Lippe tells the "Fritz" that he bought the horse at a "fair" in Grodno from a Gypsy. The "Fritz" did not negotiate a price, and paid for the horse the amount that

---

[742] The blessing appropriate for alcoholic beverages other than wine. "Blessed are You, Adonoi our God, Ruler of the universe, by Whose word all things came to be."

[743] Isaiah 1:2.

[744] A Polish nobleman.

[745] Named here as Yeshu, the usual rabbinic name for him, which is the abbreviation for "May his name and Memory be erased." Babylonian Talmud Avodah Zarah 17a: "...I found a man who was one of the students of Yeshu the Nazarene..."

Lippe asked for. On the next day, in the morning, when the manager of the farm entered the stable he saw that the horse he had sold yesterday is standing in the stable. An act of sorcery. Father used to tell that over the course of years Lippe was afraid to pass by the estate. For the Fritz the 100 rubles was no loss, but his neighbors made fun of him on how he fell victim to Lippe's ability.

In this way, Lippe was my "grandfather." Decades went by and I had a family, a father to two children; a son who was 4½ years old, and a daughter who was 1½. I was working in Egypt for a German company. On May 1, 1912, I received a vacation to travel to Europe, after an exhausting year of working in the wet heat in the area of Aswan and Luxor. My wife, may her memory be for a blessing, wanted to see her relatives in Suwalk, and I, the city of my birth, Augustow. On the day after my arrival in the city, I went to visit Lippe. The small house had aged like its owner. On the roof the wooden roofing tiles gushed with leaks. On the "*prizbah*" (a kind of bench next to the outer wall of the house, with a shielding wall of wooden planks), he sits. White as snow, his eyes almost closed, his chin adorned with a long beard, leaning on a stick, maybe sleeping, maybe awake. I approached him, took his right hand into mine, and I blessed him with peace. "Reb Lippe!" I shouted in his deaf ear. He opened his eyes and asked: "Who are you?" Before I had time to answer Tzipke, my wet nurse, came running out of the house. This was a very dramatic meeting. The two of us wept from an abundance of emotion. I asked about my friend my age, who had emigrated to America. The stable in the yard was open, there were no horses, only a wagon, on the trash heap decaying wagon parts were laying. Tzipke screamed: "This is our Kivele, the son of Reb Leib!" He recovered: "Your father is in the land of Israel. I envy him. The land of Israel. Jerusalem! {p. 256} He is happy. I would have wanted to be buried on the Mt. of Olives, and be exempt from the rolling tunnels[746] in the coming of the Messiah." "Lippe" – I asked – what about the virtue of "wine will gladden the heart of a person?"[747] "Tzipke the wicked doesn't give." I remember, how I used to hitch the lions and travel with your father to Suwalk. In every public house I drank brandy in a tea cup, 92 proof, I used to feel a tickling in the belly. There are no proprietors like those now. In the "*kloiz*" tailors and shoemakers sit now, ignoramuses. "Do me a favor – I said to Tzipke - here is money, go to the "*Monopol*" (a government store for beverages) and buy him a bottle of brandy, but the strongest, that he should drink to his health." She brought the bottle, and poured him a large cup. He took the cup with trembling hands, gulped, and said: "This is brandy? "The pony" (a derogatory name for the Tsar's government) knows how to make brandy? Thieves! They dilute it with too much water, I don't feel any tickle in the belly." "Nu, Lippe" I said, "be healthy, until 120."[748] "Feh,[749] it is boring – Lippe sighed "soon the "*hetzel*" will take me (a professional who kills sick horses and strips the hides from them).

Abba Gordin, May His Memory Be For a Blessing
By Chaim Dan

Secluded and isolated, he used to sit alone in his abode in Ramat Gan, with his weapons upon him. His quill in his hand, bent over his manuscripts, ready for battle and for creation – and he was more than seventy.

---

[746] Babylonian *Talmud Ketubot* 111a: "Abaye said: Tunnels are prepared for them in the ground, through which they pass to Eretz Yisrael." Those buried on the Mt. of Olives, facing the Temple Mount on the east, will already be in place for the arrival of the Messiah, who will come through the eastern gate of Jerusalem. In Ezekiel 46:12 we read that there is one person, a "prince," who may enter via the eastern gate: "When the prince provides a freewill offering to the LORD . . . the gate facing east is to be opened for him...Then he shall go out, and after he has gone out, the gate will be shut."
[747] Psalm 104:15.
[748] It is traditional to bless someone that they live to be 120 years old, the age of Moses at his death.
[749] An exclamation of disgust.

A remnant of the generation of illegal immigration that the Jewry of Russia and Poland established at the beginning of the present century,[750] a generation that wrestled with beings Divine and human…[751] A personality rich in spirit, a wise scholar son of a wise scholar, expert and sharp. In his articles and books, he integrated words of the first and the last together. A swimmer in the sea of the *Talmud* and the "*Zohar*,"[752] with a hand in Marx and Kropotkin, and frequently quoting from all sides, without a barrier. His furrow delved into various fields: science and philosophy, prose and poetry, essay and story, article and feuilleton.[753] Intellectual curiosity that did not know satiation, and that had no limit to its range.

The man knew many incarnations. From Poland to Russia, from Russia to America, and from America – in old age – to Israel. From piety to heresy, and to piety in heresy, until anarchism.

In Russia, in the days of the revolution, he was one of the first of the speakers of anarchism, who competed with the Bolsheviks over the seizure of power. He came into personal contact with the greats of the revolution: Lenin, Kamenev, Dzerzhinsky, etc. An opponent of their tactics in the name of revolutionary consistency… How he, the son of a rabbi, a seeker of morality and splendor, careful with the honor of every person, encountered this milieu – the irony of fate.

By a miracle, he left there and sailed for America. Keeping faith with the ideas of anarchism, there too he found his place in the elite of the anarchists, of the generation of the veteran emigres, and became their teacher.[754]

Full of wandering and disappointment, he left there and reached Israel.

When you came in his presence you saw how tragic was the fate of the part of the Jewish intelligentsia {p. 257} in the generation that passed by. And among all of them, wasn't the fate of the part that held fast to this discarded movement that served anarchism on the street of the Jewish workers more tragic? What is the face of that same faction today? A movement without successors, without heirs, a movement whose horizon is sealed by the erosion of time. In effect, it shrank altogether in groups of individuals above middle age, without a public, without a living reality.

His liveliness stood him in good stead – and the fire of his youth did not go out despite the changes in the times and the changing climate on the landscape and in the surroundings. At the end of his days he aroused his spirit in worlds that were closer to him than the dawn of his youth. In the last years, he was given to the writing of a novel from the period of King Solomon, and monographic books about the Maharal,[755] Rashi, and the Holy Ari.[756]

Old and weakened, he did not know fatigue in his literary work until his last day. All who knew him were surprised by him, and in their eyes the matter was a symbol of the supremacy of spirit over the material. And while he still carried in his heart rich worlds, and sought to bequeath them to many, he was taken, and is no more.

He died August 21, 1964. He was 77 years old at his death. Peace to his dust.[757]

---

[750] The 20th century.

[751] Genesis 32:29 "Said he, your name shall no longer be Jacob, but Israel, for you have striven with beings divine and human, and have prevailed."

[752] The primary work of Jewish mysticism.

[753] A part of a newspaper or magazine devoted to criticism, light literature, or fiction.

[754] This phrase, "*moreh-hora'ah*," generally refers to a teacher of Jewish law. Its use here seems ironic.

[755] Judah Loew ben Bezalel, 1520 - 1609, known as the *Maharal* of Prague, or *The Maharal*, the Hebrew acronym of "*Moreinu Ha-Rav Loew*" ("Our Teacher, Rabbi Loew").

[756] Rabbi Yitzchak Luria, 1534-1572, is commonly known as the Ari, an acronym standing for *Eloki* Rabbi Yitzchak, "the Godly Rabbi Isaac"; *ari* is also the Hebrew word for "lion." Isaac Luria was the father of Lurianic kabbalah.

[757] May he rest in peace.

Members of the Enlightenment and *Chovevei Tzion*
by M. Tzinovitz

The Hebrew Writer Yisrael Ze'ev Sperling

A zealot for the enlightenment, and battling with the conservative "rebels against the light,"[758] who were afraid that the enlightenment would weaken the foundations of the religion and change the traditional ways of life. In his articles in "*HaMelitz*" he sharply attacked the young Rabbi Reb Katriel Natan, the local *Av Beit Din*, who stood on guard for the life of the patriarchal[759] religion, so that it would not be harmed by the enlightenment.

At the end of the seventies of the previous century,[760] he was renowned as a Hebrew translator. Within two years, 5637-5639 [1877-1879], he published translations of two books by Jules Verne: "In the Depths of the Sea" and "In the Belly of the Earth," which achieved great attention in the groups of Hebrew readers.

In the opening to the translation it is written that the book contains: "stories of knowledge of the nature of the sea and its wonders in the deep, wrapped in a charming, even pleasant, story from a journey around the globe of the earth in the heart of great and small seas, under the cover of the water and awesome ice. They derive from the language of France, and were copied freely to the language of *Ever*, clearly and simply, for the benefit of the youth seeking enlightenment."

The second book, "In the Belly of the Earth," contains: "geologic knowledge and wonders from the workings of nature in the lap of the inner land. Wrapped in a charming, even pleasant story from a journey to the center of the earth, by way of volcanic channels carved by fire. They derive from the language of France, and were copied freely to the language of *Ever*, clearly and simply, for the benefit of the youth seeking enlightenment."

With the occurrence of the pogroms in south Russia, Y. Z. Sperling was disappointed and sobered, as an example of other Hebrew writers, in "heavenly education."[761] He joined the "*Chibbat Tzion*" movement, which was developed in the Jewish public in Russia, and was one of its heads in Augustow, the city where he resided.

{p. 258} When he died in the year 5670 [1910], an article in his memory was published in the daily Hebrew newspaper "*Hed HaZman,*"[762] which appeared in Vilna, edited by Ben-Tzion Katz. The writer of the note, the *Shaliach Tzibur* and *Shochet U'bodek*, Yosef Chaim Ratner, writes: "another one of the enlightened of the old generation in our city went to his eternity. One of these types that are becoming fewer in our generation. The writer Yisrael Sperling translated the French writer Jules Verne's "In the Belly of the Earth" and "In the Deeps of the Sea." The deceased sage was great in *Torah* and God-fearing, and expert in research books. He dedicated a great part of his time to general sciences. He knew the German, Polish and Russian languages well. The deceased left behind a book which is still in manuscript, by the name "Validation of Wisdom on the Science of Physics," that the sage Chaim Zelig Slonimski (founder, editor, and publisher of "*HaTzefirah*") supported. The deceased was 90 years old at his death. The members of our community accorded him great respect. All the shops were closed, and many thronged behind his bier."

Yisrael Ze'ev Sperling served for decades as "Rabbi on behalf"[763] in Augustow. He also became the speaker and the advocate of the Jewish community of the city of his residence in relation to the Russian authority and the district officials of Augustow, which included the Jewish

---

[758] Those who opposed the light of the enlightenment.

[759] This word is missing one letter, but can only be "patriarchal."

[760] The 19th century.

[761] Enlightenment.

[762] "The Echo of the Time."

[763] The Rabbi appointed by the community and ratified by the Russian governor.

town of Sapotzkin. When Rabbi Katriel Natan left Augustow, he served as rabbi in Bodki and Sapotzkin. He supported the invitation of Rabbi Leib Gordin from Michaelishok to be the Rabbi Av Beit Din in Augustow. Y.Z. Sperling ascribed great importance to Rabbi Gordin and emphasized this matter in his letters in "*HaTzefirah*."

Reb Arieh Leib Glikstein

Born in Grayevo in 5594 [1834] to his father Yaakov. He received a traditional education in *cheder* and *yeshiva*. He was a merchant in Augustow and one of the activists of "*Chovevei Tzion*" in the place. In correspondence on the "*Chibbat Tzion*" movement," his name is always mentioned. He went up to the land in the year 1904. He engaged in public needs on the *moshava* Zikhron Yaakov. His daughters were Esther, the wife of Chaim Margalit Kalvariski, and Rivka, the wife of Dr. Hillel Yaffa. His son Akiva was born in the year 5641 [1881]. Akiva completed university in engineering. He went up to the land. He built many buildings in the land. He helped his brother-in-law, Dr. Hillel Yaffa, in cleaning and drying out the swamp that was adjacent to Merchaviah.

In the year 1912 he established the Institute for Irrigation, the first in the land, next to the Yarkon. In the First World War, he built buildings and roads in the Sinai Desert for the Turkish army. In the year 1919 he established the Institute for Water on Allenby Street in Tel Aviv. He also built the school building for teachers in Beit Karem, and the "*Keren Kayemet L'Yisrael*" building in Rechavia, Jerusalem. In World War Two he worked as a contractor for the British Army in Syria and Lebanon. (According to the "Tidhar" Encyclopedia).

The Writer and Enlightened One E.Y. Shapira

Elazar Yitzchak Shapira was born in the year 5596 [1836] in Seirijai to his father Reb Moshe. In his youth he learned in the *yeshiva* of Sejny. When the *yeshiva* was closed he moved to Augustow, and continued to learn with his uncle, who was the Rabbi of the city.

{p. 259} With the influence of his relative Tuvia Pesach Shapira, who was a Hebrew teacher, Reb Elazar Yitzchak became a Hebrew teacher in Augustow and preached the Enlightenment. When the place in this town, where his uncle officiated as Rabbi, became too restricted for him, he settled in Warsaw, in the year 5624 [1864]. There he opened a bookstore, which was famous as a meeting place for sages and writers. He also became one of the first Hebrew publishers. A. Y. SH. [his initials], the nickname "*Ish*,"[764] for some time edited the "*Boker Or*,"[765] of A.B. Gotlover, and contributed to "*HaMaggid*," "*HaTzefirah*," "*HaMelitz*," "*HaYom*," "*HaAsif*," with articles, feuilletons, and translations. In "*HaAsif*" of the year 5646 [1886], He published a story about Daniel Deronda, and translated the story of the German-Jewish writer Shlomo Cohen, "The Redeemer and the Savior," which in its time was a book read widely by the youth.

Is"h also knew Polish, and published articles in this language on Jewish topics in the Polish-Jewish newspaper "*Yotshanka*" that appeared in Warsaw.

One must further point out that in the year 5631 [1871], the book "Letters in a Book" was printed, which contained 100 letters to youth in addition to the story "*Rephael*," which achieved great distribution among *yeshiva* students who became enlightened, and served for them as the first fundamental material for their recognition of the Hebrew language and its grammar. In that

---

[764] "Man."
[765] "Morning of Light."

year he also published two booklets "*Meged Yerachim*"[766] and also a collection of stories "*Yad HaRotzim*."[767]

In the weekly "*HaOlam*,"[768] year two, he published his memories of A.Tz.[769] HaCohain Zweifel.

Chaim Rozental

A functionary and merchant, who went up to the land of Israel in the year 5682 [1922], and died at the age of 93. He was born in Augustow on 13 Tevet, 5626 (1865). He learned in "*cheder*" in Augustow, continued his studies at the gymnasia in Suwalk, and afterwards at the University of Warsaw. He was crowned with a Master's degree in law.

In the year 1890 he was appointed as the agent of a kerosene and oil company. Afterwards he became the owner of a soap factory in Odessa. He took to wife Miriam the daughter of Eliyahu HaCohain Kaplan, a well-known lover of Zion.

He was drawn further to Zion when he sat on the benches of the University of Warsaw. He administered intensive Zionist propaganda among the Jewish students. When the "*Bnei Moshe*"[770] organization was found in the year 5649 [1889], he joined it.

For many years he dwelt, for the purpose of his business, in cities that were outside the area of "the Pale of Settlement." And in every place that he resided, he served as a faithful one of Zion.

In the year 1893 he served as the Deputy Chief of the community and attorney for "*Chovevei Tzion*" in Saratov. When he moved to Gur Levko, he was appointed there as head of the community council (in the year 1901). He was always taking care of great ventures, yet he always found time for communal and Zionist action. In the year 1906 he moved to live in Odessa, and was chosen as a member of the "*Chovevei Tzion*" Council. In the year 1911 he visited in the land and travelled its length and its breadth. When he returned to Odessa M. Ussishkin appointed him to be the publisher and official editor of the weekly "*HaOlam*," which was transferred to Odessa at the beginning of 1912. Besides this he was active in Zionist educational and cultural institutions in Odessa, and also was a member of the community council. In addition, he founded the "*Kinneret*" book publisher, which published books about Judaism and Zionism.

In the year 1919 he was imprisoned together with a group of Zionists in Odessa (among them: Ze'ev Tiomkin, the attorney Pen, Yaakov Vasserman). Only thanks to the investigator Svarny, a friend of his son-in-law Dr. Leib Tshartkov, {p. 260} they were saved from a death sentence. In the year 1920 he reached the land of Israel and immediately undertook public action. He was chosen for the administration of "Savings and Loan" in Tel Aviv, and served as the administrator of the institution over the course of 10 years. With the outbreak of the events of 5681 [1921], hundreds of Jews that lived in Jaffa were left without a roof over their heads. At his initiative, and the initiative of Dr. Bogroshov, they organized and founded the society of "The Homeless." Thanks to his action and his energy (he was the head of the association), the association succeeded in obtaining land from "the *Keren Kayemet*," and mortgage loans for building, and the neighborhood was erected with a speed outside of the regular restrictions. In the year 1929, at his initiative, the monthly "Cooperation" was founded, in which he participated for a long time as writer and editor. His articles were translated afterwards in the literature of the

---

[766] "The Bounty of Moons." Deuteronomy 33:14 "With the bounteous yield of the sun, And the bounteous crop of the moons;"
[767] "The Hand of Those Who Want."
[768] "The World."
[769] Eliezer Tzvi.
[770] "Children of Moses."

Cooperation in Poland. He was the head of the "Covenant of the First Ones"[771] after the death of Alter Druyanov. He died in Tel Aviv, 24 *Tammuz* 5706 (July 23, 1946), and was buried in the old cemetery. His descendants: Lydia (Leah), the wife of Dr. Leib Tshartkov (doctor of the "Herzliya" gymnasium); Aharon, a lawyer in Tel Aviv.

Reb Shaul Mendel Rabinovitz

The son-in-law of Reb Dovid Mordechai Markus. Learned in *Torah*, an enlightened Hebrew and veteran Zionist. He dwelled for a number of years in Augustow. He moved afterwards to Pinsk, the city of his birth, and became the manager of a factory of the house of Luria in that city.

He was a quintessential Zionist. A delegate to the 7th Zionist Congress. Head of the local Zionist organization. He died in the year 5679 [1919] in Pinsk. His wife Malkah (Regina),[772] was born in Augustow, and was head of the WIZO[773] organization in Pinsk, and head of the orphans' homes in that city. Their son was Dr. Ze'ev Rabinovitz, the doctor of the Haifa municipality, a researcher of Chassidism, who won a prize for his book "The History of Chassidism in Lithuania."

Yosef Guviansky

Born in the year 5607 [1847] in Lipsk, which is adjacent to Augustow. He became enlightened in the *yeshiva* of Volozhin and settled in Augustow. The enlightened writer Y. Z. Sperling drew him near. He supported himself by the teaching of *Tanakh* and Hebrew to a small group of youth who were the sons of householders in the city. His influence on the young *yeshiva* students was great.

From Augustow he moved to Krynki, his wife's birthplace. The zealots pursued him, and on account of them he wandered from place to place. He found a few years of calm in Plonsk, where he succeeded in implanting knowledge of the Hebrew language and literature in wide groups of youth of the generation. He published articles in the Hebrew press of those days. Finally he settled in Warsaw as a modern teacher of the children of the Lithuanian "*Mitnagdim*"[774] that were settled in that city.

Yosef Guviansky died close to the outbreak of the First World War.

Kalman Avigdor Perla

Kalman Avigdor Perla was born in Kolno. One time he saw letters that were not Hebrew in the gate of a book. It aroused in him the desire to know what these letters were. He began to follow men who knew {p. 261} foreign letters, and with their help he learned the Polish and Russian letters. He connected the letters into words, and succeeded, after much labor, in learning to read.

He married a wife from the daughters of Lomza. When he was dependent on his father-in-law's table, he made the acquaintance of the teacher Shvartzenberg, who used to lend him books to read. When the matter became known to his father-in-law, he began to make his life miserable, until he was compelled to flee from his house and move to Augustow, where his brother-in-law the doctor Yazlovski lived, who he called "seedling doctor." In Augustow Kalman Avigdor learned Polish, Russian, German, French, Italian, and Greek well.

He engaged in teaching in various places for many days. Finally, he settled in Lublin, and founded there a school for young men.

---

[771] Leviticus 26:45 "I will remember in their favor the covenant with the ancients, whom I freed from the land of Egypt in the sight of the nations to be their God: I, the LORD."

[772] Regina is a translation of the Hebrew name *Malkah*. Both mean queen.

[773] The Women's International Zionist Organization.

[774] Opposers.

His book "Treasury of the Language of the Sages" is a study of the Hebrew language. In his last years he composed his book "The Interpreter and the Translator," a study of the "foreign" words in Rashi's commentary.

Kalman Avigdor Perla died in the year 5673 [1913]. He was 84 at his death.

According to *HaTzefirah* 1913 No. 93

Dovid Arieh Aleksandrovitz

A Jew of the "*amcha*" type. He lived by the fruit of his labors, from his work in tanning leather. A man of action, and industrious. He did not withhold time and effort for the good of the collective and the private. For a certain time he served as Head of the Jewish community in Augustow.

In the year 1920 a serious war was fought between the Russians and the Poles, and the Russian army had already reached the gates of Warsaw, the capital city of Poland. The Russians conquered city after city, and tarried in our city for about a month of days.

The Polish army wore strength and succeeded in driving the Russians out to Minsk in White Russia. The Russians fled in panic, starving and thirsty. While in flight they threw off their weapons. A situation was created between them: the Russians left the Polish cities, and the Poles had not yet entered. Then hard days came to the Polish Jews, a situation "between kings, a time when each person did what was right in their own eyes."[775]

Jewish youth from all the cities of Poland accompanied the fleeing Russians from all the cities of their retreat. The Jewish youth fled from fear of the Polish army, which was likely to make false accusations against them… the number of Jewish refugees reached the thousands.

The goal of those fleeing was the border of the neutral country of Lithuania. This border was signposted a few kilometers past Augustow, on the way to the town of Ratzk. Many of them, however, succeeded in crossing the border and reaching the place that they sought. However, those that did not succeed remained stuck in Augustow.

{p. 262} The Lithuanian border was suddenly closed and placed under meticulous guard. Among the Jewish refugees were youth from all the echelons: intelligentsia, workers, *yeshiva* boys. All of them were miserable, hungry and thirsty, their feet were swollen and wounded from much walking. All of them were terrified and desperate with fear for the future.

The Polish army reached Augustow, the regiment of General Heller, who was notorious as the quintessential anti-Semite, and also his soldiers did his will. The soldiers scattered in all the Jewish houses, on the pretext of searching for Bolsheviks, and in the meantime arrested all the refugees that they could.

After a certain time, when their spirits calmed down a little, the Jews came out of their hiding places. Most of the people began to worry about their livelihoods, and how to get back their looted property. However, Dovid Arieh Aleksandrovitz preferred the communal worries to the private worries.

He shut the doors of his workshop, and engaged in opening the doors of the prison. He enthusiastically took care of freeing the Jewish boys – among them were people without a name, lacking passports, who were expecting severe punishments. He did not hesitate and entered with

---

[775] Babylonian *Talmud Chullin* 57b "Or perhaps it was between king and king, as it is written: "In those days there was no king in Israel; every man did that which was right in his own eyes" (Judges 17:6)."

devotion into a bad and dangerous business, and this in a warlike atmosphere, days of emergency, when every Jew was suspected of spying and of Bolshevism.

At a time like this, Dovid Arieh Aleksandrovitz found pathways between the people of the regime and the Polish secret police. He acted and he succeeded. The doors of the prison were opened, and the arrested Jewish refugees went out to freedom, group by group, in order that the evil eye of the high windows would not control them.

He was respected by all the residents of the city, for they knew his faithfulness to the public, and the work of his hands – was magnificent.

Reuven Rotenberg
By Zelda Edelstein (Koshelevski), daughter of the rabbi.

He was a magnificent figure, a good man who did good, ran like a deer and brave as a lion to do the *mitzvot* between a person and God, and between people. He was always ready to extend help to others. In every event of tragedy or saving a life, Reuven Rotenberg always stood out, at the head of those offering help. Even in the middle of the night, in the cold, in the rain and snow, he hurried to the bedside of the sick and lonely. Even before they had time to summon a doctor, Reuven Rotenberg would roll up his sleeves, put wood in the stove, heat water, wash the sick with alcohol, etc. He was expert in offering first aid, and was not afraid of contagion. He believed with complete faith that "the keeper of *mitzvot* will not know evil."

There was an incident when a respected Jew turned to Reuven Rotenberg with a request to provide him with *gemilut chasadim*,[776] on condition that it remain a secret, and he would not let his wife know about it. He was in need of money in order to marry off his sister, a poor and lonely orphan. Reuven hurried, went out to the market, and found a Jew that gave him *gemilut chasadim* without asking even for an IOU. In this way {p. 263} Reuven R. provided the needed amount, and kept the secrecy over the course of many years, until the payment of the debt. Reuven was happy that he merited to do two *mitzvot* at one stroke: the *mitzvah* of bringing in the bride, and the *mitzvah* of *gemilut chasadim*.

Reuven R., who was enthusiastic about doing *mitzvot*, took an active part in the *mitzvah* of accompanying the dead,[777] as President of the "*Chevra Kadisha*."[778]

The crowning glory of his activity was the *mitzvah* of rescuing captives.

At the end of the 19th century, there were a few *yeshiva* boys in the regiment of the Russian Infantry that camped in Augustow. These were entirely unable to serve in the military, but they were unable to be freed, due to the lack of money for paying a bribe.

Reuven Rotenberg befriended the military doctor of the regiment. He began to provide old wine to his house from his wine cellar, the work of his own hands, something to be proud of. (He would sell his wine, and other beverages, to Jews – for *Shabbatot* and festivals, for the four cups of the *seder* night, for *Kiddush* and *Havdalah*.[779] The gentiles purchased sharp beverages for

---

[776] An act of lovingkindness; sometimes a gift of money, sometimes a loan, sometimes other assistance.
[777] Burying the dead.
[778] Literally "The Holy Society," this refers to the Burial Society.
[779] *Kiddush* is the sanctification of *Shabbat* recited over wine, and *Havdalah* is the ceremony that marks the end of *Shabbat*, which also includes a blessing over wine.

guzzling into drunkenness.) He began to be a regular visitor in the house of the military doctor. Once he entered into conversation with him about the beverages, about his friends, the officers of the regiment, who were valiant men who knew how to drink, as well as the soldiers of the regiment, who were commendably brave, except for an insignificant number of "*Yehudunim*" of feeble strength. The doctor agreed with the opinion of Reuven Rotenberg that it was not worth spoiling the good name of the regiment, and that the unsuccessful soldiers should be freed.

In order to strengthen the decision of the doctor, R. Rotenberg increased the sending of gifts to his house. The soldiers, the *yeshiva* boys, received an order to appear for a medical examination, and were declared unsuitable for service in the army.

In the period of the regime of Tsar Nicholas, the period of the pogroms and the dispossession of the Jews of their economic positions, masses of Jews streamed from the Russian cities to the Prussian border, in order to cross it and reach America, the free land.

Augustow is a border city, which sits next to the eastern Prussian border. Smugglers of illegal immigrants transferred migrants from it across the border by the masses. It happened that the border patrol caught infiltrators like these, and arrested and imprisoned them.

He alleviated the gate of people's suffering.

Reuven R. did not rest and was not quiet. He ran around day and night until he succeeded in redeeming and freeing these unfortunate ones. He was friendly to all the clerks and under-clerks who visited the tavern in his house, and filled their throats at every opportunity, free, without paying.

In his twilight days he merited going up to the land of Israel. On *Shabbat*, before he left Augustow, after the reading of the *Torah* in the *Beit Midrash*, Reuven R. kissed the *Torah* scrolls, exchanged kisses with all the worshippers, and wept greatly. All of them wept with him, as if their hearts prophesied for them the Holocaust that was about to come and destroy all of the Jewish community in Augustow, without leaving any remnant of it.

{p. 264} Fania Bergstein

Fania was born on 10 Nisan, 5668 (11 April 1908), in the town of Stutzin, Lomza District in White Russia. In her father's house, a teacher and Hebrew *Maskil*, the first seeds of love of the Hebrew language and literature are buried in the aware and impressionable soul of the child. In her wanderings with her teacher-father from town to town, with the outbreak of the First World War, the family reaches the city of Sumy, which is in the Ukraine. Here Fania attends the White Russian gymnasia, learning the Russian language and its literature. Here also are revealed the first sparks of her ability, the first fruits of her attempts at writing.

When it was decreed, after the revolution, against the teaching of the Hebrew language in the schools of Soviet Russia, the parents' decision was made to return to Poland. In the year 1922, the family settles in the city of Augustow.

In Augustow Fania, fourteen years old, encounters the Zionist movement. She joins "*HeChalutz HaTzair*," and afterwards, "*HeChalutz*," taking an active part in the work of the branch and carries the burden of the *mitzvot*.[780] Fania tells: "Simple wooden steps led to the dwelling place of the "*HeChalutz*" branch. Here there blew an enchanting wind of

---

[780] She takes on observance of the *mitzvot*.

far-off places, here there peeked from the eyes of all these simple young men and women the mute and radiant light of satisfaction that the soul so desired to be let into its secret.

As the place of precious light, "The House of the Pioneer" called at the edge of the town. And the heart called forward, to the fields of toil, to the road, to the road. For isn't it incumbent on the pioneer to be the first, to go, to march. Immediately, without delay." From the time that the first seminar of "*HeChalutz*" was organized in the year 1926, Fania was called to participate in it. From a late impression, at the end of years, Fania brings up something from the memory of those years: "The influence of the house, the town, was still impressed on us, the young people, and in our tender souls. Much of the old still clung to the hems of our garments, to our words, and in our thoughts. And especially we, the young women, the web of the dreams of youth hung on our brows, and the soul still shrank, shied away from, the crowded group, the happy circle of friends."

Yet the heart was beating, the song was captivating, the words of the lecturers were received like seeds on the soil of the hearts, and slowly, like the fading of fog in the face of the sun, the lines begin to become apparent, the dream removes the shining finery, the path awaits, the command is clear, and the heart is prepared and ready."

Fania returned from the seminar drunk from the pioneer *Torah*. But there was not enough in that. Fania faced towards the realization of the imperative of the movement. And first of all, going out for training. Tcharlona was set at the place of her training – an estate on the banks of the River Niemen.

{p. 265} In Tcharlona, during a visit to the doctor, the heart disease that had settled in her first became known to Fania. This was the disease that in the future would hang a dark shadow over all of her life.

With her return from the training Fania was called for work in the administration of the movement. She visited the towns, the branches, guiding and lecturing in the summer settlements, establishing new branches and conquering hearts for pioneering.

In that period Fania began to write and participate in the journalism of the pioneer youth, "*Lahavot,*"[781] and "*HeChalutz HaTzair.*" In the newspaper "*HaYom,*" which was published in Warsaw, the first fruits of her poems were published.

In the year 1930, when she was 22 years old, she built her family house and went up to the land with her life companion, Aharon Viener (an Israeli), a man of the pioneer movement, from Pinsk. And their home here was the group named for the martyrs of Pinsk, Gevat, which is in the Jezreel Valley.

From the year 1932 her poems "Word," "On the Ascent," "From Within," "The Matter of the Woman Worker," were published in anthologies of the Writers' Association and others.

In the year 1945 the condition of her health worsened. From then she was confined to her bed and did not get up from it again in the last five years of her life. Despite her great suffering, her spiritual awareness did not weaken, her deep interest in all that was going on in her settlement, in the movement, and in the land, did not dissipate. She never let her quill fall from her hand.

On the 7th of Tishre, 5710 (September 18, 1950), her soul departed.

Fania Bergstein gave her strength primarily to the poem and to writing, but she also wrote stories and plays for children. Until now 14 of her books have appeared, 7 of them in her lifetime, and all of her literary legacy has still not been completely extracted.

On Fania's gravestone, which is in Gevat, are engraved the opening lines from her poem "Gift":

---

[781] "Flames."

I said to give the gift
The big one, the one.
To carry it with head upright,
With lucid eyes smiling,
With hands spread out before me,
And with a happy step, spring-like…

{p. 266} My Parents' House
By Mina Ampel – (Volmir)

The Volmir-Rotenberg family was one of the extended families in Augustow. My father, Mordechai Arieh, was known for his diverse communal activity.

With the outbreak of the First World War, a significant part of the Jewish residents of our city were drafted into the Russian army. Among them my father, Shmuel Meir Goldshmid, Omburg, Pelkov, Ratsitsky, Moshe Rotenberg and Mordechai Lev.

All of them served in the Augustovi regiment. Mother was left by herself with five small children.

When the Germans surrounded Yanova, we returned with Mother to Augustow. On the way we passed Shivtin. It was entirely destroyed and burned. When we reached our city we found that German horses were standing in our store.

We received information from Father that he was in German captivity, in a camp not far from Kassel. With outbreak of the revolution in Russia, many families that spent the years of the war in Russia began to return to the city. Father returned from captivity, and immediately began to take care of the refugees.

In 1925 Father and Manya Kantorovitz founded a union of craftsmen. Elected to the council were: Manya Gipstein, my father, and Dovid Arieh Aleksandrovitz. Vertzelinska was the first Secretary. After her Hinde Stein served in the position.

My Father was also a member of the City Council, and the Commission of Taxes that it was responsible for. In his role he tried to help all who were in need.

Who could have imagined that from an extended family like this one, from a flowering and rooted population, that only a very few would remain?

There are no consolations – only the assemblage of the nation of Israel in its land would light up the darkness for its children.

{p. 267} A Candle for the Soul of M. B. Eizenstadt
The Name
By Tz. Z. Weinberg

20 years old, talented and good-natured, Moshe Ber was beloved by people, and his acquaintances and friends appreciated him. But no one knew the suffering that this modest young man suffered in his house. His stepmother, a simple and respectable woman, who related to his brothers and sisters honestly and also with affection, kept concealed hatred for him, from the day she came to their house, and at every opportunity she brought her defamation of him to his father. It is possible that his gaze, which restrained inside him a spark of orphanhood that was not extinguished, was his undoing. With her intuition, this good woman kept silent about the rebellious foundation that was in his nature. She saw his existence solely as a kind of a continuation of the existence of the trouble that she had renounced for herself. Moshe Ber would casually dismiss his

255

stepmother's frequent complaints and his father's numerous protestations, and did not see fit to justify himself before them. With an easy smile and a nod of the head he would pass by it all, as if the matter did not affect him. His stepmother and his father boiled from the abundance of complaining, while he conquered his spirit and maintained a rebellious silence. He forgave his father's wife for her warm care of his brothers and sisters, his mother's orphans, for also in her relationship to him she was more honest than his father, even if she did not relinquish her injustice towards him. There were many with him especially in matters of "fear of heaven." His father, a pious and courageous *chassid*, pursued him with his exaggerated religious claims, and his stepmother, a believer in meaningless words, followed him with her foolishness with each and every step. And Moshe Ber, even though he trembled over the fundamentals of religion, could not put up with their insipid demands, and objected to them openly.

In order to put an end to the conflicts that had finally worn them out, Moshe Ber's parents tricked him and began to seek a proper match for him. Moshe Ber was educated on the knees of *Torah*, in *cheders* and *Batei Midrash*, in the way of all the sons of the religious in Poland, and private teachers completed his knowledge with a little bit of general studies. He was not satisfied with this, and worked diligently and with a great desire to deepen his knowledge, and since he had an open mind and a developed intellect, he acquired for himself a fair amount of wisdom and knowledge. He, the enlightened one, despised the young women that the matchmakers offered him, and always found in them a reason to view them as defective. His parents saw the hand of the "enlightenment" in this opposition of his, and his frequent deliberate obstinacy to deprive them of their good desire. However he, when he saw that there was no path before him, and all his acquaintances and those who came to their house annoyed him with their arguments, finally admitted that, contrary to his habit, there was more there, since he had already found one young woman who found favor in his eyes, and only her would he take for a wife, and no other.

The young woman was the daughter of one of the small grocers, a man of inferior rank; however, Moshe Ber found in her a woman like his own heart. The connection that was between them strengthened slowly, over a long period of time, and in secret. {p. 268} The best of the excuses and reproaches of the members of their families and relatives were not helpful. Moshe Ber was as solid as a rock. From his pursed lips only one answer escaped:

This one, only this one.

This time his father also insisted, and fought with all his might against "an indecent match" like this. His wife helped him. The two of them pressured Moshe Ber and embittered his life, and demanded of him with entreaties to stop his relationship with "a girl like this." The house became a hell for him. The arguing and the confrontations became stronger, and Moshe Ber left his parents and moved to live in his uncle's house, his mother's brother.

However by standing on his own, Moshe Ber felt the difficulties, which stood like an adversary on his path. The frequent altercations in his parents' house destroyed his health and exhausted his strength. His bride blossomed, charmed with her grace, her gentleness, and womanly tenderness, and like a young woman who reached marriageable age, demanded what was hers. And he, terrified by his fear of life, and by the burden of marriage, deferred her demands with various excuses, and yearned for a good future, in which his situation would be established, or then the voice of his heart would be answered and he would acquiesce to her.

"A man directs his way gradually, with intelligence and consideration, and is not hurried in his deeds, and knows also to overcome the feelings of his heart, when the hour calls for it…" he said to himself, and silenced the confusion of his soul, and ignored the quiet expectation that emerged from the eyes of his beloved.

"It's nothing, she will at the end come to an understanding, and she will know that I did not do this from malice or lack of love."

256

*

The father and son were like two mortal enemies. One would not speak a word of peace to the other, and one would not concede his own even a bit.

- If he will not leave this one alone, he will never have a house or a father…

With many efforts, Moshe Ber aimed towards his future. He was convinced that, according to the situation of his health, he would not succeed at physical labor, and according to his nature, he was not able to carry a job in a store or in a factory. Therefore, he chose to learn a free profession, and became a diligent extern, studying day and night. His purpose was to reach one of the universities that was outside of the land, in order to learn the theory of law and economics, his desire from then on. And for the present time, he would support himself there by the teaching of Hebrew and *Talmud*, which he knew well. And when he succeeded in graduating, then he would marry his partner and settle in the land of Israel.

This path, which was so clear to Moshe Ber, seemed far from reality in the eyes of his betrothed Mila. She tried to oppose him, argued with him and said he was making a mistake, and that the matter was an illusion. Indeed, when she was convinced that all of her words were not entering his heart, she stopped bothering him and put herself in the hands of fate.

Moshe Ber went on his way unresigned. His father tried many times to return him to his house, but he was not accepted. Then his father set his face towards deception, and sent messengers to Mila's parents, and offered them a large sum of money to break their agreement with Moshe Ber. When this too did not succeed, he spread made up charges[782] about the young woman Mila, in order to blaspheme her name in Moshe Ber's ears. After Moshe Ber also did not pay attention to this, his father stopped his weekly support that he had set for him upon his departure from his house, and cut off all ties with him.

At first Mila's parents consoled him, and stood with him in the hour of need. Mila herself made it pleasant for him {p. 269} to accept their help. Because in this war against his parents, Moshe Ber strengthened his faith in her heart, that in its way knew how to overcome the obstacles and reach its goal. The days dragged out, and Moshe Ber was placed on her parents as a yoke and a burden, his strenuous studies depleted him, he became thin and a broken vessel,[783] and the military council disqualified him as a soldier. Nevertheless, Moshe Ber did not budge from his opinion, and as before described his future to his betrothed in brilliant colors. Only then did the young woman shake off her dream, and in clear speech demanded from him to put an end to his hallucinations, and to consider his path like all men, who walk the face of the earth with open eyes and looking at life face to face.

Secret and stinging disagreements began between them. This was no longer the same gentle and soft Mila, who was devoted to spoiling him, subordinate to him and his authority. She matured, and slowly became freed from his influence. From now on she saw an obligation to herself to take the reins of their lives in her hands, in order to repair a little the years-old twisting and to sweeten the bitterness that had accumulated in her heart. She tried with all her might to bring her partner into the circle of reality, as the way of the world.

This change of Mila's in her relationship to Moshe Ber brought arguments and quarrels between them. Mila's parents, who were not able to see their daughter's distress, and increased the confusion in the house, also became involved. They were unable to bear Moshe Ber's difficult nature, which did not diminish at all even by means of Mila's yielding and the abundance of her love and her devotion to him, and their complaining about their daughter's torment and the disturber of her life increased.

---

[782] Deuteronomy 22:14 "and makes up charges against her and defames her, saying, "I married this woman; but when I approached her, I found that she was not a virgin.""
[783] A shadow of his former self.

She fell into a trap…. They banished her and her fate, and suffered their pain in secret, without finding a way out of the thicket.

And Mila went on her way by herself, opposed Moshe Ber's spirit with gentleness and with firmness, used all of the weapons to bend him to her will, and to make him capable of compromising, and for life in a group.

*

Moshe Ber saw himself as placed in chains, and his nature, which did not accept authority, now encountered the hardened manner of his betrothed.

Difficult days arrived for Moshe Ber. The suspicion of and the disgust for the members of Mila's household grew stronger in his heart from day to day. Every deed, every word from them, aroused his irritation, and once it erupted:

- From today on, your parents' house is forbidden. We must meet in my room, or in any place that you want.

- For what reason? – Mila asked, and all her limbs were trembling, for she knew well that all speech of this kind, in which a decree comes out of his mouth, is the kind that there is no changing.

- For the reason that your parents are like my parents, only the good of their enjoyment is before their eyes, and they are completely strange to me…

- But I indeed am of one mind with my parents… Mila expressed openly, muttering each and every word angrily.

- Then, then… - Moshe trembled in his place, and he held his tongue.

- Then what? Mila shot up, as if ready for battle.

- Moshe Ber was silent, bit his lips, and looked at her with harsh bitterness, which made the veins of his cheeks and the pupils of his eyes bulge.

- Say where, didn't you start…Mila teased him deliberately.

- Moshe Ber did not answer. He turned his face,[784] wrapped himself in his coat, and took hold of his walking stick.

- This is therefore your answer – she shot at him with poison – you are fleeing, in your usual way…as it were, from my parents' house, and since this is fleeing from my house, from me….

{p. 270} Moshe Ber turned at once. His sad gaze fell on her inflamed face, which expressed a woman's insult and irritation blended with pleas. He delayed for a moment, as if debating to remain. Afterwards he regained his composure and turned to go out.

- You are going out, doing your own… a cry of sadness burst out of Mila's mouth, her face was twisted, and her body swayed, as if falling.

Moshe Ber hurried to support her, peeked in silence into her tearing eyes, and softened. He smoothed her hair, and with a pleasant expression on his face let slip:

- You will go with me where I go. I will not leave you alone here.

This speech, new in Moshe Ber's mouth, was like balm for her heart. She did not demand more from him. Moshe Ber acceded to her and became bound to her instructions and her advice, and suffered with her in her parents' presence. Even if within himself he was making various plans, how to distance her from her parents' house and remove her from their destructive influence. Nevertheless, all his attempts to change his situation did not succeed. He was a dreamer by nature, not practical in general matters.[785]   He distanced himself in his learning for all intents and

---

[784] There is likely a typographical error here. The word in the text is *kenav*, כניו, which makes no sense in this context. The change of the letter *chaf* to *pey* renders *panav* פניו, his face, which makes total sense in this context.

[785] Aramaic, Babylonian *Talmud Bava Metziah* 59a: "and that proverb maintains that one should follow her counsel in general matters."

purposes, and his exams were always completed with total failure. Nevertheless, he did not give up, and still held on to his opinion and pleaded with Mila that she should not steal from him his faith in the best of his aspirations, and that she should not force the issue.

However, Mila's parents demanded deeds. Five years went by from the day that Moshe entered into the betrothal agreement with Mila, and the matter had still not come to anything. The war took place between them. They spoke with Moshe Ber clearly, that they should take their daughter to wife, and if not – he should leave her alone.

- And what will I do after the wedding – Moshe argued pleasantly, as was his way.

- Like all men. You will open a store, seek a position.

- I am unable.

- You will be able, when you take a wife…

- I will take a wife for my own sake and not for your sake. He cut with his voice.

- And we, we are not asking anything from you, only that you should not confuse Mila's head and that you not ruin her life.

Now Mila too was convinced that there was no place for Moshe Ber with her parents, distanced him from their abode, and became a regular guest in his house. Whereas her parents did not stop bothering her and insistently demanded that she break her agreement with her betrothed. She opposed them with all her might, and did not allow in any way to defame Moshe Ber, even though deep in her heart she agreed that their admonitions were right. And when the quarrels intolerably increased, Mila did not see another way before her, except to leave her parents' house. For this purpose she learned a trade, so that she could stand on her own and also help Moshe to some degree.

She suffered a long time, until she learned the trade well, and transferred her residence from her parents' domain and guardianship. She received Moshe Ber in her special room radiant with happiness.

- From now you will not worry about support – she hurried in joy to greet him.

- The matter is still far off, Mila.

- What? Are you still hesitating?

- Still….

- From what?

- Because you are earning and not I…

{p. 271} - Is that too a shortcoming?

- Shortcoming no, not at all, but also not an advantage.

- And therefore, we must again sit and wait…

- To wait, to wait patiently, my friend…

Mila cast confused eyes on him, and her spirit couldn't take it. Moshe Ber grasped the palm of her hand and passed it across his face as an affectionate apology.

- For you the marriage is essential, the wedding; and for me, not so… aren't we already like a married couple for a long time... devoted and faithful to each other…Let's get ourselves out from before the burden, and then certainly everything will change for the better…

*

As previously, Moshe Ber continued in his studies out of diligence, and did not pay attention to the many obstacles that stood in his way, and Mila, who followed him every day, was convinced that there was not in his work a real basis, tried from time to time to wound the essence of his faith and divert him to practicality, but did not succeed. His strange ways, which were like a riddle to her, with his zealous outbreaks of intense and strange love, which came frequently as an appeasement for the suffering that she suffered in his presence – all these stood her in the passage of days in a grave suspicion that he was not right in spirit, and that there was in him a mental impairment.

With a woman's guile, and with various temptations, she took him from doctor to doctor, and investigated and demanded of the doctors that they tell her the truth about the nature of his illness. The doctors determined that his health was deficient, that a serious and difficult illness came to him as a result of his bad living conditions, from his constant anger, and from his maternal heredity, but they did not admit to a mental illness, or in any defect in his spiritual strengths. On the contrary, they specifically found him healthy in spirit, since with great effort he carried his severe illness and did not collapse beneath it.

From now on Mila strove with all her might to adjust to him, to his suffering, to his craziness, to his depression and misfortunes, and to protect the quiet in their troubled presence, for his fate – her fate – and his tortured life - her lot. She stood in open conflict with the members of her family, rejected with disgust every suggestion of a marriage match that they made, and every attempt to separate her from Moshe Ber. With the fitness of her work and with great toil she succeeded in standing on her own, and supported Moshe Ber as much as she could. At last she succeeded in taking him out of his uncle's house, and moved him to her own dwelling, to a special room that she added for him. She organized his room, his meals, managed his clothing, and was a faithful friend to him in all. Moshe Ber, too, changed a little, took upon himself the yoke of a livelihood, and earned a little money giving hourly lessons, and carried the work together with her, in the house and outside of it. In his free time he drew his strength and vitality by being within her "4 cubits,"[786] as if he had nothing in his world except this corner, and this single soul, Mila.

However, in intimate matters, there was still something like a barrier between him and her. Moshe Ber permitted himself hugging and caressing and kissing, but he never lost control of himself, and knew how to place a rhythm and a measure to his feelings and his passion. Mila, on the other hand, was entirely like a raging storm, a fire consuming her bones, and a woman's inner humiliation raged in her eyes and within her, and troubled her spirit, the health of her body, and her joy. All the years she suffered in silence, carried the depression of her temperament alone, for she hoped to find an outlet in marriage. However, in the last days, {p. 272} when she was convinced that Moshe Ber was still far from this, and the flame of her desire consumed the remnant of her vitality, she began to harass him in her dealings, and demanded improvement with allusions

- Indeed, I am like your wife, whether permitted or forbidden. We became betrothed and also married in the crucible of life.

- Indeed so, indeed so... Moshe replied, and bit his fingernails in confusion... but the hour has not yet come.

- What hour? Why do we have an hour? Our parents in any case will not bless us, we have already suffered as a man and woman, enough!!

- Indeed so, indeed so, Moshe added, and his face was distorted from pain. The justice is with you, Mila, but I for one am not permitted...

- Because of what?

- Because I am not yet a husband, I am not yet able to be a husband...

- She did not understand his words, and again suspected him of a hidden deficiency, discussed it with the doctors that healed him, and they corrected her mistake. The stubbornness of her partner, who was knowingly torturing himself and her, for the sake of some distant and imagined purpose, infuriated her to the core. She continued in her suffering for some time more, finally she could not find strength and decided to put an end to her suffering and to speak with him openly.

---

[786] The four cubits (six feet) that the rabbis articulate as one's personal space. Babylonian *Talmud Eruvin* 48a.

- Moshe Ber – she said to him – I abhor my life. I am a woman. I was not born for greatness, and not for a man's insanities. I demand what is mine, and you are torturing me for nothing…

- But…but…Moshe Ber apologized and changed his tune, and his face paled.

- This time answer me clearly – Mila held on to him – you will not mislead me. I want to know, what will be herein after? No one is here, not my parents, not your parents. They have given up on me. But I too do not find satisfaction with you. I too see in you strangeness and extreme reversals, what would not be possible with any man in the world.

Moshe Ber turned around in the room this way and that, and did not find a place for himself. A cold sweat covered his whole body, and he did not know what to answer. Finally he controlled himself and responded:

- You are right, Mila, you are suffering on my account for no reason. I am your undoing. You need to free yourself from me…

- Like that…like that…Mila burst out in restrained sobs…for this I suffered days and years – for this I got to this point…

- But there is no suggestion…

- What "there is no suggestion"?

- Why should you lose your mind and destroy our lives? I am not demanding from you impossibilities, rather, what is owed to me as a woman, as your wife…

- But I want this to come with our parents' agreement, with their blessings, with their good will…

- We will never achieve that…My hair will turn white and we will never achieve that… you have patience, my friend, extra patience…while the power of patience has failed me. I can't anymore, I can't anymore…

She spoke with pain and bitterness. And he heard with a lowered head and downcast eyes as if guilty. {p. 273} This time he did not find the right words nor the courage to quiet or placate her. He felt himself entirely obligated to her.

*

They lived together for a few months pleasantly and peacefully, peeked with yearning gazes, as if each one was drinking their happiness from their overflowing cup,[787] until on one of the days Mila expressed to him her hidden secret, a woman's secret. He was excited and quiet, trying to subdue his feelings and speak with her truthfully.

- Good, Mila, good. Here they will stone us, both my parents and yours. We will leave here, travel the world. There we will live our lives properly, without fear.

- Here too I am not afraid…Mila answered coldly, and in her eyes there shone a strange gleam.

- What does that mean?

- It is my business… she hinted.

- Ach, so…Moshe Ber wondered, and took her hint - and I will never agree to that, never.

- How's that?

- Because it is my child, the first of my vigor[788]… since it is forbidden to destroy the seed…

- Nonsense! - Mila interrupted – this is my business and not your business...

---

[787] Psalm 23:5 "You spread a table for me in full view of my enemies; You anoint my head with oil; my cup is overflowing."

[788] Deuteronomy 21:17 "Instead, he must accept the first-born, the son of the unloved one, and allot to him a double portion of all he possesses; since he is the first fruit of his vigor, the birthright is his due."

- It is our business... Moshe Ber corrected – I ask you, Mila, that you will not do such a thing, you will not do it...

He bent over and kissed her, and the pleas of his gaze wrapped her whole being.
- Remember please, Mila, remember this...

However, she did her thing. Once when he came to her room, he found her friend, a midwife, tending her at her bedside. Mila was pale and melancholy, and in her eyes there burned a hidden fear.

- A simple accident, an accident...Mila apologized quietly.

Her friend also confirmed this, swore to him faithfully that it was just an accident, neither she nor Mila were not at fault for it. Moshe Ber sensed the deceit of their words, shot a look at Mila and at her friend, and got out of the way.

- Murder, murder, his heart pounded within him, an enmity mixed with compassion emerged from him for Mila and for himself, who did not properly appreciate their mutual lives and their strange situation in which they were placed. He primarily blamed himself, who caused this sin, and decided to immediately do something, that would have in it some appeasement for her and her abject maternal feelings. And very soon, as soon as she got up from her bed, he drew her to the office of the rabbinate and married her according to the law, and gave his marriage public validity, and invited their many friends to a celebration of their wedding, and even to their parents, on both sides, arranged letters of apology and appeasement and asked them to forget the past. His parents did not answer at all, while Mila's parents came and kissed them and blessed them with a parental sweetness, and with their staring everywhere, until Moshe retired to the corner and Mila breathed deeply when they left.

From then their lives began flowing in the standard path. The distant ones began to draw near. And their abode {p. 274} that had been ostracized by those close to the family and the pure-minded among them became from now on a foothold for uncles and aunts and relatives, who saw an obligation to themselves to appease the wounded couple, who had suffered enough. Also, their inadequate livelihood improved greatly, following the involvement of the relatives, who now extended their protection over the proper couple, and from every side offered them work and wages, and also entered into the thicket of the matters to reconcile between Moshe Ber and his parents. Moshe Ber's parents agreed and made peace with him, renewed their full allowance of support for him, and accepted Mila pleasantly, as befits the wife of their son, and their daughter-in-law. Except that they avoided visiting them, due to habit and the keeping of their tradition and their protection of their traditional rights, which was stained with something. Moshe Ber went through it with his usual complete disrespect. Mila, however, even though she pretended that she wasn't concerned about them or their visits, boiled inside from suppressed insult, and saw in this, after the peace, serious damage to their honor and the honor of her father's house.

With the material comfort, Moshe Ber left work in teaching and again became engrossed in his studies and his beloved books. This time Mila approved of these actions, and herself increased the vigor of her work and brought abundance into the house. The burden of livelihood and the suffering grew lighter. Moshe Ber accepted the cessation of work in his quiet nest and cherished the seclusion of his four cubits. However, Mila was drawn now in her frantic way to the commotion of company, pursued gatherings of friends, and fun parties, and would frequently leave the house. When she parted from the passion of her blood, and warmth poured out from her, she would return to Moshe Ber as to her sheltering nest, and poured out her love and kindness on him, as if purified from her repulsive habits that clung to her, but she would immediately return to her old ways, like a drunk to his vomit, without the ability to restrain herself over her weaknesses.

Moshe Ber recognized this change that had taken place in Mila and was not angry. With an astuteness of feeling, he penetrated to the depths of her soul, and discerned what was taking place within her. The sorrow of the flesh was such that he had no remedy for, the suffering of years that disappeared without satisfaction; and it acquired a shriveled and sickly brokenness. How could he quench this flowering and thriving woman, how could he calm the stormy erupting waves of blood?! He gave her complete freedom in her actions, he dismissed, in his way, all the suspicions that crept into his heart, and uprooted them, for he depended on the sincerity of her heart, and the purity of their relationship, which were not cast in doubt at all.

- Let her enjoy herself a little and diminish the boredom in the company of her friends and acquaintances as she desires, and she will return to her home calm and satisfied; why should he aggravate her with his difficult state of mind, and why should he force on her his angry will, when she is free by herself and not imprisoned in her house?

And again Mila became pregnant, a second and a third time, and she destroyed it. Moshe Ber watched over her like every guard, cooed to her affectionately, like the moaning of a dove,[789] and pleaded with her: "please have pity on him, and on their lives, and do not destroy a gift of God…" And she, with ridicule, protested all his pleas and warnings, and insisted and did her own thing. Only then was his faith weakened within him; even her great devotion could not cover up his doubts, which bit his flesh like the tongue of a python. Out of mental distress and torturous insomnia, Moshe Ber came at last to a certain conclusion. He did not hurry to do it, he prepared in his usual way, with restraint, and at the hour of the decision, he informed Mila briefly:

This matter is damaging our relationship, and requires repair. I will keep faith with our covenant, and I will never take another wife… Mila collapsed beneath her when she heard the words coming out of his mouth. She recognized the smile in his speech {p. 275} and the cold that was in his eyes, that this was not just a warning – and burst out into sobs. Now the situation as it was it became clear to her, and with all of a woman's strategies tried to straighten what was twisted.[790]

- The righteousness is with you, Moshe Ber, the righteousness is with you… She apologized. You are allowed to demand more proper attitude to you… You are entitled to it, entitled…

She abstained from her previous way of life, and swore off enjoyment of any meetings or parties with friends, until Moshe Ber berated her and showed her error to her.

- It was not this that I intended. You do not need to be a nazirite[791] in my presence, nor bound to a spiritual path. You are a free creature. Your free time is yours to use as you desire, and I only ask one thing of you – not to repudiate your purpose as a woman, a mother, a housewife.

She nodded her head to him as a sign of agreement, and he was warmed by the light that was kindled in her eyes, as recompense for all the suffering with which she caused him. She planned her interests with intelligence and knowledge, tended the hearth flame that burned in the house, and about the matters of the friends that were outside of it. Until the tears were mended, and the rejuvenation between them was strengthened.

However, when she conceived a fourth time, and she felt clearly that she would not be influenced by Moshe Ber, if she would do something, she schemed and pretended she was sick. She sought guidance, as it were, of the doctors, she went wherever she went, for the sake of healing and recovery, and returned home when the weakness was still permeating her limbs and the pleasant expression on her face had faded a little; she returned, when her cheerful smile spread

---

[789] Isaiah 38:14 "I piped like a swift or a swallow, I moaned like a dove, as my eyes, all worn, looked to heaven: "My Lord, I am in straits; Be my surety!"

[790] Ecclesiastes 1:15 "A twisted thing that cannot be made straight, A lack that cannot be made good."

[791] In the book of Numbers, chapter 6, a nazirite is one who takes an oath to refrain from any product of the grape, contact with a corpse, or cutting the hair, for a specific period of time. The word is used here to refer to someone who swears off all of life's social pleasures, like a nun, or hermit, or ascetic.

over her lips and her arms were spread to receive her partner. Moshe Ber was well-tested; he recognized immediately, in the innocent twinkle in her eyes, and the sweetness that was in her words, the traces of hidden malice and cold-blooded murder. This time he did not object or protest, pretended not to know, and went with her pleasantly and modestly, as usual. But within himself he made an accounting with his soul, and strove to understand the circumstances of these misdeeds of hers. On the one hand, she was bound to him with a strong love, and on the other hand she did not want to have a child with him. He found that the inadequate health of his body and his poor social situation were destroying him.

For about two years Moshe Ber dwelt outside of the country and saw a reward for his toil. His illness improved over time. He excelled in his studies. From season to season, on holidays, he visited his home, and he found in Mila a wife of his own heart. The plentiful support that his parents gave him, the abundance in the house and on holidays, came from afar as renewing and invigorating, shook off the anger and the bitterness from Mila that she carried within herself, and made her comfortable and mixed with her qualities and her demands, and he rejoiced with her as to the wife of his youth, who accompanied him in his life for good and for ill. And precisely this time, when she saw herself near the goal, and her spouse going in the right way, and she longed to conceive and give birth, Moshe Ber hurried and grasped the deed of men, and dissuaded her from her desire, and appeased her with consolation: "now, in the middle of the way, certainly it is not worth it. Now this can undermine all our plans and get in our way."

{p. 276} And she acceded and didn't accede. She became immersed in her world, and diversions of hope, which emerged as lines of happiness and light within the plenty of his letters, that he rushed to her almost every day. And in the secret of her abode, devoted to her dream while awake, she forced the issue, and wanted to shorten the days and the nights and finally reach that purpose, which was desired by the two of them as one.

The World War that came suddenly caught Moshe Ber in Germany, when he was reading Mila's last letter, which did not have in it a shred of what was going on, and was entirely fraught with faith in their happy future. Full months Moshe Ber suffered internment camps, as a conscript of the Russian army, as a prisoner; and only after great effort, by the leaders of the Jews in Germany and friends of his father, he reached Berne in neutral Switzerland, and there he continued to complete his studies as a college student. In his long isolation, he immersed himself entirely in his studies, he was exemplary to his friends and his teachers, who supported him to the best of their ability. He was entirely cut off from his country and the city of his birth. He received no reply to the many letters that he sent to his house and to his father's house. One old letter, that rolled around in the cases of the mail of the Red Cross, that reached him indirectly, updated him a little on the situation. Mila's father died a quick death with the outbreak of the war. Mila went out after the death of her father to her sister's house in southern Russia to distract herself a little, and with the conquest of the borders by the German army she remained stuck in distant Russia, without the ability to return home. Moshe Ber, who saw before him his destroyed world for this third year, did not despair, and carried his suffering in silence. He completed his degree in law with excellence, and also obtained a permanent position in the area, and made an honorable living. All his efforts to discover Mila's residence in Russia and to connect with her in an exchange of letters were of no avail. The answer of the Red Cross was always negative: "She went out to Russia, and her place is not known." Moshe Ber continued with his work, and became tirelessly immersed in public cultural activism. His many acquaintances who came into contact with him were amazed at his quickness and his punctiliousness and his peace of mind, which accompanied him on his diverse activities. His honesty, his hair style and his dress, which were neatly done, proudly covered his deep grief and his troubled soul, which slowly undermined the unstable foundations of his health.

With the fourth year of the World War, sparks of hope for a rapid peace flickered, and Moshe Ber's hardships were decorated with the glow of the coming redemption. He fell to his bed on account of a light cold, to which he did not pay attention, and finally developed, as a consequence of his old defect, and his body's weakness, and the great neglect by him, into a fatal illness from which he did not recover. He lay alone on his bed and pondered the passing days with his difficult spirit, and the mistakes that he had made in his brief futile life, and the corrections that he was destined to make, if fate would favor him and return him to his home. He kept his many visitors distant from him, and even the small number of friends that he cherished, he did not allow to come to his house. He wanted to be alone, left to himself, dreaming his dream and distracting himself with his hope. He ignored his illness, in his usual way, overcame it, and even amazingly inclined the heart of his doctors, who recognized the seriousness of his condition, to believe in his rapid healing, on account of his spiritual powers that were hidden in him which provided him with an abundance of strong spiritual health. He recuperated little by little, and got up and walked about in the house on his cane, and with his banter and jokes and sayings, caused pleasure to all who were around him, and all who served in his house. He again instituted the previous order of his day, even though he still did not go outside, and read and reviewed and prepared his articles, and planned for the large amount of work that had been neglected during his illness. He also sat and attempted to write his regular letter to Mila, which he sent by way of the Red Cross, just because, to {p. 277} Russia, in his transmitting each time another presumed address, lest, lest it reach its destination, and recorded the date, and also drafted and wrote something more, and suddenly he fell off his chair.

The members of the household found him dead, with his forgiving smile on his lips, while the name "Mila" was written on the paper, put in the wrong place, crooked, ripped up, and bringing to an end the suffering of remorse – and longing engraved upon it.

*

And Mila – the forced separation shocked her to the brink of despair, and she saw in it a punishment from heaven, which she justifiably deserved. When she cheered up a little, and found interest in her strenuous efforts to connect with Moshe Ber, a new disaster fell on her. Her father died very suddenly. In her bitter anguish, in which she was entirely in pain without letup: "why did Moshe Ber distance himself from his house? Why?" She fled from her four cubits and from her pleasures, and from her mother's widowhood, to her sister in Russia.

In her sister's house, in the wide-open space of Russia, she rested a little from the fury of her sorrow, however her world darkened for her. She entered into herself, and did not come into contact with anyone, and became engrossed only in work in the house, and taking care of her sister's children, and trips saturated with delusion and dream of a distant happiness that once was, and passed by... The war and its sufferings almost didn't touch her. The closing of the borders and the cutting of the connection with her mother and the members of her household did not agitate her at all. She remained indifferent to their fate, as if reconciling herself to her misfortune and the misfortunes of the time and the surroundings. Only one point of light still flickered before her: "Moshe Ber, after all, exists, indeed he is alive somewhere and worried about her...and they will still meet, surely they will meet...."

When the World War was concluded, there immediately took place, with the old hopes that were shaken up, the terrible pogroms against the Jews of Russia, that tore her from her roots and from her little steadfastness, and she and the members of her family hurried to find themselves a refuge wherever they could. In the tumultuous and confusing whirlwind, they forgot to take one child. They forgot and they fled, they forgot and they escaped. Whereas Mila retraced her steps, returned with superhuman, driving force, without paying attention to the expected danger, and the choking cries: "Mila, Mila..." And brutal people attacked her, next to the mutilated child, to

265

quench their despicable need. From her tightly closed teeth, on living flesh that was torn in her mouth, flowed a stream of her blood, and her dimming consciousness was cut off in her final moments on a sweet, sweet, memory: "Moshe Ber" ... However, providence ordained otherwise. She awoke from her long, long, sleep in her white bed, in a room soaked with drugs and medicines, with her hazy head struggling in vain to make a connection between her world from which she had emerged and the awakening reality, when her stupefied eyes with difficulty gripped a human image, who was walking around near her and taking care of her, with worry and great fear, as if all his life was dependent on her.

When her senses returned to her, she recognized immediately the person who was helping at her bedside. He was Alexei Pavlov, their neighbor's son, an orphan, who grew up in his grandmother's house, a Russian Pravoslavie, and they gossiped about him because he was of Jewish extract. A leftist among leftists, a fervent Bolshevik, friendly with his Jewish friends as one of their own, and who always lifted his eyes towards her, with the modesty of his gaze and his silent longing, really like Moshe Ber in his gaze, and impressed on her soul a deep, deep, hidden echo of days gone by. All that she now saw around her was like a miracle in her eyes, like a dream from an imaginary world, that she almost didn't believe {p. 278} what her eyes were seeing. Nevertheless, Grandmother Masha, the mother of Alexei's father, her good acquaintance from before, who did not move from her bed the whole time, solved the riddle for her. Alexei fled with the rise of the "Whites" and hid in the nearby grove with his friend Lada, until he succeeded in being accompanied to the camp of the Bolsheviks. And when the rioters burst into the city and created destruction in it, Alexei suddenly attacked at the head of a battalion of "Reds"[792] that drove out the "Whites" like chaff before the wind, and in an opportune moment, he also saved her, the single remnant of the Jews in the city, from the hands of her predators, her torturers.

"And the members of her family?" Mila asked with terrified restraint.

The old woman uttered something, crossed herself, and groaned quietly. The weakness again encompassed her, and she sank again into a deep abyss, whole days and months, hovering between life and death, anxious over her fate and observing every change for the better in silent expectation.

When she finally recuperated and stood on her feet, and came among people, they informed her of many details, what they had kept from her in Pavlov's house, and she saw before her a new world and a different regime and a new style of people that were different in their roles. Those who were upper were made lower, and the lower ones were elevated to the level of the authority and the government. Jews were not Jews, and gentiles were not gentiles. The old people were thrust into the corner, and the young people were arrogant with the power that was given to them, and with haughtiness rejected the teaching of their fathers and connection to the past, and permitted what they forbade, and broke off every yoke of family and the tradition of the generations.

Lonely and alone, banished from her family, from her acquaintances, and from those who knew her, Mila remained redeemed and rescued in Pavlov's house, and slowly adjusted to their world and their way of life. Alexei Pavlov got a high-level position in the Soviet regime, as a supervisor for the army. He went about with her as a brother from birth, and next to him, Grandmother Masha, who protected her with devotion, like a compassionate mother. The two of them made it pleasant for her to dwell in the shade of their roof, and integrated her into their house. The habit of years and ancestral heritage still troubled her and her conscience from time to time, and destroyed her spirit and poured bitter drops into the cup of her life, which was poured anew:

---

[792] This is a reference to the Russian civil war, that took place between 1917-1922. The Reds were the communists, and the Whites opposed them.

"What is there for her here, and who is there for her here?" However, time did its own. The feeling that was in the streets and the engaging revolutionary ideas that penetrated the holes and the cracks into her consciousness slowly changed her world view, and with a concealed hand smoothed the many differences between race and nation, and stitched together the tears that were within it, and made it comfortable for the whispers of affection and the proximity that showed her benefactors to her.

But the thin webs of the conquest that were woven around her with delicate gentleness by Alexei Pavlov, the pleasant young man, who outside of the barracks did not know another pleasure except to spend time within the walls of her room, were made pleasant for her and very close, as if there had cracked open inside her a kind of emotion that she had not known and whose significance she did not know. Her heart became awakened to the erupting streams that carried away all the old and worn out, and distracted her from the past, and prepared her to greet the good and the beautiful that were in the new and the next.

Nevertheless, she was not entirely cut off from her roots. The old still fermented in her somewhere in their hiding places, in the depths. When Alexei Pavlov finally proposed that she be married to him, she still hesitated, fell into his arms with tears of joy and an outburst of emotion, as if sheltered under the shade of the only shelter, whereas this proposal of his, for various reasons and excuses, she rejected. The time was not yet right, her health was still not in order, and her spirit was not yet with her. From now on she began to strive with all her strength for contact with her mother and her relatives outside of the country. Russia was blockaded on all sides, subject to the elimination of the rebellion of its enemies from within and the continuation of {p. 279}its war with Poland, its enemy on the outside. However, after Russia quieted down from its wars and the borders were opened, the first information was received from Mila's house – a bundle of letters and notes from her brothers and sisters, each person with their own story,[793] each person and the story of what happened to them. From the outset, with the first reading, the information was lukewarm – touching on details from the lives of the members of her family that were already old news, and that did not touch her at all, as if the world still existed as before, and nothing had changed. However, she swallowed up whole pages in reading, and her heart was afraid for the essence, and she skipped over the lines with her eyes, and found on one of the sheets information, as if hinting, on the death of her mother, and restrained herself with paralysis, and searched on, and on, and suddenly she stumbled upon one vague piece of news: "Moshe Ber had completed his world in his usual way. He was a *tzaddik*,[794] and he died a *tzaddik*." Her eyes went black, and everything inside her turned upside down. With a blind sense that had still not been extinguished, she searched and found among the letters a section from his last letter, in which was written only the date and her single name "Mila," and the crooked letters danced before her likes sparks of fire, and burned her heart, and her lips glued themselves to the writing, and her eyes rose… She fell down, and again sank into a deep extended faint, placed between life and death for a long, long, time, without exit, and almost without hope…

Only after she became completely healthy and rose from her bed, abundant with grace and refined by the furnace of her suffering, like a creature that had been born anew, at peace with her fate, did she become devoted to the house of those that had gathered her in with all the warmth of her love, like a devoted daughter to the elderly Masha and like a faithful wife to Alexei Pavlov. Now she did away with the barrier, and her world was purified before her. She carried the weight of the house and participated in the toil of Alexei, and shared with him equally. And in all that she did, in the ways of the house and the delights of her spouse, she made an effort to erase the traces

---

[793] Literally, each one with their own *megillah*, scroll.
[794] A righteous person.

of the past, to cause to forget the troublesome memories and overcome the hidden emotions, so that they would not bother her and so that they would not taint the few moments of her happiness.

When she became pregnant and first felt the living heartbeat inside of her, a terrible dread immediately attacked her in anticipation of what was happening and what was coming: "indeed because of this...this...she lost Moshe Ber." But nevertheless, the uncertain vitality that was becoming integrated into her roots, gripped her and intoxicated her senses and gladdened all of her being: "now you will give birth, you will surely give birth, you will hug a living soul to your bosom, for what else does she have in her world?"

The child, who cried next to her, gave her a sad and hopeful image. He was healthy. A strong body, and a wonderfully beautiful face. Alexei stood next to her bed and caressed her with his good glances. Sparks of happiness and joy burst out from his eyes to hers, which gripped all who were near her: "there is a reason for all the suffering, and it is worth it to continue...worth it..." He bent over her and kissed her and surrounded her with questions, and stuck in his last, fundamental, question:

- And his name, Mila?
- His name, his name...

Mila was confused, peeked at his face, alternately blushed and blanched, and stammered weakly.

- His name is...Moshe Ber...
- What? W...what? Alexei listened closely to hear.
- How? Movshe Beer?
- Yes. Moshe Ber.
- Mila, what is with you?

{p. 280} - Indeed, I said: Moshe Ber.

- Alexei examined her with his warm gaze, recognized in her tortured face pleas for compassion, and spat out a plea:

- My dove, Milotchka, indeed this is not possible...
- Because of what?
- Because my friends will make fun of me "Movshe Bir, Movshe Bir..." Have mercy on me, Milotchka...
- But... but... Mila deliberated in sorrow, and her face became embarrassed[795] with a grimace of confusion.

- Let it be like yours - Alexei was wounded by the look on her face- let it be as you say... But not "Movshe Bir," not "Movshe," let it be Bir alone, the name has the ring of an English name, "Bir," "Bir."

Mila nodded her head, straightened up, and calmed down a little. Alexei picked up the pillow on which the baby lay and waved it and shook it and laughed and sang repeatedly, "Bir, Bir." And Mila accompanied him with her weak maternal glances, with recognition of thanks and deep affection. And when he left her by herself and parted from her to go to the clerical office to register the name of the child in the birth registry book, Mila brought the tender newborn's pillow close to herself, pressed him to her heart, and her lips clung to the mouth of the chirping child, and with the devotion of prayer and joy and thanks she embraced him: "My Moshe Ber, my Moshe Ber, Moshe Ber, Moshe Ber...

---

[795] There seems to be a typographical error, here, where the word in the text is נתכרמו, which is not a word. The correct word seems to be נתכרכמו, which has a meaning of "became embarrassed." The difference in the two words is a single letter kaf, omitted in the text. The word as emended appears throughout rabbinic literature, e.g. *Midrash Tanchuma Chukat* 6: "When [the Holy One, blessed be He,] did not answer, at that time the face of Moses turned yellow (with shame).?

My Family
by Faygl Rabinovitch (Mayzler)

My mother, Khaye-Hodl, departed this world in her early forties. My brother, Yehoshua-Velvl, was already living in America by then.

Of the three girls in my father's home—Etie, Libe and Faygl—I, Faygl, was the youngest, at eight years old.

My mother's death was a devastating experience for me. I remember her to this day: shorter than average height; a tidy figure; blue eyes; pale, delicate skin; blonde hair combed up into a bun at the top of her head.

In my memory she has remained as the model of an exemplary human figure: courteous, patient, and highly capable. Not only was she an exceptional homemaker—able to sew a garment, ready to knit an entire sock from scratch on a Friday afternoon—but she was also the one who taught me how to read and write. It was she, and not my father the scholar. So that even before I was old enough to think of attending Bulke's school I could already fluently read not only the *khumesh* (for which I received a reward of a ten-kopeck piece), but also German and Russian.

That my father, Avrom-Mayer Mayzler, became a more learned scholar, and one of the best Hebrew teachers in the area are well known facts. His pupils (firstly only boys, but in later years girls too) were mostly capable learners. But he did not want to teach me. He {p. 281} hired another teacher, Sherman, who would fall asleep as I was practicing reading.

I used to listen attentively when my father taught his students and would derive great pleasure when everything went according to plan. But when a student gave an unsatisfactory response to a question, and my father began to dole out slaps, I would hide in a corner and cry in solidarity with the punished child.

One incident in particular left a lasting impression on my memory: a clever little boy, Moyshele Mints, answered back to the teacher after receiving a powerful smack.

"People are no angels," he shouted through his tears, refusing to continue studying with my father.

Summer was the time when my father would go for a stroll with his friends, after his Sabbath nap, through the woods toward the Sajno—a large, beautiful lake. Naturally I would tag along. One of the men who would walk and talk with him (they liked to carry out discussions no matter the context: walking, sitting, standing) was, I recall, Leyzer Alpern, one of Eyzenshtam's grandsons.

The winter Sabbath days were mostly spent at home. My father's friends would come, and also some of my elder sister's friends. What did they all do? They discussed all manner of issues, from global matters to Jewish matters, books, writers, *Haskalah*, Zionism—what didn't they discuss?

My father was not a healthy man. He suffered from a variety of ailments including asthma, high blood-pressure, stomach problems, insomnia, and poor eyesight.

To sooth his nerves my father liked to play a card game called "Thousand." His companion in this pastime was the lawyer Shapiro. They would play one round after another. Shapiro would tap his glass and say: "Khaye-Hodl, the tea is cold." My mother would take it, add coal to the samovar, and hand him a fresh glass of tea. Shapiro would dip the tip of his finger into the glass and say: "Ah, that's better," and would proceed to leave his tea sitting until it got so cold he could swallow it in one gulp.

My father was considered to be a miser. His reputation for stinginess was perhaps a little exaggerated, but there was some truth to it. It was at its core a fear for the future, which every Jew living in similar circumstances suffered from.

They considered my father to be a wealthy man, but to the best of my recollection the children of those who owed my father money lived better than we did. His debtors would indeed pay the interest they owed, but my father never saw a penny of the principal.

{p. 282} My father married a second time. My stepmother, Sonia, was a picture-perfect widow. She had a daughter, Maytke, from her previous marriage, who was even more beautiful than her mother. In 1915 my stepsister Brokhe (Bertha) was born. Sonia and her daughter died in the early years of the 1930s. We never heard from Bertha again; one must assume she was one of the six million.

My father managed to thwart those whose names should be erased: he died a natural death, at 75 years of age, shortly before the murderers invaded.

Ruven Sinai HaCohain (1850 - March 31, 1918)

Born in Augustow. His father, Ahren Sinai, was renowned as one of the town's great scholars. When he died (Ruven was 5 years old at the time) the family moved to Grodno. Ruven attended *kheyder* followed by *yeshiva*, and received from the Kovno Chief Rabbi Reb Yitskhok Elkhanon authorization to practice as a rabbi.

But he did not want to be a rabbi and became a private Hebrew teacher instead.

In 1894 he emigrated with his family as part of the first wave of Jewish colonists in Argentina at Baron Hirsch's colony, Moisés Ville. There he became a religious and cultural leader.

When a heated conflict arose between the Moisés Ville colonists and the directors of the Jewish Colonization Organization, Sinai traveled to Paris with a delegation to receive justice. The pleas of the delegation fell on deaf ears and consequently (at the end of 1897) Sinai and his family left Moisés Ville and settled in Buenos Aires where the Eastern European Jewish immigrants offered him a rabbinical post. He accepted the offer, but did not wish to take a salary for his work. He earned a living teaching private students from bourgeois families.

His first articles in Hebrew were published in *HaMaggid, HaKol*[796] and *HaMelitz*. Under the pseudonym BRS (By Ruven Sinai) he published in Rodzinzon's Yiddish newspaper *Kol La'am*.[797] From Argentina he wrote for the London Hebrew weekly *HaYehudi*.[798] He also worked in his son's newspaper *Vider-Kol*,[799] as well as the *Folkstime*,[800] *Yidishe Argentiner Vokhnblat*[801] and the first daily Yiddish newspaper in Argentina, *Der Tog*.[802]

He left behind a manuscript in Hebrew with the title *The History of the Jews in Argentina*. His son Mikhl Sinai passed the manuscript on to Zalman Reisen (Zalman Reisen visited Argentina in 1932 with the intention of publishing a YIVO edition on the history of Jews in Argentina, but nothing came of it and the manuscript was lost during the war).

{p. 283} Ruven HaCohain Sinai died in Buenos Aires. His son was also a writer and journalist in Argentina.   *Lexicon of Modern Yiddish Literature, Volume Six*, New York, 1965

Goldshteyn, Dovid

Goldshteyn, Dovid (born April 15, 1868, died November 24, 1931). Born in Yagestav (Yagustova) [Augustow]. He studied in *kheyder* and in a *yeshiva*. In 1882 he emigrated to England, where he worked in a sweatshop and became an active leader in the local anarchist movement. In 1885 he settled in the United States. He was an active member of the New York anarchist

---

[796] "The Voice."

[797] "Voice for the People."

[798] "The Jew."

[799] "Echo."

[800] "The People's Voice."

[801] "The Jewish Argentine Weekly."

[802] "The Day."

organization "Pioneers of Freedom." He then lived for a time in Philadelphia, where he was also active in an anarchist group, the "Knights of Freedom."

In 1889 he was the Philadelphia delegate to a New York conference of anarchists and social democrats with the aim of founding a joint newspaper. He later lived for a time in Boston. He supported himself by working in various trades: he was a tailor, ran a newspaper stand, and later ran a coffee house in New York.

On February 18, 1887 he published his first poem entitled "*Der Ekspres*" (The Express) in the *Nyu-Yorker Yidishe Folkstsaytung*.[803] He published social and lyrical poems in New York Jewish newspapers and magazines: *Der Vegvayzer*,[804] *Der Folks-Advokat*,[805] *Fraye Arbeter Shtime*,[806] the *Forverts*,[807] *Tsaytgayst*,[808] *Yidisher Kemfer*,[809] *Di Tsukunft*,[810] and *Der Veker*,[811] among others. He authored the book: *Vinter Blumen*,[812] poems (New York, 1916), pp. 112, with a foreword by Leon S. Moissief. Yoel Entin wrote of his poetry: "Goldshteyn's poems are remarkable for their powerful tone, in word choice and rhyme." N. B. Minkov characterized Goldshteyn as: "By nature a fine lyricist, he was always full of images, lines, rhythms. This gave his work a certain disquiet, one which overpowered the poet entirely, a disquiet like that on the eve of creation."

For many years Goldshteyn was all but forgotten. In 1929 he fell gravely ill, and spent his final days in a hospice for the terminally ill in New York.

Lexicon of Modern Yiddish Literature, Vol. 2. New York, 1958.

Published by the World Jewish Culture Congress.

{p. 284} Avrom Yankev Netter (1918–1842)

Born in Lithuania, lived in Augustow. He became a *Maskil* and a Socialist under the influence of the first socialist writers in Hebrew. With the group "Am Olam,"[813] he came to America in 1882. He worked as a teacher in the New York *Talmud Torah*, though he was later forced to give up his position because of his apostasy.

He was active in the Jewish workers movement. In 1897 he helped found the *Forverts*. He wrote for the *Forverts*, and the *Fraye Arbeter Shtime*. Articles about Zionism, religion, Socialism etc. In 1901 Netter was active in re-establishing *Di Tsukunft* becoming the manager of the newspaper.

In his personal relationships he was the very picture of goodness and refinement.

From the *New Yiddish Lexicon*, New York, 1965.

Liptsin, Sam (Shepsl) —

Born in Lipsk on March 13. 1893. At 13 he began to work with his father in his tailoring workshop. In 1909 he came to New York, working in a sweatshop, and spending his free time educating himself. At 16 he was active in the Socialist Party. He began his literary career in *Der*

---

[803] "The New York Jewish People's Paper."
[804] "The Guide."
[805] "The People's Advocate."
[806] "The Free Voice of Labor."
[807] "The Forward."
[808] "The Zeitgeist."
[809] "The Jewish Fighter."
[810] "The Future"
[811] "The Alarm."
[812] "Winter Flowers."
[813] "Eternal Nation."

Kundes[814] and *Di Varheyt*,[815] as well as in trade union newspapers. Together with A. Ayzen and H. Garvin, he published (1920) the monthly *Der Humorist*.[816] From 1922 onward he was a regular contributor to *Frayhayt*,[817] later *Morgn-Frayhayt*,[818] in which he published humorous sketches, poems, and stories of the sweatshop. He wrote a column "*A Vort far a Vort*."[819] He also published in the journals *Yidish Kultur*[820] and *Zamlungen*[821] in New York; *Naye Prese*[822] in Paris; *Folks-Shtime*[823] in Warsaw. His books include: *Af Laytish Gelekhter*,[824] *Royte Feferlekh*,[825] *Ikh Lakh Fun Der Velt*,[826] *Lomir Zingen*,[827] *Far Royte Ovntn*,[828] *Gekemft Un Gelakht*,[829] *Lebedik Un Lustik*,[830] *Kamflustik*,[831] *A Freylekhs*,[832] *A Gut-Yontev*,[833] *Krig Un Zig*,[834] *Mit Gezang In Kamf*,[835] *Tselokhes Di Trern*,[836] *Kvekzilbers Penshtiferayen*,[837] *Hert a Mayse*,[838] *Shpil Tsum Tsil*,[839] *Zingen Mir*,[840] *Amol iz Geven*,[841] *A Vort far a Vort*,[842] *Af Vakatsye*,[843] *Far Kleyn un Groys*,[844] *Vi Zogt Der Feter*."[845]

---

[814] "The Prankster."
[815] "The Truth."
[816] "The Humorist."
[817] "The Freedom."
[818] "The Morning Freedom."
[819] "A Word for a Word."
[820] "Jewish Culture."
[821] "Collections."
[822] "The New Press."
[823] "The People's Voice."
[824] "Proper Laughter."
[825] "Red Peppers."
[826] "I Laugh at the World."
[827] "Let's Sing."
[828] "For Red Evenings."
[829] "Fought and Laughed."
[830] "Cheerful and Alive."
[831] "Ready to Fight."
[832] "A Happy Dance."
[833] "Happy Holidays."
[834] "War and Victory."
[835] "A Song in Battle."
[836] "Despite the Tears."
[837] "Quicksilver's Pen-Games."
[838] "Listen Up."
[839] "Play to Win."
[840] "We Sing."
[841] "Once Upon a Time."
[842] "Word for Word."
[843] "On Vacation."
[844] "For Small and Large."
[845] "As Uncle Would Say."

The Economy of the Jews of Augustow
by Dr. Moshe and Eliezer Markus

The economy in the district of Augustow was based on agriculture. The city itself served as a commercial and administrative center for the many villages that were around it. All of the commerce (except for the sale of lumber), the craft and the few industrial enterprises that were in the city served, essentially, the agricultural population that was in the area.

The district of Augustow was partly covered by forests and lakes. On the open and fertile lands, there grew all kinds of grains, flax, beans, fodder, and vegetables. Other parcels served as pasture lands for cows and horses. The villages were populated by Polish farmers, mostly agriculturally based, whose livelihood was on their land. And some of them, lacking plots of land, made their living in the wood industry, fishing, building work in the summer, and all kinds of simple work.

The main branch of agriculture was the cultivation of field crops: wheat, barley, and oats. In the villages there were almost no crafts people. The crafts people in Augustow, tailors, shoemakers, hatters, smiths, leather workers, carpenters, glaziers, painters, metal workers, bakers, and more – were Jews. They were supported by the sale of their products to the farmers in the area.

Commerce was in the hands of the Jews. Only in some of the villages were there Polish shops for the sale of grocery necessities. These stores were established after the liberation of Poland, when the empowerment of the regime began to develop the movement in the state for the conquest of commerce from the hands of the Jews. However even then these shopkeepers purchased their necessities from the Jewish wholesalers in Augustow. The farmers arranged most of their purchases on the days of "the market." On Tuesdays and Fridays of the week the farmers would come to the city on their wagons; with them were the members of their families. They would sell their products, and would buy all that they needed in food, clothing, and household goods. Some of the farmers in the nearby area attended the Catholic church in the city on Sundays. They would take advantage of this opportunity to sell their products and arrange purchases in the city, to repair the wagon, to shoe a horse, to repair a harness, or order boots.

3-4 times in the year there were big "fairs." Then farmers from the near and far surroundings would gather in the city market and the adjacent streets. Travelling Jewish merchants who sold their merchandise from temporary stands would also come. On the days of the "Fair," many work animals would pass from hand to hand, animals for slaughter, wagons, sheep and goats, pigs and the like. Market days and the "fairs" were an essential source of income for the Jews of the city. The farmers would bring to the city of all the goodness of the land; {p. 286} potatoes, onions, wheat and barley, vegetables and fruits, poultry and eggs, dairy products, mushrooms and berries, etc. The products were purchased mostly by housewives, and partly by merchants who would sell it afterwards in the Jewish houses, or export it outside of the forest. After selling their products, the farmers would turn to the many shops in the market and the adjacent streets, which were all in the hands of the Jews, and would buy sugar and salt, groats and oils, kerosene and candles, tea and tobacco, salted fish, etc. As needed, they also acquired fabrics, especially for the women, although most of the garments for the men and women were self-woven. Weaving on home looms was still widespread in all of the village houses. The women primarily engaged in this on the long winter nights, when there was little work on the agricultural farm. They would bake their bread themselves from black grain flour. But for Sundays of the week and holidays, they would buy from the Jews *challot* made from white flour, and sweet baked goods.

Market days were also primary revenue days for the Jewish pubs that were in the city. On these days the farmers would enter the pubs for the purpose of drinking for its own sake, or for the purpose of marking the completion of business (the acquisition of equipment, a horse or a cow); they would drink brandy and beer, and finish it off with salted and smoked fish, eggs and sausage. On the rest of the days of the week the pubs were empty, and only a very few of the Jewish residents of the city, primarily waggoneers and porters, and some of the local gentiles, would enter them.

Augustow was a district city, and the seat of the district government. In it was the district courthouse, and the notary who was in charge of the registry of plots of land and buildings. The villagers frequently needed these authorities, and they frequently visited in the city. The commerce and the industry were, as was mentioned, in the hands of the Jews, and therefore we find that that all of the shops in the market square and the streets that branched off from it belonged to the Jews, and the matter was the same in the many workshops. It is no wonder, then, that on *Shabbat* and festivals all work and all commercial negotiation stopped, and the rest of the holy *Shabbat* was spread over the whole city. In the city there was one pharmacy, whose owner was *Ploni*, and two stores for the sale of medications made by uncertified Jewish pharmacists. Actually, the Jews and even the gentiles turned specifically to the medicine stores of the Jews. The shop owners and the craftspeople existed principally by the proceeds from the farmers. One must take into account that the residents of the city numbered about 15,000 souls, upwards of half of them Jews, whereas the residents of the district who needed the services of the city, numbered about 80,000 souls. In addition to the craftspeople that we mentioned, there were also fabric dyers who dyed fabrics and threads that the farmers would bring them, coppersmiths, and makers of metal utensils and vessels, potters, makers of roofing tiles, and roof tilers. There were also a few butcher shops, which mainly served the Jewish residents, and the *treif*[846] animal meat was only sold to the gentiles.

From fear that there would be a majority of Jews on the city council, the Polish authorities added to the city, for the needs of the elections, villages from the area that were populated only by gentiles.

Among the many and diverse livelihoods in which the Jews of the city engaged, the waggoneers and porters must especially be mentioned. The freight wagons were engaged in transporting merchandise from the train station, 3 kilometers from the city, and also in transferring merchandise and heavy equipment within, and outside of, the city. There were also carriage wagons (*britzkas*), whose main business was transporting people from the city to the trains that went out from the train station twice a day, and the bringing of those arriving on the train – to the city.

{p. 287} There were those who used these means of transportation for the purpose of trips to the forest, for example. In the winter, with the falling of snow, the carriages were replaced by sleds.*[847] Tens of Jewish families were supported by this transportation. The porters were also almost entirely Jewish. They stood out as a typical group of those with physical strength, against the background of the general human landscape of the Jewish population. A special livelihood was that of the water drawers and transporters of the city. Water for drinking and cooking was brought from the big lake on which the city**[848] was situated. A transporter of water would pour the water into a big barrel, which was loaded onto a wagon hitched to a horse, and sell it by the bucket to all those who needed it. This livelihood was, more than the rest, in the hands of the Jews, but in the last years it passed to the gentiles, for the Jews tired of it. The wood cutters were gentiles. The farmers' sons were free in the winter from their agricultural work, together with the horse and wagon that they had on the farm. They would cut the trees in the forest into individual sections,

---

[846] Literally torn; non-kosher. Exodus 22:30 "...you must not eat flesh torn by beasts in the field; you shall cast it to the dogs."

[847] Original footnote 1: A winter wagon which instead of wheels had iron runners.

[848] Original footnote 2: In many yards there were wells. They drew the water with buckets hung on ropes, by turning the handle of a wheel by hand. The water from the wells was not good for drinking or cooking.

bring them to the city for sale. After them workers would come to chop the wood into pieces suitable for heating in the ovens in the winter, and for cooking on the stovetops all the days of the year.

It should be mentioned that between the First and Second World Wars, when the Zionist youth movements were developed in the city, training groups of "*HeChalutz*," "*HeChalutz HaDati*," and "*Beitar*,"[849] were established in Augustow and the surrounding area that gripped the youth in physical work as a source of training and financial support. The sight of Jewish youth wood cutters in the yards of the Jews turned into a regular sight in the city.

Since Augustow resides next to large lakes, the profession of fishing was widespread in the city, and the Jews too had a significant part of that. The government had the practice of leasing the lakes; the tenants were mostly Jews. Jews were also engaged in the work of fishing itself, but essentially – gentiles. In addition to licensed fishing, it was widespread to fish without a license. These "fishers" would, with a rod or a small net, pull out fish from the river and sell them in the houses of the Jews. Because of the great amount of fish in the lakes (there were in them many kinds of excellent types), they were one of the primary foods of the residents of the city. On *Shabbat* in all the Jewish houses they ate fish, even in most of the houses of the poor. Many Jewish families were supported by the fish. One Jew engaged in the preparation of smoked fish from the fresh fish, and salted fish, which had a good market not only in the city, but also in the surrounding area. Another Jew engaged in making sausage and smoked meat. Soap production was also in the hands of the Jews. Although in the last years the people of the city began to use soap imported from the factories that were in the large cities, indeed the residents of the villages preferred the simple and cheap local blue, white, and yellow laundry soap. Many of the Jews from the city also continued to use it. The soap was made from the milk fat of animals, which was unacceptable for eating, and supplied by the butcher shops and the slaughterhouses.

One of the Jewish livelihoods was the rag trade. The rag sellers would buy all the rags and worn-out clothing in the city and the area, and would sort them in their store houses. Linen – separately; wool – separately. They would export the linen to Germany, and they would bring the wool to Bialystok, for the large textile industry that existed in that city.

{p. 288} The manufacture of ropes was also among the Jewish livelihoods, and for the most part it was coupled with the making of saddles and straps for the bridles of the horses and wagons.

Since the district of Augustow was rich with forests, lumber for building was relatively plentiful and cheap. For the construction of their houses the farmers used wooden beams that they bought or cut in the nearby area. The farmers' sons who still lacked independent farms, engaged in the work of building. In the city they would also build houses of wood in the suburbs and the side streets, and there too the builders were gentiles. On the main streets of the city buildings made from bricks were already raised. The Jews were building contractors, who saw to the execution, however the work itself was done by non-Jewish workers. Only in plastering, painting, and framing were there Jewish workers. There were three brick factories in the city. Their owners were Jews, but their workers were mostly gentiles.

Augustow was, as is known, near the German border. The currency of things was the smuggling of goods from one country to the other. Primarily the resident farmers of the villages adjacent to the border engaged in this. The middlemen and the coordinators of the commercial activities connected to smuggling were Jews. In the days of the Tsar's regime, when young Jews, before being called up for the army, needed to cross the border without a permit, in order to

---

[849] *Beitar* was a Revisionist Zionist youth movement founded in 1923 in Riga, Latvia, by Vladimir Jabotinsky. An acronym for *HaTzionim HaRevizionistim*, The Revisionist Zionists, officially *Brit HaTzionim HaRevizionistim*, Union of Revisionist Zionists, was a Revisionist Zionist organization and political party in Mandatory Palestine and newly independent Israel. It was founded by Ze'ev Jabotinsky in 1925.

emigrate to America and other countries across the sea, these smugglers would help them cross the border to Germany. The Jewish smugglers were known to the community, and they called them *"Mistachnim."*[850]

The manufacture and commerce connected to the wood industry occupied a special place in the economy of the city and the surrounding area. The forests that extended over thousands of square kilometers, and the network of streams, lakes, and the canals that joined them, turned Augustow into one of the centers of the wood trade in Poland. The trade in this area was entirely in the hands of Jews. But the work of cutting down the trees, bringing them out of the forest, binding them to rafts and moving them by way of the rivers, lakes and canals to Danzig, was done by the local farmers and their sons. The supervisors and administrators of the work in the forests were Jews. Most of the forests were government-owned, and only a small part of them belonged to the landholders in the area. Parts of the forest were turned over to lumbering by auction, which took place in the chief office of the forest authority in Poland, in the city of Shedlitz. The forest merchants were for the most part wealthy. In "fat" years, when the wood market in Germany was good, the profits were great. The merchants enjoyed a high standard of living, and generously distributed donations for public needs. This industry supported many Jewish families of work administrators, surveyors, appraisers, supervisors, and those engaged in secondary production, such as collecting the sap of the trees and processing it.

Industry for the most part served the local needs and those of the surrounding area, and was entirely in the hands of the Jews. 3 flour mills, one of which was operated by the water power of the Augustow canal, 2 sawmills, 2 beer breweries, 2 tanneries, 2 brick factories, 1 factory for porcelain tiles; these constituted the industry in Augustow. The flour mills were small and their owners engaged also in selling flour. Most of the workers were Polish. The sawmills employed a great number of workers, however all of them were Polish. For some reason, it was precisely in the tanneries that Jewish laborers worked.

In the days of the Russian regime the tanneries[851] would export their products to greater Russia. With the establishment of the independent state of Poland, the markets contracted and the big tannery closed.

{p. 289} In a few villages in the Augustow area at the beginning of the present century[852] there still dwelt a few Jews, who engaged in trade and in craft. Smiths, tailors, shoemakers, etc. lived in Yanovka, in Raglova, Sztabin, Lipsk, Tzernovroda, Gortzitza, Mikaszówka, and others. By virtue of a command from the Tsarist government, the Jews were expelled from the villages. Most of them moved to the cities, and some of them emigrated to lands across the sea. More than a few of the Jewish population in Augustow were of those who had left these villages. Sometimes there remained in their personal name an association to the name of the village where they previously dwelt, such as: *Ploni* the Lipsk man, or *Almoni* the Sztabin man, (The Lipsker, the Sztabiner, and the like).[853]

The Poles took the place of the Jewish shopkeepers and craftspeople.

Jews were supported also by the leasing of orchards of fruit trees etc. from landowners. A few Jews engaged in growing vegetables within the city, and this was their livelihood.

In the district of Augustow there was also one Jewish landowner (Binstein).

Within the economic system of the city, there were tens of other livelihoods. These were in craft, in commerce and services that were integrated together to provide the needs of life in the

---

[850] Self-endangerers.

[851] A typographical error here omits the letter *kuf* from the word "tanneries." The word is included once, with an alternate spelling, in the previous paragraph, and once again at the end of this paragraph.

[852] The 20th century.

[853] In Yiddish.

city and the area, such as: watchmakers, bookshops, whitewashers, metal workers, electricians, etc. Doctors, medics, lawyers etc., Rabbis and *shamashim*, *Chazzanim* and *shochtim*, officials and teachers, all of them together constituted the diverse spectrum of the livelihoods in the typical Jewish town in Poland and in Lithuania.

The Jews existed and developed despite the generally hostile relationship on the part of the authorities. As a counterweight against the actions that were intended to narrow their steps and dispossess them of their positions, the Jews established internal institutions for mutual aid. At first these were funds for *Gemilut Chassadim*. A small merchant who was in need of operating capital, a craftsperson who sought to acquire a machine or equipment, a waggoneer who was forced to buy a horse in place of the one that "fell," all had their needs fulfilled with the help of the associations for *Gemilut Chassadim* in all their forms.

At the beginning of the century, the cooperative movement began to be developed among Russian Jewry. In its footsteps a small cooperative fund was also established in Augustow, which gave small loans to craftspeople and small shop-owners.

After the First World War, with the expansion of the Jewish cooperative credit movement in Poland, a Jewish cooperative bank was established in Augustow that existed until the outbreak of the Second World War. This bank, which was greatly developed over the course of time, was an important support and protector for the economy of the Jews in the city. At the head of the bank stood important community leaders, merchants and craftspeople. Over the course of many years Reb Binyamin Markus, may his memory be for a blessing, served as head of the administration.*[854]

The economic lives of the Jews of Augustow were primarily based, therefore, on the forming of connections between the village and the city, and on the provisioning of the needs of the farmers. In this way Jewish lives developed over the course of hundreds of years, and became consolidated into a social and cultural way of life, which formed the character of eastern European Jewry.

Serious changes to this structure began after the First World War.

With the establishment of the independent State of Poland, a national movement began to act for the conquest of commerce and manufacture from the hands of the Jews. The great development of manufacturing in the cities, on the one hand, and the cultivation of the status {p. 290} of the merchants from the country with the help of the authorities, on the other hand, pulled many livelihoods out from under the feet of the Jews. The field of sustenance for the Jews contracted and disappeared. The lack of work, especially among the younger generation, increased. The governmental system, in all its institutions and activities, was closed in the face of the Jewish youth. The great and heavy industry was for the most part "purified" of Jews. The schools of higher education instituted "*numerus clausus*."[855]

The tax policy of the government was intended to weigh heavily on the Jews, and to deprive them of their livelihoods. For the Jewish young generation there were no opportunities in the state of Poland. This situation pushed the Jewish youth to emigration and *aliyah* to the land. This path also shrank with the closing of the gates of the United States and the land of Israel.

Depression and anguish reigned in the Jewish population even before the Second World War. In this atmosphere of lack of resources, a great yearning for redemption, and hope for the breaching of the closed gates[856] of the land of Israel, the Nazi vandals came and destroyed life and

---

[854] Original footnote 3: In a later period a cooperative grocery store was opened in the house of R. Rotenberg.

[855] Literally, a closed number. This was a quota that restricted the number of Jews permitted to attend university in the 19ᵗʰ and 20ᵗʰ centuries in eastern Europe and Tsarist Russia.

[856] The word as printed here is עשריה, which can mean "its tens" or "its wealth." In context, the word as printed makes no sense. What does make sense is the accidental transposition of the first two letters of the word, which would render

property. They drowned Augustow, together with the thousands of holy congregations throughout Russia, Poland, and Lithuania, in a sea of fire and blood. May God avenge their blood.

The Status of the Teachers
by Meir Meizler

When all of the teachers assembled for a proper consultation on what to do to improve our status, I then acquiesced to their request and wrote these words.

These days are not like the first days for we teachers. Days arrived that no one desired, evil days of trouble, for instead of the days that passed in which people's needs were few and the income great, now the matter has become the opposite, the income is little and meagre, and the needs are great. It is the case in this year too, where the high prices will increase from day to day, and the money that we previously spent to support our household over the course of a full month, is necessary for us at this time for one week's living, and all of us are expecting to starve, and if we are not for ourselves who will be for us?[857] Therefore we have gathered together as one, friends, to investigate and to seek the origin of the evil and the source of the trouble, maybe it will be within our hands to improve our situation, which is very terrible and horrifying, and who will give us a chance?!

Indeed, if a person becomes sick and falls on his deathbed, it will happen that, if the people of his household are quick and diligent they will hurry to call for the doctor, while most of his bones are still strong and his illness has not overcome him, his healing will quickly develop. But woe to him, to the person whose household members are indolent and lazy, and when he falls into his bed they say: "but it is an illness and he will carry it, an illness that develops and passes," for his illness will be strengthened from hour to hour, the pillars of his back will weaken, and he will reach the gates of death, until the people of his house will pull themselves together {p. 291} to call the doctor, and will also succeed with a great deal of toil and trouble to find a remedy to cure him, and also remove his very old illness from him. But what is his lot in life even after his recovery? Weak, lacking vitality, and extremely powerless, and many days will pass for him until he returns to his original strength, for his illness already consumed half his flesh, and extracted the sap of his vitality. So the matter is with us today; we have not assembled to give advice to ourselves before the damage spread within us. It can be that we have dwelt at this time quiet and serene, we did not know any worry, and in the days of the rest and the calm, we have truly rested and found serenity for our souls that are exhausted from the hard work which we worked all the summer. But the problem is, each of us turned to themselves. And not alone, but no man gets sick from his friend's disaster, except that each one built a stage for himself and says: I am a sprinkler son of a sprinkler![858] There is none like me! And for me it is pleasant, and for me it is suited,[859] and the one who is lifted above all as chief,[860] and he will not return to his heart and say: Isn't there a lie in our day? And why should all the nation say "holy" to the one who will say "I am holy"? Indeed, my friends, he too, like me, was created in the image of God; he too has to live on the face of the earth,

---

the intended word "שעריה," its gates, referring to the closed gates of the land of Israel mentioned in the previous paragraph.

[857] *Mishnah Avot* 1:14 "He [Hillel] used to say: If I am not for myself, who is for me? And when I am for myself [only], what am I? And if not now, when?"

[858] The one who sprinkles the blood of the offering onto the altar, that is, the Priest. *Ein Yaakov, Brachot* 4 "Let him sprinkle who is a sprinkler, the son of a sprinkler; he who is neither himself a sprinkler, nor the son of a sprinkler shall say to him who is a sprinkler and the son of a sprinkler..."

[859] A play on the words from the *Nirtzah* section of the *Pesach Haggadah*, which refers to God: "Since for Him it is pleasant, for Him it is suited...."

[860] 1 Chronicles 29:11, again referring to God: "Yours, YHVH, are greatness, might, splendor, triumph, and majesty— yes, all that is in heaven and on earth; to You, YHVH, belong kingship and preeminence [being lifted] above all."

and to sustain his house with bread. Of all these he will not know and will not want to know and will not relinquish what is his even for a sandal strap[861] therefore the one will assemble in his room like a flock of students, herds and herds too many to count! Indeed, he will eat meat to satiation, and for his neighbor, a person who like him was created in God's image, he will leave hunger[862] and lack of students. And therefore, this trouble comes upon us, for foreign teachers will increase their thinking that great happiness is hidden in this site, and all the more so will they take it upon themselves. If it is so for the small teachers, for the big ones how much more so, indeed their fortune will increase to thousands and tens of thousands! Happy is the man who is satisfied with his lot to be a teacher in our community, and the evil consequence that emerges to us from it is that a few of our brothers, members of our pact, born of this city, die of hunger. They don't have even food for one meal in the full sense of the word, for this is a great principle in our community; they will take out the old before the new,[863] therefore they will favor the new ones recently arrived. For these the elders became obsolete, and put their sons next to them, in their image, for they brought a new *Torah* with them, which on one foot[864] they will teach their children to put in their mouths![865] Woe to the creations from the insult of *Torah*! The honor of the *Torah* is humble and humbling, and no one takes it to heart! What is the teacher in the eyes of the fathers and sons together? He is only the scum of humanity, a subordinate and loathsome object! He eats and does nothing, etc., and how will the *Torah* be able to be beloved in their eyes, if the carriers of its flag are despised and contemptible, and who is guilty of this matter? Woe to us if we say: We ourselves! In us is the blame! For in the way of the world, each person who wants to cover their nakedness, or will want to sew for themselves footwear, will seek and inquire after the artisan, will seek him and will find him, and we? Aha! We will cover our disgrace; our shame is too great to bear![866] We like poor people will go from door to door. Seriously and hunched over, shame-faced and with trembling heart, we will come to the house of one where we will search there for food, and like a ghost from the ground so will our speech chirp [867] before him, saying: Give me children![868] Woe to that same shame! Each and every day a Divine voice emerges[869] and proclaims, saying: the teachers are scornful of the honor of the *Torah*, and degrading to the land, its glory, and its splendor! The evil outcome that comes from this is that each one will speak ill of their neighbor, each one will praise himself, for like this one and like that one he will do great deeds,[870] (hah, how evil and corrupt is this attribute!) He will desecrate the honor of his neighbor, for what will a person not do in seeking food for himself and for the souls[871] in his house, indeed for a piece of bread a man will commit a crime!

This matter which we will go by ourselves to seek a student in contract law, although the matter is very worthy of contempt, as I have proven, yet nevertheless we have no further

---

[861] Aramaic. Babylonian *Talmud Sanhedrin* 74b: "Even to change the strap of a sandal."

[862] Literally, "cleanness of teeth."

[863] Leviticus 26:10 "You shall eat old grain long stored, and you shall take out the old to make room for the new."

[864] Babylonian *Talmud Shabbat* 31a: "Convert me on condition that you teach me the entire *Torah* while I am standing on one foot."

[865] Deuteronomy 11:19 "and teach them to your children—reciting them when you stay at home and when you are away, when you lie down and when you get up;"

[866] Genesis 4:13 "Cain said to the LORD, "My sin is too great to bear!"

[867] Isaiah 29:4 "Your speech shall sound like a ghost's from the ground, your voice shall chirp from the sod...."

[868] Genesis 30:1 "... and Rachel said to Jacob, "Give me children, or I shall die."

[869] Babylonian *Talmud Eruvin* 13b "a Divine Voice emerged and proclaimed..."

[870] Joel 2:20 "For [YHVH] shall do great deeds."

[871] The letter *fey* seems to have been accidentally omitted from the word נפשות, souls or lives.

justification to comment on it, for each one's heart strikes him[872] and his life is precarious,[873] for if indeed we are believers who are the children of believers, [874] and every person knows {p. 292} that he will not take his part in his hand, and a person's food is measured for them, nevertheless every person will want to know what God has measured for them. We are not better in this than the rest of humankind, nor worse than them, and we will not be able to order a person to sit subordinate to him, and wait until the fathers will rise to open it. How much of the ugly and offensive is there in the matter, if there are found among us fools who are prominent, who arrive early to seek students in the summer days, from the day of *Purim*, and in the rainy season, from *Rosh Chodesh*[875] *Elul,*[876] and upon hearing the sound of the *shofar*[877] in the camp of Israel they proclaim liberty[878] for themselves and for the feeling of shame that is embedded in the heart of every person. They hurry to seek students and to arouse arguments with their neighbor, and the evil result that emerges for us from this is that the teacher and the student, the two of them together, will set aside their hearts from the learning. Indeed, the teachers will seek new students for themselves, and the students, for their part, will not be quiet and will not rest, and will seek for themselves new teachers, indeed will hurry to find them, and will no longer pay attention to the instruction of this their teacher, for all their interest is in the new teacher, and in this way the learning continues to be destroyed to its foundation, and what teaching will be upon it?

Augustow, the year 5652 [1892] (from his literary estate)

The Students of the "*Talmud Torah.*"

Caption In the photo: Students of the *Talmud Torah, Lag Ba'omer*,[879] 5692 [1932]

---

[872] Babylonian *Talmud Berachot* 7b: "Only one whose heart strikes him with pangs of conscience…"

[873] Deuteronomy 28:66 "The life you face shall be precarious…" The text incorrectly uses the word תלויים, while the biblical text uses the word תלואים. It is a difference of one letter, yud, instead of an aleph.

[874] Babylonian *Talmud Shabbat* 97a: "The Holy One, Blessed be, said to Moses: they are believers, the children of believers…"

[875] The beginning of the month.

[876] The last month of the Jewish calendar, which falls at the end of the summer.

[877] An ancient musical instrument made from the horn of a kosher animal, blown in the synagogue on *Rosh Hashanah* and *Yom Kippur*.

[878] Leviticus 25:10 "You shall proclaim liberty throughout the land for all its inhabitants…"

[879] The 33rd day of the *omer*, the 49-day period between *Pesach* and *Shavuot*.

A History of Chibbat Tzion and Zionism in Augustow
by M. Tzinovitz

The beginning of the "*Chibbat Tzion*" movement in Augustow was in the early years of the 80s of the previous century,[880] after the pogroms in the Ukraine and southern Russia. From a movement of individuals there developed a cohesive branch, which held a respected place, over the years, in the framework of the Odessan Council for the support of the Jews of Syria and the land of Israel.

At the head of *Chovevei Tzion* in Augustow in the 1880s and 1890s stood the teacher Reb Dovid Mordechai Markus, the brothers Shabtai and Tzvi Rosental, Gershon Mintz, Reuven Rotenberg, Moshe Arbstein, Eizik Elblinger, Efraim Friedberg, the Hebrew writer Yisrael Ze'ev Sperling, Leib Glikstein (who went up afterwards to the land of Israel), Shlomo, the son of the local *Gaon Av Beit Din*, Reb Moshe Yitzchak Halevi Segal. The names of those mentioned above always appear in lists of the donors and fundraisers for the needs of the new settlement in the land of Israel, for both monthly memberships and special collections for various actions. This branch of *Chovevei Tzion* constituted the basis of the Zionist organization in this city, with the appearance of National Zionism.

The first public action of "*Chovevei Tzion*" in Augustow was their celebration, in the year 5645 [1884], marking the birth of Sir Moses Montefiore, which was celebrated with great magnificence. Even the local *Av Beit Din* the *Gaon* Rabbi Katriel Aharon Natan welcomed it graciously. We find the following details about this celebration in the Hebrew weekly "*HaMaggid*" (from the year 1884, No. 48):

"Augustow. Russian Poland, *Cheshvan* 5645. Among the congregations of our kindred children of Israel, who took part in a celebration of the double jubilee[881] of our Lord the magnificent one of our nation, the righteous Sir Reb Moses Montefiore on the day of the completion of 100 years of his life[882] - may our community also be considered honored. In the assembly of people from our community from young to old, at the time of the afternoon worship of the Great Synagogue, to pour out speech to the One who dwells in the high places, for the length of life of this righteous Lord, may he live. After the *shaliach tzibur* had prayed the prayer of the Rabbi the Gaon, Our Teacher the Rabbi N. Adler, may God sustain him in life and protect him,*[883] the people responded verse after verse, the Rabbi the *Gaon*, the Rabbi *Av Beit Din* of our community, ascended the podium, and began his homily with the words "Moshe will rejoice in the gift of his portion, for I have called him a faithful servant,"[884] since this man Moshe is a faithful servant of God and of *Torah*, and very much desires God's commandments. "You placed a crown of splendor on his head." For among princes his honor was singular, and he stood before kings and princes and brought out like a shining light the righteousness of our kindred, the oppressed and shattered children of his people, who had done no injustice.[885]

---

[880] The early 1880s.

[881] The Jubilee is marked at 50 years, so 100 years would be a double Jubilee. Leviticus 25:10 "and you shall hallow the fiftieth year. You shall proclaim release throughout the land for all its inhabitants. It shall be a jubilee for you..."

[882] He actually lived from 24 October 1784 – 28 July 1885.

[883] Original footnote 1: Rabbi Dr. Natan Adler – the Chief Rabbi of the Jews of England.

[884] These are the opening words of a prayer from the *Shabbat* morning liturgy, part of the *Amidah*, the Standing Prayer.

[885] 1 Chronicles 12:18 "If you come on a peaceful errand, to support me, then I will make common cause with you, but if to betray me to my foes, for no injustice on my part..."

{p. 294} The Rabbi also mentioned his many travels, how he endangered himself[886] to pass over the seas,[887] and desolate wilderness places, in order to save our kindred the children of Israel who were put in trouble and distress here and there, and for all of them kept the name of Jerusalem the holy city always before him. His spiritual life was entirely in it, and he travelled seven times to Jerusalem.

The correspondent "Etzbah"[888] (Yisrael Ze'ev Sperling) adds that

"The Rabbi's words found favor in the eyes of all who were gathered for this celebration, and they entered into their hearts, and went home happy and joyful, for all the good that God did for us, to bring to life for us Sir Moshe, may he live as this day for fame and praise.[889]

On the day after the celebration, on the actual birthday of the Prince mentioned above, the great completion ceremony was held for the *Shas* society in honor of the Lord. After the ceremony, notables of the city founded the "*Chovevei Tzion* Association." And many set their hands to sign up, and also pledged to give from time to time continuing, respectable, donations. They fulfilled their promise immediately: they raised donations for the *Keren Kayemet*, and monthly fees for the support of the workers of the holy land, and each and every day the members increased, and lent their hands to the work of *tzedakah* with monetary donations."

My Ascent to the Land
by Akiva Glikstein

In the years 1900 – 1901 I served in the Russian army as a "volunteer." I volunteered at the age of 18 in agreement with my father's desire, who I admire to this day. My father was of the opinion that if we, the Jews, want rights, we must accept on ourselves all the obligations. "I want to show the gentiles" – he would say "that a Jew also can be a good soldier, brave." The "volunteer" had rights that a regular soldier did not have.

When I was in the army, there was under my command a soldier, "Tzarmis," from the minorities of the Kazan region. He converted to Christianity under the influence of Russian missionaries; before that he was a Buddhist. He was primitive, he spoke terrible Russian, and he was dirty. He had never seen a towel or a napkin. I had to teach him to wash dishes. When he brought me a meal from the kitchen for the first time, the soup and the porridge were in a dish, but he took the meat out of a pocket of his dirty coat. I reprimanded him, and I granted him the meat as a gift.

Over the course of time he learned the rules of cleanliness. He was very devoted, because to serve with a Jewish volunteer was such a privilege: he did nothing and nothing,* he did not exercise, did not accept insults. The economics were good, and he also received a ruble in salary.

When I would send him to my parents' house, he would return drunk, and would relate in his language, which I finally learned to understand: "your mother is a good mujik (farmer, masculine). He [sic] gave me a big cup of vodka, food that was ai ai good, he said, she would watch out for my meltzik (boy), that he should not get cold, and she also gave me 20 kopecks, on my life."

---

[886] Literally, placed his life in his hand.
[887] Psalms 8:9 "...the birds of the heavens, the fish of the sea, whatever travels the paths of the seas..."
[888] Finger.
[889] Jeremiah 13:11 "I brought close to Me the whole House of Israel and the whole House of Judah—declares the LORD—that they might be My people, for fame, and praise, and splendor."

282

{p. 295} He was exempt from serving duty in the kitchen; it was impossible to impose on him the cleaning of the yard or chopping wood. A volunteer, even a Jew, was permitted to join officers' school; in the barracks he lived in a room with another friend; under his command was a regular soldier; the volunteer would wear, in his free hours, a fancy uniform, which his father would pay for, resembling those of the officers. None of these rights were based in law, but on custom. The "volunteer" was obligated to have a high school education, healthy in body and with a pleasant appearance. The central purpose in this was that the volunteer was permitted to choose his place of service; the draftee was not so permitted. We were happy, my parents and I, that I was accepted to the infantry regiment that camped in Augustow. The officer appointed over me was German-Russian, a university graduate; an educated man. He almost never visited the clubhouse, in which the officers used to get so drunk that they lost their senses. He was a bachelor and liked to read science books in German and French. Sloppy in his dress, he looked like a *yeshiva* boy. He liked me. He used to invite me to his house for a cup of tea, and talk with me about all kinds of topics, even about Zionism, which was hated by the government. On *Pesach* Father would send him bottles of "Carmel" wine from Rishon L'Tzion,[890] and *matzah*s. The "*Feldwebel*" (Sergeant-Major) was a bachelor of about 45, a Lithuanian, who served for about 25 years in the army. The Sergeant-Major had more influence than the company Commander; he knew every soldier, and it was impossible to hide anything from him. He had an elementary education, at a time when the vast majority of the Russian people did not know how to read or write. The relationship to me was, therefore, excellent. My father was proud of me, but not so my mother. She would sigh and worry that it might be harmful to me. My father promised me a trip to the land of Israel if I would complete my service in the army without getting entangled in troubles. I was very happy, even though I was not then a Zionist.

My two sisters lived in the land of Israel: Rivka, the wife of Dr. Yaffa, and Esther, the wife of Chaim Margalit-Kalvariski. My father was one of the "*Chovevei Tzion*" and the President of the association in the city. Every *Shabbat* a few *Chovevei Tzion* would gather in our house. They would read articles from "*HaMelitz*" and from "*HaTzefirah*" and more. My father would volunteer in the synagogue and *Shabbat* and festivals, for the "*Chovevei Tzion*" council in Odessa. More than once I saw religious elders stick a finger in their forehead as a sign that my father was not sane, since he believed in the return to Zion prior to the coming of the Messiah.[891] Finally I completed my service in the army, and the preparations began for my journey to the land. My father drafted craftsmen to build for me two wooden suitcases. My father went about happy and cheerful, and would hum the tune "In the Place of Cedars."[892] My mother would cry and say: "Is it not enough that I have my two daughters in this desolate land of Israel, he wants to send there also the son of our old age? What do they have there, in the land of Israel? Goose fat, there is none; jam – there is none; malaria – there is plenty; they eat grass like animals; the heart of a father!" My father would laugh to himself and reply: "Fool, the land of Israel – a land flowing with milk and honey,[893] but what? Arabs ruined it. The land awaits us, as we wait for it. And if with God's help I will rid myself of the business matters that are hateful to me, of the Cossacks that live in our houses, and from all the haters of Israel, who extort bribes from the Jews, the two

---

[890] In the land of Israel.

[891] Prior to the modern Zionist movement, it was believed that only the Messiah could bring about the return to Zion and the reestablishment of Jewish sovereignty in the land of Israel. Even today there are some on the far right who believe that the establishment of the State of Israel by human hands actually delays the coming of the Messiah.

[892] A poem written in Yiddish by Dr. Yitzchak Peled, Lvov 1862-1922. Set to music, the song served as a kind of anthem for the Zionist student unions and the Zionist youth unions. The song was sung on the stage of the first Zionist Congress. Lyrics in Yiddish, Hebrew and English are readily found online.

[893] Exodus 3:8 "I have come down to rescue them from the Egyptians and to bring them out of that land to a good and spacious land, a land flowing with milk and honey…"

of us will go up to the land and there we will conclude our lives. And I have one more wish, that this son of ours will marry his wife in Jerusalem." And indeed, his wish was fulfilled; after a few years, in the year 1907, my *chuppah*[894] stood in the Kaminetz hotel in Jerusalem, and the two elders are sleeping their eternal sleep in the cemetery in Zikhron Yaakov. The wooden suitcases, meanwhile, were prepared, and in addition to them, a crate that was one meter square. Mother put into this crate tens of packages of jam, marmalade, and goose fat. This crate supplied me {p. 296} with mostly bitterness. We had only reached Costa,[895] Smyrna, Salonika, and when the sun began to warm, all the packages began to stream liquids in various colors.

When I reached Odessa, I lodged in the house of the writer Ben-Ami, who was the brother-in-law of my brother-in-law Dr. Yaffa. This Ben-Ami was a revolutionary, and hated the Tsar's regime with all his heart and soul. He had a favorite nickname for this regime: "Otto Svolotz." I asked him what did I have to do for "Otto Svolotz" to permit me to leave Russia? He answered me that maybe it would be possible to obtain a Turkish visa, and if not – I had to buy a round trip ticket. And "don't forget" he added "that Dr. Yaffa was in Yafo,[896] who had great influence thanks to the "*baksheesh*"[897] that he distributed. And regarding the return ticket, there would certainly be found a Jew in the land whose wife was embittering his life for him because there was no jam, goose fat, theatre, etc. there; he will buy the ticket from you." I did as he said, and I went up onto the ship. I found a place in third class, for there wasn't a fourth.

All the bundles around me, and in the center, the known crate, on which I sat "like the king of the regiment." Suddenly, woe is me, there suddenly appeared, as if from under the ground, a Russian gendarme. His feet – like the feet of a hippopotamus, wearing shining boots; on the boots were ringing nickel wheels. His uniform was blue, on his head there was a blue "*yarmulke*" [898] with a white "*fuftzik*."[899] He searched in the passport, and when he didn't find a Turkish visa, he respectfully[900] invited me to go with him. In the office of the gendarmerie, the officer ruled that I was right! "If the Turks will not allow him to get off the ship – he said – he will return on the same ship, doesn't he have a return ticket?" The gendarme immediately changed his spots, became as soft as butter and as sweet as honey, accompanied me back respectfully to the ship, brought me to the captain, saluted him, presented me as his sister's son, and humbly asked him to give me a place in a cabin, if possible. The captain promised to fulfill his request after the ship left the port. I invited my "uncle" to the buffet, and after drinking a cup of beer he parted from me with hugs and kisses. The ship began to whistle, to belch and yawn,[901] as is the way of every ship, and sailed to the sea. I washed myself, I combed my hair, and I returned to the captain, who welcomed me nicely. He called the head sailor, who was about 60, a "sea wolf" type, and instructed him to settle me in a cabin. The "boatsman" called for half a dozen sailors, who took my bundles, and installed me with all the luggage into a cabin, where I spent 14 days. We would travel only a few hours at night. In the days, the ship would enter ports along the way, and they would load or unload merchandise from it. With my arrival in Yafo I visited in Costa, Smyrna, Salonika, Libyan Tripoli, and Beirut. I spent time with the Arabs on the ship in the company of the Russian pilgrims who travelled to visit the Christian holy places. I was very impressed by their great love for the Holy Land. I used to meet with the "boatsman," who used to tell about the days before there were

---

[894] Wedding canopy.
[895] Short for Constantinople.
[896] Jaffa.
[897] Bribes.
[898] Yiddish for "skullcap."
[899] Yiddish for "50."
[900] This is sarcastic.
[901] Babylonian *Talmud Berakhot* 24b "Furthermore, one who belches and yawns while praying is surely among the uncouth…"

steamboats. He was 15 when he started to work, as a student on a sailing ship. "What do today's captains know?" he would say, "putting at their disposal a ship equipped with a steam engine and the rest of the devices, and they are so good as to travel when it is good for them to travel. The captain of a sailing ship was a hero, a valiant man. One must love the sailing ship, must know on what angle to set it, otherwise he will drown with all the crew." He was a beloved man, he would drink 12 bottles of beer at once, like all of them. When we reached Beirut, a youth came up onto the ship dressed like a European, but wearing a red "fez." This was a Jewish medical student from the University of Beirut, whose name was Rozenfeld. He gave me a letter from my brother-in-law Dr. Yaffa from Yafo, in which he wrote that Mr. Rozenfeld would show me all the best of {p. 297} Beirut, Lebanon. Towards evening I returned to the ship. During the night, my sleep wandered, for on the next day, early in the morning, we would reach Yafo. Indeed, finally, I daydreamed, I would see the land that was known to me from the Bible, I would see the Baron's[902] settlements, and those of *Chovevei Tzion*. I would see Jerusalem, the Holy City; the Western Wall; the Hand of Absalom,[903] the Mount of Olives, the Foundation Stone[904] that I learned about in *cheder*. I would see Arabs, members of our race, whose language resembles our language.[905] I would see the wineries at Zikhron Yaakov and Rishon L'Tzion, whose wine I had drunk on *Shabbatot* and festivals. I would see vineyards that were spoken of in the Song of Songs. I would also see my two sisters, and their husbands and children. The husband of one was a well-known physician in Yafo, Dr. Hillel Yaffa. He was the representative of the Odessan Council of *Chovevei Tzion*, a man whose deeds it was possible to read much about in letters from the land that were published in "*HaMelitz*" and "*HaTzefirah*." My second brother-in-law, Chaim Margalit-Kalvariski, who dwelt in Sejera,[906] between Nazareth and Tiberias, was a builder of settlements in the lower Galilee on behalf of the well-known philanthropist. When he was my sister's betrothed, in our city of Augustow, and I was then Bar Mitzvah age, he heard that I loved horses, and that I knew how to ride like a Cossack. He then promised me that if I would go up to the land, he would make available to me a noble Arabian horse, and a Bedouin as a guide, with whose help I would pass through the land from Dan to Beersheva.[907]

The hour was 3:00 in the morning. I was the only Jew on the ship. My heart was overflowing, and there was no one with whom to share the joy. The pilgrims woke from their sleep, and began to pack their belongings. Their priest, an uneducated Russian boor, hung his big crucifix on his chest, and said to me: "in another few hours we will step on the holy soil. Nazirites and priests will welcome us and send us to Jerusalem, the Holy City, where God is buried, where the cursed "zhidim[908]took him out to be killed." I answered him: "*Batyushka* (my father), you seem to have forgotten that I am also a *zhid*." He blushed and said: "You are not a *zhid*, you are a Hebrew. I even like the "Hebrews."

---

[902] Baron Lionel Walter Rothschild, 1868 – 1937, member of the British Parliament, recipient of the Balfour Declaration in 1917 from Arthur James Balfour, stating Britain's interest in establishing a Jewish homeland in Palestine.

[903] The Hand, or Tomb, of Absalom, one of the sons of King David, is in the Kidron Valley in Jerusalem. The monument is traditionally ascribed to Absalom, who would have lived in the 10th century BCE, but scholars date the structure to circa 1st century CE. The word "hand" is often used to refer to a memorial.

[904] The Foundation Stone is the rock on the Temple Mount in Jerusalem that is at the center of the Dome of the Rock in Jerusalem. There are Jewish beliefs that this rock was the site of the Holy of Holies of the ancient Temple, as well as the site of Mt. Moriah, where Abraham went to sacrifice Isaac.

[905] Jews and Arabs are both Semitic peoples; Hebrew, Arabic, and Aramaic are all Semitic languages.

[906] Sejera, named for the adjacent Arab village al-Shajara, was the first Jewish settlement in the Lower Galilee and played an important role in the Jewish settlement of the Galilee from its early years until the 1948 Arab–Israeli War.

[907] A biblical reference to the entire land, represented by Dan, the northernmost point, and Beersheva, the southernmost point. This phrase appears 9 times in the Hebrew Bible, in the books of Judges, Samuel, Kings and Chronicles.

[908] Russian slur for "Jews."

The hour was 5:00 in the morning. A dinghy arrived, driven by Arabs. A sailor from the ship lowered a thick rope and a squat Arab climbed on it like a cat. When he came onto the ship the Arab yelled in a loud voice: "Choga Linstein, Choga Linstein!" I understood that he was looking for me. I approached him and he took a letter from my brother-in-law, Dr. Yaffa, out of his *tarbush*.[909] My brother-in-law wrote that the bearer of the letter, Eli Chamis, was his friend and a lover of Jews, and also the uncrowned ruler of the port of Yafo. I was to unhesitatingly hand over my belongings to him. Eli and his men took my possessions, and within a short hour my brother-in-law appeared. We kissed each other. I asked about my sister's welfare, their children, etc. During the conversation the Arab took hold of me, threw me into the arms of the second, and that one into the arms of the third, and before I had a chance to cry "save me" I was already below in the dinghy. My brother-in-law descended on the steps of the ladder and seated himself next to me. The dinghy's sailors worked the oars energetically, and I pathetically began, pardon me, to vomit. I lay on the floor of the dinghy and felt that I would not reach the dock alive. Two wretched Arab officials stood on the dock. I noticed that one of them wore one regular shoe, and on the other foot, a rubber shoe. The second official was barefoot. One of the officials requested my passport. My brother-in-law had warned me beforehand not to give him the passport, suspecting that he would take it and sell it to the highest bidder. To be on the safe side, he put my passport in his pocket. Eli Chamis, upon hearing the word "pass" (passport) coming out of the mouth of the official roared: "Have you gone mad? You require a pass? Do you not know who it is that is arriving? Indeed this is the brother-in-law of the wise[910] Dr. Yaffa, who is an important *Kaimakam*,[911] *Mashallah*,[912] (without the evil eye). The official understood that I {p. 298} was responsible for the *baksheesh*, and let me go. We entered a hall that was half dark, with no floor. In the middle of the room was a pit full of rainwater, which entered by way of the leaking roof. Next to a long table stood two *barnashim*,[913] resembling the previous ones – the customs officers. One of them instructed us to open the bundles, but Eli screamed that there was no sense in their heads, they were seeking to check Dr. Yaffa's possessions, while at the same time yelling at the porters: "outside, dogs, with the baggage!" The porters carried the baggage, and we walked a respectable short distance behind them, by way of a dirty Arab market, until we reached the road. There a wagon hitched to two wretched horses waited for us, one of which was infected with eczema on its back. The spring of the wagon was broken and tied with a rope. The coachman wore torn clothing. Slowly he brought us to the apartment of my brother-in-law in Neve Shalom. In the lane stood two houses that looked alike. They belonged to an Arab of Ethiopian origin, Abu Chadra was his name, a successful merchant. Dr. Yaffa lived with his family in one house, and in the second house lived his mother and his sister Roza, who was the Director of the "Alliance" school in Yafo. She was the first, who after a difficult struggle with the first management in Paris and with the help of the teacher Yehuda Garzovsky, may his memory be for a blessing, instituted Hebrew as the language of instruction in the "Alliance" school in place of French. The house in which my sister lived was built in good Arab taste. In the entrance were two round marble pillars, which were brought from Italy, all the floors were covered with white Italian marble with black marble stripes. An enormous salon was divided by a wall decorated with white marble pillars. The height of the rooms was about 5 meters. The kitchen was in the yard, in a special building. Water was drawn from a well in the yard, upon which was hung a wheel with a rope and a bucket. Clearly,

---

[909] Or fez; a hat.

[910] In Arabic.

[911] The Turkish word *Kaimakam* is the title that was used for the governor of a provincial district in the Ottoman Empire.

[912] Arabic, "what God has willed." It expresses gratitude, joy, or praise.

[913] *Bar nash* is Aramaic for "son of a person," like the Hebrew "*ben adam*," meaning person. This is the plural form.

there was no trace of electric light. In all the land there was not even one ice factory. Water was kept in large and small jerry cans (clay jugs). They would wrap them in fabric that they would wet from time to time, and in that way they kept the water inside cold.

I had seen this sister of mine about a year before, when she came with her eldest son, one year old, for a visit in Augustow. I was happy to again see my beloved sister and her two children. We sat down to each lunch. They served dishes at the table, most of which I tasted for the first time in my life: eggplants, olives, zucchini, and tomatoes. My sister explained to me that the climate in the land was different than the climate in Russia. In the land it was warm, and therefore one ate many fruits and vegetables, and fewer meat dishes. I really ate everything, but without desire. At that time they were picking oranges.[914] Yafo was entirely covered with orchards. At that time they watered the trees in a primitive fashion: a camel or a horse would turn a wheel, which brought crates full of water up from the well. The water was spilled from the crates into irrigation channels. But there were also orchards where the water was brought up by motors and pumps. Dr. Yaffa had a friend, Saleem Salchi, a son of a wealthy Muslim family of distinguished lineage (in Yafo there is a Salchi market). This young man, blind in one eye, knew a little Yiddish, and very much liked to visit in the houses of the well-known Jews, and he would boast about it in front of his friends. I used to walk in the orchards with him a lot, and swallow tens of juicy oranges. I was only in Yafo for a month. This Yafo was then, in effect, a big village, in whose center stood a mosque with a slightly crooked tower. Three times a day the "muezzin"[915] (the chazzan), would go up on the tower, and with his monotonous voice he would call the believers to prayer. At that time I never imagined that I would get to live in a Jewish state. I left Yafo and I traveled to visit my sister who was older than me, the wife of Chaim Margalit-Kalvariski, on the Sejera farm, between Nazareth and Tiberius. I hired a dilizhnez[916] for sixty {p. 299} franks, an enormous amount in those days. We left Yafo early in the morning. We had only just left when a strong rain began to fall. It was impossible to see the road or the way. By the way, then, in the days of the Turks,[917] the roads were so bad that people preferred to travel on the ground alongside the roads. The contractor was obligated to distribute a bribe to the various government officials; he left, of course, a proper profit for himself. There did not remain, therefore, money for the paving of the road. It was a daring thing to go out of Yafo in those days when there was no road, and the way turned into a swamp. We set the course by the stars and the sun. From time to time the wagon would sink into the mud and then, as if the coachmen were playing around, there was no strength required for the coachman, only the sense to crawl under the wagon, to load it on his back in order to help the tired horses extract it from the mud. We travelled three days from Yafo to Qaqun.[918] There the wagon got stuck in a pit. We had a bachan (a kind of hotel in which people, mules, horses, camels and fleas slept together.) The next day we succeeded, with the help of farmers from the community of Qaqun, in exchange for much baksheesh, to extract the wagon from the pit. Towards evening we reached Hadera, and on the next day towards evening we reach Haifa. Tired and broken we sat, I and Avraham'ka the coachman, by a table in the hotel, and I said to him, after we drank a large bottle of cognac, "Avrahamaleh! Don't be sad, put your tired head on my shoulder, this is how we build a homeland for our people, who are scattered and dispersed among the nations. A day will come and they will remember us, the first pioneers, who laid the foundation for the state of the

---

[914] Literally, golden apples.

[915] Arabic. The man who calls Muslims to prayer from the minaret of a mosque.

[916] Stagecoach.

[917] The Ottoman Empire ruled Palestine until the end of World War One.

[918] Qaqun was an Arab village located 6 kilometers northwest of the city of Tulkarm at the only entrance to Mount Nablus from the coastal Sharon plain.

Jews, of which the fine Jew with dreaming eyes, the wonderful old semite, "Dr. Herzl,"[919] dreams. On the next day I found a German stagecoach that was travelling to Nazareth. A small town, in which, 2000 years before, lived Joseph the carpenter with his wife Miriam and their son Yeshu. On the next day I hired a horse from a Christian Arab, Nasrallah was his name. I rode on the horse, and before me walked a barefoot Arab youth, to show me the way. In Sejera I found a large house, on the lower floor there was a stable for horses, and a place for cows. On the upper floor were many rooms for the workers' dwelling. Nearby there lived families of foreigners, who my brother-in-law Kalvariski brought to teach our unmannered farmers the work of the land. My brother-in-law was not at home. He had travelled to Beirut on a horse, accompanied by his faithful head guard, the Bedouin Chamdi from the tribe of Isbach, to bring a large sum of money in gold coins. The known donor was sending his assets to Beirut, for in all the land there was no bank. The leather sack full of gold coins was hanging from the neck of the head guard, knowing that according to Bedouin custom he would not touch money that gave his bread, and would do battle with anyone that dared to touch it. At home were my sister and her two small daughters: one three years old, and the second, one year old. Helping her were a Christian cook from Nazareth, a servant expert in arranging the table and supervising the food, and additional Arab servants for work in the kitchen and the yard. The languages that were spoken in the house were Arabic and French. In that same house was the agronomist Krause,[920] who had established the farm. That same year he moved to direct the agricultural school "Mikve Yisrael." He was overwhelmed with compassion for my beautiful sister who had completed her learning in France, loved music, art, and literature – for that fact that she had agreed to settle in this wilderness only for her husband who she loved, who was a Zionist and a lover of Zion even before Herzl. For dinner, my sister dressed as if she was in a fancy salon in Paris. When I asked her why she was dressed that way when there were no guests in the house, she explained to me that if she did not pay attention to her dress in this atmosphere, she would become sloppy and grow old before her time. After a few days, my brother-in-law returned from Beirut. We were happy to greet each other. This was the same Chaim the dreamer who believed in the rejuvenation of the nation in its land. The few who believed in that seemed then like they were delusional.

{p. 300} My brother-in-law was born in the town of Pashroshli, which is adjacent to Augustow. He studied in the gymnasia in Suwalk. After he completed his army service he continued his studies in Monfalia, which is in southern France, in agriculture.

He came once on the big vacation to visit in Suwalk; this was in about 1893. I studied in the modern *cheder*, with Rabbi Donieger. On one Friday we played in the yard of the "*cheder*," and a youth of about 25 approached me, dressed nicely, adorned with a small beard, blessed me with peace, and asked in Russian where was the *cheder* of Misyah Donieger. I brought him into the rabbi's room, and I stood with my friends next to the door and listened to their conversation. We heard that the young man was telling the rabbi about the land of Israel, about a council of *Chovevei Tzion* in Odessa, about Baron Rothschild, about the settlements of Petach Tikvah, Rishon L'Tzion, etc. The rabbi enjoyed it, smiling, smoothing his grey beard. Occasionally the rabbi asked the young man a question and he responded that the Jews in the land of Israel were plowing the land really like the gentiles did here, to distinguish,[921] and the rabbi said that the redeemer is the Baron from Paris,[922] the well-known philanthropist. When the young man left, we meanwhile had fled to the yard, he came near us, politely raised his hat, and said in Russian: "Shalom to you,

---

[919] Theodor.
[920] Eliyahu Krause, 1878-1962.
[921] This is an expression used when one does not want to compare one thing to the other, such as Jews to Gentiles, making them seem equivalent.
[922] Rothschild.

children, we will see each other in the land of Israel." This was my first encounter with the man who in the future would become my brother-in-law.

The First Group of Those Who Went Up
By Binyamin Efrati

Zalman Bezant,
may his memory be for a blessing

In this memorial book we immortalize the community of Augustow, which was destroyed by the Nazi murderers in the years 5701-5702 (1941-1942). If we can write this book, indeed it is thanks to the Zionist movement, thanks to which we went up to the land and reached here, to live in the sovereign State of Israel.

In the year 1915, in the First World War, I was expelled by the Russian army to the Voronezh district, with other thousands of Jews. They suspected that the Jews were supporters of the Germans. In the year 1919 I returned. The city of my birth, Lipsk (28 viorsts from Augustow), was burnt and destroyed in the war. I moved, therefore, to live in the district city of Augustow. I found there good Jews, people who engaged faithfully in the needs of the public, in the community council, and in other institutions. I remember D. Slutzky, Dovid-Arieh Aleksandrovitz, the Elenbogen brothers, M. Vilmer, and more. Their primary actions were the offering of help and aid to the needy: monetary and medical help, wood for heating in the winter, the distribution of food to schoolchildren (they received the food from the "Joint"),[923] and the like. However, I did not find people {p. 301} who engaged in Zionist activity, even though most of the Jews of Augustow were faithful lovers of Zion. In that same year we founded, with the help of the teachers Reuven Levin and D. Boyarski, a Zionist association. Activists of the community council also joined our initiative. A club was opened in the house of Feinstein, and extensive activity in the fields of propaganda, culture, and the collection of funds for the *Keren Kayemet L'Yisrael*. Part of the youth also undertook the action. On *Lag Ba'omer* 5680, 1920, we held a rally with the synagogue to benefit "The Redemption Fund."[924] The preacher Natan Mileikovsky,[925] may his memory be for a blessing, spoke, and excited the community. Many donated. Women took off their jewelry and turned it over to benefit the fund.

With the receipt of the information on the death of Trumpeldor[926] and his friends at Tel-Hai, the first group was organized to go up to the land. In *Sivan* 5680, 1920, we left Augustow, and in *Tamuz* we reached the land of Israel. In the first group the following went up: Reb Zalman Bezant, may his memory be for a blessing, and, may he be set apart for long life, his son Yitzchak,

---

[923] The Joint Distribution Committee. Founded during World War I, the American Jewish Joint Distribution Committee (JDC) was the first Jewish organization in the United States to dispense large-scale funding for international relief. The JDC played a major role in sustaining Jews in Palestine and rebuilding the devastated communities of Eastern Europe after World War I.

[924] This was the fund of the World Zionist Organization before the establishment of *Keren HaYesod*, the Foundation Fund.

[925] Rabbi Natan Mileikovsky, 1879 – 1935. He was Benjamin Netanyahu's grandfather.

[926] Joseph Vladimirovich Trumpeldor (1880 – 1920) was an early Zionist activist who helped to organize the Zion Mule Corps and bring Jewish immigrants to Palestine. Trumpeldor died defending the settlement of Tel Hai in 1920 and subsequently became a Zionist national hero.

Yehuda Levita, may his memory be for a blessing, Tuvia Rabinovitz, may his memory be for a blessing, and Noach Borovitz, may he be set apart for a long life, Noach Varhaftig, Mendel Libernat (went back to the diaspora), Arieh Rotstein, and Binyamin Efrati. After a short time Reuven Levi, may his memory be for a blessing, went up. Other pioneers came up after us. With the passage of years, parents, brothers, and sisters joined, until we reached a camp of about 200 families that emigrated from Augustow.{p. 302} If we add to them the second and third generations, who were born in the land, our number will be about 1000 souls. So may they multiply.

The First Group of Those Who Went Up – The Year 5680 – 1920

Seated from right to left: Yehuda Levita, may his memory be for a blessing, Binyamin Efrati, Reuven Levi, Noach Varhaftig.
Standing: Mendel Libernat (returned to Augustow), Arieh Rotstein, Noach Borovitz.
Laying down: Yitzchak Bezant.
Caption in the Photo: The Augustow Group, in Rechovot, the Land of Israel, *Shavuot* 5681 [1921].

We merited that our aspirations to go up to the land were realized, to build her and to make her wasteland bloom. We mourn for those whose aspirations were not realized. This book will serve as an eternal monument to them. It will also remind our children, our grandchildren, and the generations to come, of the faithful activists who nurtured the Zionist movement in all its hues; thanks to them, their ancestors were saved from destruction and were able to help in the establishment of the State of Israel. **Tammuz 5723 [1963]**

A History of "*HeChalutz*" in Augustow
by Dr. Nechemiah Aloni
The most active movement in Augustow after the First World War was the "*HeChalutz*" organization. This was the practical Zionist movement with the clear result: to go up to the land

290

and participate in the building of the homeland in the way of self-realization. It was founded in the year 5684 [1924] and remained in existence until the year 5699 [1939], the year of the outbreak of the Second World War, the invasion of Poland by Hitler's troopers, and the destruction of the Jews of Poland by the Nazi murderers. This article was written in the year 5725 [1965] in Jerusalem, after the "*HeChalutz*" archive was destroyed together with the members of the city. There remain therefore only the memories that serve as the source for the words to come.

Augustow, whose population numbers reached the tens of thousands, was a Jewish city – typical Lithuanian. This was a district city that controlled the towns and villages that were around it. Politically it belonged to Poland, but socially and culturally it belonged to Lithuanian Jewry. This was rabbinic Judaism, which did not know the Chassidic movement. Lithuanian Yiddish was the language of speech, and its leaders were the leaders of the Jewish settlement in Belz and in Telz, in Kovno and in Vilna. The big cities that were adjacent to it were Suwalk and Grodno. It was joined to the two of them by a train that travelled in both directions once a day. The train station was a few kilometers outside of the city, and carriages hitched to horses would conduct the travelers from the train to the city in the morning, and in the evening from the city to the train on the Grodno-Bialystok-Warsaw (the capital of Poland) line. This was the main movement of travelers, while the movement in the morning to Suwalk and the movement in the evening from Suwalk, was the secondary movement of passengers.

The residents of the city were by a decisive majority Jewish, and they set the Jewish style of the city. On Sabbaths and festivals the entire city stopped, while on the ordinary days the entire city worked. And {p. 303} the Jewish settlement in Augustow had experience and a manner. The community and the heads of the community and its leaders and officers were veterans and experienced. There were a rabbi and a judge and *tzedakah* institutions, a large central synagogue and a central *Beit Midrash*, and in addition to them there were small synagogues and "*kloizim*" of various kinds. The institutions of learning were the "*cheder*," and the study of *Talmud* in the *Beit Midrash*. It seemed that the small echelon of wealthy merchants had been wealthy for generations, and the small class of poor people were poor people of the "*erev rav*,"[927] who accompanied the Children of Israel when they left Egypt. The tailors, the hatters, the shoemakers, the smiths, the carpenters, the porters and the wagon masters – their professions were inherited, passing from generation to generation. Most of the Jews of the city belonged to the middle class.

The foundations of the society and the leaders were violently shaken by the First World War. The establishment of the State of Poland after its liberation constituted the cause of the awakening of the youth movement in Augustow. The liberation and the establishment of the state aroused the national feelings also in the heart of the Jewish youth. The Zionist movement developed and a communist movement arose, the "*Bund*" was organized and also "*Tzeirei Tzion*," "*HaShomer HaTzair*," "*HaShomer* {p. 304} *Trumpeldor*," and the "*Yidisher Yugend Bund*." On the foundations of all these the "*HeChalutz*" organization was founded in Augustow. The level of modern culture was not high. With the liberation of the State of Poland a national Polish school was founded. Those seeking to continue to learn migrated to the high schools in Suwalk, Lodz, and Bialystok in Poland, and to Dresden and Konigsberg in Germany. The little additional completion of education the youth acquired, after the age of the national school, was in the youth movements. The thirst for enlightenment constituted one of the causes of the development of the various youth movements in the city.

---

[927] Exodus 12:38 "Moreover, a mixed multitude went up with them, and very much livestock, both flocks and herds."

Members of "*Hechalutz*"

First row from right to left: … Z. Leizerovski, G. Freund, D. Freitzeit, N. Lozovski, Y. Feivovorski, A. Shumski.

Second row: D. Stoliar, M. Shreibman, Y. Strozinski, Yechezkel Sherman, N. Aloni, Ratner, M. Vilmer.

Third row: Bezant, Herzl… B. Avariah, L. Staviskovski, M. Chalupitzki, A. Mintz, H. Stein.

Fourth row: Yitzchak Sherman… M. Mariampolski, T. Bidek, Ch. Friedman.

A Group of Members of "*HeChalutz*" (1924)

First row top, from right to left: Y. Roznov, Freizeit, D. Stolar, L. Staviskovski, Feivovorski… A. Borovski.

Second row: Z. Leizerovski, Alter Aleksandrovitz, Yechezkel Sherman, Nechemiah Linda, Yisrael Strozinski, Ch. Freidman. Laying down: Yosef Linda, A. Zilberstein.

292

The most important cause in the growth of the "*HeChalutz*" organization was the economic situation of the Jews of Poland in the years 1923-1925. The heavy taxes that the Polish government placed on the middle class, and especially on the small merchants, destroyed their business and their position. Members of the middle class were unable to continue their education due to a material lack, and the doors of the institutions of higher learning were closed to them by the anti-semitic authorities. The Jewish youth in Poland lacked interest, purpose, and employment. Most of them led aimless, boring lives, and sought a way out and release, a purpose and a vision. There were those who found a solution in assimilation, absorption, and self-deprecation, in *tikkun olam*[928] *and malchut shaddai*,[929] in communism and self-sacrifice for the sake of strangers. In contrast to them, {p. 305} others turned to national and Zionist organizations, and by means of them they went up to the land of Israel to build it and be built by it.[930]

In the spring of 5684 [1924], between *Purim* and *Pesach*, a group of young people age 17-18 assembled in one of the houses of the city for the purpose of founding the organization "*HeChalutz*." There were among them: Nechemiah Aloni (Linda), Tovah Bidek (today Ben-Dov), Adah Mintz, Breintza Yevreiska (Ivriyah),[931] Yisrael Strozinski, Hinda Stein, and Yechezkel Sherman.

Caption in Photo: Kibbutz Trumpeldor in Augustow

Standing from right to left: Y. Aloni, Y. Sherman, N. Aloni…
Seated: M. Stolar … Z. Leizerovski … … Tz. Glikstein …D. Stein …Z. Kalstein …

---

[928] Repairing the world; a Jewish concept that has its origins in *kabbalah*, Jewish mysticism.
[929] God's sovereignty.
[930] A popular saying from early Zionism, which made its way in a popular Zionist folksong.
[931] Both the Hebrew and Yiddish forms of this name mean "Hebrew."

In the first meeting the *"HeChalutz"* council was elected, composed of the members: Nechemiah Aloni (Chairperson), Yechezkel Sherman (Deputy Chairperson), Yisrael Starazinsky (Secretary), Hinda Stein (Treasurer), and another male or female member that I don't remember. The purpose was clear to all the participants: Ascent to the land of Israel, and participation in the building of the land as workers. For this purpose preparation and training were required, which included socialist-Zionism, Hebrew culture, and acquisition of a profession. The Council was connected with the *"HeChalutz"* center in Warsaw, and received permission for the establishment of the branch. The council organized evening Hebrew lessons and conducted conversations and groups for the teaching of Zionism. The cultural activity was primarily expressed by the reading of Mendele,[932] Shalom Aleichem,[933] Bialik[934] and Ahad Ha'am,[935] the writings of Herzl and Borochov,[936] the history of Zionism and the working settlement.[937]

Within a short time, many of the youth in the city joined *"HeChalutz,"* and among them members of the working class: M. Mariampolski, the son of a smith, and Gedaliah Freund, the son of a carpenter, who were considered in our eyes to have pedigrees, since they had professions and were accustomed to physical labor. The youth, 19-22 years old, {p. 309}at first stood on the side, but after a few months these two joined the *"HeChalutz"* organization, and we became the most important youth association in the city, numbering 50-60 people.

The matter of professional training was harder. We required of the members to choose for themselves a physical profession, but the most important profession in our eyes was agriculture. We were unable to engage in heavy farming. We leased, therefore, two plots of land for the purpose of raising vegetables. We even found for ourselves an adult man who knew agriculture, L. Staviskovski, who joined as a member and agreed to guide our members in working the two vegetable gardens.

The *"HeChalutz"* organization brought a revolution in the city and poured new ideas among the youth and even among the adults. The parents looked favorably on the deeds of their children, and did not object. They offered their houses for meetings and gatherings, and even would give their children the required pennies for the membership fee. However, they did not easily agree that their children would become workers and laborers, the growers of vegetables and agronomists. When they raised the vegetables and made the members of *"HeChalutz"* sell them to the householders, they were not easily sold; we were forced to sell them at a lower price than that demanded by the gentile farmers. The mothers and farmers came out of their houses and gazed with astonishment at how their children from a good family were taking the vegetables with a hand cart, to sell. The judge of the city, Azriel Noach Zelig Koshelevski, was among the first of the buyers. Even the rabbi of the city, Rabbi {p. 310} Kosovski, who had recently been appointed to this rabbinate, and was

---

[932] Sholem Yankev Avramovitz, 1835-1917, used the pen name *Mendele Mocher Sforim*, Mendele the bookseller. He wrote books in both Hebrew and Yiddish.

[933] Shalom Rabinovitz, 1859-1916, used the pen name *Shalom Aleichem*, a common Hebrew greeting used among Jews, "Peace to You," and also the name of a popular prayer. He wrote in Hebrew, Yiddish, and Russian.

[934] Chaim Nachman Bialik, 1873 – 1934, was a Jewish poet who wrote primarily in Hebrew but also in Yiddish. He was one of the pioneers of modern Hebrew poetry, and came to be recognized as Israel's national poet.

[935] Asher Zvi Hirsch Ginsberg, 1856 – 1927, used the pen name Ahad Ha'am, literally "one of the people." He was a Hebrew essayist, and one of the foremost pre-state Zionist thinkers. He is known as the founder of cultural Zionism.

[936] Dov Ber Borochov, 1881 – 1917, was a Marxist Zionist and one of the founders of the Labor Zionist movement. He was also a pioneer in the study of the Yiddish language.

[937] "The working settlement" was an inclusive name for the agricultural settlements in Israel, which were founded by Hebrew workers tied to the labor movement and its organizational frameworks. This nickname, as well as the principles of working settlement were established at the third conference of the Agricultural Workers' Federation in 1908.

The Balforia Group in Augustow

Caption in the photo: The Artitz Group "Balforia" in Augustow.

The "*HeChalutz*" Council (1925)

Caption in the photo: "*HeChalutz*" in Augustow
From right to left: Y. Lonshel, M. Ostrov, Y. Sherman, Y. Strozinski, L. Staviskovski.

{p. 307} **Caption in the photo: The Brenner Pioneer House in Augustow**

The "*HeChalutz*" Carpentry Shop

M. Stolar… Yehoshua Dagani, Feinstein.

Pioneers – Wood Cutters

A Group of Pioneers in Kelson's Factory

From right to left: Y. Barzilai (Gazis)… Dilon, Chositzer, A. Kelson, Mariampolski.

The Members of the "*HeChalutz*" Branch

First row, top, (from right to left): Tz. Papirovitz, Ch. Goldstein, Y. Livni, N. Levinson, Y. ..., S. Koritzki, D. Kaplan, L. Veisberg, B. Chositzer, Ch. Bialovzetski.
Second row: S. Lifshitz, Y. Blacharski, Gad Zaklikovski, Shoshana Strozinski, M. Gutman, A. Cohen.
Third Row: R. Tsherman, Y. Kestin, A. Morzinksi, Y. Gazis, Fania Bergstein, Z. Dilon, A. Kahn.

one of the men of the "*Agudah*,"[938] prepared breakfast from the vegetables of our garden. The Yevreiski family, who owned a hotel, helped us, and agreed to allow us to provide vegetables to its hotel. This was a family that had a Zionist tradition. Their daughter Leah prepared to go up to the land together with her heart's chosen one Yitzchak Sherman, and a second daughter, Breintza, was a member of our organization.

The life of the youth, and public life in general in the city, were made much more interesting: general assemblies, lectures, parties on the 20th of *Tamuz* and 11th of *Adar*, public celebrations on festival days, also the activity for the benefit of the *Keren Kayemet L'Yisrael*, whose activists were the Hebrew teacher Mr. Bergstein (the father of Fania Bergstein[939] the poet), a drugstore owner Mr. Orimland, and Mr. Papirovitz, acquired a special taste and a new momentum. The outings of the youth in the forests on the *Shabbatot* towards evening and the boating on the River Nitzko had in them a consolidating social element. From then, and always, there was no fear in our city from the "*shkotzim*" who threw stones; we would fight back in the war of stones. Ties were formed with the nearby small towns; Rigrod, Sztabin, Suchovola, Goniądz and Ratzk, and with the big cities – Suwalk and Grodno. The leaders of "*HeChalutz*" began to visit us; Eliyahu Dobkin, B. Maniv, Pinchas Rasis, and others from the "*HeChalutz*" center in Warsaw, P. Bendori and Pinchas Koshelevski (today the Minister Pinchas Sapir),[940] from

---

[938] World Agudat Israel, usually known as the *Agudah*, was established in the early twentieth century as the political arm of Ashkenazi *Torah* Judaism.
[939] Fania Bergstein was a Hebrew poet, born in 1908 in Ščučyn, Russian Empire. She was a member of the Zionist youth movement *HeChalutz HaTzair*. In 1930 she went up to the land and joined Kibbutz Gevat. She died of heart failure at the age of 42, on September 18, 1950.
[940] Pinchas Sapir, 1906 – 1975, was an Israeli politician during the first three decades following the country's founding. He was Minister of Finance (1963–68 and 1969–74) and Minister of Trade and Industry (1955–65 and 1970–72) and also held several other high-ranking governmental posts.

Caption in the Photo: A Group at the Oasis of Yad Charutzim, in Augustow
1) Tz. Papirovitz, (Chairperson), 2) D.H. Kaplan (Treasurer), 3)? Vezbotzki (Secretary)

Standing from right to left: Pinchas Lev, A. Vezbotzki, Kentzuk, W. Sheinmar, Y. Dagani, M. Stolar, R. Feinstein.
Seated: Mordechai Shreibman, Tz. Shidlovski, V. Vezbotzki, Tz. Papirovitz, D. H. Kaplan, A. Lozman, Z. Kalstein.

the regional bureau in Grodno. After some time the special emissary from the land Yitzchak Tabenkin[941] came, and others.

At the end of the summer of 5684 [1924], the problem of the lack of training locations for the members of "*HeChalutz*" sharpened. {p. 311} It was decided to establish a house for physical and professional training by the name of "*Yad Charutzim*."[942] We rented a house at the edge of the city, and assembled a group of 12 people, boys and girls. I indeed wonder today how we succeeded in organizing a house like this. The rent for the house was raised by the members of "*HeChalutz*" going out to chop wood for the homeowners, and the wages of their labor were turned over to the organization's fund. The occupation of the members of "*Beit HeChalutz*"[943] was loading wood onto the train cars at the Augustow station. It was no small struggle for our members, until they succeeded in conquering the work. At first they refused to give us the work for a daily wage, and we were forced to work under contract. The women members worked in sewing sacks and in the housework of "*Beit HeChalutz*." In addition to these jobs, the regular work in cutting wood for heat was set in the yards of the homeowners. Due to the cold winter in this place, Poland, there was much work. Members of the branch from Suwalk, Bialystok, and other towns, were also sent to "*Beit HeChalutz*." Despite everything, a deficit was created in the budget of "*Beit HeChalutz*," which caused great worry for those responsible for the branch.

---

[941] Yitzchak Tabenkin, 1888 – 1971, was a Zionist activist and member of Knesset. He was one of the founders of the *kibbutz* movement.
[942] "Diligent Hand."
[943] "Pioneer House."

The Members of the Kibbutz in the Name of "Trumpeldor"

First row, top: Yosef Linda, Yisrael Starazinsky.
Second row: Z. Leizerovski, Zenya Yones … Dora Stein … … L. Staviskovski, Tz. Glikstein.
Third Row: Nechemiah Aloni, M. Ostrov, Y. Lonshel.

The winter of 5685 [1925] passed and towards the summer of that year it was decided to organize the members of "*HeChalutz*" for real agricultural training in the houses of farmers and on agricultural lands in the area. This very extensive plan of agricultural training in the Augustow area, with the participation of members from various branches, brought our members from Suwalk, with Pinchas Sapir at their head. Our members were scattered in villages and holdings {p. 312}and with great toil we succeeded in organizing about 150 people in work. The requirements that we introduced were very modest: only room and board. In exchanged for this our members became enslaved to a long and difficult workday, up to 14 hours a day. At first the farmers and the landowners related to the Jewish youths with a lack of faith, but after that summer they began turning to the organization, who would provide them with members of "*HeChalutz*" for agricultural work in the days of summer, and they even began to pay two months' pocket money to the workers. In this way the main way to training for pioneers was paved for those who were in the future to go up to the land and to join the family of workers there.

On January 1, 1925, "*Davar*,"[944] the daily newspaper of the General Organization of Hebrew Workers in the Land of Israel,[945] began to appear. This was a holiday for us. This newspaper, the "*Kuntrus*"[946] of "*Achdut HaAvodah*,"[947] the "*HaPoel HaTzair*" of the "*HaPoel HaTzair*" party in the land, pamphlets about Yosef Bussel[948] and the group in the land, various pamphlets of the "*HeChalutz*" center and the weekly "*HeAtid*" of the *HeChalutz* center in Warsaw, served as cultural training material for our members. Thanks to our parents {p. 317}who educated us in a Jewish atmosphere and instilled in us a Hebrew education with the help of private teachers Y. Bergstein, D. Boyarski (his son Ezra in New York was tested by me after many years, in the year 5710 [1950], in the exam certificate of the Hebrew University in Jerusalem). Reuven Levi,

---

[944] Word.
[945] The *Histadrut*.
[946] Pamphlet.
[947] Labor Unity, (1919 - 1930), was a Zionist Socialist party formed as a union, "Workers of Zion" led by David Ben-Gurion. The party's magazine - Pamphlet was published in the 1920s.
[948] 1891-1919, Belarus-born Zionist activist, one of the founders of Kibbutz Degania Alef.

G. Zaklikovski, we succeeded in turning the Hebrew language into the language of speech of many in the organization "*HeChalutz*" in Augustow. A competition was developed in the acquisition of information about Zionism and the workers' movement in the land and the ways of its settlement; tests were set, and woe to the member who did not know how to respond to a question that was presented to him in these matters. There was even set between members a special fine for the "*Keren Kayemet L'Yisrael*" for every non-Hebrew word that members used in their conversation. In this way a Hebrew and Zionist cultural atmosphere was formed in the "*HeChalutz*" organization in Augustow, and our members acquired cultural training for *aliyah* to the land. As the first for *aliyah*, two of our members that had professions were presented, M. Mariampolski, the son of a smith, and Gedaliah Freund, the son of a carpenter, who were sent to the land eight months after the foundation of our organization, and they were absorbed into the work in the land. It happened that one of the sons of the householders who was an electrician and knew a little about "Singer" sewing machines, passed on to him by his father, obtained a permit for *aliyah* to the land (certificate) not from us, but straight from the land of Israel office in Warsaw. That same youth from the Chalupitzki family went up to the land, reached Haifa, served as an agent of the "Singer" company, and only a few months went by when he left the land and returned to Augustow. The *aliyah* of our members and their absorption, and the descent of that youth, were compelling proof of the rightness{p. 318} of our way, the way of cultural and professional training.

Members of the "*HeChalutz*" Branch

First row from right to left: Staviskovski, S. Morzinksi, D., Freitzeit, Tz. Glikstein, N. Lozovski, L. Veisberg, A. Borovski, Y.A. Shor.
Second row: Nechemiah Aloni, Y. Feivereski, Ch. … Y. Strozinski, D. Kaplanski, Ch. Sherman, T. Bidek, T. Linda, D. Stoliar, Y. Roznov.
Third row: H. … Ratner, G. Freund, Z. Yones, … Staviskovski, M. Mariampolski, Ch. Lozman.
Fourth row: Y. Linda, Edah Mintz, Staviskovski, B. Ivriyah, Z. Leizerovski.

Membership Certificate of Aleksandrovitz, from Augustow
March 26, 1930. Valid until 1/31.

[Hebrew] The "*HeChalutz*" Organization of Poland.

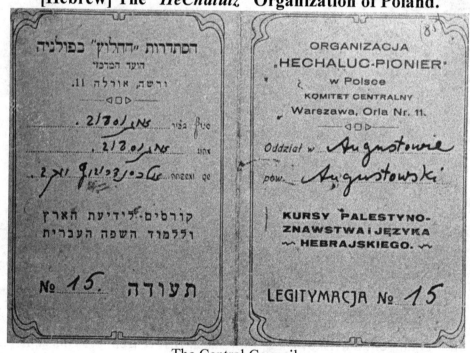

The Central Council
Orlah 11, Warsaw.
Branch: Augustow
Family Name: Aleksandrovitz Yaakov
Courses for Knowledge of the Land and the Study of the Hebrew Language
Certificate No. 15

{p. 314} **Flower Day for the Benefit of "*HeChalutz HaMizrachi*"**

Standing from right to left: Y. Blacharski, S. Zupnitzki, S. Gardovski, Y. Bilovzetzki, Batya Gizumski, Blacharski? Y. Gizumski, Meizler, A. Borovski.
Sitting: B. Bidek, Leizerovski? … Y. Shibek… Filvinsky, B. Tz. Filvinsky.

The Training Kibbutz of "*HeChalutz HaMizrachi*"

First row from right to left: A. Leizerovitz, D. Kaplan, M. Amit
Second row: B. Chozitzer, S. Leizerovitz, Y. Shadmi, N. Soloveitchik.
Sitting: A. Lifshitz, Y. Aleksandroni, R. Shadmi, P. Sarvianski.

Flower Day for the Benefit of the *Keren Kayemet L'Yisrael*
Caption in the Photo:
The Membership of the *Keren Kayemet L'Yisrael* Regiment in Augustow on Flower Day, 5
Tishre, 5687 [1927]

Standing from right to left: B. Sokolovski, Beknovitzki, H. Kaplan, Tz. Papirovitz, Y. Bergstein,
B. Koifman, A. Chalupitzki.
Sitting: A. Kleinman, Ch. Lozman, Masha Rosenfeld, Beknovitzki, F. Sarvianski, Zenya Yones.

The *Kapai* Council

Standing from right to left: Y. Feivoshvitz... R. Sherman, A. Chalupitzki, R. Bergstein.
Sitting: R. Rozenfeld, Friedman, P. Sarvianski, Goldshmidt.

At the end of the winter of 5685 [1925], eight members from among twenty from "*Beit HeChalutz*" were authorized for *aliyah* and four of them were members of the "*HeChalutz*" organization in Augustow. This time, two girls went up to the land; my sister Yonah (today Mrs. Finkelstein), and Tovah Ben-Dov (Bidek) (today the Director of the dormitory for outside of the country guides in Jerusalem). At the end of the summer of 5685, after the completion of the agricultural training period in the houses of farmers in the villages and agricultural holdings, an additional group was authorized for *aliyah*. After all the *aliyot* of members to the land, additional youth joined our organization, and the club "*HeChalutz*" on Bridge Street (*Brick Gasse*) was teeming with life and public activity. In that period the "*HeChalutz HaTzair*" movement was founded, which developed cultural activity in the young cohort of youth, ages 14-17. A few of them, and some of the members of "*HeChalutz*," were sent to the "*HeChalutz*" seminar in Warsaw, in order to serve as youth leaders in Augustow upon their return. These were: Fania Bergstein, Bracha Ivriyah, Shlomo Plotzinski, Yaakov Aleksandroni, and Zenya Yones (today Mrs. Riftin). Zenya established a branch of "*HaShomer HaTzair*" in our city. This movement gathered part of the youth who had not joined the "*HeChalutz*" and the "*HeChalutz HaTzair*" organization. After some time the "*Mizrachi*" youth movement was also founded. The city of Augustow was filled with Zionist youth movements, and was considered one of the important places in the Zionist movement. Until the Second World War, each and every year many went up to the land, and with their influence many of the adults that dwell here with us in the land were also saved, and take an active part in the building of our land.

Among the first to go up to the land from the "*HeChalutz*" organization in Augustow in the years 5684-5685 [1924-1925]

The "*Freiheit*"[949] Association

Caption in the photo: *Freiheit* in Augustow, 1936.

---

[949] Yiddish for "Freedom."

A Letter From the *HeChalutz* Organization

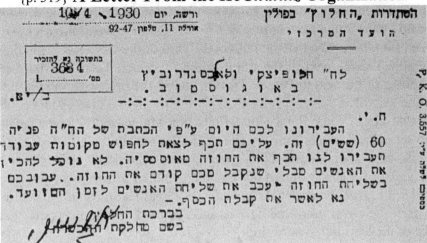

Warsaw, October 4, 1930
Orlah 11, Telephone 92-47
In replying, please mention No. L. 3684

The "*HeChalutz*" Organization in Poland
The Central Council

To Ch. Chalupitzki and to Aleksandrovitz In Augustow

Dear Friends,

    We have transferred to you today according to the dictation of the dear friend Fania this sixty (60). You must immediately go out to search workplaces. Transfer to us immediately the contract from Austasia. We will not be able to prepare the people without first receiving the contract from you. Your delay in sending the contract will delay the sending of the people at the designated time.

    Please confirm the receipt of the money.

    With the pioneer's blessing, In the name of the training division

Pioneers in the Land (1932)

307

{p. 320} were assembled a few in the *"Ma'avar"*[950] group in *"Givat HaShlosha"*[951] in Petach Tikvah. After a year these *olim* founded, together with *olim* from the same district of Poland, an independent group by the name of *"Hitamtzut."*[952] At first they went into an apartment in a built house, and moved from there to a thatched hut in the yard of the workers' council, and after a time they put up a wooden shack next to the train station in Petach Tikvah. Members of the group worked in the houses of farmers in Petach Tikvah, and in the orchards; in picking, in tilling, and in watering. In the years 5685-5688 [1925-1928], which were the crisis years of the 4th aliyah,[953] they suffered a great lack of work. Persistent deficits, constant worry for a piece of bread. However, that same group served as a center for *olim* from *"HeChalutz"* in the cities of Augustow, Suwalk, Suchovola, Ratzk, and other places. This group was a school for agricultural training in the settlements, and a place for absorption of our members in their *aliyah* to the land. In the year 5688 [1928] it merged with *"HaKibbutz HaMe'uchad"*[954] - Givat HaShlosha, in Petach Tikvah, which accepted upon itself the covering of the deficit, and acquired the little property in assets, and the great experience of the learning in suffering.

Pioneers in the Land

Standing from right to left: A. Morzinski, Y. Lonshel, Moshe Levinzon, Sender Lifshitz, D. Sherman, Y. Shadmi.
Sitting: B. Chositzer, L. Veisberg, A. Leizerovitz, Ch. Freitzeit, Z. Leizerovski, S. Plotzinski, M. Amit.

For many, Petach Tikvah served as a transit station. The members that left the *"Hitamtzut"* group became independent farmers and workers in the settlements of the land of Israel. Others turned to various professions. Because of the olim from the *"HeChalutz"* organization in

---

[950] "Passageway."

[951] A kibbutz in central Israel east of Petach Tikvah, named for the three workers from there who were accused of espionage during World War I and were sent to a prison in Damascus. They were tortured and died in 1916.

[952] "Endeavor."

[953] During the years 1926 - 1927 an economic crisis occurred in the country, the toughest the Jewish settlement had during the period of the British Mandate of Palestine.

[954] The United Kibbutz" was formed in 1927 by the union of several kibbutz bodies and was associated with the *Poalei Tzion* and later *Achdut HaAvodah* parties, and was aligned with the *Habonim* youth movement.

Augustow, Jews also went up who were not members of "*HeChalutz*," and because of them parents and elders from Poland were also saved, and even whole families settled in the land.

{p. 321} A Party of Zionist Professionals in Honor of the *Aliyah* of Yaakov Bergstein to the Land (5697) [1937]

Top from right to left: Yonah Linda, Topolski, R. Rozenfeld, Bidek, … Papirovitz, L. Staviskovski.
Second row: Tz. Papirovitz, … Kestin, Yaakov Bergstein, Gad Zaklikovski, A. Chalupitzki.
Third row: Freitzeit, Bialovzetski ….

Kibbutz "*Tel Chai*" in Augustow

{p. 322} Today Augustow is a distant city in Poland, and there are no Jews in it at all. The magnificent Jewish community that existed in it for over 400 years, which is also mentioned among the communities in the period of the "Council of the Four Lands,"[955] is destroyed. Only those who emigrated in the great stream of migration to the United States, and in the small stream to the land of Israel, were saved. Individuals ascended to it to the land in the year 5680 [1920]: Zalman Bezant, may his memory be for a blessing, his son Yitzchak, may he be distinguished for a long life, Yehuda Levita, may his memory be for a blessing, N. Varhaftig, R. Levi, may his memory be for a blessing, T. Rabinovitz, may his memory be for a blessing, B. Efrati, A. Rotstein, and the relatively many *olim*, after the founding of the "*HeChalutz*" organization in the years 5684-5698 [1924—1938]. The *olim* from Augustow and their descendants dwell in the land in settlements and in cities, in *kibbutzim* and *moshavim*. They participate in all aspects of the economy, and there are some of them who fulfill important public roles.

A Receipt for a Donation to the *Keren Kayemet L'Yisrael* signed by the agent Abba Rozenfeld.

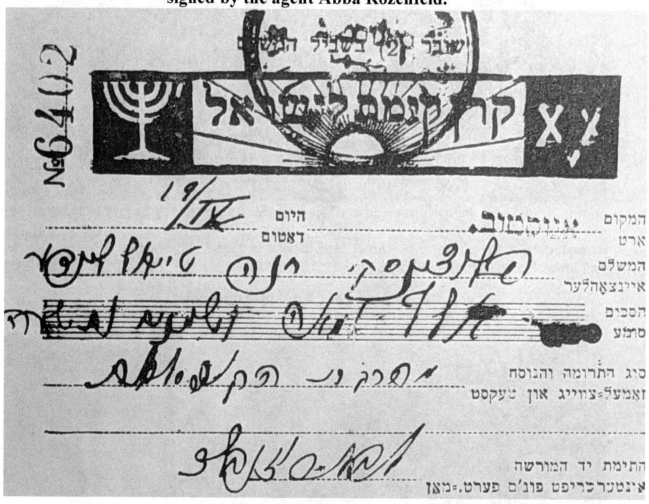

---

[955] "The Council of the Four Lands" was the central Jewish institution of autonomous governance in Poland and Lithuania. It began to operate in the middle of the 16th century and its authority was cancelled by the authorities in 1764.

Friends Tell

Yisrael Starazinsky:

"*HeChalutz*" was founded in the spring of 1924. We gathered, 12 people, and we said that we needed to do something real. We decided to lease a plot of land next to Meltzer's house and to establish a vegetable garden in it. There was an expert who took it upon himself to teach us agriculture. We sowed and also guarded the plot from animals, and from those with two legs. Our weapon was a long stick. I came once with Yechezkel Sherman in a pouring rain, to check and see if the guard was awake. To our surprise we found him standing outside, and not in the hut, despite the heavy rain. It became clear that because of the length of the stick he couldn't bring it inside, and therefore he too remained outside.

Later we put up the "*HeChalutz*" house. This was a small-scale[956] *kibbutz*. We worked mainly in cutting wood. We sought additional work and went out to the train station. Since they did not want to employ us for a daily wage, we did the work under contract. Our work satisfied the employers. From then the wood merchants would come to "*Beit HeChalutz,*" to invite us to work. The girls worked in repairing sacks and in rolling *matzah*s.

At the end of the winter of 1925 P. Koshelevski (today P. Sapir) came to us with a demand that we should look for training places on properties in the area. We turned first to the property of Binstein, who was an assimilated Jew. We met with the administrator. He claimed that he had never heard of Jews that were farmers, and rejected our request. We did not despair. We decided to meet with Binstein himself, when he would come to the city. On one of the days we saw him enter a restaurant. We approached him and explained what we were looking for. He was convinced, and put into our hands a letter to the administrator of the property that he should accept 8-10 of our workers. The workers worked, according to the practice of those days, from sunrise to sunset, about 14 hours. The payment – room and board. The young men made their best effort to fulfill the desire of the administrator. The matter became publicly known, and made it easier for us to introduce 150 more people on gentiles' properties.

Yitzchak Sherman:

A few years prior to the founding of "*HeChalutz*" in Augustow, a group of young men pondered the idea of "training." Immediately after the rise of independent Poland eight friends decided to seek agricultural work in the villages in the area. We found work in Slupsk. In this village there also lived a few Jews. To our misfortune, they were also looking for army deserters at the same time, and when we went to the work we encountered Polish gendarmes. We had no documents with us. They chose from among us two who looked more mature, me and Abba Rozenfeld, and sat us in the prison.

After efforts and convincing they freed us.

Yosef Aloni:

We helped to distribute the Zionist *shekel* and participated in the work for the sake of the "*Keren Kayemet L'Yisrael.*" We collected money for the benefit of the funds in every way possible.

At first they looked at us, at the members of "*HeChalutz,*" as crazy people. Indeed, sane people would not leave {p. 324} their good warm houses and settle in the "*Beit HeChalutz*" at the edge of the city, and work oppressively, really like gentiles. When the parents saw the calluses on our hands, they really cried: "Is a thing like this heard of that the children of Jews should be like the children of gentiles?" However, we felt that the rug was being pulled out from under our feet. We did not see another way to solve our problem, except for the way of *aliyah* to the land of Israel.

---

[956] Aramaic.

Shoshana Strozinski:

The members of "*HeChalutz*" did not only engage in agricultural work. I was the homemaker at "*Yad Charutzim*." I took care of the members, cooked and did laundry. I remember that an emissary came from the Center and demanded that I also learn carpentry, for in the land of Israel there was a lack of carpenters.

Moshe Einat:

The jobs that the members of "*Beit HeChalutz*" engaged in have been mentioned here. I remember that for the work of packing hides, which my parents sent outside of the country, they would invite a group of about 20 people from "*Beit HeChalutz*." My parents were very happy with their work.

Rachel Goldstein:

When the *kibbutz* was established in Augustow, I was the cook and launderer. The *kibbutz* resided in the house in which my parents lived too. However, according to the opinion of the members it was forbidden for me to enter our house to see my mother, in order that I not be found in a more comfortable situation than others. When all the members of the kibbutz went up to my parents, it was specifically forbidden for me to taste the refreshments that my mother served. Only after the emissary from the center visited the kibbutz were these decrees nullified.

{p. 325} *"HeChalutz HaTzair"* in Augustow
By Moshe Amit (Drozinski)

"…And the younger envied his brother. From there, from the hall of "*HeChalutz*," he surely heard song erupting, and his brother left the house of his father, and he created for himself a new life, a life of work, comradeship and freedom, and he went up to the land, to the land of Israel. And he envied him, and it came to his mind if he could not also do as he did. And he and his friends gathered and decided: let's we too be pioneers, young pioneers. And there arose – "*HeChalutz HaTzair*."

"HeAtid," **11 Adar 5688 [1928], N. Chayut**

When the young people saw that the adults were entering the club, singing and dancing, carrying out cultural and social activities, they too decided to do as they did, and established "*HeChalutz HaTzair*" in the city. We began with a very few, and we became, within a very short time, a great nation.[957] "*HeChalutz*" accepted as members those age 18 and up, while "*HeChalutz HaTzair*" accepted ages 14-18, who completed elementary school or "*talmud torah*." Members of "*HeChalutz HaTzair*" were essentially the children of laborers, shopkeepers and small merchants, whose parents did not have the means to send them outside of the place to learn in high schools.

First thing we rented a club. To cover the expenses the members paid a monthly tax, and when that did not suffice, they drafted the members for days of work in cutting wood for heating in the yards of the Jews of the city, or in helping with the baking of *matzot* and the like. The wages for the work went into the fund of the branch.

Each evening the club, in Arbstein's house next to the Great Synagogue, was full of people, young men and women, who came to learn and also to spend time.

---

[957] Exodus 50:20 "Besides, although you intended me harm, God intended it for good, so as to bring about the present result—the survival of a great nation."

The branch was divided into groups according to age. The cultural-explanatory activity included the study of the Hebrew language, the history of Israel, literature, the workers' movement in the world and in the land. The activity was based on friendly conversations, evenings of questions and answers, literary trials, singing and dancing the *horah*,[958] outings in the forests and sailing in boats accompanied by stories and legends about the land of Israel. On special opportunities celebrations were held, and receptions around long tables.

The public appearances, for example, the trials on literary topics, achieved great participation of the community outside of *"HeChalutz HaTzair."*

At the head of the branch stood a council of five members that was elected at a general assembly, and two adult members were sent by the council of *"HeChalutz"* to help the youths.

On the council were active, among the rest: D. Aloni, Y. Aleksandroni, E. Chalupitzki, H. Lenzinger, {p. 326} S. Plotzinski, M. Freitzeit, S. Koritzki, Y. Shadmi. The representatives of *"HeChalutz"* – M. Ostrov, Leibke Shreibman, Yechezkel Sherman. Fania Bergstein and Shlomo Plotzinski (they died in the land) guided and directed the cultural-educational activity. They were family members, guides in lovingkindness, good friends, and beloved to their protégés. Breintza Ivriyah and Eliav Chalupitzki, whose power was great in social games, singing, and dancing, did not get to go up to the land, and were tragically killed in the period of the Holocaust. D. Aloni and Y. Aleksandroni live with us here in the land.

In the Vegetable Garden - Caption in the Photo
The *"HeChalutz HaTzair"* Group in Augustow After the Work in the Garden

First row from right to left: S. Koritzki… M. Freitzeit, Y. Livni, R. Rozenfeld, D. Sherman.
Second row: Y. Blacharski, A. Morzinski, M. Goldshmid, A. Barglovski, A. Sheinmar… D. Roznov.
Third row: A. Leizerovitz, … … Y. Freimark, Y. Leizerovitz, A. Preisman, Y. Goldstein, R. Tsherman, N. Portnoy.

---

[958] An Israeli folk dance.

With the passage of time, the friendship tightened and formed a kind of family; the club was their warm home. Members of *HaShomer HaTzair* were, of course, partners in carrying the yoke of the practical Zionist activity (emptying the boxes of the *Keren Kayemet L'Yisrael*, participation in movie day, etc.) The goal of the cultural activity was to train the members for *aliyah*. For this purpose age-appropriate physical training for these ages was also required, so that they would become fond of work in general. For this need we rented a plot of land and we prepared it as a vegetable garden. The fact that respected householders went out to chop wood or tend vegetables {p. 328} caused a revolution in the ideas of the town. Until then only gentiles, who were considered inferior, worked in these kinds of work. Because of the "*Chalutzim*" the value of the work went up among the Jews.

At about the age of 18 we passed to the "*HeChalutz*" organization, and in a short time we reached our turn to go out for "training." The parents, of course, objected, but after difficult discussion we won, and we went out to Kibbutz Ivtzvitz next to Baronovitz. The living conditions in the training *kibbutz* were very hard. The place was cramped. In the one small bedroom about twenty youths lay side by side on primitive beds. When they awoke from their sleep, those who had returned from the night shift lay down in their places. We worked in the sawmill. The Augustov group (Y. Bialovzetski, Barukh Chositzer, may his memory be for a blessing, A. Morzinski, M. Amit) excelled at the work, and after a few months was authorized to go up to the land. After a short stay at home, we left the city, one day after Tisha B'Av, 1929.*[959] Many came to part from us with songs of joy, while our parents parted from us in tears.

On the next day, while we were still in the capital, Warsaw, it became known to our parents from the newspapers that riots had broken out in the land. They immediately sent two emissaries to bring us home. However, we were not deterred. After a long argument, the emissaries of our parents withdrew their demand and blessed us with a safe trip.

On September 6, we reached the land.

Eliav Chalupitzki

---

[959] Original footnote: At that time B. Chositzer, M. Levinzon, M. Morzinski, M. Amit, S. Plotzinski went up.

In the Vegetable Garden
Caption in the Photo: The "*HeChalutz HaTzair*" Group in Augustow
and the Shade of the Work in the Garden

In the Vegetable Garden
Caption in the Photo:
The "*HeChalutz HaTzair*" Group in Augustow After the Work in the Garden.

From right to left: M. Amit, Y. Leizerovitz, R. Kaplanski, Y. Aleksandroni, R. Tsherman, Y. Shadmi, Channah Goldstein, Y. Piastzky, A Leizerovitz (on the horse), S. Plotzinski, B. Bidek, Y. Blacharski.
Laying down: A. Drozinski, R. Rozenfeld, … Y. Blacharski.

{p. 329} **The Council of *HeChalutz HaTzair* (1925)**

Standing: M. Ostrov, Hadassah Lenzinger, Eliav Chalupitzki.
Sitting: Yaakov Aleksandroni, Yechezkel Sherman, M. Freitzeit, Shlomo Plotzinski.

The Council of *HeChalutz HaTzair* (1926)

Standing: M. Morzinski, Yaakov Blacharski.
Sitting: L. Shreibman, S. Plotzinski, D. Aloni, Yitzchak Tabenkin, Y. Aleksandroni, L. Staviskovski.

316

{p. 330} **The Trumpeldor Group (1925)**

Standing from right to left: Rivka Blechertzik, B. Ivriyah, Miriam Olechnovitz.
Sitting: G. Blacharski, A. Vidogerski, Leah Chanikovski, R. Goldstein, H. Morzinski, Ch. Kaplan.

The "*HeChalutz HaTzair*" Council

A. Morzinski, L. Shreibman, S. Koritzki, Y. Shadmi, D. Aloni, A. Chalupitzki.

My Way to "*HeChalutz HaTzair*"
by Yishayahu Shadmi (Blechertzik)

A few reasons caused the awakening of national-Zionist feelings in the hearts of young people after the First World War.

A. The Poles that were freed from the yoke of foreigners aroused the jealously of the Jews who remained in bondage.

B. The new regime immediately began to harass the Jews, to narrow their steps and diminish their lives. The young Jew began to feel that he was sitting on a volcano, that he had no future among the gentiles. This was the driving force. On the other hand, the compelling force: the atmosphere that we absorbed in the religious or traditional house, and the education that we acquired with the good teachers. The parents were good Jews, proud, healthy in their souls and their bodies, tied to the ancestral heritage. They insisted on overcoming all the obstacles, and not to surrender to their oppressors. With our mothers' milk we too absorbed these qualities. When I heard father praying with devotion "and let our eyes behold your return to Zion with compassion"[960] it would make my heart tremble. The teachers saw to not only teaching us, but also to plant in our hearts a love of nation and Zion. I am reminded of the powerful impression that the huge collection that took place in the Great Synagogue following the San Remo decision left on me and on my friends, in which our mothers donated jewelry for the redemption fund. A short time after the collection, the first *olim* from the city went up to the land, and this too aroused yearning in us.

I remember a collection for work tools on behalf of "*Kapai*" for the workers of the land of Israel. My father donated a pliers that was very dear to him that he inherited from his grandfather. It is no wonder, therefore, that we jointly searched for an outlet for our dreams. In this way the scouts' organization "The Trumpeldor Guard" arose, which better expressed the desires of the generation, and in a short time inherited the place of the "*HeChalutz HaTzair*" organization. Each evening we gathered in the club. An intensive educational activity was conducted. One of the regulations set the obligation to speak Hebrew, and whoever made a mistake had to pay a fine for the benefit of the *Keren Kayemet L'Yisrael*. We read the Hebrew journalism "*HaYom*" and "*HeChalutz HaTzair*" that appeared in Poland, and the "*Kuntrus*," "*HaPoel HaTzair*" and "*Davar*," that came to us from the land. This was not just reading, for every week we were tested on everything that was connected to the land, to the "*Histadrut*,"[961] and to the collective movement. This method spurred us to deep reading. Each one attempted to be in order and not to fail. Many members began to learn professions suited to the needs of the land, for we decided to cut ourselves off from the exilic livelihoods of our parents. Our aspiration was to be workers of the soil in the land, and we began to train ourselves by means of working a vegetable garden on a plot of land that we rented on "The Long Street." When we became adults and transferred to the "*HeChalutz*" organization, we went out {p. 332} for training, and after it we went

---

[960] From the liturgy.
[961] The General Organization of Workers in Israel, *HaHistadrut HaKlalit shel HaOvdim B'Eretz Yisrael.*

up to the land. The "*yordim*"[962] from the land that brought bad reports[963] did not dissuade us, and the crises and incidents[964] that broke out from time to time did after the son, that his brothers and sisters who were younger than him went up, and the parents with them. The chain was cut, to our great anguish, when the bitter enemy succeeded in destroying everything. Were it not for the tragedy that befell our people, we would have achieved that the great majority of the members of our city would be living with us – in the State of Israel.

Members of the "*HeChalutz HaTzair*" Branch (1928)

First row top from right to left: R. Rozenfeld, A. Vidogerski, Zaviela, G. Blacharski, Y. Otstein, D. Slovtitzki, R. Blechertzik, Z. Ampel.
Second row: D. Topolovski, A. Arbstein, P. Cohain, Y. Blacharski, B. Morzinski, Y. Freimark, A. Drozinski, R. Kaplanski, S. Lifshitz.
Third row: A. Leizerovitz, H. Morzinski, M. Amit, Fania Bergstein, A. Chalupitzki, D. Sherman, A. Barglovski, M. Kahn.
Fourth row: Sh. Gravinski, Staviskovski, R. Goldstein, S. Plotzinski, Ch. Kaplan, … L. Chanikovski, A. Aleksandrovitz, M. Olchnovitz.

---

[962] This word means "descenders" and is the opposite of the word *olim*. It is a disparaging term for those who left the land of Israel and returned to Europe.
[963] Genesis 37:2 "…And Joseph brought bad reports of them to their father."
[964] This word in this context refers to Arab riots against the Jews in the land during the period of the British Mandate, between the end of the First World War and the Establishment of the State of Israel.

The *HaShomer* branch was established in Augustow at the end of the summer of 1927. The *"HaShomer HaTzair"* movement reached us after it had already undergone a period of searching for a way.

This was already a movement on the way to its consolidation, a movement that became one of the vigorous expressions of the fermenting Jewish youth.

The world view of *HaShomer* was not for the Jewish youth a specific political program, but rather a worldview vis-à-vis all of life. The *"HaShomer HaTzair"* movement was already then founded on the connection of its members to the Jewish people, and on the principle of personal-pioneer realization. The emphasis was placed especially on the design of the nature of the person, on his nearness to nature, on his deep education that he is a part of the new human society.

This movement was the fruit of a stormy period of the beginning of the 20th century – the conclusion of the First World War, the revolution in Russia, the Balfour Declaration. This was the background in which the buds of the movement sprouted.

That same ferment that surrounded the Jewish youth in the diaspora that period did not skip over the Jewish youth in Augustow.

The hearts were full of dreams of a repaired world, of a homeland, of a proud Jewish person in the land of the ancestors, of the work of one's hands. These dreams led the Jewish youth to various political movements. There were those who saw the focus as a class war, a war of equal rights, and there were those who saw the exile as only a vestibule,[965] and the most important thing was *aliyah* to the land. And there were those who walked in the footsteps of the brilliant analysis of Borochov.[966]

Indeed, all of that mosaic of ideas found its expression in our city as well. There was some of everything in it. *"Bund,"* *"Tzeirei Tzion,"* *"Poalei Tzion,"* in its two factions, and of course also *"HeChalutz."*

{p. 334} Each one chose for himself the way that was closest to himself. The division was not according to echelon or class. It was possible to find more than a few families where each member of the family belonged to another stream. The feast at the shared table – more than one turned into a political symposium.

The *"HaShomer HaTzair"* movement was founded after other movements preceded it. It was possible to suppose that there was no living space for another movement. And yet see a wonder: with the first announcement of the foundation of the movement, tens of members of the youth immediately presented themselves in its ranks. When we come to tell the story of *"HaShomer HaTzair"* in Augustow, it is impossible not to mention the young men and women, the boys and girls, the beautiful and pure-hearted. All of them, we must remember all of them.

---

[965] *Mishnah Avot* 4:16 "Rabbi Jacob said: this world is like a vestibule before the world to come; prepare yourself in the vestibule, so that you may enter the banqueting-hall."
[966] Dov Ber Borochov, 1881 – 1917, was a Marxist Zionist and one of the founders of the Labor Zionist movement.

There were some whose path was consistent. From the movement – to training – to *aliyah* – to the *kibbutz*. And all of their lives were dedicated to this movement, until this day. To our deep sorrow they are alone.

The "*HaShomer HaTzair*" Branch

Row 1, from right to left: Yaakov Trestzenski, Channah Gotlib, Yekutiel, Feigl Sarvianski, Gershovitz, Rachel Aleksandrovitz, Kentzuk, S. Zupnitzki.
Second Row: Kestin, Peshke Aronovski, ... Fredka Aleksandrovitz, L. Blech, R. Gotstein, Z. Leizerovski, B. Rotstein.
Third row: Y. Feivovorski, S. Kaplan, Freyda Sarvinski, Z. Kentzuk, Zenya Yones, Domovitz, Esther Ivraiski, Volmir.
Fourth row: S. Kaplanski, Berta Grosberg, Beila Ratzitzki, Edah Mintz, Y. Ratzitzki, Liza Saperstein, Sonka Kleinman.

{p. 335} There were those who reached the land and for various reasons did not continue to the kibbutz. They were weak and had little faith, and were not able to live up to the ten commandments of *HaShomer*.[967]   The charms of the present overcame them, and they dropped

---

[967] The Ten Commandments of *HaShomer HaTzair*:
1. The *Shomer/et* is a man/woman of truth and stands on its guard.
2. The *Shomer/et* is an integral part of the Jewish people and strongly connected to the State of Israel. He/she is rooted in his/her culture and is a *chalutz/a* of our Judaism.
3. The *Shomer/et* finds meaning in his/her relationship to work and fights to create a world where labor is a productive expression of human creativity and freedom.
4. The *Shomer/et* is politically active and a forerunner in the pursuit of freedom, equality, peace and solidarity.
5. The *Shomer/et* is a committed *chaver/a* that works jointly with others, struggles for the progress of society and promotes *Shomer* values.
6. The *Shomer/et* actively develops and maintains relationships which are intentional, free and honest within the group and the whole Shomer community. He/She takes the responsibility to look after his/her *chaverim*.

out. And there were those who carried with them the dream of *HaShomer HaTzair* on their final path, the path of suffering, which the Jewish people walked during the years of the *Shoah*. For these, for the last, let these lines be a memorial.

Who were the youth that joined the movement? These were not those who had left other movements. This was principally youth who, for some reason, did not find their place in one of the existing movements.

There was not a high school in our city. One who wanted to continue in their learning had to wander to far-off places. Not all of them were able to withstand that. Part of these youth, who for various reasons were not able to continue in their studies or were forced to stop them, constituted the foundation of the *Shomer* branch in Augustow. Indeed, even working youth, or partly working, found their way to "*HaShomer HaTzair*." And there was in this {p. 336} great blessing. The synthesis between the working and learning youth formed, on the one hand, a folksy atmosphere, and on the other hand, caused a broadening of horizons.

HaShomer HaTzair Branch

Row 1 (from right to left): S. Kaplan, Yehuda Gershovitz, Rachel Aleksandrovitz, Drozinski, Noach Sarvianski, Y. Feivovorski, Volmir, Zelda Lenzinger, Yocheved Preis, Freydka Sarvianski, Esther Ivraiski.
Row 2: Devorah Staviskovski, Leah Strozinski, Batya Gizumski, Dora Borovitz, Edah Mintz, Feshka Aronovski, Freydka Aleksandrovitz.
Row 3: Grodzin, Zelda Grodzin, Levatinski, Dovka, Beilka, Devorah Kremer, Sheindel Kolfenitzki, Hadassah Lenzinger, Leizerovski.
Row 4: … Golda Eilender, Bilovzetzki, B. Ratzitzki, Zenya Yones, Feigl Sarvianski, Tuvia Feivoshvitz, … M. Volmir.

---

7. The *Shomer/et* respects and cares about nature; he/she gets to know it, learns how to live within it and acts in accordance with sustainable practices.
8. *The Shomer/et* is courageous, independent, thinks critically and takes initiative accordingly.
9. The *Shomer/et* strengthens his/her character and strives towards physical, mental and spiritual wholeness.
10. The *Shomer/et* is led by his/her reason and takes full responsibility for his/her actions. He/she sets a personal example.

322

The foundation of the branch encountered sharp opposition from the existing organizations, who saw it as a serious competitor for the same human material from which "*HeChalutz*" and "*HeChalutz HaTzair*" drew its members. Not so the adult Jewish female member. She accepted us with great encouragement, and even political opponents sworn as general Zionists, and Revisionists. Here Mr. Abba Orimland must be mentioned favorably. Although he was from a political aspect a rival, he was among the first that signed off on the request to receive a permit from the Polish authorities to establish the branch.

As was said, the ranks of the branch were immediately filled with young men and women of varying ages. There were male and female "Seniors," ages 17-18, the scouts, girls and boys, ages 14-16, and the young lions, the youngest, to whom the Seniors served as counselors.

The branch began its active life when the main part of the work was concentrated in the *Shomer* group, the same *Shomer* group that was like a kind of new house for the youth. In it was conducted varied activity. It began from the scouting game {p. 338} for education about the character of the individual, reading together in a book, the analysis, the dream, to the point of confession and self-examination. We conducted the activities in two areas: in the bosom of nature, and in the branch.

"HaShomer HaTzair" Branch

Vilensky, Kolfenitzki, D. Kremer, Sarvianski, Gershovitz, S. Kaplan, Levatinski, Edah Mintz, Golda Eilender, Fredka Aleksandrovitz, Freydka Sarvianski, Esther Ivriyah, Yocheved Preis.
Second row: Zelda Lenzinger, L. Starazinsky, Channah Linda, Esther Eilender, Devorah Staviskovski, Rachel Aleksandrovitz, Feshka Aronovitz.
Third row: Shmuel Zupnitzki, Selke Kaufman, Rivka Rozenfeld, Yekutiel, Feigeleh Sarvianski, Beila Rotstein, Channah Gotlib.

{p. 337} *"HaShomer HaTzair"* Branch

"HaShomer HaTzair" Branch

Caption in the Photo: *"HaShomer HaTzair"* Branch in Augustow on a One-Day Boating Expedition, 18 Tamuz, the Year 5687 [1927].

From right to left: Yoske Levatinski, Channah Gotlib, Esther Ivraiski, Freydka Sarvianski, … … Esther Eilender, Zelda Lenzinger, … Sonka Kleinman, … Berta Grosberg, Feshka Aronovitz, Fredka Aleksandrovitz, Golda Eilender, Yehuda Gershovitz, Feigeleh Sarvianski, Noach Sarvianski, Kolfenitzki, Dovka Vilensky, Leka Starazinsky, Rachel Aleksandrovitz, Channah Linda, Rivka Rozenfeld, Yekutiel, Shabtai Kaplan, Selke Kaufman, Yaakov Trestzenski. Next to the bicycles, Shmuel Zupnitzki.

The wonderful paths of the forest and the lakes that were hidden within them, no one was witness to our games, our songs, and our conversations. In the evening the *"HaShomer HaTzair"* branch was crowded with happy youth, dancing and singing. Of course, more than once we were a burden on the neighbors "that we were dancing on their heads," and more than once we were forced to wander, until we were securely housed, until the last day, in the house of the Aleksandrovitz family, who spread its wings over us, and we, in return, spread our wings over the daughters of the family (Fredka, Rachel, and Channah).

The *"Shomrot"*[968] Group

Standing from right to left: A. Eilender, M. Shumski, Ch. Lozman, B. Blacharski …
Sitting: Zenya Yones, S. B. Dubrin, Lenzinger, R. Halprin.
Third row: F. Sarvianski, Liza Borovitz, Esther Ivriyah.

The period of foundation and organization went by, and life entered a normal course. The youths sought to fulfill the "movement commandments": going out to a summer colony or for training. A clash between the parents and the children suddenly appeared; the period of the "revolt of the child" began.

The parents saw *"HaShomer HaTzair"* as a place for games, for spending time, and no more. That feeling {p. 339} that their children had, that the exile was a vestibule, that the ground was burning under their feet, that the true way was the way of realization and *aliyah* to the land, was not the parents' portion. More than once we were helped by Mother Aleksandrovitz,*[969] who placed on herself the difficult role – to influence other mothers, who would make it possible for their sons and daughters to participate in the activities of the movement, in summer colonies or in training.

---

[968] The feminine plural form of the word *shomer*, guard.
[969] Original footnote: * Chaitza.

... Shabtai Kaplan, Freydka Sarvianski, Zenya Yones, Esther Ivriyah, Edah Mintz

The movement continued to ferment. Its economic existence was based on independent actions, taxes and the organization of receptions, which became a cultural experience for the youth of the town.

The members of "*HaShomer HaTzair*" took an active part in the activities of the Zionist movement. Especially beloved to the youth was the activity of emptying "The Blue Box," the same box that was in many houses the finest ornament. With fear and love[970] they would volunteer for this work, and more than once we were welcomed warmly into the houses of the poor of the people, and the opposite – into the houses of the "Lords."

Also from the aspect of powers of leadership the branch carried itself, except for the adult echelon.

The adult echelon based its work mainly on self-education and group work. In light of the lack of a high school in Augustow, this had a special reality. Here one must mention {p. 340} especially the important role that was fulfilled by the librarian Shaika Plotzinski, may his memory be for a blessing, who faithfully and devotedly guided the library visitors, in offering to each one the appropriate book for them.

The problem of the lack of counselors was sharply felt with the *aliyah* to the land of the first counselors. However, the movement did not neglect the Augustovi branch. With the help of counselors from outside the expected activity was continued. In this way the matters of the movement were administered in an orderly fashion until the year 1931, the year of the departure of the adult echelon, the counselors, for training.

---

[970] In Aramaic.

A change of guard took place. The scouts that grew up in the movement took upon themselves the leadership of the branch. The load was too heavy, and they could not withstand it. In the year 1933, when the adult *Shomrim* returned from training they found the branch in a condition of disintegration. They energetically took upon themselves the renewed organizing. Again the branch blossomed, the ranks were filled, the groups led their lives in proper order.

A great privilege fell to me. I was able to accompany the "*HaShomer HaTzair*" movement in Augustow from its first steps. A sad privilege also fell to me – to tell the last story. In the year 1939, a month before the outbreak of the Second World War, I spent a number of weeks in Poland, and it was natural that I came to visit in Augustow. On one of the wonderful summer evenings the entire branch gathered in the forest, on the bank of a lake. Surrounded by young men and women, most of whom I did not know, I told them about the shared education on the *kibbutz*. Eyes sparkling with curiosity, with desire to know, eyes yearning, longings and dreams, accompanied my story. The conversation flowed for a long hour. The singing reverberated a distance among the pine trees. I and they – did not know that this was the end.   **Ein Shemer 5724 [1964]**

{p. 341} **The *Beitar* Movement and *HaTzohar*[971] in Augustow**
by Dr. Moshe Markus

The beginning of the Revisionist movement, *HaTzohar*, within the Zionist movement, was in 1924. In that period the first nucleus of the Revisionist youth movement *Beitar* (*Brit Trumpeldor*)[972] was also established.

The movement spread in all the countries of the exile, and achieved a significant scope in Poland.

With the conclusion of my studies at universities in Germany and Prague, I returned to Augustow. In those days I arranged a lecture, in the local movie theatre on "The Long Street," about the *HaTzohar* movement and *Beitar*. The organization of *Beitar* began as a continuation of that, and the lawyer Moshe Gotkovski from Suwalk (today he lives in Tel Aviv) was invited to the founding assembly. The lecture took place in the great hall that was on "*Zoibgasse*," and drew a large audience. Already then the Revisionist movement and *Beitar* were the topic of many arguments on the Zionist street. With the enthusiasm of the violent ideological and organizational struggle between the Zionist youth movements, the lecture went by amid great commotion and many disturbances.

After the lecture the first groups of *HaTzohar* and *Beitar* were organized. Veteran members of the Zionists joined the movement in the city, and a youth group that served as the foundation of the *Beitar* branch. Over the course of many years Mr. Abba Orimland served as Chairperson of the movement and its representative to the government.

Among the active members of *Beitar* one must mention: the Commander of *Beitar* Yechezkel Rotstein, Arieh Borovitz, Eli Noach Stolnitzki, Alter Kaplanski, Moshe Glikstein, Yaakov Gotlib, Chaim Orimland, and Bielka Papirovitz.

The first female Commander of the *Beitar* branch in Augustow, at whose head stood Yechezkel Rotstein, was active until 1938. From his hands Bielka Papirovitz received the command, and she led the branch until her *aliyah* to the land (a month before the outbreak of the Second World War in 1939). Yechezkel Rotstein was exiled in the days of the war to Russia, where

---

[971] Another name for *Beitar*, named for Yosef Trumpeldor.
[972] A Revisionist Zionist youth movement founded in 1923 in Riga, Latvia, by Vladimir (Ze'ev) Jabotinsky.

327

he was drafted into the Red Army and killed on the Finland front. Bielka Papirovitz was a student at the Hebrew University in Jerusalem, when she was killed by Arab snipers' bullets on her way to Har HaTzofim.[973]

The people of the Revisionist movement and *Beitar* in Augustow were active in the Zionist and cultural life in the city. They participated, together with the people of the other Zionist movements, in all the activities and fundraising campaigns for the benefit of the land of Israel, and engaged in pioneer training of their members in preparation for their *aliyah* to the land.

The *Beitar* branch operated in Augustow until the outbreak of the war. When the Russians entered the city, {p. 342} all Zionist activity was stopped. Many members of the movement were imprisoned, among them the Chairperson of the movement in the city Mr. Abba Orimland, who was exiled to Russia together with his family, and died there. His family returned from exile in Siberia at the end of the war, and settled in the land. His son Chaim went up to the land in the ship "Altalena."[974]

Only a few were saved from the *Shoah*. Individual members of *Beitar* found their way to the land. In this way the reaper came up against the idealistic youth movement *Beitar* in Augustow, which aspired and educated for *aliyah* and realization in the land.

HaMizrachi

HaMizrachi in our town experienced continual growth. The *Torah VeAvodah*[975] movement was also growing from day to day. Thanks to the members of the *HaMizrachi* committee, Messrs Binyomin Zhelaze (chairman), Sender Lenzinger (secretary), Moyshe Rabinovitsh (treasurer), a massive recruitment campaign was organized to increase membership. With this goal in mind, last *Peysach*, the *HaMizrachi* and *Torah VeAvodah* movements organized a grand festive celebration. The event was opened by the head of *HeKhalutz HaMizrachi*, Mr. Yoysef Gizomski, who shared the stage with Rabbi Khayim and Yoyl Grudzien. Other speakers included: Rabbi Gedalye Gizomski, Reb Yankev Tuker, and the members of the *Torah VeAvodah* movement, Binyomin Badenes (Kibbutz Mohilover), Moyshe Yehuda Grudzien (director of *Tarbut*) and Ben-Tsien Fulvinski.

Moment 1934 (No. 96)

The Great Synagogue

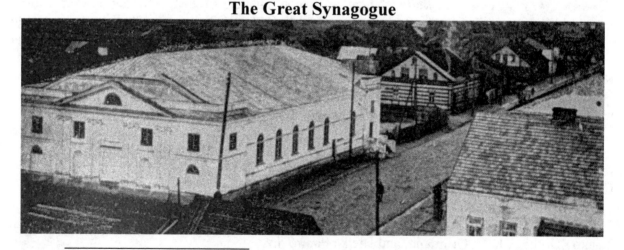

---

[973] Mt. Scopus.

[974] The Altalena Affair was a confrontation in June 1948 between the Israel Defense Forces and the *Irgun* (*HaIrgun HaTzva'i HaLeumi B'Eretz Yisrael*, "The National Military Organization in the Land of Israel"), one of the Jewish paramilitary groups, led by Menachem Begin, that was merging with the IDF. The Altalena had been loaded with weapons and fighters by the *Irgun*, but arrived during the period of the *Irgun*'s absorption into the IDF. There was shooting took place the IDF and the *Irgun*, 19 men were killed, and the ship caught fire from the shooting and the arms it contained.

[975] "Torah and Labor," a religious Zionist movement.

"… In the future, the synagogues and the study halls in Babylonia will be transported and reestablished in Eretz Yisrael…" Babylonian *Talmud Megillah* 29a

Synagogues in Augustow
By Rabbi Yekutiel Azrieli

I bring to light the synagogues and their activity on the holy days and the secular days. They concentrated around them all the members of our city, almost without exception. There, the people of almost every status found a place for themselves; the worker, the porter, the waggoneer, the craftspeople, the small merchant, the wholesaler, the forest merchant and the exporters of wood from the forests of Augustow.

In the synagogues that were scattered throughout the city, every street with its own synagogue, they prayed morning and evening. In a few of them they also set various *Torah* lessons between the afternoon and evening prayers. There Jews of the town also found for themselves a place to converse, each one with their friends, from the aspect of "speaking about his worries and it will benefit him."[976]

* The Great Synagogue was wrapped in legends. Its wonderful structure, tall in height and on a large plot, was able to contain about 2000 people inside of it. On its tall windows, artistic colored suns. The Holy Ark was double; with the opening of its doors, another two doors were opened above, which covered over a gloriously made *menorah* with its arms, its calyxes, and its flowers.[977] The synagogue served also for large public gatherings of both joy and sorrow. There were also in the vestibule of the synagogue two branches, *kloizen*, that prayed in them morning and evening, regularly every day. Formerly the large yard of the synagogue served for setting up wedding canopies for the weddings of members of the city.

* Facing each other stood two prayer houses on the one side of the street of the Great Synagogue, and across from it, on the other side of the street, a *Beit Midrash*, in which there were also two branches, *kloizen*, in the vestibule. The name of this street was The Street of the Synagogue (*Shul Gasse*).

The *Beit Midrash* served as a place of prayer every day, evening and morning, and also for lessons, and for various *Torah* learning. Also, individuals who worked diligently in *Torah* study secluded themselves in it during the course of the day in order to learn inspiration from within

---

[976] Job 32:20 "Let me speak, then, and it will benefit me…"
[977] Exodus 25:31 "You shall make a lampstand of pure gold; the lampstand shall be made of hammered work; its base and its shaft, its cups, calyxes, and petals shall be of one piece." The word for shaft is misspelled here, with a *kaf* כ instead of a *kuf* ק.

329

{p. 344} **The Remains of the Synagogue in Augustow**

"*Yatke Kloiz*" after the Destruction (1945)

{p. 345}The Great Synagogue (south side) After the Destruction

Beit HaMidrash

{p. 346}and to use the *Torah* library that was there. *Beit HaMidrash* served also as a meeting place for *Torah* sages: two groups to study *Talmud*, a group to learn *Mishnah* and *Ein Yaakov*, and a group that recited Psalms on the winter nights after midnight until the light of morning, and heard a *Torah* "*drasha*"[978] on one of the chapters of the Psalms.

      Beit HaMidrash served as a forum for the Rabbi's homilies, and every visiting scholar was honored in it with a *drasha* before the community. From the podium of the *Beit HaMidrash* all the public calls went out that concerned the public and the community, and it also served as a regular place of prayer for the local Rabbi.

The Prayer House Previously. Today, a Dairy

      The two wings that were in the vestibule served as a gathering place for prayer and learning for specific groups. They called the right-hand wing "The *Chevra Kadisha Kloiz*," and the left-hand wing they called "The Shoemakers' *Kloiz*." The left-hand wing principally served as a place for *Torah* lessons, in which the public was organized, maintained a "*maggid shiur*"[979] at its expense, and would very much multiply joy on *Simchat Torah*, and also they were punctilious to celebrate there with much magnificence the 7th of Adar, the day of the birth and death of Moshe our Rabbi, peace be upon him, in prayer and in lighting candles according to the numerical value of his name – 345[980] - in a framework made in the shape of a *Magen David*[981]and hung from the ceiling.

---

[978] A homiletical teaching.
[979] One who preached a lesson.
[980] The Hebrew letters of the name *Moshe*: *Mem* = 40, *Shin* = 300, and *Hey* = 5.
[981] Shield of David, a Jewish star.

* The synagogue that stood on the Street of the Butcher (*Yatke Gasse*), they called the "*Yatke Kloiz*." Previously they called it *Kloiz HaChassidim*. This synagogue was distinguished by a concentration of owners of important houses, knowers of {p. 347} *Torah*. The *Shamash* of the synagogue also was a man who knew *Torah*, the teller of the lesson in the *Shas* group of this synagogue.

In this synagogue they also prayed morning and evening. It served as a center for learned people, those who came out of the *yeshivot*, who made it a regular place for their studies. There was also in it an important *Torah* library.

* The worshippers of *Beit HaMidrash* and the prayer houses (the *kloizen*) carried the yoke of the financial support of the members of the *yeshivot* who came for recuperation in the days of summer, to breathe clear air in the pine forests that were next to the city. The members of the *yeshiva* persevered in *Torah* study even when they were found in our city, and left it in bodily and spiritual health to continue in their studies with greater vigor in the halls of the great *yeshivot*.

The Great Synagogue (1945)

* There were also another two prayer houses: on the Bridge Street (*Brik-Gasse*), and on the Long Street (*Lange-Gasse*) in which public prayer three times a day did not stop. And *Torah* lessons also took place in them every day, and especially on the *Shabbatot*, by tellers of lessons who knew *Torah*. They were cherished by the worshippers out of love and affection for their glory and magnificence. *Tzedakah* and *chesed* funds for every need were maintained by them, out of respect for others who were in need of *chesed*, for an hour or for a long time. A society for visiting the sick (*Leinei Tzedek*) for the time of trouble and illness.

These synagogues became the magnificence and splendor of the community of Augustow. The sound of the *Torah* that reverberated from within them {p. 348} proved that the Augustow community kept faith with the faithful Jewish spirit, which continued the Jewish tradition from generation to generation.   **Zikhron Yaakov**

The Great Synagogue
By Elchanan Sarvianski

The Great Synagogue was a tall building, whose walls were thick, and its windows tall and narrow. The windowpanes were colored and decorated with pictures, the roof and the rafters were supported by 8 round pillars, built from burnt bricks, in a diameter of about 80 x 80 centimeters, which served as a place for national rallies. They ascended by seven broad steps, to a vestibule of the synagogue. From the vestibule one would descend at a depth of seven steps, to fulfill what is said: "From the depths I called Yah."[982] In the balcony was the women's section. In the vestibule, wide open, were two small prayer houses, the *Kloiz* of the Butchers, and the *Kloiz* of the synagogue.

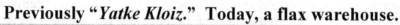

Previously "*Yatke Kloiz*." Today, a flax warehouse.

The *aron kodesh* in the Great Synagogue was a masterpiece, and work of art. It was three stories tall. On its doors and its two sides were wood carvings and images of leopards, snakes, eagles, birds, cherubs,[983] and various verses. Also on the round pillars, which supported the *aron kodesh* on its two sides, were fine carvings. On the third floor there was a *Torah* crown, with all kinds of {p. 349} carvings. On the opening of the *aron kodesh*, the doors opened at once on all three stories. On the first floor were the *Torah* scrolls. On the second story the tree of knowledge

---

[982] Psalm 130: 1 "A song of ascents. Out of the depths I call You, Adonoi."

[983] The cherubs are celestial winged beings with human, animal, or birdlike characteristics who function as throne bearers of the Deity, or guards. In the *Torah* they are found in pairs, guarding the way back to the Garden of Eden, Genesis 3:2 "He drove the man out, and stationed east of the garden of Eden the cherubim and the fiery ever-turning sword, to guard the way to the tree of life," and sitting on top of the ark of the covenant, Exodus 25:20 "The cherubim shall have their wings spread out above, shielding the cover with their wings. They shall face each other, the faces of the cherubim being turned toward the cover."

was carved, and on its branches, its fruits.[984] On the third story there was an image of an eagle[985] made of wood, standing on a small *menorah*.[986] Above it, in the dome of the ceiling, two great lions were drawn.[987]

The Remains of the Magnificent *Aron Kodesh*

The great Synagogue was open only on *Shabbatot* and festivals. Among the worshippers were: The Rabbi the *Gaon* Reb Katriel Natan, and the Rabbi the Teacher of Righteousness Reb Azriel Zelig Koshelevski. Among the prayer leaders who passed before the ark in the synagogue on *Shabbatot* and festivals were Reb Reuven Rotenberg, peace be upon him; Lobel, may peace be upon him, the *shacharit* leader;[988] the tailor Reb Mendel Kolfenitzki, may God avenge his blood; Reb Velvele Hotshein (the baker), may God avenge his blood; the leader of the *mussaf*[989] service, and sometimes the leader of *Kol Nidre*, the *shochet* Reb Gedalyahu Gizumski, may God avenge his blood. When Reb Katriel Natan served as Rabbi in the city, he was the *shaliach tzibur* for *Kol Nidre*. The *gabbai* at that time was Reb Pinchas (Piniya) Ahronovski, may God avenge his blood, and the *shamash*, Reb Moshe Dovid Morzinski, may God avenge his blood. On Shabbatot and festivals in the afternoons many of the Jews of Augustow would gather in the synagogue to recite chapters of Psalms until *Mincha*,[990] and after it. Among the regular "passers before the ark" in the

---

[984] The *Torah* is called the Tree of Life, and its partner in the Garden of Eden was the Tree of Knowledge. Its fruit is the fruit that the man and woman ate before being expelled from the garden.

[985] The eagle is a symbol of the Exodus: Exodus 19:4 "'You have seen what I did to the Egyptians, how I bore you on eagles' wings and brought you to Me."

[986] The *menorah* here is not the 8-branched *Chanukah menorah*, but the 7-branched menorah that stood in the Jerusalem Temple, its seven branches representing the 7 days of creation.

[987] The lions are the symbol of the tribe of Judah, the tribe from which the Davidic kings descend, and one of the two surviving tribes of Israel after the exile of the "10 lost tribes" in 722 BCE. Jews today trace their lineage either to the tribe of Judah or the tribe of Levi. Genesis 49:9 "Judah is a lion's whelp; On prey, my son, have you grown. He crouches, lies down like a lion, Like the king of beasts—who dare rouse him?"

[988] The morning prayers.

[989] The additional service that follows the morning service.

[990] The afternoon service.

kloiz of the butchers were included the butcher Reb Sender-Moshe Kaplan; may God avenge his blood, Reb Mottel (the *Farbrenter*[991]) may God avenge his blood; Reb Mendel Kolfenitzki, may God avenge his blood. The *gabbai* was Reb Zovel Korotnitztki. Most of the worshippers there were butchers, and with them, the *shochetim*: Reb Chaim-Zalman Kaplan, and his brother-in-law Reb Moshe-Lev Shidlovski.

On *Shabbat* night, after a festive evening meal, the butchers would gather in their prayer house, and learn the weekly *Torah* portion from the mouth of Rabbi Reb Azriel Zelig Koshelevski, may God avenge his blood. On the secular days, the *shochet* Reb Gedalyahu Gizumski, may God avenge his blood, and the *shochet* Reb Chaim Zalman Kaplanski, may God avenge his blood, would teach there the "*Ein Yaakov.*"

{p. 350} Across from the *Kloiz* of the butchers was found the *Kloiz* of the synagogue; the *shamash* was Reb Brill (the painter), may God avenge his blood, and the *gabbai*, Reb Asher Hempel, may God avenge his blood.

After the conquest of the city by the Nazis, the synagogue served them as a warehouse. In the middle of the year 1944 they fixed their headquarters there. The Russians paid attention that the Germans were in the house; they blew it up and destroyed it.

The *Beit Midrash* was open all the days of the week. On secular days, and also on *Shabbatot*, two minyanim would pray there. In the evenings they would learn *Torah* there. Reb Itshe Chositzer, may his memory be for a blessing, until his *aliyah* to the land, and after him Reb Velvel Zelivanski, served as *shamashim* in it. Not far from the entrance, for the entire width of the *Beit Midrash*, two tables were set up with long simple benches next to them. The table that was on the right side belonged to the study of *Gemara* (the *Shas* Society), while the one on the left was for the *Mishnah* Society. Next to the *Gemara* table sat the sharp-minded; the pharmacist Reb Meir Koifman, Mintz, Reb Binyamin Markus, Chefetz, Reb Yisrael Barukh Lieberman, and others. Among those who sat at the tables of the *Mishnah*s: a thin and short-statured man, but with a sharp mind, Reb Zissel Zlotnizki; Reb Sender-Moshe Lenzinger and his father; Yisrael Katzman and his father (tailors); and many more. At this table Rabbi Reb Azriel Zelig Koshelevski guided and taught. In the other corners of the *Beit Midrash*, *yeshiva* boys would learn individually. Next to the stove two scholars exalted in *Torah* and in years would sit: one blind, Reb Yaakov Rubenstein, (a tavern owner), and his partner, Katzman the elder, who merited four generation of *Torah* learners. Reb Yaakov Rubenstein used to sail in the sea of the *Talmud* by heart, and Katzman the elder would accompany him in his reading from the open *Gemara*. In the circle of friends they would review their *Talmud* until the middle of the night. Also in the *Beit Midrash* building were another two prayer houses. On the right side of the entrance, the *Kloiz* of the *Chevra Kadisha*, the *gabbai*, Friedman, (the oven builder), may God avenge his blood. Reb Chaim Yoel Grodzin used to teach the weekly portion there every day, and on *Shabbat* in the afternoon, *Mishnah*s. On the left side was found the *Kloiz* of the shoemakers, and Reb Itze Preis, may God avenge his blood, used to teach in it. The *Beit Midrash* was entirely destroyed, to the foundation, by the Nazis, and no memory of it remains.

The *Yatke Kloiz*, which was not like the other small prayer houses, was found inside a special building. A large building, pleasant enough, and in it was a new and beautiful *aron kodesh*. The building was found on Mitzkivitzke Street (*Ziava Gasse*). Its rear portion bordered almost to the old cemetery. Many prayed in it, of all classes. The *gabbai* was Reb Itze Rotenberg, may God avenge his blood, the *shamash* was Reb Meir Lozovski (Grubauer), may God avenge his blood.

In the year 1932, or 1933, the "*Yatke Kloiz*" celebrated the completion of the work of the new and beautiful *aron kodesh*. At the time of the putting of the *Torah* scrolls into it, the band of

---

[991] The "burning" or pious one.

the young men of Augustow played: Bidek; Zhimka Kaplan; the son of Shimon Rozenhof, a Ratzk man; Leibl, the son of Shaika the chimney cleaner, and Shaika himself was the drummer. The walls of the building remained intact, but within, all was destroyed. **Kfar Malal**

{p. 351} *Linat HaTzedek*
by Mordechai Aharon Migdael

To the credit of "*Chovevei Tzion*" in Augustow one must mention the matter of the founding of the "*Chevrat Linat HaTzedek*"[992] in this city in the year 1899. In "*HaTzefirah*" of the year mentioned above, (Number 41), we read:

"The excellent preacher of Zionism, Dr. Hecht, agreed to turn aside to our city Augustov, and excited the hearts with his sublime homilies that he preached about Zion and its events, and about two hundred and fifty people volunteered to participate with their *shekel*s for the support of the fund of the national council.

By the way, the correspondent informs about the activity of "*Tzeirei HaChovevim*"[993] that "In their dedication to the idea of Zionism as their hearts' desire, their hearts are aroused to every good action within our community, and they have established in it a "*Linat HaTzedek*" association, the lack of which was very much felt. About eighty youth are participating in its activities, and they purchased the necessary equipment for a proper price, for the use of the ill. And when a person from within the community became ill, even if they were not one of the members, the association would offer them its help to provide for all their lacks, and would even send two of its members to alternate spending the night next to the bed of the sick person, to keep watch over them.

Functionaries of *Linat HaTzedek* – Visiting the Sick

From right to left: Shmuel Meir Goldshmid, Mordechai Staviskovski (Mottinke the Sweet), Avraham-Dovid Rozenfeld, … Mordechai Volmir.

---

[992] The Association of the Charitable Hostel.
[993] The Youths of the Lovers.

{p. 352} In general, this institution excelled in its arrangements and its good governance, and in its management did not fall short compared to the houses of *chesed* that were in the big cities. The writer of this notice is the *shaliach tzibur* and the *shochet u'bodek* Yosef Chaim Ratner.

In "*HaTzefirah*" from the year 1911 No. 142 we read about the celebration of the completion of the writing of a *sefer Torah*. "On Thursday, *Parashat Beha'alotecha*,[994] the members of the "*Linat HaTzedek*" society, most of whom are poor workers and craftspeople, celebrated the festival of "the completion of the *Torah*," and on the evening of that day they transported the *sefer* with great pomp and grandeur to the Great Synagogue.

The celebration drew to it many of the important Christians, such as the Minister of the District and his deputy, the City Minister and his secretary, and the good arrangements and the great splendor that prevailed in the house produced pleasure for them. The Rabbi Our Teacher Reb Katriel ascended the podium and expressed to the members of the society the feelings of thanks of all of the community. On the great benefit that they were bringing to the sick of the city and its poor people, and in his warm words, he strengthened their spirits that they should add courage and valor on their path in the way of *chesed* and love of humanity."

The Pharmacy Next to the "*Linat HaTzedek*" Association, and the Pharmacist, Mordechai Ratner

*

The *Linat HaTzedek* society mentioned above continued its blessed activities in Augustow really until the days of the *Shoah*.

---

[994] Dates are often given relative to the *Torah* portion of the week.

338

{p. 353}In the one-time newspaper "*Augustower Leben,*"[995] which appeared 5 Adar 5699 (February 24, 1939), in the section "Our Social Institutions," we find the following details in connection to the "*Linat HaTzedek*" Society in the city:

"The institution for social aid for the sick, the *Lines HaTsedek* has existed since 1879. In the early years there were two separate *Lines HaTsedek* institutions: one that provided lodgings and organized home visits for patients, and another that arranged social aid for the sick, medications, material and so on. In time the two institutions merged and have remained together to this day.

The *Lines HaTsedek* brought together all the social classes of the town. The several hundred members organized in the institution formed a strong administrative body which worked with dynamism and strict discipline. One can see why the youth in particular took an active interest in the organization. {p. 354} They had their own small prayer house with its own *Torah* scroll. They were taught by Reb Gedalye Gizumski, the *shoychet*, and later by Reb Mayer Faynshteyn. That is how things once were. Nowadays, in contrast, the town and particularly the youth show little interest in this useful institution. For this reason, now, during a period when the help of a wider circle is much needed, all the work falls on the shoulders of the administration.

Dr. Yordanski and Chaya Markus in the *Linat HaTzedek* Infirmary

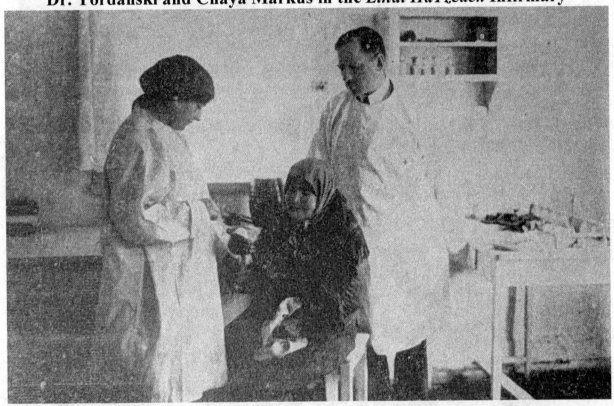

The treasury of the *Lines HaTsedek* has a monthly income of 130 *złotys*, taken from the weekly membership dues, as well as donations, traditionally collected at the reading of the *Torah* portion "*Naso.*"

The board is made up of the following people: Chairman: Khayim Mints; Members: Mss. Safirshteyn, Vilkovski, Levit, Lenzinger, Mariampolski, Shvarts; Misses Rishli Mayzler, Tsila Bernshteyn, Alta Kleynman; and Messrs. Hofnshteyn, Servianski, Khayim Arimland. In the oversight committee: Miss Arbshteyn, Mr. Zaboravski and Mr. Uzhitski.

---

[995] "Augustower Life," a Yiddish publication.

The Functionaries of *Linat HaTzedek*

Standing from right to left: P. Eilender, unknown, Miriam Cohen, B. Denmark, Chaya Markus, Y. Chalupitzki, L. Lozman, S. Bornstein, G. Lenzinger, Y. Bergstein.
Sitting: L. Patak, Dr. Shor …, M. Elenbogen, Dr. Grodzinski, Bidek, Shulkes.
Third row: P. Ofenstein, Rivka Rozenfeld.

{p. 355} Farewell Party for Chaya Markus on the Occasion of Her *Aliyah* to the Land

{p. 356} *Purim* **Ball for the Benefit of** *Linat HaTzedek*

Award for Chaya Markus Before Her *Aliyah* **to the Land**

The Foundation of a Library in Augustow

In the year 5642 (1882) a library was founded in Augustow. In the daily Hebrew newspaper "*HaYom*," (The year 1887, No. 18), which appeared then in Peterburg, edited by Dr. L. Kantor, Y. Barkat writes:

"In another few days, the young men and women of our city will celebrate the day in which five years have been fulfilled from the day that a collection house for books was instituted, and the number of books will exceed three hundred volumes, most of them written in the language of Russia, and the number of books in the language of *Ever* are few at this time." The bringer of the information gives in this "appreciation and praise to the administrators of the house for doing their work faithfully, and planning their deeds with order and authority." One must point out that in the course of time the "Folk Library" was developed from this library in Augustow, which existed until the days of the *Shoah*. According to a notice in the one-time newspaper "*Augustower Leben*," 5 Adar 5699 (February 24, 1939), we learn that in the library there were 6000 books. Of that: 1300 in Hebrew, 1700 in Yiddish, 1600 in Polish, and 1400 in Russian. In the library 160 subscribers were listed. The reading fees went up from 25 *prutah*s until 1 gold a month. Only twenty percent of the readers borrowed books in Hebrew and Yiddish.

The Library
by Meir Meizler

After I was honored, honored friends, to see you under my roof, you gathered together in my house to take counsel on what to do with the collection house of the books. I will take for myself the permission to preach a few words in your ears, but this I must tell you from the start: that you should not hope to hear from me lofty and sublime poetic phrases, you will not be able to fly very high with them on the mountains of reason. To these I have never been accustomed, and also presently for many days I have made my *Torah* a spade with which to dig,[996] to dig a grave for my ideas. In simple words that emerge from the source of my heart I will speak to you this time, and this will be my reward if they will enter your hearts too, and you my lords will be so kind as to listen, even if all the words of my mouth will not be acceptable before you.[997] Please don't disturb me, and after my words praise me or desecrate me, each person according to his spirit, for all that the master of the house will say, do!

*

We are children who are faithful to our people, faithful children and paying attention. And although we are young in days, nevertheless there is in us the reason of elders, and in their ways we will walk without leaning from them right or left,[998] and like them we will not keep from doing that which we have established with our lives. A matter fell in the camp of the Hebrew youths who did not leave their holy flag - to speak the language of *Ever*, to resurrect our dead language and to make it a living and spoken language. We hurried, we too, to emulate their deeds and speak, we too. We spoke, we preached, and our soul enjoyed pleasure but not for long, for the end of the summer of 5651 [1891] had not yet come, the summer that ended its society,[999] and also she did not fulfill her year, it became like a woman's stillbirth that does not see the sun,[1000] and found for

---

[996] *Mishnah Avot* 4:5 "Rabbi Zadok said: do not make them [words of *Torah*] a crown for self-exaltation, nor a spade with which to dig.

[997] Psalm 19:15 "May the words of my mouth and the prayer of my heart be acceptable before You, Adonoi, my rock and my redeemer."

[998] Numbers 22:26 "Once more the angel of the LORD moved forward and stationed himself on a spot so narrow that there was no room to lean right or left."

[999] Playing on the words for end, קץ *ketz*, and summer, קיץ *kayitz*. Ezekiel 7:6 "The end is coming! The end is coming! It stirs against you; there it comes!"

[1000] Psalm 58:9 "...like a woman's stillbirth, may they never see the sun!"

it a grave, and all {p. 358} our words that we spoke about the love of the language and its expansion were carried away by the wind and it was as if they never were. We founded for ourselves a collection house for books, and over the two years of its existence we acquired for ourselves many books, Hebrew and Russian, also from the other nations who speak about our nation. And we acquired for ourselves a community of readers who dedicated their time to our books, also we made many souls[1001] for our language, for the reading of Hebrew books brought the readers to an understanding of the language[1002] of *Ever*, to know all that was done in the midst of our people, to rejoice in its joy and to sorrow with its sorrow. I will not turn for even a minute but after a few years, and the youths that began to read Hebrew books will become lovers of our people, its language, and our holy land, until they become seed blessed of God, in whom Israel will be proud.

And here bad days have reached the collection house, the springs of income have diminished and dried up, and a yoke of obligations too heavy to carry hangs over it, and is it fitting for a foot to stumble and to fall from the eternal calamities, and we its first founders who lay its cornerstone fall silent? In the rest of soul and heart we will gaze at our ruin, and not even a faint sigh will come from our hearts. The thing that we are doing is not good, my brothers and friends! We are shirkers,[1003] shirkers! Be strong and strengthened[1004] for our language, and for the great building on which builders toiled and build in it! Let's participate each and every one according to his offering and the giving of his hand, according to all that his heart will offer.[1005] Here we have made for this house sockets of silver[1006] at the beginning of its founding, let's also make for it now a silver staff, maybe it will live long, be encouraged and be strengthened, and this work of our hands to be proud of will continue to make souls for our language. The youths that read when they grow up and become adults, from their great love of their language they will increase and glorify the collection house, will multiply books in it and multiply readers, and then with pride and swelling heart[1007] we will be able to look at this enterprise, for we the first founders made all this success. Also the poor blessing of our lips will come upon us, for we made an effort to establish a community of readers, Hebrew thinkers, Hebrew writers, whose hearts are Hebrew hearts faithful to their people and their language. We have the obligation to give money this time too, but those who are obligated for reading, will want to give what is coming from them, also every one of us will be so kind in their goodness to give their donation. With the collected money we will turn away from ourselves the suffering of obligations, we will also buy for ourselves new books which will also bring to us increased fruit, and by this we will save the book collection house, so that it will not go down to destruction in its youth and in the spring of its life.

Augustavo 5653 [1891] (from his estate)

[1001] It is not exactly clear what is meant by this obscure phrase found in the story of Abraham and Sarah in the *Torah*. Genesis 12:5 "Abram took his wife Sarai and his brother's son Lot, and all the wealth that they had amassed, and the persons that they had made in Haran..." In the Bible, the Hebrew word *nefesh* does not mean "soul," as it does in later Hebrew, but rather "living thing."

[1002] This word has a typographical error, spelled שפר *sfar* rather than שפת *sfat*.

[1003] Exodus 5:8 "do not reduce it, for they are shirkers; that is why they cry, 'Let us go and sacrifice to our God!'..."

[1004] Reminiscent of the expression used when one completes the reading of a book of the *Torah*, "*chazak, chazak, v'nitchazek*," "Strong, strong, and we will be strengthened."

[1005] Exodus 25:2 "Tell the Israelite people to bring Me gifts; you shall accept gifts for Me from every person whose heart will offer."

[1006] Describing the Wilderness Tabernacle, Exodus 26:32 "Hang it upon four posts of acacia wood overlaid with gold and having hooks of gold, [set] in four sockets of silver."

[1007] Isaiah 10:12 "He will punish the majestic pride and swelling heart of the king of Assyria."

The Education of the Jews of Augustow
by Yaakov Bergstein

The old "*cheder*" in which many generations were educated, and from which emerged learners and intellectuals, sages and learned people, was preserved in Augustow until the First World War. The "*cheder*," with its flaws, was that which caused *Torah* not to be forgotten by Israel. Despite its very old method, and its unmodern, anti-logical form, the "*cheder*" nevertheless succeeded in inculcating much wisdom and knowledge in the heart of the students, to guide them in the practical *mitzvot*, and to root truth and faith in their hearts, love of the *Torah* and love of Israel. In the days of the old "*cheder*" every person from Israel, even the simplest {p. 360} of the simple and the poorest of the poor, raised his sons for *Torah*. No sacrifice would compare, in the eyes of the father, to the acquisition of an education for his sons according to the law of Moses and Israel; he would save his bread, and would not withhold the learning of *Torah* from his sons. Know well that "poverty is good for Israel"[1008] and ignorance is not good for a child of Israel, and therefore it is comfortable for the father to live like a poor person rather than his child should be an ignoramus. One who cannot afford to pay the fees for learning that are placed on him by the teachers would turn his son over to the "*Talmud Torah*," which was supported by the community. The year was divided into two "times:" from after *Pesach* until *Rosh HaShanah*, and after the festival of *Sukkot* until 8 *Nisan*. The Rebbes[1009] were diverse, as were the types of learning. Rebbe Chaim Bayar was a teacher of young children; he lived on the street of the synagogue. He was bad-tempered. He would beat with a belt on the bottom part, and also pinch the cheeks. The children learned the "*aleph bais*"[1010] with him and finished with the *Chumash*. He knew Russian, German, and Polish. The Tsar's regime required the teaching of the Russian language in the "*chadarim*." Reb Chaim himself would give this Russian lesson. Another teacher of young children was Tzvi Sherman. The children of the wealthy learned with him. Kantor taught the Russian language. The Rebbe Abba taught *Chumash* and *Nach*[1011] and a little *Gemara*. The Rebbe Yisrael Rotblit (from Stavisk) taught *Chumash*, *Nach*, *Gemara* for beginners, and also Hebrew, and even Yiddish. He was helped by his sons: Zhimmy, Nissan, Moshe and Dovid. The "*cheder*" of the teachers D. Boyarski and Eizerski was more modern.

They were stricter about the learning of the Hebrew language. There was also a girls' school with two classes. Its owners and also its teachers were Bulkin and his wife. Another school was directed by the teachers Reuven Levin and his wife Miriam. They taught Hebrew and also Russian in it. There was also a Russian gymnasium, with four divisions, in which only daughters of the wealthy learned. In the "*cheder*" of the Rebbe Filivinsky (the teacher from Sapotzkin) older children learned *Chumash* with Rashi's interpretation, *Nach*, *Talmud* and also Hebrew. He was a somewhat modern Rebbe and also very knowledgeable in *Torah*. He also knew foreign languages. A group of parents specially brought from the town of Lazdie the teacher Elyakum Levinzon, and they set a condition with him, that he would not accept more than 15 children. He did not keep this condition, since the children were drawn to him, because of his method in the learning. He taught everything in melody. They would sing the *shacharit* prayers, and likewise *Tanakh* etc. Rebbe Pesach taught only *Talmud*. Rebbe Betzalel Grader also gave lessons in *Gemara*. He would come to the student's house or would teach in the "*Ezrat Nashim*"[1012] that was in the Beit Midrash and in the *Kloiz* of Reb Chaim Zalman Shub. Boys learned in the "*chadarim*" until age 12-13.

[1008] Babylonian *Talmud Chagigah* 9b "Shmuel said, and some say it was Rav Yosef: This explains the folk saying that people say: Poverty is good for the Jewish people like a red bridle for a white horse...."
[1009] Rebbes are teachers, not Rabbis.
[1010] The Hebrew alphabet.
[1011] An acronym for Prophets, in Hebrew *Nevi'im*, and Writings, in Hebrew *Ketuvim*.
[1012] The women's section of the Jerusalem Temple, and also of the synagogue.

{p. 359} **The Students of the "*Talmud Torah*"**

The Elementary School Building

345

The Students of the "Hebrew Courses" (1917-1918)

First row from right to left: Roza Kolfenitzki, Boba Boyarski, Sonia Bramson, Lazdeizka, Sonia Poniminski, Devorah Bramson, Shulamit Grinberg, Rechtman, Channah Starazinsky, T. Beker.
Second row: Yedidiah Ivraiski, Meir Vezbotzki, Borovitz, Leah Ivraiski-Sherman, Sarah Gershovitz, Channah Finkelstein, unknown, Golda Goren, Abba Rozenfeld, B. Tz. Boyarski.
Third row: Shimon Feinstein, Mendel Borek, Moshe Markus, the Teacher Boyarski, the Teacher Levin, Ratner, Sheinmar, Patek. Laying down: Borovski, A. Grinberg, A. Markus

{p. 361} **Teachers of the Elementary School in the Period of the German Conquest**

Standing from right to left: Dovid Levinzon, Ch. Veisbord, Glikstein, P. Rabinovitz, R. Levi
Sitting: D. Boyarski, A. Meizler, the German Director, S. Soloveitchik, Elyakum Levinzon

346

Some of them continued their studies in the government school, and some of them traveled to the yeshivas of Slobodka, Lomza, Radin, and more. Girls who finished the two classes continued their learning in the Hebrew language in private lessons with the teachers D. Boyarski, R. Levin, M. Meizler. They learned foreign languages with the teachers Dina Frankel, Malkah Rotblit, P. Gutel, {p. 362} Borovitz (from Rajgród). Boys and also girls learned Russian with Ziman, Rabinovitz, Mintz. The boys that attended the Russian government school learned Hebrew in the afternoon with Meizler, and *Gemara* with the Rebbe Betzalel. When the Germans conquered the city, they set the requirement for learning German in place of Russian. The German regime confiscated suitable apartments and opened schools in them; a girls' school, and a boys' school. Mrs. Yones, Rabinovitz, Meizler, and the teacher Reuven Levin were accepted as teachers. As administrator of the school a German teacher who served in the army was appointed, at the rank of Corporal or Sergeant. He brought into the schools, which were administered according to the program of elementary schools in Germany, also sports and agricultural work. In that same period the teachers Boyarski and Levin founded evening courses for Hebrew.

The last is the most beloved – the "*Talmud Torah*." The Rebbes of that time were Reb Betzalel Grader and his son-in-law Reb Avraham Yitzchak. Rabbi Azriel Zelig Koshelevski saw to the *Talmud Torah*, assisted by Reb Reuven Rotenberg, who with heart and soul devoted himself to public activism day and night. He actually did not have to worry about his livelihood, for his wife, who was a woman of valor, saw to it; he only helped her. He was also helped by Reb Yehuda Arieh Levatinski, who was a wood merchant; and Dov Bergstein, owner of a manufacturing store, a donor and contributor. {p. 363}He would go out to the villages during the week of *Purim* and

The Girls' Class (1921)

First row standing: (from left to right) Kaplanski, Stolar, Denmark, Preis, Olchnovitz.
Row 2: T. Viniski, S. Stolar, M. Zupnitzki, R. Lutinski, A. Gotstein, Tz. Levinzon, G. Beder, P. Ofenstein, A. Burak, Eilender, Soloveitchik, A. Ivraiski.
Row 4: S. Rechtman, the Teacher Domovitz, the Teacher Bertishovna, the Teacher Bartish, B. Ivraiski. Sitting: Y. Stolnitzki, the Teacher Kolinski, D. Linda.

gather donations from the village Jews for the benefit of the "*Talmud Torah.*" Yaakov Ze'ev Otstein, a baker, would neglect his store and engage in this *mitzvah.* He would voluntarily collect the tax money that the Jews owed to the Community Council. He would transmit the money to the "*Talmud Torah*" fund, and the list of payers, to the Community Council, which would issue receipts. This task was not easy and even not so pleasant.

In the last years, before the outbreak of the Second World War, the "*Talmud Torah*" became a modern school with 8 classes. The Director of the school was Zilber from Galitzia, who taught the Polish language. Vasserman, born in Augustow, who completed a Polish government seminar for teachers, also taught Polish. Yehoshua Bergstein was a teacher of *Tanakh* and Hebrew in the upper grades. The teacher Diskin taught *Tanakh* and Hebrew. The teacher Yismachovitz taught *Torah* and Hebrew in the lower grades. Efraim Maletz served as secretary of the institution and also was a teacher of laws and *Gemara.*

The Girls' Class in the Year 1917

Row 1, from left to right: Gritzen, Blacharski, Viedenboim, Kolpitzki, Donieger, … Staviskovski, Staviskovski, … … … … Rozenfeld.
Row 2: … Gotstein, Giteleh (and Chaneleh), … Preis, … … … … … Popkin, Denmark, Grodzin.
Row 3: Levin, Boyarski, Povembrovski, Veisbrot, Meizler, Soloveitchik, Rabinovitz, Levinzon, the Supervisor.
Sitting: … … … Eilender, Kronenrot, Zupnitzka, Levinzon, … … … Kleiman, Viniski, Popkin.

{p. 366} Our Communal Institutions

The People's Bank

When we attempt to describe such an important institution, which in today's world plays such a vital role in our difficult economy of our daily life, we must first provide a brief overview of its origin in order to be able to appreciate the great rise and quick development of the aforementioned institution.

The People's Bank in Augustow was founded in 1922, at the initiative of several people, with an initial capital of several hundred *zlotys* collected locally and with the assistance of the Joint.

{p. 364} The Girls' Class in the First World War

Female Students 1917

The teachers sitting from right to left: R. Levi, D. Boyarski, Feigl Rabinovitz, Chaya Veisbord, Povembrovski, A. Meizler, A. Levinzon, Tzovak – the Director of the School by Order of the Germans.

Honored Sir: Teivel Linda
We are Honored to Request His Honor to Participate
In a Banquet That We Are Arranging in Honor of Our Teacher
Mr. Dovid Boyarski
On Wednesday 13 Elul 5682 [1922] in the Home of H. Rozenfeld
at the Hour of 8:00 in the Evening.
With Complete Respect and the Blessing of Abundance[1013]
The Students of the "*Orah*"[1014] Courses
Augustow, 12 Elul, 5682

The following episode is typical: a certain member of the initiative-group, Mr. Monush Kantorovitsh, turned to the accountant Mr. Nakhman Freydberg, of blessed memory, to see if he would like to pay to replace the small electric lamp in their small office whereupon the latter flew into a rage: "You want us to go into deficit just to buy a bigger lamp?"

The steady development of the bank over the course of sixteen years means that we now see it as one of the most stable banks in the whole region, one which stands on a solid foundation and which still, at times, supports the smaller banks in the area. All thanks to the devoted and energetic work of the management as well as the capable employees.

The bank currently boasts 267 members and possesses a capital of 70,000 *zlotys*. The highest loan that it offers is 5,000 *zlotys*; deposits in the bank amount to 220,000 *zlotys*; it is worth noting that all kinds of transactions are facilitated by the bank, from the smallest to the largest.

The bank distributes 1,200 *zlotys* annually for philanthropic purposes, of which 250 *zlotys* for Zionist funds.

Chairman of the bank: Monush Kantorovitsh. Council members: Dovid Simner, Alter Ravidovitsh, Dr. Shor, Alter Polak, Ariye Aynshtat. Management — Chairman: Binyomin Markus. Members: Shaul Kelzon, Mordkhe Rekhtman, Yoysef Gifshteyn, Yitskhok Varhaftig.

[1013] A typographical error, the substitution of a letter *heh* instead of a letter *ayin* at the end of the word, has the word *hasafah*, השפה, the language, in place of the word *hashefa*, השפע, the abundance.
[1014] Light.

The Boys' Class in the Elementary School

First row standing from right to left: M. Zborovski (Einat), ... Kaplanski, ... A. Kaplanski, P. Levin, Ratzkovski, M. Volmir, M. Borovitz, L. Blech, R. Kaplanski.

Second row standing (from right): ... Barglovski, A. Chaliupitzki, Y. Feivishovitz, Y. Bernski.

Third row sitting (from right): ... Ch. Bilovzetzki, A. Glikstein, A. Levinson, Vilkov, Veisbort, Beka Blech, ... Y. Feivovorski.

Fourth row sitting (from right): M. Glikstein, Ch. Orimland, S. Relski, D. Inonovitz, Y. Aleksandroni, Y. Trestzenski.

{p. 367} *Talmud Torah*

The *Talmud Torah*, which is our only Jewish school in town, traces its history back about 50 years to the time when Mr. Yehuda Kohen built the premises on Kopernika Street. As is usual, it was divided into several sections according to the old system. It was administered by the *gabbai*s Reb Avrom Yankev Shilevski, of blessed memory, and Reb Yankev Leviush, of blessed memory, who took an interest in its fate and existence. During the world war it survived only thanks to American money and stood under the supervision of our esteemed rabbi Reb Azriel Zelig Noyekh Kushelevski, long may he live, who together with the dedicated activists Reb Ruven Rotenberg, may his light shine, and Reb Yehuda Leyb Levantinski, may his light shine, stood guard and worked for the survival of the *Talmud Torah*.

From 1920 it began to have the characteristics of a school, but for a certain period it only had four classes; experience showed that it was not enough to provide students with only an elementary education, as once they had graduated from the four classes of the *Talmud Torah* they would need to continue their education in the public schools. It turned out that it could not remain as a half-school and it was necessary to develop it to the same level as a public school. And so, thanks to the determined work of the parents' committee under the leadership of the rabbi, long may he live, together with the Jewish community, a class was added each year until in 1934 it had achieved the status of a seven-class public school with government approval. The school now provides a religious, national education to around 230 pupils from the town; in the preparatory class and in the first three classes girls are also taught. The teaching staff is made up of eight teachers: 5 in Hebrew and 3 in Polish.

The budget of the school is around 15,000 zlotys annually; student's fees make up 10,000 zlotys, and there is also a stream of small donations meaning that the school runs with a deficit of 25% though it is the only Jewish school in town.

In the school there is also a small library of Polish books which was created to meet the requirements of the school inspector.

"CENTOS"

The important charitable institution "CENTOS" feeds and clothes thirty poor children in our town. It has existed for three years now, founded as an offshoot of the Bialystok branch. In the beginning {p. 368} of its formation it took the form of a boarding house where children between the ages of 5 and 7 would be provided with all their daily meals and a special teacher would take charge of their education. Recently the setup has been changed to a half-boarding house, meaning that children from the other schools go there after their regular lessons to receive lunch and an evening meal as well as help from the teacher with their homework.

The local CENTOS is funded by a monthly subvention from the Bialystok branch, as well as subsidies from the state itself. With the arrival of winter it also receives an allowance from the magistrate's office called, so-called "winter aid." All of this would not be enough to cover the running costs if it weren't for the energetic work of the administrators who raise the remaining funds through various initiatives such as children's spectacles and events.

The administration and auditing commission are made up of the following individuals:
Management: Mrs. Niuta Tenenboym—chairwoman. Members: Sore Safirshteyn, Rokhl Kelzon, Khiene Levit, Yudis Lazman, Libe Shvedzki, Golde Lenzinger, Mashe Stolar, Bronie Stolar, Zelda Vazbutski, Miss Rishel Mayzler. And the auditing commission: Messrs. H. Lap, A. Shevakh, M. Shteyn, I. Gizumski.

Gmiles-Khesed Fund

This fund was founded in 1927 thanks to the work of a number of community activists in Augustow who established it under their own initiative. The founding capital was made up of registered promissory notes, donations from local townsfolk, as well as several foreigners, who happened to be visiting at the time, as well as credit from the Joint.[1015]

By the first quarter of 1938 there were 357 members, or whom 218 were active, who paid their debts on time in addition to their regular membership dues, as well as 139 passive members with combined debts of 14,860 zlotys. To this is added the Joint's long-term credit of 8,640 which came in yearly payments of 900 zlotys to reimburse loans underwritten by the management. The "Tsekabe"[1016] also received 400 zlotys a year paid throughout the year with promissory notes.

Their own basic capital was 5,820 zlotys, which had been saved over the years thanks to the volunteer work of the accountant and the manager of the fund.

{p. 369} From the founding of the fund to January 1st 1939, 4,860 loans were given out. The unpaid loans of about 5,000 zlotys paralyzed the fund. The management did everything they could; the question of whether to chase up the loans through the courts or by gentler means, as was the normal modus operandi of the *Gmiles-Khesed*, took up a lot of their time and energy.

Social Club

The Social Club in Augustow, which was a focal point of the high society of the town, developed a broad span of cultural activities during the one year of its existence. Thanks to it the

---

[1015] The Joint Distribution Committee, a Jewish Relief Organization based in New York City.
[1016] Central No-interest Loans' Office.

townsfolk had the opportunity to meet a variety of celebrities in the club's meeting hall, such as Roman Brandstaetter, the newspaper editor Mark Turkow, Hertz Grosbard, Rochel Holzer etc.

Also noteworthy is the wide selection of press material that they made available from all the Polish-Jewish daily newspapers and literary periodicals. They also had a well-developed ethos of philanthropy with which the club distinguished itself this year with its generous donations to various causes.

The management of the club is currently made up of the following people: Chairman: Mr. Nosn Varhaftig; administrator: Khonen Kantsiuk; treasurer: M. Lap; secretary: A. Vaksman; members: Dr. Grodzieński, Frayshtern and H. Y. Zalkind.

"*Tiferes Bakhurim*" by **Khayim Bialobzyski**, Tiferes Bakhurim Chairman

On Wednesday, during the week of the *Torah* portion Beshalakh in the year 5693, our *Tiferes Bakhurim* was visited by Zalman Gradowski from Suwalki. A meeting of the community council was called straight away with the participation of the guest, at which it was decided to hold a general meeting on Thursday. There was also consideration given to the creation of a spiritual council. With this in mind invitations were sent to the best spiritual minds in the community to attend the meeting along with the esteemed guest, in the rabbi's house.

On Thursday evening the general meeting took place. The esteemed guest gave a report on the *Tiferes Bakhurim* conference in Baranovits. The next *Shabbes*, during the week of the *Torah* portion *Yitro*, the *Tiferes Bakhurim* held a gathering in honor of the *yeshiva* council made up of local friends.

{p. 370} Shepsl Sandler (Falander) spoke before *Kries-HaToyre* several words about the importance of the *yeshiva*s in our modern times. We quickly said *Mishebeyrekh* and many of us promised to contribute each according to his means.

Tiferet Bachurim (5691) [1931]

First row standing from right to left: Aharon Cohen, Ch. Yachnish.
Second row: B. Lazovski, A. Arbstein, A. Borovski, A. Gritzen, A. Krinitzki, D. Freitzeit, B. Sherman, M. Staviskovski, Y. Grodzin, Freund, Z. Ampel, M. Lazdeiski.
Sitting: Tz. Shumski, Shibek, Y. Blacharski, R. Tsherman, B. Tz. Filivinsky, Rabbi Koshlevski, the Rabbi's son Arieh, S. Zebla, Ch. Bialovzetski, Y. Melamed

353

{p. 371} A City in Its Destruction

{p. 372} Crematorium

The Memorial at "Yad Vashem" Jerusalem 5724 [1964]

A short time before the outbreak of the war, the Poles felt that it was approaching with giant steps. The newspapers wrote much about the "*Prozdor*" (Danzig, the free port city), and informed that the Germans were drafting an army and stationing it around the Prussian border, Pomerania, and Upper Silesia. In Augustow they already felt that something was about to happen. In those weeks it was possible to see that the Polish government began to implement means of self-defense after it came to know that it had been deceived by the Germans, and the Beck-Ribbentrop Agreement[1017] did not help it. The Suwalki foot brigade abandoned Suwalk, and reached Augustow in the night. It crossed Bridge Street (*Brik-Gasse*), entered the market (*Plotz Pulsodskiago*), and to Krakovska Street. From there, I do not know – if to the Osowiec Fort, or to Grodno.

The police, fire-fighters, and the other types of "patriots" occupied the produce warehouses of the Levit brothers, and directed the produce of the area there and to the other warehouses that had been nationalized.

They began to catch people from the houses and the streets, for the digging of positions. The people hid. They went, therefore, from house to house and searched for men. I was curious and I went out to the balcony (an open veranda). They immediately sensed me. I fled to the upper roof of our house and I hid behind the chimney. They caught me, took me outside, and transported me together with a few other men to the excavations. The custom was: if you finished digging your quota, they freed to you to go home. On the way they caught you, and – back to the excavations. Tens evaded this, as usual, with the help of a bribe.

The excavations were dug in three separate places. At first, they dug simple military posts for the foot soldiers on the way to Ratzk, 5 kilometers from Augustow, next to two windmills, in a place {p. 374} that was called Slepsk. This was, apparently, the first line against the invasion from Prussia, by way of Gabrova or Ratzk. The second line was next to the train station, not far from the sawmill and the "Lipavitz" electric station. The third line was on the way to Grodno, on the 5th-6th kilometer on the deep Sajno River.

Friday, September 1, 1939, was a market day (there were two market days every week in Augustow, on Tuesdays and Fridays). I arose at 4:00 in the morning and I walked to the Grayevo-Grodno crossroads. This was the place to which the small Augustow merchants would come out to meet the farmers' wagons, laden with various merchandise. Suddenly a tremendous noise of airplanes was heard. Hundreds passed over us. They came from Prussia. At the hour of 7:00 in the morning, approximately, all the residents of Augustow already knew that war had broken out. The Germans attacked Poland without advance notice. Meanwhile it became clear that the squadron of airplanes that passed over us had already shelled Grodno and Warsaw. On their return, they flew so low that I worried that they would destroy the chimneys of our houses with their wheels. A few of them bombed the train station, which was full of soldiers preparing to travel to

---

[1017] Known more widely as the Molotov-Ribbentrop Pact, a non-aggression pact between Nazi Germany and the Soviet Union that enabled them to divide Poland between them. It was signed in Moscow on 23 August 1939 by German Foreign Minister Joachim von Ribbentrop and Soviet Foreign Minister Vyacheslav Molotov.

Grodno. They were killed. That same hour information was received that in Garbova the Poles struck a German plane with a machine gun. The plane crashed, but two German pilots escaped from it. I remember that they brought them, slain, to the Polish hospital on "Posbiontny" Street, and all Augustow, the Poles and the Jews, went to see slain German pilots.

On the second day of the war there was announced a partial army induction; there were not enough arms for a general induction. A few names remain in my memories: Tuvia Brizman, who went and did not return; Feivel Lavozitzky did not return; Yaakov Blacharski returned and was killed in the Shoah; Berkovitz (Tzirski) was seriously wounded in Grodno; Lieske Gutman returned and was killed in the *Shoah*. The men wanted to fight, requested to enlist, and were answered negatively. Time went by quickly, and the Germans did not conquer Augustow, they preferred to go by way of Grayevo and conquer the "Osowiec" fort, and from there to go up against Warsaw. In this way Warsaw was left without rule.

At that same time I completed 20 years. My parents were afraid that if the Germans entered they would kill all the men of army age. They began to pressure me, that I should flee with the Polish army and not fall into the hands of the Germans. I did not want to listen to them, since my father was sick. They decided, therefore, to act behind my back and spoke with Hillel Rotenberg, the brother-in-law of Abba Popkin. He came to me, spoke with me, and convinced me to flee. This was on Friday, exactly a week after the outbreak of the war. On the *Shabbat* day, September 9, 1939, I came to Hillel Rotenberg. In his yard there already stood four wagons, each with a wagon hitched to a team of horses. We loaded various merchandise onto the wagons, and turned to the road that went to Suchovola. From there we wanted to continue to Bialystok.

We left Augustow with broken hearts. We crossed the bridge, and travelled and travelled in the direction of Bialobrega. Before Bialobrega we met a small group of 4-5 Augustovian Jews, and at their head the old Rabbi Reb Azriel Koshelevski, may the memory of the righteous be for a blessing. We requested of the Rabbi that he come on the wagon, but he refused. Towards evening we reached Suchovola. We spent the night there and regained our strength. On the next day towards morning we moved our caravan in the direction of Korotzin-Yasinovka. The Rabbi and the Jews from Augustow that accompanied him remained in Suchovola. We passed Koritzin, Yasinovka, and reached the Knishin forests. Suddenly soldiers and Polish officers emerged from the forest, and asked where we were coming from. We told them that we were from Augustow, and fleeing from fear of the Germans.

{p. 375} They were so confused that we really took pity on them. On the next day before noon we reached Bialystok in peace. We unloaded the merchandise by Hillel Rotenberg's sister, rested a little, and went out to buy a few casks of oil. Hillel had enough money for his needs. We came to the factory, and there they informed us that they were no longer selling. But, since Rotenberg was a customer of theirs for years, they took it into consideration and sold him one cask. We tried to buy as much as possible, but they were not selling for Polish money. The economic situation got worse. It was impossible to buy any needed food for money, but only in barter, that is to say, for salt, kerosene, matches and soap. We did not have that merchandise. We were a little hungry, however, even though we had money. A day or two after our arrival was *Rosh HaShanah*.

*

On *Rosh HaShanah* eve the Germans bombed the storehouses at the Pulaski train station. When the Poles saw that the Germans were getting close to Bialystok, they opened the storehouses, and called to the public to take as much as they wanted, only that the goods should not fall into the hands of the "Swabians."[1018] I too ran there, and took as much as I could carry. On the way back,

---

[1018] Swabia is a cultural, historic and linguistic region in southwestern Germany.

the German planes came and began to bomb. A few people were killed. I was saved by a miracle but I lost part of my booty. Meanwhile the neighbors came and told that on Staroviarsk Street they opened the storehouses of tobacco and cigarettes and everyone could take as much as they desired, so I also went there and brought tobacco and cigarettes. On the next day on *Rosh HaShanah* in the morning, we went to pray by one neighbor who had gathered a *minyan* in his house. Before the *Torah* reading, the son of one of the worshippers came and called: "Jews, in this moment the Germans are entering the city." We stopped praying, and we scattered, each one to their house. We shut the gate and the shutters, and did not go outside.

On the next day, the hunger began to bother us. Neighbors told that on a Polish street they would distribute bread, one kilogram to everyone who would stand on line in front of the bakery. When my turn arrived the bread was gone. On the next day, I stationed myself on the line at 2:00 in the morning. A great many people were there. The Germans kept order. This time I was able to get a kilogram of bread. It was like clay, and without salt. But, since we were hungry, we swallowed it. I got used to going outside. I would take tobacco in my pockets, a bottle of oil or vodka, in order to trade for foodstuffs. Sometimes I succeeded, and sometimes, not. *Yom Kippur* arrived. We went to pray. This time, in the cellar of a neighbor. One of the worshippers told that his son was listening to Radio Moscow and heard that on that same day, that is to say, September 17, 1939, Russian troops advanced towards the Polish border. They had already crossed the border in a few directions, in order to liberate Poland, and they had already conquered Baronovitz, Stolpce, and were approaching Bialystok. Great joy burst out among us. Meanwhile the Germans caught tens of people, most of them Jews, loaded them onto a vehicle and brought them to the Jewish hospital on Varshavski Street, tasked them with removing the straw from the mattresses and to fill them anew. At the conclusion of the work, they stood them next to the wall and shot all of them, and buried them there in the yard.

On the next day the Russians entered Bialystok, and the people began to emerge from their hiding places. The joy was great. They danced out of great joy. The young people jumped on the Soviet tanks, and circled the city on them.

{p. 376} I said to Hillel that I didn't want to remain in Bialystok anymore, that my heart was drawing me home. I took a little food in a rucksack and went with the Russian army to Augustow. I came home and I was happy that I found them all. During the whole time of my absence the Germans did not enter Augustow. The border stabilized as follows: Ratzk, Suwalk, Filipova, and all the area were under Russian rule; 8 kilometers before Augustow the border stood on the bridge from Suwalk to Augustow in Shtzavra-Olshinka. On the other side, on the dirt road to Ratzk, Bianovka, the border remained as in the time of the Poles; Grodno, Bialystok, Grayevo, Osovitz, were in the hands of the Russians.

From the time that the Russians reached Augustow, they quickly found helpers for themselves. Many Jews found upper- and middle-level jobs with them, in both the police and the N.K.V.D.[1019] Many felt the power of their arm.[1020] They informed on party activists of all streams, who were exiled because of it to Russia. They revealed storehouses. They found a big storehouse in Popkin and Rotenberg's attic.

In this way they confiscated produce, stores, sawmills, flour mills, and more.

The Russians entered Augustow, continued to advance to Ratzk, and stayed there 3 days. They were in Suwalk for a day or two, and then they retreated, and were stopped at the new border, as I detailed in the previous paragraph. Before their retreat, most of the Jewish officers, and also the Russians from the Red Army, advised that the Jews come with them, since the Germans would

---

[1019] The People's Commissariat for Internal Affairs, abbreviated N.K.V.D., the interior ministry of the Soviet Union.
[1020] Isaiah 30:30 "For the LORD will make His majestic voice heard, and display the power of His arm in raging wrath…"

enter these towns according to the agreement that was signed between the Russians and the Germans. They put at the disposal of every family that did not want to remain with the Germans, a vehicle to transport their possessions and people. In this way, a stream of refugees began to stream from Suwalk, Ratzk and more, towards Augustow. Very quickly the city filled with refugees, and the crowding was great.

In the month of April 1940, the order came from Moscow that all the refugees had to distance themselves from the German border by 100 kilometers in the direction of the old Russian border, to the area of Baronovitz and Slonim. Whoever wanted was able to cross the border to Russia. In this way the refugees were forced to leave Augustow. Part of them wandered to Russia, but most remained in the area of Baronovitz-Slonim. This part was slaughtered in the first days of June 1941, by the Germans, with the outbreak of the Russian-German war.

*

At the beginning of the year 1940 it was publicized that everyone who wanted to, could travel to Russia on condition that they would obligate themselves to work in it for a year or two. They promised the volunteers everything. Part of the Augustovi youth signed the agreement, and after a short time they travelled to Russia. When they reached Russia, they were sent to work in the coal mines, which were in the distant Ural. Some of them fled from there by all kinds of ways, and returned to Augustow. Among these, I remember only a few individual names: Pshashtzalski (the son of Mushke Dundah), the youngest son of Hershel Meltzer, my uncle's daughter Shulamit Sarvianski. A few weeks after they returned from Russia, they were sentenced by the Russians to imprisonment, until the period of each one's volunteering was complete, according to the work contract that they signed.

{p. 377} There were also those who did not flee from their work, and completed their period of obligation in peace. There are at least three of them in the land: Shayna Zielaza, and the Levinski sisters.

*

In February 1940, the expulsion began, and it continued in March and April. The Russians were deported to Russia, the party activists, business owners, and those with money. People were also deported who could not afford to pay taxes. People closed stores, butcher shops, etc. In their place new businesses sprung up, mostly buffets, and shops for writing materials, which were supported by the army that was camped in the city. Most sought work or a job with the authorities, in order to be saved from the expulsion. I too was among the latter. After I closed my shop because of the tax burden, I got work as an administrator of the second shift, at the flour mill of the Borovitz's who were exiled to Russia. The director of the first shift was Stein, who before the war was a shop-owner for writing implements. I worked at the flour mill until they drafted me into the Red Army.

*

In the Second World War

On *Yom Kippur* eve in the year 1940, I was drafted into the Red Army, together with a few other friends from Augustow: Chuna Rudnik, the son of Moshele the tailor; Tzvi Pozniak, the son of Shmuel the blacksmith; Moshe Kravitz, the son of Beinish the porter; Barukh Brenner; Feivel Zeimanski, the brother-in-law of Tziporah and Friedka Sarvianski; Beinish (I no longer remember his family name), the son of a shoemaker who lived with Aleksandrovitz; me, and Elchanan Sarvianski, the son of Itshe from Charnibrod. The assembly place for the inductees was the third house from ours, in the house of Chaim Leib. We stood to go out on the train at the hour of 1:00 in the morning, on *Yom Kippur* night.

358

With a heart full of sorrow and with tears I parted from my mother, from my two sisters, and from the rest of the relatives. I set out, broken and shattered, for the assembly place. A few hundred Poles from Augustow and the area were gathered there, and us - 7 Jews. There remained much time before the train would go out, and everyone attempted "to kill the time" according to his understanding. Many went to get drunk. I directed my steps to the synagogue, for the "Kol Nidre" prayer, and for "kaddish" after my father my teacher, may his memory be for a blessing.

The synagogue was full from mouth to mouth. Here the Jews of Augustow gathered, with their wives and children, to pour out their conversation[1021] and to throw down entreaties before their Master. Holiness saturated everything. All of them were dressed in holy day clothing, wrapped in *tallitot* and white "*kittels.*"[1022] Here were ascending to the podium Rabbi Azriel Zelig Koshelevski, the *gabbai* Reb Fenya Ahronovski, and the "*ba'al tefillah*" with the pleasant voice, the *shochet* Reb Gedalyahu Gizumski at the head of a choir of boys (among them, his youngest son Shlomkeh). Reb Moshe Dovid Morzinski the *shamash*, wrapped in a "*kittel*," his beard coming down on it,[1023] knocking on the table, and a hush is sent throughout the whole synagogue. They open the *Aron HaKodesh* and take out the *Torah* scrolls. Reb Asher Hempel passes from bench to bench with the *Sefer Torah*, and each one kisses the *Torah*. They finish the *hakafah*[1024] and bring the *Torah* scrolls to the *bima*. Here they are placed in the hands of the Rabbi, Reb Fenya, and the *Chazzan*. This last one opens with the singing of *Kol Nidre*, and every Jew in the synagogue is helping {p. 378} beside him and singing together with devotion. I lift my head and I look at the Jews of Augustow for the last time. Here is Doctor Shor; here is Shevach, the brother-in-law of F. Aharonovitz; here is Dr. Grodzinski; here is Paklof; standing next to me my uncle Leibl Steindem, Velvel Starazinsky, and Reb Mottel Leib Volmir with his sons; next to them, Shmuel Sosnovski; behind me, Vilkovski (Manoly the porter), Mottel Staviskovski, and the tailor the "*baal tefillah*" Reb Mendel Kolfenitzki, and the smith with the beautiful beard; and here – Dovid Leib Aleksandrovitz with his two sons, Alter (Zalman Tzvi) and Aharon; on the other side of the *Aron Hakodesh* stand Reb Itshe Rotenberg, Manush Kantorovitz, Mordechai Lev, the Lozmans, Shmuel-Yehuda Zborovski and Hershel Meltzer, Yehuda Rinkovski, Chaikel Morzinski with his two sons; and below, "the simple people." The *chazzan* concludes the "*Kol Nidre*" prayer, they put the *Torah* scrolls into the ark, and all the *klei kodesh*[1025] descend from the *bima*. The *chazzan* Reb Gedaliah and his choir approach the prayer "*amud*"[1026] and the Rabbi Reb Azriel Zelig Noach Koshelevski approaches the *bima* that is in front of the *Aron Kodesh*, opens the *aron*, and begins his sermon. I turn my head towards the *Ezrat Nashim*. There too it is full from mouth to mouth, and the sound of the women's weeping is heard...

The rabbi concludes his sermon and returns to his place. The *chazzan* opens with the "*Barechu*"[1027] prayer and all the holy nation prays with devotion. There are not secular thoughts now, everything speaks holiness. We reach the "*Aleinu L'Shabayach*,"[1028] and I say the "*kaddish*." Tears glisten in my eyes; my heart is broken within me.

Slowly the synagogue empties out. People bless each other with the blessing "May you be signed and sealed for a good year." I emerge from the synagogue and return to the gathering place. I wandered around there for an hour or two, and there still remained about an hour and a

---

[1021] Pray. Psalm 102:1 "A prayer of the lowly man when he is faint and pours forth his plea before the LORD."

[1022] A white linen or cotton robe worn by religious Jews on holidays.

[1023] Psalm 133:2 "Like goodly oil on the head coming down on the beard, Aaron's beard coming down over the opening of his robe."

[1024] The procession of the *Sefer Torah* around the synagogue.

[1025] Holy implements. This can refer to sacred objects, and is also used to refer to the clergy and the prayer leaders.

[1026] Lectern.

[1027] The "call to worship:" "Bless the Eternal the One who is Blessed, blessed is the Eternal Forever and Ever."

[1028] The concluding prayer, "It is upon us to praise the Master of all…"

half, the last ones, of my stay in Augustow. I decided to approach our house, in which I grew up and in which I lived for more than twenty years. I entered the yard and I looked in the windows for the last time. My whole family was sleeping. Our puppy sensed me and jumped on the window. I opened the kitchen window and went inside. I listened to the sound of the rhythmic breathing of my dear ones and I went out again. I went around and looked in all the corners of the yard and I went with a broken heart to the induction place. After some time they loaded us on the vehicles and transported us to the train station. Young men and women who came to accompany us waited there. We parted. We went out of Augustow to an unknown land.

*

The train had already left the sawmill and the "Lipavitz" electric company behind it and was racing quickly towards Grodno. After about two hours it stopped in Grodno. A few wagons loaded with inductees from Grodno, Grayevo, Shtutzin, Vonsozh and their surrounding areas were already waiting for it there. They were joining their cars to our train. The signal was given, and the train moved from its place. We were arriving at Breinsk, and here too they connected cars with inductees to our train. We were passing Volkovisk, Slonim and Baronovitz, in every place the same sight recurring over and over. From Baronovitz the train was skipping to the old Russian border, and we were on Russian soil. All of us were sticking our heads out of the windows, and gazing at the Russian scenery. We were passing by giant factories with tall chimneys. We were arriving in Minsk, the capitol city of Belarus, and continuing to Kiev, Charkov, Dnieper-Petrovsk, Zaporozhe, Tula, Oryol. We travelled a few weeks on the train until we reached {p. 379} Rostov on the River Don. We stayed there about half a day, they put us onto vehicles, and brought us a distance of 40 kilometers to Novi Tzarkask.

*

In Novi Tzarkask, which before the revolution was the capital city of the Don Cossacks, the journey meanwhile was concluded. There were me and another 3 Augustovians: Barukh Brenner, Chuna Rudnik and Beinish, living in the barracks that before the revolution was a palace of Ottoman Cossacks. In a palace-barracks like this, an army battalion entered. The soldiers of our division were from various nations, and there were almost no Russians in it. When we came to the division I said to my friends from Augustow that most of the people in the division were Jews, according to the appearance of their faces. We did not recognize until then the various members of the nations from east Asian Russia, who were partly of the Semitic race. Therefore, I approached them and asked them in Yiddish if they were Jews, and from where they had come. They stared at me and answered in halting Russian that they were Armenians, Azerbaijanis, Turkmans, Tatars, and more.

After some time they finally assigned us and I remained in my platoon with one and only one Augustovi, with Chuna Rudnik. To our luck there were another 3 Jews with us: one from Grayevo, one from Shtutzin, and one from Vansosh. Barukh Brenner and Beinish were transferred to another battalion. They were in another barracks in the same yard, and we would meet each day. After a few days they began to turn us into soldiers. We received clothing, rifles, and all the rest of the equipment. At first they taught us to march, and after a few months – military tactics and shooting. One day followed another, and month followed month. The training became harder from day to day. Time moved slowly. In this way 8 months of my being in the army went by, and only another sixteen months were left to the completion of service.

In the middle of the month of May 1941, our division received an order to gather its people and its "property," get up onto wagons, and travel. To where? No one knew. We travelled for 6 days until we reached Kiev. In Kiev we got down and went by foot to the area of Biala Tzarkiev. In the forests we dug posts and put up big tents, 16 people in each one. On the next day the battalion

360

went to the bathhouse in Biala Tzarkiev. In the city I encountered many Russian Jews. From them it became known to me that the Germans drafted an army and stationed it on the Russian border. I began to understand why they had transferred us, together with all the northern Caucuses' corps. On *Shabbat* June 22, 1941, we received an order to put on a full battle belt and to prepare for a race with full military equipment, a distance of 10 kilometers, with gas masks on our faces. The generals of the division and the "*Politruk*"[1029] gathered to take counsel.

*

Ten minutes before the hour of 12:00, the Lieutenant-General got up and opened with these words:

"Friends! Today, the *Shabbat* day, towards morning, June 22, 1941, the dark, armed[1030] forces of the German Hitlerists attacked our country, without a declaration of war. They bombed Grodno, Berdichev, Minsk, Kiev, and more. They crossed the border, entered Lithuania, Latvia, {p. 380} and Estonia. They also crossed the border to Belorussia (that is to say, they crossed the border from Prussia and entered Poland, in the area of our city). The Germans threw into battle thousands of tanks that they plundered from the conquered countries in Europe and from the enormous "Skoda" factories (factories in Czechoslovakia). Our soldiers retreated. It is our job, the soldiers of the Red Army, who are always ready to defend our soil, to enter the battle and hold back the enemy."

Exactly at the hour of 12:00 they activated the radio, and from it burst out the voice of Molotov, calling to the soldiers and the nation to defend their soil. A shiver passed through my body upon hearing the "message." All of us were despondent. It was immediately agreed among us, the Augustovians, that if one of us would see his friend killed in the battle, then the obligation fell to him, if he remained alive, to inform the parents of the slain the day and place of his falling, so that the parents would know on the day of the memorial (*yahrzeit*)[1031] to say *kaddish* for him. At night we went to see a movie that they were showing in the forest. The fabric was hung between two trees, and the movie was military, showing how the Russians were chasing the Japanese Samurais from their soil. During the time of the screening, there suddenly burst out a few German jets. Panic arose. They stopped the screening of the movie. We scattered in the panic, but to our luck they did not bomb us. On the next day with dawn, the brigade distanced itself a few hundred meters from the place, and began to entrench itself.

*

After a few days an order was given to our brigade to march to Kiev and get on the train that was already waiting for us. We loaded the cannons, the tanks, and the rest of our implements of destruction. On the roofs of the wagons we positioned machine guns to protect us from the planes of the enemy. It was known to me from the officers (I was involved with them, and I became endeared to them) that the objective of the journey was Lvov. The journey progressed slowly, and continued for many days. At every station we were forced to wait a long time. The road was loaded with military that travelled to the various fronts. In all of the stations I encountered trains with Russian and Jewish refugees, who had fled from Poland and Bessarabia. The engines and the wagons were punctured by bullets and shrapnel, the roofs were full of holes and dirt. Trains loaded with machines arrived, whole factories, that the Russians managed to dismantle in order to move them to Oriel and Siberia. Finally our train moved. Towards morning we reached Smolensk. The station was full of thousands of soldiers, and various weapons, which were loaded on the trains.

[1029] A supervisory political officer responsible for ideological education and organization.

[1030] This word, *mezuyanim*, מזוינים, is more likely to be translated here as "f**king, which a Russian officer might well have used to describe the German soldiers.

[1031] Yiddish for the anniversary of a death.

The soldiers from the nearby trains told that they were already waiting in Smolensk for a few days and could not move forward.

*

Towards morning a German reconnaissance plane appeared that flew very high above the station. Our cannons and machine guns opened fire at it. It flew above us for about ten minutes, and fled. Not an hour had passed when hundreds of German planes appeared above us, and began to rain from their machine guns, and to bomb us and the trains that stood in the station. Panic prevailed. The trains, the cannons, and chunks of human flesh – flew up into the sky. All around the German jets sowed death, and there was no one to give {p. 381} an order. I called to my friends that they should jump to the ditches that were at the edges of the tracks. I ran first, and they after me. We somehow hid ourselves until the planes emptied all their munitions and left, leaving after them death and destruction.

From our battalion about 70 men were left. I suggested that we get away from the place before the Germans returned with new munitions. We fled from Smolensk station and directed our steps far from settlements, by way of fields. We passed about 10 kilometers and sat down to rest. And here we see that tens of planes are nearing, from two directions, and flying over us. To our surprise we noticed in one squadron the identifying marks (a star) of Russian jets. In the second squadron were German jets. An air battle developed really right over our heads. Tens of planes went up in flames, and fell next to us with tremendous thunder. The German pilots that were left escaped. The Russians returned to their bases. We decided to flee, but we did not know to where…

*

After consultation we decided to retreat in the direction of Moscow. We were nearing the main Minsk-Moscow highway. This broad highway was full of soldiers, tanks, and cannons that were retreating from the German military corps. The movement was conducted with great slowness. The beginning and end of the long line could not be seen. On the way one could see tanks and vehicles that overturned on their soldiers when they fell from the high highway to the ditches that were at the edges of the highway. Killed people were seen with every step and pace, and no one was paying attention to them.

There was no room for the retreating infantry on the highway, and with no choice we walked by way of the fields that were next to the highway. After many hours of walking, we decided to sit and rest a little. Russian floodlights lit up the sky, and revealed a number of German planes. You could see the planes well, cannons against planes shooting at them, and always, missing. The German planes were shooting fireworks in the air, illuminating the whole area, and sowing panic. The tankists jumped from the tanks and fled, the vehicle drivers left their vehicles and fled, and we too fled a distance from the highway as much as possible, in the direction of the forest. We hid ourselves at the feet of the hills and in pits, and we waited for what was to come. After some time the sound of a great explosion was heard. At the time that the German planes lit up the highway and its surroundings, and sowed panic within the retreating army. Other planes parachuted saboteurs onto the Dnieper bridge who blew it up. The whole line that was moving on the highway was stopped, for it was not possible to move forwards or backwards. With dawn the German planes came and destroyed everything.

We, the infantry, remained in the forest and dug ourselves in. The hunger bothered us a lot. Over the course of weeks we did not see bread, and human food did not enter our mouths. We existed on wheat, rye, carrots, onions that we found in the fields. We also did not have water. We drank water from the swamps, which was crawling with all kinds of bugs, and stank. I became very weak, and I did not have the strength to continue to flee. My friends were also in the same condition. The day passed, and in the evening we placed our steps in the direction of the town of Dorogobuzh. In the nights we walked on the highway; before dawn we would go down from the

362

paved road, get a few kilometers away, and hide ourselves in the forests all day. The German planes were flying full hours over the forests. Suddenly there was someone from the retreaters shooting fireworks towards the planes, and they were immediately bombing the forest.

{p. 382} In light of these facts we decided not to allow soldiers that we did not recognize to follow behind us, but this did not help. We saw that German planes were parachuting on the outskirts of the fields, parachutist-saboteurs, in groups of 4-5 men equipped with 85- or 86- millimeter mortars and sub-machine guns that were shooting expanding bullets. We destroyed more than one group like this while they were still in the air. The Germans were parachuting saboteurs day and night, dressed in the clothing of Russian generals and officers. Next to the train stations saboteurs were parachuting in the clothing of train workers, or in the clothing of Russian policemen, and the like. These were destroying bridges and trains, and shelling the army that was hidden in the forests. We finally reached Dorogobuzh. I requested of our one officer that he should put at my disposal a few soldiers and I would go and look for a bakery. My request was granted. I took Chuna Rudnik and another two Russians with me. We found one and only one bakery. It worked for the army, the manager was a Jew, and he was also an army man. In Yiddish I told him our troubles, and that we were hungry, and that bread had not entered our mouths during the course of the entire retreat. He immediately gave each of us a loaf of bread, and we devoured it on the spot. He told us that the Germans were nearing Dorogobuzh, and in another few hours he was abandoning the city. He gave us as much bread as we were able to carry. We returned to our friends and told the news. We ate and rested until the evening.

*

Towards evening we went out and walked in the direction of the highway that went to Yartzevo. We met many soldiers that had fled for their lives after their defeat at the hands of the Germans in additional places. From them it became known to us that there was no other way to retreat but the road that led to Yartzevo, Yazma, and from there to Moscow. We went tens of kilometers until we reached Yartzevo. Next to Yartzevo we encountered barricades and next to them officers. They called to our officer and asked him where we were coming from and where we wanted to go. The officer explained that we were hit in Smolensk and were retreating to Moscow. The general informed us that we had to remain in Yartzevo. He called to the *Polkovnik* (Major-General), and commanded him to show us the section of the front that we had to hold. They told us that two days before the Germans had taken Yartzevo, the airfield, the ammunition storehouses that were across the river, and we had to chase them from their new bases. In the evening we would receive reinforcement, and it would be on us to attack. Our officer did not panic, he informed that first of all he had to feed the hungry young men, that food had not entered their mouths for a few weeks, and they had to give them a few days to rest. Food was not given to us, and we did not attack.

*

After a few days they brought food, weapons, and ammunition, and they also added men in order to bring the battalion up to full size. At the end of July 1941 towards morning the General visited our trenches with his staff. He said that on the next day in the afternoon we would receive an order to attack, jointly with other units, Yartzevo and the airfield that was about two kilometers on the other bank of the river, in order to destroy the German "bridge" behind our line. He asked if we would fulfill the order, and we answered as one: "Yes, Comrade General!"

On the next day, our artillery began to shell the German commando posts. Exactly at 12:00, we began to attack Yartzevo, and at evening time we captured it. We dug ourselves in and waited for reinforcements, {p. 383} which arrived after a few days. At the beginning of August an order came to cross the river at night and attack and conquer the airfield and the rest of the areas that were in the hands of the Germans. We went out towards evening for the attack. We crossed

363

the river and advanced without shooting, until we got about 200 meters before the German trenches. Then the Germans sensed us, or maybe they allowed us to approach deliberately. Suddenly they lit up the area, and opened heavy fire from automatic weapons and from tanks that were entrenched in the ground, and created havoc among us. When darkness fell, and the shooting stopped a little, I got up and ran for my life. On the way I heard someone calling my name. By the voice I recognized that it was my old friend, the Uzbek Chadirov. I approached him and saw that he was seriously wounded in the belly. I tore his shirt and his undershirt; I took out a bandage and I bandaged him. I left him in his place, and I ran to the place from which we attacked. On the way I found another friend who was also seriously wounded. Finally I reached the river and crossed it. There I met about another twenty men, among them Chuna Rudnik. I told the officer about the two seriously wounded men, our good friends, who were lying in a place a distance of a kilometer from where we were. He put at my disposal 6 men, and charged me with bringing the two wounded. I went with the "group" by way of the field that bordered the main highway, where it was possible to walk upright. When I felt that we had reached the place across from where the wounded Chadirov was lying, I ordered the "chevre"[1032] to cross the road behind me. Not one of them moved. The four Russians announced that they would remain in their place and provide cover for us. I explained that in another half hour it would be dawn, and we would be unable to return. They insisted, for they were afraid. I threatened them that I would tell the officer that they did not want to fulfill an order, but despite this they were frightened, and remained. I and another two – one of whom was Maniak Grayevsky – climbed to the edges of the highway (the highway was 15-meters high in that place, and I deliberately chose that place).

With the "Shma Yisrael"[1033] prayer in my heart, I crossed the road peacefully, crawling. I waited for the other two to cross also, but they were afraid and did not move. I was forced to return to them, and with difficulty convinced them to cross after me. We came down from the highway, loaded the wounded onto a canvas sheet (which served also as a tent, a coat, and a sheet), and we began to walk. The body of the wounded man was on the sheet, and his feet dragged on the ground. He screamed from all the pain. I explained to him that he should not scream, lest the Germans hear and open fire, but he apparently could not overcome the pain and he screamed the whole way. It was difficult for three men to carry him. The two of them held the front edges of the sheet. It was pleasant and easy for them, I held onto the two edges of the side with the lower part of his body. The feet that were dragging on the ground interfered with my walking. I made an effort and carried him with what was left of my strength. I asked the Grayevi to switch with me a little – he would in no way agree. At that moment the Germans lit up the area, shots were heard, and this Grayevsky grabbed his chest with his hand and screamed "Ma…" He did not have time to say the word "Mama" and fell on me killed. The wounded Chadirov also received a bullet from the same burst, which killed him. We left everything, the two of us lifted our feet, and fled in the direction of the river.

*

We crossed the river in peace and joined our friends. In the afternoon a special runner came from the Division Staff, bringing the news that in the evening a new brigade that would relieve us. The brigade that came was made up of men dressed in civilian clothes and their weapons were one rifle for every two or {p. 384} three. There were many adults among them. They were refugees from the towns that were conquered by the Germans. We left that section and walked along the river until we reached a giant fabric factory (the second largest in Russia). They ordered us to enter the factory and settle in there. We sent a few men to bring potatoes from the fields. The

---

[1032] A group of friends. Different than the Hebrew word *kvutza*, group, this word is based on the root *chaver*, friend. It does not really have an English counterpart.
[1033] Hear O Israel, YHVH is our God, YHVH is One.

"*chevre*" brought potatoes and a few chickens that they caught, and we prepared a meal. We ate and lay down to rest under the machines, so that we would be protected from shells and shrapnel. I was deathly tired, and I immediately fell asleep. In my dream a beautiful man came to me, adorned with a black beard and a large *kippah*[1034] on his head, and he resembled my grandfather Reb Shmuel Yosef, who I had never seen, but I recognized him from a picture that was hung on the wall of our house. He caressed me, placed his hand on my shoulder, and said: "my son, tomorrow you are going to an attack. Go, don't be afraid. Don't submit and don't hide yourself, for you will not be killed, although soon you will be wounded." I woke up terrified. A cold sweat broke out on my forehead, but I was happy, and new hopes awakened within me. Until the end of my life, I will believe in the dream.

Towards evening they sent us reinforcement. From the day that we entered the battle and until this very day, we remained 16 veteran soldiers in our brigade. We guarded each other as much as possible. We all received ranks. Some were division commanders, some were in contact with the division, and some were in the "Staff." We were very connected to each other.

Meanwhile the Germans broke through the Russian defense lines. They conquered towns and came near to Yartzevo.

The next day an order came to prepare for the attack. The engineering force prepared a crossing from rafts on the river. Half an hour before 12:00 the Russian tanks opened up with shelling on the German positions, and exactly at 12:00 in the afternoon the order came to attack. We began to advance. Part of us had time to cross on the rafts in peace. But when the turn of the second half came to cross, the Germans noticed them and opened with terrible cannon fire. Shells fell on a raft and destroyed it. There were many sacrifices. We did not wait, since we were afraid to lag after other brigades, and we attacked. We advanced quickly and conquered the train station and another few villages. We did not have time to dig in, and the Germans opened with a total counterattack, with the help of ten tanks. They were arranged in rows head-on, and began to advance towards us, while they were drunk and shooting from sub-machine guns. They didn't even duck. We allowed them to come close and then we opened fire. The first line was almost destroyed but about 100 meters after it marched a second row, a third, etc. – all of them drunk. We destroyed row after row, and they did not stop walking on the corpses of their soldiers and to come near us. We could no longer hold the position and we retreated about a kilometer. We entrenched ourselves in a four-story school. Around it we positioned mortars and machine guns. Meanwhile reinforcement reached us and entrenched itself behind us, and all of us together shattered the counterattack. The Germans suffered heavy losses and retreated. The night came. Under the cover of darkness more reinforcements of men and artillery came to us, and took positions. The next day we continued the attack. The Germans retreated and we advanced slowly. In this attack I lost the last Augustovi – my friend Chuna Rudnik. I did not see him again.

*

On September 12, 1941, on *Shabbat* before the afternoon, when I advanced in the attack with my friend the last Jew, about 40, from Minsk (I no longer remember his name), a shell exploded next to us. My friend {p. 385} was thrown into the air and torn limb from limb, and I fell wounded and unconscious on the ground. After some time I began to feel cold, and slowly my eyes opened a little. There was no one around me. I got up from the ground and felt myself, to convince myself that I was still alive. I felt the injuries; the mouth and the bottom half of the nose were torn, the upper jaw was broken, and also eight upper teeth. Shrapnel penetrated my cheeks and the area of the eyes. I took out a handkerchief that was dirty with ash, put it on the torn mouth, and began to run with the remains of my strength towards the river that was next to the forest. I

[1034] Skullcap.

knew that the Division Staff was there in the forest, and a temporary hospital. On the way I met a compassionate brother and requested that he bandage my wound. He put a bandage on my mouth, but it was dropping and falling. I was forced to hold my hand on my mouth. I requested that he help me to go and show me the way. He refused. He was afraid because there was heavy shooting in the area, and it was impossible to walk at full height. I took out the pistol that was with me, aimed it at his chest, and said that he would go with me or I would shoot him, and the two of us would die here. He was terrified, and so with difficulty I got to the bank of the river and fell. A few soldiers caught me and took me across the river on their backs. They brought me to an underground clinic or hospital. My face swelled up and shut my eyes. I became blind and deaf. I also could not speak. The hunger troubled me greatly. For two days food did not enter my mouth. Finally someone came, patted me on my shoulder, and said something to me. I requested that he speak loudly. He asked if I needed to go out. He supported me and I walked after him. Afterwards he returned me. After some time he came back and took me to the office. There they asked me what brigade I was from, what was my name, and the name of my family. They did not understand me, so I requested paper and a pencil. With one hand I opened the eye and with the second hand I wrote. At night they loaded me with other wounded onto a vehicle and brought us to the forest. Underground were two hospitals. There they sutured the wounds and took out the shrapnel and I began to see again. The next day they took me, with a group of severely wounded, and brought us to the airfield, a distance of a few hundred meters from the hospitals. They put me and another wounded man on a plane (every plane took two wounded people), and transferred us to Kondrova. After the emergency room they transferred me to Murmas and from there to Viksim in Gorky district. I lay there for two weeks.

*

The front got closer to Moscow. They began to evacuate the military hospitals that were found in the areas of the range of the bombs of the enemy. For this purpose a sanitary train came. They transferred all the seriously wounded to the train. After two days it went out to the long way to Siberia. The sanitary train was equipped with beds, with doctors and nurses, and they performed operations in it. The wounded who were able to walk would pass from car to car looking for acquaintances. I too was among the walkers. The Russians recognized that I was a Jew, would belittle me, and ask "why aren't you like all the Jews, who sit themselves far from the front in offices and live it up? You, loser, went to the front, and here, see what shape you are in." They liked me and would share with me in everything. On the second day of travelling, during a friendly conversation with the wounded, I discerned in one that his hand was put in a cast. I "suspected" that he was a Jew, I approached him, and asked him if he was "*amcha*" (this is a sign of recognition between Jews). He denied it. The next day I asked him where he was from. He answered that he was from Belorussia. I pressured him to tell me from exactly what place, and then he clarified that he was from Lomza.

{p. 386} The train swallowed up the vast distances of Russia. Here we were in Kazan, and here is Orel. On all the roads were trains loaded with soldiers. The Siberians were travelling to defend Moscow, the capital. In every place our train was delayed a few days and allowing the military trains that were hurrying to the front to pass. Very slowly, after a journey of six weeks, we arrived at Novo-Sibirsk. They took some of the wounded off the train and moved them to hospitals, and I too was among them. The hospital that I arrived at was new and stood on the main street, across from the unfinished opera building. In the hospital they received us warmly, since we were the first wounded that reached Siberia.

*

In February 1942, my wounds were healed. They also made me eight false teeth, but while eating they would fall out. I almost swallowed them. I went to the doctor and demanded that they

366

make the teeth on crowns for me. She refused. I got agitated and I hurled at her: "Is this my reward for coming from Poland and spilling my blood to fight for you? I will not go to the front again." Not an hour went by, when a messenger came and invited me to the Commissar. The Commissar began to interrogate me about what I said to the doctor. I told him that I requested that they make me good teeth. He said that I slandered the government and I said that I would not go to the front. He commanded to bring my clothing, and put me into a room whose only furniture was two wooden beds without mattresses. The cold in it was terrible. They locked the room, and outside the door they posted a guard. Hours went by. I very much regretted the slip of the tongue that had brought this kind of trouble on me. My mind began to work vigorously. Suddenly there flashed in my mind a wonderful idea, which indeed was what saved me. I knew that the Director of the hospital was Jewish, an adult woman at the rank of Colonel. I decided to go see her, be what may. I knocked on the door of my cell and asked the guard to bring me to the bathroom. On the way I noticed the room of the hospital Director. In the blink of an eye I opened the door and entered the room, running, when the guard grabbed me by my robe. I said that I wanted to speak with her about an important matter. She ordered the guard to go out, and the two of us remained in the room. I began a conversation with her in Yiddish, and I told her that I was a Jew from Poland, that I was wounded in battles, and the Germans murdered all the members of my family, etc. I added that the division administration was anti-semitic, and that I was worried about my fate. The speech greatly influenced her, and tears glistened in her eyes. She quieted me and promised that tomorrow they would free me from imprisonment. I returned to my room, but I could not find rest for my soul. My worries and my fears were very great. I closed my eyes, but I could not fall asleep. And here I hear that the door to my room was opening, and a person in civilian dress was entering. He seated himself on my bed and asked why I was placed in detention. I told him everything, he said goodbye, and he left.

On the next day they freed me. I wandered around in the hospital about another ten days. On February 27, 1942 I went out of the hospital with a group of soldiers to a selection place.

*

The selection station was full of soldiers who had recovered from their wounds, with Soviet soldiers from the areas of the German conquest, with soldiers that came from the areas that the Russians had conquered from Poland, in Serbia, Lithuania, and more. All these the Soviet regime returned from the front, or did not allow to travel to the front, since it did not trust them.

{p. 387} In addition to these, there was a Polish battalion from General Andres' army, that was preparing to travel to Iran. In one of the corners of the selection station was a buffet that sold various drinks and sauerkraut. I stood in line to buy cabbage. I felt someone put his hand on my shoulder, turned my head around and was amazed. Before me stood the Lomza'i with whom I travelled in the sanitary train. This time he did not deny that he was a Jew, and added that they called him Yoske (he is in the land). We became friends. We walked around together in the station, and found many Jews from Lvov, from Stanislavov, from Kishinev, and more. I was afraid lest they send me to the front again, and I decided on a daring step. I told my new friend about my plan, to enter the office of the station commander and demand from him a transfer to the Polish army. He hesitated, but in the end he agreed. I approached the door of the commander's office, opened it, and entered, and after me, my friend. Across from me sat the Station Commander, the Major-General. I saluted, and requested permission to speak. When I made my request, I told him that we were from Poland, that we volunteered for the Red Army, that we spilled our blood for the Soviet homeland, and now we were requesting that he transfer us to the Polish army, in which our relatives were found. After a short consultation, the General responded that for the time being we would work in the rear, and when there would be an additional recruitment to the Polish army, they would inform us. We were also happy with this answer, and we went out in peace. The next day the managers of factories, construction works, and army storehouses came to the sorting station to recruit workers. Each of them passed before us, while we were standing in a row, and asked for various professionals, or someone who graduated elementary school. My friend and I were in one group. They loaded us on a vehicle and brought us, by way of the forests, to the Anskaya train station. There they gave us food, money, and clothing, and sent us to the bathhouse.

The next day the manager explained our role to us. He said that it would be good for us if we would work in order. He asked each one about his education, and according to the answers assigned to each one his place and type of work. They set me up as helper to the manager of the division. In the division worked hundreds of civilian women, who would arrange and bind and count the army clothing, shoes, etc. Over the course of two weeks they called me to the office and said that they were thinking about appointing me manager of the division, but I had to know, that I would need to check the women workers each day, that they had not stolen something and tied it on their bodies. If God forbid something should be missing from the monthly stock, then I would be responsible. I heard these words and immediately answered that I did not accept this kind of responsibility on myself, since I struggled with Russian writing. They transferred me, therefore, to the role of guarding the main exit. I was obligated to check and to count the fabrics, the shoes, etc., that were registered in the transport certificate of every truck and also to feel in the clothing of all the workers and the officers that were going out. My friend stood in the passageway behind me in the same role. We agreed between us that we would not get entangled in unkosher activities. It happened, that they loaded onto one truck more than had been declared on the certificate, and the officer who was responsible for the truck would come and offer me a bribe. I always rejected such offers. My work was interesting, I earned well, the food was excellent, I received clothing, and it was very good for me.

Half a year went by and I became ill with fever. For about two months they treated me without success. Finally they dismissed me. My friend quit, since he did not want to part from me, and they sent the two of us back to Novo-Sibirsk, to the sorting station.

In the sorting station they drafted me and my friend to a work battalion. This was a big government company. Its role was to serve all the army brigades in Novo-Sibirsk and the surrounding area. I and my Lomza friend were sent to building work, to carry bricks and more. We saw that it was nasty business, and did not {p. 388} go out to work. When the supervisor threatened us, I told him that we were not political convicts, but rather, wounded, and that we would not work unless they arranged guard duty for us. Meanwhile all of them were assigned to various work, but for me no suitable place was found. I began to walk around in the market. I met Jewish merchants from Kiev who fled to Novo-Sibirsk during the time of the war, and managed shops for cotton wool. The dealings were not kosher. Most of the managers of warehouses and shops in the city were connected to each other, and supported by each other. I entered into this "commerce," and I earned a great deal, until they informed on me that I was not working, and gorging myself on everything good, while they, the Russians, were working hard and didn't have enough food. I was invited to the Commissar. There were with him another 7 men who didn't want to work. He asked me from where I had money and clothing and so much food, in a time when I wasn't working at all. I denied everything, but he sent all of us, accompanied by guards, to the police commander, and asked that he arrest us as "refusing work." The commander asked each of why we did not want to work. I answered that I was severely wounded, and that I could not carry bricks, and that I was ready to engage in guard duty or something like that.

I was appointed as a supervisor of a large stable. My job was to feed the horses, to clean the stable, to distribute to the waggoneers, etc. There were six workers who worked in three shifts. I worked with one other 24 hours straight, and then two days we would rest. On the free day off I would engage in selling. I also brought the Lomza'i into the business, since his situation was difficult. Selling was more than enough for all of us.

*

One day I returned from the market feeling unwell. My head was feeling dizzy, my appetite disappeared, and my knees were collapsing. I lay down to rest. My temperature went up and I almost lost consciousness. My friend Yoske ran to call the medic. He came, checked me, and determined that I was sick with a type of typhus. He filled out a questionnaire, and sent me to the hospital for infectious diseases. I went by foot. I reached the hospital with difficulty, and there was no room, and they directed me to another hospital. It too did not accept me. When I reached the fifth hospital I collapsed, and fell unconscious. I returned to consciousness over a course of two weeks. Since in the nights I would get up from my bed and wander around the room, they would tie me to the bed. After two weeks, the crisis passed and a binge of ravenous hunger attacked me. I would eat all the portions of the unconscious soldiers in my room. The water that was in the bottle was not enough for me, I always asked for more. A fire burned within me. After a month they permitted me to go out of my room. I went into the bathroom, opened the faucet, and drank a lot of cold water. The next day I was sick with dysentery, and I lay another month. I left the hospital in the middle of the winter and went to the "barrack." I did not have the strength to walk upright, the wind and the ice hampered me. I preferred to crawl on my knees to the shared apartment. There my friends met me, and immediately cooked potatoes in a large pot for me, which I swallowed quickly. They told me that after I got sick, a wave of typhus broke out in the "barrack." The medic got infected from me, and he infected almost all of them. They took him to the hospital and he died there, and another few men died. My friends went to visit me in the hospital where I had first been sent, and they told them that I was not there. They thought, therefore, that I had died. Slowly, slowly, my strength returned to me.

*

{p. 389} The months went by. I, with my partner, engaged in selling in our free time, until on one bright day, my friend Yoske was caught with a cargo of merchandise. The policeman confiscated the merchandise, and invited him to walk behind him to the police. In this way the policeman gave, intentionally, an opportunity to my friend to flee, in order that the merchandise remain in his hand, and he would not have to turn it over to the government. The matter recurred over and over each day. Things reached a point that my friend could not engage in selling in that city, and moved to sell in another city.

Immediately after I got well, I left the barrack and moved to live in a private house, with Russian people. The landlord and the members of his family were good-hearted people. They did not agree to receive the rent; sometimes I even found, when I returned home, that my work clothes had been laundered.

One day, at the end of the year 1943, I met with my friend from Grodno, Yasha Kobrinski. He told me that he met one Augustovi in the draft office, and his name was Alter Kaplanski. I was very happy, for not only was he from my city, but he and his parents lived near us for many years. I succeeded in finding him, and from that day we would meet very frequently. He told that he was working as a fuel warehouse man. Once, he told me and my friend, that he could sell fuel, and that the drivers were prepared to pay any price. We advised him not to engage in this.

Alter was a regular guest by me and by friend over the course of about half a year. Suddenly his visits stopped. When two weeks went by and he didn't come, I went to his apartment. His landlady told me, weeping, that about ten days before emissaries from the N.K.V.D. came in the night and took him. We tried to investigate his fate, but it was told to us by a friend of his that we should not look for trouble…in this way I lost my neighbor and my fellow townsman.

369

The war was continuing. The front required reserves. Already they were drafting almost everyone, even the "politicals." Men from the draft bureau were coming to the factories, the warehouses, and the like, closing the gates in order to not let anyone evade the inspections. They were also stopping men in the markets and streets of the city and checking their release papers. Only those who had great "*protectzia*"[1035] succeeded in being released. In an atmosphere like this, my turn came, too, to present myself for inspection. In the medical examination I was classified as fit for the front; in the political examination, as unfit, since I said that I was from Suwalk, which did not belong to the Russian protectorate, but to Poland. The chairman, a Major-General, looked at the map that was hung on the wall, and ruled to free me and three other Jews, since we were from Poland. We remained to wait until we received our release papers. After the chairman and the doctors had gone their way, an officer nevertheless ruled that we had to present ourselves in three days at the train station, in order to be sent to the front. We were afraid to open our mouths and we went to pack our belongings. I succeeded in selling part of my possessions, part I left for my good landlords.

{p. 390} At the appointed time we presented ourselves at the train station. On the next day we reached Kamarova. There they trained us without a pause.

After two weeks of difficult training, the order was given to go out to the front.

*

The train went out on a long road. It travelled with great speed to the front, in order to crush the Nazi animal. We went by Novo-Sibirsk, the city where I spent 2 ½ years. We passed Omsk and Tomsk, reached Kazan, and from there to Moscow. Day and night I was sitting by the window, and looking at the wonderful scenery of Siberia and Oriel, and my eyes could not get enough of seeing. In every direction, from Vyazma on, one could see the traces of the Germans, who burned or cut down the forests and the settlements, in a diameter of a kilometer or more, from two sides of the iron tracks, from fear of the Russian Partisans, who blew up and took down the German trains that were loaded with soldiers and tanks. The train went by Smolensk, Minsk, Hummel, and was approaching Vitebsk. The front was already very close. Before the old Russian-Polish border, from before 1939, the train was stopped. We got off next to the Molodizhna forest (if I am not mistaken), which only a few days before was conquered by the Russians. The forests were full of thousands of soldiers and thousands of modern implements of destruction. Here they divided the soldiers into brigades that were needed for reserves, after they had been thinned out in the battles. I, and about a dozen[1036] Jews from Stanislavov and Bessarabia were joined to the 695 Foot Brigade, from the 221st Division, which belonged to the Belorusian Third Army. The Commander of the Army was the Jewish Marshall Tchernichovsky. We rested in the forests for three days. Each one received his weapon and all the equipment of a battle soldier. On the next day the order was given to go out to the front singing.

*

We crossed the old border. We entered the towns of Soly, Keni, we conquered Smorgon, Oshmyani, and Stara-Velika. We advanced towards Vilna. The Germans began a speedy retreat. It was really a "pleasure" to see how the "heroes" were fleeing, and leaving everything behind them. We did not have enough time to chase after them. A battle over Vilna developed. Our brigade conquered the train station and the surrounding streets, and the rest of the brigades completed its capture. After the conquest of Vilna, we got a day off. After a day of rest, we entered the battle

---

[1035] Connections that protected them from the draft.
[1036] Aramaic.

and conquered a few villages, we crossed the old Polish-Lithuanian border, and advanced towards Kovno. We crossed the river Niemen quickly on rafts, and entered the city together with other brigades. We received a few days of liberty to fill in our brigade, whose men had dwindled in battle. I went with my friend to the Kovno market to buy brandy and various foods. I noticed there a Jew and a Jewess. I asked them in Russian if they were "*amcha*" (Jews). They answered that they were not, but when I began a conversation with them in Yiddish, they told me that they were Jews, and that they had emerged from the forest only two days earlier. They looked in every direction, gripped by fear, asked me not to speak with them, and left. After we rested, the Major-General came for a visit and announced that our brigade had been given the job of conquering Mariampol. On the next day {p. 391} the cannons and the Katyushas opened up with great noise, and in face-to-face battle we conquered the city. As a reward for our heroic acts, they called our division The Mariampol Division. The corpses of the Nazis lay everywhere, and there were very many captives in our hands. We didn't know what to do with them.

After the capture of Mariampol, we advanced quickly to Kalvaria. We entered into very heavy battle, since Kalvaria lies on high hills. Within the hills were reinforced concrete fortifications. We advanced in the tanks to Kalvaria, and in face-to-face battle we conquered it. The Germans fled in every direction, we pursued them, and we also conquered Vierzblova. We reached the Lithuanian-Prussian border, next to the great Masurian lake. We had no more strength left to pursue. We remained few, and tired to death. Over the course of weeks we almost didn't sleep, and we didn't take off our shoes. On our toes great wounds developed from sweat and decomposition; the men fell and fainted from the super-human effort. When Marshall Tchernichovsky saw that his boys were unable to move from their places, he gave us another day's rest, and commanded to bring a military band. Afterwards he began to speak to us. In his surveying the long way that we had crossed until we reached the border of the Nazi animal's lair, he said to us, that here, in its lair, we needed to destroy it once and for all. When the sign was given, the band began to play, the soldiers arose, and the feet began to march by themselves.

*

To the sound of the music of the band, we crossed the German-Lithuanian border and entered Prussia. Every house in their villages was built in strategic fashion. In every house, a reinforced concrete basement, which was able to withstand artillery fire. The most effective weapons against fortifications like this were grenades. One had to capture house after house. In conditions like these we advanced towards the holding of the German Air Marshal, the Nazi Goring. We conquered the bridge, made of concrete, adorned with statues of lions and stags, that was on the river, and advanced about two kilometers by way of a thick and well-kept forest, to Goring's palace, which we conquered at night, in face-to-face battle. We rested there and in the morning we advanced forward and conquered villages and farms. In those villages and towns we did not encounter even one German citizen. They fled a few weeks before this, when they heard that the Russian army was rapidly advancing, and when they saw that the German army was retreating. We approached Goldap without resting, pursuing the fleeing German army.

We received an order to get up on the tanks. We entered Goldap, which was full of German citizens and army men who did not expect us at all. We jumped from the tanks and began a face-to-face battle. The tanks destroyed mercilessly. Finally we conquered Goldap. After a few hours the Germans recovered and moved to a counterattack, and reconquered Goldap. We retreated about two kilometers from the city, fortified ourselves, and dug ourselves into the German cemetery. We did not have enough men with which to attack. The men and the weapons dwindled in the battles. We waited for reserves.

At the end of October 1944 an order was received that the whole battalion would go out for a day tour, in order to check the German strength and equipment that were arrayed against us, and to catch German soldiers alive from whom it would be possible to extract information. The Major-General himself oversaw the operation. He commanded to bring very many cannons and Katyushas, which opened heavy fire on the German positions. Under cover of fire we dashed {p. 392} forward and we reached the German posts. We threw grenades and created havoc among them. The captive soldiers told that they were from a Hungarian brigade, while others were from a battalion of Poles (*folksdeutchen*).[1037] We understood that arrayed against us this time were not Germans, but rather their Hungarian and Polish partners. They revealed to us where the brigade staff was. Our Commander asked who volunteered to go out about thirty meters forward from our posts, to be a sniper. My friend, who was a commander of a squad, volunteered and went out with a sniper's rifle. The next day he came and told me that he discovered the place of the German staff, and that the way was possible under his sniper fire. He suggested that I go with him to see how he was destroying Germans. I acceded to him. And indeed, we would only see one German on the way – a bullet was expelled, and the German was no more. This "game" very much found favor in my eyes. I immediately requested a sniper's rifle, and I remained with him to hunt "Fritzes."[1038] We sat together in that cemetery for about three weeks and sought prey. When German appeared in "our territory," we immediately killed them. The Germans noticed this, and started seeking us with the help of shelling. In the last two days they covered our approximate territory with hundreds of shells, which exploded in front of and behind us.

*

On November 29, 1944, the German shells found us. When a German shell crashed right next to me, on the left side, I was wounded and fell covered in my blood and unconscious. After a time, when I returned to consciousness, I stood up in great pain and I saw my friend Dmitry Bogoslavitz from Stanislavov sitting in his place at the post. I yelled to him that he should bandage my wound. When he did not answer I kicked him, until I saw that blood was dripping from his head and congealing on his forehead. I understood that he was not alive. I ran in the direction of the posts, which were full of mud from the rain and the snow, until I reached my friends. An orderly bandaged me, and transferred me to the hospital that was next to the division. I felt strong pains in my head, which was wounded, as if hammers incessantly pounded in it, and in my back, which was wounded by shrapnel to the depth of the left lung from above, and in my left hand, which was paralyzed. They immediately tore off my shirt, which was red with blood. I lost consciousness.

*

When I regained consciousness, after three weeks, I was in the hospital in Kovno. Next to my bed stood 6-8 doctors who asked me how I feel, and what hurt me. They consulted among themselves and told me that they would give me a blood transfusion, and that after two days they would operate on my head. I asked them what happened to my head, and they answered that the skull was fractured, and inside, until the membrane of the brain, there were many shards of shells of all sizes. Besides that there was also shrapnel in the skull bones, and they had to at least remove these, for they were endangering my life.

After two days they gave me various injections and took me to the operating room. Among the surgeons I recognized that one was a Jew. He had a typical Jewish face with an eagle nose. I saw that they wanted to tie me to the table, and I said that I would be quiet and ready for everything, and that they should not tie me. I began a conversation in Yiddish with the surgeon, and I asked him to spare my life. I told him who I was, and from where {p. 393} I came. I saw that

---

[1037] In Nazi German terminology, Volksdeutsche were people whose language and culture had German origins but who were not German citizens.
[1038] Germans.

372

my story touched his heart. They put a sheet on my head, with an opening, and I immediately felt that something was stuck into my head, and was cutting. The whole time the surgeon was talking to me in Yiddish and asking me about my home, and who remained there, and I answered him with difficulty. I felt strong pains, and I asked the surgeon to do something to quiet them. Afterwards I felt that the surgeon was working with "tweezers" and saying to me that I should not move my head even one millimeter, since he was removing shrapnel from the membrane of my brain, and if I moved, the tweezers was likely to puncture the brain, and then I would be lost. When I heard these things, I tried with all my strength not to move my head. When he finished taking out the shrapnel, they stitched the skull, bandaged it, and put me into a room for the severely ill (two in a room). Meanwhile my face and my head swelled up, and I couldn't see anything for a few days. I couldn't walk around or move, and when one side hurt from prolonged laying on it, I asked the nurse to turn me to the other side.

Days passed, the swelling went down, and I was already able to sit up in bed. Very slowly, I began to get off the bed to go to the bathroom, holding the wall with one hand, and my head with the other. Very slowly I got stronger, and I began to walk around in the hallways. The doctors decided then to send me to the rear.

*

On one of the cold days of December of the year 1944, they transferred me from the hospital in Kovno to a sanitary train that was collecting all of the severely wounded that were being sent to the rear to the various hospitals.

Me they brought to a giant hospital in the center of Ivanovo, near Moscow, which only took care of head wounds. Immediately the wounded who had been there for a long time surrounded me, and asked me where I was from, and from which front I came from, and what was going on at the front, and how we beat the "Fritzes," etc. We became friends. We played dominos, chess, and checkers. We would go to see a movie, a performance, comedians, a band of singers or musicians that would very frequently come to entertain us and lighten things for us. Delegations would come from various organizations and from factories and bring small gifts: notebooks, envelopes, pouches for tobacco (*Makhorka*)[1039] that were made by hand and embroidered by hand. Every gift had a small letter included, with an address, asking the wounded man to reply to the sender of the gift. In this way the wounded found friends among the citizens that would come to visit them; after their recovery the wounded would visit in the houses of their friends.

The wound on my head continued to heal. The hand and the back healed on their own, without the care of doctors, but there remained in my back much shrapnel, and one piece was next to the left lung. They are there to this day. Another two weeks went by, the wound in my head was almost healed, but there remained a wound the size of a match head, which according to the calculation of the doctors should have already formed a scab, but it remained open and was oozing pus. The matter aroused the doctors' suspicion, and one day I was called to the doctors' room, in which was also the Director of the hospital, an adult Jewish woman, who recognized me from her visits to my room (she knew that I was the only Jew in the hospital). The doctors had reached the conclusion that they needed to send me for Roentgen pictures.[1040] After I had the Roentgen pictures, I returned to my room. Together with me in the room there was a Ukrainian by the name of Tzervinski. When I arrived at the hospital, he was already walking around and they thought to send him home, but he had a wound like mine, and they decided to operate on him again. And so, {p. 394} they operated on him that same day, returned him to the room, and towards morning he died. The orderlies who came to the room in order to transfer him to the morgue made a mistake,

---

[1039] Coarse tobacco that was high in nicotine, especially grown in Russia and Ukraine.
[1040] X-rays.

and approached me. I was in deep sleep, but when they took hold of me with their hands and wanted to put me on the stretcher, I opened my eyes, looked at them, and asked them what they wanted. They were confused and stuttered that they sent them to take Tzervinski to the morgue. After I explained to them that my name was Sarvianski, they let me go, and took the dead Tzervinski.

*

After two days a nurse came to shave my head before the operation. I refused. The surgeon called me to his room and explained that the operation was necessary. I did not agree and returned to my room. After some time, the Director of the hospital, the Jewish woman, sent to call me to her room. I answered her and came. I told her that I was very afraid of a second operation on my head, and the main part of the fear was because of the surgeon, that he was young, and in all the operations that he performed, the patients died. The Director explained to me that pus had accumulated in my head, between the membrane that enveloped the brain and the inner bone of the skull, as a result of shifting shrapnel. Since the external wound had healed, no path remained for the pus to emerge, and there was a danger that the pus would burst the membrane and be spilled into the brain, and then there would be no saving me. She advised me, for my own good, to be operated on that same day. I turned to the Director with a request that she operate on me. She answered that she and the surgeon would operate on me together. That relieved me and I agreed.

They immediately shaved my head, and towards evening of the same day I entered the operating room by myself. There the Director and the young surgeon were already waiting. I got up on the operating table. They injected a few local anesthetics, put the sheet with the opening on me, and after a few minutes I felt the scalpel at work. Blood dripped from my head and went into my left eye. I lay without fear, without moving my head. The Director spoke to me in Russian the whole time. After they finished their work and stitched the wound, they lay me on a stretcher, and brought me to the room. My head immediately swelled up, but after a few days the swelling went down. Two weeks went by, and the wound was healing nicely. After a month I was already walking around without a bandage. Every few days I would go to the doctors' room, where the Director always was, for an examination. Once I complained that a large piece of shrapnel which was exactly next to my left eye was bothering me. They knew about it from the Roentgen pictures. The surgeon offered to operate, but informed that he was not responsible for the eye. I passed on the operation.

Very slowly the time went by. I stayed in the hospital a little longer, and on March 27, 1945, they gave me instructions how to behave in daily life, dressed me in old army clothing, gave me dry food, a product card for the way, documents, and sent me home.

I left the hospital and walked to the city Commander. I requested a free travel ticket to the city of my birth and a permit to cross the border to Poland. He gave me the permit and a free travel ticket to Lublin. In a letter that he sent in my hand to the Commander of the 9th Infantry Brigade of the Polish Army, which resided in the buildings of the Majdanek extermination camp (3 kilometers from Lublin), was instruction to hold {p. 395} me in his brigade for 3 weeks in order to guide a division from the Polish Army. I travelled to Lublin on the train and from there I walked on foot to Majdanek. I remained there three weeks.

On the festival of *Pesach*, all the Jewish soldiers went to "Peretz House" in Lublin, where a public *seder* was held.

The next day we went to visit the museum in Majdanek. The Germans did not have time to blow up this extermination camp. We entered the area of the warehouses. One of them was full of shoes of every size, glasses, people's hair, all kinds of clothing, *tallitot*, etc. We went to another area, and in it were the shacks in which the death camp prisoners lived. We saw two-story wooden beds, upon which were carved Hebrew and foreign names. Outside, between the shacks, in the

374

small yards, all kinds of miniature castles and mansions were made from small stones, works of art, and also on them were engraved Hebrew names, like for example: this is the handiwork of Ploni… We entered the crematorium. The ovens were open like baking ovens. Next to every oven was an iron wagon the length of a person, which moved on an iron track to the oven. Under the oven was a very thick steel screen, by way of which the ashes fell. I wept. Others fainted.

We went down to the cellar, about 15 meters from the crematorium, and we saw the arrangement of pipes by way of which the fat of the burned dripped, straight to the barrels. A little farther on, the "RIF" soap (*Rein Iddishe Fats*).[1041] At the other end stood a surgical table made of cement, on which they would open the belly, take out the stomach, and search for diamonds and gold. Next to the surgical table was a dentist's chair, also made of cement, on which they would extract gold teeth. There was no grass around, everything was covered with ash and human bone fragments.

We passed on to the gas chambers. A very low building made of cement, with no windows. Only in the steel door was there a small window, through which the executioners could see if the victims had already suffocated. I entered with the guide in the rear door of the crematorium, by which they would bring in the victims "to bathe." When one enters this doorway, one gets the impression of a bathhouse, with faucets and showers. Hermetic doors divided between this room and the gas chambers. The victims passed through these doors to the gas chambers (the murderers would lie to them and tell them that by way of these rooms was the exit to the outside). When all of them had entered inside, the doors were shut, and within about half an hour, all were poisoned by the gas.

From the crematorium we went to the area of open trenches (the Poles had opened the communal graves), and next to them was a giant heap of the skulls of the murdered, the bones of arms and legs. About ten meters from the trenches stood four or five gallows, on which they hung the managers of the camp who did not have time to flee. I emerged from this museum with a broken heart.

*

Three weeks went by. The soldiers that I guided were sent to the front. The wounded guides, and I among them, were sent to their homes. I got on a train in Lublin, and in peace reached Warsaw, which had been destroyed down to its foundation. From Warsaw I travelled to Bulumin. There were the bridges of the Russian railroad tracks, and it was impossible to move forward. I reached Radzymin by wagon. There I got on a train, and came at night to Bialystok. I spent the night in the destroyed train station, which was packed, with no room to spare. {p. 397} I recognized there a "shaygetz" from Dombrova, who returned from a concentration camp. He told me his troubles and I told him mine, and both our suffering brought us close to each other, and we became friends. For a full day food did not come to my mouth, also I had no money. Morning came, and from the mouth of the station manager it became known that this was the final station, since all the bridges that were on the rivers in the direction of Augustow were destroyed by the bombing. I had no choice. My heart was drawn home. I decided to traverse on foot the 140 kilometers from Bialystok to Augustow with my friend. I went out on the road with the "shaygetz," the two of us, hungry and weak. The longing gave me added strength, and we walked very fast. We covered about 40 kilometers, and from a distance we saw Knishin. 3 kilometers before Knishin 3 bicycle riders went by us. One of them looked at my face, got off his bicycle, and asked if I was a Jew. He told me in Yiddish that in Knishin there were many Jews that the "Katzafs" (a sect of bearded Belorusians) had hidden in the fields and forests, and saw to their sustenance. They called him Mottel. We agreed that he would wait for us on the corner of the street that led to Yashinovka.

[1041] Yiddish: Pure Jewish Fat.

Plunder of Eyeglasses in the Extermination Camp

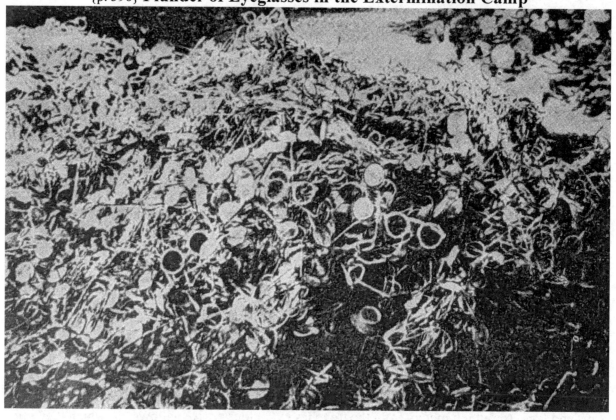

Plunder of Shoes in the Extermination Camp

We reached Knishin in about half an hour. Mottel brought us into a Jewish house and they gave us food. Many Jews were gathered. Each one asked questions, and finally they advised me that God forbid, I should not go to Augustow, since there was not even one Jew in all the surrounding towns, except for Yashinovka. I answered them that I must go, and that I could not believe that in Augustow not even one Jew remained. They wanted to also give me a little money, so that I would have something to buy food with, but I refused. (The truth is that I needed money, but I was embarrassed.) We parted from them, and set our steps towards Yashinovka. We walked another few hours until it got dark, and entered a village, in order to scout out a place to spend the night. In the house that we entered (it was the house of a rich man), we requested a place to spend the night in the barn, but the homeowner chased us, saying that every day refugees came to the village, asking for food and a place to spend the night, and that he was already fed up with the whole thing. We went a little farther, and the daughter of the homeowner who had chased us caught up with us and asked that we return to their house. We returned, of course. This time the homeowner received us with welcome. All kinds of good things were laid out on the table. A few other gentile neighbors came, drank brandy in cups, and also honored us. Afterwards they chatted about the Partisans (the bandits from A.K.[1042] and A.N.Z.) who were in the forests, and about their murdering activities. (From the words of the homeowner it was possible to understand that he apparently shared actions with them, and he knew all the bandits). Afterwards the conversation turned to the Jews. My friend the "*shaygetz*" knew that I was a Jew. When we were leaving Knishin, after the Jews warned me, I requested that he not reveal to anyone that I was a Jew. He promised me, and I believed him, since he too suffered much. He kept his promise the whole time. My friend would also answer in my place, in order that they not recognize in the Polish in my words that I was a Jew. We finished eating. My friend said that we were very tired and wanted to sleep. They arranged a straw bed for us on the floor, and we immediately fell asleep. When we got up in the morning they gave us breakfast, and also provisions for the way. We accepted, we parted, and we went.

On the second day our walking became very difficult. The legs wouldn't obey after we did 60 kilometers the day before. We were resting every few kilometers, but we reached Yashinovka. I had in my hand an address for a Jew in Yashinovka that I received from the Jews in Knishin. We went to him, of course. The matter immediately became known, and other Jews came. Each one asked, and I answered. We ate and rested a little. Here too they advised me to stay. Again I did not heed their warnings. I told them that I had to reach Augustow. I parted {p. 398} from them. We received provisions for the road. They nodded their heads and had great sorrow. Towards evening we reached Koritzin. This time I sought a place to spend the night not in the village, but on a farm. The owner of the house was Belorusian, not wealthy. He received us gladly, brought us into his small house, and fed us. Afterwards he brought straw, scattered it on the floor, and prepared for us a place to lay down. The day in the morning we feasted on his yogurt, received food for the road, and parted. There still remained about 32 kilometers to Augustow, but, *oy vavoy*,[1043] the feet hurt so much, and the heart was about to burst from longing for my city and my family. In Suchovola we parted ways. My friend the "*shaygetz*" requested of me that I go with him to Dombrova, and I would remain with them a few weeks until I grew stronger, and he would drive me to Augustow in a wagon. I explained to him that my heart would explode inside me if I didn't reach Augustow on that same day. There remained 25 kilometers to Augustow. I mustered all my strength on that last section of my journey. I was already not walking, but running. Every limb of my body was enlisted in this one lofty goal. I reached the edges of the forest. Another 18 kilometers

---

[1042] The Home Army, in Polish *Armia Krajowa*, AK, was the dominant Polish resistance movement in Poland during World War II.

[1043] The long form of which *oy vey* is the short form; "woe is me!"

separated me from my city. I was crossing the forest, and I was in the area of Kolnitza. My strength was almost gone. From afar I saw a wagon hitched to a horse leaving the city on the dirt road, and approaching the main highway. I forgot my pain and fatigue and I ran a distance of a kilometer with all my strength until the intersection, and I got there before the wagon. I sat on a rock and waited. When the wagon drew near, I requested of the gentile that he drive me to Augustow. He asked me who I was. I answered that I was the son of Yitzchak Sarvianski; when one enters Augustow, the first two-story house is ours. On the way I asked him how many Jews there were in Augustow, and he answered me that there wasn't a single Jew. I didn't believe him. We got close to the city. My glance flew to see the houses that were known to me, that stood out above, and I didn't see the crosses on the church, not even the city tower, etc. I asked the gentile, what is the meaning of this, and he answered that in their retreat the Germans blew up the tall buildings.

Finally, after five years of absence from Augustow, I return to her. Here is our street – Krakovska. I get down from the wagon, and I look at the destruction. There is no sign of our house. I stand next to our gate, I try to reconstruct the house, the entrances, the windows. Suddenly I felt terrible. My head spun, I fell, and I fainted. When I awoke there were "gentiles" next to me. I recognized a few, and they recognized me. They brought me into the house of Reb Chaim Kaplan, peace be upon him, gave me something to eat and drink, and requested that I rest a little. Now I knew that there was no memory of a Jew in Augustow.

*

When I left Kaplan's house, I didn't know where to go. For me everything was lost, all my hopes were proven false. I remained an orphan alone. I reached the market. I looked at the gentiles, a large part of whom were not Augustovians, but rather came from the surrounding villages that were burned, and settled in the houses of the Jews of Augustow. They looked at me as if at a Russian soldier adorned with medals, possibly normal, possibly not. From time to time some gentile acquaintance stopped me, and talked with me. I decided to go to Starostavo, whose offices were in Blech House (the Starosta Building which was on the Long Street, which was blown up and destroyed to its foundation). When I entered the Starosta offices, then the first who recognized me was the Secretary Zushka Choroshevska.

{p. 399} She fell on my neck and began to weep bitter tears. She told me that the Germans killed her sister too. Many gentiles gathered around me, and each one approached, pressed my hand, and asked from where and how I arrived. Zushka Choroshevska requested of those gathered that they not bother me, since I was weak. She brought me into her room, and went downstairs to the kitchen (the kitchen was in the place that previously had been the bakery shop of Kalart) and ordered that they prepare me a meal. She prepared a table full of everything good, and requested that I eat slowly, otherwise I was likely to be sick. When I was done eating again there gathered around me many gentiles. A few said to me that I should not worry, they would not let me fall. About a dozen of them asked me to go with them to their homes, and they would take care of me. There were those who claimed that they worked for my grandfather Shmuelke, and transported trees for my father, and they specifically were entitled to the honor of helping me. One of them would not cede in any way, took me by the hand and said: "Come, Panya[1044] Chunka,[1045] with me. It is true that I am a beggar, but I will split everything with you, since more than once I worked for your father, and he helped me." They called this gentile "Adam," and he lived in the cellar in proximity to Issachar-Abba the shoemaker (Dr. Shor lived in the same yard). He was a waggoneer for Shaya-Ruvke Staviskovski, and he used to distribute beer. He pulled me after him. I didn't

---

[1044] Polish for "Mr."
[1045] Short for Elchanan, the author's name.

think much, I was sick, and I had nothing to eat. I told the other gentiles that I would also come to visit by them, and I went with Adam to his house. He lived in the same cellar as before the war, and lived a life of poverty. He supported himself, with difficulty, by the raising of 8-10 pigs (not his own), for the kitchen of the clerks of the Starosta. But he was a good-hearted person, he, his wife who was a little lame, and his only son. He turned his bed over to me, and slept with his son. They would share everything with me. They took care of me as if I was their son. And would that God would reward them for their good deeds! Thanks to their devoted care I returned to my strength.

Two weeks went by and I said to him: "Listen, Adam, I can't remain in your house. I see that you are a poor person, and I can't steal your piece of bread from your mouth and the mouths of your wife and son. I have nothing to pay you, nor will I have. You see my situation. I will go to another "gentile." He looked at me and answered, that I was not stealing anything from their mouths, and that I should not speak that way, and that God would pay him for me, and he would not let me go.

I went to the Starosta to request that they return to me our garden, which the gentiles worked for the public city kitchen. The Starosta immediately ordered to return the land to me. I came to Adam, and I said to him: "Here you have land, work it, and I will help you, and we will have something from which to be sustained." Since he was never a farmer, he measured about twenty paces in length and width, and said that would be enough for him for a garden. The remainder I leased to a gentile on a "third"; that is to say, he would give me a third of the yield. I did not deserve this third, he claimed, since the yield did not even cover the cost of the seeds, and I yielded to him. A few months went by, and I got a little used to my situation. The relationship to me was good and proper, I always visited the tenants who once lived with us, and all the neighbors, and mere acquaintances, and I attempted to find out from them about the fate of my family, about my relatives, and about the Jews of Augustow in general. I would sit for whole days on the steps of the shops on Shia Bas, or Popkin-Rotenberg, and dream and contemplate about my lost world.

In those times, May-June-July of the year 1945, near-chaos prevailed. From Augustow and until Bialystok, from Kovno to Grodno, a huge area sprawled over many hundreds of {p. 400} Kilometers; all kinds of "Partisan-Bandits," Lithuanian murderers, Poles and Germans, ruled, and dared to attack the regular Russian and Polish army, and to kill among them. The police stations were fortified at night. Sometimes the Partisans from A.K. or from A.N.Z dared to attack the police stations in the day, to kill the police officers, and to plunder the weapons storehouses. Events like these occurred not far from Augustow, in the town of Ratzk. Twice, in the months of May and June, they attacked the police station in Ratzk, killed and hung the policemen together with their commanders in the middle of the day. In Suchovola 2 Jews came to their acquaintances in the morning when they were travelling back on the way to Yashinovka. The bandits attacked them, and murdered them. A Jew, a freed officer, came to Sztabin to seek his family. In the night the murderers took him out of the house and murdered him. On one of the days of June 1945, gentiles came from Sztabin and told the police Commander that there were a few bandits by them who were plundering and killing, and that it was possible to catch them because they were drunk. The Augustow policemen went out in two trucks to capture the bandits, but the murderers ambushed them in the forest and killed them.

On one of the days in the month of July, they served a festive dinner at Adam's house, my landlord. They killed a pig, and the Starosta came (he was from Grodno), the secretary, and a few other people. They roasted cuts of meat, and of course drank much "l'chaim."[1046] I too was among them. When they were a little drunk, the Starosta turned to me and said: "Look, Chunka,

---

[1046] "To life," a common Jewish drinking toast.

in Sztabin they killed a Jew, in Suchovola, two Jews, in Ratzk they killed the policemen, when the police went out from Augustow to capture the bandits they attacked them and killed 48 men. I am not sure that one of the murderers will not come and kill you. I am in the role of Starosta, the father of the city, I would be embarrassed that I could not watch over you. Right, you are unfortunate, you fought and helped to free our homeland, you became disabled, what will people say if God forbid they kill you? I will give you a letter to the Jewish Council in Bialystok, and they will help you until the anger passes…tomorrow morning our car is travelling to Bialystok, and is ready to take you." When I heard this speech I broke into weeping and I said: "I am bereaved of all my family and relatives, I gave my health and my blood, I have nothing in the world, and I have nothing to live for, let them come and kill me, and redeem me from my troubles…" All those assembled and the Starosta also broke into weeping. They were helpless. Adam (the landlord) the generous-hearted, said: "Chunka, you will not go from here, I cannot leave you to moaning. Remain with us. I, my wife and my son, will protect you at night, we will guard outside with axes and knives in hand, and if God forbid we will need to die, then we will die, all of us.

But the words of the Starosta penetrated into my mind and didn't give me any peace. I began to be scared to death. I couldn't sleep at night. After a few nights of insomnia like these, I went to the political police, told them the words of the Starosta, which resulted in a fear that gripped me at night, and I asked that they allow me to sleep a few nights by them, on a table or on the floor, until I decided what to do (the police were located in Rechtman House). After consultation they decided to permit me to sleep in the house of Chaikl Morzinski, may God avenge his blood, which bordered the police (Morzinski's house also belonged to the police). They set up for me two armed policemen outside, who would protect me "from the evil eye," but the two nights that I slept in this house also did not diminish my fear.

*

{p. 401} I decided to flee. Early in the morning, this was on a Sunday, I went to Adam and told him about my intention to go to Bialystok, and I asked him to bring my satchel to our garden, in order that the gentiles would not sense my intention. First he wanted to stop me, but when he saw that this time he would be unable to, he asked me to wait, in order to have time to borrow a few "zlotys" from acquaintances. After he returned (he did not obtain money, for who would lend to a beggar?), he packed my backpack, and put into it all the stock that he had in his possession: half a liter of brandy, about half a kilogram of tobacco leaves, bread, and all the pennies that were in the family's possession. We went out to our garden, and we parted there. I left Augustow not on the King's Road, but by way of the fields of the gentile Stzashani, from behind Lisa-Gora. This time I went the longer way - Rigrod, Grayevo, Osovitz. I chose this way because it was quieter. Three kilometers from Grayevo I met a Pole dressed in festival clothing who was going to church. I asked him show to me the way to Osovitz. We entered into conversation. I told him that I was a wounded soldier, that not long ago I had come from Russia, and that I was going for a check-up to the hospital in Bialystok. The gentile told me that the Russians drafted his brother into the army, and that he had no news of him. I asked him what his name was, and he answered me that his name was Maniak Grayevsky. I told him that the one mentioned above served in Novi-Tzarkask, in the 29th Brigade in the 2nd Battalion. We were together in the army and at the front, and he was killed at the end of August 1941. Overwhelmed by emotion, the gentile didn't know what to do with me. He invited me to his parents' house to tell them about their son. I told him that I would go to them when I returned. I reached Osovitz, where there was the famous fortress on the Bobra River, and the dug stream that surrounded the fortified town from all sides, and the bunkers whose walls were two meters thick. This fortress was entirely destroyed by the Russian saboteurs. I walked on the highway for fear of mines. I left Osovitz and passed Goniądz. The sun began to set, I entered a

380

solitary house, and asked permission to spend the night in the barn. The people permitted me, and also fed me. The next day I feasted with them to my heart's content, and parted. Night fell about 20 kilometers before Bialystok. I found shelter with a Belorusian, there too I dined and slept. On the next day before noon I reached Bialystok. I asked the passers-by where the Jewish Council was located. The Council's yard was full of Jews, survivors of the ghettos, concentration camps, forests, and more. Two young men approached me and asked me what city I was from, and how was I saved? I answered them that I was from Augustow, and one of them said that in Bialystok there was one Jew from Augustow, and that he was a partner in a butcher shop and his name was Zanvil. I guessed that it was the butcher Zanvil Korotnitztki. The young man volunteered to show me the place of the butcher shop. On the way to Zanvil I ran into him. We fell on each other's necks and wept. We went to his house to eat lunch, afterwards we began to tell each other all that had happened to us. From then and until this day, we are friends in heart and soul.

Zanvil Korotnitzki was bereft of his wife and his daughter. This Jew had a heart of gold. And therefore, Zanvil Korotnitzki gathered to his apartment in Bialystok a number of solitary people without a place to live. There were three adult women there who were saved from an extermination camp; Kagan from Kovno, Yehudit Gotkovski and Bernstein from Suwalk, Yankel Gamrov from Baklerove, two brothers from Bialystok, and a few other people. Zanvil would bring meat every day, and Mrs. Kagan from Kovno would cook and distribute it to all of them. When the evening came, all of them {p. 402} gathered and began asking me various questions. When they heard that I was in Augustow for more than three months and that I had land, they began to make fun of me that I didn't sell it. I suspected that they were sorry that I came lacking everything, and was eating on their account. The next day I went, therefore, to eat in the public kitchen. There they gave all the new people 400 grams of bread a day, soup in the afternoon, and tea in the evening. In the evening I came to Zanvil. He asked me if I had eaten lunch in the house, I answered him that I had eaten at the Council's kitchen (I didn't tell him the reason), and that I was full. The next day I took the bottle of brandy that I got from Adam, and went to the market to sell it (at that time there was no brandy to be found). I exchanged the brandy for sewing thread. I sold the thread and I earned 500 *zloty*s. I again bought thread and profited. After a week of selling I permitted myself to buy a big chicken, butter, cheese, and a big loaf of bread. I brought all this home and I said to the "*chevre*" that from today I would join as an equal partner in the kitchen in rights and obligations. Three weeks went by. I saved a sum of money, but the earnings from the sale of thread decreased, because many were dealing in this business. On one of those difficult days, a Jew from Suwalk appeared and his name was Podroznik (previously a partner of Osovitzki in the movie house). He was going around with an Aryan identity card, and buying all kind of merchandise and sharp beverages (homemade) in Bialystok, and selling them in Suwalk at astronomical prices. There was no transportation to Suwalk, and anyone who succeeded in bringing any merchandise to Suwalk would earn nicely. This Jew requested that I buy brandy for him. He had acquaintances in a village that were producing the brandy. I ordered a large quantity from them, which they brought the next day. I requested from the Jew that he take me to Suwalk, but he did not agree. But he told me that next to Bialystok there was an airfield, and that an airplane flew from it three times a week to Suwalk, transporting items of mail. I went to the airfield, I showed the officer the Russian permit documents from the hospital, and I told him that I had no transportation to return home, from which I had already been absent for 5 years. He brought me into the Commander of the airfield, who answered that if the pilot would agree to take me, he would not oppose it. The pilot agreed (the plane was a 2-story Piper). I purchased sewing thread, helped the pilot to power the engine, and we flew to Suwalk. When we arrived I took out money to pay him, but he didn't want to accept it, since I was disabled. With difficulty I put the money in his pocket, and asked him to permit me to fly with him each time, with a little merchandise, so that I could earn my

381

subsistence. He promised. In Suwalk I walked around in the streets to find Jews. Across from me on Skolna Street, I heard voices in Yiddish coming out of a shoemaker's workshop. I went inside and I found five Jews, and a few Russian Jewish officers who were joking around in Yiddish. They all turned to look at me, and I told them my story in Yiddish. They honored me with tea, and Mottel Plonitzki from Filipova asked me if I had a place to spend the night. When I answered in the negative, he took a key out of his pocket and gave it to me. He also went with me to show me the apartment, which he took from *folksdeutsch*, a nice apartment, big, and fully furnished. He had for himself another apartment.

After a short rest I went out to sell my wares. I entered two stores, showed them the merchandise, and sold it in a minute. After two days I flew back to Bialystok. I purchased merchandise with all my money and returned to Suwalk. I sold my merchandise at a great profit. At that time a curfew was placed on the city, and the great pursuit of the Partisan bandits began in the city, and outside of it. In this way I was stuck in Suwalk for a protracted period.

{p. 403} Partisans: A) Noach Sarvianski

In the Partisans in Polesia, the Partisans Zerach Kraman, Arich Stein, Sarvianski and Lieker were known for their achievements and their bravery.

Noach Sarvianski moved from the city of his birth, Augustow, to Slonim in 1929. With the German invasion, he worked as a welder in a German warehouse, and assembled a rifle for himself that he took with him to the Jewish company in the "*Shtzurs*" regiment when he fled after the slaughter in Slonim. Sarvianski acquired a name for himself among the Partisans as a person without fear or dread, who would walk in the face of death at the time of battles with a smile on his face, with a feeling of self-confidence that a German bullet would not wound him, and he would occupy the first position at the time of battle and fight with level-headedness.

In August 1942, the "*Shtzurs*" regiment attacked the German garrison force in Tzamiuli (in the Bitan region), which guarded the bridge over the Stzara stream[1047] on the Brisk-Moscow road. The attack was conducted by surprise, at night, and the German sentry who stood on guard was killed, but the Germans had enough time to recover and open fire. A German officer took a comfortable position in the attic of the building, and with deadly fire from his machine gun blocked the Partisans' approach to the building. The regiment command ordered: to take the officer alive or to burn the building down around him. The Jewish Partisan Sivash (Warsaw), who attempted to approach the house, fell, covered in his own blood. Sarvianski did not pay attention to the danger, snuck over to the building, and burned it down around the head of the German officer that was inside it.

In the hour of the great battle next to the 10th dam of the Dniepro-Bug canal (November 14, 1942), Sarvianski first attacked the German ambush (more than 100 Germans and Lithuanians), which had entrenched itself on the opposite bank of the river. He crossed the narrow bridge that was above the dam first, amid cries of "hooray!" The rest of the Partisans came on his heels, and in face-to-face battle the Germans were destroyed.

Sarvianski participated in the explosion of a significant number of trains, and in all the battles that the regiment conducted. He used to joke that: "the bullets are afraid of me and skip over me," and truly he got lucky. In the battles next to Tzamiuli and the 10th dam, the enemy bullets punctured the clothing he was wearing, but did not wound his body. Despite his regularly endangering himself, he walked the Partisan path whole and arrived at the day of liberation.

[1047] The word for stream is נחל, *nachal*; the word in the text is נהל *nahal,* manage. This seems to be a typological error, a difference of one letter, *chet*, easily confused for the other, *hey*.

Badges of the Order of "The Red Star," "The Red Flag," and the "1st Degree Partisan of the War of the Homeland" medal were granted to him. He lives today in Grodno, which is in Russia.

A publication of "*Ayanot*," 5714 [1954] from the book "The War of the Jewish Partisans in Eastern Europe" by Moshe Kahanovitz.

B) Shmuel Zupnitzki*[1048]

According to the Hitler-Stalin agreement Augustow fell into the hands of the Russians. The Germans were in the city for only two hours, and then left it. When the Russians entered the city they immediately exiled the wealthy and the Zionists to Siberia. {p. 404} They exiled the less wealthy to a distance of 100 kilometers from the border. It was difficult to obtain work. I succeeded in being accepted as a driver by the head of the Russian police. The Jewish leaders in the city in that time were Leibke Vilkovski and Elke Orimland, who were freed from prison, in which they sat during the period of the Polish regime. The Jews were organized into *artel*s,[1049] which worked for the Russians. The private stores were closed and food needs were purchased in the cooperative store. Of course, the salaries were not adequate for existence. They sold, therefore, everything of value.

On June 20, 1941, the Germans entered the city. The Russians were surprised and only a few of them succeeded in fleeing. The Jews were shut up in their houses. Already on the next day the Germans caught 200 men, transferred them to the Hunter's Club, and from there to the Shtzavra road, and shot them. Only one was saved, Yisrael Leizerovitz, who jumped into Biala Lake. After a short time he was destroyed too. The remaining Jews put on, at the command of the Nazis, a white ribbon with a blue *Magen David*, and were sent to various work. The Polish police helped the Nazis. Before they came I was taken from my house, and I succeeded in fleeing to Burks, near Nitzko. From there I turned to Białobrzegi, Sztabin, Suchovola, and I reached, after moving from place to place, Bialystok. This city too was in the hands of the Germans. I hid myself in the cemetery and I was saved from being grabbed. When the hunger started to bother me, I entered the barbershop and offered myself for work. I was accepted. I worked to the best of my ability and in exchange I received food.

The ghetto was established in Bialystok. The Jews were desperate and numb. On each Jew was hung, front and back, a yellow *Magen David*. I happened to meet Abush Zupnitzki, who worked as a translator in the German hospital, and also wrote the letters of the wounded German soldiers to their families. He accepted me as a barber. My situation was then excellent. I received a lot of food. I would also bring necessities to the ghetto when I returned after work each day. After the order went out forbidding leaving the ghetto, I met Reuvka Rozenfeld by chance. He was the work manager in a German factory. He brought me into this factory. I worked there for 6-7 months. I met, meanwhile, a woman who was a Jewish artist from Warsaw. She brought me a pistol with bullets; I felt that our end was near. I suggested to Reuven Rozenfeld that we flee to

---

[1048] Original footnote: These things were recorded from his mouth in the time of his visit to the land. He told it in Yiddish, and Y.A. recorded the events in Hebrew, and also brought them to publication.
[1049] Cooperatives.

the forest. He hesitated. I made a connection with a Jewish *Komsomolka*[1050] in the ghetto, and through her I reached a group of Russian Partisans, with about 18 people in it. Another two youths came with me. The Russians did not receive us with a warm welcome. We had the impression that they coveted our weapons and our clothing. I joined a company named for Suvorov. I wandered with them for about two years in the swamps of Polesia, in the area of Pinsk. Among about 4000 Partisans there were about 20 Jews. We engaged in ambush attacks on the Germans, and in blowing up trains. I would shoot standing up, since I didn't care if I was killed. I continued to live only out of a desire for revenge. Once, {p. 405} I almost drowned in the swamps, with difficulty they took me out with a rope. I also engaged in the work of haircutting and shaving with the Partisan commanders. While I was in Brisk, I read in the announcements that emigres from Poland were permitted to return to their places, but I was worried to take care of it, because I heard that the end of these – to Siberia.

On one of the days I met a Jewish soldier who was employed as a messenger (courier). He told me that in Warsaw there were about 20,000 Jews, and suggested to me that the two of us move there. I did not know if it was possible to put my faith in him, but I took a risk. He set up a meeting for me with a Russian officer. I claimed that I wanted to take revenge on the Poles who had abused me. The officer enabled me to reach Bialystok, where I was arrested and returned to Brisk. From there I fled and reached Lodz.

Jews from various places were gathered in Lodz. I looked for people I knew and I found only Moshe Yitzchak Vidogerski. In a short time, he disappeared too. Until today I do not know where he is. When the Jews again became many in the city the Polish Antisemitism party again raised its head and began to bother the Jews. My wife and I decided to leave Europe, which was covered with blood, be what may. With the help of Yitzchak Tzukerman, one of the Warsaw ghetto fighters, we went out on the way – to the land of Israel. We travelled to Krakow, from there to Hungary, Czechia, and Austria. Here we were forced to again see the murderers' faces.

On a cold and rainy night, we were asked if we were ready to go out on the way. We did not hesitate for a minute. We wandered in the mountains of the Alps a day and a night. It was very difficult, but we succeeded in crossing the border. In Italy it became easier for us. We lived with a thousand refugees in barracks in the city of Cremona. Every now and then a ship would go out to the land of Israel, the British would catch it, and bring its people to Cyprus. In this way three years of our being in a camp went by. We were sick of it. In that same time we received a letter from a friend who had migrated before this to Argentina. He urged us to come to him. We travelled to Paraguay, for we did not receive permission for entry to Argentina. We sat there for three months. Meanwhile a revolution broke out there. Again we heard the whistling of bullets and we suffered hunger. We therefore took the walking stick in hand, and went out on the way. We wandered for 14 days, without human food, in forests that no human foot had stepped in. Wild animals endangered our lives, mosquitos sucked our blood. We were shaken about in a boat on the Parana River without seeing a shred of land. We saw death before our eyes. A miracle happened and our boat ran onto dry ground. It was a small island. We went up onto it in order to rescue our aching bones and to rest from our terrible fatigue. To our luck, a ship that was on its way to Argentina passed by the island. The Captain brought us up onto the ship, offered us medical assistance, and brought us, illegally, to the port in the city of Sadeh. From there we arrived, after troubles, to Buenos Aires.

Then a new chapter of suffering began. My wife and I worked very hard. We went through the seven levels of hell until we reached rest and the homestead.

[1050] A female member of the Komsomol, a Russian youth movement.

The Town is Burning!!
by Mordechai Gevirtig

Fire, brothers, a burning!
Our poor town, alas, is burning.
Raging winds there tremble[1051]
Force and breaking have taken hold of it -
Flames of destruction growing higher
Fire in all the city.

And you sit with your hands folded,
Without doing anything
And you sit with your hands folded,
At the time that the city will burn!

Fire, brothers, a burning,
Our poor town, alas, is burning.
Already in these flames
All the houses of the city are consumed
And the fire still rages,
And strength increases.
And you sit with your hands folded,
Without doing anything
And you sit with your hands folded,
At the time that the city will burn!

Fire, brothers, a burning!
There is still likely to come
God forbid, an evil moment
That the city entirely with us
Will go up in flame,
We will be smoked out,
Only black walls.

And you sit with your hands folded,
Without doing anything
And you sit with your hands folded,
At the time that the city will burn!

Fire, brothers, a burning
Only you to hasten help
If the city will still be dear to you
Hurry put it out let it not burn more!
Grab vessels, hurry put it out
With your blood!

Don't sit with your hands folded!
Without doing a thing
Grab vessels,
The fire, put it out
Let our city not burn!

Hebrew: Mordechai Amitai

[1051] Exodus 15:14 "The peoples hear, they tremble; Agony grips the dwellers in Philistia."

{p. 407} Our Town is Burning!

It's burning! Brothers, it's burning!
Oh, our poor town, alas, is burning!
Angry winds with rage are tearing, smashing,
blowing higher still the wild flames—all
around now burns!

And you stand there looking on with folded
arms,
and you stand there looking on—our town is
burning!

It's burning! Brothers, it's burning!
Oh, our poor town, alas, is burning!
The tongues of flame have already swallowed
the whole town
and the angry winds are roaring—the whole
town is burning!

And you stand there looking on with folded
arms,
and you stand there looking on—our town is
burning!

It's burning! Brothers, it's burning!
God forbid, the moment may be coming
when our city together with us will be gone in
ash and flames,
as after a battle—only empty, blank walls!

And you stand there looking on with folded
arms,
and you stand there looking on—our town is
burning!

It's burning! Brothers, it's burning!
Help depends only on you:
if the town is dear to you, take the buckets,
put out the fire.
Put it out with your own blood—show that
you can do it!

Don't stand there, brothers, with folded arms!
Don't stand there, brothers, put out the fire—
our town is burning…[1052]

[1052] Translation of the Yiddish by Murray Citron, found at the website of the Yiddish Book Center. Used by permission of Murray Citron.

The Destruction of the Jews of Augustow
by Elchanan Sarvianski

On June 22, 1941, the Nazis breached all of the borders of the Russians in the territories which previously had been parts of Poland. Without a declaration of war, they attacked the Russians on a very broad front. Simultaneously, they marched to the 3 Baltic countries (Lithuania, Latvia, and Estonia) from one side, and by way of Poland on the other.

At 4:00 in the morning, the Nazi German march began from Prussia towards Augustow, and at 4:30 in the morning they entered the city to the sound of drums. Most of the people of the city were still asleep, and Russian officers ran around in pajamas, terrified and afraid. Most of the Russian army was not in the city or in its vicinity. They had gone out a few days earlier "for training." Therefore, there were almost no battles. When the people of the city awoke from their sleep, and saw the German army, panic gripped the Jews. Many tried to flee, by foot or by Russian vehicle, to Rigrod, Grayevo, to Suchovola and to Grodno, but all the roads were cut off. There was nowhere to flee to. All was lost. The only open road was to the forests. Those who tried to run for their lives by Russian vehicle or on foot to Grayevo also did not succeed. German shells came upon them next to Lissa-Gura. There my cousin Shmuel-Chuna Steindem (the only son of Leibl Steindem) was mortally wounded; in the crashing of a shell next to their vehicle, his arm and leg were severed. When the matter became known to his mother Reina, she almost lost her mind. When she got to Lissa-Gura he was no longer alive. Also, my brother Shmuel Yosef Sarvianski, may God avenge his blood, attempted to run for his life with the Commissar of the Wienkomt who lived next to us. They attempted to flee in the direction of Grodno, but they did not succeed.

The Germans spread throughout the city, caught people, and shot them in the streets. They entered Rechtman's yard, in the place that used to be the restaurant of Mitzeiyevski, and in the time of the Russians, the restaurant of the N.K.V.D., took out of there my uncle Hershel Bobrik and killed him on the spot. Afterwards they took Berl Kaplanski out of his house, and shot him next to his store at the corner of the market. In this way, they caught and killed more people, whose names, to my great sorrow, I no longer remember.

On the next day, the Germans went with the help of a prepared list, to the houses of people with deformities and the defectives, and killed them by shooting. In this way, they killed my cousin Yankel Sarvianski, Avigdor (Vigder the Lipsker), Daniel who was a porter for Markus, Max who used to polish the floors, Shachne, and others.

The Jews began to hide themselves in the fields and in the forests. Next to our house, in the fields of the gentile Stzashani, Mottel Pogomfri the smith and his brothers hid. After a few days the Germans pasted up an announcement, which called {p. 409} to the Jews to come out of their hiding places, promising that nothing bad would happen to them, they would only be sent to work. The Jews came out of their hiding places, which they were already sick of. One night Germans came to Gershon Kolnitzki (the owner of the fur store. In his courtyard lived Bazialiya the Redhead Velb, the husband of the eldest daughter of Shai Bas and one other, Shmerl, a Suwalkian) in a military car, loaded all of them into the car, brought them to the cemetery in the forest, and killed them.

After a short time, they began to conscript the men for all kinds of work. The Germans employed most of the men in various work in the castle of the "Yacht Club" which was next to Lake Biala, and would return them each day to their houses. One day they transported them to the Shtzavra Forest, about 9 kilometers from Augustow, on the way to Suwalk. Behind the small church that stood on the hill, the dug pits were already prepared. There they shot to death most of the Jewish men from Augustow.

After some time the Germans decided to establish a ghetto in the city, and chose for this purpose the Barkai suburb, which sprawled the length of the dug canal (the Augustovi Canal), and

The Barracks – a Suburb of Augustow

The Place of the Ghetto During the Period of the Destruction

the whole width between the canal and the Netta River, until beyond the waterfall which is next to the Varhaftig flour mill. The residents of the suburb were transferred to the houses of the Jews, and the Jews were transferred to the ghetto.

They would bring the people of the ghetto to work every day in the city. They employed them in cleaning the streets, and more. Next to the barracks stood a brick house, which previously belonged to the Polish army. The Germans {p. 411} turned it into a prison, and a place of torment and death for many of the Jews from the ghetto. Those in charge of this place of torture were two Poles from Augustow. The first was, in the period of the Poles, assistant head of the city of Ardziyevski, and the second, a smith, a murderer, by the name of Klonovski. This was told to me by my friends the "*shkutzim*," with whom I studied in school, and who afterwards became security officers. Together with them I searched for the two of them in Prussia in the year 1946.

On November 1, 1942, the day of an important Christian holiday, the end of the ghetto came. The Germans conscripted horses and wagons from the Polish residents of the city, and began the expulsion from the ghetto. Men, women and children of our beloveds were commanded to walk on foot, under a rain of blows, in the direction of Bogushi, between Rigrod-Grayevo and the Prussian border. Among those marching at the head, was Malkah Shor (Dr. Shor's wife), and her friend Kielson. While the weak, the children and the old people were loaded on the wagons. Dr. Shor sat on a wagon, next to the weak ones, and helped them as best he could. Thus they marched and traveled in the direction of Bogushi. Many were shot on the way. Afterwards, the Poles from that area showed me a large communal grave of the Jews of Augustow who were shot there.

After the troubles of the road, those that remained arrived, finally, to Bogushi. There was an extermination camp there, {p. 412} and there too many were destroyed. The rest were sent to Treblinka, and a few to other death camps. Fewer than a dozen lived to be freed.

Gentiles, including the maid of Yasha Rosianski (the Kadish family), told me that after the expulsion from the ghetto, when there were already no Jews in Augustow, Rosianski's son Yudke, would appear at night during the course of a week, by the maid, and receive food from her. Afterward he disappeared. There were in Augustow a few converts, who became Christian before the war, and married Polish Christians. In the middle of the summer of 1943, the Nazis put their hands on them too. They took out of their beds during the night Merke Pogomfri, the wife of Kashivinski (who had a printing press and a bookstore next to the church), the lawyer Yazi Korl, and Kleimashevski, brought them to the Jewish cemetery, and shot them. Two succeeded in escaping, and remained alive. One was the wife of a Russian Cossack, the owner of a haberdashery store, and the second, the wife of the manager of the "Lipavitz." After the war she married Max Rechtman.

The Cemetery in the Ghetto. Rechtman and the Guard.

A Section of the Ghetto

The Memorial to the Nazi Victims in Klonovnitza next to Augustow

In This Place About Two Thousand Jews Are Buried.
On the Monument Jews are Not Mentioned at All.

*

For half of the year 1944 the front came closer to the Augustow area. The great Russian advance was stopped on the banks of the river Sieno (about 6-7 kilometers from Augustow in the direction of Grodno). The front stayed there for about 6 months, while the two sides were dug into the two banks of the river.

{p. 413} **The Communal Grave in Shtzavra**

The Ghetto

{p. 414} The German murderers used that period of time to cover up the traces of the mass murder of the Jews in the Shtzavra forests, and to hide their deeds from the eyes of the world. They brought a group of Jews, who specialized in opening killing pits and graves and in the burning of murdered corpses. These Jews opened the pits, took the bodies out of them, and arranged them in a special barbaric German way – they first put down a flat layer of trees, and on these trees they lay a row of bodies, and on the bodies they placed another layer of trees, and afterwards again bodies, and so on. Afterwards they set fire to the giant pyramid. For full months the Germans and the special Jewish command engaged in the burning of murdered bodies (here I must add that in addition to the Jews of Augustow, there were also found there the bodies of Russian prisoners, and about 500 Poles, from the Augustovian intelligentsia, who were taken as hostages and killed as recompense for the fact that the Partisans killed a few German officers in the Sejny forest). For a few months the smoke rose and ascended from the burning of the bodies of the murdered.

After they completed their work, the Germans enlisted the men of the villages in the area, with their horses and plows, and for full weeks they plowed the forest, until they flattened the place. The Germans thought that by also killing the Jews who engaged in the burning of the bodies of our martyrs, it would not be made known to the world about their murders, but fate did not agree; individual Jews from those who engaged in the burning of the bodies of our martyrs understood in the last days of their work that their end was also near, and succeeded in fleeing. Two or three of them remained alive.

{p. 415} According to the stories of the Poles in the Augustow area, and the city of Augustow, and from a description of the horrors from the mouths of the Jews of Bialystoki, I succeeded in drawing up a map of that place.

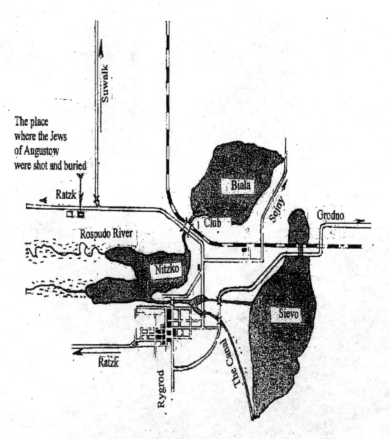

The Valley of the Killing

392

The German barbarians also did not skip over the Jewish cemetery that was across the river, and they desecrated it as well. They uprooted the monuments, and transferred them to all kinds of places in the city. They blew up the lion's share of the monuments, and with the shattered pieces they repaired the roads in the city, and made sidewalks. When I was in Augustow, and when I walked on those sidewalks, I was able to read clearly the names, or parts of family names, or other details on the sidewalks. The second part of the monuments, which were still whole, were collected on the other side of the river, and were designated for building. The Germans, when they finished uprooting the monuments, conscripted people and plowed the cemetery, and levelled it, and they did not leave any memory of it.

In this way the life of the Jewry of Augustow, which flowered and flourished over the course of hundreds of years, was brought to an end.[1053] A mother city [1054] in Israel whose Jews were destroyed and are extinct forever.   **Malal Village, Rosh HaShanah eve, 5725 [1965]**

{p. 416} The Destruction of Augustow

Dr. Shor, who served as a doctor in Augustow, describes the destruction of the city in his letter to Dr. Z. Rabinovitz in Haifa, as follows:

1650 men, of the residents of Augustow, beginning from age 14 and up, mostly sick and elderly, were shot and murdered in the Shtzavra forest on August 15, 1941. The rest of the community was confined to the ghetto, in the part of the city that was known by the name Baraki. On November 1, 1942, the ghetto was liquidated and its inhabitants were deported to the German border, a place where there was a prison camp. They were confined there for about a month and a half, together with Jews from Grayevo, Stutzin, Goniądz, Rigrod, Kolno, Staviski, and others, and their food – 100 grams of bread a day, and watery soup. Two thirds of the camp were transferred afterwards to the gas chambers that were in Treblinka, and a third – 250, plus 90 women, to Auschwitz. Of all these there remained alive: Bornstein (Shreibman's grandson), the driver Kalstein, the daughter of Noach Levinzon (the butcher), and the writer of the letter, Dr. Shor.

From among the families who were deported by the Soviet army to Siberia, there remained alive: Yaakov Borovitz and his wife, Nissl Borovitz, their daughter and son, Batya Blacharski and her husband, Max Rechtman, his daughter and her daughter, Dr. Raphael and his wife, the Kestin family, and Musya Varhaftig.

From within the testimony of Amiel Shimon, the son of Yosef and Sarah, 35 years old, a merchant from Bialystok (translated from Polish):

"- - - In the middle of May 1944, they took our group out of the Bialystok prison and transported us in a closed vehicle in which they transported to destruction, to Augustow. Armed gendarmes with machine guns and grenades guarded us. We were commanded to uncover the mass graves, to take out the bodies, to arrange them in piles, to pour pitch and benzene on them, and to burn them. In one pile, whose size was 6 x 7 meters, we arranged 1000 bodies. In Augustow we burned 6 or 7 piles like that. After the completion of the burning we were forced to crush the bones to dust with special work implements, and to sift the dust with a screen in order to make sure that there were no gold teeth, rings, or earrings in it. All these the Gestapo men would take immediately.

In Augustow we uncovered three large graves, and one smaller one. The big ones were 15 meters long, and the small one 5-6 meters.

[1053] The Hebrew idiom for "came to an end," that "the burial stone was rolled closed," is an especially apt one here.
[1054] 2 Samuel 20:19 "… you seek to put to death a mother city in Israel!..."

In the graves Jews, Poles, and Soviet soldiers were mixed. All of them were murdered by shooting. We found hundreds of bullets in the graves. In the graves we found more than 100 prosthetics of elderly disabled people. That these were elderly we were able to see from their long grey beards.

We were in Augustow 10-11 days (from May 17 – May 28, 1944). When we finished burning the bodies in Augustow, they transported us 10 kilometers in the direction of Prussia. There we uncovered 10-12 graves, 400 people on average in each grave. There we were engaged in the burning of the bodies for five or six days. We spent every night in a barn in Augustow, while the gendarmes lived in houses."

October 12, 1945   **The testimony was given before the Historical Council of Polish Jewry.**

{p. 417} From within the testimony of Avraham Karasik in the Trial Against the Bitter Enemy Adolph Eichmann.

Avraham Karasik, a resident of Rechovot, told of the underground actions in the Bialystok ghetto. After the liquidation of the ghetto the Germans attached the witness to the "Sonder-commando" unit which was employed until the middle of July 1944 in the covering up the traces of the destruction in the Bialystok area.

The men of the "Sonder-commando" were forced to burn 22,000 corpses, which were taken out of tens of mass graves.

In May 1944, at the beginning of May, I was working in the welding workshop of the prison.*[1055] An officer came and ordered 40 chains with rings at the end, at a length of two meters each. Also, a number of short and long hooks, and iron rods. He ordered this and it lay in a side room of the welder's shop.

The Presiding Judge: What?

Answer: They ordered it but didn't take it. It remained there. In May, I don't remember the exact date, Fridl came again – he was the one in charge – he was our regular visitor. We knew that if he came, something new had to happen. And to be expected. He took us out to the yard, he looked at us, and he said: You still look good enough. You will travel to work in building. They separated 10 men from us and left them in service in the prison, and the rest they told to go into the sewing workshop, and they tore a 10-centimeter hole in our clothing, and in its place they sewed a white fabric on the back and on the right knee. Afterwards they put us into the famous vehicle. They also told us to take the hooks and the chains, and we started to travel.

The Legal Advisor: Where did you arrive?

Answer: When the doors were opened, we saw that we were in the courtyard of the Gestapo on Senkavitza Street. There we underwent an additional search, and they took from us all the things that remained from the prison, pencil stubs, shoelaces.

Question: To where did they transport you?

Answer: We arrived in Augustow. There we found a place prepared for us: two cowsheds, and around it was a wire fence.

Question: Did they let you eat?

Answer: They gave us as much to eat as we wanted: bread and honey and pig meat, and they let us rest a few days. Afterwards they took us out to work.

Question: To what work?

Answer: To building work, however they said. They gave us digging shovels, brought us to a certain place, and indicated that we needed to dig.

Question: Who indicated the place to dig?

[1055] In Bialystok.

Answer: Our escorts, the S.S.[1056] men and the "*Motorgendarmerie*" (Motorized Gendarmerie). SS men were the ones responsible and the "*Motorgendarmerie*" were only guarding us. {p. 418}

Question: Who was the one responsible?

Answer: The name of the man who seemed to be the responsible one, they called him Heman, I don't know if that was his real name.

The Legal Advisor: Yes, there is one Heman, exactly according to the prepared form.

The Witness A. Karasik: That's what we heard from the mouths of the Germans that spoke, for we saw him a few times. On the first day that we began to dig.

Question: One minute, Mr. Karasik, you began to dig.

Answer: Yes, first of all we fenced the area with a wire fence and we made a camouflage of young trees in order to hide the place.

Question: Afterwards you began to dig in the place they ordered you to. They told you that you were digging for a building foundation.

Answer: They only said to dig.

Question: You dug. What did you uncover?

Answer: We came across something hard. And each one that encountered something hard moved to the side, but there too was the same thing, at a depth of about 25 centimeters. We uncovered the remains of bones. We told the Germans that something was laid here, and they answered: it's nothing, these are horse corpses. Take them out. We began to whisper with each other, because for us it was a complete surprise. We didn't know what it was. And then the Germans entered the pits and began to hit us. This Heman came specifically to me and began to hit and commanded that I throw the dust on his feet. I dug and I threw, and he didn't stop hitting. One of the "*Motorgendarmes*" saw this; afterwards his nickname among us was "The Boxer." He called me to bring trees, and with this he saved me from certain death. All the S.S. men were drunk in that moment.

The Presiding Judge: The "*Motorgendarmerie*" were S.S. men?

Answer: No.

The Presiding Judge: You said: "the S.S. men."

Answer: Yes. There were S.S. men and there were "*Motorgendarmerie*." They took part of the men to saw trees. We sawed trees a length of about 8 meters, and they ordered us to make a square pyre, and onto this pyre we needed to afterwards take out the people's remains, the remains of the people's bodies.

The Legal Advisor: What was revealed before your eyes was a mass grave?

Answer: Yes, this was a mass grave.

Question: What was its size?

Answer: Its length was 8 meters and its width was 2 meters. In a grave like this there were usually 250-300 bodies.

Question: And you were ordered to take out the bodies?

Answer: We were ordered to take out the bodies and put them on the planks of the fire. On every layer they added wood in a length of 1 meter, and in that way we made the pyre.

Question: How many bodies did you take out on the first day?

Answer: On the first day we took out about 1700, for the Germans ordered us to count every body, and if the body was disintegrated, they ordered us to count the skulls. {p. 419}

Question: In the graves you also found objects – *talleisim* and *tefillin*?

[1056] The Schutzstaffel, "Protection Squadron," was a major paramilitary organization under Adolf Hitler and the Nazi Party in Nazi Germany, and later throughout German-occupied Europe during World War II.

Answer: Yes, there were all kinds of graves. It depended on the soil. In sandy soil the bodies were better preserved, and if the soil was black, the bodies were more disintegrated.

Question: What did you do with the bodies?

Answer: Afterwards the Germans set fire to the pyres and burned the bodies. The extra things that remained from the pyre we had to pound with the iron bars so that no bone would remain. We had to pass it through a sifter. Of course the gold that remained, teeth and also rings, chains and so on, the Germans commanded us to give to them.

Question: I understand that this agitated you and that you wanted to kill yourselves.

Answer: That is a very human word.

Question: But you didn't do that.

Answer: Because we couldn't, they didn't let us. They guarded us inside and they guarded us outside. Even if one entered the toilet, a guard immediately entered to see what he was doing there.

Presiding Judge: How many Jews were in this unit?

Answer: In this unit there were 40 Jews, afterwards a few more were added.

The Legal Advisor: Over the course of time did it become known to you what the unit was called?

Answer: No. They called it the *Sondercommando*. They indicated every time that we too would go up in the last pyre, for it was forbidden for the secret to become known. This the German Gendarmes said. We came to Grodno…

Question: Slowly, slowly, on the next day you continued with the same work?

Answer: We continued with the same work. We even uncovered a special grave outside of the wire fence that we made. In the special grave there were 10 corpses, and before we uncovered them one of the gendarmes said: on top there should be a woman with a flowered dress. Afterwards it became clear that this was correct, it was so. And again they joked amongst themselves: "You remember how this woman did somersaults, turned upside down, rolled around (I think that in Hebrew this is the correct translation) at the time that she received the first bullet?"

The Presiding Judge: What was the word in German?

Answer: "Somersaults." We took out these bodies and added them to the pyre.

The Legal Advisor: When you finished digging in it, to take out the bodies, what were you ordered to do with the open pit?

Answer: We were ordered to cover it and afterwards to camouflage it with trees and grass.

Question: Who showed you where to dig each time?

Answer: The S.S. men who were inside with us.

Question: When you finished the work in that place you were transported to another place?

Answer: We were transported to another place, not far from the first place, also still in Augustow, not far from the train tracks. There were 8 or 9 graves like those there.

The Presiding Judge: How many graves like these did you open in the first place?

Answer: In the first place there were also 7 or 8. After a year I wrote all the numbers, because I still remembered from each and every place. Afterwards, when I was wounded in the hospital I wrote it down on paper, so that I would have the numbers. {p. 420}

The Legal Advisor: How much time were you in this Sondercommando unit?

Answer: Until its elimination on July 13, 1944.

Question: That says in total?

Answer: Two months, two months and something.

Question: And how many graves did you open in that time?

Answer: I did not keep a sum of the graves.

Question: How many bodies did you burn?

Answer: 22,000 bodies, according to the facts that I have from each and every place.

Judge Halevy: This is all in the area of Bialystok?

Answer: Bialystok, Augustow, Grodno.

The Legal Advisor: Afterwards you reached the area of East Prussia?

Answer: Yes. Our place was in the Gestapo yard of Grodno. From there we would go out to the surrounding area of Luna, to the surrounding area of Grodno. We dug next to an ancient fort and there we found bodies with gold rings on the hands. Apparently they were not Jews, people who been kidnapped on the streets and they exterminated them.

Presiding Judge: This was in the territory of Poland or East Prussia?

Answer: I cannot indicate exactly. Once we saw the border post. On the border post was the symbol of Prussia.

The Legal Advisor: Did you find the bodies of children?

Answer: Of children. Of old people and of women. We also found the bodies of Polish officers, and with these Polish officers the hands were bound behind them with telephone cords. From a grave like this we once took out 750 officers.

Presiding Judge: They were in uniforms?

Answer: In uniforms, exactly. In uniforms and in boots, so that we could even tell their ranks.

The Legal Advisor: Once they also exterminated people next to bonfires?

Answer: Yes, this was exactly on the festival of *Shavuot*, and this was the second time that I saw this Haman.[1057] They took the vehicle in the middle of the work and travelled to some place. After about an hour they brought 8 people, farmers, and they shot them on the spot.

The Presiding Judge: Poles?

Answer: Yes, Poles.

The Legal Advisor: And you had to burn them?

Answer: Yes, we had to burn them. And they said that we should also take off the clothing, whatever we needed. Of course no one touched it. If it is permitted to describe this sight – then it was worth it. At the time that they brought the vehicle – the vehicle was closed, the same vehicle that transported us to work and the vehicle that transported hundreds and thousands of people to death – of course in the driver's cabin Haman sat, the driver sat, and one more "Gestapovitz," they opened the doors and the men began to come out. Apparently they were not ready for this. Then Haman took a sub-machine gun and began to shoot at the men. The people were surprised by the shooting and began to scream and beg, but the additional bullets put an end to the men's convulsions.

{p. 421} This Haman approached and with his fingernails he grabbed the flesh of a young woman whose dress was slightly raised.

The Presiding Judge: These were women and men?

Answer: Two women and six men, apparently a whole family. Afterwards we asked the meaning of the thing, and the Germans said that they went to take pigs for us for the holiday.[1058] For them and for us, and these apparently objected and did not want to give, so they brought them to the forest and exterminated them.

The Presiding Judge: All the time of the work in this unit they gave you to eat?

Answer: Yes, as much as we wanted, and also to drink hard liquor, this was the well-known *samagon*.[1059] They also drank, but not *samagon*, liquor.

[1057] This name is originally spelled האמן, *hey aleph mem nun*, Heman, in the text. The spelling changes here and remains changed to המן, *hey mem nun*, which is the spelling in the Bible of the name of the villain Haman in the Book of Esther, the *Purim* story. Whether this is conscious or unconscious is impossible to know, but it is surely curious and worth noticing.

[1058] It goes without saying that pork would not exactly be the traditional *Shavuot* meal.

[1059] In folk Russian, homemade vodka.

397

Question: And now, tell us, were there many graves of Jews that you found with the "*Magen David*"?

Answer: Yes, there were also graves that we found with the ribbon and a *Magen David* on the hand. This was a surprise for us. In these graves the eyes of all of them were bound with strips of fabric. In all the graves we did not find that. In one grave we found it.

Question: Mothers, children?

Answer: Yes. It happened once when we uncovered a grave in the area of Luna. The grave was adjacent to a village that once was. At that time it was no longer a village, but rather chimneys that stood in the place of the village. In this grave there were only women and children. There were no men at all. Afterwards it became known to us that the Germans said that the men fled to the Partisans, to the forest. At the time that we uncovered this grave we saw on top one woman who lay with a baby in her arms and a small girl on the side and one baby on the back, tied on with fabric. This was a shocking picture. And this boxer began to cry, tears ran down from his eyes, but the rest of the friends began to make fun of him…

Question: What friends?

Answer: His friends, they began to make fun and laugh at him, and with that it was finished.

Question: Mr. Karasik, you worked in this work until the date that you reported?

Presiding Judge: This was until July 1944?

The Witness: On July 13, 1944, they liquidated us.

The Legal Advisor: And on that same day?

Answer: On that same day we worked in Zelonka next to Bialystok, it's about 6-8 kilometers.

Question: I will guide you with questions, be so kind to confirm for me if it is correct or not. In the middle of the work they ordered you to stop the work… to burn the stretchers?

Answer: Yes.

Question: You asked the guards if it was already your end?

Answer: Yes.

Question: They too were nervous?

Answer: Very nervous.

Question: They took the tools from you, ordered to stand three by three and walk in the direction of the open pit? {p. 422}

Answer: Exactly.

Question: You saw that the Germans were walking behind you with automatic rifles cocked?

Answer: Not behind us, but in a semi-circle, in a horseshoe.

Question: You reached the open pit?

Answer: Yes.

Question: What happened then?

Answer: I was in the first row. I saw that from the side there came Machon and someone else who the trees hid, I didn't exactly see him, and he took out a small pistol and fired a shot. Together with this we heard a cry: "Friends! Run!"

Question: In what language?

Answer: In Yiddish. One of our friends called out. I jumped into the pit, afterwards I jumped out of it, I jumped again and crossed the fence, and I began to run at full height.

Question: And you were wounded?

Answer: Yes, suddenly I received a few shots.

Question: Do you have to this day a scar from this wound?

Answer: Yes. Here (on the shoulder) I received a bullet.

Question: Finally you crawled to the Russian lines?

Answer: Yes, over the course of 9 days. On the first night there was another friend with me, we walked all night. Towards morning we saw the light. We very slowly came close to the light, and it was again the place from which we had emerged. The campfire burned. We lay there all night and on the next day at night we began to go by way of the forests in an easterly direction. Over the course of 9 days, with all kinds of adventures, we crossed the border. My friend was killed, and I was taken to a Soviet hospital, scientific.

Presiding Judge: Killed by what?

Answer: We don't know, this was on the last night.

The Legal Advisor: You were inducted into the Soviet army, you still participated in battles in Czechoslovakia?

Answer: Yes, thanks to an acquaintance, the director of the hospital that I was in.

Question: At the end of 1945 you were freed from the Soviet army and in 1947 you went up to the land, you were deported to Cyprus, and in 1949 you went up to the State of Israel?

Answer: Correct.

Presiding Judge: Dr. Servatius,[1060] does my lord have questions for the witness?

Dr. Servatius: I have no questions.

Presiding Judge: Thank you very much Mr. Karasik, you have completed your testimony.

{p. 423} The Voice of the Forest
by Eliezer Aronovski

Like a child in its mother's arms the town of Augustow lies nestled in the surrounding pine forest.

The forest, like a blue dream, has always captivated the youth, drawing them to it. Especially in the spring—when the world awoke to the cracking of the ice, the blooming of the lilac, the sprouting of flowers, and the small town was enchanted by the smell of acacia— the youth would follow the currents of spring and make their way into the forest.

There is no tree that did not hide a secret love under its branches. The initials carved in their barks are testimony to this.

During the summer the forest was full of vacationers. From tree to tree, they would stretch their hammocks. Lying in them, the people sought to draw as much of the fragrant odor of the pines into their lungs as possible.

Men bathed in the canal as naked as the day they were born, diving under the piers, smearing themselves in the tar and turpentine that oozed from the planks, like blood from wounded bodies. Further along the women enveloped their young wriggling limbs in the currents, blushing modestly as though ashamed before the daylight itself.

By the lakes Sajno, Necko, and Biale the youth wandered into the depths of the forest. Canoes slicing quietly through the water. Boy snuggling up against girl. Heart joining to heart. Lip to feverish lip. The forest was full of love and song. Every voice resounded in the distance, and the echo made it sound as though the forest were teasing - I can also sing just like you, with the self-same voice.

All this looked like God's Song of Songs come to life, as though each person were a verse, a word, in the great, creative composition, lived by the forest of love . . .

This is how life had gone for generations. Until the outbreak of the Second World War, where the song of life was drowned out by the screams of the tortured, by the death rattles of the tormented. The Red Army saved the town for a short time. But it did not last for long.

[1060] Robert Servatius was a German lawyer, known for his defense of Nazi war criminals, including Adolf Eichmann.

In the night of the 22nd of June 1941, the town was torn from its sleep by the crack of shelling and machine-gun fire, through the buzzing and {p. 424} whistling of bullets and a howling of terrified people who did not know where to run . . .

German tanks broke the stone paving of the streets under their heavy passage. The Jews knew that the worst lay in store for them. And however dark was the night, it was darker in their hearts, sadder in their spirits. Some were resigned, preparing to go to their deaths, like hundreds of thousands of Jews before them. The young sought to save themselves in the darkness. Amid the gunfire they ran off into the forest, joining hidden paths to meet up with the partisans of the Red Army. Others succeeded in escaping outright. Some fell into the hands of the Nazi tormentors, and were tortured for several days with all manner of barbarian methods, beaten half to death, compelled to divulge who the leaders of the town were. Where were they hiding? Who were their friends? But the bloodied and battered faces, the torn wounded bodies and broken limbs did not give up a single word; they merely waited for the moment of redemption—for the peace of death.

The Nazis, seeing that they would get nothing out of them, decided to hang them near the forest. The whole town was driven to witness the execution, in order to sow the seeds of terror. Surrounded by armed Nazi troops with bayonets on their rifles, crushed one against the other, clothes caked in their own blood, faces covered in bruises, bloodshot; blackened eyes; bodies hacked. They were led to the forest on swollen feet, barely able to move.

Behind them the townsfolk were driven to follow them to the gallows. They watched their own funeral procession on the way to the hangman. They also heard the sobbing and the choked back cries that tore at their hearts, of those who were afraid to weep aloud because the Nazis threatened: those who dared cry would hang on the trees along with them. Their hearts broke; they wanted to scream for the world, but fear of death forced them to hold back, like iron clamps, the wound in their breast, and they suffocated on the pain within.

One by one, the victims were strung up on the trees. Each, in their last minutes, said farewell from afar to their father and mother, their brothers and sisters, their friends and loved ones, and in sight of death, new energy flared up inside them—they {p. 425} cried out like people whom death cannot separate from the world, because they already stand on the other side, where life is eternal. And with contempt for their executioners, purified by pain, they forged words from their feelings and thoughts with the flame of their souls, and the forest was full of noise—our spirit will live forever! Freedom cannot be choked with a rope! The Jewish people is eternal! —You'll never destroy us! —God will avenge our blood! —You Nazi dogs! Cowards! Weaklings!

The Nazis were enraged by this display of Jewish audacity, of Jewish strength, enraged by the courageous words and scorn expressed on the very threshold of death—and so they ordered everyone else to return home; they herded them away, beating them with the butts of their rifles, threatening to open fire if they did not leave without delay.

Above in the trees—bloodied, blue, swollen—hung the martyrs of the town. The wind brought them the sighs in their bloody coattails, of all those who mourn them and what they experienced.

But the forest rustles with the last words of the hanged, which transformed into thousands of echoes, spreading from tree to tree, from the forest to the town, from town to village, calling and rousing with courage and faith: that mankind—the victor, purified from all this hell, would build a better, more just world for themselves and for all future generations.

A Visit in Augustow After the Shoah
by Moshe Einat, (Zborovski), Attorney at Law

The 4th day in July 1944 is engraved in my memory, for on it occurred the big turning point that determined my fate for the future. That day the Russians again captured from the hands of the Germans the cities of Savir and Zshavizh in northern Poland. I belonged at that time to the Polish underground organization A.K. (Armia Krajowa – the land army) in this area of the country, after I underwent many wanderings crammed full of events which were bound up more than once with mortal danger.

On that day I felt with all of my might that I had returned to be a human being like every person, and that I had no need any more to hide myself and to search for shelter, like a hunted animal, or to put on a face that I am an "Aryan" and to deny my Jewish origin.

I was indeed liberated from the discomfort and the choking sensation that encompassed me all the period of the Nazi conquest, however the nightmare that was revealed before my eyes after the great destruction, which was many times more terrible and terrifying than what I thought, did not leave me alone.

Although I knew that almost no living soul remained of my relatives, my friends and the people of my city, my soul yearned to visit Augustow. This aspiration did not give me any peace during the two years that I worked in the Military Legal Service in Poland.

This was at the end of the summer of 1946. I sat behind a table loaded with files in the Staff Military Attorney's District office in Lodz. There were among them files of "*Folksdeutsche*" that infiltrated the Polish army and by chance were discovered. Most of the crimes of the "*Folksdeutsche*" were connected to the abuse of Jews. When it came into my hand to gather enough material to put the criminals on trial, and to demand their punishment in agreement with the law, I felt that I did a deed that my murdered brethren placed on me.

After my completion of the attention to the files of the murderers' I was unable to return to regular work. The thought {p. 427} that I had not yet visited in my city after I was saved from the claws of death, did not leave me alone. I was finished saying that I would travel to Augustow. The next day in the morning I went out on the road.

I traveled dressed in civilian clothing, and for greater security I took a pistol with me. These were the days after the Kieltz pogrom, and travel by train was fraught with mortal danger. Gangs of nationalist extremists, members of the N.S.Z. (Naradowe Sily Zbrojne – The Armed Nationalist Forces) had organized in the forests in order to fight in the National Regime in Poland. When they succeeded in stopping a train, they took high officers off it, men of the P.P.R. (The Communist Polish Workers' Party), and Jews.

The fate of the latter was known ahead of time – they transported them to the forests and after they abused them they murdered them.

I went out on the train from Lodz and I travelled by way of Warsaw, Bialystok, Osovitz, Grayevo, Prostki, Alec, Margravova, Ratzk and Suwalk, by way of East Prussia that was annexed to Poland. There was no longer the possibility, as before, of travelling to Augustow by the shorter way – by way of Grodno. This city, like Brest-Litovsk, Lvov, and others, had been annexed to Russia. In Alec, Dr. Shor from Augustow served as a doctor. At that time I didn't know that, and it was a pity. Dr. Shor accompanied the Jews of Augustow almost to the last moment of their lives.

I reached Suwalki in the morning hours of the next day. When the train neared the approaches to the city, I saw the station that was very well known to me. At first glance it looked like no change had occurred here. Everything stood on its foundation – the same buildings, the same train station, and even the same carriage owners, who waited for travelers, in order to transport them to the city.

However, where did those masses of Jews disappear to, who in the regular years filled the train cars with tumult and noise, and who would leave it in haste when it stopped?

Only a few travelers got off the train: solitary farmers, and the rest, Christian residents of the city. The carriage owners waited in vain. These travelers were not pressed for time; they preferred to make their way by foot. I too joined this community.

While walking on the paved road to the city, I exchanged words with an elderly Christian woman, and from her story it became known to me that a few Jews remained as a remnant in the city of Suwalk, and one of them was Yishayahu Kirshkovski from Yatkova Street.

The information that Yishayahu remained alive, encouraged me and filled my heart with joy, since Yishayahu was a faithful friend of my parents. I decided to immediately go to his house.

I passed by streets and houses that were in the past populated mainly by Jews. The houses stood on their foundations, they were not damaged, for the city of Suwalk almost didn't suffer from the air raids in the time of the war. The only change was that the Jewish foot was eliminated from its streets, and the voice of Jacob[1061] was silenced in its houses.

I met Yishayahu in his house, in which his mother had lived in the past. Traces of the war had left their imprint on his face, which was plowed with deep furrows. Old age jumped upon him before its time. His dress was poor, his home appeared forlorn, and dreariness burst out of every corner.

Yishayahu received me with his characteristic warm-heartedness, while tears flowed from his eyes, and invited me to have lunch with him. {p. 428} Next to a small beverage cup and fried liver that Yishayahu prepared with his own hands, the two of us sat in his desolate room, and all of me alert to his story about his events and troubles in the period of the *Shoah*.

From his words it became clear to me that he had been in Kazakhstan. His brother, Asher, was killed in Warsaw, while his sister-in-law, Asher's wife, and her children found their death in Vilna. Only one of Asher's sons, an 18-year-old youth, remained alive, and resided in the area of the British conquest in Germany. Yishayahu took out a letter that he received from this young man, in which he pleads that he should leave Suwalk and come to him, in order that the two of them together should continue their way to cross the sea, in order to join the remnant of their family.

To my question, why in truth would he not fulfill the request of his brother's son, Yishayahu indicated the iron bed that he was sitting on and said:

"You see the iron bed. This bed accompanied me in all my wanderings. I even dragged it throughout Russia, and I brought it back to my poor and desolate room. One thing I did not bring with me – my strength, my disposition, my life force, and my will to live, which characterized me before the war. I decided, therefore, to finish the remainder of my life in this bed of mine in the city of Suwalk."

[1061] Genesis 27:22 "So Jacob drew close to his father Isaac, who felt him and wondered. "The voice is the voice of Jacob…"

Towards evening a few Jews entered Yishayahu's house: Vinitzki (I met with him and his wife after some time in Uruguay), Lovovski the elder, and also Vilkoviski. Mr. Vilkoviski arrived in Suwalk from the city of Lodz, for the purpose of selling his house and parting from the city. He had set his face towards *aliyah* to the land of Israel, together with his daughter and son-in-law. All of them were of the opinion that there was nothing more absurd than for Jews than to bind their fate in the Poland of after the war.

I spent the evening in the house of the engineer Trotzky. Trotzky and his wife (of the house of Smolenski) were saved from the bitter fate that visited the rest of the Jews of Suwalk by the fact that they spent the years of the war in the Soviet Union. In his return to Poland after the war, he was appointed to the role of the one responsible for the management of the electrical station of Suwalk and the surrounding area. In Trotzky's house I met his daughter-in-law, Mrs. Edelson, who made preparations in anticipation of her emigration, together with her son, to Paris. Her sister lived there. I also met the Karmersky brothers, Mr. Solnitzki with his two sisters, and a few more Jews. This was the surviving remnant of the magnificent Jewry of Suwalk.

All of them, except for Yishayahu and Trotzky, expressed a wish to leave Poland as soon as possible, in order to join relatives of their families, in the lands across the sea.

The next day in the morning I continued on my way to Augustow. Yishayahu accompanied me to the bus. A few minutes after the emotional parting, the bus had already carried me onto the road that was well known to me.

Pine trees on both sides along the road passed quickly before me. The road was entirely in the shade of the tall trees, and their smell gave pleasure to the travelers. More than once, when I was a youth, I went out on a bicycle trip on this beautiful road, to the lakes and the forests. When I returned on it at a late hour of the evening, it seemed to me that the road, by the pale light of the moon, was the Milky Way from the legend. I didn't know, in my travelling this time, that this pleasant road became a road to death for the Jews of the city. The residents told me afterwards that a short time after the Germans entered Augustow, all the Jewish men were ordered to present themselves at the city's town square, and after they underwent a selection and only a handful of men were taken out of their rows, {p. 429} people with a trade, the rest made their final way on this road. In the Shtzavra forest they were shot by the Nazi murderers.

The trip by bus from Suwalk from Augustow is not long. Within an hour I was in the city. When I passed Długa Street I saw through the window of the bus that the city had suffered badly from the war. The destruction was obvious. The houses, the sidewalks, and even the large building of the Catholic Church and its magnificent spire had become islands of destruction. People of the place told me that near the end of the war, after the city had passed into Russian hands, the Germans bombed it from the air.

The bus was stopped in the center of the city. I was emotional when I stood in the market square. Indeed, in this beautiful city, surrounded by forests and lakes, I spent the best days of my youth.

I stood in its plaza and I looked at all sides of the square. I recognized it only with difficulty. Half of it was destroyed. The houses on the southern side, including the municipality building, remained on their foundations. Likewise, the houses on the eastern side, whose sidewalk served in the days of my youth as a promenade, remained standing. But in these there were substantial signs of the damage that was caused by the serious bombing.

I set my steps, by way of the city park, to Kosciuski Street, where my parents' house stood. The park was abandoned, most of its trees were uprooted, the benches were missing. I was reminded of the fine games that I played with my friends in this park, when I was a boy.

I crossed the park quickly and with a pounding heart, I approached the place where our house stood, and I saw that only the foundations and the remains of the destroyed building stood out among the grasses that covered the empty lot. A vision of the house arose before my eyes. This was a two-story house, built of bricks of two colors – red and white – with a thin, delicate, black line that passed between their rows.   The house was not big, but solid and pretty. My father and my uncle Hirsh Meltzer, who erected it in the year 1924, saw to it. Within a second I saw all the members of my family who lived in this house. Now, I stood as if before a gravestone. I thought about my parents and the members of my uncle's family who were killed.

I don't remember how much time I stood, head up, entirely in sorrow. Suddenly I felt that someone was approaching me. It was one of the non-Jewish residents of the city that I knew. The man requested of me that I sell him the lot that was beneath the destroyed house. I refused, even though he offered me a high price. The place was too precious and close to my heart.

Despondent, I left the place. I stepped with slow steps along the length of the fence that they had recently put up around the yard of "The Monopoly House" across from our house.   The fence was built from the colored bricks of our destroyed house. Slowly I approached Skolna Street. I remembered that on the corner there stood Breizman's house, in which was also his bakery. On the upper floor lived Rabbi Azriel Zelig Koshelevski, may his memory be for a blessing. The house was entirely destroyed. I continued on Skolna Street until the end of Koprinika Street. The buildings of the electric flour mill of the Borovitz brothers, the houses of Nisan Borovitz and many other Jewish houses, were all destroyed. I continued to walk until Zigmuntovska Street, and I stopped next to the place of the *Beit Midrash*. The house in which the Jews of Augustow prayed and learned *Torah*, during the war went up in flames. The same fate also visited the Great Synagogue, which was not far from me, on Polna Street. Only the walls of the synagogue remained. I passed Rigrodska, Mitzkovitz (*Zhava Gasse*), {p. 430} Krakovska (*Zoib Gasse*), Glinki Alley, and others. In all the places the destruction was great. I went back out to the market square.

I had only taken a few steps on the sidewalk and suddenly I was stricken with shock. I saw something that made my heart tremble. Before my eyes Hebrew letters burst out from the sidewalk. I didn't believe what my eyes were seeing. I thought that I was still liable to passing thoughts, and that I was dreaming. I strained to see but it was not magic. After I felt the stones with my own hands I was convinced that they were really Hebrew letters. At first I didn't understand what was going on here. I didn't get where these letters came from. However, when I came across a full name that I recognized, it became clear to me, and the shocking abominable deed was revealed– the sidewalk was paved with gravestones of the Jews of the city.

While my spirit was still in me I hurried to the cemetery. The cemetery was previously a distance from the city. One had to walk a few kilometers on foot before reaching it, there in the forest across the River Netta. However, when the bridge over the river was built in the year 1935, the way was shortened. I passed Mostava Street almost running and went by the bridge; before me the place that used to be the cemetery was revealed. I remembered that only a few tens of meters separated the Jewish cemetery from the Christian cemetery. But when I got to the place I didn't find one gravestone. The area was plowed. Only the foundation stones of the "*Ohel HaTzaddik*"[1062] stuck out from the ground, and they testified that the Jewish cemetery was here.

I stood like a stone. I did not utter a sigh, I didn't shed a tear. I was gripped by rage and I shrank from an abundance of anger and pain.

[1062] "Tent of the Righteous." This generally refers to the structure built around the tomb of a righteous person, usually a great teacher or rabbi of the community.

A Gravestone from the Destroyed Cemetery

Gravestone of Reb Avraham son of Meyrim Soloveitchik

{p. 431} I returned to the city with a difficult feeling. Despite the fact that my legs were tired, I began to walk around in the streets of the city. I wanted to see everything.

I realized that all the houses of the Jews were occupied by the gentiles. Also, the houses of business passed into their hands. I was reminded of the vigorous life of the city before the war. Indeed, it appeared to the eye that the residents of the place acted for the sake of the rejuvenation of the city, especially in the economic area, however they did not succeed in doing it.

I walked from street to street, from alley to alley, and I looked at the people, the houses, the stores – everything was foreign to me. The faces of people entirely unknown to me looked at me through the windows. All the atmosphere was foreign to me. On the streets I indeed encountered many of the residents of the place, but not Jews. Sometimes I encountered glances that expressed amazement that they were seeing a Jew. A few that I knew approached me and asked the purpose of my coming, and only in the words of a few did I sense a tone of humiliation and self-justification for what had occurred.

I was tired and wanted to rest. Inadvertently, I found myself again on the street where I lived. It seemed that out of habit I had returned to the place that once had been called "my home," however the appearance of the desolate plot, its wild vegetation and its destruction returned me to the lap of reality.

I remembered that in an alley not far from our house a Christian woman lived who was a friend of my mother. I decided to approach her house. The woman welcomed me warmly. Her wrinkled but magnanimous face expressed joy that I passed through the difficult days in peace, and that I remained alive. The woman told me that my parents were not in the Augustow ghetto, and that she didn't know what their fate had been. Only my aunt, my mother's sister Basha, who was married to the leather merchant Meltzer, she frequently saw sweeping the market square together with other Jewish women, who had been brought by the Germans from the Barkai ghetto.

405

The woman expressed to me sorrow that she couldn't help my aunt, except that she would secretly give her bread for her and her children who lived with her in the ghetto.

In the evening, I stayed with the Polish woman Zusha Choroshevska, who served before the war as a clerk in the district administration of Augustow, and was a friend of my friend Liza Borovitz. At the time of the Nazi conquest she lived with her relatives in the village, since she was afraid of the Germans in the city, as she was known as a patriotic Pole.

From her I heard the terrifying story of the Jews of Augustow and their fate in its destruction without exceptions.

Mrs. Choroshevska told me that immediately after the Germans entered the city, the abuse of the Jews began. Some of the Christian residents of the place also helped the Nazis. A few of them were put on trial in the courthouse in Suwalk after the war, and one was even sentenced to death.

Many of the Jews of Augustow, mostly the men, found their deaths in the Shtzavra and Klonovnitza forests. They were transported there in vehicles – after they were ordered to present themselves in the city square – and all of them were shot by men of the SS with automatic weapons.

The rest of the Jews were confined to the ghetto in Barkai, in a suburb at the edge of the city across the Augustow canal. The non-Jewish residents from the suburb were evacuated to the city. The Germans enclosed the area of the ghetto with a wire fence, and placed guards around it. The situation of the Jews in the ghetto was exceedingly difficult. They were all starved for bread and were gripped by despair. Their tragic lack of power and the information about the terrible fate {p. 432} that was expected for them, brought them to this situation of despair. Only a few overcame it and succeeded in escaping from the ghetto. They found shelter in the forests, but there too danger also lay waiting for them.

The Jews of the ghetto were brought each day, group by group, to various workplaces in the city. Those whose strength ran out made desperate efforts to withstand the yoke of forced labor, for otherwise they expected blows from the whip at the hands of the German guards, and even shooting.

On one bright day in the summer of 1942 the SS men surrounded the ghetto and the Jews were all loaded onto vehicles and transported on the road that led to Grayevo. The Germans brought them to the work camp in Bogushi, and from there they were sent, after selections, on the "death trains" to the gas chambers in Treblinka and in Auschwitz.

Mrs. Choroshevska told me that her friend Liza Borovitz died in the ghetto after an extended illness. Dr. Shor, the Augustow doctor, took care of her.

Destiny wanted, that after years, by chance, there fell into my hands a letter written in the Polish language, in which Dr. Shor briefly reveals to Liza's father the chapter of the events in our city.

In light of the importance of the letter, I here bring it in its fullness in Hebrew translation:
"Dear Mr. Borovitz,

I am very happy that you remained alive. Please sir, try to come to me, and I will tell you everything that relates to the city of Augustow.

Liza*[1063] gave birth, after two days of labor, to a baby girl, beautiful and lovely. At the beginning she managed well in the ghetto, and even obtained work from the Germans (mainly handwork), however at the end of 1941 she fell ill with an illness whose symptoms resembled those of the disease of malaria. At the first stages of the illness I myself took care of her, although afterwards I referred her to the hospital. There were better conditions for healing there. It was, however, an unusual event that she was admitted to the hospital, since the Jews were outside the

---

[1063] Original footnote: * The daughter of Nisan Borovitz and the wife of Alter Aleksandrovitz.

zone of care in the hospitals. After a few months' stay in the hospital, she was sent home. She continued to live for only another three weeks. I would visit her and take care of her daily in her home, while my wife would bring her hot meals, and that was because her mother-in-law and her sister-in-law were prevented from coming to her and taking care of her. Before her death she expressed her deep sorrow that not one of you was by her bed in these moments. The Aleksandrovitz family took it upon itself to take care of her child. Liza died in June 1942.

Liza's husband, Alter Aleksandrovitz, Mr. Ofenstein and also your son**[1064] were taken from Augustow by the Germans in an action that they carried out in July 1941. All the Jewish men, residents of Augustow, were ordered at that time to present themselves. They were loaded onto vehicles and transported to the basements of the sailing club,***[1065] and on the 15th day of August 1941 they were shot by the Germans in the Shtzavra forests. Ofenstein's wife and their daughter were sent on December 18, 1942, from the Bogushi camp to Treblinka, and there they were put to death by gas. Shmuel Borovitz found his death in the prison in Bialystok, while his wife and children died in pogroms in Slonim. Leivush Borovitz stayed in Grodno. Asnah and Rivka****[1066] - in Bialystok. When they died I do not know. Of those who were in the ghetto in Augustow during its time, there remained alive, in addition to me, the driver Kalstein, Dr. Herman and his daughter and also the daughter of Noach Levinzon (Noach the butcher).

{p. 433} Of the members of my family, on the one hand those close to me, and also others who were more distant, there remain alive my brother's wife and their two sons, who appear as "Aryan" in all the papers. On December 18, Mrs. Zelazo and her children were killed. The Jews of Augustow were killed in three stages: on August 15, 1941, in the Shtzavra forests, on December 18, 1942, in Treblinka, and on July 1, 1943, in Auschwitz. My wife was also among those who found their deaths on July 1, 1943 in Auschwitz. Those who remained alive after the actions mentioned above, found their deaths in the death camps in the months of January and February 1943 in Auschwitz. The members of the Vezbotzki family were killed in January.

Alter and Liza Aleksandrovitz

[1064] Original footnote: ** Enoch Borovitz.
[1065] Original footnote: *** "Yacht Club" which was established in 1935.
[1066] Original footnote: **** The daughter of Zalman Bramzon, may his memory be for a blessing.

The last people of Augustow, Elko Elenbogen and Domovitz, were killed in March 1943 in Auschwitz. At the beginning of the year 1944 Yechezkel Piastzki*[1067] (Fishtzok) was still alive in Auschwitz, and Elko Kantorovitz – in Sachsenhausen which is next to Berlin. If they succeeded in remaining alive, I don't know.

And regarding what happened to me, myself. There were times went my weight went down to 35 kilograms,[1068] and I stood on my own feet, which were wounded, only with great difficulty. I remained alive only by way of a miracle. Fate apparently wanted that at the time of my old age, all the horrors would always stand before my eyes, the suffering and the torture mentioned above. I have no doubt that you would not be able to recognize me, I have changed to such a great extent.

After I was liberated from the last concentration camp next to Dachau, I was employed as a doctor in the Jewish displaced person's camps. In the last year I worked in a sanatorium for those ill with tuberculosis in Genting.

With blessing, Dr. Shor"

NOTE: The letter carries a date of October 25. As the Borovitz family informed me, the letter was received in the year 1945. - Moshe Einat

{p. 434} The hour was already late when I left Mrs. Choroshevska's house. With nightfall I didn't go to sleep. I was still under the difficult impression of the story of the Polish woman. I walked on the promenade and the knocking on the stone pavement aroused in me echoes and memories from the days that went by without returning. I remembered Augustow from before the war when it was teeming with social, economic and cultural life. I was reminded of the youth of Augustow, who were counted among the first of *"HeChalutz,"* in its tendency towards enlightenment and knowledge. I was reminded of the lectures, the arguments, and the fine orators who left their impressions on the youth and planted in them good qualities and a desire for advancement, and also – a yearning for national and personal redemption.

All of us loved our city, we cleaved to it because of its beauty and the scenery of the forests and the lakes that encircled it. At every opportunity that I had, although I was studying and spent a lot of time outside of it, I always preferred to spend my free days in Augustow.

Given over to reflections, I did not at all sense that I had reached the Augustow canal on the promenade. Out of the fog the bridge that was suspended on iron chains stood out. Signs of the air raid were considerable here too, and the floodgate that was next to it was badly damaged.

I returned to the city after midnight. I spent the night in the hotel that had previously been called "Rosianski Hotel," for the name of the husband of Zlatka Kadishs, the owner of the famous public house in Augustow. I was very tired and my nerves were stretched tight. I couldn't fall asleep. I waited for dawn, so that I could get up and quickly leave the city that had become, due to the circumstances of the time and the *Shoah*, foreign to my spirit and my soul.

*

The idea to publish a memorial book for the Augustow community, which would constitute a *yahrzeit* candle[1069] for the thousands of souls, holy and pure, who were tortured and murdered, and no one knows their burial places, motivated me to reminisce and describe what my eyes saw and what my ears heard in my visit to the city of my birth, after the *Shoah*.

[1067] Original footnote:* Yechezkel Piastzki lives in the United States.
[1068] A kilogram is 2.2 pounds, so 35 kilograms would be 77 pounds.
[1069] Literally, a soul candle.

In order to integrate my personal impressions with documentary material that was based on testimonies of survivors of the *Shoah*, I turned to my friend from the days of my youth, Berel Mark, the Director of the Jewish Historical Institute and a history professor at the Warsaw University, and asked him to deliver to me material on the destruction of the Augustow community.

On July 5, 1963, I received a letter from my friend Mark, in which he wrote (translated from Yiddish):

With regard to the book about the Augustow community, I will be able to help you very little, because there remains almost no documentary material. The certificates and documents of the city were burned and the information about the period of the conquest is vague, since the Jews of Augustow were destroyed within a very short time. However, I will do my best to offer you my help in the matter at hand.

And indeed, within a short time Professor B. Mark sent me a few protocols from within testimonies that were reported before Historical Councils. I bring here two testimonies in their exact words. The first testimony is from a son of our city Ze'ev Kalstein from the day April 27, 1947, before the Central Historical Council which is next to the Central Council of the Jews who were liberated in the area of the American conquest in Germany, in the city of Regensburg. The second is the testimony of Moshe Gershoni, born in Bialystok, which was given on June 9, 1944, before the Regional Jewish Historical Council in Bialystok.

{p. 435} Ze'ev Kalstein tells in his testimony (translated from Yiddish):

"On Sunday, June 22, 1941, at 6:00 in the morning, German soldiers were already seen in our city. They published an order, according to which all Jews were to wear a special identifying sign, a yellow patch on the chest and on the shoulder. Every morning many Jews were abducted and sent to forced labor.

At the end of July of that year, all the Jews of Augustow were forced to assemble in one of the city squares, allegedly for the purpose of registering their identity. In this gathering, 1500 men were taken and transported to the Shtzavra forests. I and another 30 Jews, who were included with excellent professionals, were sent back to their houses. The Jews were held for three full days in the Shtzavra forests, without food entering their mouths, and after that they were shot to death by the men of the S.S.

At the end of August the ghetto was established, surrounded by a barbed wire fence, and placed under the guard of the Polish police. The crowding within the ghetto was terrible, 10-15 people lived in one room. In total the ghetto numbered 70 men and 1500 women. Every day we were forced to go out to work.

On one of the days of June 1942, in the morning hours, the ghetto was surrounded by men of the S.S. and the Polish police. All residents of the ghetto were taken out of their houses and transported to Bogushi, next to Grayevo.

There about 7000 Jews from all the forests and settlements in the area were gathered.

Over the course of 6 weeks that we were held in the camp we received a portion of food that contained from 100 grams of bread and half a liter of soup. In this period of time about two thousand Jews died.

At the end of August a selection was conducted by the Germans, the result of which was that about 3000 Jews were transported to the Treblinka extermination camp, and two thousand were sent to Auschwitz.

Only three Jews from all these that were in the camp remained alive, and I am among them."

Mr. Moshe Gershoni tells in his testimony (translated from Polish):

"On May 15 (the intention is to the year 1944 – Moshe Einat), they transported us, a group of professionals and experts in various work that numbered 20, and me among them, to the Gestapo headquarters at 15 Shenkvitz Street.*[1070] Iron handcuffs and chains were put into the vehicle in which they transported us. It was promised to us that they would not harm us, but that we had to perform difficult work and it was up to us to work and be quiet.

We travelled on the road. Our vehicle stopped twice on the way. A heavy guard of 50 Germans accompanied us on our way.

On the next day we continued our journey a few kilometers and we drew near to the forest (I was able to identify the place, even though the route that we took was not familiar to me).

We had to dig in the ground and when we reached a depth of 1.5 meters, many bodies were revealed to us. Six men from our group, me among them, were commanded to cut trees down to their roots. 12 trees, each one 6 meters long, were arranged horizontally and vertically. The men of the guard, who were drunk, cruelly urged us on. They ordered us to arrange the bodies on the pile of trees (we took the bodies out in handcuffs, which were prepared in the prisons). From three ditches, of which the length of each {p. 436} was 30 meters, 2 meters wide and 1.5 meters deep, we took out about 900 bodies. We counted them according to the German instructions. The bodies in the ditches were arranged in three layers, one on top of the next.

We did this work for 3 days, 12 hours a day. We burned the bodies over the course of a day and a half. The ashes and the bones were passed through a sieve. Afterward they returned the bones to the ditches, covered them with earth and for the purpose of camouflage covered the area with tree branches. The bodies in the ditches were mostly men.

The Germans sought and found things made of gold. Likewise, they found various sacred accessories and Soviet army clothing. There were bodies of Jews, Poles, and Soviets.

After about 3 days they transported us to a second place in the direction of Augustow, and again in a place near a forest and train tracks. There were 7 ditches there, of the same dimensions as described above. The bodies were in a state of complete disintegration. Most were men, about 2000 people.

In the course of this work, a vehicle approached from the direction of the city, and on it were twelve bodies that were still bleeding. The wounds were deep, and they were caused by shots from automatic machine guns, whose bullets mostly struck the heads and the upper parts of the bodies. The bodies were naked. Nine of them were young women, one was an elderly woman, and two were men. These bodies were burned together with the bodies that were taken out of the ditches, and the smoke rose from this burning over the course of 8 hours.

The burning of all the bodies continued in the two places for about two weeks."

The Desecrated Gravestones
By Aleksander Yosefsberg

My origin is from Drohobycz, and my profession in the past was photojournalism. Six years ago I went up to Israel from Augustow, after I lived there with the members of my family for one year. I was, except for Dr. Sadovski, the only Jew in the entire area.

My wife (Polish) had two married sisters who lived in Augustow. Her father, her brothers and her sisters live in the village of Garbova, which is adjacent to Augustow.

We lived by the brothers Edmund and Yosef Bartoshvitz, on May 1st Street. One day a frightening picture was revealed before my eyes, when my wife showed me a number of gravestones that were uprooted from the Jewish cemetery in Augustow and were lying next to a

---

[1070] Original footnote: * In Bialystok.

pile of trash. My wife was filled with fury about the heartlessness and the denial of the residents of the place. When she commented to them about this in a sharp fashion, they answered her that the gravestones would serve as cornerstones for the new houses that they would be putting up in the future.

The next day my wife returned from the market extremely agitated. She discovered an abominable deed that was frightening and shocking. She showed me that on a number of streets sidewalks were paved with Jewish gravestones, on which the names of the dead were displayed.

In Augustow ignorance still prevails, which is an inheritance from the previous century, and {p. 437} exceptional anti-semitism, even in the conditions that exist at this time in Poland. This is also the reason that until now there is not a person in Poland who would see to gathering to an appropriate place the gravestones that were uprooted by the Hitlerist animals and their assistants.

Apparently, the doctor could have engaged in this matter, but he was interested, apparently, in hiding his Jewish origins.

I was also convinced that most of the Jewish houses were stolen by the residents of the place – despite their knowledge that the legal heirs remained alive.

Moshav Meliah, January 1963

A Street in Augustow Paved With Jewish Gravestones

I Am the Daughter
by Fania Bergstein[1071]

I am the daughter
For generations of hunched over Jews, bowing down
Under the burden of heavy days,
The terror of every Staraznik[1072] and every abomination upon them,
Trembling at the sound of the barking of the neighbor's dog,
Clearing the way for the small one among the street brats
And saying hello to the miserable and the drunk,
And shivering like the shiver of a leaf
With the echoes of pogroms and killings
Of their brothers.

I am the daughter
To terrified and silent mothers
Whose lives' years slipped away
As if in a long hallway, dark and narrow,
By the gleam of two flickering candles on the Sabbaths,
Nourished by their dreams of pleasure from children,
And from the prayer of a pure tear flowing from the heart.

I am the daughter
To Jews with an empty mind upon their faces,
Emitting a silent thank you, whispering a terrified pardon
To each trouble of their lives;
I am the daughter
To those who carry in the Holy of Holies of their hearts
A dream of distant and comforting light
On a wing Tzion erases the grief of her children,
About the *Shekhina*[1073] who weeps on a distant shore,
And sighs for the welfare of her prisoners.

I am the sister
To all who go out every day towards death
{p. 439}   And don't know if these are their last,
This is his day on earth
And this is the brightness of the setting of the sun.
And the kiss of his boy,
And his prattle: goodbye,
And this is the silent and trembling handshake,
While pressing the rifle with his other hand,
This is his last friend and the remaining one –
In the still of the nights there are indeed terror and murder.

I am a sister
To all who direct their gaze every day to the road,

[1071] Many thanks to my colleague Sarah Radovici for her help with these translations of Fania's poems.
[1072] An informant for the Tzarist government.
[1073] The feminine personification of the Divine that dwells among the people Israel on earth.

While the hand grips the steering wheel of the car,
To steer it with every turn of the wheel,
Towards death,
As the heart guesses in its trembling,
Day by day, hour by hour, and minute by minute.
To all who served up their joyful lives
With two generous hands to the maw of death,
Which doesn't ask, doesn't choose, doesn't distinguish;
To all who placed at the feet of sweat-drenched boulders
And at the heads of mountains wrapped in seedlings
Their lives, their pure souls –
I am a sister

I am the mother
To all of these little children,
Who hang their bright eyes
On the faces of big ones with one question
Silent and piercing in amazement:
Why? For what? Until when?
To these babies who with their footing kissed
This soil step by step
Its countenance with rejoicing every clod of earth
Sanctified every green shoot in its bud;
To these soft hands in which is secreted
Every treasure of glory of the tomorrow;
To these the pure eyes
Which were opened under these heavy skies
{p. 440}   On the tidings of the paper, the forest and the garden,
For the disasters of the sands of the desolate desert –
I am the mother.
For all these tiny children
That would not be demanded of them
Not the strength to forgive, not the bravery to be quiet
And also not the bravery to die;
For all those that would still walk
On the face of this small earth
Without that which will weigh down,
Press in dread,
The crown of the holy ones on their heads,
I am the mother.

5696 [1936]

Four Songs for My Father
by Fania Bergstein

A

My father,
Do you remember the hour of the parting?
The train moving slowly
And you hurrying by its side
With a teary gaze…

The train is swept away, slipping away,
In the window my hand waves,
And you are receding more and more
And are left alone.

The whole world – shining tracks
Leading only to you, my father.
Moving between the sailing of letters
And wandering back to my heart…

B

Your handwriting is still clear and pleasant,
Without embellishments and ornamentation,
As you taught me to write
Then, in the days of the childhood.

Your clear handwriting, serene,
Each letter in it pouring out confidence
Like them your image still stands erect
And the house is strong and true.

I will bend over your letters
Examine the depth in them, and I will learn
That you grew tired, tired, my father.
That trembling of the hand had begun.

C

Today your word remembered me,
Today I received a letter
The address was printed, official,
Crowned by the redness of the cross,
(Blessed be the cross to me,

{p.441}
My cruel and terrible hater,
Because it turned a friend to me,
Carrier of the blessing of peace)

To your voice in the language of the state,
As if through the lowered screen
I will lend an ear,
My father with every letter,
With every tag and with the trembling in hand.

And as if you raised
My hair to kiss my forehead -
So I will raise the screen of the translation
And your phrase will rage in me and will live.

D

My father, give a hint, bring a sign!
…there is no sound and no utterance through
walls.

My father, between me and you are great
distances.
The days are stormy, the waves are calling out.
Across the borders bristling spears
Are drowned out in hundred-year-old shadow.

You are covered in shade, endless returning
shade,
And one sun in it – the yellow patch!

My father
How will I pass over distances,
How will I pass deep seas,
How will I breach borders and walls
Until I return to you
Fatigued to death.

Again a little girl is in the community of your
students,
Squeezed around you
Tightly cheek-to-cheek,

To hear in the secrecy of innermost rooms
Your voice that still teaches the language of the
Hebrews
And to help your trembling hand to write
By the light of the yellow patch
My father!...

Forever

A

All the books of the world will not contain
your one word.
All the ways of the world will not lead
To your path that is lost.
The silence will not listen closely
When I think: Father!
I will never again tell you
What is in my heart.

B

Your distant days are concealed in a cover of
Heavy fog and moving shadow.
A silent wing spread over the last of your
words,
And there is no redeemer.
Your white head that I did not see will not
express
The snows of the north.
Your sighs that I did not hear
Will not contain
The mountains of sorrow.

C

Legends of wonders you once told me,
Legends in abundance.
Only the embarrassed legend of your days
You did not tell until the end.

But it, the only one, still yearns in me
And arouses interest.
All that you didn't tell me
Will sing in me
There are no words.

D

Into the cup that awaits you I poured a little
joy,
And the table is set.
Come, father, sit a little to rest from your way,
And may your coming be blessed.

You have had enough of going
And carrying upon yourself
The blowing night wind.

Illuminate please the shadow of my house with
your sitting,
And sit with us.

- -

The cup of my joy is poured
Embarrassed watches still,
It is only designated for your mouth.
It is my prayer, it is my trembling,
It is my yearning for you,
It is my tear of thanks.

On an Ancestral Grave

My heart led me in the thick darkness
Among graves without gravestones,
I came today to prostrate myself alone
On an ancestral grave.

I came today, and my soul is silent.
What can I throw pleading and say?
Will I pray for the peace of my house
Before you, those who dwell in the dust?

If you will be the good intercessors on high,
And hasten help to me in distress?
Complete healing to the sick of humanity,
A blessing for the wandering to a foreign country?

I will tell nothing.
I will prostrate myself and be silent
And my silence he will give ear to and hear
The voice of the dead that breaks through to me
From the depths of earth.

Thus came the voice of my father and the voice of my mother
To me, to the living, to request:
About a great sickness, about an unhealable pain
About a wound that will burn with none to bandage it.

They will give weeping
That no person will perceive,
The anguish of their rebuked old age,
And they will ask, request a blessing, of me
For the way they went out without returning. - -

I will tell nothing. There is no answer in my heart
For a last softening under their heads.
From the dust of their graves I will only take a handful
And I will place it as a seal upon my heart.[1074]

If Only I Was Permitted

If only I was permitted to come to your grave,
On the face of its dust I will prostrate myself,
As if I sought a hiding place
In your compassionate and tender lap.

To this pure stone
On which your name is engraved in black letters,
To lift my eyes with a tear,
As to the light blue of your pure glance.

If only I was permitted to come to your grave…

[1074] Song of Songs 8:6 "Place me as a seal upon your heart…"

{p. 443} The Martyrs of Our City
by Zelda Eidelstein (Koshelevski)

What memorial monument, what gravestone, shall we erect to their memory?

The territory upon which their bones and their ashes are scattered spreads over vast distances! Will there be enough stones of the cursed region to impress on them all of our feelings about them, to draw their profiles and the ways of their lives?

We will not know their last moments, the time when they were put to death in strange and cruel deaths. No one comes to us to tell how they fought and how they struggled with the vile Nazis. Even though we are certain that there were among them those who wore strength and courage and fulfilled "the one who comes to kill you, get up early and kill him first,"[1075] To our great sorrow, there does not remain a remnant or refugee[1076] who can tell or reveal who struggled heroically with the tyrants. The place of their burial has vanished from us – we will try, therefore, to raise in the Book of Memory for the Community of Augustow, memories of the days gone by, which will be preserved for many generations.

What will give and what will add the monument stone that we erected on foreign soil? The monuments were uprooted from their places and served as materials in the hands of gentiles to pave the sidewalks of the city; they are soaked with the blood and tears of our ancestors, our brothers and sisters, our elders and our little ones.

Who can recount and who can tell the praises of our ancestors of all the groups, beginning with the laborers, the porters and the water drawers, and until the notables whose place is on the eastern wall?[1077]

All of them as one are loved and clear, and their memory for us is a sign of pure and exalted lives. May their souls be bound up in the bundle of life,[1078] and may God avenge their blood.

A Tear Shed for the Destruction of our Town
By Khayim Lazdeyski

The smallest drop of water reflects the mighty ocean. So it was with our little towns in the old country: each one reflected the fruitful and glorious Jewish life in Poland.

So it was too in our dear, unforgettable town of Augustow (a.k.a. Yagostov, or Avgustov). Among the hundred or so families that occupied the small town situated between Suwalki and Grodno, between Lithuania and West-Prussia, one could find a microcosm of everything that Jewish life in Poland represented. The good along with the bad, {p. 444} the positive alongside the negative. Certainly the light far outshone the darkness . . .

It's been over twenty years since our Jewish settlement in our old home was destroyed. The compatriots of Augustow, scattered in the four corners of the Earth, have received only fragmented reports, never the full story, concerning the tragic demise of about seven thousand Augustow Jews. On the fingers of one hand we can count those few who managed to escape death

---

[1075] Babylonian *Talmud Sanhedrin* 72a.

[1076] Joshua 8:22 "…Now the other [Israelites] were coming out of the city against them, so that they were between two bodies of Israelites, one on each side of them. They were slaughtered, there was no remnant or refugee."

[1077] The most precious seats in the synagogue are those on the eastern wall, closest to Jerusalem.

[1078] 1 Samuel 25:29 "the life of my lord will be bound up in the bundle of life…"

during those gruesome days of slaughter and horror. It is not possible to know with complete certainty where our nearest and dearest spent their last days, where their final stop was, in which death camp or gas chamber they gave up their holy souls. There are various reports on these matters. I've heard contradictory versions from compatriots in Mexico, the United States, Uruguay and Argentina. But what difference does it make in the end? The sad and terrible toll remains the same: in Augustow not one single Jew was left alive.

*

Augustow was more to us than just a little point on the Polish map. It was our beloved home, which we warmed and protected. It was the home of our parents and grandparents. The love of one's hometown, where one was born, and took one's first steps in life, as a child and an adolescent, cannot be dampened by the passage of time.

Today there is not a single Jew in Augustow. But we are not thinking about the sad present. In our imagination we wish to see our town as it was twenty-five years ago, thirty years ago, when we could not have predicted that the murderous Nazi thugs would wipe out Jewish life in Poland with such ferocity.

I wish to see our beloved hometown as I left it in the summer of 1936. We wish to see the glorious dense woodlands surrounding the town and the large lakes, the canals and rivers, for which our town was renowned throughout Poland. It is tempting to close our eyes and allow ourselves to be carried on the wings of fantasy.

Here we see our hometown in its full amplitude. We see the hundred needy and downtrodden Jews, the merchants and shopkeepers who just about scraped together enough to keep their heads above water, to provide for their families and celebrate *Shabbes* in a manner befitting God's will. The shopkeepers and merchants from the Market Square, and from Broad Street, the artisans and handworkers from Synagogue Street and from Bridge Street. We see the pale and harried children of the *Talmud Torah*, {p. 445} the little Moyshes and little Shloymes, who could not all come to school with something to eat . . . We see the Jewish bourgeoisie, the Chasidim with long beards and thick *peyes*, who never missed a prayer service in the large synagogue, in the main prayer house, or in one of the smaller prayer houses where it was always so warm and welcoming.

Chaim Lazdeiski with His Friend Chaim Vodovoz

418

{p. 446} Who could forget the town intellectuals and the well-read youth who silently and secretly sympathized with the liberation movement? Who could forget the glorious *chalutz* youths who left comfortable homes to go to Palestine and work the land, chopping wood and carrying water? Who could forget the young children of the Zionist Youth Organization who, against the wishes of their parents, went to their colonies to work clandestinely?

How could we forget the rustic folk-types of our town? How could we forget Avigdor the Lipsker, Shakhne the Beer Carrier? How could we forget the hard-working, down-trodden Jews who used to carry bags on their backs to the marketplace near Bridge Street, where the automobiles would stop on their way from Grodno to Suwalki?

It's impossible to forget the Jews of our town who, each in their own way, symbolized Jewish life in Poland, with all its bright and dark aspects.

It's also not possible to forget all the lovely places in Augustow where Jewish children and young adults would go to dream of a better life in a better world, about a future in the Land of Israel and about a better standard of living for their parents, brothers and sisters.

With the power of our imaginations we can see the city gardens and the very center of the Market Square. The clock-tower on the roof of the magistrate's office dominated its surroundings and when the bells rang out it was to indicate a fire. Sunday amusements in the gardens were not for Jews. Cavalrymen from the town garrison would often get drunk and run wild. Jews knew better than to stray too close. At the point where Long Street came to an end there was a park, or the "monument" as we called it because of the memorial for Polish heroes that was there. In the park the fragrant scent of lilac and acacia was positively intoxicating in May and June. Young couples in love would walk further: to the rampart by the shore of the canal under the bridge on the Suwalki Road. On the Grodno Road it was not so romantic. There only the Zionist youth organizations would go marching—*Hashomer Hatzair*, *Beitar* and others—singing Hebrew marches and Polish songs. But not late at night. It was not safe.

We see the winter snows heaped over our town in great mounds. The youth would go skating on the ice rink. The children from poor families did not have it easy; they did not have warm woolen {p. 447} coats or jackets. But our young blood warmed us more than our clothes . . .

Who is the equal of those children who in winter could slide on the snow in the frosty and sunny days, skating in a row, tethered to a horse (that was a luxury in its own regard) throwing balls of tightly packed snow?

After *Purim*, when milder winds began to blow, and when one began to feel traces of the breath of Poland's glorious pre-spring in the air, it would be a celebration for the children. Even the slippery paths and thick mud could not hold them back. The snow would grow weaker and thinner, revealing more and more patches of green fields and woodlands.

And on the eve of *Pesach*? The preparations for this important and beautiful holiday; scrubbing and koshering the tables and chairs, rinsing the dishes and glassware, beating the carpets and bedding, and most importantly of all—bringing *matzo* into the white-washed houses . . . how beautiful it all was. How it ignited the childish imagination.

*

In June 1936 I left Augustow and travelled to Uruguay, South America, where my two older brothers were already living. For a few months—in 1932—my third brother had also been there. But it seems he was destined to fall victim to the Nazi's slaughter. He travelled back to Augustow after spending six months in Montevideo.

419

Poland at that time was still reeling from the pogroms in Przytyk and Minsk Mazowiecki. The policy of *"owszem"*[1079] weighed heavily on the Jewish population. We felt it vividly in our town.

Being in Uruguay, we—a group of compatriots and recently arrived refugees from the old country—suffered from afar, observing the course of events in Poland. Most of us were consumed by yearning for our old home and our family members who had remained behind.

Then came the tragic first of September 1939. In early September, a Uruguayan newspaper published a list of Polish towns bombed by the German air force on the first day of the war, and there I saw the name of our town.

Several weeks later our town was "liberated" by the Red Army. Only one letter from my "liberated" mother, sister and brother {p. 448} arrived to me in Montevideo. It was the only letter, on dark thin paper, in a dark thin envelope—a sign of the new order, implemented in the Soviet style . . . it was hard to make anything of a letter like that. But worse was still to come. The Nazi murder machine was already preparing to consume all the Jews of Eastern Poland and all of Europe. The German-Soviet war followed, bringing the worst calamities down on the heads of millions of Jews.

Our hometown suffered the same fate as all towns and villages in Poland. The Jews of Augustow were killed by the German murderers.

*

With a holy tremble, we hold and honor in our hearts the memory of our parents, our brothers and sisters, all of our family members who perished as martyrs. May this publication prepared by the Augustow compatriots in Israel serve as a gravestone on the tomb of the dead.

We will never forget them! May their holy memory be blessed until the end of all generations.

{p. 448} Uprooted and Desecrated Gravestones

[1079] Owszem: Name given to the policy of economic boycott of Jewish businesses.

{p. 449}**From "*The Song of the Murdered Jewish People*"**

Scream from the bottom of the sands, from under every stone, scream,
Scream from every dust, from every flame, every plume of smoke —
It is your blood and your sap, it is the marrow of your bones,
It is your flesh and your life! Scream, shout at the top of your voice!

Howl from the entrails of the beasts in the forest, from the fish in the river —
They have devoured you, scream of furnaces, screams large and small,
I want to hear your voice, give me a cry of pain, a howl of anger,
I want a clamor: shout, murdered Jewish people, shout, shout! — — —

— — Come all, from Treblinka, from Sobibor, from Auschwitz,
Come from Belzec, from Ponar, from other places, and others and yet others still!
With bulging eyes, a frozen cry, a voiceless scream, from the marshes come,
From the muddy depths where you have sunk, from amid the rotten mosses — — —

Come, you desiccated, you crushed and scraped, come take your place,
Form a circle around me, one enormous ring —
Grandfathers, grandmothers, mothers with infants in their arms —
Come, Jewish bones, ground to powder, flakes of soap. — — —

Yitskhok Katzenelson

{p. 450} Letters from Survivors

My Best friend Khatskl Murzinski,

You cannot imagine my immense joy in receiving this letter from you. We simply wept for joy and from pain and suffering, reading again about the terrible misfortune that befell our mothers and fathers, brothers and sisters and the whole Jewish people. May the murderers be cursed for all eternity. I and my family—that is to say, my father, mother, and three sisters—were saved by the fact that we had left immediately for Russia. My younger brother was doing his military service at the time and was taken captive by the Germans. He was also saved by this fact, as he also fled to Russia. We lived in Augustow between October 1939 and April 1940 after which we all went to Russia, all except for one of my sisters who remained behind in Augustow. She worked as a teacher in the Jewish school. She married a certain Wasserman, whose father was a baker. My sister and her husband, as well as their two small children, stayed in Augustow and perished along with all of Augustow's Jews. They lived across the way from Khaykl, and stuck together the whole time until the very end. I tell you, my dear friend Khatskl, that it breaks my heart to remember all of this, and I believe that until our dying day we will never forget our great misfortune. For the time being we are living in Wroclaw. I received your letter from the Jewish Committee in Rychbach[1080] via an acquaintance from Suwalki. I thank you a thousand times. Let us stay in contact. My dear friend, Khatskl, we do not yet know for sure if we will stay here or for how long. For the moment I have no request for you, though truth be told I could use some help. But I know myself that by the time my letter reaches you, and you send aid back, I may already have left Wroclaw, because we are thinking of leaving Poland altogether. For now I'm working as a baker and I make it through the days as best I can.

My sisters and brothers-in-law send their warmest regards.

Wroclaw, August 10, 45   **Ruven Lentcheski**

[1080] Modern day Dzierżoniów.

421

My Best friend Khatskl Murzinski   **Cremona 4.6.46**

I'm writing to respond to your last letter. It is hard for me to write because your family was as dear to me as brothers and sisters. Now I will write to you frankly. Your father died during the registration of the men. It happened on July 2, 1941 on the day when 800 men, including your father and my brother, were gathered together. They were all shot 3 kilometers from town in the forest by the Suwalki Road. Very few of us men remained, only women and children enclosed behind wire fences in a ghetto. Out of 2,500 people there were only 60 men, one of whom was your brother Khaykl with his children, along with your sister Dobke and her husband Osher and their children. Your brother's eldest son would have been a rabbi; he studied in the Suwalki *yeshiva*. One of the daughters had studied in a gymnasium, and all of them were very gifted. Now I will tell you about your sister's children: the daughter was a friend of mine; her name is Lubke. She had a boyfriend, also a friend of mine. She was one of the prettiest girls in town, and the sons too were handsome children. It pains me to remember it all. We lived together and worked together in the ghetto, helping each other, until the terrible order came to liquidate the ghetto. It was carried out by the Starosta and the mayor, whose names were: Pon Namen and Richter. With the help of the police we were loaded into train cars and sent to Auschwitz, where the final tragedy began. This was on January 6, 1943. They loaded us off the train cars and split us into rows where the Gestapo began to select young men, and also women, for purposes unknown. Naturally no one wanted to be separated from their families, and so they took a small number of men and women and loaded everyone else onto jeeps and drove them to the crematorium where they were gassed and incinerated. This is where your brother and sister died together with all their children. The handful of selected men and women were taken into the camp for hard labor. Most could not survive more than a few days of being starved and beaten with heavy clubs that flew over our heads—there remained only me and a girl from our town. She was with me in the camp. She is Noyekh the Butcher's daughter; Rokhl Levinzon. She will write a few words herself, as will Shmuel Zupnitski and his wife. He was saved by joining the partisans. No one else remained from our town, aside from those who were sent to Russia in 1940.

Now to the questions asked by Moyshe Khayim son of Hershl the coachman. You didn't mention their surname, but I think they must be from the Poznanski family.

{p. 452} His father is Hershl, his brothers were called Itshe, Binyomin and Dovid. Before the war we shared a car. Hershl would always talk about his loyal son Moyshe Khayim. I understand that you served in the military with my brother Avrom? If you are from the family I think you are then your father and his three heroic brothers died along with the 800 men on July 7, 1941. If I am mistaken, send me the names and I will answer you in a second letter.

Concerning Isser the carpenter's son and Leybl the cobbler's son I will not write to you now. Send me the family names first.

I will finish up now. May my letter find you in the best of health. Give my regards to my brother, sister and son.

I received the two dollars.

I would ask you, if it is not too difficult for you to help the two Augustow compatriots to do so. The best is with a letter, because money lasts about two months but a letter can have everything cleared up in seven days.

From me, your friend, **Yekheskl Piastski**

My Best friend Khatskl Murzinski   **June 23, 1946**

We received your letter, for which we are very grateful, Piastski and I. I thank you for taking an interest in me. Thank you too for the 5 dollars, you can imagine how useful it was, as you understand what life is like in the camps. I believe we will someday meet and I will repay you then. First you want to know who I was in Augustow. Your brother Leybl was my friend. My name is Shmuel Zupnitski. My mother was called Tsivie, and my father was called Velvl. I am thirty-six years old. No one special. I send a hearty greeting to all my compatriots.

On another occasion I will write more. For now I thank you for everything and look forward to your response.

From me, your friend, **Shmuel Zupnitski**

Dear friend Khatskl!   **Wroclaw, October 21, 1946**

It has been a long time since I answered your letter. And yet I have not received a response. Not awaiting or expecting a response from you, I write to you again. Dear Khatskl, as you know from my first letter we had planned to leave Poland. But last month we unexpectedly received letters from our brother Moyshe, who is now in Uruguay—you must remember him, though he was only a young lad when you knew him. He plans to bring a few people over to him and is currently working to that aim. And so we have decided to stay put for the time being and wait until we receive the necessary documents for my sister to travel to Uruguay. We have also made contact with Mexico, where our uncles—Avrom Dovid Rozenfeld's two sons, Abke and Yudl—are living. They also want to help someone emigrate to them. For now they have been sending packages for my sisters and their children. Dear Khatskl, living with us at the moment is the hat-maker Sender Moyshe Lenzinger and his wife, who is our uncle's daughter. His name was Itshe Krinitski, a tailor. They arrived not long ago from Russia and plan to continue on further, to their friends in Palestine. It was only by accident that we found out they were here in Wroclaw. I brought them back to our place and now they are living with us. The mood is a little lighter to see some relatives from Augustow, given that all the others perished at the hands of the Nazis, may they be cursed for eternity. Dear Khatskl, perhaps it is not too hard for you to bear because you are so far from here. But we find ourselves here in Poland and every day we find out more information about people; when and how our fathers, mothers, brothers, sisters and children died. This makes it harder for us to bear; though we know there is no hope, our heart bleeds from the pain of it. Where I can I continue to make inquiries: perhaps someone else has survived the slaughter in Augustow. But alas, to this day we have not heard of anyone. We have only heard news of Augustowers who were sent away to Russia before the outbreak of war. In this way Sender Moyshe Lenzinger and his wife returned from Russia. So as you can see we are staying in Poland for the time being. I'm waiting for my brother Moyshe in Uruguay and my cousins Abke and Yudl in Mexico to bring some of us over to them. Then I will see about leaving for somewhere, because it is heart-breaking here, and you know as well as I do how they look upon us Jews . . . Dear friend, you wrote me that you would be able to help me in some way but that you did not know what I needed. My dear friend, what should I tell you; I work in a bakery as an employee. You'll understand that the prices being what they are I cannot afford everything I {p. 454} need. So I would ask you, if you can, to send me a parcel of goods. The favor would serve me well and I would be very grateful to you. Be well, your friend — Rufke

My Best friend Khatskl Murzinski

Yesterday I read your letter to Ruven with the greeting for us. We thank you for thinking of us, dear friend. Many years have passed since you left Augustow. Over the years we have lived through so many things, particularly in the last years of the war. It is very hard to write about whom we've lost, the best and the brightest. Not to mention our own parents and sisters, and also such friends as your brother Khaykl, of blessed memory, and your father, of blessed memory. It is very difficult for me to say their names without shedding a tear. But the wells of our tears have long ago run dry. It is as though we have been turned to stone. But a pain, a great pain has stayed behind in our hearts, and emptiness which cannot be filled. Since the time I was taken from my home, on October 30, 1939, I have only once had occasion to see my dear friends again. On the way to an interrogation they drove me past Khaykl's shop and at that moment he happened to come outside. Our eyes met; but we had no chance to speak. When, a year later, I was sent to the desolate north for eight years' hard labor, I would often receive letters from him, and even parcels. Golde, having been sent to Siberia received the same. Then that devil Hitler declared war on Russia. Then I was freed, while they, those unlucky ones who were left under Hitler's control, they all died—our best, most trusted friends, the likes of which we will never have again. It is sadder still when one does not even know where their bones lie so that they can be given a proper burial. Thanks to the fact that I was arrested I survived. Though I was left permanently disfigured. In the distant North I spent the best part of a year in a hospital. There was even a time when the doctors had given me up for dead. But as fate would have it I survived, but as an invalid, having lost an eye. I was left half blind, with an untreatable heart condition along with kidney and liver damage. There are times when the pain is so bad that I envy the dead. That's what my life is like. Naturally this was all very hard for Golde {p. 455} and she too is ill. You would not recognize us if you saw us. And what now? What will happen to us now, I do not know. You write that you remember Golde has brothers in America: Pinye and Khatskl. I probably also knew Kopl, he is also in America. We have their addresses and if not for their aid, even when we were back in Russia, we would long ago have starved to death. It's truly thanks to them that we are still alive. But how much more can they help us? If I were able to work, I might be able to get back on my feet with a little help. But not being able to earn so much as a penny the whole time, and the expenses are so high, because treatment and medicines are very expensive here. The strict diet they have me on is also very expensive such that we are dependent on other aid from good friends. You will excuse me writing like this, explaining my situation to you . . . Now I would like to ask you who is this chairman of the Augustow committee Sol Lang? Is that Matie Langrevits the medic's son? We're guessing from the changed surname that it's either Shaul Langrevits or Shepsl Langrevits. If yes, do they receive letters from their sister Khayke? She's on the other side of the border, in Estonia, I think, with a daughter-in-law and grandchild.

We've read your call to organize eulogies for the fallen martyrs. That made a strong impression on us, but unfortunately we cannot do anything much to help, because there are so few of us left in Augustow, and there's no one to do it with. I will write to you about that another time. You also mention a cooperative encompassing Suwalki and Augustow; that is alas impossible. There is a lot to write about the whole matter. If ever someone else comes along who expresses an interest in it you should know that they have an ulterior motive. I'd ask you not to tell anyone else about what I write to you. I will end my first letter to you and hope that our correspondence will continue. We would be very grateful to hear from you again.

Be well. We wish you a joyous *Pesach*. Regards to your wife, your children and all of our compatriots. *Wroclaw 18.3.47.*
Your friend, **Sender Moyshe** and **Golde Lenzinger**

{p. 456} **Best friend Khatskl**

Received your letter from the 3rd of the 4th. We thank you for your swift response, and particularly for taking such an interest in us all. Dear friend, reading your letters we learn things that we would not otherwise hear being in Poland. About our parents, brothers and sisters, where and when they perished. When we were in Russia we could not fathom returning to Poland and not being in Augustow. But the bitter truth has shown us that such is possible. Firstly, because in Augustow there is not a single Jew left, and at the time the situation was such that going to Augustow would have meant certain death and none of us had wanted to risk our lives. The area was rendered so alien by the Nazis; in all of Bialystok *voivodeship*, apart from Bialystok itself, there are no Jews at all. There are a few Jews in Suwalki too, but there is no question of being able to go to Augustow. There are people who went there such as Baravits, also the Rekhtman brothers were there, and the Vaksmans, who left behind many houses there, have no intention of going there to sell the houses, that's how bad the situation is. Before '39 the whole area was already poisoned enough. That the German murderers were there when Jewish blood and property was abandoned, that was enough to ruin things to the present day. It's true that the government is trying to combat antisemitism, and to a large extent it has had an effect. But the negligible number of Jews who remained alive would prefer to live somewhere else where there are Jews. And generally even searching for the graves is futile, because the murderers have poured petrol on the gravesites and burned them, wiping away every last trace. Even the old cemetery has been plowed into the ground, the headstones used to pave roads and as foundations for buildings. Such atrocities have never been committed since the beginning of time. Nowadays the world has more sympathies for the murderers, the Germans, than for the eternally misfortunate Jews. That's how our situation appears. How long can we live like this? No one had an answer to this question. You asked why there were so few Augustow Jews in Russia. I will tell you that the only Augustowers who found themselves in Russia were there because they had been sentenced for various reasons. For example Kestin and me were sentenced for being Zionists. For the same reasons Eliav Khlufitski and Abba Arimland, may peace be upon him, were exiled, but they never returned. Others were sentenced because they were big time businessmen, others because of illegal trade. Then there were also a few who served in the Soviet army. The families were sent out in 1940. The people who saved themselves {p. 457} were in distant places such as Siberia, working such jobs that none of them had ever imagined they would ever do. Selling all their possessions in order to survive as best they could, hoping they would someday find their way back home and somehow be able to live some semblance of a normal life again. The dream was short lived, and the bitter truth soon revealed itself to have something else in store. It's depressing to look back on all this. Now whoever comes back in one piece, though no one comes back entirely unscathed, can expect to get straight to work for very little pay. And to find some extra aid is also painful. But someone like me, who's lost one eye in the prisons and camps, who's suffered heart failure and severe kidney disease, an entirely broken man, must depend entirely on aid. And believe me I've sometimes envied Khaykl, of blessed memory, and other dear friends who died as martyrs, but what can one do? One struggles to live, though life holds no appeal. I know I'm not the only one who's been left like this, but we each feel our own pain. True, Golde's brother Pinye supports us, and Kopl a little, but can one ever fill a sack that's full of holes? It's only thanks to their aid, and the aid from the Augustow committee, that we manage to survive. And who knows, perhaps with God's grace we can manage to emigrate to Palestine or America, and spend whatever years that remain in the company of our own people. You ask if it is true that there are those who take aid even though they do not need it? I can tell you that whoever comes begging must receive something. As the saying goes, you can never tell whose shoes are tight. We can never know 100%. Everyone has suffered and everyone suffers still— some on a great scale and others on a lesser scale. That's why we appealed to you concerning the Vaksman affair. I believe one must be accommodating.

Be well. Your friend **Sender Moyshe** and **Golde Lenzinger**

P.S.—I would like to add: if you are in contact with our Augustover brothers and sisters in other cities, can you warn them not to give any money, or goods, to the Suwalki committee, because wherever there are joint Suwalki-Augustow committees we receive nothing from Suwalki. We've seen cases of this before. Here in Lower Silesia the delegate of the Suwalki association, Mr. Gedalye Smitshekhovski, received money from Chicago and Argentina (where there is a joint {p. 458} committee) and we never received a single penny of it. At the same time things came from Augustow—also from a joint committee—and their delegate in Wroclaw told us that after winter those from Augustow would receive a portion. In the end they never gave us anything. So we ask that our Augustow compatriots should not take part in joint aid campaigns with those from Suwalki.

You can even publish this warning in the press.

With respect and thanks, **Sender Lenzinger** (Secretary)   **Wroclaw 20.4.47**

{p. 459} 1426/260
Central Historical Commission
at the Central Committee of the Liberated Jews in the American Zone

Historical Survey of Ruined Jewish Settlements and Deceased Jewish Personalities

1. The city of Augustow. District library. Poland.
2. How old was the Jewish settlement?
3. How many Jews lived there before the war? — around 4,000[1081]
4. What were the main occupations? — handworkers 70%, small traders and merchants 30%.
5. Which and how many community institutions, cultural organizations, associations and clubs were there in the town, and what has become of them today?

(Such as synagogues, prayer houses, *yeshiva*s, cemeteries, old-age homes, orphanages, hospitals, *Lines HaTsedek*, schools, libraries, evening courses, drama clubs, cooperatives, banks, Gmiles-Khesed, professional and artisan unions, political parties etc.)

A large synagogue, a prayer house, cemeteries, *Hakhnoses Orkhim, Bikker Khoylim*, Talmud Torah, Jewish library with 10,000 books, drama club, cooperative bank, *Gmiles-Khesed*, Small Traders' Union, Artisans' Union, "*Chalutz*."

The Germans destroyed everything in 1941; during the Russian occupation everything was active.
6. What rarities were in the possession of the community and in private hands, and what has become of them now? (such as: buildings, gravestones, *pinkeysim*,[1082] ritual objects such as: *poroykhes*[1083], *atores*,[1084] spices, holy books, paintings etc.)
7. The most important events in the town from the start of the war (1.9.1939):

a) Since the Nazi occupation.

—The Red Army occupied our town at the beginning of the war. They arrested 4 Zionist activists; one by the name of Hershl Papirovitsh. He {p. 460} was freed after 8 months of captivity, I don't remember the other names. They were deported to Russia.

b) Under Nazi occupation: (date of arrival, the first decrees against Jews, fencing, tribute, confiscations, ghetto—open or closed—torture, beard cutting, badges, forced labor, evacuation of Jews from the town to other places or the contrary, pogroms, executions, looting, how did the final liquidation of the settlement come about? —date).

—Straight away, on Sunday June 22, 1941, 6 a.m. the German army had already entered our town, they issued a decree that all Jews had to wear a special sign, and every day Jews were taken and put to work on various tasks. At the end of July the same year all the Jews had to go to a certain spot, allegedly to be registered. Then 1,500 men were taken to Szczebra in the forest. I and thirty other Jews were chosen as skilled workers and taken back to town. They kept the Jews there 3 days without food, and then they were all shot in the forest by S. S. men.

At the end of August the ghetto was created, where 15 people were housed in a single room. The ghetto was surrounded by a barbed-wire fence and guarded by Polish police. In total there were 70 men and 1,500 women in the ghetto. Every day we had to go to work. In Early July

---

[1081] Original Footnote: There were more than twice as many people in the town.
[1082] Community Ledgers.
[1083] Curtains for the *aron kodesh*.
[1084] *Torah* mantles.

1942, the ghetto was surrounded by Polish police and S. S. men. We were driven out to Bogusze near Grayevo where 7,000 Jews had been gathered from the surrounding settlements. We stayed there for six weeks. We received about 100 grams of bread with half a liter of soup per day. During those six weeks 2,000 of us died. At the end of August they made a selection: 3,000 were sent off to Treblinka and 2,000 were sent to Auschwitz. In all three Jews from the camp survived.

8. Relations and interactions with the non-Jewish population.

—Very bad. They had a direct hand in all things.

9. Did the Jews in this town organize a resistance?

—No.

10. Number of survivors from the town.

—15.

11. Notable people: (name, age, profession, role, area, date and manner of death).

Place: Regensburg.

April 23, 1947   **Ze'ev Kalshteyn** (witness)

{p. 461} **Jewish Provincial Historical Commission**

Bialystok February 20,1947

L. G. 35/37

Communicated by Yekheskl Fendzukh, born 1901 in Bialystok. Lived in the Bialystok ghetto during the occupation. On 14.8.43 transported to Augustow, and following the liquidation brought back to Bialystok prison. Survived in Działdowo[1085] camp. Now located in Bialystok.

On August 14, 1943, at 3:30 in the morning, the Gestapo, escorted by the Jewish police removed me from my home and in a windowless van took me out to the outskirts of town. I didn't know where they were taking me. It was only after Knyszyn, when they stopped to refuel that a man in the vehicle behind me, Klein, told me they were taking me to Augustow for a work detail.

Arriving there I soon met carpenters from Bialystok who had already been working there for some time: Yoyne Lis, Furmanski, Mayer Markhovki and Gelman, I don't remember the others' names, six men altogether. They were bruised and battered, because a few days earlier the Augustow camp commander had caught them, led them into the camp where each one received 25 lashes and finally they were forced to eat hot potato soup for two minutes which left blisters on their mouths . . . they were very sorry to see me. Mr. Lis said to me: "Yekheskl, they brought you here as a victim too?..."

Our task was to finish building a villa for General Kanarius.

A few days later we went into town to a Polish hairdresser for a shave. He told us that in Bialystok he had seen the ghetto burn, and watched them evacuate all the Jews; where they were taken he did not know. Later a construction technician called Lenkovitser was brought on, and he told us exactly how the liquidation proceeded, and how 140 workers who had been working for the Gestapo led people to Lomza prison, while others were taken to Lublin (Majdanek). When I asked him about my wife and children he confirmed that they had also been taken. It is pointless recounting my experiences. From that moment on I went gray, and though I am only 46 years old, I am as gray as a dove.

Then we began to think about how to escape. Escaping into the nearby woods was impossible, because there was a group of Polish partisans there {p. 462} who called themselves "Młoda Polska." On every tree in the forest was the slogan: "*Polska bez żydów i bez Rosjanów*"[1086]

[1085] Soldau concentration camp.

[1086] Polish: "Poland without Jews and without Russians;"

We began to dig a tunnel in the cellar of our workplace, but many of us believed that we would not be able to acquire the necessary supplies of food and water.

Jewish Provincial Historical Commission

Bialystok 10.11.1945

L. G. 97

Nr. 1267

Memoirs written by Fania Landau, born in the year... In Bialystok. Lived in Bialystok ghetto. Brought out on work detail two days before the definitive liquidation of the Bialystok ghetto. Awaited liberation in Auschwitz camp.

I lived in the Bialystok ghetto and worked together with a group of Jews outside the ghetto in S.R. The work was led by a Jewish engineer Zigmunt Lenkovitser from Warsaw.

On August 13 Lenkovitser passed on the order that two women and four men were needed to travel to Augustow, because the villa of inspector Kanarius had to be completely finished by August 15, 1943. I also wanted to see the inspector's villa for myself. His mission was—the annihilation of Jews in Europe. There was no question of refusing the order to go. It was enough to hear the order for my fate to be tied up in theirs.

The following morning, at 9 a.m. on August 14, 1943, I left Bialystok for Augustow. Driving out of the ghetto I must admit that I could breathe more freely. Straight away the engineer removed our yellow badges which we had been wearing for two years. As we drove further away from the ghetto I could no longer see the deeply anguished faces; the small children selling cigarettes in order to earn a morsel of bread; the boys stooped down toward the earth lugging a bundle of wood from outside the ghetto in order to earn a mark for their families. I did not hear the daily news: another *aktion*, or more dead in Treblinka, a fresh victim, Auschwitz, Majdanek—the news upon which we {p. 463} subsisted in the ghetto. We approach Augustow and it looks like we're entering an entirely different world. People are moving around freely, knowing nothing of a ghetto. I must remark that they also seem to know nothing about Jews because there had been no Jews there for almost a year. They also perished in Treblinka and Majdanek. We see forests, fields, lakes and finally the inspector's villa. There I meet several Jews from Bialystok, working on getting the villa finished.

They briefly tell us about how good life is there. They've been in Augustow for two weeks now. I quickly get acquainted with my surroundings. The workers prepare me a place to sleep where I can stay for the few days I am scheduled to be here. The first day is truly pleasurable: we worked for a few hours and afterwards we walked around like free people, taking in the lakes, the glorious forests; everything was so beautiful to us as we had spent the last two years unable to go out and enjoy the beauty of nature. We had no desire to go to sleep.

The next day, August 15th, 1943, Inspector Kanarius arrived with his murderous Anita. They amused themselves for half a day, rowing boats, catching fish and gathering them . . .at 4:00 in the morning two of the murderers come to us and say we should no longer go anywhere near the building where his friends will soon be gathering, or should I say the pogromists will soon be gathering. Then began the meeting—the preparations for the bloody Monday. Yes that's where they planned how they could most easily fool the Jews and lead them to their deaths.

Their meeting lasted a long time. Afterwards they came to visit us in the dilapidated building opposite, where we were staying. There they told us ironically that our Judaism did little to serve us, that they would serve us better. In the evening they went off on a hunt where they caught several wild ducks and a rabbit. That was all a preparation, and now, in the middle of the night they drove off for the real hunt, to Bialystok. This time it was not birds they were going to catch but people, to snatch children from their mothers, sisters from brothers, wives from husbands: destroying all that people hold dear - taking the lives of innocent, unarmed people.

Then came Monday. We were waiting impatiently for a truck from Bialystok in order to travel home. But it was in vain: the truck never came. We believed that we would be able to go back on Tuesday. But then rumors reached us that the ghetto was burning. Several regiments of soldiers went to surround the ghetto and evacuate the Jews. But our companions reassured us: it was a lie; the Christians were saying that to scare us. On Wednesday we find out that it was not a lie, it was the bitter truth.

{p. 464} And now the worst began for us: no more home, no more loved ones, no more families. Gloomy and terrified we sat there waiting for our turn to come. We were now almost continually silent, except when a voice spoke from a corner: "My wife, my little children . . ." then another: "My mother and my sick father." Then from the other room: "I thought I would die with them, such a terrible death—gas!" Day after day passed in this manner, each one harder than the last. We were running low on food, and there would be no more supplies coming. The wind started to howl; it was growing cold. Our group had no more than the work clothes on our backs, and those were beginning to fall apart. We no longer worked 8 hours but 10 hours and each day we had to present ourselves to the Gestapo.

Now we heard a cry of pain—death! But hurry up! When you want to live the German says—for you there is only death! And when you want to die, he says—drudgery! That's how it was for us. We had toiled for two months already and there was no end in sight. Every day the Christians would tell us that 23 Jews had been found and shot right then and there; on Petrasz Square they had found 35 Jews in a cellar and shot them. We knew that the fate of our group of ten would be no different. So why did they continue to torment us? Another week passed, then another; but this week brought something new.

It was Thursday the 12th of November and we lay down again to sleep on the cold floor with nothing but our fists for pillows. We did not reckon with any change in our circumstances and then suddenly there was a clatter on the door, all but taking it off its hinges. A Gestapo man came to us and announced that the next morning, Friday, 5 a.m., at daybreak, that we were to go to the Gestapo square and each of us was to take a shovel with us. He noted coolly that he was tasked with keeping an eye on us, but seeing as he knew us, and trusted that we would not try to escape he would go to sleep and come back to pick us up before dawn. Despite being convinced that death awaited us the next morning, and that we would have to dig our own graves, none of us gave any thought to escaping because we were already so exhausted. Despite being entirely apathetic I could not sleep a wink those few hours.

5:00 in the morning. Each of us has prepared a shovel. Our executioner comes to take us. We walk. A deathly silence reigns. No one says a word, not even Mayer, who had always been so kind to me, always sharing his last portion of bread. He does not speak to be because he has nothing to {p. 465} say to me before death. Then I decide I want to say something to him. I try to open my mouth to say something. No. Useless. Something catches in my throat, and no word can come out. Now I understand Mayer; he wants to speak, but cannot. We approach the square. It's surrounded by police. Seeing us, the police deploy themselves and hurry us onto the square. And there we see death before us. The bandits inform us that in 4-5 hours we must each dig a trench 180 centimeters long, 90 centimeters wide. All manner of thoughts begins to rush into my mind. What if I don't dig? They'll shoot me and then they'll have to dig the grave themselves. And maybe I could run away? That way I would not see as they shoot me. I have to spit in their faces before I die, I thought. And then I hear my colleague next to me say: "Children, time to atone before death." Then I felt bewildered. What should I do? Scream? Scream and maybe atone for my sins? But then I see that all the others have already dug large pits, and I have not even started. But then when I look down

429

again at my own pit I realize it is actually deeper than the others. I barely noticed how quickly I had dug my own grave. Another minute and it would all be over. Once all nine graves were ready they would shoot us and no trace would be left to show that nine innocent young people had stood there just a moment before, shot because they bore the name Jew.

Thinking this, I hear Mayer say to me, with a voice unlike his own:

"Fania, is it true they are going to shoot us? And you too, Fania? But you're so young, you're not even 18 years old."

"And you're only 23," I say to him. "You've not even begun to live. Let's stop talking; the bandits are coming already."

"Are you finished?" one of them says.

"Shoot these dogs," shouts another. And all the others laugh heartily. We are not laughing. We're thinking only of how to get a bullet faster so as not to have to hear their ironic laughter, or look in their loathsome faces. But then something unexpected happens; they take the men from our group. Were they not going to shoot them along with us? We see that they are given full sacks and they come back to the pits and are told to empty them into the pits. Something strange is happening: are they going to bury us with these potatoes? But then we hear the boss's voice: "When you've finished go back home." We all stare with half-crazed eyes . . . Is it true that they're not going to shoot us? Was it all just a game for them? . . . Yes. This time it was all just a joke—they were playing with our lives! We filled the pits with the potatoes and went back {p. 466} to the dilapidated villa and for our efforts we each received a loaf of bread.

We go back to our quarters. Each of us seems to have lost our minds: one laughs, the other gobbles down his bread; Estherke screams: Because we prayed, God spared our lives. We would have a few more days after which they were going to shoot us anyway. And that's exactly what happened.

We stayed there another two weeks. Each day was terrible. Yes, it was Tuesday. It had been a successful day for the bandits. They found some partisans whom they shot, and in celebration they had gotten drunk. Then when they were drunk they met our five men who they began to toy with. This time they played a different game: they beat them—each of them received 25 lashes! Exhausted and broken they returned to their quarters. We administer compresses to their wounds and tell them to take heart; perhaps we would one day look back on all this as ones who had been through it all. But we could not console ourselves in this way for long.

Friday came. This time they took us out and separated us from the men—but for good this time. It was daybreak. A knocking on the door. We get up to open the door. But then we see that the building is surrounded by Gestapo men and some of them were already inside the building. They give an order that in half an hour everyone must be ready because we were leaving. We were ready and believed that we would all be traveling together. But no. Climbing onto the truck they separate us from the men. They don't let them board the truck, and tell them to stand to one side. "You're going to a different work detail," they tell them. Mayer begins to plead, my sister is there, he says, I want to stay with her. As an answer he receives a punch. He is bleeding and they push him aside. I'm confused, standing on the truck, not knowing what to do. Should we say goodbye? But it's no use—the truck begins to move. We begin to feel dizzy. We're moving away from them. I see Mayer, bloodied and crying and he calls out: "farewell! Maybe you'll survive?" Our ears buzz, our minds are foggy. We look at each other and every face tells the same story: Where was fate taking us now? And yet Fate did want me to live after all.

Chairman of the Provincial Historical Commission
Mgr. Turek

Dedicated to the Memory of the Heroes and Martyrs of the Augustow Jews

The First Little Candle
By Eliezer Aronovski

It trembles, the poor, Chanukah candle...
No more is the heroic Maccabean strength,
of a people that fought and died like lions,
in a land made holy, and free.
Extinguished is that flaming fire,
which hurls its people into death to liberate!
The wee flame of a candle remains,
and before its own shadow it cowers and shakes...

Come down from the window! – scream the stars –
you foolish, faded, *Chanukah* candles;
not to free a people – but to dupe them!
Energy ebbs and sits forged in place!...
Suffering in exile fettered and fixed;
bound in grief waiting on bliss...
blinding a people with tears in their eyes–
but you know this already – no more and no less...

We still remember them, us stars in the sky,
heroic, tigerish, Hasmonean battles,
where not with candles – but hearts of flame
thrown into battle, the enemy bested!
Indeed candles were kindled! – when this people triumphantly
danced in the streets of a holy victory.
Then, the lights showed the world,
that in the heart of this people, there burns a holy blaze!

What do you have to show for it, you candles? – Frozen fire!
The tremble of our people at every step?
That blackened, bloodied Jew in exile?

431

The oceans of tears that don't help one bit? –
Extinguish forever and don't burn again!
If my heart must be black as it's always been;
and like eagles, should this people not fly to be free –
it should be dark in the window! If it is night in my heart . . .
Augustow, December 1923

How can I grieve...
How can I grieve, how can I properly lament,
the murder of my people, since if I start to obsess; –
The tears in my eyes will all soon be spent
on one corpse, or two – so what of the countless?

We are far too used to slaughter, to butchery!
Pogroms in every land, that threaten every home;
of auto da fe is hallowed the memory,
of our martyrs in fire and brimstone.

Not a death untried upon us –
not a tyranny, not an anguish in the world;
we are airless, we are breathless,
the light of our sun cloaked by a curtain unfurled...

{p. 469}

Yet we're quite accustomed to all that's been done –
since we've lived thousands of years this way...
But today's hellfire – spares no one –
we burn by the millions... like stalks of hay!...

And whoever remains – alack and alas –
ashes and grave sites, a coyote's cry –
in mad howls, and shouts to shatter glass
will call, will wail: Adonai, Adonai!...

And he who will hear his voice, his moan,
his heart will burst, and his head will unhinge...
he will fashion himself a heart, hard as stone...
and shut every window and door before him...

A loner, his howls heard the whole world through...
a surrogate voice from the graves for their strife –
so that a fatal chill should come to imbue,
all that prepares to come into life...

And what rest there is in the world won't last –
a million souls – all's not forgiven! –
Bile will drip in every wine glass...
and in every temple shadows of dread will be driven...

To a world that allows millions to be slaughtered –
joy and rest should not be given! –
And however its fate may be secured,
its being remains, a being in question...

432

I Will Never
I will never hear from you again;
no sense in searching, or trying to pretend.
It won't help, this looking high and low –
there is no savior, there is no hero!

{p. 470}

They burned you up, my dear mother, in the barn,
along with all the Jews of the shtetl,
you with your son, in fire, arm-in-arm
devoured by flame, like a heap of dry nettle.

No ash left behind – the wind carried it away,
now through distant lands it's borne in bluster,
and when it comes – you can hear the lament...
from Yaakov's tents, a mournful mutter.

And there in another shtetl is shot to death
your daughter with her children,
her blood poured together with
all the Jews, the kosher flesh...

And flowing in rivers, through streets, and down drains
an ocean of blood, that boils and brews,
and in heaven, God can't contain
the cries of the tormented Jews!...

The winds blow through this very shudder,
casting dread on everything and everyone;
so who now isn't an orphaned daughter?
And who now isn't an orphaned son?

We carry sorrow withheld in our soul,
shed sometimes a tear we tried to keep in,
which covers the abyss, that deep dark hole,
but is soon wiped away – not to be seen again...

There is no comfort, no comforter, no consolation,
and no one can get a moment's relief;
so better to stick the pain down deeper,
in holy torment, to choke, and to grieve . . .

{p. 471}

The Tenth Day
On the tenth day of *Elul* my father died,
a young tree – in the spring of his life.
It was the year 5673,
for four orphaned children and one widowed wife.

I was the oldest, but no more than eight,
my sister, the youngest – and too young to know.
I remember the night, the glimmer, his face...
when we all mourned that terrible blow...

433

Who would believe that now it would be
such a gift from God, that he died when he did –
An autumn night when they buried his body,
that held him like a flower, a flower gone wilted...

At least I know where my father spends his days,
I saw his headstone, through the fence, not long ago...
where a tree arched over him piously sways,
sending thanks from afar – with a silent "hello" ...

Where is my mother?! My brother?! – My sister?!
Where do they lie? And when is their *yahrtzeit*? –
Did no small bone remain from the fire? –
Of the barns full of Jews burned for sheer spite!...

Do any trees still stand there today,
That witnessed without protest or uproar,
how all the Jews were driven away
from their cities and villages – like never before?...

Scorched in the stable, burned in the byre,
choked and smothered in rooms full of gas; –
will a small branch, singed from the fire,
show me that place, where lies their ash?

Might not a tree turn to me and say "hello",
call over and point out: Here they lie!...
And might I keep walking and not even know,
my heart should've burst for those I walked by...

{p. 472}   **Yisgadal V'yiskadash Shmey Rabo**
Yisgadal v'yiskadash shmey rabo,
every soul that I used to know...
tormented, gassed, devoured by flame,
rend your garments – cry out in vain!

Sit *shiva* – take off your shoes,
lament that you're still alive,
and how you don't feel that you are a part
of the people encamped, who met their demise.

So you don't feel that you need to try
to hallow all the life left to come,
like they – in that torturous time –
hallowed the pain of their martyrdom...

The light was snuffed out –
the fire, the fire, it burns! –
Take a moment to look at yourself,
deep in the eyes – try and discern…

that you are their heirs,
children of martyr and hero! –

434

should your hearts be pure as their prayers,
and your conscience clear, as it crows...

They have no grave, no burial shrouds,
the wind wafts their dust up above,
just a soul fluttering about,
like a poor, bloodied white dove...

Take her in as one of your own,
offer the rest she's been kept from,
then you will see that you will be shown
the light that leads to the world to come.

Make sure your life has an aim,
even when it splits at the seams;
let the pure light of dawn be the flame,
that shows you what it all means . . .

{p. 473} **My Cities and Towns**
By the Bobra, by the Niemen, by the Vistula,
by the Netta, by the Biala, by the Sajno,
in thousands of cities and towns,
there were more than you could know...
Jews that lived by the millions,
through labor, commerce, and travail,
from a needle, a pin with some thread,
to fields full of cattle and cattails.

Jews were dignitaries,
with comforts, with lavish estates.
And out and out beggars,
in hardship, starvation, and straits.

Yet together we fashioned a life! –
A Jewish city or town;
through the tyranny and oppression,
it's a miracle we're still around.

Those gray days that turn into weeks,
that encase the heart and harden like clay,
Jewish faith and devotion,
turned those weeks into months of May...

And that's how we weathered
the days of terror and bloodshed;
through black clouds that hover over
we saw the light up ahead...

Hundreds, thousands of years,
Jews, the bookish and learned.
Generations birthed generations,
The kernels of *Torah* and *Talmud*...

{p. 474}   We taught our children
to be good honest Jews is an art,
in school, in the study and prayer halls,
with God's word etched in their hearts.

It used to ring out in the shtetl
Of *Chumesh* and *Gemora*, a song...
Tell me, when was the last time you heard it?
And has it been very long?

Now on *shabbosim*[1087] and holidays –
the world gets its rest and relief!
and for each and every person
God kindles courage, belief...

And alone in every dwelling
There rests the presence of the divine,
when the *shabbos* lights are lit,
how stunning, how sacred, how fine!...

2
A dark curse from the heavens
suddenly fell to the ground:
they came in from Germany –
brown beasts and bloodhounds! . . .

And over peaceful people
descended the terror of war.
The world crashed in the flames,
of their carnage and gore.
The blood filling up
the earth, the rivers, and seas.
The flames are still burning,
with no sign the killer will cease...

{p. 475}
But he did destroy us
eternally and forever so;
he built death factories,
and torched us like willows . . .

From all of the cities and towns
he drove cattle cars of millions –
to Treblinka, to Sobibor, to Majdanek –
to slaughter not cow – but civilian.

And standing there nakedly
mother and child, kith and kin,
they all suffocated together. –
But for what crime, and for what sin?

[1087] Sabbaths.

And as if that wasn't enough,
then they set their bodies to burn.
God! If you're really there,
how could you pay no concern?!

And even the bit of ash left over
not let to rest – au contraire! –
Scattered by wind through farmland –
earth be fertile, fruit to bear . . .

My cities and towns!
Ruins, graveyards turned to dust! –
And me with my heart full of tears,
who's most deserving of my disgust?

For they took your life,
your Jewish life and strangled it,
casting clouds above you,
blackened, bloodied, desperate . . .

Where there were thousands,
not a single Jew left;
inscribed on each footprint
those murderers, consigned them to death! . . .

{p. 476}

Now the sky looks to me like it's crying,
even through rays of sun;
not seen nor heard up til now,
it seems they've escaped everyone: –

To massacre kith and kin,
to choke to death, to burn into ash,
And to build factories for it,
no one will recognize death after that!...

A shudder runs through me –
how can we live after this?!
how much better if my heart
could just burst – for all its distress.

And there, together with them,
could my soul, in salvation,
in holy, divine torment,
receive comfort, and commiseration . . .

{p. 477}   **My Mother**
There by the Bobra,
in a small town,
lives my sickly mother,
alone in her decline.

A pile of skin and bones,
And a head of gray hair,

And those black eyes –
growing colder each day.

Children, worlds away,
far, scattered, strewn...
driven out, forced to carry on,
by hunger, torment, and ruin...

From time to time
comes a letter from afar –
and a humdrum day becomes divine,
and the world – restored...

She kisses every word
as her tears escape her...
traded in those children –
on tiny scraps of paper...

They write: they're quite well.
but aren't they just saying that? ...
They just don't want to hurt her –
or give her a heart attack...

She senses, she feels –
The children are suffering over there!
though in the letters –
no sorrows, nor cares...

So she reads them
over and over again,
until she sees a secret message
in every piece of punctuation...

{p. 478}   **My Village in the Flames**
My village in the flames
of bombers and cannons,
and I hear my mother's moans
amid the moans of millions!

Is her voice from the ruins,
that still remain here?
or from the wild wilder-wander,
where they all were led by fear?

Were she and the children
bombarded by bombs?
Or did they all get split up,
then had to forge their way on?

How many days has she been starving?
And does she still have her health?
Perhaps she's laid up sick
some place all by herself?...

438

My dear mother, my dear mother!
Would only that one day I'll hear –
that you got out alive –
In some letter, drenched in tears...

{p. 479}   **Who Wiped My Village off the Map?**
Gone through all the lists
looked through every name –
who took my poor faint-hearted mother,
who took her away?

Who took my poor brother,
So humble, so sweet,
A worldly young man
And beat him bloody?

Who threw my beautiful sister
to the wild unsheltered
with her dear little children
in swamps, in heavy weather –
then forced them yet again
to march to death together?
Who took my family,
of good, pious people,
and laid out every last one –
so that their blood would boil?

Who took my village
and wiped it off the map?
which menacing devil
took it into his grasp?

Were they all led there
to the altar on the mount? –
the whole of everyone!
the whole damn town!

In the confines of a train car
to the death factories,
tricked to the showers
with no air to breathe?

{p. 480}   Did they get each one,
at home, under the staircase,
in the yard or in the attic,
in the stable, in a crawl space –

And work them all:
with the butt end of a gun,
with the blade of a knife –
to torture just for fun?

439

Where is their resting place?
Where is their gravesite? –
down in the earth,
or up in the sky?

Does their dust blow about,
their ash carried by wind?
woe to me, my God,
woe to me, and to them...

I'd like to give
their dust a gravestone –
and rest in their row,
when they bury my bones.

So my life of sin
will also carry on: –
and then I'll lie with the martyrs,
when I'm dead and gone . . .

{p. 481} After the Nightmare
by Shmuel Eliezer Aplebaum

Some of the Augustow Jews may have survived, but of the beautiful and rich Jewish social and cultural life in the city, there remain only memories—nothing more. Hitler's brutes destroyed everything that was, and that could serve to commemorate any of the martyrs; they even desecrated and turned the cemetery, that holiest of places, into a field for cows to graze.

They paved streets and thoroughfares with the gravestones. And as a testament to their barbarity and inhumanity—the gravestones were paved with the letters facing up, to be desecrated without end.

I'd like to turn back time to those beautiful, candid memories of a thriving Jewish life in Augustow, the memories from the earliest years of my childhood. In Augustow there was well-organized, systemic work on the part of the Jewish community to manage its vital institutions. One of them was the *Talmud Torah* School. The school had five classes, but offered much enrichment. The students didn't just learn *Torah* and Hebrew, but also acquired a secular education at the school. We fondly recall the Principal of the school Zilber, the beloved Hebrew teacher Bergstein, the teacher Levinson, and the superintendent Efraim who taught us *Gemara*, may they all rest in peace. There was also an "almshouse" in Augustow, where a traveling Jew without means always had a place to eat and a bed to sleep in.

And that wonderful library, which benefited young and old; the great selection of books—historical, scientific, and belletristic; and the librarian Yishayahu Plotshinski, who worked there many years, who knew everyone, and was a friend to everyone.

With great reverence we remember the *shul*, the prayer houses—all the holy places which were built and preserved at great sacrifice to the Jews of Augustow; where we, during prayer, revitalized our national pride and {p. 482} tenacious perseverance against the difficulties of life in exile, and asked God for a return to Zion.

The political life in Augustow was rich and diverse, most of all the Zionist organizations. It was like a holy duty to contribute to the Jewish National Fund; to redeem tokens for the Jewish Congressional elections. The youth were a part of "*HaShomer HaTzair*," "*HeChalutz*," "*HeChalutz HaTzair*," and other organizations that led developmental and educational work. We recall with honor the youth activist Eliav Chalufitzki, and the cultural house in which the Zionist groups did their work; the beautifully arranged youth center and the *erev Shabbes* gatherings when emissaries used to come, telling of the noble work of the first settlers, about the obstacles and successes of conquering and developing our land. The youth would visit this house by the masses. The song of the youth would resound through the street where the cultural house was located. It was in these organizations that the youth received their initial education as pioneers of the Zionist movement. Many of these youths went through "training" and immigrated; they experienced the War of Independence, and helped fight for a free fatherland—the State of Israel.

In Augustow there was also the athletic club "*Maccabee*," where the handsome Jewish youth would, after the school day or a hard day's work, engage in sport. In the athletic club, all strata of political affiliation were as one. The motto of the club was, "A healthy spirit in a healthy body." The athletic exhibitions would spark envy from the Polish youth.

So came the year 1939, the year when Germany invaded Poland and the humanitarian catastrophe for Polish Jewry began. It was the first of August 1939 when Germany invaded. The Jews of Augustow received the news with great angst and trepidation. Though even before that life in exile had started to become unbearable. The people of Poland had more plainly and more forcefully displayed a negative attitude towards the Jews through boycotting Jewish business and enacting other restrictions. For several days, Augustow remained without any military personnel. The Polish military capitulated, and the police deserted after hearing that the Russian army was advancing. Everyone sensed, and feared, that the Christians would use the chaos to spread anti-semitism, so we sat in our houses listening in confinement to the news on the radio. News came from Suwalk and from the surrounding villages, that Polish vandals were targeting and pillaging Jewish businesses. There was tension in the air. When the Russians finally came, the Jews could breathe a sigh of relief—but life was veering down a new path, and certainly one like {p. 483} nothing before. Suffice to say the traditional organized Jewish life which dominated for years, vanished like a dream. The chasm between Jews and Christians grew larger. Jews quickly adapted to the new reality, began working in cooperatives; Jewish youth even took up jobs in city council, and it strengthened hope that we would get through it all.

But soon the sky went black again. Refugees who escaped the Germans began to arrive from Suwalk and they told of the atrocities committed by Hitler's army. The Jews of Augustow were shaken to the core by news that the Zionist activist Eliav Chalufitzki was arrested and imprisoned. And early one morning, we learned that just that night the Russians had led families like the Rechtmans, Borovitches, and many others to an undisclosed location. Augustow was known to the Russians as a stronghold city, so all the refugees, the arrivals, had to leave. Some Russians came soliciting work deep in Russian territory. Among the refugees who volunteered, there were also some Augustowers who joined up, thereby saving themselves and outliving the atrocities of the war. Many months before the invasion of Russia by the German brutes, I too left Augustow. Far off in Siberia, in various work camps, I survived the war. The Jews that outlived the brutal war in Russia eventually turned back—they led us to Lower Silesia, where the Polish military would establish the Jewish colony. After traveling for several hours, the train came to a halt. A bridge was blown up and it would be a long time before we'd be able to travel any further. I knew that we were close to Augustow. I turned to a crew member, an old Pole, and I tried to get him to buy Russian cigarettes from me. Then I told him that I wanted to travel to Augustow so long as the train was stopped, and I didn't have any money. The Christian agreed and told me to wait. He came back, "I'm getting on a cargo train transporting lumber; the train is going through Augustow," he told me, "you can even come back with me."

I was in Augustow. I ran quickly, and first I saw the mill. Then there was the forest; soon I would see the Jewish cemetery. I was very close to the Polish "churchyard." But what was that? I stood there, I couldn't believe my eyes, no more "holy place"! I saw cows grazing, a shepherd sitting with a dog; there were still signs of the graves, and one great stone (the wall of a tomb) in the corner. Everything was soiled by cattle... and the tears obscured my vision . . . The shepherd came over to me, "what are you standing there for? Why are you crying?" he asked me. I didn't answer.

{p. 484} Suddenly I heard, "Aren't you Mulki Khaim Itshe's son?"

Yes, that's me, and you are Pavel, Mikhal's son?" "Yes, I am Pavel," he answered.

"So Mulki, why did you come here? I see that you survived." ... I did not know how to answer him.

I went over the bridge, arrived at Bridge Street number 22—the house where I was born. The house was roofless, deserted; I stood and stared, I didn't know what to do with myself. Christians surrounded me, looking at me as though I were a specter from the afterlife... They asked me if I was hungry. I walked further, feeling as though they were mocking me... no trace of the prayer house on Bridge Street! I walked further; it was hard to recognize the city. It was neglected, in shambles... Yes, Pavel wasn't lying. At the stairs of Tzali the Baker was a stone with Hebrew letters, "May his soul be bound in the bundle of life." Some passersby laughed; others expressed their sympathy.

I wanted to see more. Something compelled me. No more *Talmud Torah*... and as for the *shul* and the study house, nothing but pieces of wall remained as a "remnant of the temple"—a remnant of a Jewish life which was demolished and desecrated; a remnant of a people who lived and created for years only to be destroyed by those brutes masquerading as humans!

I'm upset at myself for having walked with my head hanging just because I was crying...

I left Augustow with the decision that I would never set foot there again!

But I was in fact in Augustow once more, in 1956, before I immigrated to Israel, with my wife and son. It was in the heat of the Sinai Campaign. I needed to find a birth certificate. Naturally, I did not find any Jews that time either.

I saw that the gravestones with the letters facing up had been removed from the sidewalks and no one mocked me, not publicly at least. I proudly looked the Poles in the eyes; I was proud to be a person, to be a Jew, traveling to his country, a country whose military defeats its enemies and protects the national honor of the Jewish people.

{p. 485} The Path of Sorrows
by Yitskhok Bialobztski

A bundle of memories from my hometown Augustow, of the war and aftermath of the war, 1946–1950.

Of my childhood years I remember that I learned in *cheyder* with Hershl Papirovitsh, Avrom Khlupitski, and many others, and alas I am the only one of them left alive. On Broad Street, where I lived, there lived many fine and dear Jews; the late Yankev Sheye Panos, a Chasid, a scholar; Shimen Eli Barman, who would study for nights on end. The Germans, may their names be erased, shot him when he refused to let go of the *Torah* scrolls. The Grabover Rebbe, scholar and a fine leader of prayers; lumber merchants—Lozman with his large adult sons, who did not know them? Who did not know the large family of Gushe the baker?

442

On *Shabbes*, after eating and having a nap, all the Jews would set off for a stroll in the town gardens or to the garden where the monument stood, or even go to lie beside the canal, by the Grodno Bridge.

When the Russians came the village of Szczebra on the road to Suwalki was where the border lay, following the pact between the Germans and the Russians. The Russians hated rich Jews, and so they sent the rich Jews to Suchowola. Only a small number of them were sent to Russia—these were the only ones who survived.

I myself, Yitskhok Bialobztski, was sent to Russia, but without my family. The Germans entered Augustow on the very day the war broke out, and the Jews had no chance to escape.
In 1946 I returned to town and my gentile acquaintances told me everything that had happened: first, the Nazis picked out several Jews and tortured them terribly. Later they gave an order that all men over 16 years of age should come to the magistrate's office. When the men arrived they were led to the park and the S.S. took them from there to the hunting club. There the Jews were tortured and {p. 486} starved. Later they were taken out to the Szczebra Forests. They had to dig their own graves and were all shot by the S.S. There were a few men left, people said, Shulik Koyfman, a shoe stitcher; Doctor Shor; Kantorovitsh the watchmaker; Beder. I met Dr. Shor myself after the war in Augustow. He told me {p. 487} almost exactly the same story. Later the Nazis erected a ghetto where the barracks was, a separate workers' quarter. The Jews lived there in cramped conditions until the 1st of November 1942. They were brought into town every day, along Mill Street, and put to hard labor. On the 1st of November in the morning, the ghetto was surrounded and everyone was taken out to the Grodno Road.

Those who couldn't walk—the old, the sick—were killed on the spot. The Jews were led along over Grodno Bridge to Grayevo as far as the Bogusze camp, carrying their baggage in their hands. It was very cold; the screams were heard as far as the town; the gentiles of Augustow ran out and tore the baggage from their hands.

They stayed in the Bogusze camp for two months in very difficult conditions. Those who were still alive were taken to Treblinka and Majdanek.

This is how Dr. Shor told it, a survivor of the Majdanek death camp. Our town was entirely cleared of Jews.

In early 1946 I arrived in Augustow by train. I all but fainted when I saw that all the carriages and cab drivers waiting at the station were gentiles. All of them tried to offer me a ride, but I went on foot.

I passed the watermill where I spent 15 years with Nosn Varhaftig and Rosental. The mill is there to this day. Under the mill I saw a mound of gravestones from the Jewish cemetery piled in a heap. The cemetery was empty, without a single gravestone. I saw many of the headstones on the paving on the market square. The main synagogue and prayer house had started to be dismantled, but the Butchers' synagogue was still intact.

The houses that were still in one piece had, naturally, been occupied by gentiles. I walked with Max and Leybl Rekhtman to the magistrate's office and asked that the few remaining graves standing near the barracks be fenced off. They promised to do so.[1088]

[1088] This promise was not kept. This year Rekhtman visited Augustow again. He went to the magistrate's and made the same demand again.

The Front of the Former Cemetery. In Place of the Cemetery – a Forest.

Standing are the Town Secretary and Mark Rakovski.

The *Taharah* Room.[1089] At the Entrance – L. Rechtman

[1089] *Tahara*, purification, is Jewish preparation of a body for burial.

444

Next to the Monument L. Rechtman. The Jews are Not Mentioned at All.

{p. 489} A Letter to a Mother . . .
by Esther Tuker (Glikshteyn)

I went to Bridge Street to say goodbye to my old friend.

My old neighbors were dear to me. I wanted to hear the hearty farewell: "Safe road!"

On Bridge Street where the prayer house bordered the large Jagiellonski Gardens there stood an old tree which could have told many stories about the sufferings and joys of our dear Jews.

It kept the Jews company as they prayed—three times a day—and when they studied the holy *Torah*.

That same tree shook its leaves sadly when the Jews were brought to the sacrificial altar.

I met a mother standing there, and she asked me: "If you see my boy, tell him he should write his mother a letter."

By the time I found him to pass on the message—there was no one left to write a letter to.

{p. 490} Memorial Candle

Gad Zaklikovski
by His Wife Dina Zaklikovski

Gad Zaklikovski came to Augustow in the year 1922 at the invitation of Berl Eylender, a friend of his from Skidziel. He was accepted in the *Talmud Torah* as a teacher of Hebrew, but after a short time he was dismissed as they found issue with his not being religious. He did however continue to give private lessons. In 1923 he helped to establish "*HeChalutz*" and began a variety of cultural involvements. He held talks, directed children's plays, and organized excursions through the woods and boating trips out on the lakes. The income from this was reserved for charitable causes.

In 1931 he travelled to Argentina at the invitation of a childhood friend of mine. In about two years, he returned. In 1938 we immigrated to Israel. The beginning of our time there was very difficult, until he was taken on by The Jewish Agency as an official in the Department of Immigration. He worked there until his retirement. In 1948 we moved from Tel Aviv to Petach Tikvah. That's where he helped organize night classes for the new immigrants, something in which he remained involved until his death. He also helped to create quite an impressive library. He participated in the newspaper *Letste Nayes*[1090] and in various journals. At the end of his life he began to collect materials for the book *Kehilat Augustow*[1091] but unfortunately, he never completed it. He passed away on the 9th of May, 9 Iyar, 1960. May he forever be with us in me.

Petach Tikvah

[1090] "Latest News."
[1091] "Community of Augustow."

Gad Zaklikovski
by Esther Eilender-Veinberg

Who doesn't know the teacher Gad Zaklikovski, and who doesn't sense his cultural activities in the period of his time of our city? But few are those who know how he reached the town.

It is this that I desire to tell about. While doing this I will also place a memorial monument to my dear parents, who were killed together with very many in the terrible days of the *Shoah*.

After the liberation of Poland from the yoke of foreigners and the proclamation of its independence, a national Zionist awakening was aroused in the state. Its reverberations reached us as well. Many of the parents felt the need to found a progressive Hebrew school. However, despite all the efforts they did not succeed in this.

My parents, may their memories be for a blessing, began at that time to look for a teacher who would instill in us, me and my sister, the Hebrew language in a more modern form.

In those days, in the middle of the 1920s, my brother Dov (Beryl), may his memory be for a blessing, was, for the purpose of father's business, in the town of Skidel. There he met the teacher Zaklikovski, who taught Hebrew in private lessons. My brother persuaded him {p. 492} to move to Augustow. He agreed to the suggestion and came to our house. We gave him full hospitality for 6-7 weeks. My father, may his memory be for a blessing, obtained for him additional private lessons, and also a position as teacher in the "*Talmud Torah*." But he did not last in the school because of his secular perspectives and his novel style of teaching, which did not befit the traditional manner of the institution. He continued, therefore, only in private instruction and put down roots in the place.

The Chassidic way of life was entirely foreign to us, for our house was a typical house of *Mitnagdim*, like all the others in the city. Zaklikovski, as the son of a *shamash* or *gabbai* with the *Admor* from Sokolov, little by little brought us into that world which was new for us, by means of *niggunim*[1092] of the *Chassidim*, and the stories of his life in his previous environment.

Children's Drama Group

[1092] Wordless melodies.

Gad Zaklikovski was a lively and invigorated man. He stimulated the young people, organized and concentrated the youth around him, led a drama group and put on the play "The Kidnappers." This was a period of many experiences, and it is preserved in memory until this day.

Fania
By Sarah Berliner

I met Fania in Augustow. We were neighbors, houses next to house. Her family lived in a large and beautiful house, entirely decorated with climbing plants. Compared to it, our house was small, poor, and dilapidated. I was always jealous of the beautiful house. Her father was a teacher in Augustow and was considered a good and enlightened teacher. The students admired him and also were afraid of him, for he was very strict and loved order.

In 1928 when I turned 14, I completed grade school and stopped learning. The means in the house were meagre, my mother was already not alive, and I was forced to devote myself to the neglected house. I was sad. In those days Fania met me and advised me to enter "*HeChalutz HaTzair.*" A ray of light in my life. It was as if I was in a dream. I was overcome by pride, pride that Fania, the teacher's daughter, was my friend. The thing was considered a great honor in my eyes. I was drawn to the movement. I will admit to the truth that I didn't understand much of what they taught in the movement, but Fania aroused in me the love and the yearning for the land of Israel and brought a breath of life into me.

In her group there were other young men and women, some of them daughters of the wealthy, but of all of them she chose me as her friend. She used to read her poems aloud to me. I forgot them. Is it not so that a lot of time from then has already passed? In my childhood I was shy, and when I sat with Fania a great respect would come over me. I did not know my soul. I remember how she taught us "Masada" by Yitzchak Lamdan. Her words abounded with hope and enthusiasm, and they entered the heart and inspired it.

"The person" she said has to rise above the pettiness that is in daily life. One needs to live a lofty life, and always to create something from nothing."[1093]

In one meeting she said to me: "A person who does not give to and help society is like a speck of dust that is worn away and no memory remains of it. Therefore one should try to be helpful. By this an eternal memory is promised." And my opinion was different: "Better to be an ordinary simple soldier, to withdraw into a corner. The easiest." I knew that I caused her disappointment. I was not able to do otherwise.

{p. 493} She published a lot in "*Lahavot,*" the newspaper of "*HaShomer Hatzair.*" Not everything is preserved in my memory, only their significance is engraved on my heart. Fania wrote about the idea that guides a person on the path and compares it to a high and steep mountain that is difficult and exhausting to ascend. Happy is the one who succeeds in ascending and reaching the summit; only then does one feel the "true" value of life. From then, I aspired to reach a summit like this. My life in her company had a special value. In her company a person became elevated.

How much integrity was hidden in her. She did not tolerate any lie. You deviated – and she immediately felt that something was not right with you.

1929. The period of the events in the land. Fania was the Director of a settlement of directors of "*HeChalutz HaTzair*" in Lomzitza. I had the privilege of participating in the settlement. In the settlement we discovered a new Fania: Fania the organizer, good hearted, who had much diverse information. What a wealth of information! No wonder! For she was always, always learning. And in all, surrounded by love and appreciation from the members of her youth

---

[1093] This is the concept of creation ex nihilo that is described in the first chapter of Genesis, and that subsequently flows throughout Judaism.

group and her acquaintances. I am certain that all these who got to be in her presence continue to love her even now.

And from the settlements – visits in the towns without end, meeting with the youth, lecturing, conversing, telling and conquering hearts for the movement with enchanting grace. More than once I would say to her: Fania! Protect your health! A waste like this! But Fania would laugh to herself, and tirelessly continue her work.

Who would be able to believe now that this Fania, confined for years to a deathbed, was in her youth powerful, healthy, beautiful, hopping and skipping like a running goat?

Fania leaves Augustow and moves to Warsaw to work in the "*HeChalutz HaTzair*" center. For many days Fania is missing from the house and the town. In my hearts are strong yearnings for her. Without her – life is worthless. Fania only comes, even for a few days, and there is a different spirit with me, life takes on a cheerful and rejoicing hue.

In 1930 Fania goes up to the land. Sad, sad without her. I commune with her picture that she left for me, upon which is written – "Don't despair! Inasmuch as you must remember that we will meet again!" From distances I sensed Fania, I felt that I still had support in life.

The hoped-for day arrived – and we met. The land. Fania receives me like a mother and sister. She alleviates my worries, worries about my health, gives advice, and drives out despair. About herself, her pains and her illness, she never spoke. How easy it was in her presence. What heartwarming humor accompanied all her conversations. She was truly loftier than any and all.

When one of her books of poems or children's poem would appear I was really happy. I would read and read aloud to the children. And they felt some kind of closeness and sympathy flowing from me to her. And when I received a letter from her – there was no end to our happiness. "Isn't it right, Mother, that Fania the poet writes this?" Like me, they loved her. More than once fear assailed me from the thought of her unstable health. The heart wanted a miracle. Wanted and believed, but… her soul is indeed immortal.

Ein HaYam

{p. 494} Yisroel (Zelyah) Bergstein

Yisroel, Fania's brother, was a doctor with status in Warsaw. Drafted, with the outbreak of the war, into the Polish army, and fell captive to the Russians. He was liberated and received the position of doctor in Bialystok. With the entry of the Nazis he was taken to a concentration camp and there he served as a doctor On the day that the Red Army neared the place of camp representatives of the camp were called to present themselves before the Nazi commander. Friends advised that he hide, but he refused, maintaining that "as a doctor, I am obligated to remain at my post." On that very day, the commander took the representatives who had presented themselves out to be killed, and among them, Yisroel Bergstein. With evening the Red Army liberated the prisoners of the camp.

Shlomo Plotzinski
by Chinah Shraga (Bergstein)

When I am reminded of Shlomkeh, I see the town of Augustow, the house of my mother's sister Raizl, Uncle Meir, and their children: Chinah, Yishayahu, Shlomkeh, and Berele the youngest. I see in my mind's eye their haberdashery store in the market square, under the large awning. The apartment adjacent to the store – clean. I see Chinke,[1094] my good friend, the beautiful young woman; and Shaya,[1095] the serious lad, immersed in books, and devotedly taking care of the library; and the third son in the family, Shlomkeh, always happy and always jesting. I am reminded of the days of the "fair," which took place twice a year. Masses of farmers came to buy, and we, the children, helped the adults with the transactions. Shlomkeh was then with us. I remember how

---

[1094] "Little" Chinah.
[1095] Short for Yishayahu.

all of us were infected by his happiness and from his "wisecracks." He was active in "*HeChalutz HaTzair*," and afterwards in "*HeChalutz*." He 1928 he went out for training. When he would come home for a short vacation, he was full of enthusiasm and preoccupied with worries about the company in which he was training himself for *aliyah*. He came to take leave from us, and he honored me with his photograph. On the back of the photograph he wrote: "Remember Chinah that without darkness there is no reason for light, and without pain there is no reason for joy."

He died in Givat HaShlosha October 17, 1952. May his memory be blessed! **Beit Hashita**

With Shlomekeh in Training
by Rivka B.

The days of the training, before the *aliyah* to the land, constituted an important part in all of our lives. We were young and fresh, and therefore the heart was open to see the human in its various manifestations.

I met Shlomkeh in *Kibbutz* "Tel Chai" at the beginning of the year 1928. Full of vigor, gentleness, humor, entirely lively, he stood out in the life of the *chevre*. He came to the *kibbutz* after he finished the seminar of "*HeChalutz HaTzair*" in Warsaw. He was a son of Warsaw. He was very active in the branches of "*HeChalutz HaTzair*" that were in the Grodno-Bialystok region.

With the passion of his youth he was prominent in all the departments of the social and cultural activities on the *kibbutz*.

{p. 495} The situation on the *kibbutz* was not easy. The winter has hard, snow and ice. We worked in the sawmill. Sometimes we lacked work. The gates of the land were closed and more than once the anguish spread among the friends. But Shlomekeh was full of hope and faith, encouraging, jesting, and helping to dispel the anguish.

He ascended to the land among the first of "Tel Chai," in the last ship before the outbreak of the events in 1929.

Givat HaShlosha

Yisrael Levi   **Shlomo Plotzinski**

Yisrael Levi

Born in 1914 in Augustow to parents who were the Hebrew teachers Miriam and Reuven Levi, may their memories be for a blessing.

He went up to the land in 1922, with his mother and his sisters. His father had gone up two years before that. In his *kibbutz* Ginosar he was commander of *PL''M* (The Special Division) in the period of the War of Liberation. On Sunday, Iyyar 28 5708, [1096] June 6, 1948, in the middle of the night, he went out at the head of a division to conquer a post above the Arab village Juer. From

---

[1096] The Hebrew date in the text has an error, showing a hey ה, which equals 5, rather than a chet, ח, which equals 8.

450

there they shot at the workers in the fields. With dawn, after the division had become established, and before the start of the attack, he stood up to survey the area, and was wounded by a bullet to the head. Under a rain of fire, they brought Yisrael to the hospital, and there his soul left him.

For fourteen years he gave his all to the building of the farm and the society on Kibbutz Ginosar. May his memory be blessed.

Tzila Bezant

Tzila, may her memory be a blessing, was born on 19 Cheshvan 5704 (November 17, 1944),[1097] in the village of Varburg to her parents Meira and Yitzchak. On her mother's side there is a third generation in the land, the granddaughter of Reb Eliyahu Glazer, one of the first builders of Rechovot. {p. 497} Her father was one of the first to make *aliyah* from Augustow. She finished kindergarten and elementary school in the village of Varburg, and went out to acquire additional knowledge in the high school in Rechovot.

With the completion of the matriculation exams and until her induction into *Tzahal*[1098] in October 1961, her literary and artistic abilities suddenly flowered. Notebooks of literature and poetry were filled by her; drawings that express emotional beauty and various handiworks filled the house.

In *Tzahal* she successful passed a clerks' course and was posted appropriately to her profession – until the bitter day that the cord of her life was cut off in a highway accident. She died on 29 Sivan, 5722 (July 1, 1962).

May her soul be bound up in the bond of life.

Tuvia Rabinovitz
by His Brother Yisrael Rabinovitz

Tuvia Rabinovitz, may his memory be for a blessing, was born in Augustow to Yechezkel and Chaya Tzippa (of the house of Plotnovski). He learned in *cheder* and after that continued in the Kagan's Hebrew gymnasia in Vilna.

In 1920 the first group of *olim* to the land of Israel went out from Augustow. He was among them. His first work in the land was in Rechavia. Within a short time, he moved together with his friends to Rechovot, and worked in the orchards there.

In the orchards in Rechovot companies of workers were organized for jobs for the British government in Sarfand.[1099] Tuvia joined one of them.

From there Tuvia went on to work in the Office of Public Works, today "*Solel-Boneh*."[1100] His group was called by the name T"U, corresponding to the number of its members.[1101] After that he worked in the city of Ganim, today Ramat Gan. From building worked he returned to agriculture, this time, in the orchards of Gan-Chaim. At that time, the agricultural workers began to organize themselves in settlement organizations, which were afterwards called by the inclusive name "The Settlement of the Thousand."[1102] That is to say, all together 1000 families were settled in that period in various settlements. This was an enormous operation in those days, and Tuvia took an active part in it.

In 1933 Tuvia settled in *Moshav* Tzofit. He planted an orchard of seven dunams,[1103] put

---

[1097] Either the Hebrew date or the Julian date is off by one year.
[1098] *Tzva Hahaganah L'Yisrael*, the Israel Defense Force.
[1099] Sarfand al-Amar was an Arab village destroyed during the War of Independence. Today it is the Zrifin IDF camp.
[1100] "Paving-Building"
[1101] 15.
[1102] This refers to two Zionist plans, in 1926 and 1932, to settle 1,000 Jewish families on farms in Mandatory Palestine.
[1103] About 900 square meters.

{p. 496} **Bielke Papirovitz**   **Tzila Bezant**

Killed by Arabs on her way to
the university on Mt. Scopus

Barukh Chositzer   **Tuvia Rabinovitz**

up a cowshed, and also worked outside of his farm. In the events of 1936,[1104] he fell at his post in Tzofit. He left behind a pregnant wife, a six-year-old boy, a farm in construction, and mourning friends and family.

Over the years his wife left the place and moved to the city. The farm she left to the guardianship of the village council until the children grew up. 20 years after Tuvia's death his elder son, Yechezkel, returned to the farm in Tzofit, and continued on his father's path.

Moshav Cherut

Barukh Chositzer, May His Memory be For a Blessing

Born in Augustow in the year 1910. The eldest son of Yitzchak and Rachel. After he completed elementary school, he continued to learn in a "*yeshiva*." Despite his traditional education, he joined "*HeChalutz HaTzair*." Since he tied his future to *aliyah* to the land, Barukh understood that he had to train himself by learning a profession, and chose painting.

{p. 498} In the days of the events of 5689 (1929),[1105] he decides to go up to the land of Israel. Despite his love for his parents, he does not accede to their request to defer his *aliyah* until after the land quieted down. In the land, he works hard, in order to save up the means to bring up the family. In the year 5696 [1936], he succeeds in the matter. He is very active in the "*Haganah*."[1106] In the year 5696 he enlists into the Police of the Hebrew Settlements, and serves in effect as secretary to the commander in the Ra'anana district. A poetic soul dwells within him, and in his free time he devotes himself to drawing and music.

With the declaration of the State he is transferred to the staff of the General Staff.[1107] On June 4, 1948, Egyptians planes bombed the General Staff. His friends in the work asked him to go down to the shelter, but Barukh didn't want to stop his work. Bomb shrapnel hit him and killed him on the spot. In the command of the General Staff from September 29, 1948, Barukh was granted the rank of First Lieutenant, befitting his role in service to the "*Haganah*."

Reb Shimon Varhaftig   Reb Yaakov Yevreiski (Ivri)

[1104] The 1936–1939 Arab revolt in Palestine, was a nationalist uprising by Palestinian Arabs in Mandatory Palestine against the British administration, demanding Arab independence and the end of the policy of open-ended Jewish immigration and land purchases, and the stated goal of establishing a "Jewish National Home."
[1105] In the August 23-24, 1929 Hebron massacre, Arab rioters massacred 67 Jews and wounded 60 others; 435 Jews survived due to the shelter and assistance offered them by their Arab neighbors, who hid them. On August 29, 1929, the Safed massacre occurred. 18 Jews were killed by Arabs and 80 others were wounded. The main Jewish street in Safed was looted and burned.
[1106] The nascent Jewish defense force.
[1107] Of the Israel Defense Force.

Father
By Esther Eger (Ivriyah)

Our father, Rabbi Yaakov Yevreiski (Ivri),[1108] was a scholar. He learned in the Slobodka *Yeshiva*, and received his rabbinical ordination in the Volozhin *Yeshiva*. He excelled in unusual memory and diligence. His heart was not drawn to a rabbinical position, and he turned to the selling of wood, but he always found free time to study *Torah*. He walked in friendship with the scholars in our city, and especially with Rabbi Kosovski, the rabbi of Augustow. He was very active for the sake of the "*Talmud Torah*" in the city, and saw to the support of the children of the poor by means of making arrangements for them with wealthy families. He travelled to America as an emissary for the *Yeshiva* of the RI"M[1109] in Vilna. During his time there he became beloved to the Jews of Brooklyn, and they appointed him as their rabbi. He sat in the rabbinic seat in Brooklyn for seven years. He died there replete with good deeds.

{p. 499} Father
by Noach Varhaftig

My father Shimon son of Reb Shmuel Varhaftig went up to the land in 1922. After a year, he returned to Augustow in order to transfer the printing presses to the land. In 1925 he went up a second time and settle in Haifa. In the year 1926 he began to officiate as rabbi in the office of the Haifa Rabbinate, not in order to receive a reward.

He passed away in good old age on the Fast of Gedaliah[1110] [September 19], 1936. He was 80 years old at his death. He was brought for burial to the cemetery in Haifa.

My Father and My Brother
By Esther Tuker (Of the house of Glikstein)

My father, Reb Yosef, a businessman, a contractor for buildings and bridges in the Russian period, set times for *Torah*. In spite of his annoying business affairs, he studied the *Talmud* every day, until a late hour of the night. In the days of the war, when danger lay in wait for those who went outside at night, Reb Yosef would get away from his house, and hurry to the synagogue that was on the street where he lived, "Bridge Street," in order to learn his *Gemara* lesson without being disturbed. He worked for the renovation of the synagogue in which he prayed and in which he also gave lessons in Talmud.

Two of his daughters merited to ascend to the land of Israel. Their aspiration for *aliyah* developed in their father's longing mentions of Zion and Jerusalem in the *Birkat Hamazon*.[1111] His only son Moshe Arieh, one of the activists of "*Beitar*" in our city, was not able to make *aliyah* in time, and was killed with his family in the *Shoah*. May God avenge his blood.

My brother was Chairman of the student organization in Vilna, and engaged in research on specific Jewish communities. He also used to write in the newspaper "*Der Tag*"[1112] about the problems of Jewish students.

*

Sender Moshe Lenzinger was Chairperson of the "*Mizrachi*" in the city. He and his wife Golde, of the house of Krinitzki, acted greatly for bringing men and women pioneers up to the land. When the Bolsheviks captured Augustow, they exiled them to Russia. He returned to Poland

---

[1108] The name means "Hebrew."

[1109] Rabbi Yitzchak Meir Alter.

[1110] The Fast of Gedaliah is a dawn-to-dusk fast observed on the day after *Rosh Hashanah*, which commemorates the tragic death of Gedaliah, governor of Judea

[1111] The blessing after meals.

[1112] Yiddish for "The Day."

broken and crushed.   They merited to ascend to the land, but he could only hold up for a short time.

My Father's House
by Yitzchak Sherman

On the margins of the Jewish city of Augustow, near the developments of the houses of the gentiles, stood my parents' house. In this house many descendants of my mother's family saw the light of the world. In my time, it already seemed that the house was unstable. My father came to Augustow from the *yeshiva* of Slobodka. After he married Mother, he went to live in her family's house. His livelihood was from a small store. He was a modest and quiet person, distanced himself from involvement in public affairs, and was happy with his lot.[1113] We were five brothers and sisters. A guest was always seated at our table. Mother would receive every guest hospitably. The pioneers, who received their training in carpentry in the yard of our neighbor Poniminski, were desired guests in our house.

In the year 1925 we left the house, my brother Yechezkel and I, and went up to the land. After that we brought up our sister Rachel. The parents, my sister Friedka, and my brother Eliezer, were killed in the Shoah. May God Avenge Their Blood.

{p. 500} My Father
by Elchanan Sarvianski

My father, Yitzchak son of Reb Shmuel-Yosef Sarvianski, may his memory be for a blessing, was born in 1889 to wealthy parents in the village of Charny-Brod, next to Augustow. A few years before the First World War, they sold their land in the village, and bought a two-story house in Augustow.

My father managed large businesses. He was a contractor for the German army, and afterwards for the Russian army. He acquired trees in the forest of the "Fritzes" and of the government. Workers from the villages would cut down the trees, and roll them down the hill, to the water. There they would tie them to rafts, and then tie raft to raft, to a length of about 148 meters. In Nitzko, Rospuda, Sieno, and Biala lakes, the rafts were drawn by horses, or were pushed by workers holding thin straight sticks a length[1114] of 5-6 meters, with a hook attached at the end. On the rivers Narew, Bug, Niemen, and Visla, the rafts floated with the power of the strong flow, until they reached the port of Gdynia on the bank of the Baltic Sea.

My father was a handsome person, tall, broad-framed, strong, and good-hearted. In our yard there was a gigantic stable that we built for the Cossacks' horses. Before the Second World War Jewish beggars from the area and also from afar, wandered, with wagons harnessed to horses (like the Gypsies), from city to city to collect donations. In our city there was one hostel, "*Hachnasat Orchim*," or "*Hekdesh*,"[1115] but it was occupied by the beggars of our city. And therefore, Father permitted these wanderers to enter our stable with their children and the horses. When strong rain came down Father and Mother would send me to invite the children and the sick people among them to our house.

In the year 1939 Father became ill with diabetes. Insulin medication was impossible to get. On *Rosh Chodesh* Adar 2, he gasped out his life-breath[1116] and was brought to burial. He merited to be buried in a grave of Israel, still before the coming of the Nazis.

[1113] *Mishnah Avot* 4:1 "…Who is rich? He who is happy with his lot…"

[1114] There is a typographical error here, giving orek, אורק, which is not a word, instead of the word for length, *orech* אורך.

[1115] Sacred property, an old name for a poorhouse.

[1116] Jeremiah 15:9 "Forlorn is she who bore seven; she has gasped out her life-breath."

My Mother

My mother, Mrs. Liba the daughter of Aidel and Reb Elchanan Steindem, was born in Ratzk near Augustow in the year 1896, to a family of wealthy merchants. In the year 1918 she was married to Father and settled in Augustow. Two sons and two daughters were born to them. I the eldest remained alive by a miracle, but the rest of the children and my mother were killed or burned at the hands of the Nazis.

My mother was religious, a righteous woman, a woman of valor, and good-hearted. In those days there were in Augustow *yeshiva* boys who fled from Russia, and also some born in Poland, whose souls desired *Torah*. They studied in the *Beit Midrash* or in the "*Yatke-Kloiz*," and ate "days" in the houses of the Jews. One of them was Yankele. He lived in our house for four years. More than once he was sick and Mother would take care of him. Another *yeshiva* boy was a refugee from Russia. He was in Augustow for many years, and of them, four years in our house. He was small, thin, and sick. Mother took care of him with great devotion. And another one of Mother's deeds: Aunt Chana Bobrik, Father's sister, died, and left behind two small orphans. Mother would go to them every day, feed and wash them, and take care of them like a mother.

{p. 501} My Brother

My brother Shmuel-Yosef Sarvianski was born in the year 1924. He was sick for the lion's share of his life. When he reached the age of 11, he got better. He was murdered or burned by the murdering Germans at the age of 17.

My Sister Leah

My sister Leah was born on *Rosh Chodesh* Iyar in the year 1922. She learned in the Talmud Torah, and afterwards in the Polish grade school. She was the counselor for "*Freiheit*" until the year 1939.

My Sister Vela

My sister Vela was murdered by the Germans when she was 6 or 7 years old. **Kfar Malal**

Rivka Yaffa, widow of Dr. Hillel Yaffa, died yesterday in Jerusalem. Rivka Yaffa, of the house of Glikstein, was born in Augustow. She went up to the land in the year 1895, was married to Dr. Yaffa, one of the pioneers of medicine in the land, and accompanied him in all his work. She left behind two sons and a daughter.

Shabtai Kaplan son of Yitzchak Eizik the Cohain
by His wife – Pesya daughter of Yoel

He served as *gabbai* in the synagogue that was on the "Long Street."

In the First World War, every *Shabbat* evening he would collect foodstuffs in the bakeries and the grocery stores, and distribute them among the families whose heads of households were at the fronts. May his memory be blessed.

*

To our brother Dovid-Hillel, his wife Chaya of the house of Panos, and their five children; to our sister Sarah, her husband Chaim-Leib, and their two small children. The hands of impure ones cut off their lives.

Their souls are bound up with the martyrs of Augustow.

You are a compassionate God! You looked down from your holy high place, at the time that like a flock of sheep your children were transported. Nurslings in their mothers' arms, babies of *Beit Rabban*,[1117] without a sin in their body, and elders with "I Believe"[1118] and the "*Vidui*" on their lips. All of them together quivering, and with the calling of "*Shma*" their holy souls removed. The ground was reddened with the blood of a grandfather and his grandchildren! Why did you not say to Satan Stop! And impure hands you did not cut off!

Ground! Do not cover up their blood!

Look down from heaven and see how they harmed Israel your people?

To the children of your people – the quality of mercy you bequeathed – and for yourself, you did not leave over even a drop of mercy?

{p. 502} And after everything – we are gathered here in the land of the ancestors, rescued firebrands. We stand with bowed heads and with reverence proclaim "*Yitgadal y'yitkadash shmay rabbah…*"[1119] Is it possible?

Daniel Kaplan

Reb Shmuel Grinberg the Cohain, May His Memory be For a Blessing
By Aminadav

A scholar and enlightened. An enthusiastic Zionist. Scion of an illustrious family from the Brisk of Lithuania area. He learned *Torah* in his youth from the mouth of Reb Chaim Soloveitchik, may the memory of the righteous be for a blessing, from Brisk (a relative of the family). He married a woman in Augustow and immediately began in blessed activity. Despite his business as a provider of hides to the Russian army that camped on the border, he dedicated some of his time to communal affairs. He was the agent of the *Keren Kayemet* in the district, and among the first activists for the Jewish Colonization Society. He was active in "*Linat HaTzedek*" and sustained the learning of the Hebrew language. He was a pleasing singer. His emotional prayers, when he passed before the ark on the *Yamim Nora'im*, aroused trembling. He went up to the land of Israel in 5697 [1937] and died in Tel Aviv in 5716 [1955].

Golda Grinberg, May Her Memory Be for a Blessing

Born in Augustow to her father Reb Natan Zelig Samuel, may the memory of the righteous be for a blessing, righteous and a pursuer of peace, who spent his days and nights in the study of *Torah* and deeds of lovingkindness. Plucked in his youth by the cholera disease when the epidemic raged in the city. His wife, Sarah Tzivia, may her memory be for a blessing, was Augustow born, a woman of valor, who saw to the support of the household so that her husband could dedicate his life to *Torah* and good deeds. Golda walked in her parents' ways and modestly did many acts of lovingkindness for those near and far, and also for the gentiles. In Israel too she continued to offer spiritual aid to many of the surviving remnant. She died in the year 5722 [1962] in Tel Aviv

Reuven Levi

Born in the year 1888. Died in November 1965. He was 77 years old at his death.

With the death of Reuven Levi a pioneer of popular Hebrew librarianship in our generation went to his eternity. He came to the Center for Culture and Education at a not very young age, when there was already behind him a long period of activity in various areas of life. But it seems that only in the last cycle of his life he found complete redemption for himself and full expression of his ability. He immersed himself in learning the skills of librarianship, acquired them completely, and became a popular teacher in this field with the best understanding of the concept.

[1117] Schoolchildren. Babylonian *Talmud Shabbat* 119b ""Do not touch My anointed ones," these are the schoolchildren, who are as precious and important as kings and priests…"

[1118] From Maimonides' 13 Principles of Faith: "I believe in complete faith in the coming of the Messiah, and even though he delays, nevertheless, I will wait for him to come every day."

[1119] The opening words of the Mourner's *Kaddish* "May the great Name be magnified and sanctified…"

To his credit: foundation of the department of libraries in the Center for Culture and Education, the editing of the bibliographic pamphlet, methodical organization of courses for librarians, the foundation of many libraries throughout the land, the publication of books and booklets in the field of librarianship, the development of an active relationship between the national libraries and the university libraries, and the main thing, the cultivation of real enthusiastic work connections with the community of librarians in the land. There was not a person who was not fond of Reuven Levi, if he only had a chance to act in his presence. The Center for Culture and Education and the community of librarians were blessed by him all his days.

In his last years he lived in *Kibbutz* Ginosar.

The Minister Yigal Allon,[1120] Betzalel Shachar,[1121] and Dr. Kurt Vorman,[1122] the Director of the National and University Library,[1123] among others, eulogized him. In the Memorial Gathering of Augustow emigres, Binyamin Efrati eulogized him.

{p. 503} Seven Martyrs
By Binyamin Tzemekh
In memory of my father Rov Meir Yosef Tzemekh, may his memory be for a blessing.

Fifty years ago, on the second day of *Rosh Hashanah*, in a private house in our small village, we formed a *minyan* to do the afternoon prayers. Between the afternoon and evening prayers, a gentile came to the house holding a *siddur*. Huffing and puffing, he told us that as he was walking along the dirt path through the woods, he saw a dead soldier lying under a tree with the *siddur* at his side.

We hadn't done the evening prayers yet, so we took up shovels and all ten of us went out to find the spot the gentile had told us about, and sure enough we found the dead Jewish soldier lying there. After we buried him, we began to do the evening prayers and said *kaddish* for the mysterious Jewish victim. With heavy hearts, we all went our separate ways home.

Six months later, before *Pesach*, in the year 1915, the Germans rose up in a fierce attack against the Russians and yet another gruesome battle seized our village of Tsharnibrod. But after a week, the Russians made a counter-offensive and beat back the Germans.

At nine o'clock in the morning on Sunday, the *Starosta* accompanied by two Russian officers came into our home. They promptly arrested my father without reason or explanation, and took him back to headquarters, a kilometer away from our house in the village of Zhilini. There were already another six Jews there: my father's nephew, three of his cousins, and two of his brothers-in-law. Another three Jews were brought from the neighboring village Sukhazhetzko, a father with a son and another nineteen- year-old young man. At the request of the "writer," as they're called, my father (who was the only one who spoke Russian) gave everyone's names and ages: Meir Yosef Tzemekh, 55 years old, Leizer Sarvianski 64 years, his son Aharon Sarvianski 25 years old, Eliyahu Bartshevski 70 years old, Hershl Borovski 71 years old, {p. 504} his son Boruch Borovski 34 years old, and the 19-year-old young man, all members of the same extended family. They were promptly shoved into a pigsty and two armed soldiers were assigned to guard them. We never heard from them again. My mother, peace be upon her, on the second day, wanted to find out what happened to everyone that was arrested. She was unsuccessful. The road to the village had been dug into trenches, which were occupied by armed soldiers, and sadly she turned

---

[1120] He was a founder of *Kibbutz* Ginosar, served as Minister of Labor, Deputy Prime Minister and Minister of Immigrant Absorption, Deputy Prime Minister, Minister of Education and Culture, and Minister of Foreign Affairs.
[1121] Author of "Workers' Education in Israel," "Culture and Education in the Histadrut," and more.
[1122] Austrian national library manager, ca. 1955.
[1123] Today the National Library of Israel.

back home empty-handed. An hour later, soldiers armed with guns burst into our house and took us all to headquarters.

We were greeted by the other families of the detainees, altogether 29 people—small children and people young and old. The older women and the five children were put on a wagon led by a couple of horses; the rest of us were forced to go on foot. And that's how we began our march to exile, accompanied by two horse-riding Cossacks, one in front and one behind. After five hours of trudging through dense forest, we arrived in the village Krasnibar. We were led into a room so small there wasn't even enough room to stand. Just about to collapse from exhaustion, that's where we spent the first night, not even knowing what they were going to do with us and for what crimes we and our fathers and brothers had been arrested for.

At five in the morning, they dragged us out again and ordered us to march further. We trudged all day long, frozen and hungry, accompanied by the cries of the small children, until we arrived in the village of Kurinka. There stood the headquarters of the battlefront. The Cossacks told us that the general had traveled closer to the front on an inspection, and we had to wait for him to come back.

About an hour later, the general came back in a terrible mood. Apparently things weren't so peachy at the front. The Germans were closing in. He considered us with a scowl and asked who we were and what we were waiting for. The soldier who was guarding us told him that we were the families of the seven spies who were hanged yesterday in the village Zhilini, and that we were sent there at the disposal of the general.

When he heard this, the general flew into a terrible rage. His face flushed red and he screamed, "Take them away immediately, two kilometers away from here and shoot them dead like dogs and bury them on the spot."

Having heard that our fathers had been hanged under the presumption of being spies, {p. 505} and they were going to kill us too, all bedlam broke loose. The women, followed by the children, erupted into a bitter wail which was to be heard by everyone around. Even the gentiles they had rounded up cried along with us.

At the same time, the Cossack who had led us there sat calmly in a house nearby eating his lunch without a care in the world. But when he heard our shouts and bitter wails, he ran in and then over to the general and handed him an envelope which he had taken out of his hat. In the letter it was stated that the Jews were to be sent out from the front by order of His Majesty, the Great Duke Nikolai Nikolayevich—and that was all. The general, who was startled by our cries, and probably also a bit touched, delivered the Cossack two passionate wallops and promptly ordered that we should be put on two wagons and led all the way to the fortress in Grodno. A couple of minutes later, he handed the Cossack an envelope of his own for him to bring to the commander of the fortress.

And so we were saved from the brink of death. The Cossack accompanied us further on our path. That spring night was quick to fall, and a dark blue sky was soon cast over us. We bobbed about in the wagons until midnight, with the Cossack accompanying us humming a Russian melody under his breath. We placed a Nikolaevski twenty-five-dollar bill in his hand, with the hopes that he'd behave a bit more humanely towards us. He was quite pleased with this, especially after how bitter he was about the wallops he had received from the general. Sometime after midnight, we arrived at the first outposts of Grodno. They received us with hospitality, gave us bread to eat and warm tea to drink. After two days without anything to eat, to us this was a feast. At about three in the morning they sent us on our way. The night was cold. At six in the morning, frozen and weary, we arrived in Grodno, but nobody wanted to take us in, so they sent us from one place to another. The Cossack was awfully tired himself, so he thought for a moment, and then threw us in jail and took off.

The warden did not know what to do with us. So he split us up: He threw the older children and the men into one room and gave the women and the small children a separate one. When my mother was allowed to go out on her first walk, she met a Jewish woman who had come to visit her father. My mother asked her to let the Jews of Grodno know about our situation, how we had been brought here without knowing why, and how she hoped they would have mercy on us and come to our rescue.

Apparently they did not spare a moment, because at ten at night {p. 506} we were set free, and they handed us over to those dearest Jews of Grodno. Five weeks later, they sent us to Kremenchuk. We were the first of the refugees that the Russians exiled from Poland, Lithuania, Latvia, and Estonia.

*

Two years later, we found out what happened that dreadful day, when our parents were arrested. That evening, a court martial was promptly formed of the general of staff, two colonels, another four high officers, a prosecutor, and a defender—everything according to "law." The seven Jews were sentenced to death. This gruesome sentence was carried out at dawn. The Jews weren't even given a chance to defend themselves. And so seven innocent Jews were murdered. They were alone when their souls escaped their lips, abandoned by God and by man, somewhere in the woods; seven martyrs who gave their lives for one solitary sin, the sin of being Jewish . . .

*

After the Germans regained control of the area, one morning, with permission from the German military, a long wagon with a group of ten Jews traveled out to the forest. They dug up the burial pit and took out the seven bodies; then they traveled to the lone gravesite of that mysterious Jewish soldier who was shot to death on that fateful *Rosh Hashanah*, and all eight Jews were given a proper Jewish burial at the Jewish Cemetery of Augustow.

My Father
By Khane Arimland

Reb Yaakov Yishayahu Panos

My father Reb Yaakov Yishayahu Panos, of blessed memory, was a Jew, a scholar, a philanthropist, and in a measure of modesty he was without equal. He was beloved by everyone who knew him. Many would come to him for advice or questions in matters of *Torah*. Often Jews would come to my father for a shoulder to cry on, and they would always leave soothed and consoled. Reb Yaakov Yishayahu was a remarkable man, may the memory of his righteous character never be lost.

{p. 507} **Yizkor**

We will elevate the memories of the people of our city,
The Jews of Augustow and the area,
The holy and the pure,
Men, women, and children,
Who were put to death, killed, slaughtered, burned,
choked, and buried alive,
For the sanctification of the Name
At the hands of the Nazis and their followers
Earth, do not cover their blood!
Magnify their names forever and ever,
and sanctify their memory,
For eternity.

Memorial Monument
For the Martyrs of the Community of Augustow and the Area
Who Were Destroyed by the Nazis
May God Avenge Their Blood
In the Years of the Shoah
5699 – 5704
[1939-1944]
May Their Souls Be Bound Up in the Bundle of Life
Scroll of Destruction
The Organization of Augustow Natives

{p. 509} **On Memorial Day**

Who will light a candle there for the elevation of their souls?
Who will set up a stone, and who will fence off their grave?
Beneath clods of earth, the bodies lay silent.
No longer will the storm of the monsters guide their repose!

Elders and children, pregnant women and toddlers,
Brothers and sisters, all of them together as a group,
The enemy transported them – into the pit threw them!
Like a predator in the forest, he carried out his atrocities,
He tore, shattered heads, and the blood flowed like water.

And the earth? With your clods you covered all of them!
The earth too was brought low with the degradation of their malicious
deeds.
The outcries of earth! For it will not be expiated!
Great is their transgression.
And we here, in the land of the ancestors, will engrave a memorial,
In a book, on marble, and an eternal candle in the basement of the *Shoah*,
Which will tell the generations: about fathers and sons,
Perfect and pure, who were murdered by impure hands.
We will not forget! We will never forgive the murderers!
And on their brows for eternity,
Will be engraved the sign of the murder for disgrace!

D. Kaplan
Kfar Saba

463

For the Requiter of blood recalled them;
He forgot not the cry of the lowly.
Psalms 9:13

So that the last generation might know,
Children yet to be born might arise and recount
to their children. Psalms 78:6

Scroll of Commemoration

On the 3rd day of *Shabbat* 29 Tevet, the year 5721 [1960] from the creation of the world, the thirteenth year of the State of Israel, and the 20th year since the destruction of our community the community of Avgustov (Yagostov) and its region, we gathered, the natives of Augustow and its region, in Israel at the Mt. of Zion in Jerusalem and we erected a memorial monument to the martyrs of our city and its region who were killed by the hands of the oppressors the Nazis and their followers in the years 5701-5703 [1941-1943] and were buried in foreign soil and the place of their burial is not known.

In this scroll we perpetuate the names of our relatives and dear ones in order to raise their memories before God who dwells in Zion.

May this monument and this scroll be a memorial to the holy and pure ones, the cord of whose life was severed in such a horrific and cruel way, and may their souls be bound up in the bond of life, and may this monument and this scroll be an eternal mark of disgrace for the shame and disgrace of the impure murderers who spilled innocent blood.

Our Father our Sovereign avenge before our eyes the spilled blood of your servants.

"Pour out upon them your wrath,
and your fury blazing fury overtake them."[1124]
"Oh, pursue them in wrath
and destroy them from under the heavens of the LORD!" [1125]

The Organization of the Natives of Augustow and the Region
in Israel and in the Diaspora

[1124] Psalms 69:25
[1125] Lamentations 4:64

The Slain of the Holocaust, May God Avenge Their Blood

- Aleksandrovitz [Soundex A425], Dovid Arieh son of Aharon, Chaya Rivka daughter of Reb Barukh, their sons Alter, Zalman Hirsh and Aharon, their daughter Channah.
- Aleksandrovitz, Leah (of the house of Borovitz) daughter of Reb Nisan, the wife of Alter, and their young daughter.
- Aleksandrovitz, Yosef and Basha.
- Ampel [Soundex A514], Chaim Asher son of Reb Shmuel, Chaya daughter of Reb Dovid, their daughters Miriam Tziporah and her children, their son-in-law Dovid son of Reb Azriel Kropinski [Soundex K615].
- Apleboim [Soundex A141], Tzerka.
- Arbstein [Soundex A612], Avraham Berel, his wife Golda, their daughter Rivka, their son Alter, their daughters Etke, Mashka, their son Moshe, their daughter Shula.
- Arbstein, Elke and her sister. - Aronovski [Soundex A651], Pinchas and his wife.
- Aronovski, Rachel daughter of Reb Mordechai, Moshe Berel son of Reb Avraham, Ozer son of Reb Avraham.
- Avigdor [Soundex A123], Man of Lipsk.
- Avka [Soundex A120] (the gravedigger).
- Barshatzevska [Soundex B623], Channah Etel.
- Bass, [Soundex B200] Gershon.
- Bass, Yehoshua, Hinda, Yaakov, Channah.
- Bass, Yehoshua, Malkah, their daughters Stirka, Golda, their son Shlomo.
- Beder [Soundex 360], Binyamin, Rachel, Manya, Genia, and Aharon.
- Beilovitz [Soundex B413], his wife and their seven sons.
- Beilovitz, Naftali, his wife and children.
- Beilovitz, Sheike, his wife and children.
- Beker [Soundex B260] and his family.
- Bergstein [Soundex B623], Dov son of Reb Ze'ev, Chaya daughter of Reb Arieh, their daughter Tzila, their son Reuven.
- Bergstein, Yehoshua Mordechai, his son Yisroel.
- Berliner [Soundex B645], Yehuda, Rivka, Avraham, Chaim, Yechezkel, Arieh.
- Berman [Soundex B650] and his family.
- Bezuzovski [Soundex B212], Dovid son of Reb Moshe, his wife Basha, their son Moshe, their daughter Gita.
- Bialovzetski [Soundex B412], Dov Berel son of Reb Shmuel.
- Bialovzetski, Doba and her two daughters, Rivka and Shulamit.
- Bialovzetski, Dovid and his wife.
- Bialovzetski, Reuven.
- Bialovzetski, Shlomo Zelig, his brother and sister.
- Bialovzetski, Yitzchak and Moshe.
- Bidek [Soundex B320], Yaakov son of Reb Ze'ev, Sarah daughter of Reb Yaakov, Stein Rachel daughter of Reb Yaakov, Stein Yaakov son of Reb Zalman, their daughter Shulamit.
- Bidek, Leib and his family.
- Bidek, Moshe son of Reb Yaakov, Shoshana daughter of Reb Yaakov.
- Bidek, Yisrael Yosef son of Reb Yaakov, Zelda daughter of Reb Chuna, their daughter Sarah, their sons Dov Berel, Ze'ev.

- Bilogorski [Soundex B426], Eizik and his family.
- Binstein [Soundex B523].
- Blacharski [Soundex B426], Avraham son of Reb Nachum, his wife daughter of Reb Yaakov, Yehuda, Nachum, Salek, Ben-Tzion son of Reb Gershon, his wife Eiga daughter of Reb Manes.
- Blacharski, Channah.
- Blacharski, Dovid, Sarah-Esther and their children.
- Blacharski, Yaakov.
- Blech [Soundex B420], Binyamin Chaim son of Reb Yosef, Rachel daughter of Reb Arieh Bramzon, their children Arieh, Yosef, Sarah, Niuta, Moshe son of Reb Yosef.
- Blofrov [Soundex B416], Dovid and Hinda.
- Bobrik [Soundex B620], Hershel and his wife, Zelig, Chaya.
- Bornstein [Soundex B652], Tzvi, his wife Sima, the daughters Shulamit, Henya Leah.
- Borovitz (of the house of Grinberg) Shulamit daughter of Reb Shmuel and Golda, Shmuel son of Reb Yaakov and Tzarna, their daughter, Tzarna.
- Borovitz [Soundex 613], Yosef.
- Borovitz, Henech son of Reb Nisan, Gita daughter of Reb Binyamin, Rivka daughter of Reb Henech, Tzila daughter of Reb Henech.
- Borovitz, Moshe, his daughter Friedka and her family.
- Borovski [Soundex B613], Beila, and her daughter.
- Borovski, Chaim, Riva-Rachel and their children.
- Borovski, Neta and his wife.
- Borovski, Tzvi son of Reb Shmuel, his wife Yaffa, their children, Altinka, Eliezer.
- Brenner [Soundex B656], Golda, Brenner, Mottel.
- Brizman [Soundex B625] and his family.
- Brizman, Tuvia.
- Burk [Soundex B620], Tuvia son of Reb Zalman, Esther daughter of Reb Arieh, Shmuel son of Reb Arieh, Esther daughter of Reb Hillel, Rachel daughter of Reb Shmuel, Mina daughter of Reb Shmuel.
- Chalupitzki [Soundex C413], Eliav, Metushalach, Avraham.
- Chapnik [Soundex C152] and his family.
- Chefetz [Soundex C132], Etke and her husband.
- Chefetz Yaakov and his brother(s).
- Cohen [Soundex C500], Yechezkel son of Reb Yosef, Gitl daughter of Reb Tzvi, their daughters Chasha, Sima, Peshke.
- Cohen, Freida, daughter of Reb Yaakov.
- Cohen, Yaakov son of Reb Nachum Tzvi and his wife.
- Darstavianski [Soundex D623].
- Darvinski [Soundex D615] and his wife.
- Denmark [Soundex D562], Tzvi son of Reb Noach, Batya daughter of Reb Yisrael, their son Noach.
- Denmark, Reuven and his son's family.
- Dlogoshelski [Soundex D422], Gershon son of Reb Yaakov, Shaina Esther daughter of Reb Tzvi, their son Chaim, Toyve daughter of Reb Efraim.
- Dolovitz [Soundex D413] and the family.

466

- Domovitz [Soundex D513], Meir, his wife Breina daughter of Reb Yaakov Ivri, their daughter Chaya Beila.
- Doniger [Soundex D526], Mottel, his parents and his sister.
- Drozinski [Soundex D625] Menachem Mendel son of Reb Nisan, Breina daughter of Reb Avraham, their son Nisan, his wife Hadassah, their son Yehoshua, his wife Channah and their children.
- Dubrin [Soundex D165] and the family.
- Efrat [Soundex E163], Hirsh and his family.
- Eilender [Soundex E453], Chaim Dovid son of Reb Moshe Leib, Chaya Alta daughter of Reb Eizik, Dov son of Reb Chaim, Alte son of Reb Nachum (Blacharski), Nachum son of Reb Dov, Eizik son of Reb Dov.
- Eilender, Yosef son of Reb Elkanah, his wife Sarah daughter of Reb Ben-Tzion, their son, Gershon, their daughter, Esther-Miriam daughter of Elkanah.
- Eilender-Kaletzki [Soundex E453, K432] Eliezer son of Reb Nisan, Peshe daughter of Reb Chaim Dovid, their son Nisan.
- Eizenstat [Soundex E252], Leon, Shifre, Niuta, Henech
- Elenbogen [Soundex E451], Yehuda.
- Elenbogen, Roza Shoshana daughter of Reb Mordechai, Shmuel son of Reb Shlomo Aleksander, their son Eliyahu, his brother Mordechai, sister-in-law Leah daughter of Reb Yitzchak.
- Einenovitz [Soundex I551], and his family.
- Falk [Soundex F420], Yaakov.
- Falkov [Soundex F421], Mirtza, Mina and Beila.
- Feinberg [Soundex F516], Moshe son of Reb Zalman, Binyamin son of Reb Yitzchak, Zalman son of Reb Binyamin, Golda daughter of Reb Zalman, Shmuel son of Reb Yosef.
- Feinstein [Soundex F523], Tzvi.
- Feivorsky [Soundex F162], Dov, Yaakov, Dovid, Eizik.
- Feivushvitz [Soundex F121], Chaim Ze'ev, Rochel daughter of Eizik Luria.
- Feivushvitz, Tuvia and Ita.
- Filivinsky [Soundex F415], Mordechai Yitzchak, Tzirl Leah, Shaina Itka, Ben-Tzion.
- Finkelstein [Soundex F524], Dveitchka.
- Fisher [Soundex F260] and his family.
- Fisher, Shmuel.
- Fishman [Soundex F250] and his family.
- Fogel [Soundex F240], Moshe, Simcha, Rochel.
- Freitzeit [Soundex F632], Avraham Nisan and Chaya, Eidli, Zundel and his family, Barukh Leizer, Malkah and her family, Pesach, his wife and children.
- Freitzeit, Mina, her son Zelig and his family. His wife Devorah, the son Lipman, Isser and his family, his wife Tzipa, the son Shmuel, Kadesh and his family, Fruma and the children Dovid, Shmuel, his wife Marka and her family.
- Freund [Soundex F653], Ze'ev son of Reb Eliezer, Liba Ahuva daughter of Reb Yaakov Yedidiah, Yitzchak, their daughters Sarah, Batya.
- Friedenberg [Soundex F635], the woman and her child.
- Friedgot [Soundex F632], his wife and children.
- Friedman [Soundex F635], Peshe daughter of Reb Shmuel Yehuda Lonshel [Soundex L524], Chinah Zak daughter of Reb Eliezer Dov.

- Friedman, and his two daughters.
- Friedman, Chaim.
- Friedman, Feigl and Meir, their son Daniel.
- Friedman, Yehoshua son of Reb Shalom, Golda daughter of Reb Avraham Mordechai, Channah (Borovitz) daughter of Reb Yehoshua, Masha daughter of Reb Yehoshua, Roshka daughter of Reb Shalom Darvianski [Soundex D615], Zavel Darvianski, Moshe Borovitz.
- Friedman, Zaydka.
- Gak [Soundex G000], Chinah.
- Galanti [Soundex G453], Shmerl and his family.
- Gardos [Soundex G632], Liuba daughter of Reb Yaakov.
- Gardovski [Soundex G631], Chaim Leib, Rivka, Chaska, Esther, Moshe-Aharon Malkah.
- Gershovitz [Soundex G621], Yishayahu Meir and his family.
- Gibstein [Soundex G123], Yosef son of Reb Betzalel, Tzarna daughter of Reb Berel, their sons Moshe, Betzalel, their daughter Devorah.
- Girshfeld [Soundex G621], Chuna.
- Gizumski [Soundex G520], Gedalyahu, his sons Chanan, Dov, Sholom, his daughter Malkah.
- Glikstein [Soundex G423], Moshe-Arieh son of Reb Yosef and Mina, his wife, Asiya, Chana, Leah, Chaya, and Alter.
- Glikson [Soundex G425], Yehoshua and his family.
- Goldstein [Soundex G432] and her three children.
- Goldstein [Soundex G432], Sarah-Leah daughter of Reb Moshe, Beila daughter of Reb Efraim, Chuna son of Reb Efraim, Tzirl daughter of Reb Efraim.
- Goldshmid [Soundex G432], Abba, Breinka and her daughter, Yehuda, Chana Etke and her children: Tzerka and Chaim-Yitzchak.
- Gordon [Soundex G635], Shimon, Rachel and their daughters. Beyers [Soundex B620] Chana, her son-in-law Yehuda Cohen, his wife, Bat-Sheva and their children.
- Goren [Soundex G650], Eli, his son and his three daughters.
- Gotlib [Soundex G341], Eliezer son of Reb Moshe, his wife Marisha daughter of Reb Menachem Mendel, their daughters Channah, Chaya.
- Gotlib, Eliezer, his wife daughter of Reb Yisroel Grosberg, their son Yasha, their daughter Niuta.
- Grader [Sounder G636], Liba.
- Gritzan [Soundex G632], Channah, Rachel, Barukh Aharon.
- Grodansky [Soundex G635], Leah and her two daughters.
- Grodansky, Shlomo.
- Grodzin [Soundex G632], Chaim Yoel and his family.
- Grodzinski [Soundex G632], Dr. and his wife.
- Grosberg [Soundex G621], Niuta, Livsi and Berta, the daughters of Meir and Rivka Grosberg.
- Gutman [Soundex G350]and his wife, Yitzchak, Sarah, and her sister.
- Gutman, Sender and his wife, Leishka (Eliezer), Chana, Malkah, her brother, her sister and sister-in-law.
- Halpren [Soundex H416], Fruma (of the house of Aronovski [Soundex A651] daughter of Reb Avraham.
- Hermenshtat [Soundex H655], Nechemiah, Esther, and their son, Chaim Dov.

- Hochman [Soundex H255], Aharon son of Reb Alter and his daughter Sarah.
- Homberg [Soundex H516] and his family.
- Kadish [Soundex D320].
- Kalstein [Soundex K423].
- Kantorovitz [Soundex K536], Monya, his wife Rochel, their sons Tzvi (Asha), Eliyahu, their daughter Esther.
- Kaplan [Soundex K145], Arieh son of Reb Meir the Cohain, his wife Basha Gitl daughter of Reb Dov, their son Tzvi, their daughters Rivka, Rochel.
- Kaplan, Bendet son of Reb Yedidiah and his family.
- Kaplan, Dovid Hillel son of Reb Avraham Yitzchak, his wife Chava, their children Yenta, Devorah, Betzalel, Naftali-Hertz, Golda-Eti, Voronovski [Soundex V651], Sarah daughter of Reb Avraham Yitzchak, Chaim Leib son of Reb Yosef HaLevi, Batya Tzvi.
- Kaplan, Sender Itshe, Breinka, Zsachkah, Chaska and her two daughters.
- Kaplan, Shabtai son of Reb Yitzchak the Cohain, his wife Peshe daughter of Reb Yoel, their son Moshe Simcha, Zidke and his family, Chaim Dov son of Reb Moshe Simcha, Rishi-Rivka daughter of Reb Moshe Simcha, Dovid son of Reb Shabtai the Cohain, Tzerka daughter of Reb Shabtai the Cohain, Yitzchak Eizik son of Reb Shabtai the Cohain, Shaina Yaffa daughter of Reb Shabtai the Cohain, Ana Leah daughter of Reb Shabtai the Cohain, Esther daughter of Reb Shabtai the Cohain.
- Kaplanski [Soundex K145], Chuna, his parents and his sister.
- Kaplanski, Chaim Zalman Shochet U'bodek, Devorah, Mordechai and his family, Leah and her family, Chaya and her family, Rochel and her family.
- Kaplanski, Yitzchak and Sarah Rivka, Dov Berl, his wife and the child.
- Kasmoivitz [Soundex K251] and her daughter.
- Katzman [Soundex C325] and his family.
- Kentzuk [Soundex K532], Sarah, Alter, Eli, Velvel, Avraham, Altzah, Hinde, Chuna.
- Kfolek [Soundex K142] and the family.
- Kfolir [Soundex K146], Rishka and her husband.
- Kimen [Soundex K500], Tzvi, Beila Breina, Tuvia, Gushi.
- Kirshenbom [Soundex K625], Moshe and his wife, Shlomo, Leizer, Efraim and his brother(s).
- Kirstein [Soundex K622], Moshe and his wife Nacha.
- Kleinman [Soundex K455], Zalman and his wife, Simcha, Eli, Shlomkeh, his wife and their children.
- Klinsky [Soundex K452], Devorah daughter of Reb Shmuel, her husband Yehoshua, their daughter Sarah.
- Kolfenitzki [Soundex K415], Pesach and his brother(s).
- Kolnitzki [Soundex K453], Gershon.
- Kopresht [Soundex K162], his wife and her children.
- Koritzki [Soundex K632], Eltke and Shmuel.
- Korotnitzki [Soundex K635], Dovka, Channah, Rivka.
- Korotzinski [Soundex K632], Devorah, Chaim and their children.
- Koshelevski [Soundex K412], The Rabbi the Gaon Azriel Zelig Noach son of the Rabbi My Master Yitzchak Tzvi, his daughter-in-law Leah Rochel daughter of Reb Yitzchak Tzvi, his granddaughters Zehava, Rivka, Yehudis (the daughters of The Rabbi the Gaon Yisrael Arieh).

- Koyatkovski [Soundex K321], Aidel, Malkah, Bashke.
- Kravitz [Soundex K613], Beinush and his family.
- Kravitz, Friedka and her family.
- Kronrot [Soundex K656], his wife, his daughter, and their family.
- Kuk [Soundex K200], Efraim.
- Kupler [Soundex K146].
- Langerovitz [Soundex L526], Masha.
- Lap [Soundex L100], Binyamin son of Reb Arieh, his wife Miriam, Chinah, Mordechai, Moshe.
- Lap, Chaim, his wife, and their two sons.
- Lap, Mottel.
- Leizerovitz [Soundex L261], Avraham, Devorah, Yisrael, Zhenia.
- Leizerovski [Soundex L261], Avraham and Mina, Yosef and his wife, Channah and her husband Efraim Piastzky [Soundex S232], Yitzchak and his wife, Dora.
- Leizerovski, Arieh, Leah daughter of Reb Gershon, and the members of the household.[1126]
- Lenzinger [Soundex L525], Yaakov, Rachel.
- Lev [Soundex L100], Chaim and his wife.
- Lev, Cheinka.
- Lev, Mordechai.
- Lev, Naftali.
- Lev, Peshke, Feivel, his son Betzalel.
- Lev, Pinchas.
- Levin [Soundex L150] and his family.
- Levinshel [Soundex L152], Eliezer and Bat-sheva.
- Levinzon [Soundex L152] and his family.
- Levit [Soundex L130], Eli and his family.
- Levit, Yehuda and his family.
- Levitzky [Soundex L132] and his wife.
- Levitzky, Feivel.
- Levyush [Soundex L120], Leib son of Reb Yaakov, and Yitzchak.
- Libernat [Soundex L165], Mendel and his family.
- Lichtenstein [Soundex L235] and his wife.
- Lichtenstein, Leibl, his wife and children.
- Lieberman [Soundex L165], Asha, Dina, Yaakov, Cheftzi and his sister.
- Lifshitz [Soundex L123], Arieh, Chitza, and Tziporah.
- Liponski [Soundex L152], Leib and his wife.
- Lizovski [Soundex L212], Nachum, Avraham, Catriel and his sisters.
- Lozman [Soundex L255], Ze'ev, Raizl, Luba, Binyamin, Yehudit, Eliyahu, Netanel, Esther of the House of Lev, Chaya of the house of Lev, Tzvi, Fruma, Mina daughter of Reb Yisrael Yaakov.
- Ludvinovski [Soundex L315].
- Markus [Soundex M622], Binyamin son of Reb Dovid Mordechai, Rachel daughter of Reb Yechezkel Mendel Berman [Soundex B650], Etiah daughter of Reb Yaakov and Zlata Frenkel [Soundex F652], Shifra daughter of Reb Yisroel Grosberg [Soundex G621].

[1126] The abbreviation used here, ב"ב, in this context can mean "member of the household" or "the son of his son."

- Mariampolski [Soundex M651], Rivka, her husband Moshe.
- Melamed [Soundex M453], Moshe and his family.
- Meltzer [Soundex M432], his wife and three sons.
- Meltzer and his family.
- Meltzer, Efraim.
- Meltzer, Nachman, his wife and sons.
- Meltzer, Tzvi son of Reb Yehuda, his wife Basha daughter of Reb Sholom, their sons Barukh, Shmuel, their daughters Etel, Yacha, Rachel, Yehudit.
- Michelson [Soundex M242], his son and his two daughters.
- Michelson, Paltiel.
- Minkovski [Soundex M521], Ben-Tzion.
- Minkovski, Moshe and his family.
- Mintz [Soundex M532], Chaim, Aharon son of Reb Chaim.[1127]
- Mishkovski [Soundex M212 or 221] and his family.
- Mistivovski [Soundex M231], Yisrael son of Reb Efraim, Klara daughter of Reb Efraim, their daughters Niuta, Marta, their son Chaim.
- Monshein [Soundex M525], Gedalyahu, his wife, his sons and daughters.
- Morzinski [Soundex M625], Moshe Dovid, his wife Sarah, their son Chaikl and his family, their son-in-law, Asher Indik [Soundex I532], Sima Leah and her family, Henya-Mindel.
- Oeron (Soundex O650], Shimon, Masha, Shmerl.
- Ofenstein [Soundex O152], Alter, Channah and Feshka.
- Orimland [Soundex O654], Elka
- Otshein [Soundex O325], Velvel and his wife.
- Otshein [Soundex O325], Yosef and the whole family.
- Panos [Soundex P520], Yishayahu Yaakov, Chava and Raizl.
- Papirovitz [Soundex P161], Tzvi.
- Patak [Soundex P320] and his family.
- Plotchinski [Soundex P432], Channah daughter of Reb Avraham Meir, Yitzchak son of Reb Tzvi-Avraham, Batya daughter of Reb Tzvi-Avraham, Sima daughter of Reb Tzvi-Avraham, Yehoshua Nisan son of Reb Avraham, Dov Ber son of Reb Avraham.
- Podtchivi [Soundex P321], Yosef, his wife Dina, and their children.
- Pogomfri [Soundex P251], Binyamin and his family.
- Pogomfri, Mottel and his family.
- Popkin [Soundex P125] the mother, the wife of Abba and the daughter.
- Poznanski [Soundex P252], Hershel, his wife Bluma, and their family.
- Pozniak [Soundex P252], Shmuel, Liba, and the daughters.
- Preis [Soundex P620], Yitzchak son of Reb Mordechai, Gita daughter of Reb Yaakov Dolovitz [Soundex D413], Miriam daughter of Reb Yitzchak, Mordechai son of Reb Yitzchak, Fradl the wife of Mordechai, Shraga son of Reb Yitzchak, Rivka Cagan [Soundex C500] daughter of Reb Yitzchak, Shraga Cagan.
- Preisman [Soundex P625], Leizer-Berl and his daughters.
- Preisman, Mottel, Gitl, and Eltke.
- Pshashtzilki [Soundex P223 or 232], Feivel, Channah and the children.
- Pshashtzilki, Moshe.

[1127] There seems to be a typographical error here. Instead of ב"ר son of Reb, the text has ברח׳ which makes no sense in this context.

- Rabinovitz [Soundex R151], Yonatan and Pesya, their daughter Hadassah, his sister Rivka.
- Rabinovitz, Moshe, Rochel, Henya, Chaya, Reichel, Berl.
- Raigrodski [Soundex R263] and his family.
- Rap [Soundex R100] and his family.
- Ratzitzki [Soundex R323], Yisrael Mordechai, Yehuda, Sholom, Esther, Rivka.
- Ravidovitz [Soundex R131] and the family.
- Rechtman [Soundex R235], Rivka, Boaz, Esther, Genya, Malkah Dubrin [Soundex D165], Tzvi Dubrin, Rishka Spielkovski [Soundex S142], Sarah Baila Glatstein [Soundex G432], and the children.
- Rentzman [Soundex R 532], Dr., and his family.
- Reznik [Soundex R252], Chuna, Hendl.
- Rinkovski [Soundex R521] and the family.
- Romsisker [R522], Yaakov son of Reb Shlomo, Sarah daughter of Reb Chaim Dovid Eilender, Shlomo son of Reb Yaakov.
- Romsisker son of Reb Efraim and Ana, Gitl daughter of Reb Shlomo.
- Rosianski [Soundex R252] and his wife Yudke.
- Rotenberg [Soundex R351], all of the family.
- Rotenberg, Esther Feigl.
- Rotenberg, Hillel, Shoshka, Itche, Gedaliah.
- Rotenberg, Moshe, Keila, Bluma, Chaya Leiba.
- Rotenberg, Shabtai.
- Rotstein [Soundex R323], Yehuda and his wife, Shulamit and her brother(s).
- Rozenberg [Soundex R251], Gitl.
- Rozendorf [Soundex R253], Yaakov and his family.
- Rozenfeld [Soundex R251], Hinde daughter of Reb Reuven Anshel, Masha, Alter, Shulamit, Shemaryahu, - Folk [Soundex F420], Rivka, Reuven, Berta – his wife, Shlomo – Rozenfeld.
- Rubinstein [Soundex R152].
- Rudnik [Soundex R352], Meshel and his wife, Yitzchak, Chinke.
- Saperstein [Soundex S162], Sarah daughter of Reb Dovid Markus.
- Sarvianski [Soundex S615], Velvel son of Reb Noach Yosef.
- Sarvianski Yitzchak, Liba, Leah, Shmuel Yosef, Vela.
- Sarvianski, Feivel, Maita, Natan, Rut, Chaim.
- Sarvianski, Leah.
- Sarvianski, Nechemiah, Sarah, and their children.
- Sarvianski, Sarah, Yaakov, Shulamit.
- Sarvianski, Yankel Hershel and his wife.
- Savitzky [Soundex S132], Miriam and Mordechai.
- Shachna [Soundex S250], his wife Ita, daughters Channah, Leah, Chaya, son Alter.
- Shalmuk [Soundex S452], his wife and their children.
- Sheinmar [Soundex S560] and his family.
- Sheintzeit [Soundex S532], Eliezer Hirsch son of Reb Gusha, Rochel daughter of Reb Gershon and her family.
- Sheintzeit, Shmuel Yosef son of Reb Gusha, Gitl daughter of Reb Gershon, their son Barukh Hershel, their daughter Chashl.
- Sherman [Soundex S650], Arieh son of Reb Tzvi, Etke, Rochel and Nelly.

- Sherman, Mordechai son of Reb Menachem Mendel, Miriam daughter of Reb Yitzchak, their daughter Freidl, their son Eliezer.
- Sherman, Nachman, Nechama, Esther, Rivka, Malkah.
- Shevach [Soundex S120], and his wife.
- Shidlovski [Soundex S341], Moshe Arieh Shochet U'bodek, and his family, his son Avraham Aharon.
- Shmulian [Soundex S545] and his family.
- Shnigvitz [Soundex S521], Golda.
- Shor [Soundex S600], Malkah.
- Shreibman [Soundex S615], Sarah Beila, her daughters Henya-Leah, Hertzliah.
- Stein [Soundex S350], Yaakov son of Reb Zalman, Rochel daughter of Reb Yaakov, Shulamit daughter of Reb Yaakov, Keila daughter of Reb Zalman, Hinda daughter of Reb Zalman.
- Steindem [Soundex S353], Leibl, Shmuel, Chuna.
- Shtiblman [Soundex S314], Chaya daughter of Reb Avraham.
- Shulkes [Soundex S420], Yaakov Dov, Sarah, Binyamin, Hillel.
- Shumski [Soundex S520], Yosef son of Reb Eliyahu, Tzippa daughter of Reb Dovid, their sons Arieh, Yitzchak, their daughter Elke.
- Sinmer [Soundex S560], Dovid and his wife.
- Sinmer, Yaakov.
- Slovtitzki [Soundex S413], Eliezer and Golda.
- Slovtitzki, Dovid and his wife, Arieh and Tzvi.
- Slovtitzki, Leibl and his brother(s).
- Slovtitzki, Zaydka and his family.
- Sokolski [Soundex S242] and his family.
- Soloveitchik [Soundex S413], Meyrim and his family.
- Sosnovski [Soundex S251] and his family.
- Specht [Soundex S123], Menashe son of Reb Itshe Meir, his wife Eta daughter of Reb Shlomo, their daughter Sarah.
- Staviskovski [Soundex S312], Yishayahu Reuven, his wife, Sarah, Chaika, Chatzkel.
- Staviskovski, Meir.
- Staviskovski, Rochel.
- Staviskovski, Shaina Dina, and her three daughters.
- Staviskovski, Tzippa and Alter, Eliezer, Chaim and his wife Rivka, Channah and her husband Chuna, the children Raizl, Moshe, Issachar, Devorah, Betzalel, Sonia.
- Staviskovski, Tzvi, his wife Rochel, their sons Binyamin, Yitzchak.
- Stolar [Soundex S346], Shimon son of Reb Dovid, his wife Etke. Their son Dovid, their daughter Sarah.
- Stolnitzki [Soundex S345], Yaakov and Noach.
- Stolnitzki, Shabtai son of Reb Yehuda, his wife Dovrosha, their son Dovid, their daughter Sarah.
- Stolovski [Soundex S341], his brothers and their families.
- Strozinski [Soundex S362], Breina.
- Strozinski Shlomo Velvel, Shaina, Leah, Shulamit, Etke.
- Strozinski, Liba, Betzalel and Bilka.
- Strozinski, Tzvi and Chaya.

- Strozinski, Yoel his wife and their children.
- Topilovski [Soundex T141], Moshe, his wife, his three sons and his daughter.
- Tzervitz [Soundex T261], Alter son of Reb Tzvi, Malkah and their family.
- Tziovska [Soundex T212], Esther, Kmalkhovsky [Soundex C542].
- Tziovska, Doba.
- Tziovska, Golda-Sherman.
- Varhaftig [Soundex V613], Yitzchak, his wife and family.
- Vasserman [Soundex V265], his wife and their family, his son and his wife.
- Veikselbom [Soundex V241], Alter-Yitzchak son of Reb Menachem.
- Veisberg [Soundex V216], Eliezer and Shoshana Gitl.
- Veishiski [Soundex V220], Yitzchak and his family.
- Vezbotzki [Soundex V213], Hershel and his wife, two brothers.
- Vidogerski [Soundex V326] and his family.
- Vidonbom [Soundex V351] and his family.
- Viltchevzky [Soundex V432] Yosef, Feige, Zina, Roza, Hirsh.
- Volf [Soundex V410], Efraim.
- Volf, Yitzchak and Bluma.
- Volmir [Soundex V456], Mordechai son of Reb Yechezkel, Devorah daughter of Reb Menachem, their sons Menachem, Moshe Aharon, Gershon, Yechezkel, their daughter Aidel, their daughters-in-law Etel, Devorah.
- Vostonitzki [Soundex V235], Bashke and her two children.
- Yismachovitz [Soundex Y252], Daniel and his daughters, Tziporah and Channah.
- Yones [Soundex Y520], Sonia daughter of Reb Ze'ev.
- Zak [Soundex Z000], Yosef son of Reb Hershel and Shaina, his wife Aliza.
- Zak Sheima, Rachel daughter of Reb Yaakov Ivri, their son Yehuda, their daughter Gitla.
- Zelivanski [Soundex Z415], Velvel, his wife and their children.
- Zelkind [Soundex Z425] and his family.
- Zelazo [Soundex Z420], Binyamin, Channah, Chaya, Gitl, Rivka, Hinde, Esther and Masha.
- Zborovski [Soundex Z161], Shmuel Yehuda son of Reb Moshe, his wife Leah daughter of Reb Shalom Demel [Soundex D540].
- Zimanski [Soundex Z552], Masha, Velvel son of Reb Noach Yosef.
- Zlotnizki [Soundex Z435], Zissel, Etkel, Hershel, Sarah.
- Zufintzki [Soundex Z153], Abba.
- Zufintzki, Zivia, daughter of Reb Shmuel, Nachum son of Reb Ze'ev, Boruch son of Reb Ze'ev, Chinke son of Reb Ze'ev, Ze'ev son of Reb Nachum.

The list of slain of the *Shoah* is not complete.

Passed Away in the Land and in the Diaspora

Aleksandrovitz, Sarah and Aharon
Aleksandrovitz, Ze'ev
Assur, Reuven
Beker
Bergstein, Fania
Bergstein, Yaakov
Bezant, Meira
Bezant, Tzila
Bezant, Zalman
Bialovzetzki, Basha Gitl
Binstein, Sala
Blechertzik, Zaydel
Bornstein, Sarah
Borovitz, Nisan
Borovitz, Rivka
Borovitz, Sarah
Borovitz, Yaakov
Borovitz, Yosef
Buchalter (Dlogoshinski) Mariashel
Chositzer, Barukh
Chositzer, Rachel
Chositzer, Yaakov
Cohain, Barukh and Sarah
Cohain, Yaakov
Domovitz, Moshe
Drozinski, Avraham
Efrati, Chava, of the house of Stolar
Freitzeit, Leah
Friedman, Batya
Rabbi Gibstein
Goldshmid, Avraham Moshe
Grinberg, Shmuel and his wife Golda Heichl
Grodzinski, Moshe
Grosberg, Yisrael
Hochman, Aharon
Kaplan, Alta-Golda
Kaplan, Avraham Yitzchak
Kaplan, Chaya Mala
Kaplan, Moshe Chaim
Kaplan, Naftali-Hertz
Kaplan, Rivka

Koitel, Chaya
Langervitz, Zelda
Lenzinger, Sender Moshe
Lenzinger, Zelda
Lenzinger-Krinitzki, Miriam
Levi, Miriam
Levi, Reuven
Levi, Yisrael
Levita, Yehuda
Lieberman, Yisrael Barukh
Lifshitz, Esther
Lifshitz, Menachem Mendel
Lobel (Dlogoshelski), Rivka
Lonshel (Jak), Helen
Lonshel, Eliezer Dov and Miriam
Lonshel, Yudel
Ludvinovski, Eliezer Dov and Nechama
Markus, Chaya
Olchnovitz (Efrati), Yehudit
Orimland, Abba
Orshanski, Chaim
Papirovitz, Bila
Plotzinski, Meir
Plotzinski, Shlomo
Popkin, Abba
Rabinovitz, Tuvia
Rotstein, Bela
Rozenberg, Michael
Rozenberg, Sarah Esther
Rozental, Chaim
Sandomirski, Barukh
Sherman, Dina
Strozinski, Aleksander
Varhaftig, Shimon
Yevreiski, Chaya
Yevreiski, Nechemiah
Yevreiski, Yaakov
Yevreiski, Yedidiah
Zaklikovski, Gad
Zilberstein, Hillel

{p. 526} The Organization of Natives of Augustow and the Region in Israel
by Binyamin Efrati

As is known, in the completion of the First World War,[1128] on the great tragedy that came down on the Jews of Europe, when six million Jews were destroyed by the accursed Nazis and their helpers, may their names be erased, the natives of our city in the land assembled to weep for the slain and to consult on how to assist the surviving remnant.[1129] At that time there arose an organization of natives of Augustow and the region, which includes also the towns of Lipsk and Sztabin. Among the first in this action were Dr. Moshe Markus, Yaakov Bergstein, may his memory be for a blessing, and G. Zaklikovski, may his memory be for a blessing.

The beginning of the activity of the council was to conduct a survey of the survivors, to find out where they were, and what was their fate? We contacted those from our city in the United States and in the lands of South America, and it became clear, to our sorrow, and regretfully, that only a few remained alive.

The Council drew up a list of natives of Augustow in the land, and set a Memorial Day for the slain of the Holocaust. Within a year all of them were gathering and raising the memories of the martyrs of our city. In general the memorials took place in Tel Aviv, where most of the members of the organization lived. Two years ago, we went up to Jerusalem and communed with our loved ones in the Chamber of the Holocaust[1130] and on the Mount of Remembrance,[1131] where there is also found, among the gravestones of cities and towns, the monument to the members of our city, which the council took care to erect. We listed the names of the slain of the Holocaust on a parchment scroll, which will be preserved forever, within the monument, in Jerusalem the Eternal City.

The Council also established a fund for the offering of emergency aid to those in need from our city. Over the course of time the Council was expanded, and we approached the great undertaking of memorialization of the martyrs by the publication of the book "The Community of Augustow" in which the men, women and children who were slaughtered for no fault of their own would be memorialized. In it would be told of the vibrant life of the wonderful community, and about its bitter end, in it we would also raise a Memorial Candle to those who fell in the defense of the homeland, and to those who died in the land and in the Diaspora, word of whose death reached us.

We turned to all the natives of Augustow once, twice, and every time, and requested that they should inform us of the names of their relatives who were destroyed. We also requested written material about life in the town and valuable communal photographs. To our sorrow, only a few responded. We know that the book which is offered before you is not complete. However, the fault is not in us. The financial aspect also troubled us a great deal. We are few, relatively, in the land, only about two hundred families. There are no wealthy among us. To our luck a son of our city, Mordechai Goldshmid and his brother in Mexico, undertook the matter with enthusiasm.

[1128] Although the text indicates the First World War, the writer must have intended to refer to the Second World War.
[1129] 1 Chronicles 4:43.
[1130] A small Holocaust museum on the Mount of Olives.
[1131] Known as *Har Herzl*, Herzl's Mountain, on the west side of Jerusalem next to the Jerusalem Forest.

They contributed a significant sum, but the sum that is still lacking is also significant. We hope that all natives of our city will include themselves in the memorialization project and will bring into their homes {p. 527} the book "The Community of Augustow," that it will also be remembered by our children, our grandchildren, and the generations to come. Our dear ones are deserving of that.

For the sake of the advancement of the activity to publish the book, the Council established a few actions, besides the many written memoirs by natives of the city. We arranged a fine party in honor of Mordechai Goldshmid, his wife, his daughter and son-in-law. Abba Rozenfeld recounted the praises of the guest, and related, among the rest, that also in Mexico, where he lived, he was distinguished in his giving, and that he saw to the education of his children in the spirit of Israel. The party's guest of honor replied to those who blessed him and announced his donation to the memorialization of the community of Augustow.

We held another party with many participants for the purpose of motivating natives of the city to write down their memories on paper. Y. Aleksandroni outlined the plan of the book, and the veteran, aged, and beloved son of our city Mr. Akiva Glikstein amazed the party-goers with his reading aloud from the creations of Shalom Aleichem.

We also held a symposium on the "*HeChalutz*" movement in Augustow. Dr. Nechemiah Aloni opened and other members added after him. The material is brought in the book.

With the publication of the book the organization does not complete its activity. On the contrary, we will seek ways and means for the strengthening of the activity among natives of Augustow in the land and in the Diaspora. **Tel Aviv, Kislev 5726 [1966]**

The Editor: In these days, 70 years were fulfilled for our friend Binyamin Efrati, the supporting pillar of our organization. The Council presented him with a Certificate of Registration in the Gold Book of the *Keren Kayemet L'Yisrael* for his blessed activity. All the people of our city wish for our Chairperson that he should continue for many more years in his devoted and blessed activity.

Memorial at "Yad Vashem" in Jerusalem.

{p. 528} **Party in Honor of Mordechai Goldshmid and his family (1963)**

From right to left: Dr. M. Markus, Abba Rozenfeld (speaker), Y. Aleksandroni, M. Goldshmid, his wife, his daughter, his son-in-law, M. Amit, B. Efrati.

The Members of the Council and Their Wives

From right to left: Ula and Eliezer Markus, Leah and Yitzchak Sherman, Bela and Moshe Einat, Sarah and Abba Rozenfeld, Rachel and Moshe Markus, Hadassah and Binyamin Efrati, Dora and Yaakov Aleksandroni, Sarah and Moshe Amit.

{p. 529} Memorial at Yad Vashem, Jerusalem

On the Mountain of Memory in Jerusalem After the Memorial

Bidek, B. Gibstein, Ch. Lifshitz, S. Lifshitz, D. Viltzevski, A. Morzinski, Y. Aleksandroni, A. Gardovski, M. Amit, R. Kaplanski, F. Finkelstein, R. Goldstein, Sh. Amit, M. Denmark, Y. Rinkovski

479

{p. 530-535} Natives of Augustow in the Land

Aleksandroni, Yaakov, Tel Aviv, Derekh HaShalom 91.

Aloni, David, Tel Aviv, Sirkin 1.

Aloni, Nechemiah, Jerusalem, HaMelech George 41.

Aloni, Yosef, Petach Tikvah, Meginei HaGhetto.

Alter, Dora, of the house of Borovitz, Kibbutz Ramat HaKovesh.

Amit (Drozinski), Moshe, Tel Aviv, Bodenheimer 4.

Ampel, Mina of the house of Volmir, and Ze'ev, Kfar Varburg.

Ampel, Moshe, Kvutzat Kinneret.

Aplebaum, Shmuel, Tiberias, Shikun 3, B/591.

Ariav, Beruriah of the house of Ravidovitz, Kibbutz Ein Charod Ichud.

Arnon, Yocheved of the house of Preis, Tel Aviv, Bikurei HaItim 1.

Arzoni, Rachel, of the house of Mistivovski, Chadera Givat Olga, Shikun Olei Sin.

Ashkenazi, Yaffa of the house of Friedman, Haifa, Ruth HaCohain 6.

Ashur, Chuna, Tel Aviv, Levinski 103.

Atzmoni, Masha of the house of Denmark, Givat Brenner.

Avramovitz, Yaffa, Tel Aviv, Yehuda the Maccabee 64.[1132]

Azrieli, Rabbi Yekutiel (Koshelevski), Zikhron Yaakov.

Barzilai, Pesya and Yosef, Ein HaKarmel.

Beitel, Pesya, Bat Yam, Ramat Yosef 3.

Ben Yosef, Channah, Tel Aviv, Lachish 1.

Ben-Dov, Tovah of the house of Bidek, Jerusalem, Yehoshua Bin Nun 43.

Bergstein, Chinah, Kibbutz Beit Hashita.

Bergstein, Shulamit, Tel Aviv, Ibn Gabirol 184.

Bezant, Yitzchak, Kfar Varburg.

Bialovitzki, Avraham, Haifa, YL"G 2.

Bialovitzki, Yitzchak, Kiryat Bialystok.

Bidek, Mordechai, Rishon L'Tzion, Herzl 44.

Biurnski, Yisrael, Tel Aviv, Hahaganah 4.

Blech, Beki, Haifa, Machanayim 4.

Blacharski, Yaakov, Haifa, Shderot U"M 53.

Blacharski, Yitzchak, Tel Aviv, Dizengoff 255.

Blecher, Rivka of the house of Staviskovski, Petach Tikvah, Arlozorow 13.

Blechertzik, Safrisha, Kibbutz Shfayim.

Bornstein, Yehuda, Kibbutz Lochmei HaGeta'ot.

Borovitz Noach, Ramat Gan, HaRoeh 43.

Borovitz, Rivka, Gadera.

Borovitz, Shayna, Ramat HaKovesh.

Borovitz, Tanya, Tel Aviv, Kehilat Varsha 133.

Borovitz, Zelig, Ramat Gan, Tashi[1133] 3.

Borovski, Avraham, Bnei Brak, Biryah.

Borovski, Golda, Netanya, Mordei HaGeta'ot 24.

Boymel-Mertzki, Petach Tikvah, Nordau 20.

Briger, Rachel of the house of Sherman, Kfar Yedidiah.

Bukashnovski, Shlomo, Tel Aviv, Sokolov 50.

Bunt, Sarah, Jerusalem, Saray Yisrael 3.

Burk, Menachem, Ramat Gan, Yahalom 17.

[1132] In the format used for Israeli street addresses, the house or building number appears last.

[1133] There is currently no Tashi Street in Ramat Gan, but there is a Rashi Street. This may be a typographical error.

Chen, Moshe, Kfar Saba, Weitzman 9.

Cheruti, Masha of the house of Kotler, Yokneam.

Chositzer, Chaim, Kfar Saba, Shikun Lampert.

Cohen, Dov, Tel Aviv, Balfour 28.

Cohen, Aharon, Givatayim, Gush Etzion 14.

Cohen, Arieh, Tel Aviv, Chovevei Tzion 40.

Cohen, Chaya, Tel Aviv, Dubnov 29.

Cohen, Miriam, Tel Aviv, HaGedud HaIvri 55.

Cohen, Rivka of the house of Blechertzik, Ramat Gan, HaDekalim 11.

Cohen, Shalom, Haifa, Tachanat Min.

Cohen, Yaffa, Netanya, Shikun Chayalim.

Cohen, Zaydel, Tel Aviv, Pinsker 68.

Dagani, Esther and Yehoshua, Tel Aviv, Elkharizi 15.

Dilon, Avraham, Jerusalem, Tachkemoni 4.

Domovitz, Channah of the house of Lozman, Afikim.

Dveltuv, Golda of the house of Eilender, Kfar Menachem.

Edelstein, Yitzchak and Zelda, Jerusalem, Rashi 31.

Efrati, Binyamin, Tel Aviv, HaYarkon 272.

Eiger, Esther of the house of Ivri, Kibbutz Shaar HaGolan.

Einat (Zborovski), Moshe, Tel Aviv, Yiftach 18.

Elenbogen, Siuma, Ramat Gan, HaGat 4.

Eshkol (Lozman), Barukh, Tel Aviv, Mandelstamm 25.

Even Chen, Yaakov, Jerusalem, Shikun HaPoel Mizrachi.[1134]

Feinberg, Yaffa of the house of Linda, Kiryat Haim, Chet 39.

Feivoshvitz, Yaakov, Ramat Gan, Rashi[1135] 6.

Fingerhut of the house of Zelazo, Tel Aviv, HaKovshim 73.

Finkelstein, Pesya, Givatayim, Halamed Hey 54.

Finkelstein, Yonah of the house of Linda, Tel Aviv, Dov Hoz 3.

Flint, Bilhah of the house of Lifshitz, Tel Aviv, Rashi 50.

Freimark, Yerachmiel, Rishon L'Tzion, Nachalat Yehuda.

Freitzeit, Chanan, Tel Aviv, Glikson 2.

Freund, Gedaliah, Tel Aviv, Dubnow 29.

Fridels, Ramat Gan, Sha'anan 20.

Friedman, Fania of the house of Sarvianski, Tel Aviv, Herman Shapira 11.

Futterman, Dorit, Haifa, Chaviva 47.

Gardis, Nachum, Tel Aviv, Netzach Yisrael 3.

Gardovski, Eliyahu, Ramat Gan, HaMelech Yosef 40.

Gardovski, Gershon, Ramat Gan, Aminadav 5.

Gazit, Yosef, Chadera, Bialik.

Gibstein, Betzalel, Rishon L'Tzion, HaKarmel 19.

Giiar, Hinda, Gadera.

Glikstein, Akiva, Jerusalem, Beruriah 9A.

Gonen, Liza of the house of Markus, Haifa, Megiddo 10.

Gorodnitzki, Netanya, Amidar 3/9.

Gotlib, Devorah of the house of Staviskovski, Herzliya, HaKesem.

Gottesforcht, Friedka of the house of Sarvianski, Kibbutz Shfayim.

Grinberg, Aminadav, Tel Aviv, Ben Yehuda 97.

[1134] *HaPoel HaMizrachi* built housing developments for its members in several cities in Israel in the 1950s.

[1135] This has the same typographical error as previously, substituting Tashi when it should be Rashi.

Grinberg, Emanuel, Tel Aviv, Neve Avivim.

Grinberg, Natan, Tel Aviv, Lachish 4.

Grodzin, Channah and Emma, Rishon L'Tzion, Ezra U'Batzron 273.

Grodzinski, Chaya Gitl of the house of Rotenberg, Tel Aviv, Neve Sha'anan 28.

Gurval, Miriam of the house of Orimland, Kiryat Chaim, Ayin" Bet 36.

Hochman, Channah of the house of Linda, Tel Aviv, Ibn Gabirol 137.

Holtzer, Yehudit, Rishon L'Tzion, Nordau 7.

Ivnitzki, Devorah, Tel Aviv, HaNatziv 42.

Kalzon, Avraham, Kiryat Chaim, Shderot Varburg 3.

Kaplan, Daniel, Kfar Saba, Aharonovitz.

Kaplan, Shabtai, Tel Aviv, Yisrael's 19.

Kaplan, Yerachmiel, Gadera.

Kaplanski, Moshe, Magdiel.

Kaplanski, Reuven, Tel Aviv, Derekh Haifa 29.

Karbatchinski, Beruriah of the house of Lonshel, Petach Tikvah, HaYarkonim 2.

Kasher, Miriam, Kfar Saba, Shikun Eliezer

Keli, Moshe, Holon, Professor Shor 21.

Kentzuk, Chanan, Ramat Gan, Arlozorov 39.

Kestin, Arieh, Haifa, Remez 120.

Klimnonvski, Leah, Kiryat Bialik, Pinat Keren Kayemet L'Yisrael 49.

Kloid, Channah of the house of Blechertzik, Shfayim.

Kornblit, Channah of the house of Strozinski, Tel Aviv, Gotlib 1.

Krinitzki, Arieh, Tel Aviv, Remez 10.

Krupnik, Yaffa, Kibbutz Alonim.

Kugel, Chaim, Tel Aviv, Mercaz Mischari 91.

Kugel, Chaya of the house of Shidlovski, Tel Aviv, Mozinson 20.

Leizerovitz, Arieh, Haifa, HaYearot 7.

Leizerovski, Ze'ev, Chadera, Rachash 6.

Lengvitz, Leah, Haifa, Yehuda Halevi 47.

Lenzinger, Hadassah, Kibbutz Ein Shemer.

Levinzon, Moshe, Haifa. Arlozorov 122.

Levitan, Golda, Ramat Gan, Nachalat Tzvi 53.

Levitov, Gita, Kiryat Motzkin, Zevulun 15.

Lifshitz, Aleksander, Kfar Saba, Beilinson 9.

Lifshitz, Ze'ev, Holon, Yitzchak Halevi 14.

Linda (Aloni), Channah-Alta, Tel Aviv, Sirkin 1.

Livni, Binyamin, Ramat Gan, Donesh 1.

Livni, Yishayahu, Ramat Gan, Jabotinsky 75.

Lizovski, Yonah, Jerusalem, Yemin Avot 4.

Ludvinovski, Yaakov, Gadera, Remez 15.

Machsanai, Tzipora, Tel Aviv, Shderot Yehudit 22.

Markus, Dr. Moshe, Tel Aviv, De-Haaz 13.

Markus, Eliezer, Tel Aviv, Geula 25.

Markovitz, Mina of the house of Kestin, Netanya, Dizengoff 36.

Mikolinski, Moshe, Petach Tikvah, Gutman 28.

Milgalgrin, Rachel of the house of Goldstein, Ramat Gan, Yahalom 102.

Morzinski, Arieh, Petach Tikvah, Dr. Shiffer 39.

Moshkovitz, Sarah of the house of Berliner, Kibbutz Ein HaKarmel.

Movshovitz, Bracha, Herzliya, Yafo 1/4.

Nafcha, Miriam of the house of Chositzer, Shikun Eliezer.

Orimland, Chaim, Haifa, Beit El 21.
Orimland, Channah, Kiryat Chaim, 59 Street 9.
Orshanski, Tovah of the house of Kaplan, Gadera.
Oshrovski, Batya, Tel Aviv, Rashi 41.
Ostrov, Mordechai, Kiryat Chaim, 23 Street 12.
Otstein, Yerachmiel, Ramat-Gan, HaShoshan 9.
Pincus, Rachel of the house of Aleksandrovitz, Kfar Menachem.
Plaskovski, Channah, Tel Aviv, Pinsker 46.
Plotzinski, Rayzel, Givat HaShlosha.
Pozniak, Tzvi, Haifa, Meir 37.
Rabinovitz, Hinda, Ramat Gan, Neve Sha'anan 20.
Rabinovitz, Yisrael, Moshav Cherut.
Rechs, Batya of the house of Gizumski, Givatayim, Katznelson 118.
Rechtman, Ovadiah, Holon, Maimon 12.
Renen (Rinkovski), Yisrael, Haifa, HaTzofim 7.
Riftin, Zhenia of the house of Yones, Kibbutz Ein Shemer.
Rotstein, Arieh, Tel Aviv. Sokolov 8.
Rotstein, Batya, Tel Aviv, Yonah HaNavi.
Rozenberg, Sali, Bat Yam, Weizmann 26.
Rozenfeld, Abba, Tel Aviv, La Guardia 53.
Rozenfeld, Aidel, Ramat Gan, HaTanaim 5.
Rozin, Shoshana, Givatayim, Katznelson 101.
Sansani, Etke of the house of Gotstein, Haifa, Rashi 4.
Sarvianski, Arieh and Zehava, Rishon L'Tzion, Neve HaChayal 570.
Sarvianski, Elchanan, Kfar Malal.
Sarvianski, Noach, Haifa, Noga 12.
Sendovski, Yocheved of the house of Kestin, Kfar Saba, Chatzerot Hadar G11.
Shadmi (Blacharski), Yishayahu, Haifa, Chenkin 14.
Shapira, Chaya, Hadera, HaGiborim.
Shapira, Leah, Kiryat Gat, HaKaloniyot 12/361.
Shapira, Tzivia, Tel Aviv, Amiel 21.
Sheintzeit, Yechezkel, Afula, HaTzaftzefa 5.
Sherman, Dov, Tel Aviv, Kikar Masryk 16.
Sherman, Yechezkel, Tel Aviv, Vitkin 9.
Sherman, Yitzchak and Leah of the house of Ivri, Tel Aviv, Ben Yehuda 141.
Shulkis, Mordechai, Kiryat Chaim, 9 Street 35.
Shumski, Tzvi, Tel Aviv, Pincus 37.
Soika, Sarah, Yehud, 22 Street No. 3.
Soloveitchik, Naftali, Ra'anana, Gordon.
Steinman, Leah of the house of Leizerovski, Tel Aviv, Dubnow 21.
Strozinski, Yisrael and Shoshana, Petach Tikvah, Rambam 4.
Surasky-Stein, Dora, Kiryat Motzkin, Usha 8.
Sverdlik, Tzipora, Petach Tikvah, Volfson 12.
Tapuchi, Sarah of the house of Slovtitzki, Hadera, Bialik.
Tarshish, Rishka of the house of Preisman, Kibbutz Gevat.
Tolkovski, Esther of the house of Sarvianski, Tel Aviv, Sutin 11.
Tuker, Esther of the house of Glikstein, Haifa, HaNasi 58.
Tzernovroda, Esther, Holon, Avodah 1.
Tzesis, Channah, Tel Aviv, Ruth 16.
Varhaftig, Noach, Haifa, Machanayim 10.

Veinberg, Esther of the house of Eilender, Ramat Gan, Herzl 51.
Veisberg-Cohen, Leah, Petach Tikvah, Kfar Ganim.
Vilensky, Tzila of the house of Glikstein, Tel Aviv, Borochov 10.
Vilin, Freida of the house of Aleksandrovitz, Kfar Menachem.
Vofshovitz, Bracha, Moshav Bat Shlomo.
Yardeni, Miriam, Tel Aviv, Daniel 17.
Yashir, Nachum, Tel Aviv, Netzach Yisrael 3.
Zak, Devorah and Shayna, Chadera, Givat Olga 154/2.
Zahavi, Simcha, Givatayim, Kaplanski 17.
Zilberfenig-Zboznik, Netanya, Yoav 3.
Zilberstein, Avraham, Tel Aviv, Modiliani 13.
Zilberstein, Menachem and Bela, Bat Yam, Arlozorov 66.
Zinger, Charna of the house of Borovitz, Ramat Gan, Cherut 13.
Zufnik, Brunia, Ganei Yehuda.

{p. 536-537} **Augustow Natives in the Diaspora**
Barglovski, Eliyahu, South America.
Bass, Chaim Hillel, United States.
Beyer, Ben Tzion, United States.
Blacharski (Bloch) Feivel, Australia.
Blacharski (Kahana), Batya, Australia.
Brizman brothers, Mexico.
Brizman sisters, United States.
Cohen, Channah, United States.
Cohen, Moshe, United States.
Feldman, Channah, United States.
Finkelstein, Zerach and Mina of the house of Zupnitzki, United States.
Freer, Sonia, Mexico.
Friedman, Luba, United States.
Gardovski, Gershon, Sweden.
Gardovski, Shlomo, United States.
Gotstein, South Africa.
Kestin, Australia.
Lazdeiski, Chaim, Mexico.
Leibl, Tzvi Mordechai, United States.
Lein, Sima of the house of Lifshitz, United States.
Levin, Chanan, United States.
Levin, Roza, United States.
Levinzon, Chanan, United States.
Levinzon, Rachel, United States.
Levinzon, Tzila, Rhodesia.
Lonshel, Zelig, United States.
Markus, Channah, United States.
Morzinski (Mor), Yechezkel, United States.
Olchnovitz, Aharon, Mexico.
Olchnovitz, Mordechai, United States.
Olchnovitz, Moshe, Mexico.
Olichnovitz, Miriam, Mexico.
Piazetzky, Yechezkel, United States.
Poznanski, ? United States.
Ptak, David, United States.

484

Ptak, Edah, United States.
Ptak, Liuba.
Rabinovitz (Meizler), Feigl, United States.
Rechtman, Arieh, Austria.
Rotblit, Moshe, United States.
Rotenberg, Chava of the house of Borovski, Sweden.
Serna, Dania, and her brother(s), United States.
Shacham, Shoshana of the house of Linda, United States.
Shreibman, Arieh, United States.
Shumski, Rephael, Sweden.
Tsherman, Reuven, United States.
Tzemach, Binyamin and Frieda, Mexico.
Vaksman, Sonia, United States.
Vodovoz, Chaim.
Zborovski, Yitzchak, Argentina.
Zeligzon, Yehuda and Yechezkel, South Africa.
Zupnitzki, Shmuel, Argentina.

{p. 538} We Will Not Forget Those Who Were Lost!

The Eilender Family

Sitting: Chaim Eilender, Alta Eilender.
Standing, from right to left: Peshe Eilender-Kletzki, Dov Eilender, Sarah Eilender-Romsisker.

485

We Will Remember the Living!

{p. 539} Aleksandrovitz Family

The father- Dovid Arieh; the grandmother, Sarah; the mother, Chaya Rivka; Chaneleh, Fredka, Rachel, Alter (Zalman-Tzvi), Aharon.

{p. 540} The Borovitz Family

Standing from right to left: Zelig, Dora, Liza, Chanoch, Tzarna.
Sitting: Nisan, the father; Shayna Chaya, the mother.

486

Nachum and Rivka Blacharski

{p. 541} **Avraham and Masha Blacharski and their children**

Julius Blacharski (Blok)

{p. 542} The Gizumski Family

Top row, from right to left: the daughters Malka and Esther Rivka,
Esther Rivka's son Chaim Berla, her husband Nechemiah Hermenshtat.
Second row: the son, Chanan Dov, Reb Gedaliah, his wife Leah of the house of Adamstein.

488

Shmuel and Golde Grinberg

{p. 543} **Gershon son of Reb Yaakov,**
Shayna Esther daughter of Reb Tzvi Dlogoshelski (Dagani)

Denmark Family

From right to left standing: Noach, Masha, and her husband Aharon.
Sitting: Hershel, the father; Bashel, the mother.

The Zelazo Family

Chaya, Gitl, Channah-Aidel the mother, Binyamin the father, Rivka, Shayna.

{p. 545} Shmuel-Yehuda and Leah Zborovski

{p. 546} The Yevreiski-Sherman Families

From right to left:
Top row 1. The parents, Chaya Beila and Yaakov Yevreiski (Ivri); 2. Rachel the daughter and her husband Sheima Zak; 3. Mordechai Sherman, the father; Friedka, the daughter; Eliezer the son, Miriam, the daughter; Middle row 1: Breintza Ivriyah (Domovitz); 2. Chaya Beila, the daughter; 3. Meir Domovitz, Yehuda Zak , the son of Rachla and Sheima; 4. Sarah; 5. Zaydka-Nechemiah; Bottom: 6. Yedidiah, the son of Yaakov Yevreiski.

491

The Lonshel Family

From right to left: Miriam, the mother; Chena (Helen), daughter; Shmuel Yehuda, son; Eliezer Dov, the father.

{p. 547} The Lozman Family

First row top from right to left: Chaya of the house of Lev, Eliyahu, Binyamin, Yocheved Eshkol, Yehudit, Netanel (Sana).
Second row: Ze'ev, the father; Rayzel, the mother; Luba, Esther of the house of Lev, Channah.
Third row: Iziah, Eliezer, Chaim.
Fourth row: Daniel Eshkol, Avraham.
Bottom, from right: Yaakov son of Yehudit, Fruma, Eliezer Tzvi her husband, Mina, Moshe Domovitz husband of Channah.

492

The Sarvianski Family

From right to left: Yitzchak, the father; Leah, daughter; Elchanan, Shmuel Yosef, a son; Liba, the mother; Vela, a daughter.

{p. 548} The Freund Family

Ze'ev, his wife Liba, their son Yaakov-Yedidiah, their daughters Sarah and Batya.

493

The Family of Yehoshua Friedman, may his [their?] memory be for a blessing

From right to left: Masha, Golda the mother, Yehoshua the father, B. Sandomirski, Channah Friedman-Borovitz, Zavel Drovianski, Rozka Friedman-Drovianski.

{p. 549} The Family of Reb Shabtai Kaplan

494

Hinda, Avraham-Dovid, Rivka, Shlomo, Shulamit Folk, Masha and Alter Folk, Reuven Rozenfeld and his wife Berta.

{p. 551} **Appendix A:** Not originally included in Sefer Augustow, the materials in this appendix were submitted by the Soloveitchik family at the time of the preparation of the translation of the book into English.

Memories of Shalom-Naftali Soloveitchik
of his dear and beloved family in Augustow
Collected by his daughter, Nava Marom-Soloveitchik,
Eulogy by Shalom-Naftali Soloveitchik
About his family who perished in the Holocaust and whose place is unknown

"And who like your people Israel is one nation in the land,"[1136] until the dazzling lightning and the thunder shone on the community of Israel in the exile.

And here in the darkness of exile, in the light of the terrible deadly lightning, the masses of Israel who are sitting on a dangerous slope are revealed to the masses and the slope is uprooted and rolls with them into the deep abyss, gaping down with no savior and no deliverer. Yes, now we felt how unnatural it was to sit in the exile and maintain our uniqueness as Jews. And we have paid for this sin in all that is dear to us and in what he has and will never have in return.

And now a few words to commemorate my family. A family that was completely lost in the storm of war, in the storm of horrors that befell a large part, a third of our people in general of which most were in continental Europe. One of the many families whose thread of life was cut off so cruelly, so tragically, without it a why? Or a wherefore?

Much have I struggled with myself whether I am permitted to raise their memory. Their holy memory, and if so whether I am able to restrain myself and write quietly while they appear to my mind in the last moments of their lives as they stand before their strange death, eye to eye with their murderers, in their standing all together, or lonely and lonesome, calling for help in the great desert around them or accepting the terrible judgment with apathy. And I see before me a large family of sisters and brothers-in-law with their sons and daughters and infants of *beit rabban*,

---

[1136] 2 Samuel 7:23, and included in the daily liturgy.

uncles and aunts with their families. The stone plunged into the water with a horrible noise and again the silence prevailed.

A family of *talmidei chachamim* on both sides. My father, Reb Meyrim, who was less than twenty years old, was an ordained rabbi, but his natural modesty, such was his nature, he did not turn the *Torah* into a spade to dig with but studied the *Torah* for its own sake. God was gracious to my father and did not prolong his days, because close to the war and before even reaching the age of sixty, he died a natural death among his family and was privileged to be buried in a Jewish burial. Above everyone was my mother Chaya-Rashel who was created by the Creator of the world to reach old age so that she would be present in all the cruelty. She perished in the Holocaust with her four daughters, her sons-in-law and her grandchildren.

I had four sisters, all of whom were teachers. The eldest, Sarah, was a teacher in the German schools during the first war and the youngest, Dina, a teacher in Grodno at the outbreak of the last war. All my sisters got married and started families, they had sons and daughters, who were all destroyed leaving no trace. The eldest Sarah and her family in Ivanitz, near Minsk. Feitzi and her family in Vizian near Suwalki. Batya and her family with her mother in Augustov. Dina and her family in Grodno.

And in my imagination now I add piles of corpses, pure corpses of saints, family members closest to me, men, women, and children. Slaughtered, stabbed, and shattered, their only sin being that they were devoted children of a stiff-necked people who were not allowed to come to the grave of Israel, and I do not know the place of their burial.

May their soul be bound in the bundle of life!

Shalom-Naftali Soloveitchik Writes and Relates

My father's house was undoubtedly a traditional house, but not a Chassidic one, we were "*Mitnagdim*," like all the Jews of Lithuania, even though as an example of the traditional education that I received the fact will serve that when our dwelling place resided on the Lithuanian-Polish border and belonged to Poland, I used to climb on to the roof of the buildings in the yard in front of my friends; I did not once miss the reading of "*Shema Yisrael*" aloud as if for the sanctification of the Name. Love of Jerusalem and the belief in the return to Zion were imprinted in my blood. When I progressed with studies and reached the study of geography and I studied the map of the Near East and I reached the eastern bank of the Mediterranean Sea, and here what do I see? Could it be? Jerusalem? Black printed on white the explicit name of Jerusalem on a map?

As if I received a shock. The city of Jerusalem appears on the map like the other secular cities of the whole world. And also the exact place where it resided! This means that everything we learned about the Land of Israel, about a Jewish state, a Jewish kingdom, in which the kings and also the prophets ruled, and everything written in the *Tanakh* was once a reality! And not like the stories about the Garden of Eden and Gehenna and the like. The shock was very strong, to this day I cannot forget this moment in my life. Then I started looking for the direction and the way from where I was, by way of the different countries to Jerusalem. In order to prove how you can really get there physically, and breathe the air of the Land of Israel. The longing was so great that at that moment I was jealous of the dogs and cats that I described to myself in my imagination, that even these were there and roaming the streets of Jerusalem. How happy they were, and what a great privilege fell to their lives! The path of life and the purpose of my life became clear to me, and that was to reach *Eretz Yisrael*!

Meanwhile the First World War broke out, the Russians retreated, and the Germans arrived. The language of instruction was henceforth German. The Germans advanced with giant steps into Russia. Finally after the defeats at the front, the communist revolution broke out in Russia. After the hoped-for peace, Poland was liberated from the Germans and was made independent. After declaring war on Communist Russia, it wanted to expand its borders to reach the Black Sea, according to all the announcements. I was then drafted into the Polish army.

After ten weeks of training in the army, I was sent to the front past Kiev. The success did not brighten the face of Poland for a long time and the great retreat began in which I was captured by the Bolsheviks. Here I went through a period of time that imprinted the stamp of life on me and according to which I would behave. A perspective of life, values, and a special perception of life and everything around it. This is the line that guides me to this day. These values are austerity, contentment with little, avoiding waste and so forth. Until they collected a large number of captives, they just held the captives in prisons. In post-revolutionary Russia, there prevailed in that period literally a hunger for bread. People died of starvation and disease. The epidemics of typhus and jaundice claimed more casualties than the battlefield.

When they permitted me once with a few more prisoners to go out into the yard to refresh myself, I saw in the distance a woman coming to visit her husband who was imprisoned, apparently, as a counter-revolutionary, (an enemy of the revolution) serving him a basket of food she had brought for him. The man holds a slice of bread in his hand and with a knife peels the hard crust and charred bread and it falls to the ground. He takes a cucumber, peels it and the peel also falls to the ground. My eyes nearly popped out of their sockets. Seeing this, the saliva came to my mouth, I swallowed it and licked my dry lips. I walked around here and there. I checked if there was no one else of the prisoners who noticed my actions. I waited anxiously for the prisoner to finish his meal and leave. When the long-awaited moment came I leaped to that place as long as my spirit was in me, and collected a crumb of crumbs from the bread, the peels, and a little of the grass that grew there, and I swallowed it all before I could chew. In the meantime many prisoners were collected and transferred to a prisoner of war past Krakow. Since I knew the Russian language well, I was authorized to be a head prisoner in the prisoner of war office.

I had just returned home, I entered the "*HeChalutz*" movement which was only in its beginning. I went out with the group for training, I was the head of the group. At the beginning of 1926 I came to Israel as a kibbutz member. A new page in my life history that not everyone achieved."

At 60, My Father Makes His Voice Heard With His Paintbrush.
Memories of His Family and the City Augustow

The shadow of the Holocaust clouded my father's life, and what he wrote in 1960 he did not want to give for publication in the "*Yizkor*" book to the city of Augustow. The people who came out of Augustow told the truth, who among you does not miss the landscape of Augustow? A landscape that nature had endowed with an abundance of water and green forests.

"Who has not once stood in in the evening by the light of the moon by the Sheliza bridge and not enjoyed the foam of water and the rumbling erupting from the cracks of the wide gates, the heavy wooden gates that were closed and opened that were designed to balance the lake surface in front of the canal at the time of the passage of the wooden rafts. Who had not travelled in the wonderful forest and reached the wide lake leading to the Sajno. When I remember this, two swimmers appear before my eyes, not of the same age but equal in the art of swimming, and here they are before me. Moshe Leib the shochet, may his memory be for a blessing, in the section of the river by the Great Flour Mill, not far from the waterfall. And, may he be set apart for long life, Leizer Aronovski (in Cuba) in Lake Sajno which is in the depths of the forest. Two amazing swimmers who, with their movements and agility greatly affected me with their abundance of beauty and grace. Between the forests and the lakes, Sajno, Netta, and Jakli, was the location of the city. Augustow was founded according to a plan prepared in advance by the Polish king in the 15th-16th centuries and was also named after him. It had a square, a large and beautiful public garden in the center, and around the beautiful garden with the Pravoslavie Church, in the center on

497

the eastern border. The city was built by the Jews with its beautiful straight streets, facing each side. It was a beautiful and clean city in a wonderful natural landscape inhabited by Jews, and in the neighborhoods around were the Polish population.

The livelihood of the city's Jews was no different from the livelihood of the Jews of the other cities in the area, where the majority made a living from trade and shops, and the minority from handicrafts. The two market days, Tuesdays and Fridays, were what helped the Jewish inhabitants in the war for their existence. Those who took more and those who took less all existed to the extent that they existed, and saw their existence among the Gentiles as temporary, until the miracle should occur or the Messiah would come. And didn't they wait for the Messiah every day, and the sign for this: they did not involve themselves with the Gentiles, they did not eat their bread nor drink their wine and if a gentile God help us (God forbid) touched a bottle of Jewish wine, then it became forbidden and had to be poured away, for it was forbidden to enjoy it. Their faith they nullified as the dust of the earth,[1137] their saints ended. A gentile's funeral was for a "carcass" and the church symbols were as rags. The church - parasitic, (insipid) and their holidays were horrors. (But) three times a day they said, "And let our eyes see your return to Zion, the Valley of Mercy" (from the liturgy). On holidays - next year in Jerusalem, and on Shabbat - "You chose us," "And who like your people Israel is one nation in the land,"[1138] (from the liturgy) until the dazzling lightning shone and the thunder roared on the community of Israel in the exile.

And here in the darkness of exile, by the light of the deadly threatening lightening, there is revealed to the masses, the masses of Israel who are sitting on a dangerous slope, and the slope is uprooted and rolls with them into the deep abyss, gaping down with no savior and no deliverer. Yes, now we felt how unnatural it was to sit in exile and maintain our uniqueness as Jews. And we have paid for this sin in all that is dear to us and in what we have and will never have in return.

And now a few words to commemorate my family. A family that was completely lost in the storm of war, in the storm of horrors that befell a large part, a third of our people, in general most of whom were in continental Europe. One of the many families whose cord of life was cut off so cruelly, so tragically, without it a why? Or a wherefore? Much have I struggled with myself whether I am permitted to raise their memory? Their holy memory? And if so whether I am able to control myself and write quietly while they appear to my mind in the last moments of their lives as they stand before their strange death, eye to eye with their murderers, in their standing all together, or desolate and alone, with a call for help in the great wilderness that surrounds them or accepting the terrible judgment with equanimity. And I see before me a large family of sisters and brothers-in-law with their sons and daughters and infants of *Beit Rabban*, uncles and aunts with their families.

And at the head of them all my mother, who the Creator of the world merited to reach old age so that she would be present in all the cruelty. Yes, the argument with the Creator is great and profound, but this is not the place. The stone dove into the water with a terrifying noise, and again the silence prevails. The sun shines, the acacia blooms, and the world goes on in its usual way.

A family of *talmidei chachamim* on both sides. On both the mother's side and on the father's side. Proficient in *Talmud* and rabbinic literature. Rooted in the Jewish tradition. My grandfather on my mother's side, R. Yosef Glikstein, was a merchant. He used to buy forest plots from the authority, formerly the Russians. He also leased grazing lands and subleased them to Polish farmers. He was a man with an imposing appearance, and was respected by human beings. *Yeshiva* students and those who had left home to study *Torah* who made the "*kloiz*" (the family synagogue) their lodging ate at his table, as was the custom in those days who ate "days" with the homeowners.

[1137] In Aramaic.
[1138] 2 Samuel 7:23, included in the liturgy.

Among them and in his time was also the *Dayan* of our city in his youth, Rabbi Koshelevski, peace be upon him, whose first name escapes my memory. His son, Rabbi Yekutiel Koshelevski, one of the survivors of the slaughter at the Hebron *Yeshiva* in 1929, now serves as a rabbi in Zikhron Yaakov.

My grandfather on my father's side, Reb Tzvi Soloveitchik, was a baker and grain trader. A learned[1139] Jew. A gentle soul and with dreamy qualities. He fulfilled it and meditated on it day and night,[1140] literally. He was entirely immersed in Talmudic issues and their commentaries, to the point that in many cases while sleeping he would mumble passages of Talmud.

He sent his eldest son, my father, Reb Meyrim (Meir), to study at the Telz *Yeshiva* in Lithuania. There he excelled in his diligence and became a prodigy (a genius in the *Torah*). At less than twenty years old he was ordained as a rabbi. But in the abundance of his modesty, such he was by nature, he did not turn the *Torah* into a spade to dig with, and studied *Torah* for its own sake.

After Reb Yosef Glikstein took him as a bridegroom for his only daughter, supported him at his table, and added him as a partner to his various businesses, including contract work such as: building bridges, road sections, buildings for military use and more. After a while grandfather Reb Yosef Glikstein was widowed and married for a second time. From her were born two daughters, who are in Israel, and a son who managed to finish the Teachers' Seminar in Vilna, but the cord of his life was cut off by the Hitlerist murderers before he had time to go up to the land.

I had four sisters. The eldest Sarah was a teacher in German schools during the First War. And the youngest Dina, a teacher in Grodno at the time of the outbreak of the last war. All my sisters got married and started families. They had sons and daughters, all of whom were destroyed without leaving any memory. The eldest Sarah and her family in Ivanitz in the area of Minsk, Feitzi and her family in Vizian in the area of Suwalki, Batya and her family with her mother in Augustow. And Dina and her family in Grodno.

The Holy One Blessed Be did righteousness for my father and did not lengthen his days, because close to the war, before he reached the age of sixty he died, among his family, a natural death and was privileged to come to the grave of Israel. In the last years of his life he was stricken with paralysis of the limbs of his body, his right hand and leg. They told me that he would go to the "*Yatke Kloiz*" synagogue, leaning on his cane, with my sister Batya accompanying him to teach the daily *Gemara* page between *Mincha* and *Maariv* in front of the listeners. May their souls be bound in the bundle of life.

In order to emphasize the family's connection to the Land of Israel, I must point out that as early as 1870-1880, there were a few individuals from many families, from both the Glikstein family and the Soloveitchik-Friedgot family, faithful to their national conscience and lacking peace of mind to continue their daily lives in exile, guided by a subtle internal force, who got up and made the great step and immigrated to Israel. This is to be known: that *aliyah* to Israel at that time, during the period of Turkish rule and the conditions in Israel then, was completely different from our *aliyah*, and even mine from more than thirty years ago (1926), which was still a period of the conquest of labor. The period of the wars of Hebrew labor in Zikhron Yaakov, Petach Tikvah and the other old settlements. The period of conquering the swamps and the construction of the first roads in the country. To appreciate this act, the Nachshoni[1141] leap (of *aliyah* in 1870, the period

---

[1139] Aramaic.
[1140] Joshua 1:8 "This book of the Torah shall not depart from your mouth, but you shall meditate on it day and night."
[1141] Mekhilta D'Rabbi Yishmael 14:22:1: Because they stood and deliberated, Nachshon the son of Aminadav leaped into the sea. Of him Scripture writes "Save me, O G d, for the waters have reached my soul.

of Turkish rule in Israel) we must know that Petach Tikvah and Zikhron Yaacov themselves did not exist in those days.

This shows the great love for Zion that beat in the heart of the ancestors of my family, the Glikstein-Soloveitchik family, a love of Zion in the version of Rabbi Yehuda Halevi, a love of Zion that drew its vitality from a source that was not disappointing. From a source that was not in need of Zionist propaganda. A love of Zion that decreed that people would leave their environment and family and take the staff of wanderers in hand. This was a longing to pair their bodies to the holy soil. *Aliyah* to the land of Israel, if not for the sake of the continuation of life in it, at least to die in it and be buried on the Mount of Olives in Jerusalem. And by means of this to continue the continuity of the Jewish people in their land, until God had mercy on them, according to their own conception.

One of the fathers of the family who advanced to Israel was my father's grandfather on his mother's side, Reb Shmuel Friedgot, who according to what was told in our house prepared himself to be worthy of the great privilege before which he stood, by self-denial and midnight prayers and studying books of *Kabbalah*. He also added to his *aliyah* the *aliyah* of one of his sons who was married then, and together with his son Reb Shalom and his young daughter-in-law they prayed that his son would be able to strike roots in the Land of Israel and build a family there, that would build the land and the people, and expiate with the good deeds the sin of those who stayed in exile. And indeed this quest was completely fulfilled; this shoot succeeded in being accepted in Jerusalem at the time, participated in the building of the Meah Shearim neighborhood, and the synagogue he built with his money is still named after him, the synagogue of Reb Shmuel. Descendants of this family are scattered all over the face of the land, involved in the life of the state and working for its existence, and theirs.

While Rabbi Shmuel and his son were engaged in the building of Jerusalem, a second son of his, Reb Shlomo-Ze'ev Friedgot in Johannesburg, South Africa, was listening to the footsteps of the Messiah, which were approaching the redemption of Israel, and he had no other worries besides preparing a building plan for the Temple, for there was no doubt this would be the first act of the Messiah. There he became a partner not to another, but to Ezekiel son of Buzi the priest in the land of Kasdim, on the River Kevar, who had preceded him by two thousand and five hundred years. He received from him all the details as written in the book of Ezekiel. And after an extended time of exertion, and after joining line to line and order to order, he brought out from under his hand a detailed and printed plan, on paper illuminated with colors. He goes up to the land, and only the answer of the rabbis and the great ones in *Torah* "it is not yet proper"[1142] (not yet kosher, proper, the time). It returns him slowly to the world of reality. It should be noted that while living in South Africa he was in constant contact with his father and brother in Jerusalem. One of his sons, Reb Shlomo-Meir Friedgot, also went up to the land from South Africa and settled in Magdiel.

Such were my ancestors on my father's side, a typical Augustovian family who lived there for generations. That even in their dwelling among the gentiles they not only dreamed of the return to Zion but were among the hasteners towards the end. "I believe with complete faith in the coming of the Messiah. And even though he is delayed despite this I will wait for him." This principle is one of the thirteen (the Principles of Maimonides). It was not just a principle that the Jew must have in his faith, for them this way was the essence of their lives. It filled their whole existence, and it was that which gave them the strength and vigor to overcome all life's misfortunes in the exile until the last generation, the last generation of bondage and destruction.

[1142] Aramaic.

The ancestors of the Glikstein family were also among the dreamers and fighters for the return of Zion and the hasteners of the end. One of the descendants is Mr. Akiva Glikstein, one of the founders of Hadar HaCarmel, one of the famous contractors in the country in the days of the British. Who had not heard of the firm "Glikstein and Katinka" in those days? I too in the year 1927 once worked on the road he built in Petach Tikvah without making myself known to him, even though I spoke to him face to face at the time. Because as a member of the kibbutz "Givat HaShlosha" I did not want to get *protectzia* ... that is how it was then.

Descendants of the family succeeded and it merited to stand out among the tapestry of the revival of the Jewish settlement in the land in all its hues, with famous personalities such as Dr. Hillel Yaffa in Zikhron Yaakov or Mr. Kalvariski from "Brit Shalom[1143]" and more like these famous people who live with us in the State of Israel. In terms of the historical descent of the family as a whole, the Soloveitchik-Friedgot-Glikstein family lives and exists under the original or other names and participates in the building of the land and the nation. Like an ants' nest after a devastating flood or a destructive conflagration. But if we divide the family into its cells, then personally and numerically most of the family was destroyed.

Yes, I raise memories and see myself in the company of my family on sought peaceful coexistence between Arabs and Jews, and I am ten years old, 50 years ago in Bridge Street *Kloiz*, which was our family *kloiz*; here next to the *aron kodesh* in the east on the right in first place, stands the father of grandfather Reb Leizer Glikstein, already over ninety years old, when the glittering whiteness of his kittle blends with the whiteness of the hair of his head and beard. This in turn highlights the parchment color of his wrinkled face.

In the second place, his son Reb Yosef Glikstein, prayed with hand movements and aloud forcefully to his Lord in heaven, with hand gestures and as one who demands what he deserves according to the promise.

The third is Reb Meyrim, my father who, out of humility and modesty, prays in a whisper and warm-heartedly, in his garments and wrapped in his tallit. I see myself, his only son. After him is my uncle Reb Yisrael Yaakov Friedgot and then my grandfather on my father's side Reb Tzvi Soloveitchik and all the uncles, the family members all dressed in white.

And in my imagination now I add heaps, corpses, the holy and pure corpses of my closest family members. Men, women, and children, slaughtered, stabbed and with shattered heads, whose only sin was to be devoted sons of a stiff-necked people, who did not get to come to the grave of Israel, and I do not know their burial place. May their soul be bound in the bundle of life! If I were in the position of Rabbi Levi Yitzchak of Berdichev, I would turn to the Holy One, Blessed Be, and say: With forgiveness from your Honor, Master of all worlds, with your permission we want to cancel the contract you imposed on us by force because there is testimony that says: "He forced upon them a mountain like a roof and said if you accept God's teachings it is better, and if not, this will be your grave."[1144]

And if you claim that we accepted it voluntarily, accept this sacrifice because you love sacrifices. Accept the six million killed and slaughtered only as the last slaughter, here they are in front of you and be satisfied with that. And from now on let us live as all peoples live, without privileges and without burdensome duties towards you, for we will never be able to stand with you in judgement, for you are a God of vengeance and make you make heavy your hand on us. And if not for us, do it for the sake of the slaughtered for the unification of your name in every generation, for our souls are weary of the slaying, and may peace be upon Israel.

Shalom Naftali Soloveitchik

[1143] Founded in 1925, Covenant of Peace was a group of Jewish Zionist intellectuals in Mandatory Palestine who sought peaceful coexistence between Arabs and Jews
[1144] Penei Yehoshua on Shabbat 88a:1

The Soloveitchik Family, Augustow 1926, before Shalom-Naftali's *aliyah* to Eretz Yisrael

Standing from right: Frieda (Vartelski), Sara (Kivevitz), Shalom-Naftali, Batya (Staverski), Dina (Zilberfenig). Sitting: Meyrim, Chaya-Rachel

Frieda (Feitzi) Soloveitchik and Betzalel Vartelski

Batya Soloveitchik and Yisrael Staverski

Chaya-Rashel Glikstein Soloveitchik with her grandson Meyrim Stavelski, 1931

Dina Soloveitchik and Mentchik Zilberfenig

July 1,1932

Standing from right: Dina Soloveitchik and Sara Soloveitchik-Kivevitz
Bottom from right:
Yentele Kivevitz, Miriam Kivevitz with Avraham Kivevitz, Itale Kivevitz

Appendix B: Glossary of Hebrew, Yiddish, and Aramaic Terms
All terms are in Hebrew unless indicated otherwise.

- *Acharonim:* "The recent ones." The leading rabbis and decisors living from about the 16th century to the present, and more specifically, since the writing of the Shulchan Aruch.
- *Achdut Ha'avodah:* Labor Unity.
- *Adon Olam:* Lord of the world.
- *Aggadah:* Jewish legend, or storytelling.
- *Agora,* plural *agorot:* A penny.
- *Aguda:* Association, often short for World *Agudat* Israel.
- *Admor,* pl. *Admorim:* An acrostic for the Hebrew *Adoneinu Moreinu veRabeinu* – "our Master, our Teacher, our Rabbi".
- *Aleinu L'shabayach:* The concluding prayer, "It is upon us to praise the Master of all…"
- *Aleph-bais:* The Hebrew alphabet, in Ashkenazi pronunciation.
- *Aliyah:* Ascent, referring to going up to live in the land of Israel, or going up to recite the blessing for the *Torah* reading.
- *Amcha:* The folk; the everyday people.
- *Amud:* Lectern.
- *Amidah:* The standing prayer, also known as the 18 benedictions or the *Shemonah Esray.*
- *Amoraim:* The explicators of the *Mishnah,* from the time of the death of the patriarch Rabbi. Judah I. (219 CE) to the completion of the Babylonian *Talmud* (about 500 CE)
- *Apikores:* A Greek word from the *Mishnah,* literally an epicurean, but used by the *Mishnah* to refer to a heretic.
- *Aron Kodesh, or Aron HaKodesh:* The Holy Ark, where the *Torah* is kept in the synagogue.
- *Atchalta De'geulah*; Aramaic: The beginning of the redemption.
- *Av Beit Din:* The Head of the Rabbinical Court. This is the designation of the principal of the *yeshiva* who made halakhic rulings and took part in the communal administration; in particular, it was used as the title of the district rabbi of a large community.

- *Ba'al Koreh:* The person who reads the Torah aloud for the congregation during prayer services.
- *Ba'al Tefillah:* The prayer leader.
- *Bachurim:* Young men.
- *Bachurot:* Young women.
- *Barechu:* The "call to worship:" "Bless the Eternal the One who is Blessed, blessed is the Eternal Forever and Ever."
- *Barnash,* pl. *Barnashim*; Aramaic: Son of a person, a human being.
- *Beit Din:* A Rabbinical court.
- *Beit Din Tzedek:* A Rabbinical Court of Justice.
- *Beit Eked:* Collection House, an old term for library.
- *Beit HaBechirah:* The Temple. Also the name of a section of Maimonides' *Mishneh Torah* on the topic.
- *Beit HeChalutz:* House of the Pioneer.
- *Beit Midrash:* Study House.
- *Beit Rabban:* Used in the expression "Children of *Beit Rabban*," meaning, young children who study *Torah.*
- *Beitar:* Brit Trumpeldor.
- *Belfer:* Yiddish. The traditional assistant in the *cheyder.*
- *Ben Adam:* A person.
- *Beshert;* Yiddish: Destiny.

505

- *Bikkur Cholim:* Visiting the sick.
- *Bima:* The raised platform in the synagogue where the prayer leaders, Torah readers, and preachers stand.
- *Birkat HaMazon:* The blessing after meals.
- *B'nai Tzion:* Children of Zion.
- *B'racha*; Ashkenazi *brokhe:* A blessing.
- *Brit;* Ashkenazi *bris:* Circumcision.
- *Bulke*; Yiddish; A soft bread roll.
- *Bund:* Federation or union in Yiddish and German

- *Challah*, pl. *challot:* Special bread for Shabbat.
- *Chalutz*, pl. *chalutzim:* Pioneer.
- *Chametz:* Foods that have become leavened which are therefore prohibited for Passover use.
- *Chanukah:* The 8-day festival that begins on 25 Kislev, celebrating the recapture from the Greeks and rededication of the Temple in Jerusalem in 165 B.C.E.
- *Charedim:* Tremblers, or Orthodox Jews on the far right of the religious spectrum.
- *Charoset:* A mixture of apples, walnuts and red wine eaten at the *Pesach seder*, symbolizing the mortar that the Israelites made in Egypt.
- *Chassid*, pl. *Chassidim:* Pious ones.
- *Chassidut:* Chassidism.
- *Chazal: Chakhameinu Zikhronam Livrakha*, "Our Sages, may their memories be for a blessing," refers to all sages of the *Mishnah, Tosefta and Gemara.*
- *Chazzan*, pl. *Chazzanim:* Cantor
- *Cheder*, pl. *chadarim*, Ashkenazi *kheyder:* a school for Jewish children that teaches Hebrew and religious knowledge. Literally, a room.
- *Cheder Metukan*; Ashkenazi, *kheyder mesukn:* An improved school that combined traditional studies in *Torah* and *Talmud* with secular studies taught in Hebrew.
- *Chesed:* Lovingkindness.
- *Chevra Kadisha*, Aramaic: The Holy Society, which is the name for a burial society.
- *Chevre:* A group of friends.
- *Chibbat Tzion:* Love of Zion.
- *Choshen:* The breastplate attached to the ephod worn by the High Priest, which are understood to be oracular devices.
- *Chovevei Tzion:* Lovers of Zion.
- *Chumash*, Ashkenazi *Chumesh:* A book containing the five books of the *Torah.*
- *Chuppah:* A wedding canopy.
- *Chutzpah:* Cheek, insolence, audacity.
- *Cohain.* pl. *cohanim:* a descendant of the priestly caste of Aaron, the brother of Moses.

- *Dayan*, pl. *dayanim:* a judge.
- *Derekh Eretz:* Literally, the way of the world, refers to good manners.
- *Divrei Torah:* Words of *Torah.*
- *Dorshei Tzion:* Seekers of Zion.
- *Drasha:* A homiletical teaching.
- *Dunam:* A unit of land area used especially in the state of Israel equal to 1000 square meters or about ¼ acre.

- *Eretz Hatreifa:* The unkosher land, that is, America.
- *Erev Rav:* A mixed multitude.
- *Eshet Chayil:* A woman of valor.

- *Etrog,* pl. *etrogim:* Citron, waved on Sukkot together with the *lulav.*
- *Ever:* Hebrew.
- *Ezrat Nashim:* The women's section of both the Temple in Jerusalem and the synagogue.

- *Freiheit;* Yiddish: Freedom.
- *Fuftzik;* Yiddish: Fifty.

- *Gaon,* pl. *Geonim:* Literally means "genius", but in this context, it is used as an honorific for the spiritual leader of the town, who decided questions of Jewish law, headed the Jewish courts and rabbinical academies, and ultimately had the final say in the religious life of the Jewish community.
- *Gabbai:* The collector. In this context, it was the title given to a person charged with collecting funds. In synagogue context, it refers to the person who follows the reading of the Torah to catch and correct any errors.
- *Gemara:* Rabbinic commentary on the *Mishnah,* composed from 200 – 500 C.E. The *Mishnah* and the *Gemara* together comprise the Talmud.
- *Gematria:* A code that uses the numerical value of a Hebrew word instead of its letters.
- *Gemilut Chassadim; Ashkenazi, Gmiles Khesed:* Acts of lovingkindness, also the name of a fund that provided interest-free loans..
- *Get:* A Jewish divorce.
- *Golem:* A creature created by magic, often to serve its creator. Legend holds that Rabbi Judah Loew ben Bezalel, the Maharal of Prague (1513-1609), created a *golem* out of clay to protect the Jewish community from the Blood Libel.
- *Goyim:* Literally means "nations," but it is regularly used as a derogatory term for non-Jews.
- *Grush:* An obsolete Israeli coin, worth the smallest amount, like a penny.

- *Habonim:* The builders.
- *Hachnasat Kallah:* Bringing in the bride; creating a bridal dowry.
- *Hachnasat Orchim:* Welcoming guests.
- *Haftarah,* pl. *haftarot:* Readings that are excerpted from the Prophets (*Nevi'im*) and accompany each weekly Sabbath *Torah* reading, as well as readings for special Sabbaths and festivals.
- *Haganah:* The nascent Jewish defense force.
- *Hakafah:* The procession of the *Sefer Torah* around the synagogue.
- *HaKibbutz HaMe'uchad:* The United Kibbutz.
- *Halakhah.* pl. *halakhot:* Jewish law.
- *HaNoar HaOved,* in Yiddish *Arbeits Kreiz:* The Working Youth.
- *HaRav:* The Rabbi, used for the title that in English is rendered simply as "Rabbi"
- *HaRav HaGaon HaGadol;* Ashkenazi *Harov Hagoen Hagodl:* The Great Rabbi the Gaon.
- *Hashomer HaTzair:* The Young Guard.
- *HaShomer Trumpeldor:* Trumpeldor Guard.
- *Haskalah:* The Enlightenment.
- *Haskamah,* pl. *haskamot:* Letters that appeared at the beginning of a book from various rabbinic authorities, stating their approval of a book. They served as rabbinic seals of approval.
- *HaTikvah:* The Hope, Israel's national anthem.
- *HaTzohar:* An acronym for *HaTzionim HaRevizionistim,* The Revisionist Zionists, officially *Brit HaTzionim HaRevizionistim,* Union of Revisionist Zionists.
- *Havdalah:* The ritual marking the end of *Shabbat.*
- *HeChalutz:* The Pioneer.
- *HeChalutz HaDati:* The religious pioneer.
- *HeChalutz HaMizrachi:* The *Mizrachi* Pioneer. (See *Mizrachi*).
- *Hekdesh:* Sacred property, an old name for a poorhouse.

507

- *Histadrut*: The General Organization of Workers in Israel.
- *Hitamtzut:* Effort.
- *Horah*: An Israeli folk dance.

- *Ilui*: Prodigy.
- *Irgun*: *HaIrgun HaTzva'i HaLeumi B'Eretz Yisrael,* The National Military Organization in the Land of Israel.
- *Isru Chag*: The day immediately following the three pilgrimage holidays—*Pesach, Shavuot* and *Sukkot*—is called *Isru Chag*, which literally means "bind [the] festival."

- *Kabbalah:* Jewish mysticism.
- *Kaddish:* The prayer for the dead recited by mourners.
- *Kahal*: A community, a congregation, or the head of the community.
- *Kamatz:* A Hebrew vowel.
- *Kapai: Kupah L'Poalei Eretz Yisrael,* The Fund for the Workers of the Land of Israel.
- *Kapparot*: Expiations. This is a riddance ritual where a Jew symbolically transfers their sins onto a chicken, in advance of *Yom Kippur.*
- *Kapote;* Yiddish: A caftan.
- *Kashrut*: All the laws concerning kosher food.
- *Kav:* About 1.3 liters.
- *Keren HaGeulah:* The Redemption Fund.
- *Keren HaYesod*: The Foundation Fund, established in 1920 at the World Zionist Conference in London.
- *Keren Kayemet L'Yisrael:* The Jewish National Fund.
- *Keset;* Yiddish: Keep, as in financial support.
- *Kesitah:* A unit of money mentioned in the Bible.
- *Ketonet*: Tunic.
- *Ketuvim*: Writings.
- *Kippah:* A skullcap.
- *Knesset*: The Israeli Parliament.
- *Kvutza*: A group.
- *Kibbutz*, plural *kibbutzim*: A collective settlement.
- *Kiddush*: Sanctification; the blessing over wine on *Shabbat* and festivals.
- *Kitnyot*: Little things; a category of food that one might mistake for the five grains that may be consumed on Passover. These have traditionally been forbidden for Ashkenazi Jews on Passover, until the last decade or so.
- *Kittel*; Yiddish: A white linen or cotton robe worn by religious Jews on holidays
- *Klei Kodesh:* Holy implements. This refers to sacred objects, and is also used to refer to members of the clergy and the prayer leaders.
- *Kloiz;* Yiddish, Hebrew plural *kloizim,* Yiddish plural *kloizen:* A "Beit Midrash" (Study House) associated with and led by a recognized and accepted strictly orthodox and scholarly rabbi usually as part of the synagogue complex.
- *Kol Nidre:* All Vows. The prayer for which the *Yom Kippur* evening service is named.
- *Kollel:* a men's institute for full-time advanced study of the *Talmud* and rabbinic literature. While it resembles a *yeshiva* in that it offers lessons, it is different from a *yeshiva* in that most of the students are married.
- *Korech*: The "Hillel sandwich," eaten at the Passover seder.
- *Kries-HaToyre*; Ashkenazi: The liturgical reading of the *Torah*.
- *K'vod HaRav:* A title of respect for a Rabbi, along the lines of "Your Honor, the Rabbi."

- *Lag Ba'Omer*: The 33rd day of the *omer*.
- *Lakchan*: A taker, a thief.
- *Lashon Hara:* Evil speech. There is an entire body of *halakhah* that governs speaking about others, even saying nice and/or truthful things, when they are not present; when it is permitted, when it is forbidden, and when it is required.
- *Lashon Kodesh, or Lashon HaKodesh:* Holy language – Hebrew.
- *L'Chaim:* To life! A common Jewish toast.
- *Linat HaTzedek;* Ashkenazi *Lines HaTzedek*: a hostel for the poor.

- *Ma'avar:* Transfer, or passage. A group for workers, largely those newly arrived to the land of Israel, who were looking for work in collective settlements.
- *Maccabi:* Maccabee.
- *Magen David:* Shield of David, commonly called a Jewish Star.
- *Maggid:* A storyteller or teacher.
- *Maggid Shiur:* One who preaches a lesson.
- *Malchut Shaddai:* God's sovereignty.
- *Malekh*: Ashkenazi; angel.
- *Ma'ote Chittin:* A charitable fund to buy flour for Passover matzas.
- *Mara D'Atra:* Aramaic for "the Master of the Place," that is, the local rabbi who has the sole rabbinic authority to decide local cases of Jewish law and practice.
- *Maror:* Bitter herbs, eaten at the Passover Seder as a symbol of the bitterness of slavery.
- *Maskil*, plural *Maskilim*: An adherent of the Jewish enlightenment movement that began in Eastern Europe in the early nineteenth century and was active until the rise of the Jewish national movement in the early 1880s.
- *Matan B'seter*: Giving in secret.
- *Matzah:* Unleavened flat bread eaten during Passover in place of bread. Also called "the bread of affliction."
- *Matzah farfel*: Small broken pieces of matza used in cooking.
- *Mazal*: Luck. Also refers to the signs of the zodiac.
- *Megillah*: Scroll.
- *Meylech*: Ashkenazi: King.
- *Menorah*: Refers to both the 7-branched candelabrum that stood in the Temple, and the *Chanukah menorah*, which holds 9 candles.
- *Mezuzah:* A doorpost; also, the parchment placed on the doorpost of a Jewish home.
- *Mikvah*: Ritual bath
- *Mincha:* The afternoon prayer service.
- *Minyan*, pl. *minyanim*: A quorum of ten Jews, in this context men, which is required to recite certain prayers in the liturgy.
- *Mishebeyrekh*: Ashkenazi: The prayer for healing, literally, "the one who blessed."
- *Mishnah:* The first part of the Talmud, compiled between ca. 0 and 200 C.E.
- *Mitnaged* (m.s.), *Mitnagedet* (f.s.), pl. *Mitnagdim:* Opposers, referring to those opposed to the Chassidic movement
- *Mitzvah*; Ashkenazi *Mitzveh*, Hebrew pl. *Mitzvot:* Commandments.
- *Mizrachi:* An Orthodox Zionist movement whose name was derived from the words *merkaz ruchani* (spiritual center), and whose slogan was "the Land of Israel for the People of Israel according to the Torah of Israel.
- *Moreh hora'ah*: A teacher of Jewish law
- *Moreh Tzedek:* Righteous teacher, that is, a decisor of Jewish law.
- *Moshav*, plural *moshavim*: A collective settlement.

- *Mussaf:* The additional prayer service on Shabbat afternoon.
- *Mussar:* The Mussar movement was developed in 19th century Lithuania by Rabbi Yisrael Salanter. It promotes the development of inner virtues and characteristics.

- *Nach:* An acronym for the last two sections of the Bible, the Prophets (*Nevi'im*) and the Writings (*Ketuvim*).
- *Nevi'im:* Prophets
- *Niggun,* pl. *niggunim:* Wordless melody.
- *Notarikon:* Using one word that is composed of the initial letters of an entire phrase.
- *Nu:* Yiddish: So? or Well?

- *Ohel HaTzaddik:* "Tent of the Righteous." Refers to the grave of a *Tzaddik*.
- *Oleh, olah,* pl. *Olim:* One who goes up, i.e. makes *aliyah* to the land of Israel.
- *Omer:* A sheaf of grain, also the name of the 49-day period between *Pesach* and *Shavuot*.
- *Oy Vavoy;* Yiddish: The long form of which *oy vey* is the short form; "woe is me!"

- *Parasha:* A weekly *Torah* portion.
- *Parochet;* Ashkenazi *poroykhes:* the curtain that covers the open of the *Aron Kodesh*.
- *Patach:* A Hebrew vowel.
- *Pesach:* Passover.
- *Peyot;* Ashkenazi *peyes:* Sidelocks; the "corners" of the beard. The biblical commandment in Leviticus 19:27 forbids the rounding off of the corners of one's beard, or one's field when harvesting.
- *Pikuach Nefesh:* The saving of a life, which supersedes almost all Jewish laws.
- *Piyyut,* pl. *piyyutim:* A liturgical poem, from the Greek *poietes,* poem.
- *Ploni Almoni:* sometimes just *Ploni:* So-and-so.
- *Poalei Tzion:* workers of Zion/
- *Protectzia;* Slavic imported into Israeli Hebrew: Connections that allow a person to pull strings.
- *Prozdor*; Greek: A corridor or vestibule.
- *Purim:* The holiday when Jews celebrate the foiling of the plot of the evil Haman to destroy them, described in the Book of Esther.

- *Rabbanit; Rebbetzin: Yiddish;* The title for the Rabbi's wife.
- *Reb:* The honorific "Reb" is generally used for all Jewish men in Sefer Augustow, and means "Mr."
- *Rishonim:* The first ones; the leading rabbis and decisors who lived approximately during the 11th to 15th centuries, in the era before the writing of the Shulchan Aruch.
- *Rosh Chodesh:* The head, or first day, of the month.
- *Rosh HaShanah:* The head, or first day, of the year.

- *Seder:* Order The name of the ritual event that is held by Jews to celebrate the festival of Passover. It which follows the order, *seder,* of the *Haggadah,* the book that is used to tell the story of the exodus from Egypt.
- *Sefer:* Book
- *Sefer Torah: Torah* scroll.
- *Shabbat,* plural *Shabbatot,* Ashkenazi *Shabbes*: Sabbath
- *Shabbat Shuvah:* The *Shabbat* of Return, the *Shabbat* between *Rosh HaShanah* and *Yom Kippur*.
- *Shacharit:* The morning prayer service.
- *Shaliach:* Emissary.
- *Shaliach Mitzvah:* An emissary for the performance of a *mitzvah*.
- *Shaliach Tzibur:* The "Public Emissary," which is the term for the prayer leader.

- *Shamash:* Ashkenazi *Shammes,* the sexton, or caretaker of a synagogue. It is also the word used for the candle with which we light the eight candles of Chanukah.
- *Shas:* The Six Orders of the Mishnah.
- *Shavuot:* The festival of Weeks that occurs 7 weeks after Passover. It is one of the 3 biblical pilgrimage festivals.
- *Shaygetz*; Yiddish: a non-Jewish man. This is a slur derived from the biblical Hebrew word for abomination.
- *She'ailah ve-Teshuva:* Question and Answer, a process by which a question is brought to a rabbi who then studies all the relevant halakhic material to make an informed decision. Also known as a Responsum.
- *Shekel:* The ancient Hebrew coin, the *shekel,* was introduced at the time of the First Zionist Congress and became an iconic "Membership Badge" of the Zionist movement.
- *Sheketz,* pl. *shkotzim:* Abomination. Source of the Yiddish words *"shaygetz,"* used to refer to a non-Jewish man and *"shiksa,"* a non-Jewish woman.
- *Shekhina:* The feminine personification of the Divine, who dwells on earth.
- *Sheol:* The place underneath the ground where the Bible believes people go when they die.
- *Shidduch:* Arranged marriage.
- *Shiksa:* Yiddish; A non-Jewish woman. This is a slur derived from the biblical Hebrew word for abomination.
- *Shiva:* The 7 days of mourning following the death of an immediate family member.
- *Shlit'a:* An abbreviation for "May he live a good long life, amen."
- *Shma Yisrael*: Hear O Israel. The prayer which is the statement of God's oneness.
- *Shmendrik*: Yiddish; a stupid person, a fool.
- *Shmura matzah:* *Matzah* that has been watched over by a *kashrut* supervisor from the time of harvest through all of the steps of it processing into *matzah.*
- *Shoah:* Holocaust
- *Shochet;* Yiddish *shoychet:* kosher slaughterer.
- *Shochet U'bodek:* A kosher slaughterer and meat inspector.
- *Shofar*: The horn of a kosher animal, sounded on *Rosh HaShanah* and *Yom Kippur* in the synagogue.
- *Shomer, Shomeret, Shomrim, Shomrot*: m.s., m.pl., f.s. f.pl. Guard(s)
- *Shul;* Yiddish: Synagogue.
- *Shulchan Aruch:* "The Set Table." An influential Jewish code of law written by Joseph Caro (1488-1575).
- *Shushan Purim:* Shushan Purim falls one day after Purim, on Adar 15, and is the day on which Jews in Jerusalem celebrate Purim.
- *Siddur*: Prayerbook.
- *Sifriyah*: Library.
- *Simchat Torah:* Rejoicing of the *Torah.* The festival that celebrates the conclusion and recommencing of the annual cycle of *Torah* reading.
- *Sofer St"m:* A *sofer,* Ashkenazi: *soyfer,* is a scribe. The acronym *ST"M* stands for the Hebrew words for *sifrei* (scrolls of) *Torah, tefillin* (phylacteries), and *mezzuzot,* the parchments that are affixed to the doorposts of Jewish homes.
- *Sukkot;* sing. *Sukkah:* The festival of Booths that is the third of the 3 biblical pilgrimage festivals, which occurs in the fall.

- *Taharah*: Purification. Jewish preparation of a body for burial.
- *Tales-kotn;* Ashkenazi: A small *tallit* worn as an undergarment.
- *Tallit,* Ashkenazi t*allis:* A prayer shawl with *tzitzit* attached to the corners.

511

- *Talmid Chacham:* a student of a sage, used to refer to a scholar.
- *Talmud:* The compendium of rabbinic interpretation of the Torah compiled between the year 0 and 500 C.E.
- *Talmud Torah:* a Jewish school for boys that places special emphasis on religious education. Some *Talmud Torah*s concentrate on Talmudic studies as a preparation for entrance into a yeshiva.
- *Tanakh:* The Hebrew Bible, composed of three sections; the *Torah*, the Prophets (*Nevi'im*) and the Writings (*Ketuvim*), whose initial letters comprise the Hebrew acronym.
- *Tanna*, pl. *Tannaim:* The sages of the *Mishnah*.
- *Tefillin:* Phylacteries.
- *Tiferet Bakhurim*, Ashkenazi *Tiferes Bakhurim*: The splendor of young men.
- *Tikkun olam:* Repair of the World.
- *Tisha B'Av:* The ninth day of the Hebrew month *Av* – the day on which the Second Temple was destroyed in 70 CE.
- *Torah:* The Five Books of Moses.
- *Tosefta.* pl. *Toseftot*: A compilation of the Jewish oral law from the late 2nd century, the period of the *Mishnah*, that was not included in the *Mishnah*.
- *Treif*: Torn, meaning not kosher.
- *Tum'a:* A state of ritual uncleanness.
- *Tzaddik*, pl. *tzaddikim*: A righteous person.
- *Tzahal:* An acronym for *Tzva Hahaganah L'Yisrael*, the Israel Defense Force.
- *Tzamday sadeh*: 165 dunam.
- *Tzedakah:* Frequently translated as "charity," actually means "righteousness," because giving to a cause or a needy person is considered a commandment, the righteous thing to do, not out of the goodness of one's heart, as the word "charity" implies.
- *Tzeirei Tzion:* Zion Youth.
- *Tzitzit*, in Ashkenazi Hebrew: The ritual fringes attached to the corners of a prayer shawl.

- *Vidui:* The confession said by, or for, a Jew who is about to die.

- *Yad Charutzim*: Diligent hand.
- *Yahrzeit*; Yiddish: the anniversary of a death
- *Yamim Nora'im:* The Days of Awe, also called the High Holy Days.
- *Yarmulke;* Yiddish: Skullcap.
- *Yeshiva*, pl. *Yeshivot*: a school of higher Jewish learning.
- *Yidisher Yugend Bund*; Yiddish: The Jewish Youth Union
- *Yiddishkeit*; Yiddish: Jewishness.
- *Yishuv:* The Jewish settlement that existed in Israel before the aliyah of the modern period, usually referred to as the "Old *Yishuv*."
- *Yom Hillula*: Day of festivity.
- *Yom HaDin*: The Day of Judgement, *Yom Kippur*
- *Yom Kippur:* The Day of Atonement.
- *Yored*, pl. *Yordim*: Descender. A pejorative term used for one who leaves the land of Israel permanently. It is the opposite of *oleh*.

Months of the Jewish Year

1. Tishri	5. Adar (In a leap year, there is also Adar II)		
2. Cheshvan	6. Nisan	9. Shevat	12. Elul
3. Kislev	7. Iyar	10. Tammuz	
4. Tevet	8. Sivan	11. Av	

INDEX

Entries in **bold**, People, Places, Jewish Books and Publications, Zionist Organizations, and Jewish Organizations and Institutions, are category headings that contain many individual entries.

Jewish Organizations and Institutions

Amit, Moshe, 16, *See* Drozinski
Amit, Moshe and Sarah, 582
Amit, Moshe Drozinski. *See* Drozinski
Amit, Sh., 584
Amitai, 10
Amitai, Mordechai, 468
Ampel, Chaim Asher son of Shmuel, 560
Ampel, Chaya daughter of Dovid, 560
Ampel, M.. *See* Volmir
Ampel, Mina. *See* Volmir
Ampel, Mina of the house of Volmir, and
    Ze'ev. *See* Volmir
Ampel, Miriam Tziporah, 560
Ampel, Moshe, 584
Ampel, Shachne, 238
Ampel, Z., 389, 432
Andres, General, 448
Aplebaum, Shmuel, 584
Aplebaum, Shmuel Eliezer, 11, 19, 530
Apleboim, Tzerka, 560
Arbshteyn, 415
Arbstein, 380
Arbstein, A., 389, 432
Arbstein, Avraham Berel and Golda, 560
Arbstein, Elke, 560
Arbstein, Moshe, 99, 162, 340
Arbstein, Rivka, Alter, Etke, Mashka,
    Moshe, Shula, 560
Arech, 238
Ariav, Beruriah of the house of
    Ravidovitz. *See* Ravidovitz
Arimland, Abba, 514
Arimland, Khane, 554
Arimland, Khayim, 415
Aristobulus, 282
Arnon, Yocheved of the house of Preis.
    See Preis
Aronovitz, Feshka, 394, 396
Aronovski, E., 10, 264, 266
Aronovski, El., 9
Aronovski, Eliezer, 11, 19, 485, 521
Aronovski, Feshka, 391, 393
Aronovski, Leizer, 609
Aronovski, Moshe Berel son of Avraham,
    560
Aronovski, Ozer son of Avraham, 560
Aronovski, P., 244
Aronovski, Pinchas, 560

Aronovski, Rachel daughter of
    Mordechai, 560
Arzoni, Rachel, of the house of
    Mistivovski. *See* Mistivovski
Ashkenazi, Yaffa of the house of
    Friedman. *See* Friedman
Ashur, Chuna, 584
Assur, Reuven, 577
Astrin, A., 200
Atzmoni, Masha of the house of
    Denmark. *See* Denmark
August II, 32, 37
August III, 32
Augustus II, 37
Auvtzinsky, Rabbi Levi Yonah, 103
Avak'eh, 167
Avariah, B., 354
Avigdor (Vigder the Lipsker), 470
Avigdor the Lipsker, 507
Avigdor, Man of Lipsk, 560
Avigdor, Rabbi Shmuel, 104, 128, 129,
    130, 132
Avigdor, Rabbi Yitzchak, 132
Avigdor, Shmuel, 129
Avigdor, Yitzchak, 132
Avka the gravedigger, 560
Avraham Sholom son of Shimon, 160
Avraham son of Shimon, 161
Avraham Yitzchak, 423
Avraham Yitzchak Cohen. *See* Grovetz
Avraham, Reb, 128
Avraham'ka, 348
Avramovitz, Yaffa, 584
Avramowitz, Sholem Yankev, 356
Avramski, Eliezer, 99
Avramsky, Mrs., 170, 213
Avramson, 96, 97, 98
Avrech, A., 200
Avresha, 179
Aynshtat, Ariye, 428
Ayzen, A., 330
Azriel Zelig Noach, Rabbi, 148
Azriel Zelig, Rabbi, 142, 155, 220
Azrieli, Rabbi Yekutiel, 8, 17, 162, 401
Azrieli, Rabbi Yekutiel (Koshelevski).
    See Koshelevski
Azrieli, Yekutiel, 10, 220
B., Rivka, 11, 542

Blacharski, Channah, 561
Blacharski, daughter of Yaakov, 561
Blacharski, Dovid and Sarah-Esther, 561
Blacharski, Eiga, daughter of Manes, 561
Blacharski, Feivel, 175
Blacharski, G., 238, 386, 389
Blacharski, Julius (Blok). *See* Blok
Blacharski, Nachum, 99
Blacharski, Nachum and Rivka, 20, 596
Blacharski, Y., 361, 368, 382, 384, 389, 432
Blacharski, Yaakov, 231, 386, 435, 561, 585
Blacharski, Yehuda, Nachum, Salek, 561
Blacharski, Yitzchak, 585
Blacharski, Z., 244
Blech, Arieh, Yosef, Sarah, Niuta, 561
Blech, Beka, 429
Blech, Beki, 585
Blech, Binyamin Chaim son of Yosef, 561
Blech, L., 391, 429
Blech, Moshe son of Yosef, 561
Blech, Rachel daughter of Arieh Bramzon, 561
Blecher, Rivka of the house of Staviskovski. *See* Staviskovski
Blechertzik, R., 389
Blechertzik, Rivka, 386
Blechertzik, Safrisha, 585
Blechertzik, Zaydel, 577
Bloch, P., 54
Blofrov, Dovid and Hinda, 561
Blumental, Sarah, 152
Blumental, Yehoshua son of Reuven HaCohain, 152
Bobrik, Chana, 550
Bobrik, Hershel, 470, 561
Bobrik, Zelig, Chaya, 561
Bogoslavitz, Dmitry, 453
Bokovski, 72
Bona the Queen, 31
Bordani, 218
Borek, Mendel, 422
Bornstein. *See* Shreibman
Bornstein, Rabbi Eliyahu, 142
Bornstein, S., 415
Bornstein, Sarah, 577

Bornstein, Shulamit, Henya Leah, 562
Bornstein, Tzvi and Sima, 562
Bornstein, Yehuda, 585
Borochov, 356, 390
Borochov, Dov Ber, 356, 390
Borovitch, 532
Borovitz, 20, 220, 422, 423, 438, 490, 493, 495, 595
Borovitz (of the house of Grinberg) Shulamit daughter of Reb Shmuel and Golda. *See* Grinberg
Borovitz Noach, 585
Borovitz, Arieh, 400
Borovitz, Chanoch Henech, 220
Borovitz, D., 244
Borovitz, Dora, 393
Borovitz, Dovid Yitzchak, 221
Borovitz, Enoch, 493
Borovitz, Friedka, 562
Borovitz, Gita daughter of Reb Binyamin, 562
Borovitz, Henech son of Nisan, 562
Borovitz, Leivush, 494
Borovitz, Liza, 397, 492, 493
Borovitz, M., 429
Borovitz, Miriam, 219
Borovitz, Moshe, 221, 562, 565
Borovitz, Nisan, 99, 113, 220, 490, 493, 577, 596
Borovitz, Nissl, 479
Borovitz, Noach, 8, 14, 219, 351
Borovitz, Rivka, 577, 585
Borovitz, Rivka daughter of Henech, 562
Borovitz, Sarah, 577
Borovitz, Shayna, 238, 585
Borovitz, Shayna Chaya, 596
Borovitz, Shmuel, 220, 493
Borovitz, Shmuel son of Yaakov and Tzarna, their daughter Tzarna, 562
Borovitz, Tanya, 585
Borovitz, Tz., 238
Borovitz, Tzila daughter of Henech, 562
Borovitz, Tzvi, 220
Borovitz, Y., 238
Borovitz, Yaakov, 99, 220, 479, 577
Borovitz, Yosef, 99, 562, 577
Borovitz, Zelig, 230, 585

Borovitz, Zelig, Dora, Liza, Chanoch, Tzarna, 595
Borovski, 422
Borovski, A., 354, 366, 368, 432
Borovski, Altinka and Eliezer, 562
Borovski, Avraham, 585
Borovski, Basha Leah, 166
Borovski, Beila, 562
Borovski, Borukh, 553
Borovski, Chaim Dov, 237
Borovski, Chaim and Riva-Rachel, 562
Borovski, Channah Alta, 165
Borovski, Golda, 585
Borovski, Hershl, 553
Borovski, Moshe, 231
Borovski, N, 99
Borovski, Neta, 237, 562
Borovski, Tzvi son of Reb Shmuel and his wife Yaffa, 562
Borovski, Yisrael Yehuda, 99
Boyarski, 173, 422, 423, 425
Boyarski, B.Tz., 422
Boyarski, Ben-Tzion, 173
Boyarski, Boba, 422
Boyarski, D., 213, 215, 228, 241, 350, 365, 420, 423, 427
Boyarski, Dov, 99
Boyarski, Dovid, 18, 98, 99, 170, 172, 212, 427, *See* Der Vishaiyer
Boyarski, Ezra, 365
Boyarski, Tzvi Hirsh, 105
Boymel-Mertzki, 585
Bramson, Devorah, 422
Bramson, Sonia, 422
Bramzon, Asnah and Rivka, 494
Bramzon, Devorah, 176
Bramzon, Sh. Z., 238
Bramzon, Zalman, 99, 494
Brandstaetter, Roman, 431
Breiman, Chaim, 76
Breintsa, 226
Breizman, 490
Brenman, Yerachmiel, 99
Brenner, Barukh, 230, 438, 440
Brenner, Golda, 562
Brenner, Mottel, 562
Briger, Rachel of the house of Sherman. *See* Sherman

Brill, 410
Brizman, 231, 562, 592
Brizman, Tuvia, 435, 562
Broide, Y., 148
Broidy, Rabbi Tzvi Hirsh, 128
Broman, V., 239
Brustein, 164
Buchalter (Dlogoshinski), Mariashel. *See* Dlogoshinski
Bukashnovski, Shlomo, 585
Bulke, 327
Bunt, Sarah, 586
Burak Dr. Menachem, 289
Burak, A., 424
Burak, T., 238
Burak, Tuvia, 288
Burk, Esther daughter of Arieh, 562
Burk, Esther daughter of Hillel, 562
Burk, Menachem, 586
Burk, Rachel daughter of Shmuel, 562
Burk, Shmuel son of Arieh, 562
Burk, Tuvia son of Zalman, 562
Burstein, Avraham Aharon HaCohain, 152
Burstein, Rabbi Gaon Reuven Dovid Hachen, 153
Bussel, Yosef, 365
Caliph Abd al-Malik ibn Marwan, 284
Caro, Joseph, 128
Catherine II, 59
Chadirov, 444
Chaim Leib son of Yosef HaLevi, 567
Chaliupitzki, A., 429
Chaliuptzki, Eliav, 531
Chalupitzki, 365
Chalupitzki, A.., 216, 224, 371, 372, 376, 381, 387, 389
Chalupitzki, Ch., 374
Chalupitzki, Channah, 216
Chalupitzki, Eliav, 16, 381, 385
Chalupitzki, Eliav, Metushalach, Avraham, 562
Chalupitzki, M., 354
Chalupitzki, Metushalach, 168
Chalupitzki, Y., 178, 415
Chalupitzki, Yoel, 180
Chamis, Eli, 346
Chanikovski, L., 389

Eilender, A., 397
Eilender, Alta, 594
Eilender, Alte son of Nachum
    (Blacharski). *See* Blacharski
Eilender, Chaim, 237, 594
Eilender, Chaim Dovid son of Moshe
    Leib, 563
Eilender, Chaya Alta daughter of Eizik,
    563
Eilender, Dov, 594
Eilender, Dov son of Chaim, 563
Eilender, Eizik son of Dov, 563
Eilender, Esther, 394, 396
Eilender, Esther-Miriam daughter of
    Elkanah, 563
Eilender, Gershon, 563
Eilender, Golda, 393, 394, 396
Eilender, Nachum son of Dov, 563
Eilender, P., 415
Eilender, Sarah daughter of Ben-Tzion,
    563
Eilender, Yosef son of Elkanah, 563
Eilender-Kaletzki, Eliezer son of Nisan,
    563
Eilender-Kaletzki, Nisan, 563
Eilender-Kaletzki, Peshe daughter of
    Chaim Dovid, 563
Eilender-Kletzki, Peshe. *See* Kletzki
Eilender-Romsisker, Sarah. *See*
    Romsisker
Eilender-Veinberg, Esther. *See* Veinberg
Eilender-Weinberg, Esther. *See* Weinberg
Einat (Zborovski), Moshe. *See* Zborovski
Einat, Moshe, 379, 495, 497, *See*
    Zborovski
Einat, Moshe (Zborovski). *See*
    Zborovski, *See* Zborovski
Einat, Moshe and Bela, 582
Einenovitz, 563
Eirhohn, Shimon, 232, 233
Eisenmenger, 138
Eisenstadt, Noach, 237
Eisenstadt, Sh., 140
Eisenstadt, Shmuel, 76, 99
Eizenberg, 218
Eizendorf, Avraham Barash HaCohain, 84
Eizenstadt, M.B., 312
Eizenstadt, Moshe Ber, 275

Eizenstat, Arieh, 173
Eizenstat, Leon, Shifre, Niuta, Henech,
    563
Eizenstat, M.B., 15
Eizerski, 420
Elblinger, Eizik, 340
Elchanan, Rabbi Yitzchak, 81, 135, 146
Elenbogen, 350
Elenbogen, Eliyahu, 563
Elenbogen, Elko, 494
Elenbogen, Leah daughter of Yitzchak,
    563
Elenbogen, M., 180, 415
Elenbogen, Mordechai, 563
Elenbogen, Roza Shoshana daughter of
    Mordechai, 563
Elenbogen, Shmuel son of Shlomo
    Aleksander, 563
Elenbogen, Siuma, 586
Elenbogen, Yehuda, 563
Eliaszon, Rabbi Yehoshua Heschel, 135
Eliezer ben Hyrcanus, 161
Eliyahu son of Ezra, 122
Elyakum, 206
Entin, Yoel, 330
Erbstein, M., 238
Eshkol (Lozman), Barukh. *See* Lozman
Eshkol, Daniel. *See* Lozman
Esne daughter of Sheyne Yudis, 245
Estherke, 520
Even Chen, Yaakov, 587
Eyzenshtam, 327
Ezerski, Simcha, 99
Falk, Yaakov, 564
Falk, Yishaya Tuvia, 169
Falkov, Mirtza, Mina and Beila, 564
Fania, 374
Faynshteyn, Mayer, 414
Fein, SH.Y., 104
Feinberg, Binyamin son of Yitzchak, 564
Feinberg, Golda daughter of Zalman, 564
Feinberg, Moshe son of Zalman, 564
Feinberg, Shmuel son of Yosef, 564
Feinberg, Yaffa of the house of Linda.
    See Linda
Feinberg, Zalman son of Binyamin, 564
Feingold, 164
Feinstein, 350, 360

Frenkel, Rosa, 276
Frenkel, Y., 9, 15, 238
Frenkel, Yaakov, 8, 24, 76, 87, 88, 89,
   155, 201, 205, 211, 274, 275, 276, 277,
   279, 281, 287
Freund, 20, 432, 604
Freund, G., 353, 366
Freund, Gedaliah, 356, 365, 587
Freund, Liba Ahuva daughter of Yaakov
   Yedidiah, 564
Freund, Sarah and Batya, 564
Freund, Yaakov-Yedidiah, Sarah and
   Batya, 604
Freund, Yitzchak, 564
Freund, Ze'ev and Liba, 604
Freund, Ze'ev son of Eliezer, 564
Freydberg, Nakhman, 428
Fridels, 587
Fried, Rabbi Eliezer Yitzchak, 132
Friedberg, A., 238
Friedberg, Ch.D., 131
Friedberg, Efraim, 340
Friedberg, Rabbi Nachman, 169
Friedenberg, 564
Friedgot, 564, 613
Friedgot, Shalom, 612
Friedgot, Shlomo-Meir, 612
Friedgot, Shlomo-Ze'ev, 612
Friedgot, Shmuel, 612
Friedgot, Yisrael Yaakov, 613
Friedkovski, Yaakov, 237
Friedkovski, Yosef Shimon, 86
Friedlander, David, 55
Friedman, 20, 372, 411, 564
Friedman, A., 238
Friedman, B., 179, 180
Friedman, Batya, 578
Friedman, Ch., 354
Friedman, Chaim, 565
Friedman, Channah (Borovitz) daughter
   of Yehoshua. See Borovitz
Friedman, Cheyne, 238
Friedman, Chinah Zak daughter of Eliezer
   Dov, 564
Friedman, Daniel, 565
Friedman, Dov, 177
Friedman, Dovid. See Katonti

Friedman, Fania of the house of
   Sarvianski. See Sarvianski
Friedman, Feigl and Meir, 565
Friedman, Golda and Yehoshua, 605
Friedman, Golda daughter of Avraham
   Mordechai, 565
Friedman, Luba, 592
Friedman, Masha, 605
Friedman, Masha daughter of Yehoshua,
   565
Friedman, Peshe daughter of Shmuel
   Yehuda Lonshel. See Lonshel
Friedman, Refael, 239
Friedman, Roshka daughter of Shalom
   Darvianski. See Darvianski
Friedman, Sh., 239
Friedman, Yehoshua, 605
Friedman, Yehoshua son of Shalom, 565
Friedman, Zaydka, 565
Friedman-Borovitz, Channah. See
   Borovitz
Friedman-Drovianski, Rozka. See
   Drovianski
Friedrich-August, 55
Friedrich-Wilhelm, 55
Friedrich-Wilhelm II, 54
Fuchs, 170, 172
Fulvinski, Ben-Tsien, 401
Furmanski, 517
Futterman, Dorit, 587
Gak, Chinah, 565
Galanti, Shmerl, 565
Gali, 167
Gamliel, 206
Gamrov, Yankel, 463
Gardis, Nachum, 587
Gardos, Liuba daughter of Yaakov, 565
Gardovski, Chaim Leib, Rivka, Chaska,
   Esther, Moshe-Aharon Malkah, 565
Gardovski, A., 583
Gardovski, Eliyahu, 587
Gardovski, Eliyahu and Devorah, 159
Gardovski, Gershon, 587, 592
Gardovski, S., 368
Gardovski, Shlomo, 593
Garnist, Chaim, 80
Garvin, H., 330
Garzovsky, Yehuda, 347

Gatsky, Avraham Yaakov, 68
Gazis, Y., 361
Gazit, Yosef, 587
Gelman, 517
Gershon of Siemiatycze, 51
Gershon son of Yaakov, 20, 598
Gershoni, Moshe, 496, 497
Gershovitz, 391, 394
Gershovitz, Sarah, 422
Gershovitz, Yehuda, 393, 396
Gershovitz, Yishayahu Meir, 565
Geshori, M.S., 8
Geshori. M.S., 29
Gesundheit, Rabbi Yaakov, 150
Gevirtig, M., 10
Gevirtig, Mordechai, 467
Gibstein Rabbi Betzalel Ze'ev, 157
Gibstein Rabbi Betzalel Ze'ev, 157
Gibstein, B., 583
Gibstein, Betzalel, 8, 159, 587
Gibstein, Moshe, Betzalel, Devorah, 565
Gibstein, Rabbi, 578
Gibstein, Rabbi Yehoshua, 8, 14
Gibstein, Tzarna daughter of Berel, 565
Gibstein, Yehoshua, 158
Gibstein, Yosef son of People, 565
Gifshteyn, Yoysef, 428
Giiar, Hinda, 587
Gilboa, D., 200
Gilda, Sarah, 145
Gilda, Y., 238
Gilda, Yehuda, 145
Ginsberg, Asher Zvi Hirsch, 356
Ginzburg, Baron, 72
Ginzburg, Yitzchak Eliyahu, 160
Gipstein, Manya, 312
Gipstein, Rabbi Yehoshua son of Betzalel
  Ze'ev, 158
Girfalovitz, A., 237
Girshfeld, Chuna, 565
Gittele, Aunt, 193
Gizomski, 242
Gizomski, Rabbi Gedalye, 401
Gizomski, Yoysef, 242, 401
Gizumski, 20, 597
Gizumski, B., 244
Gizumski, Batya, 368, 393
Gizumski, Chanan Dov, 598

Gizumski, Chanan, Dov, Sholom,
  Malkah, 565
Gizumski, Gedaliah, 163, 598
Gizumski, Gedalyahu, 409, 410, 439, 565
Gizumski, Gedalye, 243
Gizumski, I., 430
Gizumski, Leah of the house of
  Adamstein. See Adamstein
Gizumski, Malka and Esther Rivka, 598
Gizumski, Shlomkeh, 439
Gizumski, Y., 368
Gizumski, Yashke, 231
Glazer, Eliyahu, 543
Glazer, Sh., 238
Glikshteyn, Esther Tuker, 489
Glikson, Avram'eleh, 169
Glikson, Avram'eleh son of Chaim, 87
Glikson, Chaim, 99, 400
Glikson, Dov, 99
Glikson, Yehoshua, 565
Glikstein, 423, 550, 611, 613
Glikstein Soloveitchik, Chaya Rashel. See
  Soloveitchik
Glikstein Yaffa, Rivka, 343
Glikstein, A., 9, 429
Glikstein, Akiva, 8, 9, 14, 24, 181, 290,
  302, 342, 580, 587, 613
Glikstein, Arieh, 236
Glikstein, Arieh Leib, 302
Glikstein, Asiya, Chana, Leah, Chaya,
  and Alter, 565
Glikstein, Esther Tuker, 302, 343, 489,
  499
Glikstein, L., 238
Glikstein, Leib, 140, 182, 340
Glikstein, Leizer, 613
Glikstein, M., 429
Glikstein, Mina, 565
Glikstein, Moshe, 238, 400
Glikstein, Moshe Arieh, 548
Glikstein, Moshe-Arieh son of Yosef, 565
Glikstein, Reuvele, 291
Glikstein, Rivka, 302
Glikstein, Sender, 290, *292*
Glikstein, Tz., 355, 364, 366
Glikstein, Y., 239
Glikstein, Yaakov, 302
Glikstein, Yankele, 291

Kalshteyn, Ze'ev, 516

Kalson, Shaul, 100

Kalstein, 479, 494, 566

Kalstein, Z., 11, 355, 363

Kalstein, Ze'ev, 496

Kalvariski, 348, 613

Kalvariski, Chaim Margalit, 302

Kalyer, Rabbi Shlomo Tzvi, 160

Kalyer, Shlomo Tzvi, 160, 161

Kalzon, 286

Kalzon, Avraham, 588

Kamenev, 300

Kaminetz, 344

Kanarius, 518

Kanarius, General, 517

Kantor, Dr. L., 235, 417

Kantorovitsh, 533

Kantorovitsh, Monush, 428

Kantorovitz, 238

Kantorovitz, Avraham, 239

Kantorovitz, Elko, 494

Kantorovitz, Manush, 439

Kantorovitz, Manya, 312

Kantorovitz, Monya and Rochel, 566

Kantorovitz, Rivka, 173

Kantorovitz, Tzvi (Asha), Eliyahu, Esther, 566

Kantorovitz, Yosef Tzvi Maihomon, 78

Kantrovitz, Mrs., 100

Kantrovitz, Yosef Tzvi, 235

Kantsiuk, Khonen, 431

Kantzok, Chanun, 290

Kaplan, 164, 460

Kaplan Family, 12

Kaplan, A.Y., 239

Kaplan, Alta-Golda, 578

Kaplan, Ana Leah daughter of Shabtai the Cohain, 567

Kaplan, Arieh son of Meir the Cohain, 566

Kaplan, Avraham, 239

Kaplan, Avraham Yitzchak, 237, 578

Kaplan, Basha Gitl daughter of Dov, 566

Kaplan, Batya Tzvi, 567

Kaplan, Bendet son of Yedidiah, 566

Kaplan, Breinka, 567

Kaplan, Ch., 386, 389

Kaplan, Chaim, 459

Kaplan, Chaim Dov son of Moshe Simcha, 567

Kaplan, Chaim-Zalman, 410

Kaplan, Chaska, 567

Kaplan, Chava, 566

Kaplan, Chaya Mala, 578

Kaplan, D., 361, 370, 558

Kaplan, D. H., 362, 363

Kaplan, Daniel, 8, 12, 14, 164, 224, 551, 588

Kaplan, Dovid Hillel, 168

Kaplan, Dovid Hillel son of Avraham Yitzchak, 566

Kaplan, Dovid son of Shabtai the Cohain, 567

Kaplan, Eliyahu HaCohain, 304

Kaplan, Esther daughter of Shabtai the Cohain, 567

Kaplan, H., 371

Kaplan, Miriam, 304

Kaplan, Moshe Chaim, 578

Kaplan, Moshe Simcha, 567

Kaplan, Naftali-Hertz, 578

Kaplan, Peshe daughter of Yoel, 567

Kaplan, Pesya daughter of Yoel, 11

Kaplan, Rabbi Naftali Hertz, 164

Kaplan, Rabbi Shmuel HaCohain, 139

Kaplan, Rishi-Rivka daughter of Moshe Simcha, 567

Kaplan, Rivka, 578

Kaplan, S., 391, 393, 394

Kaplan, Sarah, 225

Kaplan, Sarah daughter of Avraham Yitzchak. *See* Voronovski

Kaplan, Sender Itshe, 567

Kaplan, Sender-Moshe, 410

Kaplan, Shabtai, 11, 20, 164, 396, 397, 588, 606

Kaplan, Shabtai son of Yitzchak Eizik the Cohain, 550

Kaplan, Shabtai son of Yitzchak the Cohain, 567

Kaplan, Shaina Yaffa daughter of Shabtai the Cohain, 567

Kaplan, Tzerka daughter of Shabtai the Cohain, 567

Kaplan, Tzvi, Rivka, Rochel, 566

533

Kilson, 15
Kilzon, Shaul, 170
Kimen, Tzvi, Beila Breina, Tuvia, Gushi, 567
Kirshenbom, Moshe, 567
Kirshenbom, Shlomo, Leizer, Efraim, 567
Kirshkovski, Asher, 488
Kirshkovski, Yishayahu, 488
Kirstein, Moshe and Nacha, 567
Kleiman, 425
Kleimashevsk, 472
Klein, 517
Kleinman, A., 371
Kleinman, Simcha, Eli, Shlomkeh, 567
Kleinman, Sonka, 392, 396
Kleinman, Zalman, 100, 567
Kleynman, Alta, 414
Klimnonvski, Leah, 588
Klimontowski, Weiczyk, 33
Klinsky, Devorah daughter of Shmuel, 568
Klinsky, Sarah, 568
Klinsky, Yehoshua, 568
Kloid, Channah of the house of Blechertzik. *See* Blechertzik
Klonovski, 471
Kobrinski, Yasha, 450
Kohen, Yehuda, 429
Koifman, B., 371
Koifman, M., 170
Koifman, Meir, 156, 289, 410
Koitel, Chaya, 577
Kolfenitzki, 394, 396
Kolfenitzki, M., 70, 176, 178, 179
Kolfenitzki, Mendel, 409, 410, 439
Kolfenitzki, Pesach, 230, 568
Kolfenitzki, Roza, 422
Kolfenitzki, S., 244
Kolfenitzki, Sheindel, 393
Kolinski, 424
Kolnitzki, Gershon, 470, 568
Kolpitzki, 425
Konstantin the Great, 46
Kook, Avraham Yitzchak HaCohain, 160
Kook, Rabbi Abraham Isaac, 153
Kopciovski, 288, 290
Kopciovski, Zalman, 77
Kopciovski, Zalman Arieh, 76

Kopciovski, Zalman Leib, 287
Kopresht, 568
Koptziovski, 155
Koptziovski, Eliezer, 239
Koptziovski, Yechezkel, 237
Koptziovski, Z.L., 238
Koptziovski, Zalman Arieh, 155
Koptziovski, Zalman Leib, 100
Koritzki, Eltke and Shmuel, 568
Koritzki, S., 361, 381, 382, 387
Korkovski, Menachem, 151
Korkovski, Menachem Ben Tzion, 151
Korkovski, Tzvi, 151
Korl, Yazi, 472
Kornblit, Channah of the house of Strozinski. *See* Strozinski
Korotnitzki, Dovka, Channah, Rivka, 568
Korotnitzki, Zanvil, 463
Korotnitztki, Zanvil, 463
Korotnitztki, Zovel, 410
Korotzinski, Devorah and Chaim, 568
Korybut, Michal, 32
Kościuszko, 37, 53
Kościuszko, Tadeusz, 53
Koshelevski, Arieh, 432
Koshelevski Edelstein, Zelda, 308
Koshelevski, Azriel Zelig, 150
Koshelevski, Leah Rochel daughter of Yitzchak Tzvi, 568
Koshelevski, P.. *See* Sapir
Koshelevski, Pinchas, 362
Koshelevski, Rabbi, 610
Koshelevski, Rabbi Azriel, 435
Koshelevski, Rabbi Azriel Noach Zelig, 357
Koshelevski, Rabbi Azriel Ze'ev, 103
Koshelevski, Rabbi Azriel Zelig, 228, 231, 409, 410, 423, 438, 490
Koshelevski, Rabbi Azriel Zelig Noach, 8, 13, 102, 103, 144, 145, 231, 439
Koshelevski, Rabbi Yekutiel, 610, *See* Azrieli
Koshelevski, Rabbi Yisrael, 231
Koshelevski, Rabbi Yitzchak, 143
Koshelevski, The Rabbi the Gaon Azriel Zelig Noach son of Rabbi Yitzchak Tzvi, 568

Levinson, N., 361
Levinson, Shlomo, 173
Levinzohn, A., 238
Levinzon, 425, 569
Levinzon, A., 427
Levinzon, Chanan, 593
Levinzon, Dovid, 423
Levinzon, Elyakum, 420, 423
Levinzon, M., 382
Levinzon, Moshe, 375, 589
Levinzon, Noach, 479, 494
Levinzon, Rabbi Elyakum, 168
Levinzon, Rachel, 593
Levinzon, Rokhl, 511
Levinzon, Tz., 424
Levinzon, Tzila, 593
Levit, 414, 434
Levit, D., 238
Levit, Eli, 569
Levit, Khiene, 430
Levit, Yehuda, 569
Levita, M., 238
Levita, Yehuda, 351, 377, 577
Levitan, Golda, 589
Levitov, Gita, 589
Levitt, Y.M., 239
Levitzky, 569
Levitzky, A., 238
Levitzky, Feivel, 569
Leviush, Yankev, 429
Leviush, Zalman, 76
Levyush, Leib son of Yaakov, 569
Levyush, Yitzchak, 569
Leybl the cobbler's son, 511
Leyter, Khaye, 243
Leyter, Tsvi Hirsh, 242, 243
Libernat, Mendel, 351, 569
Lichtenheim, Professor, 136
Lichtenstein, 569
Lichtenstein, Leibl, 569
Lieberman, Asha, Dina, Yaakov, Cheftzi, 569
Lieberman, B., 77, 241
Lieberman, Yisrael Barukh, 156, 410, 577
Liebermann, A.D., 89
Liebermann, A.S., 84, 85
Liebermann, Rabbi Eliezer Dov, 84
Lieker, 464

Lifshitz, A., 370
Lifshitz, Aleksander, 589
Lifshitz, Arieh, Chitza, and Tziporah, 569
Lifshitz, Ch., 583
Lifshitz, Dovid, 156
Lifshitz, Esther, 577
Lifshitz, Menachem Mendel, 577
Lifshitz, P., 238
Lifshitz, Rabbi Ber Wolf, 135
Lifshitz, Rabbi Yaakov, 102
Lifshitz, S., 361, 389, 583
Lifshitz, Sender, 375
Lifshitz, Yaakov, 60
Lifshitz, Yisrael, 134
Lifshitz, Ze'ev, 589
Liftzianski, Ch., 239
Lilienblum, M.L., 66
Lilienblum, Moshe Leib, 66
Linda (Aloni), Channah-Alta. See Aloni
Linda, Channah, 394, 396
Linda, D., 424, See Aloni
Linda, Naftali Hertz, 165
Linda, Nechemiah, 354
Linda, T., 178, 366
Linda, Teivel, 427
Linda, Y., 176, 178, 366
Linda, Yonah, 376
Linda, Yosef, 354, 364
Lipman, Yom Tov, 76, 132
Liponski, Leib, 569
Liptsin, Sam (Shepsl), 330
Liptzin, Sam (Shapsel), 9
Lis, Mr., 517
Lis, Yoyne, 517
Litinsky, Yisrael Leib, 171
Liubel, 238
Liubel, Shmuel Yitzchak, 99
Livni, Binyamin, 589
Livni, Y., 361, 382
Livni, Yishayahu, 14, 589, See
    Bialovzetzki, See Bialovitzki
Liza, 176
Lizovski, Nachum, Avraham, Catriel, 569
Lizovski, Yonah, 589
Lobel (Dlogoshelski), Rivka. See
    Dlogoshelski
Lobel, D., 176
Loinshel, Shmuel Yehuda, 175

Loite, Arieh Leib, 99
Lonshel, 20, 70, 602
Lonshel (Jak), Helen. *See* Jak
Lonshel, Chena (Helen), 602
Lonshel, Eliezer Dov, 602
Lonshel, Eliezer Dov and Miriam, 577
Lonshel, L., 70
Lonshel, Miriam, 602
Lonshel, Shmuel Yehuda, 602
Lonshel, Y., 179, 358, 364, 375
Lonshel, Yudel, 577
Lonshel, Zelig, 593
Lovovski, 489
Lozman, 20, 237, 238, 439, 533, 602
Lozman, A., 363
Lozman, Avraham, 603
Lozman, Ch., 366, 371, 397
Lozman, Chaim, 237
Lozman, Channah, 177, 180, 603
Lozman, Chaya of the house of Lev. *See* Lev, *See* Lev
Lozman, Eliyahu, Binyamin, 603
Lozman, Esther of the House of Lev. *See* Lev
Lozman, Fruma and Eliezer Tzvi, 603
Lozman, Henya Channah, 237
Lozman, Iziah, Eliezer, Chaim, 603
Lozman, L., 415
Lozman, Liba, 99
Lozman, Liuba, 173
Lozman, Luba, Esther of the house of Lev. *See* Lev
Lozman, Mendel, 237
Lozman, Mina, 603
Lozman, Mina daughter of Yisrael Yaakov, 569
Lozman, Netanel (Sana), 603
Lozman, Rayzel, 237
Lozman, Shaul Eliezer, 237
Lozman, Tzvi, Fruma, 569
Lozman, Yaakov son of Yehudit, 603
Lozman, Yehudit, 603
Lozman, Yisrael, 99
Lozman, Yisrael Yaakov Elchanan, 237
Lozman, Yocheved Eshkol. *See* Eshkol
Lozman, Ze'ev, 99, 237
Lozman, Ze'ev and Rayzel, 603

Lozman, Ze'ev, Raizl, Luba, Binyamin, Yehudit, Eliyahu, Netanel, 569
Lozovski, Meir (Grubauer). *See* Grubauer
Lozovski, N., 353, 366
Lozovski, Nachum, 180
Ludvinovski, 569
Ludvinovski, Eliezer Dov and Nechama, 577
Ludvinovski, Yaakov, 589
Luria, Rabbi Moshe Betzalel, 91, 161
Luria, Rabbi Yitzchak, 301
Lutinski, R., 424
M.Tzinovitz, 8, 9, 148, 157, 340
Ma'ayan HaMitgaber, 161
Machon, 484
Machsanai, Tzipora, 589
Maciej Zaskowski, 33
Madianovski, Isaac, 99
Maggid of Posvola, 169
Maharal, 202, 301
Mahler, Professor R., 200
Mahler, Raphael, 37, 52
Maimon, Aleksander Ziskind, 149
Maimon, Rabbi Aleksander Ziskind, 133
Maimonides, 128, 289, 550, 613
Malbim, 201
Maletz, Efraim, 425
Malletski, General, 46
Maniv, B., 362
Manor, Aleksander, 103
Margalit, 238
Margalit, A., 200
Margalit, Rabbi Shlomo Perla, 63
Margalit-Kalvariski, Chaim, 343, 345, 347
Margolin, Mr., 96
Margoliot, Yosef Barukh, 77
Margolis, 201
Margolis, Barukh, 201
Margolit- Kaloriski, Chaim, 218
Mariampolski, 361, 414
Mariampolski, M., 180, 354, 356, 365, 366
Mariampolski, Rivka and Moshe, 569
Mark, Berel, 496
Markhovki, Mayer, 517
Markovitz, Mina of the house of Kestin. *See* Kestin

Rabbi Elazar ben Azariah, 233
Rabbi Elchanan Tzvi, 155
Rabbi Levi Yitzchak of Berdichev, 614
Rabbi Yitskhok Elkhanon, 328
Rabbi Yochanan, 142
Rabbi Zadok, 418
Rabbi Zeira, 134
Rabinovitch, Faygl (Mayzler). *See* Mayzler
Rabinovitsh, Moyshe, 401
Rabinovitz, 172, 423, 425
Rabinovitz (Meizler), Feigl. *See* Meizler
Rabinovitz, B., 179
Rabinovitz, Dr. Z., 478
Rabinovitz, Dr. Ze'ev, 305
Rabinovitz, Feigl, 427, *See* Meizler
Rabinovitz, Hadassah, 571
Rabinovitz, Hinda, 590
Rabinovitz, Malkah (Regina):, 305
Rabinovitz, Meir Micha'el, 105
Rabinovitz, Moshe, Rochel, Henya, Chaya, Reichel, Berl, 571
Rabinovitz, Nechemiah, 290
Rabinovitz, P., 423
Rabinovitz, Rabbi Eliezer Simcha, 135
Rabinovitz, Rabbi Mordechai Eliyahu, 156
Rabinovitz, Rabbi Sh. Y., 94
Rabinovitz, Rabbi Yehoshua Leib, 130
Rabinovitz, Rabbi:, 170
Rabinovitz, Rivka, 571
Rabinovitz, Shalom, 356
Rabinovitz, Shaul Mendel, 305
Rabinovitz, T., 377
Rabinovitz, Tuvia, 11, 19, 351, 544, 545, 578
Rabinovitz, Tzvi Hirsh, 146
Rabinovitz, Yechezkel and Chaya Tzippa. *See* Plotnovski
Rabinovitz, Yisrael, 11, 544, 590
Rabinovitz, Yitzchak Leib, 151
Rabinovitz, Yonatan and Pesya, 571
Rabinovitz, Ze'ev, 290
Rabinovitz-Markus, Regina, 290
Rachel-Leah'ke, 168
Raguler, Eliyahu, 134
Raigrodski, 571
Raizl, 542
Rakovski, Mark, 535

Rambam, 128, 141
Rap, 571
Raphael, Dr., 479
Rapoport, Rabbi, 142
Rapoport, Shlomo Yehuda, 154
Rashi, 160, 212, 246, 301, 306, 420
Rasis, Pinchas, 362
Ratner, 354, 366, 422
Ratner, Chazzan, 221
Ratner, Mordechai, 17, 173, 413
Ratner, S., 178, 179
Ratner, Shlomo, 175
Ratner, Volf, 173, 178, 215
Ratner, VV., 176
Ratner, Yosef Chaim, 92, 99, 239, 302, 412
Ratsitsky, 312
Ratzitzki, B., 393
Ratzitzki, Beila, 391
Ratzitzki, Y., 180, 392
Ratzitzki, Yisrael Mordechai, Yehuda, Sholom, Esther, Rivka, 571
Ratzitzky, Yisrael Mordechai, 100
Ratzkovski, 429
Rav, 205
Rav Hamnuna, 135
Rav Ketina, 82
Rav Yosef, 419
Ravel, Rabbi Nachum Shraga, 135
Ravid, 159
Ravidovitsh, Alter, 428
Ravidovitz, 571
Ravidovitz, Avraham Shlomo and Shayna, 159
Ravidovitz, Chaim Yitzchak, 159, 160
Ravidovitz, Rabbi Zalman Yitzchak, 126, 130
Ravidovitz, Shabtai, 130
Razin, Stenker, 183
Reb Abba, 255
Rechs, Batya of the house of Gizumski. *See* Gizumski
Rechtman, 18, 422, 462, 470, 473, 531
Rechtman, Arieh, 593
Rechtman, L.., 19, 70, 535, 537
Rechtman, M., 70
Rechtman, Malkah Dubrin. *See* Dubrin
Rechtman, Max, 472, 479

Shumski, Tzippa daughter of Dovid, 573
Shumski, Tzvi, 591
Shumski, Y.G., 238
Shumski, Yaakov Tzvi, 100
Shumski, Yosef son of Eliyahu, 573
Shustarski, 238
Shvarts, 414
Shvartzenberg, 306
Shvedzki, Libe, 430
Shveida, 72
Sigalovitz, A.M., 238
Sigmund August, 32
Sigmund August II, 31
Sigmund I, 31
Sigmund the Old, 31
Sikorsky, 55
Simner, Dovid, 99, 428
Sinai, Ahren, 328
Sinai, Mikhl, 329
Sinai, Ruven, 328
Sinai, Ruven HaCohain, 328, 329
Sinetzki, M., 241
Sini, Reuven, *9*
Sinmer, Dovid, 573
Sinmer, Yaakov, 573
Sivash (Warsaw), 464
Skliar, Rivka, 100
Slomon, Avraham Yitzchak, 237
Slonimski, Chaim Zelig, 302
Slonimski, Rabbi Chaim Zelig, 89
Slouschz, Dr. Nachum, 77
Slovtitzki, Arieh and Tzvi, 573
Slovtitzki, D., 389
Slovtitzki, Dovid, 573
Slovtitzki, Eliezer and Golda, 573
Slovtitzki, Leibl, 573
Slovtitzki, Zaydka, 573
Slutzky, 238
Slutzky, D., 241, 350
Slutzky, Dovid, 76, 170
Smitshekhovski, Gedalye, 515
Smolenski, 489
Smolenskin, Peretz, 66
Smolinksi, Avraham, 237
Sobieski, Jan, 49
Sobleski, Yitzchak, 104
Sofer, Moshe, 152, 163
Soika, Sarah, 591

Sokolov, Nachum, 102
Sokolovski, B., 371
Sokolski, 573
Solnitzki, 489
Solnitzki, Rabbi Avraham Yitzchak, 168
Solomon, A.V., 238
Soloveitchik, 20, 172, 424, 425, 613, 614
Soloveitchik, Dina (Zilberfenig). *See* Zilberfenig
Soloveitchik, Avraham son of Meyrim, 491
Soloveitchik, Batya, 21, 607, 611, 615
Soloveitchik, Batya (Staverski). *See* Staverski
Soloveitchik, Chaim HaLevi, 161
Soloveitchik, Chaya-Rashel, 607
Soloveitchik, Dina, 21, 230, 607, 608, 611, 617, 618
Soloveitchik, Feitzi, 20, 607, 611
Soloveitchik, Frieda (Feitzi), 615
Soloveitchik, Frieda (Vertalski). *See* Vertalski
Soloveitchik, Gaon Levi, 151
Soloveitchik, Meyrim, 573, 607, 613
Soloveitchik, Meyrim (Meir), 611
Soloveitchik, Meyrim and Chaya-Rachel, 614
Soloveitchik, N., 370
Soloveitchik, Naftali, 591
Soloveitchik, Nava Marom, 607
Soloveitchik, Rabbi Chaim, 91, 551
Soloveitchik, S., 99, 423
Soloveitchik, Sara (Kivevitz). *See* Kivevitz
Soloveitchik, Sarah, 607, 611
Soloveitchik, Shalom-Naftali, 607, 608, 614
Soloveitchik, Tzvi, 611, 613
Soloveitchik-Friedgot, 611
Soloveitchik-Kivevitz, Sara. *See* Kivevitz
Sosnovski, 573
Sosnovski, Shmuel, 439
Specht, Eta daughter of Shlomo, 574
Specht, Menashe son of Itshe Meir, 574
Specht, Sarah, 574
Spektor, Rabbi Yitzchak Elchanan, 79, 129, 130
Spektor, Yitskhok Elkhanon, 260, 261

549

Sperling, 87, 211, 212, 234
Sperling, Dov Ber, 211
Sperling, Shlomo, 100
Sperling, Y.Z., 139, 234, 301, 302, 305
Sperling, Yisrael, 302
Sperling, Yisrael Ze'ev, 88, 89, 301, 302, 340, 341
Sperling, Yisrael Ze'ev son of Naftali, 89, 102
Sperling, Yosef Ze'ev, 153, 235
Sperling, Ze'ev, 211
Srulovitz, Leib, 13
Srulovitz, Yehuda Leib, 116
Stalovski, Y., 238
Stanislaw August, 32
Stanisław August Poniatowski, 37
Stanislaw Poniatowski, 46
Starazinsky, Channah, 422
Starazinsky, L., 394
Starazinsky, Leka, 396
Starazinsky, Velvel, 439
Starazinsky, Y., 238
Starazinsky, Yisrael, 356, 364, 378
Stavelski, Meyrim, 21, 616
Staverski, Yisrael, 21, 615
Staviskovski, 164, 366, 389, 394, 425
Staviskovski, Binyamin and Yitzchak, 574
Staviskovski, Chaim and Rivka, 574
Staviskovski, Channah and Chuna, 574
Staviskovski, Devorah, 393
Staviskovski, Eliezer, 574
Staviskovski, L., 354, 356, 358, 364, 376, 386
Staviskovski, M., 432
Staviskovski, Meir, 574
Staviskovski, Mordechai. *See* Mottinke the Sweet
Staviskovski, Mottel, 439
Staviskovski, Raizl, Moshe, Issachar, Devorah, Betzalel, Sonia, 574
Staviskovski, Rochel, 574
Staviskovski, S., 366
Staviskovski, Shaina Dina, 574
Staviskovski, Shaya-Ruvke, 460
Staviskovski, Tzippa and Alter, 574
Staviskovski, Tzvi and Rochel, 574
Staviskovski, Yaakov Yosef, 99

Staviskovski, Yishayahu Reuven, Sarah, Chaika, Chatzkel, 574
Stein, 438
Stein, Arich, 464
Stein, D., 355
Stein, Dora, 364
Stein, H., 354
Stein, Hinda, 312, 355, 356
Stein, Hinda daughter of Zalman, 573
Stein, Keila daughter of Zalman, 573
Stein, M., 216
Stein, Rabbi Y., 68
Stein, Rochel daughter of Yaakov, 561, 573
Stein, Shulamit, 561
Stein, Shulamit daughter of Yaakov, 573
Stein, Yaakov, 176
Stein, Yaakov, son of Zalman, 561, 573
Stein, Z., 238
Steinberg, Yosef, 24
Steindem, Aidel, 549
Steindem, Elchanan, 549
Steindem, Leibl, 439, 470
Steindem, Leibl, Shmuel, Chuna, 573
Steindem, Liba the daughter of Aidel and Elchanan, 549
Steindem, Shmuel-Chuna, 470
Steinman, Leah of the house of Leizerovski. *See* Leizerovski
Steintzeit, Barukh Hershel, 573
Stern, Natan, Rabbi, 150
Stern, Rabbi Y.Z., 93
Stern, Rabbi Yosef Zechariah, 92, 136
Stern, Yosef Gedaliah, 150
Stern, Yosef Zechariah, 150
Sternfeld, Ben-Tzion, 133
Sternfeld, L., 238
Stolar, 354, 424
Stolar, A., 180
Stolar, Abba, 176
Stolar, Bronie, 430
Stolar, Dovid, 173, 176
Stolar, Dovid and Sarah, 574
Stolar, Etke, 574
Stolar, M., 178, 180, 216, 355, 360, 363
Stolar, Mashe, 430
Stolar, S., 424
Stolar, Shimon son of Reb Dovid, 574

557